S0-BNC-311

AMERICAN HISTORICAL EXPLANATIONS

A Strategy for Grounded Inquiry

AMERICAN HISTORICAL EXPLANATIONS

A Strategy for Grounded Inquiry

GENE WISE
University of Maryland

Every force has its form.
Shaker motto

University of Minnesota • Minneapolis

Copyright © 1980 by the University of Minnesota.
All rights reserved.
Published by the University of Minnesota Press,
2037 University Avenue Southeast,
Minneapolis, Minnesota 55455
2nd edition, revised.

Library of Congress Cataloging in Publication Data

Wise, Gene.
   American historical explanations.

   Includes bibliographical references and index.
   1. United States—Historiography. 2. Historiography. I. Title
E175.W47   1980   973'.072   80-17697
ISBN 0-8166-0954-3
ISBN 0-8166-0957-8 (pbk.)

To Stuart Gerry Brown, from whom I caught the fever of ideas; and to Raymond College, where fever got transmuted into form

CONTENTS

Foreword

A writer ought to let readers know what they are in for. Some books speak for themselves, some do not. This one, I imagine, may need some help.

When a work of scholarship functions wholly within pre-established forms, readers can simply plug it into ready receptacles—say, "historiography," or "intellectual history," or "sociological theory," or "literary criticism"—and thus be prepared for what is to come. But my intent in this book is to begin outside the traditional forms of historical scholarship—not by abandoning them, but rather by trying to gain some analytic distance and critical perspective on them, then attempting to construct some supplementary forms for historical-cultural inquiry. This strategy may require some explaining.

In the chapters to follow, I try to counter three working assumptions held by many practicing historians in America:

(1) That the art of method in history studies should be to conceal method; that discussions of procedure and "how-to-do-it" problems are incidental to scholarship and best relegated to prefaces and footnotes and an occasional methodology article; and that a historian's modus operandi should be carried by how one does it and not by what one says about doing it.

(2) That the real aim of historical scholarship is to discover what happened in the past; that what happened has been recorded here and there in what historians call "primary documents"; and that true scholarship in history must be based on only those primary documents.

(3) That ideas are ideas and words are words and books are books, and that none of them presents any special problems of inquiry or interpretation for the working historian.

I challenge these assumptions by seeing each of them as problematic and not a given of scholarship; and my challenge comes out of a position similar to Thomas Kuhn's in *The Structure of Scientific Revolutions*. Kuhn contends that scientists do not go to nature pure in their inquiries, but rather they address the world through intervening filters, or what he calls "paradigms." He also says these paradigms are subject to change now and then, and he is concerned to explain just when and how that happens.

What Kuhn calls paradigms for scientific communities, I call "explanation-forms" for historians' communities. I focus on three such explanation-forms used by historians in 20th-century America; and I try to illustrate what happens in situations when one of those forms gets stretched beyond the breaking point, and disintegrates.

Conventionally, when working with ideas, American historians have used a "climate-of-opinion" mode of explanation. Such a conception tends to pick up on an idea after its vital work is over with—in completed systems of thought like "Puritanism," or "Transcendentalism," or "Darwinism," or "Progressivism." I counter that procedure by seeking to enter an idea or explanation-form while it is still at labor—when it is in the process of being created, under strain, altered, or dying. I am concerned not with "thought," then, but with "the act of think-ing." I also seek to reach below the visible surface of historians' explanation-forms— trying to see their world from the inside out, as it were. Such a procedure grows out of this book's underlying assumption—*that a historical explanation is distinguished not so much by its content as by its form.*

All this will require some alternative methods, or what I call "strategies for inquiry." To develop these, I have gone to several sources for help—to Carl Becker for some elementary historiographical questions ("What is a Historical Fact?," "What is Historiography?," "Everyman His Own Historian"); to the cognitive psychologist George Kelly and the sociologists of knowledge Peter Berger, Thomas Luckmann, and Karl Mannheim for a behavioral model of people's ideas (*The Psychology of Personal Constructs, The Social Construction of Reality, Ideology and Utopia*); to the historian of science Thomas Kuhn for a functioning model of explanation-forms and for an operative sense of how scholarly communities behave; to Kenneth Burke for a strategy of historical criticism (*The Philosophy of Literary Form*); and to John Higham, David Noble, Richard Hofstadter, and Robert Skotheim for background on my basic subject matter (*History, Historians against History, The Progressive Historians, American Intellectual Histories and Historians*).

Methodological discussions seldom have much impact on working historians. This is so because too often such discussions are left floating— hanging in the air, so to speak. Methodic proposals work best, I believe, with a visible body of materials to experiment on. I have tried to *ground* my methods, and my observations of ideas, in extended case studies— which comprise the book's latter half (hence the book's subtitle "A Strategy for Grounded Inquiry"). Methods and ideas are not merely proposed, then, but are put to work in this latter part of the study; so that part functions as a particular testing ground for the general strategies suggested in the book's opening chapters.

In these case studies, I invite the reader to begin by watching how one kind of explanation-form behaves under siege—the Progressive historical form through Frederick Jackson Turner (*The Frontier in American History*) and Vernon Louis Parrington (vol. 3 of *Main Currents in American Thought*). Then we move to enter the inner logic (and psychologic, and sociologic) of a "paradigm revolution" in the making—as the old Progressive form breaks apart under mounting pressure, and a new form begins to take shape in the 1940s writings of Lionel Trilling ("Reality in America") and Reinhold Niebuhr (*The Children of Light and the Children of Darkness*). Finally, we watch this new form—what I call the "counter-Progressive" explanation—come to establish itself in the 1950s works of R. W. B. Lewis (*The American Adam*) and Perry Miller (*The New England Mind: From Colony to Province*). We also look some at New Left historical explanation-forms, and note wherein they differ both from Progressives and from counter-Progressives.

My intent, then, is not primarily to review the forms of American historians in this book, but to try and offer *explanation* of their structure and behavior—to show how they are put together, how they respond to stress, how and when they may change, how they respond to this situation and that. I am also trying to articulate a more or less integrated field or territory for such inquiries—which territory I call here "explanation in American historical-cultural studies."

This book has been written, in the words of a recent rock hit, "with a little help from my friends." Foremost among these are three—Robert Skotheim, Richard Reinitz, and Karen Lystra. The first has given me sage advice throughout the study, and has provided a model with his own fine scholarship in American historiography-intellectual history. The second has the critical power to make a manuscript tremble when he reads it, and has done much to hold at least some of my wild flights of piety in check. The third, upon her second reading of Perry Miller's *Colony* and my tenth, politely told me I didn't understand what Miller means by "mind" . . . and was right. She also set me straight on Thomas Kuhn and got me to thinking about the whole issue of *form* in historical-cultural inquiry.

There are others implicated in this work—though responsibility (and blame) for what I have done with their ideas is, of course, mine and mine alone. John Higham, Rush Welter, David Potter, Louis Hartz, Jurgen Herbst, Arthur Schlesinger, Jr., Ralph Ketcham, David Hollinger, John Diggins, Cushing Strout, Hayden White, David Noble, Charles Crowe, David Levin, Richard Bushman, Rogers Hollingsworth, Morrell Heald, Ronald Formisano, Dwight Hoover, Brom Weber, Robin Brooks, and Robert Merideth have read early drafts in and around this study, and have given me valuable historiographical advice. Michael McGiffert, Thomas

Pressly, and Stuart Crawford read an earlier version of the entire manuscript and urged some basic revisions which led to its present form.

Peter Morales, Jerry Gaff, Mike Wagner, Margaret Payne, Warren Martin, Park Goist, Richard Evans, David Trousdale, James Gilreath, and Gabrielle Miller have also given me useful suggestions for this volume. And my graduate students in American Studies 501–502 at Case Western Reserve have offered valuable stimulation and insight, as well as a dialogue-environment where ideas can get challenged and grow. Such students deserve the title "colleagues in inquiry," for I have learned from them at least as much as they from me.

Finally, the book is dedicated to a great graduate teacher, and a great undergraduate institution for teaching. Without them, this would not have happened.

February 1973   Gene Wise

Prologue, 1973: The Imperative of a New "Territory"

Every generation of history graduate students confronts twice as many books as the generation which preceded it.
> David Hackett Fischer
> *Historians' Fallacies*

Man is not differentiated from the lower animals by any increased capacity for intake of information. Human eyes and ears are not much better than those of other mammals, and the human nose is almost certainly worse. It is the capacity for organizing information into large and complex images which is the chief glory of our species.
> Kenneth Boulding
> *The Image: Knowledge in Life and Society*
> (University of Michigan Press, 1956)

The human species, it is said, is distinguished by its history. That is not true. Dogs and mountains have a history too. Humans distinguish themselves not by their history, but by their capacity to *talk to* their history, through constructed forms.

Academic historians, I believe, have not sufficiently emphasized this distinction. They have thereby constricted one potentially rich branch of historical understanding. Many historians have a peculiar sense of priorities. Using a set of assumptions that we shall explore more thoroughly with David Donald in chapter 3, they feel one should go out and *do* history-work before thinking much about the *forms* through which one does it.

As contrasted with, say, some disciplines in the natural or social sciences, the profession of history has not been notably self-conscious of the conventions through which its scholarship functions. With a few striking exceptions, the historian's craft has tended toward that of the literary artist—to tell a story well, with a minimum of side forays into how and why and through what he or she is doing it. One branch of history's scientific tradition—that concerned to recover "history as it really happened"—has merged with another of its literary strains—"the art of method is to conceal method"—to block any substantial growth in the profession toward critical self-awareness of its modus operandi.

I am hardly the first to note this. Just since the mid-1960s, we have seen John Higham's *History* (1965), David Noble's *Historians against History* (1965), Robert Skotheim's *American Intellectual Histories and Historians* (1966), David Levin's *In Defense of Historical Literature* (1967), Richard Hofstadter's *The Progressive Historians* (1968), the essays in Marcus Cunliffe and Robin Winks, eds., *Pastmasters* (1969), Robert Berkhofer's *A Behavioral Approach to Historical Analysis* (1969), Martin Duberman's *The Uncompleted Past* (1969), David Hackett Fischer's *Historians' Fallacies* (1970), Howard Zinn's *The Politics of History* (1970), Lee Benson's *Toward the Scientific Study of History* (1972)—and all are concerned to make visible our forms for inquiry in American history studies. The critical student of historians' forms—be he behavioral methodologist (like Berkhofer or Benson), or historiographer (like Higham or Skotheim), or radical critic (like Duberman or Zinn)—can take heart that he is not wholly alone in his concerns. But we can hardly grow sanguine about the prospects for any imminent revolution in the profession's understanding of itself. The inertial weight of old forms is too heavy for that yet.

I can briefly illustrate why this is true by citing two instances in the recent intellectual history of American historians. These instances set the situation to which this book and the field it proposes—"explanation in American historical-cultural studies"—are a strategic response.

The first instance happened in December of 1962 at an American Historical Association convention held in Chicago. Carl Bridenbaugh, AHA president at the time, was delivering his presidential address on the decline of traditional standards in the profession. At one point, Bridenbaugh paused to lament that an alienating materialism in scholarship threatened to inundate historical inquirers "with an overwhelming mass of data." He was fearful that the historians' cherished concern for wholeness of vision might not survive the onslaught. And, he went on to report, when a sociologist once queried of him, "What is your method of sampling?," he set the upstart in his place by responding that "those who work in the prestatistical age of history . . . do not sample, but seize upon every scrap of a statistic they can find."[1]

Where many social and natural scientists have welcomed the strategic, and metaphysical, necessity of *selection* in their inquiries, historians like Bridenbaugh resist. They long to recover the whole past, not fragments of it. We shall return to some implications of this attitude in a moment.

The second instance was really a non-instance, or rather an instance where something should have happened but did not. What did happen was that in 1953 Perry Miller published the second of his *New England Mind* volumes—*The New England Mind: From Colony to Province*. Historians immediately took note—praising the volume, accepting or challenging one or another of its findings, and generally recognizing it as a major new "contribution to historical knowledge." What did not happen was any critical recognition of *how* Miller did what he did.

In *Colony*, Perry Miller was able to say what he did about the New England mind because he worked through forms radically different from the norm among American intellectual historians. But because Miller took "mind" so seriously there, most historians simply plugged his procedure into already existing categories—"idealist," "rationalist," "monolith," "intrinsic analysis." They granted him his new information and his new insights. But they refused to recognize his new method of historical inquiry. And those few who did sense something different about his modus operandi claimed it was so private, so much the product of his unattainable genius, as to be un-transferable beyond Miller.

What happened in 1953 was a potential revolution in ways of understanding how ideas have functioned in American historical experience. But the revolution never happened. As a field of inquiry, intellectual history has waned in recent years. It has lacked forms to handle change very well, it cannot convey variety effectively, it cannot get its ideas into motion, it cannot connect ideas into concrete events of history, it cannot detect strains or cracks in an idea—*it cannot, in short, ground intellectual abstractions in the life-experiences of people*. Two decades ago, Perry Miller did do all that, yet almost no one bothered to notice how. And those few who did take notice never tried building on Miller's alternative mode of analysis. It is an added paradox that Miller is charged with intellectualist shortcomings—too idealist, too narrowly rational, too monolithic—which he, and he almost alone of American intellectual historians, has been able to break free from.

What the Miller instance illustrates is this: When someone contributes new information to our stock of historical knowledge, historians in the field are obliged to take notice. To ignore such information, if it relates to one's own concerns, is to risk being called "un-scholarly." Because of this sanction in the profession, there is some measure of cumulative growth in our knowledge of the past.

But there is little cumulative growth in our scholarly methods for knowing the past. This is so because there are few sanctions which show that concern for such methods is important. It is a damning indictment of a historian's work to say he or she has failed to consult important documentary evidence available for the subject. It is not very damning to say she or he has failed to use important forms available for interpreting the subject. Under-*researching* is frowned upon, under-*explaining* is not.

Why is it, then, that American historians seem so information-conscious, but so form-ignorant? This issue too has a history, one that we in the field might profitably spend some time reviewing. For while we have been busy urging the perspective of history on others, we have been uncritical of our own past. As a result, we work through socially constructed conventions that we are historically unself-conscious of.

II

This is not the place to consider the issue in its full depth. I can only note the problem here, and hope others may investigate the matter more thoroughly later. But W. Stull Holt has made a suggestive beginning in his 1940 article, "The Idea of Scientific History in America."

Holt shows how, late in the 19th century, American historians found themselves with a paucity of reliable information—with many gentlemen scholars who saw their work as a leisure-time sort of activity, and with an ethos that made of history-writing a literary art, with the aim to tell a dramatic story. In the early years of professionalization, scholars countered this situation with their version of a "scientific" strategy. Holt notes this strategy as it was crystallized in a 1908 AHA presidential address of George Burton Adams:

At the very beginning of all conquest of the unknown lies the fact, established and classified to the fullest extent possible at the moment. To lay such foundations, to furnish such materials for later builders, may be a modest ambition, but it is my firm belief that in our field of history, for a long time to come, the man who devotes himself to such labors, who is content with this preliminary work, will make a more useful and a more permanent contribution to the final science, or philosophy of history, than will he who yields to the allurements of speculation and endeavors to discover in the present stage of our knowledge the forces that control society, or to formulate the laws of their action. None of the new battle cries should sound for us above the call of our first leader, proclaiming the chief duty of the historian to establish *wie es eigentlich gewesen.* . . . The field of the historian is, and must long remain, the discovery and recording of what actually happened.[2]

Few historians today would state the purposes of scholarship quite in the naive form of Adams in 1908, but few have envisioned clear alternative forms either. Adams' purposes have been modified some in the intervening years, and we shall look at those in chapter 2. But what he said then defines the main intents of American historical scholarship even now, I believe.

Many historians still feel the fundamental problem of scholarship is a paucity of information; many envision that the final goal of their field is to construct some kind of scholarly pyramid, and see their own work as building blocks along the way (making "contributions to historical knowledge"); many believe their basic if not sole task is to gather more information about the past, which information has been stored only in "primary" documents. And many still believe, as we shall see with Charles Sellers in chapter 2, that the quintessential purpose of historical scholarship should be to aim for some kind of "overall synthesis" of "objective reality" in the past. As Bruce Kuklick has written of the "ideal historical observer" model which embodies all these purposes, "Emphasis will be given to the collection of all the available evidence and the citation of all the relevant facts."[3]

Such a cluster of purposes has done much in the last three quarters of a century to establish the rigor and enhance the fullness of our historical understanding. No one can reasonably argue with that. But any good strategy may produce fall-out which is not so good. In this case, the fall-out has been that historians in America have felt so pressured to produce more information that they have lacked the time and inclination and critical detachment to take note of a radical change in the historical situation of scholarship. Quite unhistorically, we are behaving as if we were still back in the late 19th century.

Historians have thus become locked in to Cotton Mather's old Puritan injunction, "Sirs, let us up and be doing"—doing in this case meaning producing more knowledge. In affairs of scholarship, we still evidently see ourselves in a *scarcity* situation—we do not have enough information—and we labor to overcome scarcity by accumulating wealth. Such a strategy was functionally relevant to the birth of the American historical profession in the late 19th and earlier 20th century. It becomes dysfunctional now, though, unless it is countered by some alternative—or rather supplementary—strategy of scholarship.

We need a supplementary strategy because in American historical studies today we confront a changed situation. We have been fixated on how to produce more, and more quickly, when our situation instead is an embarrassment of riches—*how to order and make sense of an overwhelming abundance*. Abundance, not scarcity, characterizes our lot in American historical scholarship today. In knowledge as in the economy, our root problem now is not production, but *ecology*—which means more conscious concern for making fresh connections among existing things; more looking outward to the wider consequences of our information; more serious attention given to questioning why we are doing what we are doing, and through what forms; more effort given to structuring our productive activities into humanly manageable patterns.

III

Which, in a word, means added *methodic* concerns—not only doing more things in history study, but giving more aforethought (and hindthought) to what we do. We are, it seems, experiencing a general crisis of ecology in contemporary scholarship, what Alvin Toffler calls a situation of "information overload."[4] In such a situation, data may crowd up on scholars' minds, and, as David Brion Davis remarked recently, it threatens to "engorge the historian with indigestible detail."[5]

If our minds are to conserve their energies and exercise some control in such an abundance situation, we must invent new strategies for slowing down the rush of productive activity around us, for finding and holding focus amid the flux, for sorting information into meaningful patterns and thereby gaining leverage on it. One way of doing this is to concentrate on the *forms* of historical inquiry—moving away from preoccupation with content to focus more on underlying structures, on social and psychological functions, and on dynamic processes of inquiry.

If we look beyond the boundaries of professional history over to other disciplines, we find whole fields of concern doing just that. In one way or another, Robert Merton and Alvin Gouldner and Talcott Parsons and Robert Nisbet and Ralf Dahrendorf and Robert Brown and Abraham Kaplan and John Madge are doing "ecological" scholarship in and around sociology; so also are Eugene Meehan and Vernon Van Dyke and Robert Dahl in political science. And Daniel Bell has used a sociological perspective on this information overloaded situation to propose a fundamental restructuring of our modes for inquiry, and our education for inquiry. Bell writes, "Training cannot deal with techniques in the narrow sense, but with the foundations of knowledge itself: i.e., how a particular discipline establishes its concepts; how these concepts, seen as fluid inquiry, need to be revised to meet new problems; how one establishes the criteria of choice for one, rather than another, alternative patterns of inquiry."[6]

When we look back from these other disciplines to our own, we are immediately struck by the contrast. We do not have a field of scholarship in history devoted to . . . scholarship in history. Indeed, not only do we lack such a field, I do not know of a single American historian who is identified first as "historiographer," or "methodologist." The most likely candidate—John Higham—has written that his two decades of labor in American historiographical studies "had always in my mind been secondary to my research interests," and he has recently vowed to guard against "the occupational narcissism of the historiographer."[7]

We have many fine studies in American historiography and historical method—several by John Higham—but they are all done by scholars who consider them a kind of professional avocation, secondary to their real research interests in "primary" subject materials. And courses taught in this area—typically bearing the label "History and Historians" or some such—are routinely ill-defined and form-less affairs. Since almost no one considers such a course "his" or "her" specialty, they are usually passed around in the department from one professor to another, and seldom grow or are refined much as a result. Jurgen Herbst, who recently completed an extensive study of such courses in American universities, comments that his results "do not attest to a very highly developed and sophisticated level of self-consciousness or self-awareness among historians. It expresses a rather vaguely felt appreciation for the desirability and vaguely felt lack of the presence of such self-awareness." "The most common criticism of theory of history," Herbst concludes, "is that the field is vague, ill-defined, overly ambitious, and not very relevant to many."[8]

In short, work in American historiography and historical method is still produced by individual curious adventurers; it does not comprise a clearly defined field, and it has done little to affect work done elsewhere by practicing American historians. Although some historiographical and methodological works are very good indeed (e.g., Richard Hofstadter's *The Progressive Historians* or the scholarship of John Higham or David Noble or Robert Skotheim or David Levin or Cushing Strout or Richard Reinitz or David Hackett Fischer or Lee Benson or Robert Berkhofer or Bruce Kuklick or Thomas Pressly), they do not feed into any fellowship of similarly concerned scholars who dialogue often with each other and grow cumulatively from the interchange. In essence, work here lacks *identity* and it lacks *a visible community of interests.*

IV

These two parts of our present historical situation—the burden of information-overload and the absence of any community in the profession trying to cope with it—sound the imperative for a new kind of "territory" in historical scholarship. The field that I propose in this book—"explanation in American historical-cultural studies"—is one response to such a situation.

The book is a study of historical inquiry grounded in the practice of American historians. It focuses on how historians have tried reconstructing experience in America, and it calls these reconstructions *explanation-forms.*

As a preliminary to considering particular forms constructed by particular communities of historians, it analyzes four general historical forms—the *idea*-form, the *reality*-form, the *document*-form, and the *explanation*-form. It also proposes some new, grounded strategies for entering and handling these forms—"situation-strategy" analysis of ideas, a "perspectivistic" approach to historical reality, "strategic" reading of documents, "pivotal moment" analysis of explanation-strain and explanation-change.

All this comprises the first half of the book, chapters 1 through 6. Then, in chapters 7 through 9, the book moves into the case studies—investigating particular historical forms in action, and putting into practice the general methods proposed earlier. There I analyze three explanation-forms used by historians in 20th-century America—the Progressive, the counter-Progressive, the New Left—and show in detail how one form cracks open under pressure and another comes to replace it.

I do not intend this work to "represent" the entire territory that I propose here—"explanation in American historical-cultural studies." I intend rather to work with some care through one small part of the territory, and suggest others. I hope this procedure, plus the imperative of our larger "abundance" situation in historical studies today, may encourage future scholars to enter the territory and concentrate their own labors here.

NOTES

1. "The Great Mutation," *American Historical Review*, LXVIII, 2 (January, 1963), p. 322.

2. Quoted in W. Stull Holt, "The Idea of Scientific History in America," *Journal of the History of Ideas*, I, 3 (June, 1940), pp. 359–360.

3. "The Mind of the Historian," *History and Theory*, VIII, 3 (1969), p. 319.

4. *Future Shock* (Random House, 1970), pp. 305 ff.

5. "Some Recent Directions in American Cultural History," *American Historical Review*, LXXIII (February, 1968), p. 697.

6. *The Reforming of General Education* (Columbia, 1966), p. 157. For a brief historical review of the situation leading to this overload of information, a review rich in sociological insights, see Bell's chapter "The Tableau of Social Change—Today and Tomorrow," pp. 68–143.

7. *Writing American History* (Indiana, 1970), p. ix, 157.

8. "Theoretical Work in History in American University Curricula," *History and Theory*, VII, 3 (1968), p. 348, 346.

Prologue, 1980: Reflections on "Reflexive" Scholarship

"Boyer and Nissenbaum [in *Salem Possessed*] take their readers into their confidence; they explain their methodology, their reasons for preferring one argument over another, and the evidence which suggests that the historical development of Salem had created this important cleavage in the community. Such explicitness reflects the 'striking methodological self-consciousness' of many historians with a social-scientific orientation, and also a more general aspect of twentieth-century thought: the deliberate intrusion of the author into a creative work."

James Henretta, "Social History as Lived and Written: Structure, Problematic, and Action" (Newberry Library Conference Paper, 1977)

This book contends that what people are willing to admit as real and right and important is deeply implicated in *context*—in who sees and thinks what, when, through what preoccupations, and under what conditions. It says that people's ideas (or in the language developed herein, "explanations") have their forms, their roles, their audiences, their functions, their seasons.

Some critics of the book's first edition, committed perhaps to different contexts of explanation from mine (hence to different forms, different roles, different functions, different audiences, and maybe to a different season), were disturbed at what they sensed to be a pernicious brand of relativism—which says in effect that anything may be true anywhere, and that real and unreal, good and bad, are arbitrary, matters of personal whim. I think such critics misread the book's message, but readers can look at chapter 2—"'Perspectives' on Historical Reality: The Relativist Dilemma"—and decide that for themselves.

What I wish to emphasize now is that the book itself, or rather its form and reception, is implicated in its own message. In ways that in 1973 I did

xxi

not anticipate —and for some time thereafter did not especially welcome—*American Historical Explanations* offers an interesting episode in the contextual relativity of "American historical explanations."

The book first took form late in the 1960s, out of a mentality shaped by experiences of that decade. At first glance it might not seem so. The book's subject matter is a wholly unrepresentative and highly privileged group of Americans, intellectuals who spent their life's work mostly in college classrooms, scholarly studies, and academic committee rooms; the more visible imperatives of the turbulent sixties tended to reject such rarefied activities, in such rarefied settings, as unreal and irrelevant. Further, the book focuses on the ideas of these intellectuals; in the sixties and early seventies ideas were often held as suspect—they either distorted reality, it was said, or they obfuscated it. In either case, if you really wanted to understand what is real and true, you passed by ideas to look for power interests or institutional structures—forces that lie below and prior to insubstantial, rationalized ideas. Finally, the book is concerned not only with ideas, but with ideas about ideas—or methodology—and that would appear doubly abstracted from urgencies of the times.

Hence the late sixties and early seventies would seem the wrong context for doing a methodological study of American historians' ideas. It would seem a context, rather, for asserting that ideas are the property of insulated elites, who use them to mask their privilege and their power—as against the common people who live in the real world of empirical factuality. In short, this was not the season to be promoting a Perry Miller on mind or a Reinhold Niebuhr on irony.

Yet at the time I saw nothing incongruous about my particular intellectual passions. That I had arrived at those passions through a circuitous route did not seem untoward either. People's minds, I have felt, often move not down straight lines but along jagged and twisted ones; so my own convoluted passage appeared quite normal.

While doing my graduate studies, for example, I had not been at all attracted to methodological concerns, and had no interest whatever in historiography (the former I had been exposed to but rejected as mechanistic and contrary to the humanistic spirit, the latter I had not been exposed to at all). Events, or rather my particular response to events, were to alter those priorities.

My first teaching position was at Raymond College, an undergraduate "cluster" college of the University of the Pacific. There—in a context where most classes were small seminars and students learned mainly through dialogue—it made little sense to try and teach simply the "stuff" of American cultural history. That would be more appropriate to the normal lecture situation in larger educational settings. I also wanted students to be challenged directly by sharp minds, the quality of mind that had provoked my own thinking as a graduate student. So I asked them to read Richard Hofstadter and R. W. B. Lewis and Perry Miller and Reinhold Niebuhr and Christopher Lasch and Vernon Louis Parrington in the original; and over time we came to focus our energies not only on what, in America's history, these thinkers were talking about, but on where the thinkers themselves were coming from, how they put their beliefs together, when they agreed and disagreed with each other, and why.[1] (This is my rationalized reason for such a focus; another reason, perhaps more compellingly "real," is that my graduate education in American Studies and social psychology had left embarrassing gaps in my understanding of our cultural past, and had my effort in class been to cover the "stuff" of American history, Raymond's aggressive students were sure to have found me out!)

So that is how, slowly and with no prior conscious intent, I began backing into methodological and historiographical concerns. Impetus for my change came not from the profession (read context of "audience") but from imperatives of the classroom. As I began to read more what professional historians had written on these matters, I became less ignorant of the field, but also restive that something in their handling of historical ideas was awry. I now suspect my restiveness on this issue came neither from the classroom nor from professional concerns, but from unsettling events in the world outside.[2] That suspicion is confirmed by the event that jolted me into a transformed consciousness on such matters—the Chicago Democratic Convention of 1968.

My initial response to that event was horror—horror at the grenade launchers, at Mayor Daley and his police, at Hubert Humphrey's efforts at a "politics of joy" amid the manifest violence outside, at the general breakdown of civility and the siege of insanity in one of the culture's most cherished political rituals. But, beyond my horror at what Americans were doing, I was vexed too at my own impotence.

My vexation was not primarily substantial—that I could do nothing to affect what was happening. Everyone in America experienced that sort of vexation, nothing was peculiar to my own experience there. My own particular vexation, it turned out, was essentially *methodological*—here I was a product of years of training in American culture studies, and I had no tools to comprehend what the hell was happening at Chicago in August 1968.

I had been trained to understand America through its manifest ideas and values, and those ideas as they were formed into broad currents of thought floating through time—Puritanism, Liberalism, Transcendentalism, the Idea of Progress, the Frontier, Technology, Manifest Destiny and Mission. Now and then the culture would emphasize some ideas more than others, and these emphases would change over the years. Hence I had been taught to envision historic "climates" of intellectual opinion in America—the "consensus" climate of the 1940s and 50s, say, or the "Progressive" climate of the 1900s and 1910s.

But such intellectual tools helped me not at all in trying to comprehend Chicago in 1968. Was it that cultural ideas were simply irrelevant to the manifest action? Surely not. But here were no gently floating currents of thought or broad drifts of an intellectual weather front. Cultural ideas were in the air, to be sure, in this volatile situation—behind the grenade launchers, behind Mayor Daley and his police, Hubert Humphrey, the Yippies, and Walter Cronkite too. Cultural ideas had also been at work in other wrenching events of the decade—the assassinations of John and Robert Kennedy, of Martin Luther King and Malcolm X; student demonstrations at Berkeley, Columbia, and elsewhere; riots in Watts, Detroit, Newark, Miami; happenings at Haight-Ashbury, Woodstock, and Altamont; the continuing war in Viet Nam.

But what I lacked was a way to get ideas out of the air and onto the ground, so to speak, or rather a way to see how ideas in history sometimes worked that way. What was needed was *some strategy for catching hold of a cultural idea as it is working inside a concrete historical event*—for watching how it may enter that event and exit from it, for detecting how it may heat up or cool down as it responds to one or another circumstance in the event, for observing it change in coloration or intensity or velocity as various historical actors employ it to cope with this or that, and as they address it to one or another historical audience. Clearly, what was needed were some different metaphors for ideas, and for change in ideas; Chicago 1968 seemed to me not a weather front but an earthquake, or a potential one.

Hence I found myself moving away from atmospheric images of cultural ideas and toward what, in the book's subtitle, I call "a strategy for *grounded* inquiry."[3] My immediate concern was to find ways of coping with the August 1968 Chicago Democratic Convention. But I soon sensed my own intellectual impotence vis-à-vis Chicago was hardly unique. It simply dramatized, in one particular form and through one particular event, a wider crisis in the study of historical ideas over the last decade and a half.

It is a historiographical truism that after two decades of virtually unparalleled growth in the profession, American intellectual history has been eclipsed of late by the new social history, the new diplomatic history, econometric history—fields with a firmer grip on less vaporous subject matters.[4] The contemporary crisis of intellectual history studies has many dimensions, only a few of which I address here, or was even conscious of by 1973. But *American Historical Explanations* is a response to parts of that crisis, by constructing some alternative metaphors of how ideas function in people's historical experience, and some alternative methods for handling those ideas. I also felt, in 1973, that we needed some alternative ways to write and talk about historical ideas. And there I got into trouble.

II

Several commentators were, to put it mildly, less than enthusiastic about my stylistic innovations in the book's first incarnation. To be sure, some critics were generous in their praise for *American Historical Explanations*, calling it "creative," "exciting," "bold," "brilliant," "original, stimulating, and thought-provoking," and writing that the book was a "signal success," "one of the most provocative works in the history of American history," and "sprinkled with arresting observations."[5]

These are, of course, nice words; they are of the sort to massage the scholarly ego, thoroughly confirming an author's own rosy view of self. It would be tempting to remove these fine words from context, elevating them to the realm of objective truth about the book (similarly, the dastardly words could be lifted from context too, and cast down to the level of blatant, and mean-spirited, falsehoods).

But such temptations should be resisted (well, maybe not all the time), for they go against a main contention of *American Historical Explanations*—that all human ideas and judgments are implicated in context. And in this case the context of negative judgments about the book may be as illuminating as the context of positive ones.

One critic, for example, saw fit to instruct me in the etiquette of proper scholarly discourse, another called the opening three chapters "disastrous"; others wrote of "jargon-bound concepts," the "pretentious and stifling analytical apparatus," and the "excessively chatty . . . and somewhat rambling" style, noting, in understatement, that "the prose results are less than happy."[6] Finally, one perverse soul (or so I thought for a while) concluded her review with this comment:

It is . . . distressing that the structure of even this fairly simple argument is buried under a heavy weight of rambling, repetitive prose, sloppy syntax and repeated lists of the same names. "The work of experience is out there breeding happenings all the time," Wise writes; and again, "Though I have preferred not to work off others' scholarship in these early ruminations, I've not just struck them out of my own imagination either." The informal voice is acceptable, but here it is carried to extremes, and badly obscures the arguments advanced.[7]

These are hardly flattering words; manifestly, they do not massage the scholarly ego, and they tend toward an author's own dimmer view of self. They are, in short, the kind of words a scholar, or one aspiring to scholarship, would prefer not to hear of his own creations.

But if these are not welcome words, they were not wholly unanticipated (or, in retrospect, should not have been). Earlier, I have noted why I set out in the book to make problematic our scholarly understanding of historical ideas. Also problematic, it seemed to me, were matters of scholarly style, of voice, role, and audience in communicating that understanding. I felt that in order to develop alternative strategies for inquiry into ideas, I would have to try some alternative modes of communication. Those modes were frankly experimental, efforts to construct different *forms* for communicating about ideas, and about idea-change, congruent with the different *content* of my message. Hence my departures from what is expected in scholarly discourse were deliberate. But as often happens in such affairs, those intentions had consequences that I had not fully anticipated.

A few efforts at stylistic innovation I now regret, and admit the critics were right. I wince at a voice that is here and there too chatty, at my too frequent resort to italics for emphasis, and at my overuse of contractions in trying to strike an informal tone. Also, on occasion there is too much self-conscious backing and filing, especially in the transitions.

In this second edition, I have removed some of the less successful of these experiments. I would have revised more, but that threatened to make the book's cost prohibitive.[8] If I regret some of the consequences of my effort at innovation, however, I do not regret the effort itself or the intentions behind it.

The intent was to make visible, and therefore problematic, the dialogue between author and reader in scholarly discourse. The normal, unproblematic mode is for scholars to address only other scholars in their writings, and to allow outsiders—normally students—to overhear the message if they choose to or are assigned to. This mode is unproblematic because the scholar knows his or her audience in advance of writing, knows its social and intellectual composition, its patterns of academic socialization, its intellectual preoccupations, the fund of information, ideas, and methods with which it works, its model or exemplar works of scholarship, what it normally reads and does not read, its rules of etiquette in academic discourse, its catch words and its code words, its inner core and its outer boundaries, and much more. All these qualities of a scholar's audience may not be known self-consciously of course; indeed, "normal" scholarship (in the Kuhn-ian sense) is functioning best when such matters need not be articulated, but are simply assumed, given in the nature of things.[9]

Those assumptions—functioning far below the threshold of consciousness and therefore removed from critical examination—are among the most powerful socializing and boundary-maintaining devices wielded by the academic professions. One fascination of interdisciplinary work is to observe the striking variety of languages used, and allowable, among the several academic fields of inquiry. What is proscribed in one discipline may be prescribed in another; and behavior frowned upon as "unscholarly" in, say, a humanistic field may be honored in one of the social science disciplines (or vice versa). This, if nothing else, gives one a strong sense of the contextual relativity of scholarly judgments.

What is equally striking is that, despite their assumed givenness by adepts in the field, most of these scholarly languages are less than a century old, having grown up alongside the various professional associations to which they are attached. And for every individual in such a profession, the scholarly mode is at least a second or third language, learned—usually in one's twenties or thirties—well after primary socialization has presumably fixed one's basic values and attitudes in life. Yet these languages—so young in historical time and learned so late relatively in individual lives—wield enormous force in defining what is real and right and important for those who use them. Indeed, at some levels their use may be the single most important key to full admission into the field. The "good" scholar in history, or sociology, or literature is he or she who can use the language properly; the "poor" scholar, or nonscholar, is he or she who cannot (or perhaps does not, depending on the degree of choice involved).

By making problematic this issue of language—the medium of dialogue between writer and reader—I have also raised aligned issues of audience, of multiple audiences, and of role vis-à-vis those audiences. One of the book's most insightful reviewers noted this when he wrote,

Much of [Books I and II] seems to be addressed to students beginning their first course in historiography. Many of Wise's preliminary arguments, distinctions, and suggestions addressed to that audience will be very useful, even though his assumption of the patient, easily colloquial posture of the classroom will often seem condescending to the conventionally professional historians whom he also hopes to enlighten.[10]

I was not, in 1973, sufficiently sensitive to variations in potential audience for the book—not just the obvious variation between academic audiences in history and in American Studies (more on that later), but the much more basic distinction between the professoriat and students. I was at least sensitive enough to realize I did not wish to address the professoriat wholly through its own normal language forms; but beyond that I had no clear sense of the book's audience and its intellectual and social makeup. In retrospect, I now think perhaps some kind of ideal reader was working in me, but not at a level I was conscious of. That ideal reader was much like students I had experienced at Raymond—intensely inquisitive and responsive to intellectual experience, but with no formal background or socialization in the professional study of historical ideas. I had come to Raymond straight from graduate school, and at a time—the early 1960s—when hopes were high for what students could do in a supportive academic climate. Several of those hopes were to be realized in the college's highly charged intellectual atmosphere, and during my six years there, Raymond—rather than my professional associations—provided my basic reference point for scholarly inquiry.

In such an atmosphere, many of the hierarchical distinctions between faculty and students could be let down, and with no necessary diminution of intellectual rigor (often, in fact, with an intensification of same, for students would sometimes apply this rigor to areas that faculty might not think of). This meant, among other things, that teachers did not have to bear full responsibility for the development of their courses; in the intimate seminar atmosphere, students quickly came to identify with the class as "their" obligation too, not just "Professor X's." It also meant that students could be addressed not as empty reservoirs to be filled with knowledge, but as more or less equal colleagues in inquiry (not as wholly equal, to be sure, the professor was still first among equals, or at least tried to be when necessary). And it meant that a class from first day to last would be seen not as a straight road from ignorance toward knowledge, but as a journey along which there would be many side paths and back paths as well as the main route.

Now, little more than a decade and a half after Raymond's opening, all this sounds hopelessly quaint and naive. Nothing of the sort could work today, we are certain; yet work it did during much of the sixties— sometimes, to be sure, with consequences less pleasant than the ideals (a community of intellectually electric 17 to 20-year-olds is not always a happy, or healthy, community). In any case, when in 1968 I witnessed the Chicago Democratic Convention, I came to it freighted with the intellectual preoccupations of my previous years at Raymond. All this was implicated in the way I was to construct *American Historical Explanations*.

That may help explain, for example, why I was to choose a *conversational* mode in the book, trying to reduce the usual distance between reader and writer in a work of scholarship.[11] This conversational mode, especially in the opening chapters, was also intended to de-reify the study of historical ideas—to try and understand ideas as radically human acts of all people (save for Benjy Compson and a few others), and not the private reserve of distant intellectual elites.

The dual impact of Raymond and of Chicago also shaped my use of "ing" rather than "ion" words—verbs over nouns—in describing historical ideas. Save for chapter 4, where I was occasionally caricaturing conventional historiographical procedures, I have tried in this book always to convey the work of ideas in active language, never in the passive mode. After Chicago (and Raymond, and Kenneth Burke, and Perry Miller, and Peter Berger and Thomas Luckmann et al.), I have striven to see historical ideas as the actual work of actual people implicated in coping with actual circumstances in their experienced world, rather than the reified product of abstracted "Isms"—Capitalism, Communism, Puritanism, Liberalism, Transcendentalism—which seem to function for scholars (and for some ideologues) outside the human agents who think them.

Also, the impact of Raymond and of Chicago (in this instance, Raymond more than Chicago) helps explain why I have used variable modes of address in the book—employing an informal and casual style in chapter 1, for example, a playful and sing-songy style in parts of chapter 4, a more tightly analytic style in the case study chapters (7–9). As in an actual conversation among people, I have attempted (sometimes I think successfully, sometimes clearly not) to adjust my language and my role to varying situations inside the book, so that words do not simply flow, as in a narrative or an anecdote, but on some occasions flow (or try to), on other occasions pause, stop, meander, or backtrack.

This strategy did not sit well with a few of the book's reviewers, accustomed as they were to the uninterrupted flow of historical narrative. But again, the narrative form is congruent with an unproblematic context where writer and reader share assumptions about each other, and about the subject matter. I was attempting to make that context itself a problem, however, by examining these assumptions. The first chapter starts, for example: "It is fitting—given the dialogue-tenor of this book—that its opening chapter should begin with a question. Or rather, a series of questions. People have ideas. But why? And when? And what can ideas do for them?" (p. 3)

Hence I was obligating the book to a form different from the historical narrative. One critic—an American Studies scholar with background in literary and film criticism—took note of this when he wrote, "The book represents a printed version of a seminar or forum."[12]

Again, I imagine my Raymond experience was instrumental here. For it accustomed me to think of inquiry not along straight and narrow lines— like a superhighway—but along twisting and sometimes meandering ones—more like Route 49 in the California foothills. This "journey" mode of inquiry is evident throughout the book, but is clearest in chapters 5, 6, and 8—"Changes of Mind II: Some Strategies for Focus," "Historical Criticism and 'The Strategic Journey,'" "A Paradigm Revolution in the Making: Parrington and the 'Moments' of Lionel Trilling and Reinhold Niebuhr."

Of course, no form of scholarly inquiry—narrative, journey, or whatever—can be an excuse for losing focus and simply meandering with no clear point in mind. Where that may happen in this book, critics have every right to object. But sometimes focus is not linear—as in a tunnel— but interconnecting—as in a web. And on those occasions a different form for inquiry and explanation is needed. As Arthur O. Lovejoy has written,

The quest of a historical understanding even of single passages in literature often drives the student into fields which at first seem remote enough from his original topic of investigation. The more you press in towards the heart of a narrowly bounded historical problem, the more likely you are to encounter in the problem itself a pressure which drives you outward beyond those bounds.[13]

This raises an aligned issue vis-à-vis style in the book—in this case an issue not of how words and sentences and paragraphs and sections are related to each other, but of the words themselves. A number of historical reviewers thought there was an overuse of jargon in *American Historical Explanations*. Since the most unusual single word I characteristically employ is "paradigm," I sense the objection was not to strange words, but to familiar words used in unfamiliar ways, or to joining words that are normally encountered separately.

The critics have a point. I do habitually use some words in unfamiliar contexts. This is especially true with "form-" words—"idea-form," "reality-form," "book-form," "explanation-form." It is also true with other words or terms that I characteristically bring together and employ as tools for explanation—"situation-strategy," "anomaly-plane," "fault-line," "explanation-strain," "pivotal moment," "critical threshold," "experience-explanation." I realize such terms will prove jarring to some readers, and for that I apologize. But these words too are implicated in context, a context tied to a major emphasis of the book.

That is the concern for *grounded* inquiry—for modes of analysis enabling us to handle ideas, and idea-change, as they are enacted in concrete historical situations. I have alluded to this earlier, in discussing the impact of the Chicago Democratic Convention on my developing methodological consciousness. Having lived through much of the 1960s in California, and witnessing its incredible land forms, I naturally gravitated toward geological metaphors as a way of getting ideas out of the air and onto the ground. And living there amid a decade of incredible change, I gravitated toward the geological earthquake as a means of picturing that change.[14] It struck me that the earthquake metaphor might help in drawing a clearer picture of intellectual change as it happens, just before it happens, and right after.

All these forms, methods, and metaphors were attempts to get at underlying *structures* of historical ideas, below face-value content. It is puzzling that in the midst of a "structural" transformation in American historical studies during the late sixties and seventies, no historical critic noted this structural orientation of *American Historical Explanations*.[15]

In a brilliant historiographical essay, Samuel Hays has claimed that this emphasis on structure—even more than its concern for quantity or for behavior—is the central distinguishing trait of recent "new social histories," marking them off from older social histories of the 1920s, 30s, and 40s.[16] In the years since 1973, I have grown more aware of this structural revolution in the history profession; clearly, some of my strictures against historians on that matter are now dated.

I also should have made more in 1973 of connections between what I was proposing for the structural study of historical *ideas*, and what social historians (Robert Wiebe, Philip Greven, and Kenneth Lockridge, to name three among many) were already doing with structural studies of historical *institutions*. It was only after the book was published that I began to sense those connections, seeing how they relate to forces running through several disciplines of contemporary scholarship. I should like now, seven years afterward, to note a few of those connections—that is, to set *American Historical Explanations* in a wider scholarly context.

III

One item passed over by reviewers is the book's discussion of "information-overload." It protests the glut of knowledge produced by modern scholarship and asks that we devise intellectual strategies to cope with that glut. Although not a dominant theme in the book, the issue of information-overload is introduced early (in the Prologue), and countering it provides an underlying rationale for a good deal that follows in the analysis.

No reviewer made much of this theme, only one or two even mentioned it. Or rather, this was true with historical reviewers; American Studies commentators did take note, usually supporting the book's concerns.[17]

This fact is noteworthy, for it relates to a larger matter of the book's reception by different scholarly audiences. Historical reviewers were generally more comfortable with the case-study chapters in the latter part of the volume; where they praised the book, it was for the contributions to substantive knowledge therein. Historians were uncomfortable with the opening chapters, however, where I introduce several methodological problems, and where the experiments with scholarly form and style are concentrated. But commentators from American Studies tended to focus on these early chapters, noting only in passing the latter parts of the book. This is also true with those who have commented on the book from other scholarly disciplines.

There is a paradox, then, in the scholarly reception of *American Historical Explanations*. The book's subject matter—ideas of American historians—falls most directly in intellectual history and historiography, yet it has had but slight impact on those fields.[18] It has been recognized, however, in several other fields—in American Studies theory and method, in general social science theory and method, in American literary history, in American diplomatic history, in the philosophy of history, in early 19th-century American history, in Southern American history, in women's studies, in published reports on undergraduate and graduate history curricula. It has also been cited by quantitative historians, by psychohistorians, historians of ethnicity, students of popular culture.[19]

In a way, all this is gratifying. The book has been noted in many areas of scholarship, even if it has not had deep impact on any. But the reception is disappointing too, for I had hoped for more from academic historians, especially historians of ideas. Their praise was reserved for the most conventional parts of the book, those easiest to do, at least in form.

But they tended to ignore or reject those sections of the volume that were most challenging for me, where I felt my efforts to construct alternative forms for inquiry were not only the most basic, but the most necessary.

For some time after the book was first published, this reception proved a grave disappointment. Now, however, with the perspective of time and intervening experience, my concern has moderated some. That is because I have come to understand the matter in a different context.

In the book's first edition, I saw the information-overload dilemma in classic intellectual history terms, as a matter largely of *ideas*. But after having been exposed more to the new social history, also having sat on numerous appointment, promotion, and tenure committees in large university settings and processed numerous applications from people I have never seen but know only through the printed word, I now see this dilemma as a problem of *structure* too, as well as of ideas. Or, to put it another way, when I passed in consciousness beyond the Gemeinschaft-like college atmosphere of Raymond to the Gesellschaft-like multiversity context, I came gradually to realize that modern scholarship's "contribution-to-knowledge" syndrome has an institutional momentum which will not be affected by addressing it as an idea alone. To ask individual scholars to change their minds is one thing, to challenge the structure and the dynamics of scholarly institutions is quite another.

In short, the dilemma of scholarly over-production comes to look like any other large-scale bureaucratic problem in a modernized society. In our world, productive scholarship has many functions—most, I think, beneficial, some not. But beneficial or no, those functions are the consequence not wholly or even primarily of individual willed decisions, but of the power of organized collectivities.[20]

At the production end of the matter, institutions of scholarship have a dynamic of their own, often severed from anything outside themselves. Hence the several disciplinary associations, the scholarly convention meetings, academic journals of publication, book publishing houses, research-funding organizations, and a host of other organized groupings have vested interests in keeping up the pace of productivity, regardless of needs in the larger society for the scholarship they produce (or even of needs inside the scholarly world; that world produces far more scholarship than it can meaningfully consume).

At the evaluation end of the issue, the problem is somewhat different, but the end product is similar—more scholarship than we know what to do with. We are aware of the incredible growth of the multiversity since the second world war, but we have not sufficiently questioned how that growth has increased the pressure for scholarly production. Universities that little more than a generation ago housed, say, 5,000 students today may handle 25,000. And academic departments that a few years back housed 10 faculty members in a collegial atmosphere now may contain

50—in a context that, on the basis of size alone, makes collegiality decidedly problematic. Add to large size the accompanying specialization of scholarly labor (now one is not an *American* historian, but an American *diplomatic* historian, or perhaps a *20th-century* American diplomatic historian), add also the generational and other demographic divisions within the scholarly population which the pace of contemporary change has accentuated, and collegiality becomes even more problematic. Finally, multiply this growth by every academic unit in the multiversity, add to that the parallel growth of a cumbersome administrative bureaucracy enmeshed increasingly in academic decisions, and any semblance of scholarly collegiality is all but overwhelmed.

Then take all this machinery and address it to the evaluation of individual scholarly achievements—an issue exacerbated by the tight academic job market and the no-growth state of academe these days. The result is a situation where, to borrow from Emerson, indeed "things are in the saddle and ride mankind."

Academic administrators and department chairs may proclaim (especially for the local student newspaper audience and to state legislators) that teaching, advising, and university service count equally with productive scholarship in matters of appointment, promotion, and tenure. They may in fact believe that, and intend to act on their beliefs. But they cannot. They are assumed to be at the centers of academic power in the multiversity, yet they are virtually impotent to counter the prevailing trend (assuming they wish to, which most do not). For the issue is not so much individual will or intent, but the functional imperative to process masses of people in gigantic bureaucratic surroundings. Teaching, advising, and service may be meaningfully judged in intimate, Gemeinschaft-like settings; but they are too intangible to count much in the extra-personal, Gesellschaft-like environment of today's multiversity.

So evaluators are left with scholarly productivity, which does function as a rough index of quality, or at least it can be measured and weighed in large numbers. At the crudest level, productivity is convenient to count—two published articles make for contract renewal, a book counts for tenure, and so on (or, if the market situation allows, the ante can be upped; four articles for contract renewal, one book plus another in press for tenure). At the next crudest level, productivity can be weighed as well as counted. Perhaps not any article will do, but only articles published in the five leading journals in the field (which journals, given the sophistication of modern counting devices, can be weighed and measured too). Or not any book, but only books published by a university press, or, more precisely, one of the top ten university presses.

The point, then, is that the sheer weight of numbers, the attendant division of scholarly labor, the fragmentation of collegiality, and the need to justify academic decisions to audiences and powers increasingly remote from the scene of original action generate a momentum for productivity that feeds upon itself. The scholarly assembly line runs faster and faster, not necessarily because individuals will it to, but because no one knows how to slow it down.

A generation ago, three of the finest works of American culture studies scholarship were the first books published by their respective authors. Judged through today's operating categories, we might think it late for these authors to be coming out with their first books. Henry Nash Smith was 45 when *Virgin Land* was published, R. W. B. Lewis 38 at the publication of *The American Adam*, Leo Marx 45 at the publication of *The Machine in the Garden*. Given the pressures for speedy publication these days, it is doubtful if Minnesota, Rutgers, and Amherst would be willing to wait so long for Smith, Lewis, and Marx to get their scholarship together. Either they would be obliged to hurry up their books by several years, or they would doubtless be passed over in promotion and tenure decisions for "more productive" scholars who could meet today's timetables.

That such an eventuality would be reprehensible—especially, and ironically, for the quality of scholarship—is obvious. But I see more clearly today than I did seven years ago that protests against information-overload, and the contribution-to-knowledge rhetoric which helps generate it, are powerless unless they penetrate to social structural dynamics undergirding the issue. Or rather to social structural dynamics historically conceived. Hence my own evolution on this matter—from viewing it as problem of ideas to viewing it as a problem of ideas embedded in social structures functioning through time—is precisely an evolution from an intellectual history form of explanation to an explanation resembling that of the new social history.

IV

Manifestly, *American Historical Explanations* is not a work of new social history. Its focus is on ideas of historians, and it does little with social relations in historians' communities. Nor does it address the social systems, in academe and in the world of scholarship, within which these communities function. It does address matters in the wider culture, but mostly through ideas and events, not through underlying institutional dynamics. Although the category "new social history" was familiar to me at the time, I had read little in the genre by 1973, when my book was first published.

Yet if the book is concerned mainly with ideas and I wrote it mostly innocent of new social history categories, it is not a work wholly of old intellectual history either. I have already referred to my Raymond and Chicago experiences; their impact, plus other experiences of the 1960s and my reading in works of historians, had sparked my increasing rest-lessness with existing conventions of intellectual history. Thus I wrote in the 1973 Prologue:

As a field of inquiry, intellectual history has waned since the mid-1960s; because it has lacked forms to handle change very well, it can't convey variety effectively, it can't get its ideas into motion, it can't connect ideas into the concrete events of history, it can't detect strains or cracks in an idea—it can't, in short, *ground intellectual abstractions in the life-experiences of people.* (p. xiii)

My concern for "grounding," then, was an effort to get at the ecologi-cal settings of ideas, and this parallels new social historians' focus on the institutional contexts of peoples' lives. My analytic tools for grounding—"situation-strategy" analysis, the focus on "anomaly-planes," "explanation-strain," "fault-lines," and "threshold moments"—were ef-forts to build methodological self-consciousness and more precise modes of focus into historical inquiry; these also parallel concerns of the new social history. And my use of "earthquake" metaphors was a way to visualize structural change in historical ideas, again paralleling new social historians' concern for ways of understanding institutional change. All this means that *American Historical Explanations* resides in an intellectual history subject matter, but points toward a number of social history-like methods.

Yet it falls short on some of those methods too. From the perspective of new social history, the book's most substantial shortcoming is its lack of an institutional sense. It does ground ideas in *situational* contexts, but it does not take the further step of grounding them in *institutional* settings too. That is because by 1973 I had not yet come to understand what now seems to me obvious—social institutions have a power in human experience that is not simply an extension of ideas. Or, to put it another way, when you understand the ideas behind an institution, you have understood only part of that institution's functioning.

This, I think, is perhaps the most vital insight of the new social history, and it is missing from *American Historical Explanations*. There is, of course, nothing magic about the new social history. For a time, many in the form became overzealous about counting; the disaster of *Time on the Cross* brought them up short, and brought the profession back to a saner sense of the limitations as well as the virtues of statistical modes of expla-nation.[21] For a time also, adepts of the form overcompensated for the previous lack of an institutional sense by shoving out ideas altogether, presuming human behavior could be understood without considering the meanings people associate with that behavior.

Both excesses, I think, were salutary in their time, and were necessary to break through a wall of humanistic prejudice in the profession that hitherto had tended to block behavioral and institutional perspectives. But the excesses ran their course in the late sixties and early seventies, and in recent years we have seen a rapprochement of intellectual and institutional perspectives. The point now is not one or the other—not ideas or institutions—but the various ways ideas *trans-act* with institutions, and vice versa.

Much of the best historical scholarship over the last decade is focused on precisely those transactions. I think, for example, of Kenneth Lockridge's *A New England Town*, Darrett Rutman's *American Puritanism*, Philip Greven's *Four Generations*, and John Demos' *A Little Commonwealth* (all published in 1970); John Blassingame's *The Slave Community* and Sam Bass Warner's *Urban Wilderness* (both 1972); Daniel Boorstin's *The Americans: The Democratic Experience*, James Henretta's *The Evolution of American Society, 1700–1815*, Stephan Thernstrom's *The Other Bostonians: Poverty and Progress in the American Metropolis, 1880–1970*, and Katherine Kish Sklar's *Catherine Beecher: A Study in American Domesticity* (all 1973); Paul Boyer and Stephen Nissenbaum's *Salem Possessed: The Social Origins of Witchcraft*, Eugene Genovese's *Roll, Jordan Roll*, and Gordon Kelly's *Mother Was A Lady: Self and Society in Selected American Children's Periodicals, 1865–1890* (all 1974); Robert Sklar's *Movie-Made America*, Edmund Morgan's *American Slavery, American Freedom*, Daniel Walker Howe's "American Victorianism as a Culture" (*American Quarterly*, December), and David Brion Davis' *The Problem of Slavery in an Age of Revolution, 1770–1825* (all 1975); Herbert Gutman's *The Black Family in Slavery and Freedom, 1750–1925* and *Work, Culture and Society in Industrializing America*, Richard Brown's *Modernization: The Transformation of American Life, 1600–1865*, Linda Gordon's *Woman's Body, Woman's Right*, Burton Bledstein's *The Culture of Professionalism*, and Henry Glassie's *Folk Housing in Middle Virginia* (all 1976); Thomas Haskell's *The Emergence of Professional Social Science*, Harry Stout's "Religion, Communications, and the Ideological Origins of the American Revolution" (*William and Mary Quarterly*, October), Bruce Kuklick's *The Rise of American Philosophy: Cambridge, Massachusetts, 1860–1930*, David Stannard's *The American Way of Death*, Nancy Cott's *The Bonds of Womanhood: "Women's Sphere" in New England, 1750–1825*, Richard Horwitz' *Anthropology toward History: Culture and Work in a 19th-Century Maine Town*, Lawrence Levine's *Black Culture and Black Consciousness: Afro-American Folk Culture from Slavery to Freedom*, Lonna Malmsheimer's "Daughters of Zion: New England Roots of American Feminism" (*New England Quarterly*, September), Richard Beeman's "The New Social History and the Search for 'Community' in Colonial America" (*American Quarterly*, Fall), and Ann Douglas' *The Feminization of American Culture* (all 1977); Robert Berkhofer's *The White Man's Indian*, Anthony F. C. Wallace's *Rockdale: The Growth of an American Village in the Early Industrial Revolution*, Paul Boyer's *Urban Masses and Moral Order in America, 1820–1920*, Daniel Rodgers' *The Work Ethic in Industrial America, 1850–1920*, Joyce Appleby's "The Social Origins of American Revolutionary Ideology" (*Journal of American History*, March), and Andrew Achenbaum's *Old Age in the New Land: The American Experience since 1790* (all 1978); Jay Mechling's "If They Can Build a Square Tomato: Notes Toward a Holistic Approach to Regional Studies" (*Prospects*, January), and John Higham and Paul Conkin's anthology *New Directions in American Intellectual History* (both 1979).[22]

These works—and countless others like them—testify to a remarkable flowering of American historical-cultural thinking in recent years. They transcend old intellectual history categories in giving social structural grounding to ideas. And they transcend the most restricted of new social history categories by giving intellectual and emotional coloring to institutions and to measurable behavior. Taken together, they span almost all of America's history (least covered is the 20th century, and the pre-Columbian past). And they have illuminated transactions between ideas and institutions in the study of: *urban communities* (Warner, Thernstrom, Horwitz, Wallace, Boyer), *material artifacts* (Demos, Boorstin, Glassie), *social generations* (Lockridge, Greven, Kelly), *land use* (Lockridge, Greven, Boyer and Nissenbaum), *ethnicity and race* (Blassingame, Genovese, Morgan, Gutman, Davis, Levine, Berkhofer), *community* (Lockridge, Greven, Blassingame, Genovese, Beeman, Horwitz, Wallace, Mechling), *social roles* (K. Sklar, Gordon, Douglas, Cott, Malmsheimer), *social boundaries* (Kelly, Boyer), *academic communities* (Bledstein, Haskell, Kuklick), *ideology* (Rutman, Kelly, Howe, Brown, Bledstein, Haskell, Appleby, Stout, Rodgers), *social order* (Boorstin, Kelly, Brown, Boyer), *scenes or situations* (Rutman, Boyer and Nissenbaum), *social change* (Lockridge, Greven, Henretta, Thernstrom, Brown), *family* (Lockridge, Demos, Greven, Blassingame, Kelly, Gutman, K. Sklar), *region* (Morgan, Wallace, Mechling), *folk culture* (Blassingame, Genovese, Boorstin, Glassie, Levine), *media* (Kelly, R. Sklar), *work* (Gutman, Horwitz, Rodgers), and *death* (Stannard).

The new social history has given us powerful intellectual tools for inquiry; with these tools we can self-consciously pose questions of and gain leverage on our historical evidence, rather than simply narrating and chronicling it. And, transcending its earlier limitations, the new social history has shown promise of joining back with a previously rejected concern for ideas and values, to forge a new form of *cultural history* that respects both institutional and ideational dimensions of people's lives.[23]

V

In my 1973 Prologue to this book, I wrote that "work in American historiography and historical method is still produced by individual curious adventurers; it does not comprise a clearly defined field, and it has done little to affect work done elsewhere by practicing American historians.'' (xvi) To counter this situation, I proposed a new subfield for the profession devoted to theory and criticism in American historical studies.

That suggestion has proved most un-prophetic. If anything, with the decline in influence of intellectual history, American historiographical studies have waned rather than waxed in the profession of late. Some excellent work has been done in the seventies, by such scholars as David Hackett Fischer, Robert Berkhofer, David Hollinger, Robert Shalhope, Murray Murphey, Michael Kammen, Richard Reinitz, Kenneth Lynn, Bernard Sternsher, among others. But again these are individual curious adventurers (at least in their historiography work), and their work does not feed into any group identity of historical scholarship. In that sense, *American Historical Explanations* in 1980 as much as in 1973 exists outside any established field of inquiry in the profession.[24]

But if this is the case for the discipline of history, it is not so for American Studies. That, I think, is because my book addresses two concerns that have become increasingly visible in American Studies during the 1970s—the emphasis on methodic self-consciousness, or *"reflexiveness,"* and the emphasis on *modes of cognition*. The former emphasis has been expressed in a number of articles critiquing past scholarship in the field, and proposing new forms for inquiry; the latter emphasis is dramatized in the movement by the influence of Peter Berger and Thomas Luckmann's *The Social Construction of Reality*, and by an attraction for cognitive anthropology. These two emphases—reflexiveness and concern for modes of cognition—have developed largely in tandem over the last decade.

The reflexive movement in American Studies dates its beginnings to the late sixties and early seventies. Most instrumental, perhaps, were the founding of the ASA Radical Caucus at the Toledo national convention in 1969; Robert Sklar's *American Quarterly* essay of 1970, ''American Studies and the Realities of America''; Bruce Kuklick's *American Quarterly* article of 1972, ''Myth and Symbol in American Studies''; and the 1973 program statement of the University of California at Davis, ''American Culture Studies: The Discipline and the Curriculum.''[25]

Although Sklar's and Kuklick's essays came to reflexiveness from different locations (Sklar's imperative was wider cultural events of the sixties, Kuklick's was scholarly problems of philosophical analysis), each took issue with past scholarship in the field (particularly the symbol-myth-image explanation), and each called for new scholarly modes more appropriate to actual American experience. The Davis program statement added to this reflexive temper a specific aim for the field—that American Studies align its future to the development of the ''culture concept.''

Americanists, of course, had been talking of the culture concept for some time before the seventies. In his influential *American Quarterly* essay of 1957—"Can 'American Studies' Develop a Method?"—Henry Nash Smith had spoken of the need for such an integrating concept, but thought the movement was a long way from actually developing it. Six years later, Richard Sykes—in "American Studies and the Concept of Culture"—not only promoted the culture concept generally for the movement, but suggested what particular kind of concept was needed. He thought it should come mainly through anthropology and the social sciences, not through literature and the humanities.[26]

Sykes was proven correct—if not immediately, then a decade later when a new generation of American Studies scholars were to gravitate toward the social sciences for tools of cultural analysis. The first route was cognitive sociology, the vehicle Peter Berger and Thomas Luckmann's *The Social Construction of Reality*.[27]

Berger and Luckmann's message is deceptively simple—that human reality is defined through the social interactions and social institutions of people, and is not the product of any extra-human force. To this elementary axiom they added several corollaries—that people's ideas are best studied in actions of everyday life, and not in the abstractions of intellectuals; that different societies build and maintain their social universes in different ways, and that a key to any given society's codes is its particular mechanisms for universe maintenance; that another key to a society's codes lies in how it socializes new people (infants, immigrants, etc.) into its particular universe; that every person is a bearer of the society's codes and thus an apt subject for study.

Although the Berger and Luckmann volume was readily adopted in American Studies classrooms soon after it appeared in 1966, the authors' message was first conveyed to a wide scholarly audience in the field in 1974, through Gordon Kelly's *American Quarterly* article, "Literature and the Historian."[28] There Kelly challenged Leo Marx's earlier contention that great classics of literature embody universal truths about the human experience; Kelly said instead that such works of literature, like all humanly constructed artifacts, are products of time and place and person and milieu and institution, and are to be understood in these situational contexts, not in culturally transcendental terms. Berger and Luckmann have also been applied, in American Studies scholarship, to studies of American children's literature, to understanding New England Puritan funeral sermons, to analyses of women's role in American literature, to the dynamics of teaching introductory courses in the field, and to studies in American regionalism.[29]

Of late, people in American Studies have also taken another route toward more systematic, social science-oriented use of the culture concept—this time the more direct route of anthropology. Or, more specifically, cognitive anthropology.

Here the agents of influence have been more multiple than in cognitive sociology, where Berger and Luckmann have dominated the scene. Most influential perhaps has been the anthropologist Anthony F. C. Wallace—mainly through his essay "Culture and Cognition," later republished in his notable book *Culture and Personality*. Also influential has been the work of James Spradley—especially *The Cultural Experience: Ethnography in a Complex Society* (written with David McCurdy), *You Owe Yourself a Drunk: An Ethnography of Urban Nomads*, and *The Cocktail Waitress: Woman's Work in a Man's World* (written with Brenda Mann).[30]

Cognitive anthropologists take a perspectivistic, or in their terms "emic," approach to cultural reality—attempting to see the world from the inside out, that is, through the eyes of their informants. Like Berger and Luckmann, they seek to discover how that world is patterned, in a culture's underlying codes; and their pre-eminent concern is for the perceived everyday working reality of ordinary people. Hence their approach had fed into an increasing emphasis on fieldwork in the American Studies movement.

This mode of inquiry first appeared in American Studies scholarship in 1972, through John Caughey's *American Quarterly* article, "Simulating the Past: A Method for Using Ethnosemantics in Historical Research." There Caughey—an anthropology Ph.D. himself with extensive field experience in the Far East, the Middle East, and the United States—laid out some fundamental methodological propositions of this "new ethnography," and suggested how historians might use these in addressing documents of America's cultural past. Five years later, Jay Mechling linked the movement's future with cognitive anthropology when he wrote, "The goal of doing American Studies is to unmask the deep-structure rules which Americans use to give meaning to their environment and which they use to generate appropriate or acceptable behavior within that environment."[31]

The same year as Mechling's essay—1977—Richard Beeman took issue with use of the new ethnography in American culture studies. In an *American Quarterly* article on "The New Social History and the Search for 'Community' in Colonial America," Beeman stated that the method of "componential analysis" in cognitive anthropology—that is, its habit of itemizing the codes of a culture—is too static and mechanical. He suggested that students of American culture might better use the more dynamic concepts of anthropologists Clifford Geertz, Victor Turner, and Robert Redfield.[32]

Beeman's article joins a tradition in the discipline of anthropology critical of the new ethnography. In a notable essay entitled "Paradigms Lost: The New Ethnography and the New Linguistics," Roger Keesing lamented in 1972 that some cognitive anthropologists have engaged in "taxonomic rummaging around in the surface stuff of culture." He went on to suggest that the more zealous of new ethnographers have "often implied that things and events in the phenomenal world are only means through which an underlying cognitive code—the proper study of anthropology—can be apprehended."[33]

Keesing thus thought that cognitive anthropologists have taken an overly idealist stance, presuming that merely charting the ideas of individuals in a culture is sufficient to explain the culture's behavior. Keesing thought not. And, like Richard Beeman, he favored Clifford Geertz's dramatistic efforts at "thick description" over the componential analysis of new ethnographers. As he put it in a 1974 review essay on scholarship in the field,

Like Levi-Strauss, Geertz is at his best when he draws on general theory to interpret ethnographic particulars; unlike Levi-Strauss, he finds these particulars in the richness of real people in real life: a cockfight, a funeral, a sheep theft. His texts are not disembodied and decontextualized myths or customs, but humans engaging in symbolic action.

Keesing concluded, "Geertz sees the cognitive view of [Ward] Goodenough and the 'new ethnographers' as reductionistic and spuriously formalistic. Meanings are not 'in people's heads'; symbols and meanings are shared by social actors—between, not in them: they are public, not private."[34]

Keesing's critique—addressed to anthropologists—has proven prophetic for American Studies too. This fact is dramatized by an extraordinary scholarly session, "On the Shoulders of Giants," held at the fall 1979 national convention of the American Studies Association.[35] The "giants" under review were Gregory Bateson, Clifford Geertz, and Berger and Luckmann; standing "on their shoulders" were Jay Mechling, Karen Lystra, and Gordon Kelly, who tried to show how the work of these anthropologists and sociologists was applicable to issues in American culture studies.

Mechling focused on Bateson's concern for "the pattern which connects"—that is, the capacity to probe for the structure underlying the surface content, and to connect one underlying structure to another in the process of cultural explanation. Kelly focused on Berger and Luckmann's phenomenological approach, also on their concern for modes of socialization through institutions.

Lystra attempted a synthesis of these positions, made possible by the comprehensive vision of her author, Clifford Geertz. Like Richard Beeman and Roger Keesing, Lystra noted that for Geertz culture is not simply "knowledge in the mind" (as it is for some cognitive anthropologists), but rather it is enacted in public events in the world. The event, or the cultural anecdote, provides the central arena for cultural analysis, the point of focus from which Geertz attempts "thick description."

Noting Geertz's early training under Talcott Parsons, Lystra distinguished five different levels of force acting on humans—the cultural, the biological, the social, the psychological, and the nonhuman physical. Geertz is strongest on the cultural, the biological, and the social, she affirmed, and weakest on the psychological. This, she thought, was because he had done most of his fieldwork in relatively homogeneous societies and had not been obliged to confront individual and subcultural variation characteristic of large, heterogeneous societies. Any translation of Geertz's methods to American culture studies would be obliged to take this shortcoming into account, she noted.

Thus we find in Lystra, in Mechling and Kelly, and in Richard Beeman a trend in American Studies inquiry away from modes of cognition toward public behavior and institutional structures. Or rather, the trend is not so much away from modes of cognition in cultural inquiry as it is an effort to take into account public behavior and institutional structures while looking at cognition, and vice versa. Which trend in American Studies is almost precisely what we saw earlier in the discipline of history—from intellectual history to social history in the sixties and earlier seventies, and now toward a new form of integrating cultural history.

VI

Hence in contemporary American culture studies—both from history and from American Studies—we see increasing use of the social sciences in scholarly inquiry. This borrowing is not only from theoretical social science, as on occasions in the past, but from the institutional and behavioral side of the social sciences too.

Adepts of this form of inquiry see *culture*, and not necessarily *America*, as their pre-eminent subject of scholarship. This shift of focus, sometimes slight and subtle, is significant nonetheless in directing inquiry toward deep-structural forms and away from exclusive preoccupation with content. The shift is clearest perhaps in American Studies—whose programs in the past often aimed for a "broad training in Americana," requiring students to take courses scattered all across the academic curriculum with "American" in their titles. Now concern in the field is less for covering "things American," and more for cultivating tools of inquiry to understand "matters cultural." As Murray Murphey has written of the program at Pennsylvania that pioneered in this shift, "In every case, our emphasis is upon the systematic character of culture—upon the patterned interaction of individuals as occupants of significant social positions. We are not concerned with the unique event, if such a thing exists, but with what is typical of the group." [36]

In its concern for understanding the forms of cultural experience, this emphasis aims to *gain leverage* on its materials. It looks for the dynamic construct-ing of cultural reality rather than at a completed reality already constructed, and it seeks methods and metaphors that will illumine the processes whereby cultures construct and perennially re-construct themselves (hence the "exemplar" status of a work like Berger and Luckmann's *The Social Construction of Reality*).[37]

In some of its more belligerent pronouncements, this emphasis has tended to dismiss pre-1970 American studies uninformed by the new dispensation. A more reflexive sense of the past would indicate that such a view is short-sighted, however. For much of the "new" position— focusing on dynamic process and underlying structure rather than surface content—is prefigured in at least two works of the 1950s that have hitherto been seen as noteworthy but not especially for this emphasis. I refer to Perry Miller's *The New England Mind: From Colony to Province* (1953) and R. W. B. Lewis's *The American Adam* (1955). Neither Miller nor Lewis was much inclined to social science borrowings, and their subjects are hopelessly elitist by today's standards. Yet each has this sense of a cultural reality in the making in his respective historical era, and each devised ways to convey that sense not only in his content but in the form and style of his work.[38] That this point is absent from our present understanding is not the fault of Miller's or Lewis's scholarship, but of the poor state of scholarly criticism in the field. What Lewis wrote of American intellectual movements is apt for American historical studies too:

America, since the age of Emerson, has been persistently a one-generation culture. Successive generations have given rise to a series of staccato intellectual and literary movements with ever slighter trajectories. . . . The unluckiest consequence . . . has not been incoherence, but the sheer dulness of unconscious repetition. We regularly return, decade after decade and with the same pain and amazement, to all the old conflicts, programs, and discoveries. We consume our powers in hoisting ourselves back to the plane of understanding reached a century ago and at intervals since.[39]

And this is the final message I should like to leave with *American Historical Explanations*. Not that I anticipated or failed to anticipate this or that movement of contemporary scholarship in 1973. But that we not be so rushed in our work—either in covering our primary materials or in reviewing past scholarship in the field—that we allow important matters to get by us too quickly. Otherwise we offer not a critical perspective on our future-shocked and information-overloaded culture, but enslave ourselves to a mirror image of it.

Gene Wise
University of Maryland

NOTES

1. For more on this Raymond College experience, see chapter 3, "The Book-Form: Historians and Primary Documents," pp. 60–63, 68–71. See also my article "American Civ.

at Raymond: The 'Cluster' Academy as Radical Alternative,'' *American Quarterly* (Summer, 1970), pp. 464–488.

2. However circuitous my own backward journey into methodology may seem, it is hardly unique. Many others, particularly those around my own generation and younger in American culture studies, have gravitated toward methodological concerns not wholly because of forces inside the profession of scholarship, but because of events in the world outside too, or in the classroom.

This "reflexive" movement is no respecter of disciplinary boundaries, hence it has influenced almost every field of contemporary scholarship. But it became visible earliest in the discipline of sociology—mainly through the influence of C. Wright Mills (*The Sociological Imagination*) and Alvin Gouldner (*The Coming Crisis of Western Sociology*). It received a gigantic boost in 1962 with the publication of Thomas Kuhn's *The Structure of Scientific Revolutions*—a work whose major impact has not been on scientific communities but in the humanities and social sciences.

Strains of a reflexive temper can be found, in American culture studies, in Bernard Cohn, "An Anthropologist among the Historians: A Field Study," *The South Atlantic Quarterly* (Winter, 1962), pp. 13–28; Richard Sykes, "American Studies and the Concept of Culture," *American Quarterly* (Summer, 1963), pp. 253–270; Martin Duberman, *The Uncompleted Past* (Random House, 1969); David Hackett Fischer, *Historians' Fallacies: Toward a Logic of Historical Thought* (Harper and Row, 1970); Robert Sklar, "American Studies and the Realities of America," *American Quarterly* (August, 1970), pp. 597–605; Robert Berkhofer, "Clio and the Culture Concept: Some Impressions of a Changing Relationship in American Historiography," *Social Science Quarterly* (September, 1972), pp. 297–320; Jay Mechling, Robert Merideth, and David Wilson, "American Culture Studies: The Discipline and the Curriculum," *American Quarterly* (October, 1973); Sklar, "The Problem of an American Studies 'Philosophy': A Bibliography of New Directions," *American Quarterly* (Summer, 1975), pp. 245–262; Richard Dorson, *The Birth of American Studies* (Inaugural Address at Founding of American Studies Center at Warsaw University, Poland, October 5, 1976); Thomas Haskell, *The Emergence of Professional Social Science: The American Social Science Association and the Nineteenth Century Crisis of Authority* (Illinois, 1977); Bruce Kuklick, *The Rise of American Philosophy: Cambridge, Massachusetts, 1860–1930* (Yale, 1977); Luther Luedtke, "Not so Common Ground: Controversies in Contemporary American Studies," in Luedtke, ed., *The Study of American Culture: Contemporary Conflicts* (Everett Edwards, 1977), pp. 323–367; Mechling, "If They Can Build a Square Tomato: Notes toward a Holistic Approach to Regional Studies," *Prospects*, IV (Burt Franklin, 1979), pp. 59–78; and my "Some Elementary Axioms for an American Culture Studies," *Prospects*, IV (Burt Franklin, 1979), pp. 517–547.

3. See chapter 5 for my working out of this "situational" strategy for grounding historical ideas. The strategy is applied to actual historical, or rather historiographical, situations in the case study chapters—7 through 9.

4. For more on this earlier ascent of American intellectual history studies, see John Higham's notable essay, "The Rise of American Intellectual History," *American Historial Review* (April, 1951), pp. 453–471. For the decline of such studies in recent years and their eclipse by other fields in the profession, see my "The Contemporary Crisis in Intellectual History Studies," *CLIO* (Winter, 1975), pp. 55–71; and Laurence Veysey, "Intellectual History and the New Social History," in Higham and Paul Conkin, eds., *New Directions in American Intellectual History* (Johns Hopkins, 1979), pp. 3–26.

5. Richard King, Review in *Journal of American History* (March, 1974), p. 1083; Joel Jones, in *American Literary Realism* (Spring, 1974), p. 112; David Hollinger, Review in *The American Historical Review* (April, 1975), p. 475; Bernard Sternsher, *Consensus, Conflict, and American Historians* (Indiana, 1975), p. 4; Thomas Pressly, Review in *Civil War History* (September, 1975), p. 270; Dorson, *Birth, op. cit.*; Sternsher, *op. cit.*, p. 4; Allan Bogue, Review in *Journal of Interdisciplinary History* (Winter, 1975), p. 526.

6. Linda Kerber, Review in *Social Science Quarterly* (December, 1974), p. 805; Hollinger, *op. cit.*, p. 476; *ibid.*, p. 475; *ibid.*, p. 476; Bogue, *op cit.*, p. 527; King, *op cit.*, p. 1084.

7. Kerber, *op. cit.*, p. 805.

8. Whatever touching up of the language there may be in this second edition, I have done nothing to alter content. Nor would I want to. The book deserves to stand, or fall, on its own

message, and I believe in 1980 as strongly as I did in 1973 that that message is worth hearing. So the revisions herein are intended only to clarify the original message, not to alter it.

9. For Thomas Kuhn on "normal" scholarship, see his chapters "The Route to Normal Science," "The Nature of Normal Science," "Normal Science as Puzzle-Solving," "The Priority of Paradigms," in *The Structure of Scientific Revolutions* (Chicago, rev. ed., 1970—first edition in 1962), pp. 10–51.

10. David Levin, Review in *CLIO* (June, 1974), pp. 342–343.

11. My effort to reduce the distance between reader and writer also helps explain the too frequent resort to the pronoun "we" when I really meant "I" in the book. This was not the editorial "we" so much as an attempt to invite the reader into the intellectual journey alongside the writer, also to strike a personal voice as an alternative to the normal objectivist address in scholarship. But in an effort to reduce the distance between writer and reader, the use of "we" in effect pretended that this distinction did not even exist, and that pretense I now think was a mistake.

12. Myron Lounsbury, Review in *Chesapeake American Studies Quarterly* (Fall, 1973), p. 16.

13. Arthur O. Lovejoy, "Reflections on the History of Ideas," *Journal of the History of Ideas* (January, 1940), p. 5.

14. See Robert Iacopi, *Earthquake Country: How, Why and Where Earthquakes Strike in California* (Sunset, 1971).

15. The only critic to make much of my book as a structural study was the social scientist John Heyl, in a survey of Thomas Kuhn's impact on contemporary scholarship. See "Paradigms in Social Science," *Society* (July-August, 1975), pp. 61–67.

16. Samuel Hays, "A Systematic Social History," in George Athan Billias and Gerald Grob, eds., *American History: Retrospect and Prospect* (Free Press, 1971), pp. 315–366.

17. See Richard Dorson and Myron Lounsbury, *op cits.* See also Howard Gillette and Janelle Findley, "Teaching the 1930's: A Cultural Approach," *Chesapeake American Studies Quarterly* (April, 1974), p. 1; and Susan Tamke, "Oral History and Popular Culture: A Method for the Study of the Experience of Culture," *Journal of Popular Culture* (Summer, 1977), p. 278.

18. Two major journals of intellectual history/historiography—the *Journal of the History of Ideas* and *History and Theory*—did not review the book, nor did the *American Quarterly*.

19. If the book has been thinly received, or not received at all, in forums of intellectual history/historiography, it has been noted in several other journals dotted across the scholarly landscape—*Daedalus*, the *American Scholar, American Literary Realism, Amerasia Journal*, the *Journal of Southern History, Societas, Computers and the Humanities*, the *Social Science Quarterly*, the *Journal of Popular Culture*, the *Journal of Interdisciplinary History*, the *Chesapeake American Studies Quarterly, Journalism History, The Old Northwest, Society, Civil War History*.

20. I have written at more length on "information-overload" as a structural and intellectual problem in two essays published recently. See my "Historical Thought and the 'Invisible Governments' of Scholarship," *Reviews in American History* (December, 1974), pp. 568–575, and "Some Elementary Axioms," *op cit.*

See also, for aspects of the same problem, William Arrowsmith, "The Shame of the Graduate Schools," *Harper's* (March, 1966), pp. 51–59; Walter J. Ong, "The Expanding Humanities and the Individual Scholar," *Publications of the Modern Language Association of America* (September, 1967), pp. 1–7; and Thomas Haskell, *The Emergence of Professional Social Science, op. cit.*

21. For an account of this, see Thomas Haskell, "The True and Tragic History of 'Time on the Cross,'" *The New York Review of Books* (October 2, 1975), pp. 33–39.

22. The Higham and Conkin anthology especially indicates how much intellectual history studies have gravitated toward institutional perspectives in recent years. Contributors to the anthology have been particularly influenced by the thinking of Clifford Geertz, Thomas Kuhn, and Peter Berger and Thomas Luckmann, and their language abounds with social science terms like "social aggregate," "social constituency," "significant others," "social matrix," "cultural modernization." See especially the articles by Laurence Veysey, Gordon Wood, Murray Murphey, David Hall, and Thomas Bender, also the introduction by John Higham and the afterword by Paul Conkin. Higham and Conkin, *op. cit.*

23. I am currently at work on a sequel to this volume—it will be a while in the doing—

which will pick up on American historical-cultural studies in the early 1960s and bring the analysis to the present. It will not only—as in the current volume—look at the explanation-forms of American historians and culture critics; it will also try and handle the social systems and institutional dynamics undergirding those forms. It will also connect out more into the larger American culture and social structure affecting those forms. It will be titled *American Historical Explanations II: From Intellectual History to Cultural History*.

24. If American historians have developed no special subfield focusing on theory and criticism, that does not mean thinking in these areas has waned. Indeed, the profession has experienced a quantum leap forward in theoretical sophistication and methodic self-consciousness during the decade of the seventies. And I am inclined now to temper considerably my earlier objections to historians on these matters. Or at least this is true on history's theory and method side. Apart from fine new journals like *Reviews in American History*, however, historical criticism is still in a regrettable condition.

25. Sklar, "Realities," *op cit.*; Kuklick, "Myth and Symbol in American Studies," *American Quarterly* (Fall, 1972), pp. 435–450; and Mechling, Merideth, and Wilson, *op cit.* I have written at more length on these matters in my "'Paradigm Dramas' in American Studies: A Cultural and Institutional History of the Movement," *American Quarterly* (Bibliography Issue, 1979), pp. 293–337.

26. Smith, "Can 'American Studies' Develop a Method?," *American Quarterly* (Summer, 1957), pp. 197–208; Sykes, "American Studies and the Concept of Culture," *op cit.*

27. Berger and Luckmann, *The Social Construction of Reality: A Treatise in the Sociology of Knowledge* (Doubleday Anchor, 1967; first published in 1966).

28. Kelly, "Literature and the Historian," *American Quarterly* (May, 1974), pp. 141–159.

29. Gordon Kelly, *Mother Was a Lady: Self and Society in Selected American Children's Periodicals, 1865–1890* (Greenwood, 1974); Lonna Malmsheimer, "Genre, Audience, and Significance: Social Contextualism and the Literature-History Dilemma" (paper presented at the Bicentennial Convention of the national American Studies Association and British American Studies Association, April 3, 1976); Kay Mussell, "*The Social Construction of Reality* and American Studies: Toward a Method" (unpublished paper); Jay Mechling and Merline Williams, "Teaching Up," *Chesapeake American Studies Quarterly* (January, 1975), pp. 1–5; and Mechling, "Square Tomato," *op cit.*

30. Wallace, "Culture and Cognition," *Science* (1962), pp. 351–357, and *Culture and Personality* (Random House, rev. ed., 1970); Spradley and McCurdy, *The Cultural Experience: Ethnography in a Complex Society* (Science Research Associates, 1972), Spradley, *You Owe Yourself a Drunk: An Ethnography of Urban Nomads* (Little, Brown, 1970), and Spradley and Brenda Mann, *The Cocktail Waitress: Woman's Work in a Man's World* (Wiley, 1975).

31. Caughey, "Simulating the Past: A Method for Using Ethnosemantics in Historical Research," *American Quarterly* (December, 1972), pp. 626–642; and Mechling, "In Search of an American Ethnophysics," in Luedtke, *op cit.*, p. 245. Both Caughey and Mechling were influenced by the "culture as knowledge" approach of the Penn anthropologist Ward Goodenough. See especially Goodenough's "Componential Analysis and the Study of Meaning," *Language*, 32 (1956), pp. 195–216.

32. Beeman, "The New Social History and the Search for 'Community' in Colonial America," *American Quarterly* (Fall, 1977), pp. 422–443.

33. Keesing, "Paradigms Lost: The New Ethnography and the New Linguistics," *Southwestern Journal of Anthropology* (Winter, 1972), p. 312, 303.

34. Keesing, "Theories of Culture," in Bernard Siegel et al., eds., *Annual Review of Anthropology* (Annual Review Press, 1974), p. 79.

35. The "On the Shoulders of Giants" session was held September 28, 1979 at the national American Studies Association convention in Minneapolis.

36. Murphey, "American Civilization at Pennsylvania," *American Quarterly* (Summer, 1970), p. 497.

37. Especially in chapter 2—when articulating "the cognitive view"—and in the case-study chapters (7–9)—when analyzing the structures and planes of historians' ideas—I have employed insights from the field of psychology to make a similar point—namely, to portray a human reality in the process of being constructed and perennially re-constructed. In drawing upon psychological perspectives here to try and understand personality dynamics func-

tioning behind ideas, I have found *cognitive psychology* more useful than *psychoanalytic psychology*.

Although I have no basic quarrel with psychoanalytic perspectives—indeed, in my own intellectual biography an interest in depth psychology preceded by several years my interest in history and American Studies—I do quarrel with the contemporary presumption that "psycho-history" is necessarily psychoanalytic history. Sigmund Freud, I believe, was a modern genius, some of his followers considerably less so. But his is only one among several valuable perspectives on the psychodynamics of human behavior, not *the* required form of explanation.

For some historical situations and many historical personalities, psychoanalytic categories are enormously valuable in illuminating human motives, and in probing for the backgrounds of those motives. But because psychoanalytic explanations work at such a deep (and often hidden) level, adepts are frequently tempted to freeze their categories, reifying them into matters of faith and not tools for inquiry. Cognitive psychology is occasionally a healthy corrective to that—not only because it offers an alternative, or rather supplementary, mode of explanation, but because it cautions against the human temptation to reify ideas, even ideas of scholarly psychologists and psycho-historians. So if Jean Piaget, M. Brewster Smith, Jerome Bruner, Robert White, Milton Rokeach, Leon Festinger, and George Kelly et al. are not titanic figures of Freudian stature, they still offer valuable tools that students in American culture studies could well afford to draw upon.

For more on this, see my article of some years back, written before the rise of the contemporary "psycho-history" movement—"Political 'Reality' in Recent American Scholarship: Progressives v. 'Symbolists,'" *American Quarterly* (Summer, 1967), pp. 303–328. See also, for uses of cognitive psychology in recent American culture studies scholarship, David Brion Davis, "Some Recent Directions in American Cultural History," *American Historical Review* (February, 1968), pp. 700 ff.; Robert Shalhope, "Thomas Jefferson's Republicanism and Antebellum Southern Thought," *Journal of Southern History* (November, 1976), pp. 529–556; and Mechling, "Ethnophysics," *op. cit.*, pp. 248 ff., 270.

38. For more on this point, see chapter 9 herein, "A New 'Consensus' Forms: R. W. B. Lewis, Perry Miller, and the Counter-Progressive Explanation," pp. 296–359.

39. Lewis, *The American Adam: Innocence, Tragedy, and Tradition in the Nineteenth Century* (Chicago Phoenix Book, 1955), p. 9.

BOOK I

Encountering the Forms: The Idea-Form, the Reality-Form, the Book-Form, Historians' Explanation-Forms

The history thus written becomes a history
not of ideas at all, but of abstractions:
a history of thoughts which no one actually
succeeded in thinking, at a level of coherence
which no one ever actually attained.
> Quentin Skinner
> "Meaning and Understanding in
> the History of Ideas" (*History and Theory,*
> *VIII*, 1, 1969)

To construe events is to use this convenient
trick of abstracting them in order to make
sense of them.
> George Kelly
> *A Theory of Personality:*
> *The Psychology of Personal*
> *Constructs*

The world of external objects and of
psychic experience appears to be in
continuous flux. Verbs are more adequate
symbols for this situation than nouns.
> Karl Mannheim
> *Ideology and Utopia*

1 "Pictures in Our Heads": Symbolic Forms amid the Flux

The universe "owes no prior allegiance to any one man's construction system."
> George Kelly
> *A Theory of Personality*

Human kind cannot bear very much reality.
> T. S. Eliot
> "Burnt Norton"

There is a *fundamental* difference between the mind of man and the mind of no-man. This difference is one of kind, not of degree. . . . Man uses symbols; no other creature does. An organism has the ability to symbol or it does not; there are no intermediate stages.
> Leslie White
> *The Science of Culture**

It is fitting—given the dialogue-tenor of this book—that its opening chapter should begin with a question. Or rather, a series of questions. People have ideas. But why? And when? And what can ideas do for them? Intellectual historians have written for some decades now about "The American Mind," but few have stopped to ponder what "mind" is. And scarce anyone in the field has paused long to reflect, "Just what *is* an idea?"

Professional historians have taken it for granted that ideas exist, and have gone on to ask of them: "Do ideas have a self-generating power of their own, or do they more or less passively reflect environmental forces around them?" "Should we look for a culture's most significant ideas in their diffuse mass expression, or in the reflective thought of certain systematic thinkers?" "Is there a general 'spirit of an age' which distinguishes each particular period of history?" "How much permanence and how much change are there in the dominant ideas of a culture?"

*Grove Paperback, no date; first published 1969 by Farrow, Strauss and Cudahy.

These are not trivial questions. They are important, they need to be asked, and anyone who's worked seriously with ideas in history has been beset by them. But they all start by taking ideas as given in the nature of things and assume the only problem is how to handle them, and where.

What if we didn't make such an assumption? What if we were to start by taking ideas themselves as problematic, and query what our experience would be without them? We might then respond to our earlier question, "Just what *is* an idea?" by posing its opposite, "Just what *isn't* an idea?" And we might look for an answer not in people—who all *have* ideas—but in a being who doesn't fully make it in the people-species. Take Benjy, the speechless idiot in William Faulkner's novel, *The Sound and the Fury*.

Benjy is almost like a figure from another world. He is virtually helpless to act on his own, he cannot talk, he has a slowed-down time sense (indeed, almost no time sense), and thus behaves in a radically different fashion from most of us. Benjy might, in contrast, offer us perspective on ourselves. If he cannot quite tell us what an idea isn't, his mode of experiencing may show us something about ideas which our more normal minds might pass by.

We'll enter the novel in its closing scene, and work back from there. The time is April 8, 1928, and the location is Jefferson, Mississippi, center of Faulkner's fictional Yoknapatawpha County. Benjy is being driven for his regular Sunday visit to the graveyard by Luster, the fourteen-year-old house servant whose duty it is to look after this grown but helpless man (Benjy is thirty-three at the time). The graveyard is on the far side of Jefferson from the Compson home, and to get there they must pass through the town square. Just as Luster drives the family surrey into that square, he mischievously strikes Queenie and swings her hard around to the left, rather than taking the usual way round to the right. Let Faulkner take it from here:

For an instant Ben sat in an utter hiatus. Then he bellowed. Bellow on bellow, his voice mounted, with scarce interval for breath. There was more than astonishment in it, it was horror; shock; agony eyeless, tongueless; just sound, and Luster's eyes backrolling for a white instant. "Gret God," he said. "Hush! Hush! Gret God!" He whirled again and struck Queenie with the switch. It broke and he cast it away and with Ben's voice mounting toward its unbelievable crescendo Luster caught up the end of the reins and leaned forward as Jason came jumping across the square and onto the step.

With a backhanded blow he hurled Luster aside and caught the reins and sawed Queenie about and doubled the reins back and slashed her across the hips. He cut her again and again, into a plunging gallop, while Ben's hoarse agony roared about them, and swung her about to the right of the monument. Then he struck Luster over the head with his fist.

"Dont you know any better than to take him to the left?" he said. He reached back and struck Ben, breaking the flower stalk again. "Shut up!" he said. "Shut up!" He jerked Queenie back and jumped down. "Get to hell on home with him.

If you ever cross that gate with him again, I'll kill you!"

"Yes, Suh!" Luster said. He took the reins and hit Queenie with the end of them. "Git up! Git up, dar! Benjy, fer God's sake!"

Ben's voice roared and roared. Queenie moved again, her feet began to clop-clop steadily again, and at once Ben hushed. Luster looked quickly back over his shoulder, then he drove on. The broken flower drooped over Ben's fist and his eyes were empty and blue and serene again as cornice and façade flowed smoothly once more from left to right; post and tree, window and doorway, and signboard, each in its ordered place.[1]

That's the raw experience, as Faulkner renders it. What then to make of this experience in our efforts here to understand something of what an idea is and isn't? What happened to spark such a furious outburst in Benjy Compson? And what clues may we get here to the idea-form and to the way it works in the experience of people?

We might use this moment now, and the fictional character Benjy, to try out some working hypotheses about the function of an idea—what it is and does for people (and isn't and doesn't do). What we're aiming for are the outlines of a behavioral explanation of ideas—that is, a model of how ideas behave in human experience (or, more precisely, of how humans behave through ideas).

This is a large order to set on a fellow thirty-three years old who communicates to others in this novel mostly by moaning and bellowing and slobbering, and who can't even eat his own breakfast without help. And this may seem a strange case to open a study ostensibly about some higher uses of the human intellect. But we can see some things best by contrast; by looking into the experience of this fictional idiot, we might gain insight into the minds of actual non-idiots. Benjy may offer us something of what Kenneth Burke has called "perspective by incongruity."[2]

II

But first, some historical background, to sharpen our later look at Benjy and ideas and mind. Normally, when we've looked for the idea-form in American intellectual history studies, we've tended to stop with readily accessible ideas. We can find this even in a historian like Vernon Louis Parrington, one of the great democratizers of the American mind. Here's someone with a driving populist urge to break through the categories of acadamic formalism and feel for the genuinely democratic "main currents in American thought." Yet Parrington has written a three-volume, 1,300-page intellectual history where ideas are found not in "the people," but mainly in thinkers like Winthrop, Williams, Edwards, Melville, Twain, and Dreiser. In short, Parrington locates ideas in those uncharacteristically human minds "who have a habit of scribbling." His is an intellectual history of intellectuals, not of average people thinking. Rather, it's an intellectual history *by* intellectuals, *for* average people; the people don't normally do their own thinking in Parrington's volumes, intellectuals do it for them And when they do occasionally do their thinking, it's almost invariably offstage. With a rare exception like, say, Anne Hutchinson or Davy Crockett, it's the articulate writers who define what "ideas" are in *Main Currents*.

All this is quite understandable—it's no easy task for historians to reconstruct the thoughts of people who never wrote them down. But taking the experience of ideas only through those who've put them to paper has had its problems. For one, by picturing thought through such a form, we academicians may have slipped into defining "ideas" as simply where we've been accustomed to look for them. *Walden* expresses ideas. *Moby-Dick* expresses ideas. Trapping beaver in Oregon does not express ideas. Nor does driving around some town square in Mississippi, circa 1928. These latter two do not express mind, and are not particularly worth mind's attention. Or at least these are not what intellectual historians have looked at when they search for ideas in American experience. They *are* typical idea behaviors for cognitive psychologists and sociologists of knowledge, though, as we'll see in the chapter to come.

It's hard to get distance from this issue because ours is a culture so flooded with ideas, and so quick to rationalize its behaviors, that we lack leverage for a fresh look at the matter. We're so immersed in the idea-form that we can hardly make out its contours, or see clearly its functions. That's why Benjamin Compson can help us. He can do it, paradoxically, by confronting us with a stark situation where this idea-form is *not* operating: what makes Benjy bellow in *The Sound and the Fury* is precisely the absence of any ideas functioning in his head, at least in any normal human form. He may have *sensations* in his head, but he does not have *pictures* in his head, or ideas. With Benjy, then, we can in effect start our inquiries here *de novo,* and try to build an idea from the ground up, as it were.

Hence this particular "tale told by an idiot"—full of sounds and furies and erupting from a vacuum of mind—may nonetheless signify something about the idea-form in people; it might tell us what ideas *can* do for we people by making us experience someone who lives without them. And, since people seem to be the lone idea-using species, Benjy's moment may help us probe below the surface of ideas as such to feel for that unique quality which sets us off from other creatures in the world—the power to create symbolic forms, or what the anthropologist Leslie White calls "symboling."[3]

In an effort to get perspective on the idea-form now, we might back off from ourselves for a moment and make a simple query, *"What is it like to be people?"* From Benjy, we may get a reply which could help us develop a working anthropology of ideas for American historiography-intellectual history studies.

We mustn't of course be too confident in classifying the whole human species here. Using an idiot, and a fictional one to boot, *does* seem a bit risky to lay groundwork of a new area in historical scholarship.

But we might let the *fictional* quality of this incident work for us; it could free our minds to speculate for a while as we do some early exploring in the territory. By holding us for onto ninety-two pages inside the head of an inarticulate idiot and making this the port of entry into his novel, William Faulkner has toyed with our assumptions about experience, forcing them out of their normal routines. In effect, he's said to his readers, "Assume you're an idiot now, and let's see how you'd experience events of everyday life." In short, Faulkner has used his literary license to play a "let's pretend" game with reality; it's a game whose analogue in historical-cultural studies is the *ideal type.*

Ideal types allow inquirers to manipulate their world—that is, temporarily to act *as if* thus and so were the case for some purpose or other. This is what, willy-nilly, any poet or novelist or dramatist does, and it gives him a freedom of movement normally denied academicians. By using ideal types, however, academicians can gain a little of that freedom for themselves.

Ideal types have many useful functions in scholarly inquiry. We might note here just two: (1) They can help scholars narrow their focus to gain control over their materials (e.g., Max Weber's focus on religious motivations in *The Protestant Ethic and the Spirit of Capitalism,* or Tocqueville's focus on equality in *Democracy in America*). (2) They can free scholars to suspend disbelief about things in the world, and experiment for a time with new kinds of realities and new kinds of connections among things. They're also not quite true, and anyone who experiments with ideal-types must remind himself that he's dealing with hypothetical realities, not actual ones.

In any case, this is what we might try now with Benjy Compson. We mustn't claim his case *proves* all the speculations we'll make from it, nor even that these speculations are all *true.* I hope what we say here is a truth, but it is not the only truth. People seem to be many-dimensioned creatures—they are part animal, they are part self-seeking, they are part god, they are part lusty, they are part self-sacrificing, they are part ascetic, they are part territorial. They are lots of other things too, depending on where they are and when they are and who they are, and what they are trying to do. But in addition to all these they are "symboling" creatures, framers of symbolic forms. This book works as if symboling were the only (or at least the basic) dimension of the human species. We needn't assume this is in fact the case—rather, we can just say, "Let's suppose it is true for now and see what it helps us to explain." Our speculations in this opening chapter are simply instrumental, laying foundations for what we'll do later with the case studies.

Our strategy, then, is to cut into experience mainly around the plane of where people seek to order their world, and to inspect how ideas function along this plane. Lest anyone object that this isn't the only plane of the species, I agree. But by pretending like it is for a time, we may see things which a less focused eye might miss. In any case, the fruits of this procedure come not now, in our speculations, but when we try those speculations out on actual historical minds—in chapters 7–9.

III

Let's see what we can make now of Benjy and the experience of living through idea-forms and living without them. What follows is not an exhaustive inventory of man as creator of symbolic forms, it's rather an opening journey into the territory:[4]

1. *We get on as we do not only because we have experiences of things in the world, but also because we can create abstracted ideas or "symbols" of the things we experience.*   Normally, what people experience is not reality unmediated—the facts of the matter—but reality as filtered through our mind-pictures of it, pictures of how things connect one with another. This screening process is not mere distortion or personal bias, each of us imposing our inner desires on the world so we can make it over into our own image. We perceive as we do because we invariably see from particular locations, and to call our perceptions "bias" is merely to admit that we humans see through filters, never without them. We're not downright liars (at least not most of us most of the time); we just don't see everything, and we don't take full account of what we can see (see chapter 7 on Turner for a refinement on this). To be sure, part of what we do take account of may express wish distortion. But doubtless a much larger part is simply *selection.* If we're not full-out liars as a species, we humans rarely tell the whole truth either, and this because we don't *see* the whole, but only parts. "Objectivity"—the truth, the whole truth, and nothing but the truth—may be a worthwhile ideal in the courtroom and in some phases of history work. But however worthwhile as an ideal, it's a human impossibility, for reasons I hope to make clear as this inquiry progresses.

If these pictures in people's heads are not just wish distortions of the world, neither are they quite xeroxes of it, or even of part of it. Rather, they're some sort of ongoing compromise between the projections of mind and the givens of environment. In any case, if pictures weren't normally operating inside their heads, people might react to the unexpected much as Benjy did when Luster began his contrary route around the square. They would probably be set off crying in shock and terror at a world which failed to behave as it ought to.

From the normal human perspective, it makes no difference which route one takes around the square, he still comes out at the same place. We may fail to realize, though, the rather complicated—and highly abstract—mind process involved in reaching this conclusion. Note again how it's not there in Benjy, as early in the novel he's being driven around the square in the usual right-to-left direction:

I could hear Queenie's feet and the bright shapes went smooth and steady on both sides, the shadows of them flowing across Queenie's back. They went on like the bright tops of wheels. Then those on the one side stopped at the tall white post where the soldier was. But on the other side they went on smooth and steady, but a little slower.[5]

The shadows and that simile "like the bright tops of wheels" are out of character here; they're rare lapses by Faulkner from his effort to render the experience of a speechless idiot from the inside out, so to speak. But beyond that, we have in this passage an attempt to convey unmediated sense impressions, impressions from an eye seeing shapes flow past it as it's moved along in the surrey. With no abstracted *idea* of the square, Benjy's head is crammed with a bundle of concrete sensations, piled one upon another in a sequence which to him is not simply one possible order, but *the* order of that reality. And it appears to him here as absolute and given precisely because it's not a humanly constructed picture; rather, it's a march of serial objects, arranged in a time sequence of linked impressions, impressions which, for Benjy, could be put together in no other way.

What he sees as he passes around this square is not in fact "house" and "lawn" and "soldier's monument," but *only that part of* each house and each lawn and the monument which comes into his eye as he is moved past them from right to left. And in the given order that each part of each object passes into his vision; as it's described in the novel's closing scene, "cornice and facade flowed smoothly once more from left to right; post and tree, window and doorway, and signboard, each in its ordered place."[6]

Notice how Faulkner has subtly reversed the sense of sequence here—has called it *left-to-right* instead of *right-to-left*—to connote Benjy's passive mode of experiencing in this scene. Though he's being driven here from right to left, he has no sense that it is he who's moving. Instead, Benjy experiences these objects *as moving past him,* now (after Jason has struck Luster) in their proper left-to-right order. When they begin passing his eye in any other fashion, they literally become different things for Benjy; he didn't alter direction, they did. No wonder he reacted by bellowing and behaving as if his whole world were coming unstuck. It was.

We might cry out in similar terror if, say, we were caught unawares somewhere in a gigantic earthquake. Our fright would be not merely physical—fear of getting injured or killed—but psychic too; things which we assume are solidly grounded in the nature of things might suddenly begin moving in the most strange, unpredictable fashion. Our world's givens would become problematic for us, and we'd not be prepared for it. If we had a better *idea* of what makes an earthquake, then we'd be prepared for them when they come, and they wouldn't strike such psychic terror in us.[7]

All of which means moving with our minds' ideas past the immediate experience—be it an earthquake or traversing the town square in Jefferson—to what is *around* the experience. What is around it in space. What is around it in time. We do this automatically with something like the town square; for when we can anticipate where we want to go, then we simply project in our mind alternative future routes for getting there. And we take whichever route is most convenient for us at the time. Unlike Benjy, we won't be bothered much that this house looks different when one goes around it from left to right, or that one gets another angle on the hedge when he passes it in the opposite direction. For seldom do we take in the full detailed sensations of an object anyway. Instead, we see some form of abstracted *type-picture*. The "type-house." The "type-hedge." We may see it here from one perspective, there from another; but to us it remains a house in both instances, because we hold a more or less sustaining picture of the type "house" in our minds. And we need see only some small fraction of an actual house for that picture to flash in our heads, and for us to recognize it as this type rather than, say, the type "barn," or "church," or "fire station." Note that the picture here is not the full house, because one could never hold all the dimensions of a house in a single projection of eye and mind. Mind pictures, rather, are suggestions, compressed "representations," as it were, rather than the whole thing.

Through these pictures, or idea-forms, people are able to *assume* the surrounding context of things, even if they see only a small part of the things themselves. Benjy, however, can never get to what is *around* his experience, he's too rooted *inside* it. He thus lacks leverage to connect what he sees in the present with what could have been there in the past, or with what might be there in the future (or with what is likely there in the present, though he may not see all of it at the moment). He can never picture a general "type house," but only particular sensations of doorway and cornice and roof, never "town square," but only details of soldier and hedge and post. Lacking any transcending idea, Benjy is locked into immediacy, much as we might be with that earthquake if it took us without warning. Without idea-forms, one has no perspective beyond the moment.

2. *Frequently, we people "break up" reality in order to cope with it.* Maybe this appears obvious in a world where humans use their manufactured tools to manipulate and destroy and foul up their environments. But what we should note here is that people take apart their environments not only in acting upon them, but even in the act of *seeing* them. Again, we can watch the contrary behavior in Benjy.

Benjy's narrative in *The Sound and the Fury*, the opening quarter of the novel, is rich in the smell and feel and shape and taste of experience. His account resonates with rattling leaves, cold gates, falling roofs, steaming soup, buzzing grass, and his sister Caddy who "smells like trees." Benjy is submerged in a world of raw things, unmediated by pictures or symbols or abstracted forms of things.

Nor is his world mediated by the perspective of distance. A reflection in a mirror is not an image of something else to Benjy, it's a thing in itself. A fire seen in a mirror is a fire *in* a mirror; a room with a single fireplace and a mirror in front of it is to him a room with two fireplaces. One fireplace makes him hot as he nears it, the other does not.

Benjy, then, is so tuned in to the world of his sensations that whatever he sees is in fact just as he sees it, and (to him) could be no other way. Which, incidentally, makes him an entirely reliable "objective" historian. We can trust Benjy's *perceptions*, because they're never filtered through any *conceptions*. Whenever he shows us something happening, we can be certain it happened just like that—a xerox, if you will, correct in all its surface details. We can't be so certain with Quentin and Jason, Benjy's more normal brothers who do the other narrating in this novel. Quentin is prone to take everything he experiences as a symbol of something else and not an experience in itself, and Jason is so self-consumed that he characteristically blocks out whatever fails to touch his own particular interests. We must discover this, learn from what special angle each brother reports on experience, before we can sort out each one's self from what it is he narrates.

Their world, in other words, is a more open one; it submits itself (in part, never all the way) to the rearrangements they project upon it. With their ideas, they have power to break up some things and try putting them together again in their own forms. Benjy can't do that; he doesn't experience what the sociologists of knowledge Peter Berger and Thomas Luckmann have called "world-openness."[8]

His world is not completely closed off, though; rather, it's one where everything is tied to concretions, inevitable concretions as they appear to his eyes. All things are locked together in an unvarying sequential pattern. This happens, then that, then that. He cannot cut into reality, break it up, isolate things and then rearrange them. Instead, he must take them whole, in the exact order they appear to him. That's one thing it means to live in a world without the experience of ideas.

3. For most of us most of the time, reality is much too much to be taken in whole; instead, we use ideas to plane down our world to manageable size. We usually think of an idiot as being simple-minded. But Benjy's problem seems almost the opposite—his mind is not "simple" enough. When we read *The Sound and the Fury* through to the end, we'll find this idiot's narrative much the most complex in the book. In fact, it's one of the most difficult sections in all American literature. It's much more complicated than the tortured symbolic journeys of his brother Quentin, and far and away more complex than the no-nonsense narrative of Jason—which starts off, "Once a bitch always a bitch, what I say," and moves on pretty straightforward from there.[9]

This is so even though these three Compson brothers tell of basically the same experiences, the history of a decaying family in a decaying Southern culture early in the twentieth century. Quentin and Jason, however, have already organized their materials for us. Using their minds' ideas, they select in and select out certain things, accenting what seems to them the important facts of this history. But Benjy, lacking any selecting devices, does not sort out at all. He takes in and reports on everything he sees, feels, smells, hears. In a word, Benjamin Compson cannot *simplify*. Sometimes we wish he could. For as readers of his narrative, we have to take in everything he takes in. And it's often more than we can handle. It might give us pause about just who's simple-minded and who's not.

On some levels, Benjy is a model objective historian. He's wholly faithful to his documents, all the experienced facts are there, just as they come to him, and they're unsullied by personal bias or ideological distortion or bootlegged metaphysics. Nor does Benjy compress or predigest his data to fit his or his readers' subjective wishes. It is, within its environs, "history as it really happened."

But it is not, I think, history as it *appears to* anybody. It is not the history of mind or meaning so much as the history of artifact, the raw materials from which mind may construct meanings.

For the history of mind and meanings—that is, history as it's experienced by people with pictures in their heads—we seem to require a different strategy for inquiry. Here the kind of mind we normally call "complex"— say, Plato's, or Marx's, or Freud's, or Tocqueville's—seems to function differently from how we're normally inclined to think of it. With such thinkers, the strategy is evidently "simplify the complex"—not oversimplify, they hope, but nonetheless seek to make intelligible form out of materials which at first experience appear unformed and chaotic, too massive and confusing to be brought to the order of mind. A Tocqueville or a Perry Miller edits out much of experience in their intellections. They strive to get the reader's mind running down a single track, or two or three clearly lighted ones; and they want to insulate him from most everything else in the world. They seem to say, "We must limit, we must pare down experience if we wish to make sense of it." In matters of mind, then, this issue of what's simple and what's complex merits some further reflection.

4. If we use ideas to pare down experience, we also use them to alter it; an idea may serve as a lever to move things.   We mobilize our world with ideas, Benjy can't do that. When we get an idea of what something is and does, we can begin to work on it, using this idea to try turning that thing toward our own intents. In time, maybe we'll form a more or less controlled response to earthquakes, much as we have now with, say, hurricanes and tornados. We've had much experience of quakes, so that isn't our problem. Our problem, rather, is that we lack a clear working idea and a technology to implement such an idea. This isn't to imply that any such idea could give us full control over the thing, or that turning things to our own intents doesn't create some unexpected consequences now and then. The connection between idea and intent and between intent and consequence is seldom straightforward, as pollution and Viet Nam and the generation gap have reminded us of late. Because of this, we Americans have become slightly less missionary in our zeal that always moving things—on earth, in space—is an altogether good idea. For now, though, we're not concerned with whether this is a *good* idea, but with the point that this is one of the things we people tend to *do* with ideas when we use them to act in the world.

Again, Benjy is our negative instance. Not only did he balk at going around the square the opposite way, he could never have gotten around it himself save by repeating his past experiences. And had a single house been moved or destroyed, any object in his perceptions altered, Benjamin Compson would have been rendered immobile. The square literally becomes a new and bewildering world for him every time any item in it is altered. That's another thing it means to live in the world without the experience of ideas.

Benjy's narrative is filled with instances of this kind of impotence, this lack of intellectual leverage on experience. Whenever it's cold outside, he must be shown to put his hands into his pockets; he cannot stoop to crawl through the fence by himself; he must be fed by Caddy or Dilsey or Luster. Benjy's is a stimulus-response reality; environment is the active agent, he simply reacts to it. He cannot do anything on his own. So any behavior which requires planning and initiative—eating, stooping, protecting his hands against the cold—is out of the question for Benjy without help. He can repeat experience, accurate to the slightest detail; but he cannot *do* anything with it.

We might now rephrase our question from the opening paragraph of this chapter. There we asked, "What *is* an idea?" Now we might ask, "What *does* an idea?" And by the rephrasing imply that an idea is not so much a thing as it is a function and a process. And it's best seen at labor rather than at rest. An idea is an active process of mind, not an end product of it. And it expresses mind in its most characteristic state—*doing*.

Again, this may seem an obvious truism. And yet few of our intellectual histories are written that way. As Lionel Trilling says, most tend to treat ideas as "pellets of intellection, or crystallizations of thought, precise and completed."[10] They look in on the idea-form after its action is over with—in inert, passive "thought." They talk about "Darwinism," or "Transcendentalism," or "Puritanism" as finished productions of mind, rather than backing up to look at particular minds as they're working through a Darwinist idea-form, or a Transcendental form, or a Puritan. Thus they miss the vital work of mind as it labors with an idea-form, and tries to order its experience through that form.

In contrast to the conventional procedure, I would say that an idea is not an *is,* it's a *does*. And what it does—at least along this order-disorder plane of life—is help us compress our experience into something people can use. Just as we focus and compress our energies in the material world when we use a lever, so also in the world of functioning ideas. We concentrate a lot of energy onto a small area, and when we do that things likely begin to move.

Take an illustration from recent American history. Early in the 1960s, Clark Kerr, then president of the University of California, was casting around for some way to picture why large university complexes function as they do. In his 1963 Godkin Lectures at Harvard, Kerr hit upon an ordering form— the label "multiversity." And in the doing he helped unleash massive human energies, energies which in time cost him his job. For that picture form gave leverage to student dissidents, who were feeling disgruntled with how their minds and bodies and psyches were being managed by this institution around them, and who were delighted to be handed a weapon to get back at it. It's an added irony that the weapon was given them by the head manager himself, President Kerr.

When we read documents from Berkeley, 1964–65 (the opening shot in the recent student revolt), we get an impression that the whole affair might never have got started had there been no concentrated idea-form like "multiversity" available to mobilize students. Repeatedly, FSM manifestos play upon this image, often referring directly to Kerr and his published Godkin Lectures, *The Uses of the University*.[11]

Of course the idea-form didn't create the revolt. All the experiences and discontents were around before the image was born; doubtless that image would have floated rootless, and weightless, without grounding in those experiences. But those experiences tended to remain privatized, fugitive and impotent, until a vivid picture of what connected everything together in this university (or multiversity) world served to galvanize them into a manageable unit. Students could *move* their environment as soon as they could see it as "multiversity" in their minds' eye. Thus can ideas mobilize human experiences, compressing and connecting things which without them might lie formless and inert. In this particular case, they helped get Berkeley students a revolt, Ronald Reagan an office in Sacramento, and Clark Kerr a new position with the Carnegie Corporation.

5. *The facts of our experience don't come to us naked and isolated, they come stuck together; what mind does with experience—when it's working as we want it to—is transmute information for us from fact into meanings.* The line between us and Benjy is not absolute at all points. We share much with him (which doesn't mean we're idiots, only that he's human). And, as we'll note in a while, Benjy's very defects helped him see things which everyone else in his family overlooked. But on this power of creating pictures in our heads, the line between us and Benjy is final; it makes literally all the difference in the world which side of that line you're on.

With no pictures in his head to schematize experience, and no words to express it, Benjy cannot dialogue. His relation to environment is more or less one-way—it acting on him—rather than the normal two-way encounter of most of us. Unable to dialogue with his world, with his self, with others, Benjy can only repeat experience; he cannot learn from it, build upon it. Though he's thirty-three years old at the novel's end, his mental age is put there as three.[12] This being so, Benjy is three years old eleven times over. Though clearly his sense of experience is intense, he has no power to explain it. His narrative passes on experience largely untouched. It's we who must form and organize it, and that's not likely to come all at once. First, we're obliged to read each of the other narratives in the novel, so we can sort things out; then we must come back and go through Benjy's again, this time with some pictures in our own heads which we can plug his raw data into.

It's as if Benjy had sat through a course called "History of the Compson Family, 1899–1928," and—with total recall—had passed the final exam with the highest grade in the class, 100 percent. Yet when we ask this prize student about the family ourselves, all we get is merely a repeat of the final. He doesn't "know" this history, he's merely got the facts right.

Only when we begin to dialogue with Benjy's data (and initially through pictures supplied not by him but by other less accurate students in the course), only then can we begin forming some idea of our own about what's been happening with the Compsons. We thus learn experience, and learn from experience, not merely by taking it in, but by getting some handles on it. We thereby move it off the plane of inert facts to the level of dialogic meanings. And we thus gain power to take something outside us and move it inside—in a sense, to make "it" ours.

We don't merely *aggregate* experiences, then, we *integrate* them. That is, our life is not merely the adding of experiences, one upon another, it's the ordering of them into forms and patterns.

It is this power to schematize experience, to give form and structure to sense data, which cognitive psychologists call "learning." It underlies Jerome Bruner's recent efforts to restructure our conception of the learning process, Daniel Bell's attempt to re-form the academic curriculum around conceptual learning (what he calls "third-tier" courses), and Joseph Schwab's attempts to teach science as critical inquiry rather than as a body of knowledge. It's also basic to how Thomas Kuhn says scientific communities actually function, and, as we shall see later in the case studies, it characterizes some fundamental activities in history work too.[13] In the next chapter, we'll review some scholarship in cognitive psychology, in the sociology of knowledge, and in allied fields which focuses straight on this process. Normally, historians— even intellectual historians—have not focused straight on it, but have touched it only tangentially. Because of that, I think they have tended to misread ideas, and have failed to understand how people use them.

6. *With their picture-levers, people are enabled to manipulate time.* Because we can use our pictures to range outside the moment, projecting backward into the past and forward into the future, we can enlarge our sense of where we are now. And we can use this enlarged sense to "move" time—in effect, to speed it up (or slow it down) in tune with our images of where we'd like it to go.

Just as the absence of pictures in Benjy's head holds him immobile spatially, so also temporally. To Benjy, every change is a revolution. When his sister Caddy at age fourteen first puts on perfume, it's Benjy who most noticeably reacts; as he understates it, "I went away and I didn't hush."[14] To him, Caddy must smell like trees, not like this strange, unnatural stuff. And after the family pasture is sold later to become a golf course, Benjy never adjusts; whenever the golfers there call out "caddie," that can mean only one thing to him, his long-lost sister, and the sound always sets him to bellowing.

But through his static reaction to change, Benjy does have a power in the novel held by no other narrator, not even by Faulkner as omniscient author (a voice Faulkner assumes only in the novel's last section, and then only part of the time). Through it, he can give immediacy to past events. Although Quentin and Jason say much about the Compson past, their memories are tinged by intervening time and by their own wish projections on experience. Not so Benjy. His very lack of growth makes all time instantaneous. When some outside stimulus sparks it for him, he may recall an event two decades away just as vividly as something which happened yesterday. Since family decline is a major movement in this novel, and since that decline is from an integrated state to a dis-integrated one, it's Benjy's narrative which most graphically shows us where the Compsons once were, and how they got to where they are.

And especially does it show us where his sister Caddy was. Caddy never speaks to us directly in *The Sound and the Fury;* instead, we see and hear her only as she's refracted in the minds of one or another of her brothers. In his particular narrative, Quentin is so bound up in abstracted pictures of innocence and virginity and Southern honor that we're forced to grope for his sister there through a kind of floating symbolic haze. And Jason remembers an earlier Caddy mainly through later experiences with her daughter (also named Quentin, significantly); when he opens his narrative, "Once a bitch always a bitch, what I say," he's referring simultaneously to them both.

But through Benjy we can see a much different Caddy, one as a young, sensitive girl. She alone senses right away why Benjy cries at her perfume, and tenderly she responds by helping him give the bottle away to Dilsey ("We don't like perfume ourselves").[15] Further, it's Benjy who shows us how different are mother and daughter, Jason's contrary memory notwithstanding. When Benjy whimpers upon seeing Caddy in the swing with her beau, Charles is unaffected: "He cant talk." But Caddy responds, "Are you crazy. . . . He can see. Dont. Dont." She then runs to Benjy crying, "I wont anymore, ever. Benjy. Benjy."[16]

She doesn't keep that vow long, but her momentary response is at least more humane than her daughter's in a similar scene nineteen years later. When Benjy reacts to a like moment with Quentin in the swing by crying again, Caddy's daughter shouts, "You old crazy loon. . . . I'm going to tell

Dilsey about the way you [Luster] let him follow everywhere I go. I'm going to make her whip you good."[17]

If Benjy lacks a picturing imagination, he does have memory, and he can connect experiences along the lines of similarity. By associating in his memory these two scenes—mother and daughter, nineteen years apart—Benjy shows the decay of the Compsons in a manner not available to Quentin or Jason. Or to Faulkner as omniscient author. And by bellowing at the Compson pasture-turned–golf course, he comments on the family sellout with an empirical poignance no normal person's abstracted moral judgment could quite match.

Benjy's keen if immobilized senses help him smell out change, then; and because change in the Compson experience usually means decline, his bellowing at strategic moments becomes a kind of unwitting historical prophecy. This very quality which locks him into particulars also fixes him on moments where the decay is initially manifest—Caddy's first perfume, Caddy and her beau in the swing, the sale of the pasture. Hence in Benjy's narrative we find the most accurate sense of what's happening to the family, and the best keys to an explanation of why (though not the explanation itself). The other narrators, with their speeded-up sense of time, pass quickly over these pivotal moments in the Compson history, and thus often contribute to the very decline they all lament.

Which may suggest that this human power to create pictures in our heads isn't an unmixed blessing for people. Sometimes these pictures can wander far away from the world they're supposed to represent. And this leads to our last point from *The Sound and the Fury*—it's a warning about the human uses, and abuses, of the idea-form.

7. *If this capacity to form pictures in our heads distinguishes us in the human species, our experience is not just those pictures.* Somehow, we require feedback, ways of checking our pictures with things in the world. And when we block this feedback, our sense of experience can get as contorted on one plane as Benjy's does on another.

Here we can illustrate with Benjy's oldest brother, Quentin. In several ways Quentin is the polar opposite of Benjy. Benjy has no pictures in his head, Quentin has little else. Benjy lacks leverage even to get around his hometown square, Quentin's ideas catapult him from Jefferson, Mississippi to Harvard (and eventually into the Charles River). Benjy's narrative is direct and richly sensual, Quentin's is abstract and piles symbol upon symbol upon symbol (his section follows right after Benjy's in the novel; to adjust, the reader must shift gears quickly). Floating rootless in Quentin's narrative are his father's little homily lectures on Southern honor and time and fortune and womanhood, hundreds of ticking clocks, the idea of incest with his sister Caddy (but never the fact), imaginary confessions to his father of this imaginary incest, an absurd Western-type showdown with one of Caddy's suitors,[18] and recurring images of honeysuckle and of sleep and of time but rarely the actual experiences of them. The only sustained, firsthand experience in his entire narrative is with a little Italian girl near Cambridge, whom Quentin fantasizes as Caddy (and gets himself beat up and nearly jailed as a result); and finally he commits suicide in the Charles River "two months after his sister's wedding, waiting first to complete the academic year and so get the full value of his paid-in-advance tuition."[19]

With Quentin, the pictures in his head take on a life of their own, seldom touching much on things outside. He's just as locked in by his abstracted idea-forms as is Benjy who lacks ideas. While Benjy is inundated by a world of concrete things, Quentin floats off in a universe of general ideas. In a world composed both of things and ideas—and where effective human experience requires an on-going dialogue between them—Quentin can cope no better by remaining on one plane than can his idiot brother on the other. Faulkner renders a fitting epitaph:

QUENTIN III. Who loved not his sister's body but some concept of Compson honor precariously and (he knew well) only temporarily supported by the minute fragile membrane of her maidenhead as a miniature replica of all the whole vast globy earth may be poised on the nose of a trained seal. Who loved not the idea of incest which he would not commit, but some presbyterian concept of its eternal punishment: he, not God, could by that means cast himself and his sister both into hell, where he could guard her forever and keep her forevermore intact amid the eternal fires.[20]

IV

So much, for the moment, on Benjy and the Compson family. We might now back off from this experience, and try giving it explanation. Which means compressing it into intelligible form, framing a picture of what ideas do, as it were. What we have here with men and ideas and world looks to be something like this:

The universe experienced by humans is open, more or less. Things in this world do obey rules; but when we learn what those rules are, we can often work to alter them, or make them work for us. There's a certain pliability to the world of people's experience.

This means the place we inhabit is susceptible to change. And because it's always available for further change, it never wholly submits to any particular order we wish to impose on it (and all human orders *are* particular orders, coming from limited experiences in time). Hence the world is not merely open until we get there, it remains open even after we've tried our hand, and mind, at it. Later, in chapters 7 and 8, we'll explore how this world-openness can confound certain minds (in this case Frederick Jackson Turner and Vernon Louis Parrington), when they think they've imposed the correct form on it, but it keeps slipping out of their grasp.

The world is not just pliable, then, it's also too large, too powerful for us to control with our minds and hands and machines. It may submit to some order or form here, but that leaves much still unformed over there; and, as the incidence of pollution has shown us, when we go to impose human forms on things, our impositions frequently have impact beyond our ability to foresee at the moment.

Thus our universe is both open-ended and larger than any single human knowing, or composite of knowings. Neither intellectually nor emotionally are people big enough to capture all the reality of their experience. The world is too much for the senses to take in, or the mind to make sense of. If this were at all true in the past, such a truth has been magnified in contemporary life; for in our humanly manufactured environment we've speeded up and multiplied the number of things impacting on persons from without. Thus the burden of "information overload," which Alvin Toffler has written of in *Future Shock*.[21] All this means that the onrush of experience is too confusing, too massive and amorphous, for anyone to take in whole. To cope, mind must block out as well as take in.

Picture, then, small man in a universe larger than his power to comprehend, seeking to comprehend nonetheless, and straining to shape things to his own mind and will. What he takes in, and what he acts upon, is therefore never quite "what is there," but some small portion of what is there. To know, to do, he must invariably compress.

In western intellectual history, we've seen conceptions of man advanced as a political animal, or an economic one, or historical, or religious, or sexual, or psychological. We might now think of an additional conception—a picture of man as *simplifying* creature, who reduces his world to size so he can communicate with it and act upon it.[22]

He does this through his power of *symboling*—which, for now, we can say is merely the ability to re-construct experience. It's the capacity to form picture representations that are something less than the full march of sensation impacting upon us at any moment, yet also something beyond those sensations. To put it another way, these pictures seem to perform two functions simultaneously for us—they both reduce our sensation of experience, and they expand it. They reduce by paring down reality for whatever purpose we have in mind at the moment, editing out signal from noise, focusing it down to intelligible form. But they expand reality by elevating us outside our immediate senses. We can use our picture-making power to imagine realities we've never before experienced. We can long and wish, we can build utopias in our mind, we can make plans for redoing things as they are, and we can act out those plans. In short, we can take parts of what we've known and felt, take those parts apart, and rearrange them into entirely new orders. We can dream—that is, envision what is not there. And we can create—that is, act on those dreams, trying to translate vision into thing.

Such a power is in people, but not, to my knowledge, in tigers, or wildebeests, or sunflowers (I do know a dog which gives me pause on this now and then!). Humans transcend other species by having power to transcend their environment. Plants can grow and thus have a history, and animals can congregate in societies and form polities of a sort. Humans too are historical and social and political, but that in itself doesn't distinguish them as a species. What does distinguish them, I think, is that they seem to be the only species around with a habit of symboling. They not only procreate, but can write poetry about it; not only kill and maim, but do it for gods; not only eat, but make an art of it; not only defend their territory, but erect flags upon it. What is an instinct for an animal is a symbol for a person. Each species employs its own unique equipment for coping in its world.

It is not simply the *fact* of symboling which we should emphasize here, though. It's also the *process*—and that process grows from a dialogue, mind moving from unformed concretion to created abstraction, then back again. Because he can compress Jefferson's town square into an idea-form less complicated than Benjy's sensation of it, and because he can predict from past experience how Benjy may react to the new and unusual, Luster can act on this picture in his head, can swing Queenie around to the left, and set off in Benjy the shock he knows is likely to come. What he of course doesn't anticipate is that Benjy will overreact, will not only be upset but horror stricken, that Jason will hear and come too, will interrupt this chain of predictions, and will threaten the fires of hell if ever Luster tries such mischief again.

What happened here is that an unforeseen variable—a variable not only outside Luster's range of immediate sensation, but absent from his idea-projection of what would likely follow—enters the picture and upsets his prediction. Next time around, Luster would doubtless take heed of this unanticipated feedback from the world of experience and would include some image of Jason as terrible avenger in any future design for rearranging Benjy's world.

Now much of this should appear obvious. As an abstract generalization, it says merely that a large part of our world of experience is being created by people and that it's ongoing and never closed off. It says that humans are both sensate and symboling, and that experience in the world is a continuing dialogue between our ideas and its things. As a nostrum for coping with reality, this view urges us to think upon our experience and to let experience feed back into our thinking. In short, we should construct idea-forms, but keep them flexible. So much for the obvious.

The example of a Quentin, though, shows that our commonsensical abstractions are not universally heeded in the species. And when we move from these general speculations on the idea-form back into the particular world of history—or in this case of professional historians—such a generalization may not seem so obvious at all. It's in the *doing* of these abstractions that the issue gets complicated. Just why this is the case is our theme for the next chapter.

NOTES

1. *The Sound and the Fury* (Random House, Vintage Book, 1956—first published in 1929), pp. 400–401.

2. *Permanence and Change* (Bobbs-Merrill, paperback, 1965), p. 69 ff.

3. Leslie White has made a noun—*symbol*—into a verb—*symboling*—because he would have us think of an idea not as a thing but as a behavior, an experience, something not at rest but moving. See his chapter "The Symbol," in *The Science of Culture* (Grove, paperback, n.d.), pp. 22–39.

4. Though I have preferred not to work directly off others' scholarship in these early ruminations, I've not just struck them out of my own imagination either. They're expressed in a form unfamiliar to most historians, but they are backed up by a rigorous ongoing scholarship in such fields as cognitive psychology, the sociology of knowledge, and anthropological philosophy.

Later, in chapter 2, we'll look more carefully into this "cognitive" scholarship. For now, let me note that my working model for this chapter is especially influenced by George Kelly's incredible little volume, *A Theory of Personality: The Psychology of Personal Constructs* (Norton, paperback, 1963—first published by Norton in 1955). My sense of ideas here has also been influenced by Ernst Cassirer's *An Essay on Man* (Doubleday, Anchor, n.d.—first published by Yale in 1944); by Peter Berger and Thomas Luckmann's *The Social Construction of Reality* (Doubleday, Anchor, 1967—first published by Doubleday in 1966); and by M. Brewster Smith, Jerome Bruner, and Robert White, *Opinions and Personality* (Wiley, 1956).

Finally, my dialogue sense of mind-world encounter parallels the "transactional" model of ideas developed by Rush Welter in a splendid essay—"The History of Ideas in America: A Redefinition," *Journal of American History*, LI, no. 4 (March 1965), 599–614.

5. *Sound and the Fury*, pp. 11–12.

6. Ibid., p. 401.

7. Such an idea, by the way, would come not only from experiencing *actual* quakes, but from going below the surface of immediate events to chart prior faults and stresses in the earth which cause them and future relocations of the earth they cause themselves. And accompanying such an idea would be an operative picture of earth not as absolutely stable and rooted, but in flux—only moving at a pace measured in geologic not human time. This picture would come not from our immediate senses (save for the actual brief moments of a quake, no one ever *sees* or *feels* the ground move), but from what measurements from the past and projections into the future appear to tell us. Again, it's not just experience, it's an abstracted *picture* of experience, that makes the difference.

8. *Social Construction of Reality*, p. 47 ff.

9. *Sound and the Fury*, p. 223.

10. *The Liberal Imagination* (Doubleday, Anchor, 1957), p. 293.

11. See especially here the documents written by Richard Fellenbaum, Bradford Cleaveland, and Mario Savio, reprinted in Seymour Martin Lipset and Sheldon Wolin, eds., *The Berkeley Student Revolt: Facts and Interpretations* (Anchor, 1965), pp. 64–65, 66–93, 216–19.

12. Actually, Benjy seems younger mentally than that. A three-year-old can talk and form all kinds of pictures in his head. Benjy must be somewhere under two, nearly one, I'd guess. That is, if it's appropriate to talk of mental age in cases like this.

13. Jerome Bruner, *Toward a Theory of Instruction* (Norton, paperback, 1968) and *The Process of Education* (Vintage, n.d.); Daniel Bell, *The Reforming of General Education* (Columbia University Press, 1966); Joseph Schwab, *The Teaching of Science as Enquiry* (Harvard University Press, 1966); and Thomas Kuhn, *The Structure of Scientific Revolutions* (University of Chicago Press, paperback, 1970).

14. *Sound and the Fury*, p. 51.

15. Ibid.

16. Ibid., pp. 57–58.

17. Ibid., p. 58.

18. It's a showdown for Quentin at least, who gives Dalton Ames till sundown to leave town, or else. . . . In the midst of enacting this terrible threat, though, Quentin "passed out like a girl." Dalton was not much bothered by the threat. And he stayed around town after sundown, (ibid., p. 201).

19. Ibid., p. 411.

20. Ibid.

21. *Future Shock* (Random House, 1970), pp. 311–15.

22. For more on this "simplifying" conception of man, see Berger and Luckmann (n. 4 above), especially their section on "Origins of Institutionalization," pp. 53–67.

2 "Perspectives" on Historical Reality: The Relativist Dilemma

Truth is a ratio between the mind and things.
Marshall McLuhan
The Gutenberg Galaxy

Essential to cubism is the simple fact that objects can be perceived from a number of different angles. It rejects the idea that the only true two-dimensional reality is to be found in the selection of one perspective among the many possibilities. Rather a number of faces are presented at once on the canvas creating the sense of seeing the object from more than one angle at once.
Richard Reinitz
"Cubism and the Application of Paradigms to the General Interpretation of American History"

The whole truth, at any stage of inquiry, is an ideal that ought to be abolished from historiography, for it cannot ever be attained.
David Hackett Fischer
Historians' Fallacies

This book is about mind, through its constructed forms, encountering world, and about strategies for entering that encounter. In chapter 1, we've outlined a model where ideas function not simply to reflect peoples' experiences, but to channel and mobilize them. Seen through this model, ideas serve not as *mirrors* of external reality, but as devices whereby people try and *cope with* the reality of their perceptions.

That is how we said ideas work for people generally. In this book, however, we're concerned with one special variant of the people-species—*historians*. More particularly, American historians. Does this model apply to them too, or just to the people they study?

Obviously, the question is rhetorical. Scholars cannot construct general

23

models of how humans behave without including themselves in the model. We all know that, of course; no one would purposely exempt himself from the human species while studying the species.

But what we do with conscious intent and what we do in fact are not always in harmony. In fact, historians do often claim for themselves what they deny to their historical subjects. They do this neither from arrogance nor from conscious malice; they do it, rather, because of the intellectual forms functioning in their discipline. American historians have not constructed working forms which simultaneously acknowledge (1) how humanly limited are their own reconstructions of the past, and (2) how scholarly rigor can be protected when they *do* admit such limitations. They can hold either (1) or (2), or (1) at one time and (2) at another, but few historians can manage both at the same time.

For one indication why this is true, let's look at a case illustration of this split vision in historical minds. The case is one of the more highly thought of historiographical studies in the profession—Charles Sellers' article, "Andrew Jackson versus the Historians."

<h1 style="text-align:center">II</h1>

Sellers' is a splendid essay, and deserves its reputation. It's an insightful review of historical scholarship on the age of Jackson, and I think it represents how American historians normally tend to see and use the findings of historiography research.

Sellers spends much of his article describing what he calls "frames of reference"—pictures through which historians have viewed reality in Jacksonian America. First, he says, came the Whig frame of reference—which prevailed throughout the nineteenth century, which was elitist in temper, and which was therefore contemptuous of Andrew Jackson's populist tendencies. By the early twentieth century, this Whig view was replaced by the Progressive picture—which applauded Jackson's democratic sympathies and drew parallels between Jacksonian democracy and the liberal battle against reactionary interests of its own day. Finally, says Sellers, more recent historians have pictured Jacksonian democracy as ambiguous and paradoxical—accomplishing both good and ill and motivated by liberal and reactionary impulses at the same time.

Sellers not only describes these frames of reference on the Jacksonian past; he gives them an existential location too, in the lives of historians who held them. Thus the Whigs:

It is important to remember that the Whig historians all came from eastern or European middle-class or upper-middle-class families with traditions of education, prestige, and public service, the kind of families that had claimed social and political leadership as their natural right during the early days of the republic. By the time these men began to write the history of Jacksonian Democracy, however, their kind had been largely ousted from political leadership by the professional politicians and new-style parties that had arisen as the institutional embodiments of the Jacksonian democratic revolution.[1]

And the Progressives:

Two facts should be especially noted about these young scholars who were to transform the writing of American history. One is that nearly all of them came from rural or small-town backgrounds in the West or South, and this in itself brought a new point of view into a field previously dominated by the urban Northeast. The second significant fact is that though they came from substantial middle-class families, they lived in a period when middle-class Americans, and particularly middle-class intellectuals, were being swept into the current of reform.[2]

Thus far Sellers works with a model resembling our own in chapter 1—men view the world through particular, bounded pictures ("frames of reference"), and these pictures are connected to their own distinctive experiences as people. That's how Sellers looks upon American historians and their scholarship up through his own day.

But then just three paragraphs from the end of his essay, he suddenly switches course . . . and form. He turns away from the scholarly past of American history to glance on into the future, and in doing so he says something very peculiar. Or at least it would seem peculiar to anyone not acculturated to the normal forms of scholarship in the profession. Listen: "Viewed in this light, the frame of reference has served a valuable purpose . . . by leading historians to the different elements of the complex Jacksonian past out of which an over-all synthesis must eventually be constructed."[3]

If we take Sellers at his word here, we're abruptly jolted away from our model of mind-world encounter of chapter 1. Now, it seems, these bounded frames of reference have become only *temporary* devices for historians; in time, they may learn to transcend them. They have served instrumental purposes in the profession, highlighting experiences which otherwise might have gone unseen. They have thereby performed a valuable historiographical service for scholarship. Once scholars have finally constructed their "over-all synthesis," however, that historiographical service can be dispensed with. When the profession of history gets to that single comprehensive view of all Jacksonian America, then it can discard its past "frames of reference." For those frames of reference can tell us only *about* reality in history. Once we've put together what the whole reality in fact *is,* then we won't need such particular "abouts" any longer.

No, Sellers doesn't quite say the history profession will reach the full truth of the Jacksonian past some day. He temporizes some. But his temporizing is on particular subjective historians and not on the general objective reality of history. Witness how he closes his article: " 'Objective reality' we know we can never altogether reach, but we need not apologize for assuming it is there, or for believing that our zigzag course brings us swinging in on a circle of ever closer vantage points for discerning its salient features."[4]

Why does Charles Sellers end this way? Why does he go on for some 18½ pages of a 20-page article viewing the past only through existentially grounded "frames of reference," then in his last three paragraphs suddenly revert to a floating abstraction like "objective reality"? He does it, I think, because he's trying to cope with the intellectual dilemma we mentioned in the last section—*how to grant the human limitations of historians, yet protect the rigor of their scholarly enterprise.* This is what we might call "the relativist dilemma."

On the one hand, Sellers notes that American historians have not been gods; looking back over the history of American history, he suggests that they have seen what they've been conditioned to see. Sketching in an elementary sociology of historical knowledge, he details how this has come about—how historians' pictures of reality are connected to their social locations in time. In short, he says their explanations of the past have been *relative*. Thus his version of the "frame-of-reference" model.

On the other hand, Sellers is not willing to admit that this is the whole of historical scholarship—that the enterprise can be reduced just to the social and personal biases of limited human beings. So as he projects on into the future of his profession, he resorts to the progressive hope; historians' explanations may have been restricted in the past, but they need not continue that way into the future.

Thus for Sellers' first 18½ pages, American historical scholarship is bound into frames of reference—pictures of the past limited to the existential locations of particular people, and particular groups of people. But in his last page and a half, there emerges an ideal, "reference-less" vision of scholarship in the field. Through that vision, an "over-all synthesis" of the past can transcend the limitations of particularity, connecting on out (or almost) to the general "objective reality" of American history.

The frame-of-reference model has served scholarship well, Sellers says. But he also says that historians must try and move beyond it. If they can never wholly escape their human limitations (" 'objective reality' we know we can never altogether reach"), at least they can envision a scholarly *ideal* transcending those limitations ("but we need not apologize for assuming it is there, or for believing that our zigzag course brings us swinging in on a circle of ever closer vantage points for discerning its salient features"). This vision, as Sellers projects it, has elsewhere been labeled the "ideal-observer" model of historical scholarship. "Andrew Jackson versus the Historians" exists in tension between these two models—the frame-of-reference and the ideal-observer.

In a recent article entitled "The Mind of the Historian," Bruce Kuklick sets down some fundamental assumptions behind this "ideal-observer" model of scholarship. We might look at these now to flesh out just what it is Sellers seems to be referring to.

Kuklick writes,

Of what then does a "plausible description" of an ideal observer consist? . . . First, he has a total knowledge of all the facts. This omniscience, moreover, is coupled with extraordinarily vivid powers of imagination enabling the ideal observer to visualize simultaneously all the actual facts and all possible sequences of events. . . . The ideal observer will additionally be disinterested and will not be influenced by interests designated as particular.

He continues, showing how the ideal observer avoids the bias of particularity:

In an analogous manner the ideal observer is dispassionate. Particular emotions are those directed toward a particular person or action, toward something *as* individual, but not directed toward other persons or actions of the same kind or class. To be dispassionate is to be free from particular emotions. Lastly, perhaps as a consequence of the qualities already enumerated, the ideal observer is consistent. His evaluatively significant reactions to any particular person or action will always be identical to his reactions to any other relevantly similar particular person or action.[5]

In short, the ideal observer is wholly freed from particular ideas. He does not see reality through existentially bound frames of reference; instead, he sees *what is,* and *all* of what is, because his vision has no existential grounding and is thus broad enough to encompass the whole. Kuklick's ideal observer has the detachment to perceive Sellers' "objective historical reality," and he has the vision and power to produce an overall synthesis of it. Whatever he says is wholly true because, being freed from the bias of particulars, he will be entirely objective in his judgments. As Kuklick says,

This analysis may, in one fairly clear sense, be labelled "objective." Whereas contemporary "non-cognitivist" theories . . . are all loosely associated in some way with "subjectivism" or "relativism," the ideal observer theory cannot be so associated. According to it, there will be one correct evaluation in every situation calling for evaluation.[6]

Kuklick is quick to note that no historian would claim he *is* the ideal observer, only that this is the goal they all should *strive for.* And they believe that by working to accumulate knowledge about the past, they move their discipline progressively closer to that goal.

Kuklick suggests that this is a basic working assumption of professional historians, and implies that almost all hold it in one form or another. Whether he's right is a question we're not equipped to handle here. But Charles Sellers does seem to hold it, or part of it, and I suspect he is far from alone in the profession. I think Sellers, like many American historians, is caught somewhere between the frame-of-reference model and the ideal-observer model—the one granting existential limitations in historians, the other trying to salvage some scholarly ideal from the flux.

This compromise makes possible a working scholarship in American historiography; and Sellers' concern with frames of reference is an instance of that scholarship. But because the compromise is so uneasy and historians are not willing to rest satisfied with the frame-of-reference position, they've restricted historiography studies to a kind of second-class citizenship in the profession. They tolerate such studies, and at some points even encourage them—admitting that they've discovered embarrassing biases in history's past. But they've allowed studies in historiography to work only around the edges of their own operating assumptions; such studies have had little power to alter or even affect much how historians do their actual scholarship. Which scholarship is informed most fundamentally by the "ideal historical observer" model.

In the next chapter, we'll inspect in some detail professional assumptions which have kept historiography backstage in the discipline—held as a kind of incidental adjunct to "real" scholarship in the field. For now, let's briefly consider how this frame-of-reference/ideal-observer compromise has grown from the legacy of relativism in the profession.

III

Relativism in American historical thought flourished during the 1930s, mainly in essays written by Charles Beard and Carl Becker. The impetus for relativism came from many different directions, but one motive was to loosen the hold of "scientific history" on American historians' minds. This idea of history as an objective science had been expressed in full form back in 1908, in a presidential address to the American Historical Association delivered by George Burton Adams. Adams declared to his colleagues:

At the very beginning of all conquest of the unknown lies the fact, established and classified to the fullest extent possible at the moment. To lay such foundations, to furnish such materials for later builders, may be a modest ambition, but it is my firm belief that in our field of history, for a long time to come, the man who devotes himself to such labors, who is content with this preliminary work, will make a more useful and a more permanent contribution to the final science, or philosophy of history, than will he who yields to the allurements of speculation and endeavors to discover in the present stage of our knowledge the forces that control society, or to formulate the laws of their action.

He then concluded, "None of the new battle cries should sound for us above the call of our first leader, proclaiming the chief duty of the historian to establish *wie es eigentlich gewesen.* . . . The field of the historian is, and must long remain, the discovery and recording of what actually happened."[7]

According to W. Stull Holt, this "scientific" faith went almost without challenge in the profession until the 1930s, when Beard and Becker's relativist critique took it to task. We needn't review the whole relativist versus scientific history debate here; a brief glance at the essays of Beard and Becker should suggest its main outlines.[8]

Look, for example, at how they titled these essays: "Everyman His Own Historian" (Becker), "What Are Historical Facts?" (Becker), "Written History as an Act of Faith" (Beard), "That Noble Dream" (Beard). In these essays, they ridiculed the "noble dream" of scientific objectivity, they asserted that historical facts are not solid and irreducible but constantly shift according to people's biases, and they challenged the professionalization of historical scholarship by claiming that basically "everyman (is) his own historian."

And they wrote things like: "[The scholar] is more or less a guesser in this vale of tears."[9] Or: "The historical fact is in someone's mind or it is nowhere."[10] And: "Our proper function is not to repeat the past but to make use of it, to correct and rationalize for common use Mr. Everyman's mythological adaptation of what happened."[11]

When Carl Becker took a look at G. B. Adams' "final science" of history—at how, in our terms, Kuklick's "ideal observer" would in time perceive Sellers' "objective reality"—he was neither exhilarated nor even pleased by the possibility. He was simply bored:

If we had all the data of all events, and a mind capable of grasping the data in their actual relations, everything would be immediately understood and immediately pardoned. In this timeless existence there would be no occasion for "views," no occasion for distinction between facts and non-facts, facts and interpretations, meaning and non-meaning, good and bad, being and becoming: everything would simply be, the entire blest *wie es eigentlich gewesen sei* would just be there and nothing to write home about. We would have the Truth, and the Truth would make us free, free to do nothing—except sit and contemplate the Truth.[12]

For many historians, this was going too far. Beard and Becker didn't quite say that any statement about the past is just as true as any other, but they came close. Becker's colleague William Dodd wrote him that his "Everyman" address was a counsel in futility to younger scholars, and some wondered if relativism was implying that historical scholarship is little more than disguised propaganda.[13] A few critics charged that relativism too was historically relative, and would pass with changing times. They were proven right when, in the late 1930s and early 1940s, Beard and Becker backed away from their relativist position when they had to confront the experience of fascist totalitarianism. As Robert Skotheim has written, "In the face of totalitarianism, Becker modified his emphasis upon a theoretical relativism in favor of an emphasis upon virtually 'absolute,' 'universal' ideas or values in man's history."[14]

If relativism waned among historians after the 1930s, it did leave a legacy, and that legacy is what we've seen in Sellers. It recognizes scholarly bias in the past, and it connects that bias with the social locations and personal predilections of historians. It may further admit, like Sellers, that some of these biases might be ineradicable, that no scholar can wholly free himself from the human particulars of who he is and what he is and where he is.

But—and this is where Adams' "scientific" faith and Kuklick's "ideal observer" come into play—if scholars have human limitations, this is no cause simply to indulge those limitations. They must instead project in their minds an ideal scholarship free of bias; if they can never reach that ideal, at least it can give them something worthwhile to aim for. Thus, again, Sellers's closing lines: " 'Objective reality' we know we can never altogether reach, but we need not apologize for assuming it is there, or for believing that our zigzag course brings us swinging in on a circle of ever closer vantage points for discerning its salient features."

IV

This, I think, is the ambiguous legacy of relativism in American historical scholarship. The legacy has not been codified into explicit doctrine, because historians are not given to being doctrinaire in such matters. Nor, for that matter, are they normally given to being explicit about them. The legacy—embodying the relativist dilemma—is mostly held below the level of verbal awareness in their work, briefly surfacing now and then in a book preface or an aside or a footnote, or sometimes in a methodology article or book review.

It's an ambiguous legacy because, when confronted directly, it must admit an enormous gulf between the existing practice of history writing and the ideal objective of future scholarship in the field. But if it's ambiguous, it is not I think hypocritical. Given the dilemma it faces—how to grant the human limitations of historians, yet protect the rigor of their scholarly enterprise—it's a legitimate compromise, if still an uneasy one.

I believe, though, that there are ways to get through this dilemma, and during the rest of this chapter I'd like to explore some. In doing so, we'll range out beyond the discipline of history—moving into an area where they've been working through such a dilemma for some time now.

But first, let us root our considerations in a concrete historical situation. Too many discussions of ideas and forms in historiography scholarship are just that—ideas and forms, unconnected to any kind of grounded experience (save perhaps for Caesar crossing over the Rubicon, and that's not very grounded). I suspect this is one reason why such methodic considerations have had slight impact on practicing historical scholarship; theoreticians and philosophers of history seldom work at a level which can benefit their colleagues in the field. It is one thing to read and write and logically manipulate abstract concepts like "relativism," "subjectivity," "objective reality;" it is quite another to consider how they operate in actual historical situations. Because it is imperative that we work our methods through substance, I've thought to ground my discussion here in a concrete historical "laboratory"— Faulkner's novel *The Sound and the Fury*.

It's a fictional laboratory, to be sure. But we shouldn't let that put us off. A fiction is not necessarily an untruth. What's important here is that we have before us a sequence of experiences which happens to and through people, and that these experiences take place over time. That, I take it, is what's distinctive about historical experience, and this *The Sound and the Fury* can give us. Further, as we noted in the first chapter, its fictional nature should offer us opportunity to play with ideas for a while, and test them out in our laboratory. Such an opportunity might be resisted if we were to deal here with some "real" experience in American history.

V

Recall that this novel presents a series of events as narrated through four radically different frames of reference. First comes the narrative of Benjy, the idiot, who experiences the world without the mediation of symbolic forms. Benjy is followed by his oldest brother, Quentin, to whom symbolic forms *are* the world, virtually his only world. Then comes Jason, the middle brother, who tries to cut through abstract symbols by an act of will; his cutting tool is a hard-nosed cynicism. Finally, the novel concludes with Faulkner assuming the voice of omniscient author, narrating events which lead to a climax on Easter Sunday, 1928.

What the reader comes out with is not *a* history of the Compson family, but at least three different ones, maybe four. Faulkner writes history like most of us experience it. Most of our experiences don't have clear beginnings, middles, and ends. And even when they do, we may enter the scene some time after things have begun. Further, there's often no satisfactory way to find out what went on before we got there, or even to learn fully what's happening now. All we can do is go to various witnesses, and participants, and piece together as best we can from what they tell us. That, in brief, is what *The Sound and the Fury* is about. In language which we'll make clearer in a few moments, we see "perspectives" on historical reality in this novel, we do not see a single "objective" reality.

We've already seen what Benjy's perspective can bring us, when we were outlining some functions of ideas in chapter 1. However limited may be Benjy's experience of the world, his perceptions are not distorted by preconceived beliefs nor by wish projections; so he becomes the most trustworthy narrator in the novel. We realize that Benjy is limited in the facts he sees; but we can be sure that his facts are always real facts, for he cannot lie to us about them.

We've also seen how, lacking the leverage of symbolic forms, Benjy is rendered immobile in the world, and cannot accommodate to change. In contrast with other characters in *The Sound and the Fury,* Benjy's sense of time is slowed down, and Faulkner cleverly uses him to detect changes which no one else in the novel is very much aware of. Like his sister Caddy wearing her first perfume, or the contrasting behavior of Caddy and her daughter in the swing, nineteen years apart, or the sale of the Compson pasture to become a golf course. Others in the novel do of course experience these changes, but they're so preoccupied with their own concerns that they're not inclined to make anything of them.

Now Faulkner might have told us this through the voice of an omniscient author (which voice in a novel is equivalent to the "ideal observer" in history studies). But if he did so, he'd have to tell us *about* change being decline. We'd then know *that* this is the case, and would use a change-equals-decline pattern for reading through the rest of the family history.

Such a reading might lead us to "objective reality" in the Compson history, but it would miss something important. If it would catch the generalities of change, it would miss some vital particulars. It would not miss particular *events*—those an omniscient author or ideal historical observer can catch quite well. What they can't catch are particular *people.* They can of course catch them from the outside, their public face, but they cannot render the experience of particular people *from the inside out.*

They cannot do it by definition, or at least the ideal historical observer can't (the omniscient author has more flexibility of movement in a work of fiction, and may on occasion move down inside his characters). As we have seen, the impulse behind this ideal-observer model is to escape the bias of particularity, to gain a position outside the perceptual flux when viewing historical reality. But the people of history—history's actors—are *inside* the perceptual flux; they act as they do because of what they see. And they see from *particular* locations. An outside observer might call these particular perceptions "distorted"—that is, not objectively correct. Yet they may well be *experientially* correct, however distorted they may appear when seen wholly from the outside.

In Benjy, for example, we can note that his very limitations show us realities which a wholly detached observer could not possibly see. It may be that reality in history lies on more than one plane, and that what is objectively real from a detached position may not jibe with what is perceptually real in the experience of involved people. If this is so, maybe we have a route out of the relativist dilemma.

Let's try looking at this issue from another angle now, taking another "perspective" on it for the moment. Let's view the same historical reality as seen from the inside out by two different observers. Here is Benjy, opening the novel on April 7, 1928:

Through the fence, between the curling flower spaces, I could see them hitting. They were coming toward where the flag was and I went along the fence. Luster was hunting in the grass by the flower tree. They took the flag out, and they were hitting. Then they put the flag back and they went to the table, and he hit and the other hit. Then they went on, and I went along the fence. Luster came away from the flower tree and we went along the fence and they stopped and we stopped and I looked through the fence while Luster was hunting in the grass.

"Here, caddie." He hit. They went across the pasture. I held to the fence and watched them going away.

"Listen at you, now." Luster said. "Aint you something, thirty-three years old, going on that way. After I done went all the way to town to buy you that cake. Hush up that moaning."[15]

And here is his brother Jason later in the novel, talking of the same day:

It's bad enough on Sundays, with that damn field full of people that haven't got a side show and six niggers to feed, knocking a damn oversize mothball around. He's going to keep on running up and down that fence and bellowing every time they come in sight until first thing I know they're going to begin charging me golf dues, then Mother and Dilsey'll have to get a couple of china door knobs and a walking stick and work it out, unless I play at night with a lantern. Then they'd send us all to Jackson [the state asylum], maybe. God knows, they'd hold Old Home week when that happened.[16]

Now what would an ideal historical observer make of this? Well, he could establish certain facts of the situation independently of who reported them. There is a golf course, separated from the Compson home by a fence. Some people are playing golf, and on occasion they say, "caddie." Benjy moves back and forth along the fence, sometimes crying as he does. That at least would give us a skeletal framework of the external scene, a kind of photograph copy, as it were, of what is there and what is happening. It would be important to know these kinds of details, and on this level the ideal observer would serve historical scholarship quite well.

But what could such an observer make of the special *meanings* people associate with these events? To Jason, the golf course is simply a "damn field full of people." But to Benjy it's a pasture where they all played as children. The golfer's cry "caddie" stimulates a sensation of his lost sister, and this further sparks sensations of innocent childhood when brothers and sister and black children all played together. Jason, however, feels the burden of "a side show [Benjy] and six niggers to feed," so his mind is blocked from recalling those childhood memories. Further, he's glad there is a fence between golf course and house (perhaps built it himself), for it keeps Benjy out of the golfers' way. But to Benjy that fence is an intolerable barrier blocking his childhood sensations from being realized. Because of that blockage, and because the golfers restimulate his sensations by calling out "caddie," Benjy cries (or moans, or bellows, depending on who's hearing it).

Could an ideal historical observer produce a single objective synthesis of this reality? Perhaps. But he'd have to stick with what is publicly observable, and thus would miss things. To get to those things, he'd have to depart from his detached location, and enter the experience of particulars.

He'd have to do that because some realities in this situation are *inescapably particular,* and to uproot them from their location is to distort their meaning.

Take the golf course. On one plane of historical reality, this golf course is an objective fact, pure and simple. It is there, we can measure it and photograph it and tape record what sounds are made by people and things on it. Only a fool or a solipsist would deny its reality on this plane.

But on another plane, it's not merely a golf course at all. It's that, *plus* what varied meanings people associate with it. We've just seen what Benjy associates with it. And we've seen that Jason has quite different associations. For him, a golf course nearby is an irritation, because it sets Benjy off bellowing. The golfers also make Jason resentful, because he has "a side show and six niggers to feed," and doesn't have time for such frivolous things.

The ideal historical observer might call Jason "biased," because he lacks detachment to get outside the particulars of his situation. Such an observer might call Benjy even more biased, because this golf course is not a pasture anymore, and "caddie" isn't Caddy.

But the golf course is not only a visibly present reality, it's also a historical reality—that is, part of a sequence in time. And it once *was* a pasture. Benjy "knows" this historical fact better than anyone else, and can, through wordless bellowing, express its human meaning more vividly than could any observer with more normal expressive powers. From this perspective, that speechless idiot conveys a richer sense of the *historicity* of this piece of land than could any ideal observer. Such an observer might fault Benjy for being imprisoned in the sensations of his past, but through those sensations he can recapture that past in a way no normal (or supernormal) being ever could.

VI

Suppose we were to use *The Sound and the Fury* now as we would a "primary document" in historical scholarship. Taking this novel as a historical source, suppose we were to try and reconstruct the experiences of the Compson family as they lived through time. Suppose further that we were to try and free ourselves from the relativist compromise and its ideal-observer corollary, and view these experiences through an alternative, "perspectivistic" model of historical scholarship. How would we go about it?

Well, first, we would ask different questions of our sources. The ideal-observer model is concerned basically with *what happened* in the past. To get at that, it queries its sources to try and unravel the objective truth of history from all the distortions of particular people. The perspectivist model is concerned with what happened too, but that is not its exclusive or even basic concern. Its basic concern rather is with the question, "How do particular people *experience* what happened?" And further, "How do they *put form* on their experience?" And yet further, "How do these forms connect into their particular locations in time and place?"

With such a perspectivistic view, it is imperative to know *who sees what* in a historical situation. It is not that everything is relative and in flux with such a model. That *would* be a counsel of intellectual despair, and historians properly reject this kind of relativism. But historical perspectivism says something rather different. It says that certain realities in a situation are existentially connected to certain kinds of people who experience them, and who give form to them. It is the task of scholarship, then, *to track down those connections*. They are real, they exist in historical experience, and any scholarship which goes after them must be rigorous in its procedures.

When Benjy bellows at "caddie," for example, it is important to know that the golfers' word "caddie" is not his sister Caddy. But it is even more important, within this model, to ask *why* Benjy bellows at this word, and to search out just what the form of his expression signifies (e.g., it signifies that he is powerless to talk, that he is incapable of normal change, that he therefore suffers acutely from the loss of his sister and from the sale of the family pasture to become a golf course). No one else in the novel can inform us of certain real experiences quite as well as Benjy can, and the *form* of his expression—anguished, wordless bellowing—is absolutely essential to the kind of historical truth he is conveying to us.

Within this perspectivistic model, a basic task of historical reconstruction is to search out who can tell us best about what kinds of experiences. Hence we should ask of our sources here, "What can each person show us about himself, the family, and the events of this history that we couldn't know otherwise?" In short, *what kind of a historian is each narrator?*

Benjy, for example, is our most trustworthy source for laying out certain external facts in the family history. He forgets nothing, he distorts nothing, and if he cannot tell us everything, he can at least convey everything that he sees and feels. And also everything that he smells. With his acute nonverbal sensitivities, Benjy can spot a radical change in Caddy when she no longer smells natural, like trees, but artificial, like perfume. Benjy can also recall exactly what it was like back in the days of Compson innocence, so he's our best source for events in the past, and for a key to how the family moved from respectability in the Jefferson community to its present state of degeneration.

But because Benjy's whole past is instantaneous to him (or can be made so with the right kind of outside stimulus), he gets the *sequence* of events all mixed up. Everything is there all right in his narrative, but it's not put into a chronological form which makes sense to us. Faulkner ingeniously opens the novel with Benjy; that gives us the raw data of this history, and piques our curiosity to try and pattern it. But it doesn't set any pattern by itself.

That pattern, or parts of it, comes through Benjy's other two brothers, Quentin and Jason. Quentin, as we saw in the last chapter, lives almost wholly in his mind and imagination. In his opening narrative, Benjy gives us the raw *experience* of change in the Compson family, and his emotional resistance to same. Quentin, in the narrative which follows, gives us the abstract *idea* of this change, and his symbolic resistance to same.

That resistance takes form in his obsession with time and clocks; Quentin's narrative opens, "When the shadow of the sash appeared on the curtains it was between seven and eight oclock and then I was in time again, hearing the watch."[17] Watches and clocks and the idea of time function for him much as do smells and visual stimuli for Benjy. They key both in to the strain of change, and indicate their inability to cope with it. One ends up in the state asylum at Jackson, the other commits suicide in the Charles River.

Of the blacks, on the other hand, Faulkner writes, "They endured."[18] They endured because they neither sought change nor fought it, they simply accommodated to it. So with Dilsey, the black housekeeper, we see a picture of change which contrasts with both Benjy's and Quentin's (also Jason's). Dilsey just accepts life as it comes, one moment at a time, and she is affected neither by imprisoning memories of the past nor by wish visions of the future. Dilsey lives in time, but her mind—her picture of the world—in a sense functions outside the flux of time. "I've seed de first en de last," she says.[19] And thus, above all the white Compsons she serves, this black servant endured; and her nobility was unimpaired by the changes which over the years virtually destroyed them.

VII

We might pause now and briefly draw the contours of this "perspectives" model, and also try to condense a few basic assumptions which underlie it. We can further show wherein it differs from the frame-of-reference/ideal-observer compromise. In doing this, we'll build upon the model of mind-world encounter which we constructed in the opening chapter.

1. The "perspectives" model begins by assuming that historical reality as experienced by people is multiple, with many faces on a variety of different planes. There are several consequences to this assumption.

One is that the world is too large and complex to be seen whole. There's just too much for mind to take account of. We noted this in chapter 1 when we said people use ideas to pare reality down to manageable size, so they can take it in and do something with it. Now we can call those particularizing ideas "perspectives." Perspectives are the "pictures in our heads" which compress our experience into controllable form.

Up to this point, historical perspectivism is not at odds with the ideal historical observer model. That model would admit the above, but would claim the problem of mind is simply *quantitative*. Particular historians cannot hold enough in their minds to encompass all of reality, but a hypothetical ideal observer could.

Perspectivism has a further consequence, however, and here it *does* move away from the ideal observer model. The problem of mind vis-à-vis world, it claims, is not only quantitative, it's *qualitative* too—not only a problem of numbers but of kind. The world not only has too many faces for a single mind to take in whole, these faces also point in a plurality of directions. So even if some ideal superhuman mind were large enough to hold all these faces, it would be torn to pieces by all the varied and competing ways they move. If it tried to handle all those pieces, then it would lose its objectivity, for its whole thrust is to keep from being particularized, being torn down like this. Rather, its purpose is to envision the whole all together.

As we've seen from Faulkner's multi-perspective strategy in *The Sound and the Fury,* each narrator can, from his special location in time and place, tell us different true things about historical reality. Were we to uproot these things from their special locations, they would cease to be true. To apprehend those truths, then, we must *not* try and pull away to some ideal objective position, we must move down into where they are and see things from there.

But when we do this, we preclude our being elsewhere, seeing things from other locations. Benjy's view of the golf course is true, so also is Jason's. Yet they oppose each other. And no ideal observer could produce from this a single synthesis saying what the golf course *really* is.

We're faced here with something like the psychology textbook example of two curving lines on a white background. When a person looks at the lines one way, he sees a vase. When he looks at them another way, he sees two faces. *But no one ever sees vase and faces simultaneously.* One pattern of the lines precludes another. Yet both patterns are real, and both are true to the objective facts.

If this is the case with such a simple reality as two short black lines drawn on a bounded white background, how much more true must it be of many more complex realities we face in historical scholarship. With some of these realities, there are always alternative patterns possible for the same objective facts. Hence the "perspectives" model insists we must not look for a single block reality in our history studies; we must assume rather a plurality of angles on our materials. As in contemporary physics so in historical scholarship—a *complementarity* of interpretations seems the best way to address reality. Or at least certain kinds of reality.

2. From the "perspectives" model, historical experiences are not only reconstructed later through particular "frames of reference," many of them happen that way in the first place.   On certain fundamental planes of reality, historical experiences don't take place objectively and holistically, they take place subjectively and through particular reference positions. This, again, is where the ideal-observer model goes wrong. It proposes to reconstruct "history as it really happened" in a way wholly different from how it really happened.

Through Charles Sellers and the relativist compromise, we have seen how the frame-of-reference model was held to embody a defect of method, a fault in the minds of past historians. Though the compromise admitted they could hardly help themselves, it tended to charge them with "contaminating" objective reality by imposing their own subjective dispositions on it.

It granted there had been some instrumental value in this, for through these contaminations we'd been alerted to things we might not otherwise have seen. But it granted that almost in apology, for it felt this was hardly the ideal way to go about scholarship. The ideal situation would be an uncontaminated view of history, a detached and objective position from which an overall synthesis of the past would be seen.

Then enter Faulkner's reality in *The Sound and the Fury.* And exit the relativist compromise and its ideal observer. For when we have this kind of historical experience in front of us, we needn't apologize anymore for the bias of particular minds. Because *only* these particular minds, existentially grounded in time and place and situation, can express certain felt dynamics of what happened with the Compson family.

These minds (or perspectives) embody the *human* part of this historical experience. They reconstruct not only the physical landscape as pasture or as golf course; they also picture this scene as a subjectively remembered sensation where children once played, or as a place where the name "caddie" stimulates sensations of a boy's lost sister. They reconstruct not only the natural smell of trees or the manufactured smell of perfume, but the human associations of these two smells, and the sense of personal loss suffered when one smell is substituted for the other.

It is hard to penetrate to what "in fact" has happened in this kind of historical experience, for what in fact has happened depends on what kinds of pictures and sensations people carry in their heads of it. What we have here is not historical reality as it takes place outside people, but the experience of time and events as they come *through* people. There is no God-perspective in this novel, save in the concluding section and the appendix. And those are a considerable letdown after the intensity of the first three sections. They are necessary to render certain facts, and certain kinds of realities, which none of the Compson brothers could report by himself. But if events in *The Sound and the Fury* were rendered *only* from the God-perspective, this novel would be but a pale reflection of what Faulkner actually has done.

And here, I think, is another point where the ideal observer misses the mark. By definition, the ideal observer must keep away from the bias of particularity. As Kuklick writes, "The ideal observer will . . . be disinterested and will not be influenced by interests designated as particular. . . . [He will be] free from particular emotions."[20]

For some historical situations, that is good; in fact, it's probably good on some planes of all situations. But on other planes, keeping away from particularities means not experiencing peoples' pictures and sensations from the inside out. However objective the ideal observer might be from his detached position, his God-perspective would block him from getting in to the *human* part of experienced reality.

It is important to recognize, then, that these perspectives—or pictures in our heads—have connections. They are connected to the kind of personality we have, to our location in the social structure, to our geographical surroundings, to our place in time, to whom we perceive as our friends and our enemies, to what problems we're addressing, and to a host of other things. If these pictures don't necessarily *make* us what we are as human beings, they do in fact *express* much of what we are. Such pictures don't get into our heads just because we will them there, nor are they easily willed away. Because of this connectedness with the people and things around them, they offer valuable keys to how humans experience their world. The "ideal observer" model falls short at just the point where it would deprive us of those keys.

3. *Finally, the "perspectives" model maintains there is no such thing as "objective reality in history," at least as a holistic entity.*   And here it takes its most radical departure from the Sellers position.

We need to make the precise nature of this departure clear now, lest the perspectives approach be confused with the 1930s relativism of Charles Beard and Carl Becker. Contrary to relativism, perspectivism maintains there *are* objective facts in the world. It further maintains that it's worthwhile for historians to try and find out—with as much care and precision as possible—just what those facts are. It does not intend to counsel despair about the possibilities of scholarship in history, nor does it lead to the suspicion that any man's view of the past is just as good as any other's.

According to this model, Becker was half wrong when he declaimed, "The historical fact is in someone's mind or it is nowhere."[21] The historical fact is in someone's mind *and* it is in the world. Or at least some kinds of facts are. Regardless of our subjective dispositions, George Washington was born in 1732 and died in 1799, the Civil War broke out in 1861, the stock market crashed in 1929, and John F. Kennedy was shot in 1963. The same holds true with certain patterns of facts—like how many people voted Republican and how many Democratic in the election of 1956, or how much of the federal budget goes to defense-related activities and how much to welfare, or what John Winthrop did publicly in response to the dual challenges of Roger Williams and Anne Hutchinson in the 1630s.

Facts like this rest on firm foundations, regardless of who sees them, or his connections to time and place and situation. We might quibble about what to call the "Civil War," or just what are "defense-related activities," but the facts behind those experiences are still objectively determinable. No school of American historical interpretation—Progressive, consensus, New Left, what have you—would argue over the reality of facts like this, and the perspectives approach wouldn't propose that they do argue. Though some things seen always up for grabs with this model, not everything is.

These, then, are objective facts in history. But they do not make for a holistic "objective reality in history." They are part of historical reality, the perspectives model doesn't deny that. But it sees such facts much like that textbook picture of a vase and two faces. In both perceptions, the lines in this picture are absolutely stable and rooted. They never change, regardless of how we look at them, or who looks. In that sense they are objectively real, subject to public test and measurement. But once we try and make something *of* these objective facts, give them human meaning, then they'll be fit into different forms and patterns depending on the existential location of who's seeing them. The lines never change, but their contextual meanings in people's minds do.

Those forms and patterns don't exist *in* the things (in this case the black lines on the white background). But neither do they exist wholly *apart* from the things, as disconnected pictures in our heads. They exist, rather, in *an ongoing dialogue between human projections and environmental givens.* In this case the environmental given is the black-and-white picture. And the human projection comes from that picture's resembling two objects with which we are humanly familiar—a vase and peoples' faces. To pattern this reality, we connect what we see on the printed page with familiar references from our past experience.

Which is about all we human beings have to go on—our past experiences, the patterns and meanings we can give to same, and the materials of the world in front of us. Out of the intermixture of these three comes the sense we people make of the world. And, I should think, out of them also comes the proper enterprise of scholarship. To ask for more is to ask for a superhuman scholarship—and that's not only a human impossibility (by definition), it's also an erroneous ideal.

So this is how the perspectives model proposes a way out of the relativist dilemma. It faces that dilemma head-on by first showing how historians and their scholarship are inescapably biased—that is, grounded in time and place and situation. It further grants that certain distortions of truth may come from this grounding. But it claims certain revelations of truth will come too, for such existential grounding particularizes reality as well as distorts it. And some kinds of truth in history are experienced *only* as particulars.

That is how perspectivism faces the relativist dilemma. But it tries to get around that dilemma by claiming the enterprise of historical scholarship need not be simply the projections of a scholar's bias upon the world. Perspectivism is not the solipsistic claim that "it's all in the mind." Quite to the contrary, it recognizes the hard stuff of the world out there and seeks to root experience in that world. Indeed, this is its basic point—*that scholars and historical reality itself are invariably connected to particulars in the world, and any model for reconstructing historical experience must be prepared to move into and through these particulars.* The ideal observer leaves us short precisely because he has no such world grounding. Not living in historical reality, he lacks the human perspective to understand historical reality. Or at least those kinds of realities that come only *through* human experience.

Perspectivism further distinguishes itself from that brand of relativism which says "anything is true anywhere." It insists instead that some things *are* true here but *not* true there, and it tends to be skeptical of experiential truths rendered unperspectivistically. It maintains that certain truths in history are intimately connected to certain points of view and certain situations and certain kinds of people. The task of historical scholarship, then, is *to search out what is connected with what, and when, and how, and through what forms.*

So scholarship through the "perspectives" model is both more limiting and has more opportunities than scholarship through the frame-of-reference/ideal-observer compromise. It's more limiting because it removes the ideal observer and objective reality from the kinds of experience it works with. But it has more opportunities because it opens out new sorts of realities in historical experience, and can explore all sorts of connections among these realities and their various levels. Let us turn now to an area of scholarship which is quite familiar with these sorts of realities, and which could therefore help us in history studies to search out new kinds of connections in our materials.

VIII

It is difficult to define this area, since there's no pre-established name for it, or departmental home in academe. But if it lacks a departmental base, it nonetheless has location and direction. We can best express where it is and where it's going by citing a few instances of it. Listen, as scholars in this area convey their sense of how man connects to the world around him.

Here is the psychologist George Kelly, who has not only written analytically in this area, but was to create a whole mode of clinical therapy from it:

We look at the undifferentiated stream of circumstance flowing past us, and we try to find something about it that repeats itself. Once we have abstracted that property, we have a basis for slicing off chunks of time and reality and holding them up for inspection one at a time. On the other hand, if we fail to find such a property, we are left swimming in a shoreless stream, where there are no beginnings and no endings to anything. Thus the first step in prediction is to get hold of a solid fistful of something to predict. And this is done by construing.[22]

Here are the sociologists of knowledge Peter Berger and Thomas Luckmann, writing of man's unique powers of mind vis-à-vis world:

The origins of a symbolic universe have their roots in the constitution of man. If man in society is a world-constructor, this is made possible by his constitutionally given world-openness, which already implies the conflict between order and chaos.[23]

Here is the philosopher Ernst Cassirer, on man's dialogue with his world through symbolic forms:

No longer can man confront reality immediately; he cannot see it, as it were, face to face. Physical reality seems to recede in proportion as man's symbolic reality advances. Instead of dealing with the things themselves man is in a sense constantly conversing with himself.[24]

Here is the linguist Joseph Church, describing how men can manipulate their world through verbal symbols:

The real value of symbolic action . . . is that we can verbally rearrange situations which in themselves would resist rearrangement, as when we discuss social or political or educational reforms; we can isolate certain features which in fact cannot be isolated, as when, in criticizing a work of art, we can talk separately about the artist's technical competence and his particular "vision"; we can juxtapose objects and events far separated in time and space, as when we try to relate infantile experiences to adult personality, or look for regularities in historical events; we can, if we will, turn the universe symbolically inside out, as, in effect, such innovators as Copernicus and Einstein have done.[25]

Here is the biologist Ludwig von Bertalanffy, writing on how man, distinctive among species, confronts things in the world:

Man's unique position is based on the dominance of symbols in his life. . . . Except in the immediate satisfaction of biological needs, man lives in a world not of things, but of symbols. A coin is a symbol for a certain amount of work done or food or utilities available; a document is a symbol of *res gestae;* a word or concept is a symbol of a thing or relationship; a book is a fantastic pile of accumulated symbols; and so forth, *ad infinitum.*[26]

Here is the literary critic Lionel Trilling, suggesting wherein man's idea-forms encounter the world:

As for the origin of ideas, we ought to remember that an idea is the formulation of a response to a situation; so, too, is the modification of an existing idea.[27]

Here is Donald Schon, once a philosopher but at the time of his writing a product consultant in industry:

We must understand concepts as the fund of expectations in terms of which we structure our experience.[28]

Here is the sociologist of ideology Karl Mannheim, writing of how ideas function in their existential situations:

It is not men in general who think, or even isolated individuals who do the thinking, but men in certain groups who have developed a particular style of thought in an endless series of responses to certain typical situations characterizing their common position.[29]

Finally, here are the cognitive psychologists Jerome Bruner and Leo Postman, suggesting how men respond to stimuli from the outside world:

Stimuli . . . do not act upon an indifferent organism. . . . The organism in perception is one way or another in a state of expectancy about the environment. It is a truism worth repeating that the perceptual effect of a stimulus is necessarily dependent upon the set or expectancy of the organism. And so, in many situations the student of perception must also specify the expectancies of the organism when exposed to stimulation.[30]

There are others working in this area too—the child psychologist Jean Piaget (*The Child's Construction of Reality*), the literary critic Kenneth Burke (*The Philosophy of Literary Form: Studies in Symbolic Action*), the art historian E. H. Gombrich (*Art and Illusion: A Study in the Psychology of Pictorial Representation*), the symbolic sociologist Hugh Dalziel Duncan (*Symbols in Society*), the cognitive psychologists M. Brewster Smith, Jerome Bruner, and Robert White (*Opinions and Personality*), the philosopher Gilbert Ryle (*The Concept of Mind*), the linguistic anthropologist Benjamin Whorf (*Language, Thought, and Reality*), the biologist-educator Joseph Schwab (*The Teaching of Science as Enquiry*), the political scientist Robert Lane (*Political Ideology: Why the American Common Man Believes What He Does*), the economist Kenneth Boulding (*The Image: Knowledge in Life and Society*), the cognitive psychologist Milton Rokeach (*The Open and Closed Mind: Investigations into the Nature of Belief Systems and Personality Systems*), the symbolic anthropologist Leslie White (*The Science of Culture*), the philosopher Susanne Langer (*Philosophy in a New Key*), the sociologist Robert Merton (*Social Theory and Social Structure*), the cognitive psychologists Heinz Werner and Bernard Kaplan (*Symbol Formation: An Organismic-Developmental Approach to Language and the Expression of Thought*), the theoretical-physicist-turned-historian-of-science Thomas Kuhn (*The Structure of Scientific Revolutions*), and, before Kuhn, E. A. Burtt (*The Metaphysical Foundations of Modern Physical Science*), the psychologist of cognitive dissonance Leon Festinger (*When Prophecy Fails*), the sociologist-educator Daniel Bell (*The Reforming of General Education*).

We could go on listing like this, turning up gestalt psychologists and ethno-methodologists and symbolic interactionists and computer theorists and some sociological and political theorists and doubtless a host of others too. But this brief list should at least hint at the remarkable variety of disciplines converging here on a single area. Not everyone in this area is doing precisely the same thing of course, but once we probe below the manifest surface of their varying subject matters, we are struck by the resemblances among them.[31]

Why this striking parallel of concern? Scholarly alignments normally congeal around academic departments; yet here we have thrown together psychologists and philosophers and sociologists and physicists and economists and linguists and political scientists and art historians and anthropologists and literary critics and biologists and educators and clinical therapists and at least one product consultant in industry.

Either there's an unseen conspiracy among these scholars, with some hidden mode of communication holding them together, or, more likely, human experience is throwing up some recurring patterns which don't follow the normal routines of academe. And, in order to search out these patterns, inquirers have evidently felt obliged to push out beyond the boundaries of their respective fields.

What is it, then, that they're tuning out after? What is it in the world of human experience that they seek, and which they cannot find within existing disciplinary forms?

We might begin an answer by simply noting some common concerns among these scholars. First, they all take things which have normally been seen as inert, and picture them as dynamic. They see a world in motion and a man in motion, and they see relationships between the two as an ongoing series of *transactions*. Peter Berger and Thomas Luckmann convey this dynamic sense in their term "world-openness"; and George Kelly has given pattern to it:

The universe is real; it is happening all the time; it is integral; and it is open to piecemeal interpretation. Different men construe it in different ways. Since it owes no prior allegiance to any one man's construction system, it is always open to reconstruction. Some of the alternative ways of construing are better adapted to man's purposes than are others. Thus, man comes to understand his world through an infinite series of successive approximations. Since man is always faced with constructive alternatives, which he may explore if he wishes, he need not continue indefinitely to be the absolute victim either of his past history or of his present circumstances.[32]

As man transacts with his world, say these scholars, he tries to cope with it and make sense of it by *patterning* things, constructing schemes of reality. These constructed patterns distinguish people as a species from all others, and Jerome Bruner catches this distinguishing quality by speaking of the human "motive to categorize."[33]

Such categories and patterns don't simply lie inert in men's heads, however, for reality feeds back on them, sometimes damaging or destroying them, often altering them, but usually affecting them in some way or another. Experience—or at least the human part of experience—lies along the plane of transactions between men's pictures of the world and what the world throws up to them. Human reality is neither the pictures inside men's heads nor the objective world outside, but a continuous *dialogue* between the two.

All these scholars converge on the assumption that man is the species who seeks to impose form on things, form and routine being less given in his biological makeup than in that of other species. What other forms of life have as a blessing of nature—preprogrammed schemas for living—he must labor for throughout his existence. Where they are *creatures of form,* he is a perennially *forming creator.*

IX

Though no one in the last section is officially labelled "intellectual historian," all are concerned with the distinctive subject matter of intellectual history—*people's idea-forms,* and their interaction with the world through time. There is a paradox of sorts here, for if any discipline should be integrating the various concerns of this idea-field, it would seem to be intellectual history studies.

Indeed, some thirty-odd years ago Arthur O. Lovejoy sounded the call for intellectual history to do just that. Noting that "ideas are the most migratory things in the world," he urged his colleagues to found a new interdisciplinary field which would seek out and study ideas wherever they may be found in the world, and in whatever form.[34]

In the years since, intellectual history has been broad ranging in its concerns; but with a few exceptions like, say, H. Stuart Hughes or Richard Hofstadter, professional historians have not been informed by what's going on in cognitive psychology or in anthropological philosophy or in the symbolic interactionist school of sociology or in linguistic theory or in computer theory or in any other allied field.[35] They have made a few taps into the sociology of knowledge—mainly through Karl Mannheim's book, *Ideology and Utopia.* But these taps have not run very deep, since in that study Mannheim offered a way out of the relativist dilemma which few academic historians ever picked up on.[36]

There are reasons for this paradox in American historical scholarship, though what is cause here and what is effect I do not know. The basic reason, I think, is that professional historians have tended to concentrate their studies on *the express content of thought*—asking "What does an idea say?"—whereas these other scholars focus more on *the underlying structure and function of thinking*—asking "How do people put ideas together, and what do they do for them?"

Where intellectual historians normally focus on thought more or less as end product, this other area tries to catch an idea back while it's still in motion, being formed. Its basic concern, then, is not with "thought" but with "the act of thinking." Milton Rokeach catches this concern when he writes, "It is not so much *what* you believe that counts, but *how* you believe."[37]

This position—which we might label the "cognitive" view—seeks to understand how ideas work in the experience of people, and what functions those ideas perform for their holders (it's also interested some in what people's ideas do in the world, though it does less there than with the other concerns). In chapter 5, we'll suggest how this cognitive view might help redirect our studies in American historiography-intellectual history. There we'll distinguish between the conventional "climate-of-opinion" picture of ideas and Kenneth Burke's "situation-strategy" approach (an approach which parallels the cognitive view). But our immediate concern now is to see how this position might release historians from the hold of the relativist dilemma. This we can see by moving through Thomas Kuhn's recent study, *The Structure of Scientific Revolutions*.

X

What makes Kuhn's book so startling (and convincing) is that he challenges the objectivity of truth in an area where it had been thought solid and irrefutable—the physical sciences. In the American historical profession, the "scientific history" movement of the late nineteenth and early twentieth century had sought to emulate these physical sciences. And even the 1930s relativist critique of Beard and Becker didn't question that objective truth could be found in science; it only doubted that historians could ever claim it. If the ideal-observer model ever had any validity, it would seem to be in those physical sciences. And yet Thomas Kuhn says that here too, in this citadel of objective reality, the world isn't exactly what it seems.

Just how Kuhn came to such a view is instructive. He notes early in the book that he began as a practicing physicist. But imperatives of the classroom—he was teaching an experimental science course to nonscience majors —sparked a latent interest of his in the history and philosophy of science. As he followed out this interest, it led him into the cognitive area we've just seen —into Jean Piaget on the child's construction of reality, into the psychology of perception (especially gestalt psychology), into the work of Benjamin Whorf on language and world views, and into Arthur Lovejoy's conception of the history of ideas.[38]

Gradually, Kuhn became less interested in the content of scientific findings, and more interested in the structure and functions of scientific inquiry. Because he was interested in the *form* and *process* of inquiry more than in its *products,* he also wanted to know what happens when those forms begin breaking apart and some of the processes get blocked. When that happens, says Kuhn, a scientific community enters a stage of crisis, where some of its members seek to defend the old forms and others search for new ones. Such a situation presents the title problem of his book—"the structure of scientific revolutions."

Kuhn intends not only to say something of scientific inquiry, its nature and structure and history in his book. He also wants to use "cognitive" insights to offer a new *picture* of the scientific enterprise. As he says in the opening words of his first chapter, "History, if viewed as a repository for more than anecdote or chronology, could produce a decisive transformation in the image of science by which we are now possessed."[39]

That image, according to Kuhn, is basically the one scientists themselves hold. It says that science aims to discover the realities of nature, that those realities are wholly out there, in nature, that scientists' precise methods and measuring instruments lead them to such realities, and that the history of science reveals the progressive accumulation of irrefutable truths about the world. In short, the image says that scientists can see nature directly, and that over time they can come to know exactly what they see.

Thomas Kuhn denies this. He doesn't deny that such an image exists, nor does he doubt that it has stimulated much productive inquiry over the years. He simply claims that this image is based on social convention and faith among scientists, not on objective reality in the world.

Kuhn rests his claim on two foundations—changing scientific views of what is true in nature and the psychology of perception. Any scientist would of course admit his first point, that views of the world have changed over time. Almost all texts in the field, says Kuhn, are written from such a perception. In this sense, scientists are like "frame-of-reference" historiographers; they grant that in the past their field has been characterized by the bias of particularity. But not the present nor the future. To textbook writers and to most practicing scientists, the present view is not a *view* of nature, it *is* nature. So the history of science up to the present is a history more or less of errors; from the present on, it should be progressive refinements on objective truth. Kuhn labels this attitude, and its resulting procedure, "puzzle solving"— unravelling knotty problems within the present view but never doubting that view itself.

Kuhn doubts that view itself. Or rather, he doubts its claim to be "objective reality," or "nature." This doubt comes from his psychology of perception. Like other scholars in the cognitive area, Kuhn claims that people see things only through forms and patterns. They don't look out on the world with a naked eye, they go to it with what cognitive psychologists call a "mental set," a cluster of expectations about what they will see.

In a functioning community of scientists, that mental set is what Kuhn calls a *paradigm*—a particular picture of what the world, or some portion of it, is like. When scientists think they are looking at and measuring reality directly, they are in fact perceiving through unseen filters; they see not "nature," but rather some part of nature already bounded and patterned by their community's working paradigm.

Those paradigms mediate between the practicing scientist and nature. They establish not so much the objective facts of the world as the temporary consensus of a scientific community. Paradigms thus set *form* for a community's inquiries. In effect, they establish the mental space such communities think in.

They also establish how young scholars will be initiated into the world of science. Novice scientists are not simply urged to investigate some aspect of nature; they're urged to investigate some aspect of nature *through their community's reigning paradigm.* As Kuhn states it,

The study of paradigms . . . is what mainly prepares the student for membership in the particular scientific community with which he will later practice. Because he there joins men who learned the bases of their field from the same concrete models, his subsequent practice will seldom evoke overt disagreement over fundamentals. Men whose research is based on shared paradigms are committed to the same rules and standards for scientific practice. That commitment and the apparent consensus it produces are prerequisites for normal science, i.e., for the genesis and continuation of a particular research tradition.[40]

Unlike those scientists (or historians) who long for objective reality, and who reject all errors in that quest, Thomas Kuhn does not dismiss normal science simply because he believes it is based on misleading assumptions. Contrary to Charles Sellers', his is no "contamination" model of mind vis-à-vis world. Rather, he says that paradigms do for scientists what we said ideas do for people generally in chapter 1—they allow them to function in the world and get things done.

Kuhn starts off by admitting that scientists cannot know nature directly, and they cannot take in all of its reality. Hence, there can never be a perfect fit between mind and nature. All mind-projections are only approximations of the world; error, then, is built into his model from the beginning.

So, given that unbridgeable gap between mind and nature, Kuhn says we do what we can. Rather than try and escape mind, we use it, through our paradigms. For Kuhn, there is simply no alternative to using some kind of paradigm, or mind-picture, since "nature is too complex and varied to be explored at random."[41]

A paradigm allows a scientist to select out from the whole of reality some aspect of it salient to his own concerns, or his community's. It pares nature down to size, and gives the working scientist something manageable to focus in on.

Within that focus, inquiry can gain momentum, and a scientific community can progress to greater precision in its interpretations of nature. The question now becomes: Just what is it progressing *toward?* Most scientists and many historians would contend it's progressing toward objective reality in the world. Thomas Kuhn says not so, and in the saying offers us his answer to the relativist dilemma.

XI

Kuhn's answer here is subtle, and merits a careful reading. It comes in his concluding chapter—entitled "Progress through Revolutions" (he also adds to his answer in a postscript to the book's second edition, in a section on "Revolutions and Relativism").[42] He writes,

The developmental process described in this essay has been a process *from* primitive beginnings—a process whose successive stages are characterized by an increasingly detailed and refined understanding of nature. But nothing that has been or will be said makes it a process of evolution *toward* anything. Inevitably that lacuna will have disturbed many readers. We are all deeply accustomed to seeing science as the one enterprise that draws constantly nearer to some goal set by nature in advance.[43]

Clearly, Kuhn is boring in on precisely the issue which beset Charles Sellers. Recall again, Sellers' closing words: " 'Objective reality' we know we can never altogether reach, but we need not apologize for assuming it is there, or for believing that our zigzag course brings us swinging in on a circle of ever closer vantage points for discerning its salient features."[44]

Earlier, we said this was Sellers' answer to the relativist dilemma. Or rather, it was not so much an answer as a way of holding on to both sides of that dilemma. Finding only particular frames of reference in the past of American historical scholarship, he needed to salvage some vision of an unbiased scholarship from the flux, and "objective reality" became his strategy for doing so. Where Kuhn claims that only science is thought to be drawing closer to a preexisting reality, I'd claim many historians have a similar goal (this is also Bruce Kuklick's claim, with his ideal-observer model for the field). It's only that historians see their road to reality as rockier than the scientific one.

In any case, Sellers would have his colleagues unapologetically assume that objective reality is there, preestablished in the world, and that by accumulating more knowledge they may draw their field progressively nearer to it. Thomas Kuhn, however, counters that such an assumption is false. "We may," he says, "have to relinquish the notion, explicit or implicit, that changes of paradigm carry scientists and those who learn from them closer and closer to the truth."[45]

For Kuhn, it is better—and more scholarly—to assume that as we accumulate knowledge we are growing *away from* particular kinds of errors. This, he feels, is preferable to assuming we are also growing *nearer to* the general truth of the world. Challenging the objective reality faith, he writes,

Need there be any such goal? Can we not account for both science's existence and its success in terms of evolution from the community's state of knowledge at any given time? Does it really help to imagine that there is some one full, objective, true account of nature [read Sellers' "over-all synthesis of the Jacksonian past"] and that the proper measure of scientific achievement is the extent to which it brings us closer to that ultimate goal?

Kuhn concludes his point, "If we can learn to substitute evolution-from-what-we-do-know for evolution-toward-what-we-wish-to-know, a number of vexing problems may vanish in the process."[46]

That is Thomas Kuhn's route out of the relativist dilemma. Normally, historians have faced this dilemma by living at once in two scholarly worlds—the actual scholars' world of particular frames of reference, and an imagined world of the ideal historical observer. The one world is an admission that scholars are still human beings, and therefore biased in their understandings; the other is a pure scholarly vision which they may draw upon to diminish that bias.

But for Kuhn this second world removes the human perceiving instrument from the scholarly enterprise. Since he sees scholarship as an ongoing dialogue between the world and men's minds, *then the ideal-observer model would block mind from engaging in that dialogue.* Distrusting the biases of men, it would take their minds out of the dialogue, and allow only the world to speak.

For Kuhn, however, such an attitude would stop the vital transaction between man and nature, because it *apologizes* for man's being man. Through his gestaltist psychology of perception, he believes the human mind is inescapably particular in what it can see. But he does not apologize for mind, and man, because of this. Nor does he despair of the scholarly enterprise simply because it can never know "the world as it really is."

Like William Faulkner, Kuhn sees certain kinds of observations as coming *only* through the particularities of mind. Granted, scientists' paradigms may misconstrue and distort nature—just as Benjy's, or Jason's, or Quentin's perceptions occasionally distorted the Compson family history. But if they may distort, they also may *focus.* They can center in on parts of the world we might never see otherwise. And in a scientific community, paradigms can help us construct measuring instruments which capture aspects of nature that a generalized, "objective" view would doubtless miss. "By focusing attention upon a small range of relatively esoteric problems," writes Kuhn, "the paradigm forces scientists to investigate some part of nature in a detail and depth that would otherwise be unimaginable."[47]

As with people's "perspectives," then, so also with scientists' "paradigms"—human bias is built into them from the beginning, but through that bias, and sometimes *only* through that bias, certain kinds of understandings become for the first time possible.

XII

In the light of Thomas Kuhn and the "cognitive" area of scholarship, it might do to revise some of our language now as we go about our history studies. That is, we might alter our word-pictures of what it is we're doing. In some of our inquiries, *we might talk not of "reality" and of "truth" vis-à-vis that reality, but of "experience" and of "explanations" vis-à-vis that experience.*

Within this revised vocabulary, *experience* is simply a shorthand way to speak of things happening in the world (now and in the past), and our elementary senses of same; and *explanation* is a way of giving form to aspects of experience. Explanations, in brief, are pictures in our heads of how experience happens.

The actual terms here are not as important as the meanings they are intended to convey. By substituting "experience" for "reality," I have at least two meanings in mind: (1) Since we cannot wholly comprehend the world directly, it might be best to give up terms suggesting that we can, and to take up terms suggesting a more modest goal for some of our inquiries. We *can* know our particular experiences of the world (though never fully, I suppose), even if we cannot know the world's entire reality. Or at least we are in direct contact with our human experiences; we're only in indirect, filtered contact with the "objective" world. (2) "Experience" is a more existentially grounded term than "reality." Through it, I seek to convey not only some objective facts of the world (e.g., dates, names, places, artifacts, people, institutions, statistics), but also people's subjective sensations of same.

By substituting "explanation" for "truth," I'm also trying to convey at least two meanings: (1) I'm trying to acknowledge the cognitive insight that our constructions of the world are inescapably biased, particular perspectives rendered by particular people from particular locations. (2) I'm also trying to salvage a place for scholarship from this perspectivistic flux by saying that it can be devoted to a systematic search for connections within and among these perspectives. This search would not comprise the whole of historical scholarship, since only part of historical reality is "perspectivistic." But we do need a subfield which would focus on that perspectivistic reality; and such a field is what we're calling here "explanation in historical studies." To articulate such a field is the larger intent of this book.

This area would not then pretend to replace existing scholarship in American history. Rather, it would just supplement it at those points where the perspectivistic insight has most to contribute (some of these points should become clearer as we enter the case studies later). It would go to the past seeking not "objective reality in history," but rather a plurality of pictures of, or perspectives on, historical experience.

Its main contribution would come in and around *historiography studies*— where it might enrich what we know of the several explanations offered by historians of experience in America. In contrast to the normal view of scholarship in the field, it would not look at history works as accumulative "contributions to historical knowledge," all leading toward some overall synthesis of objective reality. Instead, it would see them as *alternative experiments with explaining historical experience in America.* It would not seek the single "definitive" explanation of an experience in history, but would rather try and see how each particular kind of explanation is existentially connected to things around it. It would look at historical reality as refracted, through mind, and would not be fundamentally concerned to assess that reality outside particular minds (such assessments are of course legitimate, they're just not the distinctive work of this area). It would, as we've said, be concerned with historical experiences as seen and formed from the inside out, pictured through the lens and windows of peoples' minds.

XIII

I'm presently at work on another book—*Experience and Explanation in American Culture Studies: An Interdisciplinary Model for Inquiry*— which will explore this "experience-explanation" strategy in more depth. For the present study, a brief sketch of its operative assumptions should give us enough to work with, in trying to free ourselves from the relativist dilemma. It should also provide a base for our case studies later. Building upon what we said of functioning ideas from chapter 1 and of the "cognitive" view and "perspectives" on reality from the present chapter, the experience-explanation strategy pictures the world something like this:

The world of experience is out there breeding happenings all the time. It does this much faster than our ability to comprehend, or even see, unless we look carefully. And when we do look carefully, we can see in only a few directions at once. Thereby, we miss what's happening over in other directions.

The world where we experience, then, is an infinitely complicated series of *multi*-verses. But people tend to pattern their world in much more limited and simplified *uni*-verses (or dia-verses, or tria-verses, but not infinite multi-verses). Experience, inevitably, surges around and past our pictures for knowing and managing it. Since our living space does not coincide neatly with our thinking space, explanation is always some considerable remove from fully comprehending experience. Explanation, in short, *filters* experience—reducing it to controllable size, and often distorting parts of it in the process of reduction. But as it distorts experience, it also focuses it; and as we've seen with Faulkner and Kuhn, it therefore illumines things in a depth and detail not otherwise possible.

The critical study of historical explanations—the study we're outlining in this book—is aimed at ways of entering this two-way encounter between experience and explanation. It's concerned with what explanation does with experience, and experience with explanation.

The whole encounter might be seen as a kind of equation. There are three basic variables—*experience, explanation, form.* Our concern is for how these three variables configure in each historical instance—how explanation works on experience through what particular forms.

Form is our crucial variable. We may call these human constructions "ideas," or "symbols," or "pictures in our heads," or "perspectives," or "cognitions," or "paradigms," or "explanations," or what have you. But what we call them is not as important as how we see them; and this model says we should see them as the patterns and structures through which people try to channel their experience.

When we work this experience-explanation strategy back through our perspectives model, we conclude that historical explanations are *invariably* perspectivistic. This is so not just because men are biased and irrational (though they are partly that too). It's because our world is open and in motion, and thus subject to continuous reinterpretation. Because each of these interpretations must come from some*where,* at some*time,* by some*one,* responding to some*thing,* through some *forms,* our task in the "explanation" field is to explore connections within and among these particular "somes."

There's much we haven't said here about historical perspectives and explanations, and we've left several questions hanging. Some will be answered as we move on through the book, but others will have to wait for the future. As we go on to develop a more systematic scholarship around "explanation in historical studies," we'll need to learn more about the logic of explanation, also about what comprises a good explanation and what is a poor one. Further, we'll need to distinguish among varying levels of experience, and varying levels of explanation. Journals like *History and Theory* and recent books by David Hackett Fischer (*Historians' Fallacies*) and Robert Berkhofer (*A Behavioral Approach to Historical Analysis*) have dealt lucidly with these issues of late; and there's a growing literature on the logic of explanation in the philosophy of science, and philosophy of social science.[48]

Also, we've only hinted at scholarship dealing with the cognitive view. We need to tap into this scholarship more at points where it can enrich our own understanding of ideas in history. There should be many such points in historiography and intellectual history studies. In chapter 5, I'll suggest how we might handle two—with the "pivotal moment" and "situation-strategy" methods of analysis. There are countless other points, however, and it will be a task of this area to locate them, and to learn just what parts of the cognitive literature might be useful to us.

These, then, are future items on our agenda in the field. Exactly where they may lead us no one can say for sure. What we can do now, though, is express our *intent.* Our intent is that further such inquiries may offer us a working symbolic for American historical studies, also a way of breaking free from the relativist dilemma and of challenging the "ideal historical observer" faith.

In place of that faith, perhaps we can substitute a working goal of our own. Revising Charles Sellers' concluding words, we might say, "It may be inefficient for us to search out every single perspective on a given historical situation, but we need not apologize for assuming that a plurality of perspectives are there; and that by trying to understand them and their interconnections, we enrich what we know of the *human* part of historical experience."

NOTES

1. "Andrew Jackson versus the Historians," *The Mississippi Valley Historical Review*, XLIV, no. 4 (March 1958), 618.

2. Ibid., p. 619.

3. Ibid., p. 633.

4. Ibid., p. 634.

5. "The Mind of the Historian," *History and Theory*, VIII, no. 3 (1969), 315.

6. Ibid., p. 316.

7. Cited in W. Stull Holt, "The Idea of Scientific History in America," *Journal of the History of Ideas*, I, no. 3 (June, 1940), 359–60.

8. Fuller accounts of this relativist debate can be found in John Higham, "Relativism," *History* (Prentice-Hall, 1965), pp. 117–31; Burleigh Taylor Wilkins, "*The Heavenly City* and Historiography: A Nearly Absolute Relativism," *Carl Becker: A Biographical Study in American Intellectual History* (MIT Press, paperback, 1967), pp. 174–209; Morton White, "Can History Be Objective?," *Social Thought in America: The Revolt against Formalism* (Beacon, paperback, 1957), pp. 220–35; and Cushing Strout, "The Revolt of Relativism," *The Pragmatic Revolt in American History: Carl Becker and Charles Beard* (Cornell University Press, paperback, 1966), pp. 11–61.

See also, for an introduction to the technical philosophy of history on relativism, Maurice Mandelbaum, *The Problem of Historical Knowledge: An Answer to Relativism* (Harper, Torchbook, 1967—first published in 1938 by Liveright).

Finally, see David Hackett Fischer's brief but brilliant critique of the relativist idea in *Historians' Fallacies: Toward a Logic of Historical Thought* (Harper, Torchbook, 1970), pp. 41–43. Fischer's integrative vision of this idea is especially striking: "A full-fledged cultural history of this intellectual movement [relativism] would embrace a major school of German historical and philosophical thought, the epistemology of Fascism, Stalin's hostility to 'archive rats' and 'bourgeois objectivism,' the great Japanese movie *Rashomon* and several popular anthologies of Hindu folk legends, the novels of Aldous Huxley, Thomas Mann and Andre Gide, the essays of Renan and Croce, the poetry of Edward Arlington Robinson and E. E. Cummings, the theology of Reinhold Niebuhr, and the aesthetics of abstract art."(42)

9. Charles Beard, "Written History as an Act of Faith," *American Historical Review*, XXXIX, no. 2 (January 1934), 222.

10. Carl Becker, "What are Historical Facts?," *Western Political Quarterly*, VIII, no. 3 (September 1955), 331.

11. Carl Becker, "Everyman His Own Historian," *American Historical Review*, XXXVII, no. 2 (January 1932), 235.

12. Cited in Strout (n. 8 above), pp. 37–38.

13. Wilkins (n. 8 above), p. 206.

14. *American Intellectual Histories and Historians* (Princeton University Press, 1966), pp. 121–122

15. *The Sound and the Fury* (Knopf, Vintage Books, 1956—first published in 1929), pp. 1–2.

16. Ibid., p. 232.

17. Ibid., p. 93.

18. Ibid., p. 427.

19. Ibid., p. 371.

20. Kuklick (n. 5 above), p. 315.

21. "What are Historical Facts?" (n. 10 above), p. 331.

22. *A Theory of Personality: The Psychology of Personal Constructs* (Norton, paperback, 1963—first published by Norton in 1955), p. 120.

23. *The Social Construction of Reality: A Treatise in the Sociology of Knowledge* (Doubleday, Anchor Book, 1967—first published by Doubleday in 1966), p. 104.

24. *An Essay on Man: An Introduction to the Philosophy of Human Culture* (Doubleday, Anchor Book, n.d.—first published by Yale in 1944), p. 43.

25. *Language and the Discovery of Reality* (Vintage Books, 1966—first published by Random House in 1961), p. 95.

26. "On the Definition of a Symbol," in Joseph Royce, ed., *Psychology and the Symbol* (Random House, paperback, 1965), p. 26.

27. "The Sense of the Past," *The Liberal Imagination* (Doubleday, Anchor Book, 1957—first published by Viking in 1950), p. 186.

28. *Invention and the Evolution of Ideas* (Social Science, paperback, n.d.—first published in 1963 by Tavistock as *Displacement of Concepts*), p. 8.

29. *Ideology and Utopia: An Introduction to the Sociology of Knowledge* (Harcourt, Brace, Harvest Book, n.d.—first published in 1936), p. 3.

30. "On the Perception of Incongruity: A Paradigm," *Journal of Personality*, XVIII (1949–50), 206.

31. In his book *The Image: Knowledge in Life and Society* (University of Michigan Press, paperback, 1961), Kenneth Boulding also notes how similar things have been said here by people working in entirely different fields. His was one of the first efforts to bring the whole area together. Boulding uses the term *eiconics* to label this field, and identifies various branches contributing to it—the sociology of knowledge of Max Scheler and Karl Mannheim, Gestalt psychology, the social psychology of George Herbert Mead and of Kurt Lewin, Clyde Kluckhohn and the anthropological study of values, Ludwig von Bertalanffy's "open systems" theory in biology, Norbert Wiener and cybernetics, information theory in mathematics. It's interesting that Boulding includes no *historians* in his list of contributors. The blockage is mutual. As historians have not contributed to this field, they've not drawn upon it either. See also, for a more recent effort to order this field, the Winter 1972 issue of *Daedalus*—which is devoted to "the study of meaningful forms."

32. Berger and Luckmann (n. 23 above), p. 47; Kelly, (n. 22 above), p. 43.

33. *A Study of Thinking* (Wiley, 1956), p. 15.

34. "Reflections on the History of Ideas," *Journal of the History of Ideas,* 1, no. 1 (January 1940), 4.

35. Among works in academic history, Hughes' *Consciousness and Society* comes closest, I believe, to work being done in this "cognitive" field of scholarship. He traces the growth of cognitive subjectivism in European social thought during the forty years after 1890, and notes that by the end of the period, " 'The nature of reality' itself 'no longer afforded a coherent totality'; the natural world and with it reality in the broader sense were now seen as approachable only through conventional fictions. . . . As Vico had declared two centuries earlier, man was capable of understanding the 'civil world' *because he had made it.* By an effort of imaginative *construction,* human thought could mimic the process of creation, and hence of understanding." (*Consciousness and Society: The Reorientation of European Social Thought, 1890–1930* [Vintage Paperback, n.d.—first published by Random House in 1958], p. 428).

36. Among works which historians are familiar with, Mannheim's *Ideology and Utopia* most closely resembles the findings of "cognitive" scholarship today. Note the parallel in Mannheim's statement below and what we're saying in this chapter: "It is not a source of error that in the visual picture of an object in space we can, in the nature of the case, get only a perspectivistic view. The problem is not how we might arrive at a non-perspectivistic picture but how, by juxtaposing the various points of view, each perspective may be recognized as such and thereby a new level of objectivity attained. Thus we come to the point where the false ideal of a detached, impersonal point of view must be replaced by the ideal of an essentially human point of view which is within the limits of a human perspective, constantly striving to enlarge itself" (pp. 296–97). For Mannheim's influence on Richard Hofstadter, see the latter's "History and the Social Sciences," in Fritz Stern, ed., *The Varieties of History* (Meridian Book, 1956), pp. 359–70.

37. Excerpted from Introduction to *The Open and Closed Mind: Investigations into the Nature of Belief Systems and Personality Systems,* by Milton Rokeach, p. 6. © 1960 by Basic Books, Inc., Publishers, New York.

Opinion study in the social sciences was not always structure-oriented. The classic "authoritarian personality" studies by T. W. Adorno et al. were almost entirely oriented to the *content* of beliefs. The Adorno authors classified their subjects basically on whether they believed this or that, and they wrote, "judgments and interpretations of fact are distorted by psychological urges." (*The Authoritarian Personality* [Harper, 1950], p. 240).

Soon after *The Authoritarian Personality* was published in 1950, a counter-trend set in—manifested especially in Smith, Bruner and White's *Opinions and Personality* (1956) and Rokeach's *The Open and Closed Mind* (1960). *Opinions and Personality* opens with the question, "Of what use to a man are his opinions?" (p. 1), and Rokeach writes, "To study the organization of belief systems, we find it necessary to concern ourselves with the *structure* rather than the *content* of beliefs." Countering the Adorno view, he says, "The relative openness or closedness of a mind cuts across specific content" (p. 6).

38. *The Structure of Scientific Revolutions* (University of Chicago Press, paperback, 1970), p. vi.

39. Ibid., p. 1.

40. Ibid., pp. 10–11.

41. Ibid., p. 109.

42. Ibid., pp. 160–73, 205–7.

43. Ibid., pp. 170–71.

44. Sellers (n. 1 above), p. 634.

45. Kuhn, p. 170.

46. Ibid., p. 171.

47. Ibid., p. 24.

48. *Historians' Fallacies,* (n. 8 above); *A Behavioral Approach to Historical Analysis* (Free Press, 1969). See also, for literature on explanation in the philosophy of science and social science, Ernest Nagel, *The Structure of Science: Problems in the Logic of Scientific Explanation* (Harcourt, Brace and World, 1961); Eugene Meehan, *Explanation in Social Science: A System Paradigm* (Dorsey, paperback, 1968) and *Contemporary Political Thought* (Dorsey, 1967); Abraham Kaplan, *The Conduct of Inquiry* (Chandler, 1964); Max Weber, *The Methodology of the Social Sciences* (Free Press, 1949), and Gordon DiRenzo, ed., *Concepts, Theory, and Explanation in the Behavioral Sciences* (Random House, 1966).

3 The Book-Form: Historians and "Primary" Documents

If, as Collingwood says, the historian must re-enact in thought what has gone on in the mind of his *dramatis personae*, so the reader in his turn must re-enact what goes on in the mind of the historian.
E. H. Carr
What is History?

Never accept a document at face value.
Robert Berkhofer
A Behavioral Approach to Historical Analysis

Historians tend to think of a book as "a building block for that imaginary tower of learning to which historical labors are always said to offer 'contributions.' "
Edmund Morgan
"Perry Miller and the Historians"

In the opening two chapters, we've maintained that ideas are not so much reflections of historical reality as they are means of coping with the world of our experience, and that in order to cope, we must invariably reduce that world to size. We haven't denied that there are objective facts in the world, but we have contended that there are no unperspectivistic, or locationless, views of those facts. Any view must come from somewhere, at some time, by someone, through some form.

That of course, is a truism in the study of history itself. We assume the *historicity* of human experience—that is, we acknowledge that experience is inevitably grounded in time and place and circumstance and social milieu. This is one of the distinguishing assumptions of history study; without it, we historians could not do our work.

But, as we noted in the last chapter, historians have not been inclined to move back one step and apply such an assumption to themselves. They have now and then of course—they acknowledge that there are various "schools" in the interpretation of history, and that some interpretations seem relevant to a particular time, but as time passes so do the interpretations. There have been superb studies of late detailing that this is the case—most notably John Higham's *History* (1965), Robert Skotheim's *American Intellectual Histories and Historians* (1966), and Richard Hofstadter's *The Progressive Historians* (1968). But if we have such individual studies in the profession, we have no systematic *field* doing this kind of thing.

There are several good reasons for this. In the prologue and in chapter 2 we've gone into some of them. We might recapitulate here, and place them in the strategic context of the present chapter.

First, we noted in chapter 1 that humans use ideas as levers to move things. So also do historians. The idea of the historian as a detached, unbiased observer of the species is a strategic lever to get useful scholarly work done. By believing he may come to *know* history while most members of the species simply *live in* it, the professional historian may be motivated to enormous labors of body and mind. He may drive himself to discover *what happened,* not what people *wish* had happened, and he may spend the bulk of his working life devoted to that task. He can take a certain justifiable pride in distinguishing himself and his colleagues from those who don't expend any such effort to know their past.

If a Carl Becker tells him that after all "everyman is his own historian," he may nod in abstracted agreement, but he can't get much leverage from such an idea while doing his own history work. For, as a teacher, he may be reminded daily that some recalcitrant students could care less about being their own historians; as critic of the culture, he may observe with pain that many people do things while wholly ignorant of their past; and as a professional scholar, he may know full well that "everyman" is not there in his study laboring over his research with him. He may grant that, of course, he is human with human limitations. But if he felt his own scholarly work amounted to nothing more than anyone else's uninformed prejudices about the past, he'd hardly be motivated to do what he does.

Which brings us to another reason why no systematic field has developed around the sociology or psychology of historical knowledge. Historians have been restive with the late nineteenth-century idea of a wholly presuppositionless, "scientific" rendering of the facts and only the facts of history. But they've been even more restive with what to put in its place. For a while in the 1930s, "relativism" enjoyed a vogue, but most historians came to reject that idea for the very good reason that it didn't distinguish much between scholarship and prejudice. What we've had since then is some kind of uneasy compromise between the relativist viewpoint and the scientific ideal. In the preceding chapter, we noted this compromise at work in Charles Sellers' article, "Andrew Jackson versus the Historians." Sellers grants the relativist view for history's past and present, but projects an ideal future where scholars can discover what *actually* happened in Jacksonian America.

That, I think, pretty much catches where many American historians are in their working assumptions today. They admit the relativity of what has been done in the field, and they grant limitations in what's being done now. But they still hold the vision of an ideal scholarly future where historians can find out what in fact has happened in the past. And, finding out, they will have discovered "objective reality" in American history.

Such a working assumption has had many consequences in the historical community. It has urged scholars out into the world to search for information on the past, it has stimulated them to try and distinguish between information which is reliable and information which is not, and it has cautioned them to remain close to their sources when interpreting the past. These are all worthwhile consequences; they are necessary to a rigorous scholarship of historical reconstruction.

But there are other consequences of this assumption too, whose worth is not so unambiguously positive. In the last chapter, we noted some of them, as they affect historians' conceptions of *ideas* and of *reality* in history. Here we might note how this quest for objective reality may affect historians' sense of their *documents*.

For one, such an assumption has made scholars uneasy with any other goal than telling what happened in the past. In chapter 2, we tried to set up an alternative—or rather supplementary—scholarly goal with the "perspectives" view. Later in this chapter, we'll see how that perspectivistic sense might re-form our picture of what a document is and does. For now, let's just say that its absence has caused historians to pour their energies into one form of documentary source for recapturing the past, but they've remained largely uninformed about another source-form.

Our understanding of those sources we designate as "primary"—original documentary evidence—is remarkable in the history profession. But our understanding of those sources we designate as "secondary"—interpretations of documentary evidence—is not very remarkable at all. We've expended much effort talking about the functions of primary source-forms, but we've not directed our minds toward learning the functions of secondary source-forms, particularly *the book-form*.

In the remainder of this chapter, we'll consider the book medium as an expressive form in American history studies. We'll do that by looking at some pictures of books held by people in and around the history profession. We'll consider three case illustrations of such pictures—two instances come out of my own personal experience as a student and as a teacher, the third is a noted scholarly controversy in the profession.

II

1. The first instance happened while I was a graduate student and was taking a course in American political theory. Students were not required to do a formal research paper for this graduate seminar, but were instead asked

to write several 5-10-page critical analyses of books in the field. These books were to be chosen from a supplementary reading list. As I recall, we were to do about ten of these book analyses during the term.

Before class one day, a history colleague and I were chatting, and he confided that this was the first course in his graduate career where he'd ever read a full book. I was taken aback. This fellow was no dullard by any measure, and I had known him as one of the most conscientious students in the department. So how could he get by without ever reading a whole book? It wasn't a matter of getting by, he replied, he'd never been required to. This was his third full year of graduate study in the history department, and no professor had ever assigned him a book to read cover-to-cover (save, of course, for a textbook or two).

I couldn't at first believe that. I'd heard him talk about Tocqueville in class, and he'd also mentioned at one time or another Daniel Boorstin and Parrington and Perry Miller and "consensus" histories, plus others I don't recall right now. So how could he talk about them?

Sure he'd read Tocqueville. Enough to know that Tocqueville said Americans were egalitarian, that he warned of the "tyranny of the majority" in a democracy, and that he's been called one of the first Western sociologists. He also knew that Boorstin was a conservative and Parrington a Progressive and Miller an idealist, and that consensus histories were being written then just as conflict histories had been in earlier years. But he didn't have to read whole books to learn that. A few sections in each was enough to give a flavor of each man's thought, or at least that's all his professors had required of him. Until, that is, he entered this course on American political theory. Why such a practice in his department? We'll try and explain why after reviewing our other two cases.

2. The second instance occurred a few years later, while I was teaching at Raymond College—an experimental "cluster" wing of the University of the Pacific. It came in an undergraduate seminar on "The Literature of American History." The course had started off slowly; I was teaching it for the first time, and we were all feeling our way along in the early weeks. By the end of a month, we hadn't got very far. And I was disappointed.

I felt the reading should be challenging students (we'd read Carl Becker's "Everyman His Own Historian," an American Historical Association pamphlet entitled *History as a Career,* Thomas Jefferson Wertenbaker's *The Puritan Oligarchy,* and Daniel Bell's *The Reforming of General Education*). But the students weren't much stimulated by any of these. I was especially disappointed with their response to *The Reforming of General Education,* which we'd just finished. Bell had suggested how the academic curriculum should be directed away from exclusive emphasis on content, to stress concepts and organizing principles; and that could have given us leverage for what we were after in the course. I'd hoped students would see this, and then we could have a fruitful discussion on alternative forms for education and on how we might structure some fresh ways of studying history at this innovating college. But students didn't see much of that at all, and we didn't have any very good discussions.

So it was with much trepidation that I looked on to the next week, for we were scheduled to read Faulkner's novel, *The Sound and the Fury*. It had all seemed so logical a few months before, when I'd laid out the course in my mind and ordered the books. We would start off by setting up Becker against the AHA pamphlet, "everyman's" history versus professional history. That should spark some talk about different ways to study history and should cause us to challenge the routine conventions of most courses in the field. We'd then go to Wertenbaker, a particular case example. After that, we'd move on to Bell, who would set our discussions in a wider intellectual and sociological context, and who—through his own idea of concept-focused courses—had framed for us a workable alternative to the narrative-based norm in history studies. This would all prepare us for *The Sound and the Fury*—where we could see a concrete historical experience as rendered from four radically varying perspectives. An encounter with Faulkner, I felt, should demolish any lingering assumptions among us about history as something separated off from experience in textbooks or about its having happened in one way and one way only. I also hoped we might see enough in Benjy there so we could do with ideas some of what we did here in the first chapter.

I hoped all that for these first weeks. I also hoped this background would set us up for the other case studies to follow in the course—Stanley Elkins' *Slavery*, Boorstin's *The Genius of American Politics*, Miller's *The New England Mind: From Colony to Province*.

But how could students handle a Perry Miller if Becker's clear prose, or Wertenbaker's stirring progressive commitments, or Bell's powerful logic, hadn't done much for them? And, of more pressing concern, what could we possibly do now with Faulkner, who was coming up the next week?

The whole situation made me restive—no, frantic is more like it. We'd just wasted the Bell book, and some of its themes were similar to what I'd intended for us to see in Faulkner. And Faulkner would be much harder for us than Bell. So I thought.

The Sound and the Fury, as we've seen in the previous two chapters, can be one of the most confusing books in all American literature. For Faulkner puts you on your own in it. He doesn't tell you the story outright, he makes you work like hell for it. And just when you're beginning to pick up on something and get moderately comfortable with it, he alters the time on you, or the person, or gives you two different people with the same name. Or he tells you about things that didn't in fact happen, but were only imagined in the mind of the narrator. But he never announces any of this, so you may be a page or two into something different before you realize he's changed the situation on you.

All this confusion has a purpose. It's part of the novel's genius, and one of the reasons I wanted students to read it. In the first chapter we watched Benjy experience similar scenes with mother and daughter, nineteen years apart, and we noted how his lack of historical imagination caused him to sense them as simultaneous. So Faulkner gives them to you as simultaneous. But he doesn't tell you they're two different scenes, or that they're separated by nineteen years. He gives them to you just as they're experienced— through Benjy, who responds to them as the same thing and as happening at the same time. When you finally discover this (*if* you do), you've learned something important—about Benjy, about mother and daughter in the Compson family, and, as we noted in chapter 1, about undergoing experiences with ideas and without ideas. But if you're not clued in to Faulkner's method here, you may not catch this at all, and you may find the whole book one irritating maze of side roads and back tracks. When this happens, you can't get your mind engaged in much of anything in the novel. After what we'd done in the first few weeks in the course, I feared that's where we might end up.

So during the week before Faulkner I racked my mind trying to figure how we could avoid catastrophe. Since the class was committed to a dialogue-seminar format, I couldn't just walk in and *tell* them what Faulkner was up to. Furthermore, I wasn't all that certain myself. I'd read the novel a few times before, enough to know its major scenes and characters and its plot and some of its themes. But I'd never really made an effort to get my mind around the whole experience—to know it in such detail and with such an understanding of its working patterns that I could satisfactorily explain what Faulkner was doing.

So this is what I tried during that week—to get my mind around *The Sound and the Fury*. I read the novel forwards and then backwards (some say it's easier to read in reverse order; I suspect they're right). I made detailed charts of what seemed to be happening at each moment in the book, and of who was experiencing what when, and how. A few things which were confusing before began to clear up for me, and that was nice. But I wondered if any teacher could reasonably expect students to put in this much effort. And what in the course had prepared them for passages like this?:

The cellar steps ran up the hill in the moonlight and T. P. fell up the hill, into the moonlight. . . . Then he fell into the flowers, laughing, and I ran into the box. But when I tried to climb onto it it jumped away and hit me on the back of the head and my throat made a sound. It made the sound again and I stopped trying to get up, and it made the sound again and I began to cry. . . . T. P. fell down on top of me, laughing, and it kept on making the sound and Quentin kicked T. P. and Caddy put her arms around me, and her shining veil, and I couldn't smell trees anymore and I began to cry.[1]

As I worked back and forth through that novel, I could in fact make most of it out—but just barely. And I kept feeling relief when working in the Jason section and the concluding section and the appendix (which had been added onto the Modern Library edition seventeen years after the book was first published). But I knew this was false comfort, for it is the first two sections— Benjy's and Quentin's—which are the novel's richest. It was because of them that I had assigned the book for the seminar. Jason's section and the conclusion are more or less conventional narrative history; and the appendix, which lays out the whole family history in neat, ordered fashion, seemed only a little short of cheating to me. It put the Compson experience into a form entirely different from the novel itself (it was "ideal observer" history); and, because it was added several years later, it tended to affront my aesthetic sensitivities about the integrity of a completed work of art. If all we could understand were these latter parts of the book, why assign it in the first place?

So I walked into class on a Wednesday morning still in a fret. I feared we must either compromise Faulkner by discussing only his easiest sections, or we'd have to compromise our discussion format by me pulling rank and lecturing on the more difficult parts.

Either alternative would be a disappointment. I still couldn't make up my mind which would be best. Or rather, which would be least worst. Finally, I just said to hell with it and decided to play it by ear, and hope something might happen to bail us out. If nothing did, I was ready to apologize to the students for assigning such a difficult book so early in the term, and hoped they wouldn't mind trying to muddle through.

So I opened class with the first question which popped into my mind, "What is Faulkner doing with history in this novel?" Three hours later, sixteen students and I walked out of the most illuminating seminar I'd ever experienced. After that first question, I'd added almost nothing, students carried the class by themselves. On their own, they figured out much of the novel's confusing chronology, they ran themselves through the maze of Benjy and Quentin and pretty well understood how each experienced things, they saw that Benjy lacked ideas and talked some about what this meant, and they caught much of what Faulkner says about the radically different perspectives people can take on a single historical experience. And what wasn't inside the mind of one or another student when he walked into class got born or clarified through the process of dialogue. In those three hours, they discussed things in that novel I had never seen, with all my labors, and when the class was over I felt ashamed that I'd so misjudged their minds. It was an example of seminar learning at its best, and I was wholly unprepared for it and did little to help it along.

I might have been ready (after the initial glow wore off) to chalk the whole experience up to a lucky historical accident, except there was another section of the same class that afternoon. An hour and a half after I'd witnessed my best seminar ever, this afternoon class proceeded to top the morning one. Which meant I couldn't simply let myself luxuriate in the afterglow of that experience, I had to try and explain it. We'll get to that in a few moments.

3. The first two instances have been on the learning environment in history studies; the last is on the actual doing of historical scholarship. It took place in 1959–60, and is to be found in *The Journal of Southern History*. It's a debate over an essay by David Donald, "Toward a Reconsideration of Abolitionists."

This essay had been published in 1956, in Donald's book *Lincoln Reconsidered: Some Essays on the Civil War Era.* In that essay, Donald had used a sample of some 106 abolitionist leaders to draw certain generalizations about the movement's social makeup. Specifically, he concluded that abolitionists were members of an old elite being displaced by a rising business economy, and that they were dominantly rural rather than urban in background (only 12 percent of his sample came from cities, he noted).

Our instance begins in August, 1959, when Robert Skotheim published a piece in the *Journal* taking issue with Donald. Skotheim didn't argue with Donald's *evidence;* rather, he took issue with how Donald *explained* that evidence. He noted that while Donald's evidence was a sample just of abolitionist leaders, he occasionally forgot that, and slipped into generalizing about the movement as a whole. He also noted that Donald lacked a control group for his sample. Without a control, Skotheim emphasized, Donald couldn't really say that persons became abolitionists for such and such reasons, because non-abolitionists might do different things for the same reasons. One couldn't know until he studied some non-abolitionist groups too. Finally, by ingenious use of census data, Skotheim showed that abolitionist leaders had come from large cities just twice as often as the population at large (12 percent against 6 percent), thus questioning Donald's explanation that abolitionism was a distinctively rural movement.[2]

Six months later, David Donald replied, in a letter to the editor of the *Journal of Southern History*. Noting in three of his six brief paragraphs that Skotheim was only a graduate student (it was not so noted in Skotheim's own piece), Donald also made evident that he was writing from Queen's College, Oxford, where he then held the distinguished title, "Harmsworth Professor of American History."

Answering Skotheim's point that he should have set up a control group alongside his abolitionist sample, Donald responded,

Of course there would be methodological validity in having a series of parallel studies made of other reform groups, and I rather hoped that my essay might provoke graduate students like Mr. Skotheim to undertake such analyses. Such work, I should warn him, however, is both time-consuming and laborious—a good deal more so than picking flaws in the writings of other historians.

Donald went on to imply that Skotheim's efforts were not really legitimate historical scholarship, and his letter closed by questioning whether graduate students should be permitted to do such things:

Mr. Skotheim's criticisms raise the general problem, which Professor David M. Potter so cogently discussed not long ago in a review in the *Journal of Southern*

History, of "how far it is possible to proceed in judging historians' interpretations without grounding these judgments in an understanding of the history which is being interpreted."

"Perhaps the teaching profession is at fault," Donald concluded, "in encouraging young scholars like Mr. Skotheim to undertake studies in methodology and historiography before he has demonstrated his competence in research."[3]

III

These are the three instances which should serve to focus our thinking on the book-form. We've seen something of what happened in each instance, now our task is to try and figure out why, to offer explanations to these experiences. Which means putting together what *picture* of a book, and of scholarship in history, seems to underlie each example. What we say here does not "prove" anything yet about pictures of the book-form in the profession. Our sample is too limited for that, perhaps too biased also. Further, we must infer our pictures, they are not obvious from each case. We cannot, therefore, be too certain of what we say at the moment; our explanations must be tentative, offered just as a start. But if we can't prove anything by these instances, we might still use them as suggestive *illustrations* of how books may appear to professional historians (or some historians). They may serve us until more reliable data and more reliable explanations come along. Which data and which explanations should come when historians bring to public dialogue their working assumptions about the book as a form.

1. Case 1 was my graduate student colleague in the history department, who was never asked to read a full book. Why not? What does this case reveal of his professors' assumptions about the book form in history studies? Again, we can't really know, but we can speculate some in a disciplined manner.

To get at their sense of the book form, we'll need to move back and consider their prior sense of the world of historical scholarship. I suspect those professors may have been informed by some variant of the contribution-to-knowledge model of scholarship in the field (which model moves off from the ideal-observer assumption). In this model, knowledge is seen as a body, an ever-growing body. It expands by the progressive accumulation of knowledge items, pieces of information which more or less accurately reflect things in the world. These individual items serve as "contributions" to that knowledge body; each scholar aims to gather many such items of reliable information, then contribute them to the accumulating knowledge of his profession.

A book of historical scholarship simply functions within this model. It's a place where information is gathered and stored. Each book is a kind of *repository,* then, for scholarship in its field. Taken collectively, all books in the field make up one gigantic Textbook, doing what Thomas Kuhn says texts do in "normal" scholarship. That is, this "Arche-Text," as it were, more or less accurately describes what is known about the world at that point in the field's accumulating knowledge. Words, sentences, chapters may over time be added or deleted, because new contributions may supersede old ones; but the basic body of scholarship remains intact and grows by this incremental process.

The locus of historical reality, and of reliability in scholarship, lies *in the particular information-item*. These information items comprise the facts of history; they are the final resource of scholarship in the field, where the irreducible truth of things can be checked out. The whole body of scholarship depends on the validity of its individual contributions, and it's there where the field's critical resources are concentrated.

What one does with a book, then, is check out these individual contributions. Subsequent scholarship in the field may have discredited some of them; if so, scholars can discard those parts of the book (or perhaps use them as examples of errors which time has corrected). Other contributions may have been validated, so in teaching and research scholars can still draw on those parts of the book.

One thus pictures the book-form as a gateway into the field's "body of knowledge." Where it leads one into that knowledge—that is, onto legitimized paths of the field—then one uses the book. Where it leads one to no-longer-useful paths, one can close it off. The book is of no value if it doesn't direct scholars to reliable information—which reliable information is found in the "primary documents" on which books are based.

Books are kind of halfway houses, then. The documents are where one really finds history. Books are simply efficient devices for compressing and representing those documents. In history studies, what one is actually after *is* those documents; a book's function is truly to represent them.

So a book is not really a form in itself; it's a device for serving another form—the documents. The historian stays with a book just long enough to get a lead into those documents (re David Donald telling Skotheim to go out and do research himself, instead of spending so much time in others' research).

Within this contribution-to-knowledge model, a book serves as a kind of stockpile where one stores information and others go to check it. In their research work, historians may lift out of books (and other documents) words, sentences, sometimes paragraphs. This way they get the book's particular information items, its individual "contributions to historical knowledge." But seldom do historians make effort to get at larger wholes—at full passages, at chapters, or at the strategy of a complete book or document. In short, they take a book as broken down, in pieces, but seldom do they address it as a structured pattern or configuration.

If our description of the model here is accurate, it might help explain why my colleague's history professors had never required him to read a full book.

He was expected to learn certain words in the field, and in his research to use sentences and paragraphs from books and documents. To do that, he was asked to read passages and chapters in books, and he was definitely supposed to read much in primary documents. But *whole* books he could do without.[4]

Which means he could also do without whole minds. He was seldom seeing a single historical mind in full labor as it was working over some dilemma or offering explanation to an experience. Instead, he was getting shards and fragments of mind, sans its larger organizing structure and patterns. And in that form, mind would come through not at labor, not in process, but as end product, over with. He was getting completed thoughts, not people's thinking. To his mind, then, "mind" in history must appear in disconnected bits and pieces, pieces which float here and there and are not grounded in strategic context.[5]

When our professor in American political theory asked us to read full books, she was challenging this picture of a book, and of professional scholarship. She felt the research-in-original-documents syndrome too often distracted minds from fully engaging other minds; so in this graduate seminar she required us not to do another research paper but to read some books. And she insisted we see a book not as a few more or less random thoughts, or items of information, but as an experience in itself, to be engaged through one's own sense of experience. That's why she wanted us to throw our selves so deeply into a single book, and to work ourselves up out of it. She felt we ought to see a mind in action, and to encounter that mind with our own minds.

Beyond that, she didn't articulate her rationale for replacing research papers with books in this course. But if we can infer her model of a book, and expand it for our own purposes in this study, it might look something like this:

A book can be one kind of moratorium on direct experience, when a person puts off other forms of involvement to engage in verbal explanation of experience (which explanation is itself an experience of sorts and is subject to further explanation by the book critic). We can see it as a time when someone sits down to give more or less full expression of what's on his mind, within certain focused limits. Those limits may be set by some immediately personal experience—for example, Alexis de Tocqueville with *Democracy in America*—or by some felt issue in the world of scholarship—for example, Thomas Kuhn's *The Structure of Scientific Revolutions* or Charles Beard's *An Economic Interpretation of the Constitution*.

These limits define the "situation," to which the book offers "strategic response."[6] In effect, the book is a gestalt upon that situation, taking certain things and symbols from it and clustering them together into distinctive patterns. What results is a particular mind picture (or perspective) of that situation, one person's mental image of it.

Among other things, then, a book is merely a convenient place for an inquisitive reader to confront the experience of mind. In the book form, we can watch just how a single mind takes in a limited experience, and tries to make order of it. The book form thus offers a bounded situation for inquiry, where the variables are more controllable than in most other kinds of mind work. So we can use a book to study how, in one medium, people may put together life (and, in a more limited sense, how historians may put patterns on the past).

We may thus go to a book not just to replace experience, or escape it, but to engage experience as it comes through in a tightly compressed form. What distinguishes the book as an experience form is precisely this fact of tight compression; it makes of the book an *efficient* medium for checking out explanation. Most other experience forms are not so tightly compressed and are thus not as efficient a place for inquiry.

We should therefore address a book not merely through its replaceable parts—its individual datums of information—but also as a whole configuration. And we ought connect this configuration to the perceived situation from which it was created and to the author's strategic response to that situation. We should allow the book to come through as an existential act, then, a drama of encounter between mind and materials, and not just as a "contribution to knowledge."

Now not all books are like this, not even all in history. Some *are* in fact intended as repositories of scholarship, and I suppose any book might profitably be seen in only that way. But some can also be seen as experiences in themselves; this is especially true with those books which form our base in this part of the territory—books in and around intellectual history and American Studies.

What we've said here is not the only way to look at books—not even at books in the territory. But it might be a useful corrective to what's apparently the norm in American historical studies. And that norm, I think, is the book-as-repository-of-scholarship model.

Had my graduate school colleague been asked to look at books in this other form too, he might not have simply associated Tocqueville with the labels "equality" and "tyranny of the majority." By reading carefully through the whole *Democracy,* he might have caught something of how *strategic* are Tocqueville's words there, and of how his fears about majority tyranny mount as he nears the book's end and loses control over his own role.

If we look at the *Democracy* not simply to find what America is like (or not like), but for the particular encounter of one kind of mind with one pattern of American experiences, then we come out of this kind of book with something far richer than a set of floating labels like "equality" and "tyranny of the majority" and the like. We can go on behind the labels to get a sense of their existential grounding; in the terms of chapter 2, we can look at one particular perspective on reality in America, and we can see that perspective from the inside out.[7]

2. Our second instance was the Raymond College students with Faulkner,

in the course "The Literature of American History." Why did they get so involved in *The Sound and the Fury,* and not so involved with things we read before that, and a few after?[8]

This could hardly be a matter of the classes' intelligence, or of "background" knowledge in the field. They were the same students all along, we were considering similar themes in every book, and *The Sound and the Fury* was the most complicated thing we read the entire semester. So logically, they should have had more problems with Faulkner, not fewer.

But psychologic, and sociologic, rather than logic was evidently at work here. Which makes it a matter not of the books themselves, but of the *expectations* students brought to those books—the pictures in their heads of what each kind of book should be.

In literature studies, you go into a course expecting to give books a close reading. You don't need to be *told* that a novel is an experience in itself, at least not by the time you reach college. You already know that, so you go right ahead and try to unravel those experiences which lie in and around and under the words on the printed page. In short, you can pour your energies into explanation—just as you might with anything else you can sense as a human experience.

Further, in the novel form, the whole experience is out there in front of your eyes. You may not know all you need to know about a given novel— about the author, or his times, or literary traditions he may be drawing upon —but information like that is extrinsic to the novel anyway. It's valuable to the degree that it helps you read more sensitively; but the words themselves are what make the novel form distinctive. And in a novel you can inspect those words at first hand. Presuming you own the book, then the "primary document" is all yours, you can do with it what you want. Some professional conventions in literary scholarship, plus "the laying on of high culture," may inhibit you from engaging the document as critically as you might. But they won't stop you from reading it on your own. In contrast to history—where most students get most of their information predigested—literature gives students immediate access to its basic materials.[9]

Academic historians are prone to believe that the basic knowledge of their field lies *in the primary documents.* And since very few students—at least undergraduate students—get into very many primary documents, most never see the field at first hand.

Further on, we'll challenge this whole picture of what a primary document is and does, and the sharp distinction historians normally make between "primary" and "secondary" sources. For now, let's just suggest that the professor who's been to the primary sources is tempted to be overly certain he's gotten to real history; and the student who hasn't been there can be made to feel he knows nothing of history at all.

This tends to build up a deference pattern of sorts in the classroom, making students rely wholly upon the professor for their knowledge of the past.

Such a pattern also will affect how students read books in history. A recruiting pamphlet put out by the American Historical Association says this about books in the field: "If you have a strong interest in history you have the most essential trait for success. Do books about historical events or personalities leave you with a desire to know more about them? Do you read history and wish to read more?"[10]

That pamphlet urges the beginning student to look not into *experience* for history, but at books—which books are written by professionals in the field according to professionally acceptable canons of scholarship. In a sense, these books "belong" to the profession; they're *its* property not the student's, and they're based on things the students rarely can see.

Where students in literature may normally assume a book is "theirs," this is less frequently the case in history studies.[11] Students are more accustomed to deferring with a history book; it's felt to be the teacher's not theirs, and they wait for him to give it the proper explanation. Which, I'm afraid, he's often quite willing to do.

Thus, both student and teacher may work within that book-as-repository-of-scholarship model we saw before. And because students can't possibly know the materials on which a book's scholarship is based, they're not very well qualified to judge it. Or can be made to think they aren't.

So the odds are stacked against a student's engaging much of himself in a history work, or at least much of his critical self. He's inclined to read books there with a "teacher-over-his-shoulder" attitude, letting the teacher's (or the profession's) imposed judgment substitute for his own experience. Because he has had history filtered through so many textbooks, he's inclined to read any book in the field *as* a kind of text.

Hence, he's not likely to read history works as intimately as he might novels. In a novel, a student's judgments may be wrong headed or ill informed, but at least it's legitimate for him to make them—testing his critical senses out on its words. But he can't make that test on words in a history work, for behind those words is a more or less unseen world of professional scholarship and primary documents, and this is a world the student knows little if anything about. Even if he can respond with some insight to the words on the page, he still might get taken in, for how can he know if those words accurately reflect the documents? A clever logician or dramatist like, say, Arthur Schlesinger, Jr., or Richard Hofstadter might persuade him of something or other, but that power has little to do with whether they're right to the facts or not.

The student simply cannot trust his own senses. So he gets accustomed to not making the experiential connection at all. That's just not his business. It's the business of the trained representative of the scholarly world—the professor, who's been to the documents and therefore knows what history is.

Up to Faulkner in our class, this is evidently much the role I'd been expected to play, and I wasn't doing it very well. The course was labeled "History," and students assumed I was going to "represent" the profession's "body of knowledge" in teaching it. What *The Sound and the Fury* did was confound that role expectation, by throwing a novel into a course of history readings.

Students knew this novel was no repository of scholarship; rather, as one young woman later noted, they saw it as a "printed experience."[12] Once they could picture it as an experience, they were entitled to engage their full selves in it. They could trust their own senses too. Not that these senses would always be right, any more than they would with any other form of experience. But at least students could legitimately exercise those senses in the experience of the novel, and share their thinking with others in the seminar. They could do this because they knew I couldn't very well assume the role of professional authority and say, "Well, what you say may seem right to you, but you've seen only Faulkner's *words*. Let me tell you what *really* happened in the South." I wasn't going to say that, for with the novel form I couldn't. In short, these students knew they could do what we've talked about before in this book—take a felt experience and exercise their species-right to try and explain it.

So they made Faulkner's novel into an arena for exploring the drama of mind engaging world. In *The Sound and the Fury,* they could see a single mind in full encounter with experience,[13] and they could involve their own full minds in trying to explain the matter. When the novel form allowed them to tap into their own sense of experience, it released a powerful source of intellectual energy in them. And that's what made those two seminar sessions go so well. The novel form broke down our role expectations, putting the students and I on an intellectual par. We all became common participants in the species-human, trying to make sense of some fellow species-partici-pants—William Faulkner and his characters.

My fears about "necessary background" for the novel were thus mis-guided. The course had been faltering not because students lacked back-ground in the field, but because we hadn't found taps to open up what background in experience they already had. *The Sound and the Fury* helped us make such taps, short-circuiting historical background by connecting di-rectly into what such background should grow out of—the experience of people acting in time.

3. Our third instance was David Donald's double put-down of Robert Skotheim—that (1) Skotheim was only a graduate student, and (2) what Skotheim did was not legitimate research but simply "picking flaws in the writings of other historians."[14]

Donald's first put-down has no substance; and we need give it no substan-tive response here. David Hackett Fischer has demolished Donald with the wit of Lewis Carroll, and I'm quite satisfied to leave it at that.[15] His second put-down does have an intellectual base, though, and we might devote some time to the assumptions which seem to inform it.

To David Donald in this case, historical explanation must evidently *follow* the sources, it cannot precede them. A scholar must not judge an explanation until he's seen the documents which it comes out of.

Further, any work which claims to make an original "contribution to historical knowledge" must be based on and in those documents. By definition, then, historiography of Skotheim's sort could not be allowed as "original" research.

So Donald urged Skotheim to do just what professional historians do so frequently. Look at an explanation in the field, take it pretty much on its face, then hurry out to the documents to check whether it's right or not. The answers of history lie *in* those sources; you'll not find much about them by looking at the words of historians. History work, then, is basically work in libraries, or wherever it is you can find caches of primary source materials.

But Robert Skotheim challenged that picture. Donald implies this graduate student was lazy because he didn't go out and labor over the sources. In turn, Skotheim implied he'd simply exercise his mind in his own way and not let the profession predefine for him what is "research" and what is "work" and what isn't. He would spend some time in his own "primary source"—in this instance, David Donald's article—and see if he might learn something there of historical scholarship which other source forms couldn't tell him.

And Skotheim would further claim that this *is* research, and that it can make original contributions to historical understanding. Which means he's using a different picture of the documents than Donald's, and which further raises the question, "What in fact *is* a 'primary document' in history studies?"

Historians seem to have established a firm consensus on this matter—a consensus so widely held and so little challenged that it has almost achieved the status of a "paradigm" within the profession. That is, it's seen as simply the way things are, rather than a set of working assumptions. John Caughey has given expression to this consensus: "All history is divided into three parts: the source materials, which we call primary; the studies based on them, which we call secondary; and the critical appraisal of these works, which we might call tertiary."[16]

A "primary" source (according to the consensus) is one produced in the time under investigation, preferably by someone(s) involved directly in what's being investigated. The Declaration of Independence of 1776 is primary. A "secondary" source is an interpretation of a primary source, produced later by someone not involved in the original action. Carl Becker's book of 1922, *The Declaration of Independence,* is secondary. A "tertiary" source is an interpretation of a secondary source. Skotheim's discussion of Becker in *American Intellectual Histories and Historians* is tertiary (and if one buys the typology, what we're doing in this book is tertiary too).

"Primary," "secondary," "tertiary" refer not only to distance from the original action, but to scholarly legitimacy in the profession too. A primary source is the purest thing one can find in history research. If he's the first to discover it, he may handle it as a virgin thing, a source untouched by the mind of man (or at least of scholarly man). It's never been filtered through others' minds, and is thus close to where real history is.

A secondary source is much less pure, and thereby less legitimate for scholarship. When one goes to the primary sources, he's getting to the original, into the actual stuff of history. But when one relies on what others have seen, he's getting to history only secondhand, predigested. Not as it in fact happened, but as somebody said it happened. It's already been filtered through mind, and is thus once removed from where history really takes place.

One merely magnifies that distance with a tertiary source. To discuss Skotheim's discussion of Becker's discussion of the original Declaration of Independence is to get lost in a haze of "abouts"; it's just too far removed from the original event to be of much scholarly value. According to the typology, it's history reflected, not history in actuality.

There is much to be said for these assumptions. They caution scholars to make their *own* judgments, and to get close to their materials in doing so. They insist that scholarly assessments be original, not derivative. But if these assumptions have a core of positive truth in them, they also have some negative fallout, and I think they tempt scholars to some profound untruths about the nature of historical inquiry.

In calling a source "primary," historians are often inclined to believe that's where history *is,* in the source. If a scholar goes to the primary documents he's into the original experience. Anything else is incidental, impure, filtered.

But a primary document is not the original experience. It may be *an* original experience—but only for the framer(s) of that document. Which means it's already filtered by the time the historian gets to it. It's not the full happening, it's someone's particular image of that happening. Just as in *The Sound and the Fury,* Benjy and Quentin and Jason give us perspectives on the Compson history, but no one—not even Faulkner—can give us the whole unfiltered experience.

I'm not sure one can ever get to the full unfiltered experience. In fact, I'm pretty sure one cannot. But if one could, going to the documents wouldn't do it. One would have to go on beyond the documents to the original experience they come out of. Like, perhaps, Hunter Thompson going off to live with the Oakland Hell's Angels for a year (and getting himself chain whipped at the end), so he could experience at first hand what the Angel world is like.[17]

This procedure does present a few obstacles, though. Historians can't very well go live with their past subjects; even if they could, I suspect most would prefer not to (especially if those subjects happened to behave like Angels). And if one could overcome that obstacle, he'd still have not the whole happening but only *his own* filtered perspective on it. Unless the historian is Fustel de Coulanges or Norman Pollack, that perspective must somehow be taken into account.[18]

Even if we wanted to stick with this conventional block typology, then, we'd still be obliged to rearrange the slots. In a few moments, I want to propose a basic reconstruction of this whole typology. But supposing for now it has some value, we might redo the slots something like this:

In our new arrangement, "primary" would no longer be an original *document,* primary would become the original *experience,* just as it happened. That experience would be our starting point for historical inquiry; and our strategic problem would then become, "How does one get into it?" In our revised typology, one could experience this experience *only* by being there; even then it would be just *his* or *her* particular experience, not the full thing. The full experience, insists this typology, cannot possibly be recaptured. All we can hope for is to catch some of its residue as it comes down to us in sources filtered through particularized perspectives.

Which residue are now changed from primary to "secondary" sources within our revised typology. They make for history filtered—not as it in fact happened, but as it was experienced in some (inevitably) partial way. Secondary sources like this are impure in their very nature. They're not virgin things, untouched by mind. Nor do they hold *the* answers to history. They hold *some* answers, but only when we know (often in advance of our going to them) what *questions* to ask of them. If one doesn't pause to consider what "rural" meant in early nineteenth-century America and one's abolitionist sample shows only 12 percent from cities, he might then claim the documents "prove" abolitionism was a basically rural movement. And, from that evidence, he might further frame a whole historical explanation of this movement. Which is what David Donald did in his "Reconsideration" essay. But if, like Robert Skotheim, one were to reflect in advance of going to the documents, or reflect beside someone else who'd already gone to them, then he might query, "What did 'rural' in fact mean back then?" And if by some checking in census data he found the population as a whole was only 6 percent urban at that time, he might challenge the basic logic of this historical explanation. He'd do it not by rushing first to the historian's own sources and checking whether he's right or not, he'd do it by pausing to reflect what pictures the historian had in his mind before he ever approached those sources. He'd thus not yield to the conventional historian's premature urge to "be up and doing" in the facts. He'd ponder some long time about what tools scholars might use to handle those facts.

Reflections like this could help us break free from the normal document/ counterdocument mode of controversy in historical scholarship. It's part of what Stanley Elkins has done so effectively in *Slavery.* Before he gets involved in his slavery materials, Elkins gives a 26-page review of the conventional debate on the issue. One side in this debate, looking at one set of documents, had claimed slavery was an evil thing. The other side, looking at different documents, said, well, it wasn't quite so bad after all. For nearly a century, as Elkins describes it, the controversy was waged in much this manner, each side arguing that its own documents were in fact truer than the other's and that, therefore, its facts were the "real" facts.

But Elkins wants to refashion the whole issue. He tries this not by going to yet another set of documents (at least not what historians would normally call primary documents); he does it by looking at what pictures each side *brought to* their documents, then taking those pictures as a stimulant to construct some fresh pictures and fresh questions of his own. Further, he brings in fresh kinds of materials (all secondary, according to the old typology)—materials from other cultures, materials from other time periods, materials from other academic disciplines.

By doing all this, Stanley Elkins has written one of the modern classics of American historical scholarship. *Slavery* is a classic not because it necessarily says the "right" thing about slavery in America. Elkins has consulted precious few primary sources (in the old sense) for his study, and we can't judge how right he is *on slavery* until we check what he says with those sources. *Slavery* is a historical classic because it's got us asking new questions about our past and because it offers us fresh kinds of pictures and tools for explanation. And it does this in a remarkably self-conscious and humble way, which makes plain that Elkins himself knows his is not the last word on the matter.

I'm not encouraging any mass exodus from the primary sources here. I'm just saying let's not fool ourselves. Documents—however many, however reliable—won't give us history *in fact;* they'll give us a few random facts *about* history. Further, any document we may use is a filter of sorts, so we shouldn't deceive ourselves that we're looking upon history pure when we work with primary sources.

To stop fooling ourselves on this issue, we need radically to rethink just what a historical source is and does. In the last page or so, we've accepted the block typology of primary, secondary, tertiary, but have rearranged the slots some. Now we might take the added step and question this whole typology, at least in its general block form. Does it really help us to predefine what a document is *generally,* or might we better see it in more operational, *situation-specific* senses?

We might better understand this issue if we simply got some perspective on where we now are and have been in the history profession. We're no longer in the same situation we were in the late nineteenth century, when this "go-to-the-documents" injunction got established in American historical scholarship. Then the problem was to counter the predominantly "aesthetic" sense of the historical form. Which sense made of history a literary art, with the historian's role to write a fine story. He was to embellish the documents, not just represent them. And he needn't always feel a strong drive to go out and look at the documents anyway.

History grew into a *professional* enterprise by opposing this sense, and developed its go-to-the-documents strategy to buttress that opposition. Such a strategy made a great deal of sense then, as W. Stull Holt has shown in his fine article "The Idea of Scientific History in America." It made historians go out and actively seek information that they didn't have before, and it made them try and tell a true, as well as an interesting, story. But it also had its drawbacks, or has since then. As Holt has suggested, the profession has been pretty much locked into that strategy ever since, and he thinks we need some alternative ones now.[19]

I think we need some alternative strategies too, for we're in a different historical situation. Our situation is not a poverty of information, or of attitudes driving us to information; our situation is an overwhelming abundance of both. We needn't overreact of course by trying to shut off the full onrush of this information—we couldn't afford that in scholarship any more than we could afford to stop producing in the economy. But we do need to ponder just how our past mind-sets got established in the profession and query if they don't serve us inadequately in the present. Among other things, they stimulate us sometimes to produce a kind of unordered information glut, simply because we're conditioned to believe that producing in scholarship is a good thing.

For some three-quarters of a century now, American historians have been urged, "Go to the originals." Now we ought to pause and reflect, "What *are* the originals?" We've been tempted to think the answer to history's questions lay *in* the documents. Now we might suggest that a document's meaning comes from what one *does* with it. "Primary," "secondary," "tertiary" are not *essences;* rather, their meaning should live *in reciprocal relationship with the document's user*. It's only a slight exaggeration to say that a historical source is as a historical source does.

Some of my colleagues in intellectual history claim that Reinhold Niebuhr, or John Dewey, or Walter Lippmann, or Randolph Bourne are in fact primary sources in the field; and, since intellectual history has now become legitimized in the profession, they're acceptable subjects for original research. But they say Daniel Boorstin, and Richard Hofstadter, and Perry Miller, and William Appleman Williams (David Donald would add David Donald too) are secondary sources, and not quite acceptable subjects for original scholarship. I've never really understood this, but I think it's based on some assumption that if you're looking at Miller what you're *really* after is the Puritans, and you're letting Miller do your homework for you.

Historiography studies have frequently taken off from such an assumption. In the last chapter, we saw part of that assumption at work in Charles Sellers' article, "Andrew Jackson versus the Historians." Sellers does a fine job of delineating historiographical "frames of reference," but eventually he subordinates them all to the quest for "objective reality" in American history. And he does it, we've suggested, because this is his way of saying historical scholarship is finally worth the effort and is not simply chasing phantoms of the mind.

But if in fact that kind of goal makes historical scholarship worth the effort, then this whole book and the field it outlines are in vain. For within our sense of the species, the dialogue between people's idea-forms and world, between explanation and experience, never ends. This dialogue does not go on just until we find the "correct" explanation, it goes on and on and on, because explanation never quite captures experience, "mind" never fully represents "world."

"Objective reality" as Sellers projects it is itself a phantom of the mind, then. It's not only not known now, it's not ultimately knowable. And it's unknowable not because of any inherent mystery in the world, but because reality always comes to us through the filter of mind, human mind. Because that mind is invariably historical, it "sees" not only what's in front of it, but what's behind it too, and what it expects in the future. It also sees from its own particular location, and human locations vary. All of which means that the reality of our experience is *human,* and always subject to the limiting perspectives of time, and place, and class, and personality, and sex and so on.

To assume that we can come to some kind of comprehensive, objective view of history is to assume we can escape our own distinctively human perceiving instrument—*mind.* And that I don't see in the offing. Failing such an escape, we're left with mind, and I suppose we'd better try and make something of it.

If we admit that mind has *something* to do with how we experience and reconstruct history, then we ought further admit that we can afford at least one subfield in historical scholarship focusing fully on that mind—which field is what we're calling here "explanation in historical studies."

We ought also grant this subfield the right to define its own original sources. Within this field, priorities might just be reversed—"primary" could mean works written by historians, "secondary," the documents those historians have used. That is, when we're concerned with the mind of a Carl Becker, then his book *The Declaration of Independence* should become an original source for us. It's in sources like this where we can watch his mind at work. The actual Declaration of 1776 should be relegated to a secondary status; we're concerned with it only to the degree that it helps us understand Becker. That Becker was or wasn't "right" about the original Declaration is important, but in this field it's important first for what it says of Becker and his mind, not for what it says of external historical reality.

We need, I think, to give up our general block definition of the documents, and substitute a more operative sense of them. The point should not be primary or secondary; it should be, *go directly to your materials,* whatever they are and wherever they are. Reflect some in advance about what kinds of things they can and cannot tell you, also about the forms they inhabit. Then go to those materials and stick with them long enough to read them through their own distinctive language.

This means that if you set out to do historiographical scholarship, you'll need to read full books and articles, and carefully. Because the conventional pressures are so strong, you'll be tempted to give them a hasty reading, move away from them prematurely, and go out to the documents to check if they're right or not. Or you'll do what's so often done when writing up historiography research—pass over large numbers of works in the field, paraphrase their conclusions, then rush to judge them by some assumed "reality" which has little base in your research itself. You'll say these works *claim* historical reality is such and such, but here's what it *actually* is (or, like Sellers, *would be, if only we knew some more*).

Now that's *not* "going to your materials"; and, within the alternative historiographical injunction we're trying to develop here, it's not very good scholarship either. That's because its base of judgment comes not from its own primary materials, but from something outside. In historiography scholarship, such a practice is almost as bad as its counterpart in regular history studies—judging an original historical experience only through reading something *about* it.

IV

Historians live in a universe of print, and some have been deceived into assuming that print *is* the history, what in fact happened. On the contrary, we must contend that it's a long way from history-as-experience to history-in-print (whether that print be in a document, book or article).

Documents *aren't* the experience, or at least they're not the exact experience they refer to. If we can keep this clear in our minds, we have a better case for taking books in the field seriously, but never confusing what historians have said with the original historical experience.

History books are not lies (not most of them at least). But, like novels, they *are* constructed. If we can see such works as people's *reconstructions* of their past, not the past *recaptured,* then we can admit that a book happens in mind as well as in libraries. And we can also concern ourselves with how the book is made, not just with what it says.

Which means that, like literature, the field of history could use a *criticism* —a subfield which gives works in the area its undivided attention. And, like literary criticism at its best, historical criticism should aim at leading us through the word to the mind behind the word and to the experience around the mind.

In building up such a field, or subfield, we may need to do what they've done over in literary scholarship. That is, we might for a time develop something equivalent to the New Criticism. New Criticism has done pernicious things for literaries, and I hope we don't repeat those in history studies. But one good thing it did was break the grip of a preexisting reality (and morality) on works of the human imagination. It insisted that these works be allowed to create their own symbolic world and need not be judged at every point by whether its constructed world fits the "real" world or not.

New Critics got into trouble when they took a good tactical strategy and reified it into a metaphysics. It's a good idea to study an expressive form on its own terms; it's not a good idea to insist that such a medium connects to nothing but itself.

We in history needn't repeat that error. We can study a book on its own terms, merely as a heuristic tactic for taking it seriously and reading it carefully. But we needn't go on to remove it completely from things outside. It's still legitimate for the historian to ask, "How well does a book's interpretation stack up with the documents?" It's just not legitimate, says the historical critic, to make that the *only* base of concern with a book.

The overarching commitment to "primary documents" has much to say for it in history studies; but that's been said so much that we needn't defend it here. However, that commitment has also had negative side effects; one is its tendency to privatize community in American historical studies, causing scholars not to listen to each other as carefully as they might. As a result, books have been getting past us too quickly. This is one cause (though not the only one) of information overload and mind pollution in the field. Perhaps the main value of the area we're suggesting here is to *slow some historical experiences down a bit* so we can get a closer look at what we're doing. It offers the possibility of sustained intimacy with a limited universe of materials, and some measure of intellectual control over them.

With the books of history, we have a *population* to work within. We can move down inside that population to look at things more rigorously, and perhaps in time try out what we find there on other kinds of historical materials.

NOTES

1. *The Sound and the Fury* (Vintage Books, 1956), p. 48.

2. "A Note on Historical Method: David Donald's 'Toward a Reconsideration of Abolitionists,' " *The Journal of Southern History,* XXV, no. 3 (August 1959), 356–65.

3. Letter from David Donald published in *The Journal of Southern History,* XXVI, no. 1 (February 1960), 156–57.

4. I suspect his professors' procedure in this instance *was* extreme. More normal perhaps—especially in intellectual history—is the practice requiring students to be *exposed* to as many books as possible. Like a professor of my acquaintance who assigns graduate students three books to read every week! He doesn't expect they'll actually "read" them. He just wants them to get "introduced" to all these books and names and terms, so they'll know something of what they're about. The end result of both procedures is similar, though—a fleeting familiarity with pieces of books and minds in history studies, never a full, considered encounter with any one.

5. This picture resembles the climate-of-opinion conception of ideas we'll see later, in chapter 5. I suspect that this conception, as it's held by working historians, is tied closely with how they're trained into the field—with their tendency not to spend much time on a single mind in action, but to move lightly over the surface of many minds. In doing this, they'll not likely catch those minds at work, but after their work is over, in finished thoughts. As a result, their picture of mind and thought may be more passive and less grounded than the model of mind we're trying to develop in this study. And the causes have to do with the dilemma of information overload and the impulse to "coverage," which we noted in the prologue.

6. These two terms—"situation" and "strategic response"—will become clearer in chapters 5 and 6.

7. In a supplementary volume to the present study—entitled *Experience and Explanation in American Culture Studies: An Interdisciplinary Model for Inquiry*—I am developing this point on Tocqueville at some considerable length. Moving back and forth between his personal life and his *Democracy,* I use Tocqueville to provide an existential base for the "experience-explanation" strategy.

8. Clearly, Faulkner was a breakthrough for us, and the course "took" after that. Which made our reading of Elkins and Miller and Boorstin much richer than otherwise. Further, these were students in an innovative college and accustomed to a seminar format where books were to be discussed and not just assimilated. Still, they never got as engaged in any other book as in *The Sound and the Fury.* And that was the most difficult work they read the whole term. Which suggests something of the point I'm trying to make here—that students bring different anticipations and different strategies to a novel than to a book in history. And what was true at Raymond is magnified in the normal academic environment, where students are characteristically less involved in the experience of learning.

9. I imagine this is one reason why the field of literature seems to draw better students than does history, and can do more with them. With the primary texts so accessible to them, students in literature can be challenged immediately by the best minds and imaginations in the field. And they can in turn challenge their teachers' minds, for both student and teacher have direct access to many of the same materials. In history, this is rarely the case; normally, it's true only in the most advanced graduate research seminars.

10. John Snell et al., *History as a Career: To Undergraduates Choosing a Profession* (American Historical Association, 1964), p. 4.

11. Granted, with Homer, Shakespeare, Milton, Melville, and other classic authors, the issue does get more complicated, and here too a deference pattern of sorts has got established. It's with these works, I suppose, where "the laying on of high culture" is most prevalent. Which attitude is the literary equivalent of the "you haven't seen the documents" put-down in history. There are differences between these two attitudes, and both in fact have some truth on their side. But one educational result is the same— to shut off the student's own experiential energies for understanding, and to intimidate him with professionalized conventions.

12. Marian Turner, Case Western Reserve University seminar paper, Fall, 1970.

13. Or rather, in this case it's four single minds—Faulkner himself and the three Compson brothers.

14. Donald (n. 3 above), p. 157.

15. *Historians' Fallacies: Toward a Logic of Historical Thought* (Harper and Row, Torchbook, 1970), p. 284.

16. "Trends in Historical Criticism," *Mississippi Valley Historical Review* (March 1954), p. 620. Caughey, by the way, doesn't buy the whole pattern of conventional assumptions here, though he understands them quite clearly. In this essay, he faults historians for slighting historical criticism, and urges the profession to develop such a field. We'll talk more about this in chapter 6.

17. *Hell's Angels: A Strange and Terrible Saga* (Ballantine Book, 1970).

18. Coulanges is the nineteenth-century French historian who, upon being applauded by students for an especially brilliant interpretation in class, protested, "It is not I who speak, but history which speaks through me." In W. Stull Holt, "The Idea of Scientific History in America," *Journal of the History of Ideas,* 1, no. 3 (June 1940), 358.

Pollack, though not applauded quite as enthusiastically (perhaps because his interpretation wasn't quite as brilliant), nevertheless claimed much the same thing in *The Populist Response to Industrial America* (Norton, paperback, 1966). In his introduction to that volume, Pollack wrote that "my interpretation, however controversial, grows directly out of the evidence itself. It was reached inductively, and not deductively" (p. 11).

19. Holt, pp. 352–53. Just why the history profession has lagged so far behind other disciplines on this point is an intriguing question. Historians often pride themselves on being "humanistic," as against "mechanistic" social scientists. Yet David Donald's posi-

tion would be laughed out of court in, say, sociology or political science. And it would be laughed at simply because it pays so little respect to *mind*.

There are extreme mechanists in both sociology and political science. But so are there respectable subfields handling the theory and method and criticism of their discipline—that is, critically applying their minds to the *forms of scholarship* in their respective fields. Indeed, some of the most noted scholars in these disciplines do almost nothing but theoretical and methodological work—scholars like Robert Merton, Talcott Parsons, Ralf Dahrendorf, Alvin Gouldner, Abraham Kaplan, Robert Nisbet, Eugene Meehan, and Robert Dahl. The result is that theoretical understandings in sociology and political science are far richer, more profound, and more cumulative in their development than are such understandings among historians. There are several reasons why this is the case, but I imagine one very powerful reason has to do with the grip of the old "scientific" idea and the "objective-observer" ideal upon historians' minds.

4 Changes of Mind: Historians and Explanation-Forms in Twentieth-Century America

Scientific theories, it must be remembered, attach to nature only here and there.
Thomas Kuhn
"Logic of Discovery or
Psychology of Research?"

In every age the illusion is that the present version is valid because the related facts are true, whereas former versions are invalid because based on inaccurate or inadequate facts.
Carl Becker
"Everyman His Own Historian"

In the first three chapters, we've talked generally about idea-forms and historical reality, and about the book-form in history studies. It remains now to look at some *actual* idea-forms advanced by American historians as a preliminary to our later controlled analyses of these forms in the case studies.

In those case studies, we'll attempt to get inside a form and view historical reality in America from there—trying to see the world as it experiences it and observing how it behaves under strain and in response to change. In short, we'll be looking for "perspectives" on historical reality there. And our intent will be to explain how particular historians behave within and through their idea-forms.

As a prerequisite to that, though, we'll need to get some elementary sense of the forms themselves. So in this chapter we'll introduce a few explanation-forms used by American historians, treating them as if they didn't change much over time, and, for the moment, minimizing the variations within them.

That should do to convey some sense of what the forms look like, if we were to stick with their outer surface. In the chapter to follow, we'll then try to move below that surface, to find ways of getting inside an explanation form. And in the chapter following that (chapter 6), we'll lay out a strategy

82

for managing explanation-forms within historical texts. Finally, in the case-study chapters (7–9), we'll attempt to put our prescriptions into action.

II

Our first venture into the world of American historical studies will follow the normal route of chronology. We'll look at three separate explanation forms constructed by historians in twentieth-century America. Telescoping the forms for a while, we can tell a story something like this.[1]

First, there were the *Progressive* historians, who had things pretty much their own way in explaining American history from 1910 or so on to mid-century. For Progressives, life in America seemed fairly straightforward. In some cases, selfish interests may have clouded over people's vision of how things worked in the country, but one had only to cut through the haze and he could see direct into the realities of things.

If one were a Progressive, what he likely saw first were classes in society and people located in these classes mainly on the basis of wealth. The real mobilizing reality to Progressives was economic; ideas, politics, religion, social forms, literature all took off from there.

Once one found that out, located the point of leverage in the world, he could go on to change things. As a Progressive historian, his role was to show that, though economics had mostly determined people's experience in the past, it shouldn't continue to in the future. And Progressives went on to promote figures in the American past who'd said so before—like Roger Williams, and Thomas Jefferson, and Andrew Jackson, and William Jennings Bryan. These heroic figures were progressive liberals who'd fought entrenched orthodoxies, and who—for a time at least—had cast forth a vision of what America might be if only regressive interests wouldn't get in the way.

Progressives were a little like a political party out of power, then. Throw the rascals out, put liberals in charge, and things will be O.K.

Progressives didn't like absolutes very well, or said they didn't, and one student of Progressive thought has called theirs a "revolt against formalism."[2] Absolutes keep people from working to correct injustices, and if there was any sin to the Progressives it was just that. Complacency, sitting back and letting things happen, was intolerable to them. Life in America could be made free and open and just if only people willed it so and labored hard to implement their wills. Progressives obligated themselves to lead the way toward a juster, more enlightened society.

Though Progressives were frequently shocked about how things had been in America, they were still cheerful about how they might be. They held much hope for the future—that's one reason why they're called "Progressives."

Progressive historians characteristically wrote things like:

It is clear enough today that the conscious reformer who appeals to the future is the final product of a progressive order of things.[3]

I print [this book] in the hope that a few of this generation may be encouraged to turn away from barren "political" history to a study of the real economic forces which condition great movements in politics.[4]

The gods, it would seem, were pleased to have their jest with Roger Williams by sending him to earth before his time. In manner and speech a seventeenth-century Puritan controversialist, in intellectual interests he was contemporary with successive generations of prophets from his own days to ours.[5]

Around 1950 or so another group of American historians and culture analysts came along, challenging the Progressives. They've been called "consensus" thinkers, though perhaps a better name is *counter-Progressives*. Looking back on the world pictured by Progressives, they felt life was more complex than that—this is one reason to call them "counter-Progressives."

These thinkers weren't as certain as Progressives that one could see straight into realities, so they spent much time studying myths and symbols and images of reality. They were also intrigued by nuances and enjoyed tracking down incongruities in American experience. Words like "paradox," "ambiguity," and "irony" sounded often through their writings.

Counter-Progressives tended to brood more than Progressives and were given to looking at the perversity of life. America's history, for example, didn't appear to them a two-party battle between ideas of progress and of regress, and even progressive change didn't always seem a straightforward victory of enlightened reason over inertia. Sometimes, counter-Progressives showed people backing forward into good things, a curious behavior one of them labelled "crablike progress."[6] Counter-Progressives also were less enthusiastic about Progressive heroes like Roger Williams, Andrew Jackson, and Woodrow Wilson, and were more sympathetic toward those who Progressives had branded as conservatives—like John Winthrop, and Alexander Hamilton, and sometimes even businessmen.

Counter-Progressives felt some things were double which Progressives saw as single (e.g., ideas sometimes pointed forward and backward simultaneously), and they rejected the Progressive doubleness of haves versus have-nots. They did this partly because they didn't think things—at least along the material plane of life—were all that bad in America; have-nots didn't seem as desperate here as elsewhere. They did it also because some felt the ideas holding Americans together were more basic than the things separating them, so they emphasized unities over conflicts (one reason they've been labelled "consensus" thinkers). Finally, they did it because they believed those things which really were quite bad couldn't be righted easily or quickly; panaceas, they contended, often made things worse.

In contrast to their predecessors the Progressives, counter-Progressives were not much for political action, but instead were mainly just curious about life, were a little resigned to the burdens of history, and were mostly put off by people who weren't. Counter-Progressives were given to writing things like:

The liberal society analyst is destined in two ways to be a less pleasing scholar than the Progressive: he finds national weaknesses and he can offer no absolute assurance on the basis of the past that they will be remedied. He tends to criticize and then shrug his shoulders, which is no way to become popular, especially in an age like our own.[7]

If . . . there were such a thing as a pure "innocence situation," it might look very much like nineteenth-century America. There, space and mobility prevented the development of a tight social structure in which one had to accept exploitation, aggression, lust, and avarice as a daily problem.[8]

Spanning a mere three and a half centuries, American history has no antiquity, few ruins, and little mystery. Moving in a fairly straight line from primitive settlements to triumphant power and plenty, it looks superficially simple. Its complexity lies below the surface and therefore makes a special demand on the historical imagination.[9]

Then in the early 1960s came yet another group of American historians— the *New Left*—who looked something like the old Progressives and a little like some counter-Progressives, but mostly tended to reject them both.

Like the Progressives, the New Left has seen things as rather clear-cut in America, but they've shifted the whole picture portside a few notches. And in the shifting they've squeezed out an entire line of Progressive heroes— notably liberals like Jefferson, Wilson, and FDR. To the extent that the New Left has had heroes (and they've had fewer than Progressives), they've tended to be blacks, Indians, unestablished workingmen, William Lloyd Garrison, Big Bill Haywood—people who resisted the controlling system of doing things in America. These people were system-changing radicals, not system-reforming liberals.

The New Left have put away the literary and philosophical concerns of their immediate predecessors the counter-Progressives, and, like the Progressives, have reached out into politics and economics again. They haven't been as much concerned with people's ideas as with systems of power; ideas, they've felt, are largely organized around power structures anyway.

America, and the American idea, has been such an organized system of power to New Left historians. America isn't really an open society; people can be free in it only down certain narrow channels. Outside those, Americans have been oppressed—and the mainstream has made it worse because when it couldn't solve its own problems it foisted them off on its marginal people. These marginal people couldn't get into the system, then, neither could they keep that system off their backs.

Progressives saw similar injustices, but said there's hope for America. The New Left has said not. The system in America hasn't been able to bail itself out. Progressives said people should work for more liberalism; New Left historians have said liberalism—corporate liberalism, cold war liberalism—

is America's problem. It's all in the system. And that system has been one of organized power. Progressives wanted to reform the structures of American experience; New Leftists have seen the only hope in replacing them. They have been radicals, on occasion revolutionaries, and they've held few hopes that in time "progress" would make things better.

New Left historians have written things like:

There is no question . . . of a "disinterested" community of scholars, only a question of what kinds of interests the scholars will serve.[10]

The United States of the mid-twentieth century might better be described as an empire than a community.[11]

I begin with the hypothesis that so intense a struggle of moral values [in pre-Civil War America] implies a struggle of world views and so intense a struggle of world views implies a struggle of worlds—of rival social classes or of societies dominated by rival social classes.[12]

III

That's how we might describe the forms if we looked only at the visible surface of historians' thought. Such a description resembles what we often see in history textbooks. The procedure makes for clarity and some ease of understanding. But by presenting thoughts as it does, it misses much of their existential vitality and intricate complexity. I've resorted to such a procedure here because, on one level, it's instrumental to our purposes later in this book. Because it's so straightforward, it gets a few things out in front of us for the case studies to come. It's a moderately useful precondition to critical inquiry in the territory; but it lies on a plane about two levels removed from the real base of that inquiry.

We've started with the level of the straightforward, then, the *what* of historians' explanation forms. Now we can move on to the next more difficult level. Where our concern on the first level was only to *describe* the forms, here we'll try to *analyze* them, breaking them apart and setting some of their differences alongside each other. The intent is to gain some of what Kenneth Burke has called "perspective by incongruity," understanding one form by noting wherein it differs from another.[13]

We needn't strive yet for tight control on this intermediate level. We *do* in time need such control; indeed, it's one of our most pressing imperatives for the effective handling of ideas. But it would be premature to insist on such control just *yet*. We have other things to do before we get there. So we'll just free-associate for a while now—picking up a form, or two, or three, turning them over and around, glancing now at this side, now at that, just to get some pictures developing of what these forms look like. In the next chapter, then, we'll introduce strategies for tightening it all up.

We could manage this kind of analysis in several ways. One is to handle the forms through the model of mind-world encounter we set up in chapters

1 and 2. Which would mean looking back at *pictures of reality in America* through each of the three explanation-forms—the Progressive, the counter-Progressive, the New Left.

The first thing we can say of the first picture is this: *Progressives* tried putting reality together so that experience became progress (in chapters 7 and 8, we'll see how they behaved when things failed to come out that way). Progress was their Master Form, the single key which explains most everything they thought and did. Any moment of history was seen in the light of how it contributed to a coming one. And the most pressing of coming moments was the present, where the allies for progress were locked in battle with entrenched self-interests, each vying for control of America's future.

As they looked back on the American past, Progressives saw a long line of liberal heroes, forthright figures who spoke out for the future against reactionary power interests. Roger Williams, Thomas Hooker, Samuel Adams, Tom Paine, Thomas Jefferson, John Taylor, Andrew Jackson, Henry George —men like these fought for the life of liberalism against antidemocratic interests defended by the John Winthrops, John Cottons, Cotton Mathers, Thomas Hutchinsons, Alexander Hamiltons, Fisher Ameses, Nicholas Biddles, and the Robber Barons.

By lining up the past this way, marching it forth in twos, Progressives could gain leverage on experience; such a procedure helped them judge what was right and what was wrong in America, and it gave them power to do something about it. By identifying with a continuous line running back and forth through time, Progressive historians pictured their heritage as a kind of simultaneous moment—all liberals from the seventeenth century to the twentieth sharing a similar vision of the land and its potential for democracy. Thus a Parrington (whose picture of America is perhaps most characteristic of the Progressive school) could write: "The gods, it would seem, were pleased to have their jest with Roger Williams by sending him to earth before his time. In manner and speech a seventeenth-century Puritan controversialist, in intellectual interests he was contemporary with successive generations of prophets from his own days to ours."[14]

Context shows that Parrington didn't in fact mean Williams was a man before his time. Or if he was, the times—not the liberal-progressive Roger Williams—were at fault. To Parrington, Williams was "a rebel against all the stupidities that interposed a barrier betwixt men and the fellowship of their dreams." And, he noted, "Those who found such stupidities serviceable to their ends, naturally disliked Roger Williams and believed they were serving God by undoing his work."[15]

If Williams—or any other American liberal—was out of tune with his times, that could be explained by conservative leaders having fought them and forced their times to postpone progress. Leaders like that, said Progressive historians, were spread throughout America's history. Like their adversaries the democratic liberals, they also shared a common heritage; and

Parrington could lay bare the motives of an entire line of American conservatives in his indictment of the Puritan theocrats: "The historian need not wander far in search of the origins of the theocratic principle; it is to be found in the self-interest of the lay and clerical leaders."[16]

Thus Progressives pictured two kinds of men in the world. First there were those who carried the hopes of mankind along with them. A juster future filled their eyes and hearts and wills. From motives not fully explained by Progressives, these men could transcend the self's preoccupations and concern themselves for the welfare of others. These others were not only in space but in time too, unconceived generations to whom the present ought leave a brighter legacy than it inherited. Such individuals could give spirit to life, they carried visions in their heads of a better world for men, and were unsparing of self in seeking to make those visions real. For Progressives, it was these men who defined the really "American" part of the country's experience.

But ranged off against these were men who, for motives rather fully explained away by Progressives, could not transcend their own selves and who carried with them the darker fears of men. The new and the different frightened them, and they were compelled to hang on to what they had. Their direction of interest was either inward—toward themselves—or backward— toward a safer past. For Progressives, it's this kind which blocked America from reaching her full democratic potential.

When we pass in our analysis beyond individuals to look at groups and institutions through the Progressive form (and thus move from a Parrington version to a Beardian), we see a similar picture. Society was divided against itself—some groups had gathered for themselves inordinate power and wealth; other groups, lacking power, were kept from enjoying their just rewards. Because of the power grasping of certain groups and the unjust distribution of America's bounty, the Progressives' picture was not a harmonious one—much oppression, poverty, ugliness, violence informed their perspective on life in the land.

Historians who looked back on the Progressives from the so-called "consensus" years after 1950 have labeled theirs a "conflict" interpretation of America's past.[17] But we might better call it a "conflict-*resolution*" model. Progressives saw much conflict in America but deplored almost all they saw; to them, conflict was not a necessary stimulant to social progress, but an unnatural barrier to it. For as James Harvey Robinson said (and most other Progressives would probably have agreed), "At last, perhaps, the long-disputed sin against the Holy Ghost has been found; it may be the refusal to cooperate with the vital principle of betterment. History would seem, in short, to condemn the principle of conservatism as a hopeless and wicked anachronism."[18]

For Progressives, real progress in human affairs could start only when this unnatural impulse to conservatism died off in the race and all people were thereby freed to become progressive, liberal, democratic. Ideas and institutions would then become purified of the dead hand of the past, and human history could take a fresh turn. No longer would the conflict between progress and reaction characterize mankind; instead, progress would have won the day.

But people couldn't real-ize their Progressive America until they knew what—and who—had held them from it all these years. So Progressive historians got engaged in a massive unmasking process, striving to lay bare the *real* interests bottling up the American vision and keeping it always on the defensive. Thus they sought out experiences in the past which most revealed this conflict between progress and regress; locating the barriers to America's promise, the people could go on to overcome them and take full hold of their destiny. Progressive historians thus characteristically focused on experiences which held out or blocked that promise—experiences like the making of the federal Constitution (Beard, Carl Becker), Jacksonian democracy (Turner, Parrington, Arthur Schlesinger, Jr. [when he was a Progressive]), the Populists (John D. Hicks, Parrington), the Puritans (Parrington, Thomas Jefferson Wertenbaker), and the egalitarian sweep of the frontier against absolutisms from the Old World past (Turner, Parrington).

Progressives make up America's first "school" of professional historians; their early history parallels the profession's developing self-consciousness in the beginning years of this century. Because they came first, they established many of the categories to which their successors would respond. Hence much of twentieth-century American history writing has consisted of dialogues in and around this Progressive tradition.

Counter-Progressives entered that dialogue by challenging the Progressives' idea of progress and by picturing change in forms different from their predecessors. This in fact might be the single master key to the counter-Progressive form—its sense of ambiguity about change. In counter-Progressive writings, that sense has taken several different shapes.

For one, counter-Progressives didn't picture a society split into two warring camps—a party opting for the future and for greater justice, another party rejecting both. Instead, they saw the ideas and motives driving men as situation-specific—on one general level, almost everyone in the culture seemed eager for progress, on other levels it depended on where and when one was as much as who he was. These locations, these situations, were constantly shifting; here one could gain by the future, there not, and here one might profit in things material, but lose in things symbolic. It was very complicated; and counter-Progressives seemed to think complication the point of it all. So they had no clear-cut consensus on what kinds of forces propel change, or how one judges whether a change is congenial to justice or not. That's one sharp difference between them and their Progressive predecessors.

For another, counter-Progressives didn't see progress as all of a piece. A favorite counter-Progressive strategy was to take some idea which appeared to point straight at the future, then keep cutting away at it until they'd bared all sorts of reactionary and primitivist counterstrains running through it. Behind and under and around this idea of progress, counter-Progressives detected vague longings for the simple pastoral life in America, and concealed desires for some kind of Adamic existence in an Eden-like world and for an escape to the free spontaneous life with no responsibilities attached. And through it all they found a strain running away from the consequences of living in a complex kind of world where interest must be balanced against interest, and idea against idea.

They also saw Americans frequently backing into their futures, accomplishing just the opposite of their intents; and they saw this temptation to irony as a persistent partner of the idea of progress. All of which—from the counter-Progressive perspective—made progress seem like an oversimplified kind of commitment, tempting people's minds away from the complicated problems of living in an intricate, interdependent civilization. If counter-Progressives had any overarching strategy in their writings, it was this drive to break through the progress form, making that their first step toward an explanation running counter to the Progressives'.

Counter-Progressives tended to be suspicious of the idea of progress, then. They also inclined away from environmental explanations of people's behavior and were given to exploring the motive forces of history inside the minds and psyches of men. They put away the Progressives' economic and political concerns and picked up on perspectives from psychology, art, literature, and philosophy. They were concerned for people's pictures of reality, as embodied through images and myths and symbols and dramatized in those psychic quests which take men's inner compulsions and project them outward. The line separating rational from irrational, altruistic from selfish, tended to blur in the counter-Progressive explanation, and all human thoughts, all actions, seemed to them a complicated blend of good and bad and reasonable and unreasonable.

At certain strategic points in time, said counter-Progressives, these private impulses were given outlet, and then the arena of public events took on fresh momentum, as life became supercharged with dramatic meanings. One such strategic point was the discovery and early history of the New World. Not all counter-Progressives would have phrased it in such grand fashion, but Charles Sanford said baldly what others in the form have implied: "With the discovery of America, Edenic expectations entered the main strain of history, assured of a prophetic fulfillment in the West. Without this westward-looking promise, the masses of Europe might never have stirred, the industrial revolution never begun, the social revolutions never launched."[19]

In the beginning, John Locke had written, all the world was America; and several counter-Progressives set out to explore this myth of the New World. They sought the image of America in the eyes of its more visionary early migrants; and these migrants saw a land open and rich with possibility, where men exhilarated in the sense they could begin all over with life and on which they could project their most compelling longings for heaven and earth. And here their longings and their actions were not held back by mediating institutions nor by ancient habits nor by all those ties and bonds and inhibitions which keep most people at most times pretty much fixed in their place. For that inhibiting net of obligations represented the Old World in these early migrants' dramaturgy; it was precisely the urge to escape such a life which motivated many of them to flee to the New World in the first place.

Whether America is *in fact* such a world was a concern to counter-Progressives, but only a secondary one. Their first concern was that many Americans *felt* this to be the case, and acted from their feelings. It was these feelings, and the pictures which gave them shape, that formed the heart of the counter-Progressive perspective on America.

This helps explain why so much of counter-Progressive scholarship focused on the early nineteenth century, at a moment when the possibilities of an entire continent seemed to open for the American imagination, and when peoples' symbolic responses came flooding out in full voice. R. W. B. Lewis saw the resulting imagery in perhaps its purest form, and has isolated one plane along which several counter-Progressives looked for their picture of America. Lewis wrote,

> The new habits to be engendered on the new American scene were suggested by the image of a radically new personality, the hero of the new adventure: an individual emancipated from history, happily bereft of ancestry, untouched and undefiled by the usual inheritances of family and race; an individual standing alone, self-reliant and self-propelling, ready to confront whatever awaited him with the aid of his own unique and inherent resources. . . . His moral position was prior to experience, and in his very newness he was fundamentally innocent. The world and history lay all before him. And he was the type of creator, the poet par excellence, creating language itself by naming the elements of the scene about him.[20]

In that early nineteenth-century situation, counter-Progressives located a recurring tendency in this New World people—the tendency to busy themselves, ironically, at re-creating the very type of Old World which they had once fled. On the level of action, their problem was that they were developing enormous power without the institutional channels for making it responsible; so often their actions doubled back on themselves, accomplishing just the reverse of what they intended. On the level of thought, their problem was how to deal with the ambiguity of their actions. Louis Hartz caught the counter-Progressive sense of this ambiguity in noting that the American liberal rhetoric reveals, "as compared with the European pattern, a vast and almost charming innocence of mind."[21]

Mostly, though, this vast innocence appalled Hartz; he was not much charmed by it. Neither was David Noble, Charles Sanford, Henry Nash Smith, John William Ward, Leo Marx, Stanley Elkins, nor Richard Hofstadter—other counter-Progressives who wrote on this theme. Marvin Meyers could tolerate it and note how it served Americans well at times. But only R. W. B. Lewis among counter-Progressives could be charmed as well as informed by this innocence in the American mind—and that because, in his dialectic theory of culture, innocence sparked counter-innocence, and when this happened, fresh ideas got created.[22]

Which leads to another difference between Progressive and counter-Progressive perspectives on America. Generally, Progressives worked in twos—life was either this or it was that. But counter-Progressives pictured things mostly in threes—they set this and that into dialogue, then out of the encounter discovered some third alternative. For Smith and Ward, this third alternative was the "middle landscape" between savagery and civilization, for Marx the "complex pastoral" between the garden and the machine, for Lewis the "party of Irony" which mediated between hope and memory.

And for all four, plus other counter-Progressives, it stimulated a search through the American past for figures who expressed a similar sense of ambiguity. Where Progressives looked back through American history to find their identity in Williams, Paine, Jefferson, and Jackson, counter-Progressives found their identity in Edwards, Melville, Hawthorne, Horace Bushness, and Henry Adams. And they went on to becloud their predecessors' picture by revealing ambiguities in Progressive heroes. Jefferson comes through counter-Progressive works as an aristocrat as well as a democrat, and a man torn between accepting or rejecting an industrial future for America. And counter-Progressives held Jackson responsible for unleashing those same capitalistic forces he claimed he was resisting—partly because he was confused, they said, partly because he too, like Jefferson, wasn't all that committed to those liberal-progressive values he claimed he was serving.[23]

Counter-Progressives saw things that way because they identified Jefferson and Jackson and other figures in the culture basically as *Americans,* and only incidentally as liberals or conservatives or Republicans or Democrats or workingmen or capitalists. Smith's *Virgin Land*—one of the earliest counter-Progressive works—opened with Crevecoeur's "What then is the American, this new man?"; and that set the question for much subsequent scholarship in the form.[24] It was after the American quest for identity, and it was curious about the culture and character types which grew out of that quest.

Perhaps this is one reason why counter-Progressive works have been labeled "consensus" by their critics. Where Progressives pictured a society through its *classes,* counter-Progressives saw *culture* as the most basic public reality. Class tends to be divisive, culture more unifying. Sometimes this quest for culture made for a rather homogeneous picture of America—we can find that in Hartz or Ward, or Boorstin or Clinton Rossiter (the latter pair saw the consensus and liked it, the former two saw consensus and deplored it). Others, like Lee Benson, pictured much variety in America, a plurality of things and ideas and people and places. But whatever, whether homogeneity or plurality, counter-Progressives tended to reject Progressive dualisms for an alternative view of how things number up.

They were not as ready as Progressives to deplore conflict either. Counter-Progressives like Lewis, Meyers, Hartz, Sanford, Marx, and Perry Miller—who saw culture *as* conflict—were not about to wish that conflict away. If there was any single fear holding this group of counter-Progressives together, it was that America didn't have enough conflict, that the country was in danger of suffocating in its own liberal consensus on life.

That consensus, they said, came from the country's distinctive advantages. Americans have enjoyed an open continent bountiful with resources. They've had no old order to overthrow as a prelude to taking over control (few counter-Progressives were concerned much with the plight of Indians, neither were Progressives; some New Leftists have been, though). They've had no hostile neighbors along their borders, and they've been protected from the Old World by thousands of miles of ocean. Because all these circumstances have been so unique and unrepeatable, counter-Progressives were loathe to proclaim America had any mission to the world. Almost the whole thrust of Hartz's *Liberal Tradition in America* or Boorstin's *Genius of American Politics* was against the belief that Americans should try and export their own experience. Beyond these two, Sanford and Elkins and others in the form wished Americans wouldn't get the categories of other peoples and themselves so mixed up. To them, America's experience was unique, and to understand themselves and others, they were obliged to learn why. If a few counter-Progressives, like Boorstin, claimed America is unique as a way to say let's keep it that way, more resembled Hartz in seeing uniqueness as America's national dilemma. This is where the New Left came in.

In some ways, the *New Left* has resembled old Progressives—they too have emphasized the economic and political in American experience, they too have pictured a society divided into classes, they too (or some of them) have seen conflicts more than unities. For all that, we might call them neo-Progressives (thus giving a kind of architechtonic unity to our labels—Progressive, counter-Progressive, neo-Progressive). Save for one thing: the New Left hasn't believed much in the idea of progress.

For Progressives, that idea meant everything. Whenever America was troubled, it was because she'd veered off the true path of progress. With enough push from enough progressive liberals, though, she could be put back on the track and return to the really American part of her heritage. At the surface, counter-Progressives rejected such a belief. Yet they also conveyed some kind of hope for the future. In their works, we find little evidence that the nation itself has sinned much, only that it hasn't understood much of sin and is naïve in the ways of the world. Counter-Progressives wanted to educate Americans to a maturer sense of tragedy in life; and though they were not overly cheerful about the prospects, most seemed willing to give it a try (otherwise, why write their books?). That's not quite Progressive enthusiasm, but it is faith of a sort.

New Left historians would have none of that. To them, the whole nation has sinned, and mightily. And these sins are no mere aberration from the norm, they *are* the norm. A return to the "really American" part of the nation's heritage will not do, for it's just that heritage which has made America such an oppressor.

Counter-Progressives pictured America as the extension of an idea, and for them that idea was innocent. However much they may have indicted the culture, they gave it the benefit of the doubt. Americans were frequently misguided, counter-Progressives felt, but they did what they did from good motives. Because of this, they blundered a lot (though to counter-Progressives, that didn't quite let them off the hook).

Not so to the New Left. In their picture, America has not been so much an idea as a structure of power. And that power is anything but innocent. The nation has not been misguided in its acts of oppression; it's been cold, and ruthlessly calculating, and has done what it's done to protect and extend itself. To the New Left, America has not been a blunderer, it's been a predator.

In framing their picture of the culture, many counter-Progressives tried re-creating how Americans envisioned their world in the early nineteenth century. Looking forward to their new land and outward away from Europe, these Americans exhilarated at the chance to start over, to build themselves something radically different from their sense of the time-burdened Old World. Counter-Progressives tried to show what that impulse meant to American culture then . . . and since then. Sometimes they were caught up by the fresh innocence of the vision, sometimes they were torn by the irony of this innocent people moving toward an Old World in their very mode of protesting against it. Either way, they placed the culture's fundamental meaning along this New World/Old World plane.

Historians from the New Left have started with a different plane. To the degree that they've moved beyond the nation for perspective, they've looked not to the Old World, Europe, but toward Asia and Africa and Latin America. These are locations outside the Old World/New World dualism. And to the degree that they've moved below surface appearances for perspective, it's not been into Melville or Edwards or Henry Adams, but to Indians, sailors, blacks, migrant laborers, the dispossessed of the country. Seen from there, America does not look innocent, New World–like at all. In fact, it's resembled the Old World picture in the demonology of nineteenth-century Americans. It's been repressive, it's been conservative, and it's offered very little opportunity or hope at all for the dispossessed.

To counter-Progressives, Americans caught their national mission from a sense they could start all over with history. They would take what they liked from their Old World heritage—certain values of personal morality, some form of commitment to reason and science and the enterprise of knowledge, but mostly a driving individualism which impelled them to believe that society is arranged to serve themselves, mainly in things material. And they would discard what they didn't like from the Old World—a net of institutions which restrained people from doing things and which held their imaginations in check, and a situation where wealth was not just theirs for the taking.

The New Left has pictured an America hard up against the consequences of this acquisitive ethic. Individualism and open land have meant wealth for some, but poverty for many more. And the race has not been to the swift but to those who already began with power or who could tap into existing power structures quickly, and ruthlessly. *Power*—that's the key to much New Left history.

Where counter-Progressives looked back on early nineteenth-century America and saw ideas of innocence and myths of paradise and of the independent yeoman, New Leftists have seen in it power structures. They've either concentrated straight on those structures—as with, say, Eugene Genovese's *The Political Economy of Slavery*—or they've focused on dissenters who fought (usually without success) against them—as with Aileen Kraditor's *Means and Ends in American Abolitionism,* or parts of Staughton Lynd's *Intellectual Origins of American Radicalism,* or the essays in Martin Duberman's *Anti-Slavery Vanguard.*

More often, they've looked for other periods in the American past where the nation's drive to power, and the expansion of power beyond its borders, has been made manifest—as in the late nineteenth century (Walter LaFeber's *The New Empire,* William Appleman Williams' *The Roots of the Modern American Empire*), or in the years from World War II to the present (Lloyd Gardner's *Architects of Illusion,* LaFeber's *America, Russia, and the Cold War,* Gar Alperovitz's *Atomic Diplomacy,* Kolko's *The Roots of American Foreign Policy,* parts of Christopher Lasch's *The Agony of the American Left*). The nation was not driven on to Cuba and Hawaii and the Philippines and Viet Nam from any misguided moralism, they've said; America has gone there because of the inner imperatives of its market-place economy and the ideological and political structures accompanying it. Williams called this perpetual impulse to expand "the great evasion"; and in his book of that title he wrote,

America's great evasion lies in its manipulation of Nature to avoid confrontation with the human condition and with the challenge of building a true community. . . . the escape hatch of the frontier . . . directed Americans down a path that carried them ever further away from the great opportunity they enjoyed to create a truly human community. And, unless it is shortly modified and ultimately reversed, the subtle process which shifted the image of the frontier from the continent to an overseas economic empire will transfer it once again, this time to space itself, and the evasion will become literally projected to infinity.[25]

What Progressives and counter-Progressives saw as opportunity—new frontiers always opening—Williams pictured as evasion. And what Progressives took as a "safety valve," Williams called an "escape hatch." Americans, he said, are unwilling to hang in there and confront themselves, but are always, like Huck Finn, "lighting out for the territories." Only they lack Huck's innocence. For behind them they've left problems still unsolved and people powerless to light out themselves. These people are the discarded of America, those who couldn't be fit into the system, but who couldn't get away from it either.

Opportunity in America hasn't been opportunity for all, then, it's been opportunity for some. And a study like Gabriel Kolko's *Wealth and Power in America* has contended that the balance of opportunity with locked-in poverty hasn't altered much over the years. Contrary to the "consensus" belief, Kolko charged, America is a stratified, top-down society.[26]

A characteristic New Left strategy has been to take a time when Progressives thought good things happened and claim they didn't. Thus Kolko looked at what's been called an age of reform—the Progressive years of 1900–16—and relabeled it "the triumph of conservatism." The American business system was not much threatened during those years, said Kolko, it was merely centralized, made less anarchic and more efficient. "It was no coincidence," he wrote, "that the results of progressivism were precisely what many business interests desired."[27]

And Christopher Lasch said that those who Progressives suppose had benefitted from reforms during that period—workingmen, blacks, women—in fact got in far short of a basic redoing of the system. Only the most organized of groups got power, and then because they cut back drastically on their goals so they could be co-opted. Unorganized, marginal people were left out then, and have been ever since.[28]

And Barton Bernstein—who felt FDR had opportunity to radicalize the American system in 1933 but instead turned to big business—has had go at another favorite progressive "age of reform":

The New Deal failed to solve the problem of depression, it failed to raise the impoverished, it failed to redistribute income, it failed to extend equality and generally countenanced racial discrimination and segregation. It failed generally to make business more responsible to the social welfare or to threaten business's pre-eminent political power. In this sense, the New Deal, despite the shifts in tone and spirit from the earlier decade, was profoundly conservative and continuous with the 1920s.[29]

What's come out of all this is a New Left picture of America as a gigantic consensus, a bulky and oppressive middle feeding on itself and upon others, and a less numerous, unorganized, and therefore oppressed marginal people who've never been let in on the benefits, and never will be under the present arrangement. They've been discarded in the rush of things. The frontier, social welfare, technology, education—all supposedly liberalizing influences in the progressivist picture—have done little to disturb that system, or right its inequities. They have all accommodated with poverty and the ghetto and racism and have easily adjusted to an economy dominated by large corporations and by imperatives of the cold war.

Most New Left historians have seen little hope from the American past either, or in trying to salvage the system from within. As Christopher Lasch has put it, and several (though not quite all) New Left thinkers would agree, "The history of American radicalism . . . is largely a history of failure and therefore not a source of comfort to those who look to the past to find ancestors and heroes."[30]

And therein the New Left, or a major strain in it, has departed from their predecessors. Progressives said Americans could get a fresh start if only they could rearrange this or that. And counter-Progressives often pictured people who saw America's destiny in just that sort of opportunity (counter-Progressives were less hopeful themselves, but they weren't thoroughgoing cynics about the matter either). But New Left historians have in effect abandoned the national covenant, with its sense of mission and progress. America has neither offered such fresh beginnings, from their perspective, nor has it symbolized any really fresh beginning itself. It has become everything Americans claimed they were getting out of when they fled the Old World. It too has become a kind of Old World, according to New Left historians, and therefore requires wholesale rebuilding, from the bottom up.

IV

This is one way to handle the three forms—by seeing how historians' pictures have framed up the American past. There are other procedures we could use too in trying to build up some elementary working models of these explanation-forms, and in developing a sense of variety in the perspectives historians have used for explaining American experience. One is to look at their *anthropology of ideas,* doing for these historians what we did for humans generally (and Benjy particularly) in chapter 1.

When *Progressives* looked out on their world, they saw it in evolution. At any point in this evolving process, the world necessitated certain adaptive responses from people. In the pre-Progressive past, most men were too unenlightened to learn these responses, or too bound in by entrenched interests and dogmas. This made them adapt poorly to their environment. And it caused enormous time lags between where their ideas were at any time and where their environment signaled they ought to be.

In the Progressive present, however, things were different. Informed men had discovered what was adaptive and what wasn't, and they'd armed themselves to do battle with the uninformed and the self-interested. For the first time in human history, men had gained power to take control of this evolutionary process, to shape their future with their ideas instead of floating aimlessly into it.

Progressives assumed the world of men and things can be *known.* For them, no tragic lot binds the destinies of men; men could know and they could do if only they willed to. Ignorance was an evil for men, because where there was ignorance there was also an unjust distribution of the world's benefits, and someone, or ones, grasping on to their more-than-deserved share with all the power they could command. Progressives strove to break through these power fronts, laying open the real realities behind them. Thus their "revolt against formalism." In that revolt, they took things once deadened in a shroud of abstractions and tried to make them come alive again. Like Charles Beard with the Constitution of 1787. To him in 1913, that document had become barren with time. It had grown into a body of absolute legalisms which condescended to men from some Superhuman Mind, and was presumed to embody "justice." Beard took his role as bringing it back to life and people again—making it a human creation—by revealing how it came from no transcendent Power but out of the interests and passions of involved men. Beard was trying, in effect, to de-reify the abstracted form.

Thus, to Progressive historians, there was unreality and there was reality. The division between the two was clear, the task of mind being to break through the one into the other. Reality was what the Progressive aimed at, unreality was what got in his way.

Because of this passion for breaking through to "reality," Progressives tended to suspect ideas. Or at least some ideas—those which, debris-like, had to be cleared out of the way before people could see straight into things. Ideas like that have served only to falsify, they've beclouded people's minds about what's actually happening in the world.

We've already seen Parrington explaining away ideas of the Puritan theocracy: "The historian need not wander far in search of the origin of the theocratic principle; it is to be found in the self-interest of the lay and clerical leaders."[31] Listen also to Beard comparing the American Constitution to the aftermath of the Norman Conquest:

It does not follow that the vague thing known as "the advancement of general welfare" or some abstraction known as "justice" was the immediate, guiding purpose of the leaders in either of these great historic changes. The point is, that the direct, impelling motive in both cases was the economic advantages which the beneficiaries expected would accrue to themselves first, from their action.[32]

When used by certain kinds of people, said Progressives, ideas function only as masks. They're ideological defenses of things, deflecting people's attention away from the things themselves.

But other ideas, used by other kinds of people, may connect into reality quite differently. Thus Robinson: "The idea of conscious progress [is] the greatest single idea in the whole history of mankind in the vista of possibilities which it opens before us."[33] An idea like that has functioned at least two stages removed from some such idea as "conservatism." Where conservatism has lagged behind reality and distorts people's pictures of it, progress brings them to reality and through it, then finally causes them to leap ahead and well beyond. With ideas like progress, not only could people see things straight in the present, they could lead things from where they are now to where they might be in the future. With such ideas, people could get leverage to reform things.

When Progressives came across an idea like conservatism or stratification or original sin, immediately they could explain it away by the interests or fears it masked. But ideas such as progress and democracy and liberalism and equality required no explanation at all. They were the elementary common sense of the matter, and their meaning was obvious to anyone committed to mankind and against selfish, particularized interests. The Declaration of Independence proclaimed such ideas as self-evident, and it was right. The role of Progressives was to make these self-evident truths into reality.[34]

A Progressive schema of ideas, separating the good off from the bad, might look something like this:

Ideals	v.	Ideas
Transcendental origins	v.	Economic origins
Self-evident	v.	Self-interested
Altruistic	v.	Selfish
Forward-looking	v.	Defensive
Progressive	v.	Reactionary
Hopeful commitment	v.	Apathy
True	v.	False

In such a scheme, any single idea could go in only one direction at a time. It couldn't be both progressive and reactionary, it couldn't be both self-interested and altruistic. It had to fall on one side of the chart or the other; otherwise the whole scheme could get tangled up (in chapters 7 and 8, we'll see how Progressives behave when this happens). By using such a model, Progressives could gain leverage on experience. For example, they could take hold of one idea in a pair and play it off against its opposite. They could build much drama into their picture of the past that way. They couldn't do that very well if ideas tended to melt into each other, and opposites shared common qualities.

Take Parrington, for example, and look at his section titles in Main Currents: "Master John Cotton: Priest," "Thomas Hooker: Puritan Liberal," "Roger Williams: Seeker," "Edgar Allan Poe: Romantic," "John C. Calhoun: Realist," "Andrew Jackson: Agrarian Liberal," "Herman Melville: Pessimist."[35] Each label is crisp and clear and, to him, self-evident. A pessimist was not, could not be, an optimist too, and an agrarian liberal could not harbor capitalist or conservative strains in his thought.

An idea was all of a piece for Parrington, and one piece necessarily precluded another. Alexander Hamilton, for example, was one "from whom our democratic liberalism has received nothing," and Cotton Mather had "not a grain of liberalism in his make-up."[36]

When Progressives put "-ism" or "-ion" onto the end of a word, they made it into an idea, and they meant for it to connote one thing and one thing only. And for every such -ism running in one direction, there was an opposite (though not necessarily equal) -ism running in the other. Thus, for Parrington, conservatism ran opposite to liberalism, the French tradition opposed the English, romanticism opposed realism, agrarianism opposed capitalism, the Jeffersonian tradition opposed the Hamiltonian.

With a dualistic strategy like that, Progressives structured conflict into their story, and could sharpen and clarify a maze of experience which otherwise might remain merely fuzzy or confusing. They could also make clear their stand on ideas and events, coming out forthrightly for the ones that count.

Counter-Progressives were just not that sure of things. Or rather, they were quite sure of this: things are rarely that clear-cut in human experience. Progressives, as we've seen, worked with a straight-line logic. This followed from that, this was opposed to that. They were not much taken with ambiguity; and they had almost no concern at all for searching out the paradoxes in life, for watching human virtues abort, and vices become virtues.

Counter-Progressives, on the other hand, used a dialectic logic. Things often traveled in a circle for them. And opposites—love-hate, liberal-conservative, future-past, adventure-security—were not mutually exclusive of each other. However much they may have been separated logically, psychologically they have often joined in the counter-Progressive form. Where opposites battled each other in the Progressive form, in the counter-Progressive form opposites were held in counterpoised tension.

To counter-Progressives, then, the reality of human experience was tensed with ambiguity. Rather than the either-or of Progressives, they saw a both/and. Where Progressive reality was *dualistic,* counter-Progressive reality was *dialectical*. It often doubled back on itself, joining things rather than setting them off against each other.

Counter-Progressives tended to begin where Progressives left off (another reason to call them "counter"-Progressives). Progressives were given to setting up this as opposed to that and casting their vote for one side or the other. Counter-Progressives had little such interest in trying to elect things. They were, though, concerned that Americans conventionally see their world this way—dividing reality into twos, and labelling one good, two evil. To counter-Progressive historians, this habit of moralizing recurred often in American experience, and to them it was a habit with a long mischief life. For only cursorily did it address the ambiguity of things, and it thus offered a single-minded explanation of experience in the world. Counter-Progressives believed its anthropology was all wrong (or at least half wrong), so also its metaphysics.

They proposed to replace it with a picture of experience something like this: The world is open. It is not fully known by men, nor is it knowable, in any fundamental sense. For to know it wholly would be to close it off, damming up its perpetual energies. Men will never do that, though they are characteristically driven to try.

But an open world does have its problems—for men at least. Although they may enjoy the freedom of opening things here and there, they're still confounded by the basic uncertainty of it all. They demand to know more than it tells them, and they'd like to find out who and where they are, and where they are going, more than they're able to.

Because they don't know as much as they need to, people are anxious. And the New World environment has multiplied their anxieties, because it's been so boundless, and it's constantly shifting, altering. Men in America live in a state of perpetual "future shock." That's the counter side of their being so free.

In this gigantic, oceanic world of uncertainty, people seek to create islands of meaning, resting points which will tell them who they are and what they are and what things are like and where they are going. That's where *ideas* come in. Ideas serve as the identity channels of men. In contrast to Progressives—who saw ideas as either true or false descriptions of "reality"— counter-Progressives pictured them as dialogue-probes into experience, efforts to communicate with things and people in the world.

Take Marvin Meyers, and look at his chapter titles in *The Jacksonian Persuasion:* "The Old Republic and the New," "Venturous Conservative," "The Judges and the Judged," "A Puritan Version," "A Free-Trade Version," "A Progressive Version," "A Dialogue of Parties."[37] These are not Parrington's one-directional labels on experience. Rather, they're tensed opposites—old/new, venturous/conservative, judges/judged—and also "versions" of reality, competing perspectives on what the world of politics and people is like.

Meyers wrote of small men seeking to make do in a world larger than their power to comprehend, and of "a troubled mind groping for names to fit its discontent."[38] Unlike both the Progressives and the New Left—who saw some men in control of other men—Meyers pictured no one in control in Jacksonian America. But men were after control—seeking it not so much through power as through mind, grasping for things with their ideas. All this resulted in what Meyers called a "persuasion"—"a half-formulated moral perspective involving emotional commitment."[39]

For counter-Progressives, it was these intangibles of the world which compelled men. Progressives had seen most people ruled by economic motives, things. Not so for counter-Progressives. To them, men were mobilized by the drive for status, the desire to recover some lost innocence, or to master a virgin continent. Psychic quests were what impelled men to do what they do.

Progressives had envisioned two kinds of ideas—those which connected directly into reality, and those which didn't. But counter-Progressives saw even the most blatant of falsehoods shaping the behaviors of men. They felt these "myths" had a reality which couldn't be explained away simply by proving them untrue.

Take the faith that the American West beyond the Mississippi was destined to become "The Garden of the World," and the aligned faith that "rain follows the plow." Neither idea was very true to the facts, as evidenced by much suffering, tragedy, and waste of human life in the late nineteenth century. American historical scholarship after Turner detailed all this, and labeled the whole set of ideas a myth, a demonstrable falsehood.

But, in his *Virgin Land,* Henry Nash Smith insisted historians should take another look, rather, another kind of look. If men believed falsehoods, then acted from those beliefs, they must have had their reasons. Even the irrational in men has its logic, said counter-Progressives. It wouldn't do to dismiss irrational ideas as rationalizations of power interests, or of people's subjective desires. To counter-Progressives, *all* ideas have roots in interests and desires; otherwise, they wouldn't engage men as they do. So to say an idea is irrational is only to acknowledge that it's been created by people and that it appeals to people. An idea might be true to facts outside it or it might not, but its power to affect men often lies along other planes. And the student of human behavior, said the counter-Progressives, would do well to learn the logic of those planes(also the psychologic and the sociologic).

That's where they thought their predecessors had gone wrong. Progressives, they contended, were so caught up in judging whether everything in experience was true or false that they couldn't reflect much on the existential uncertainty of it all.

There was something of the Gatsbyesque "world's-foundation-on-a-fairy's-wing" attitude among counter-Progressives. Below the manifest substance of things, below the power, the brute strength, the visible solidarity of the world lay an insubstantial driving energy which made it (or much of it) go. Such an energy could not be weighed or measured or even seen directly, but somehow it moved and gave form to those things which could be weighed and measured and seen. Where Progressives tried unmasking ideas to see the real driving things below, counter-Progressives tried unmasking things to see the real driving ideas below.

That isn't true of all counter-Progressives. It does get to much of Smith, Ward, Marx, Alan Trachtenberg, Sanford, Hofstadter, Meyers, Lewis, Hartz, Miller, David Noble, and Merrill Peterson. But it misses most of Boorstin and Rossiter and much of Elkins and David Potter. On one level, these latter don't even fit into the same school as the above symbol-myth-image writers, for they share little of their anthropology of ideas. In the next chapter, we'll confront more directly this question of how to group thinkers into a "school." For now, let's just say that however much these latter depart from their counter-Progressive contemporaries on the function of ideas, they differ even more from Progressives. They differ especially with the Progressives' assumption of ideas as clear-cut and unidirectional, and with their faith in the self-evident truths of liberalism, democracy, and equality.

Daniel Boorstin has been the most noted spokesman for this other strain in counter-Progressive thinking. He's been much impressed with the formlessness of experience in America and has felt efforts to make it all congeal into ideas and formulas are innocent and wrong headed. "It was life, and not thought, which would excel here," Boorstin wrote in his *The Genius of American Politics;* and much of his scholarship has been taken with proclaiming the cheerful uncertainty of things and life in the land.[40]

Boorstin opened his first volume of *The Americans* with this challenge to the progressivist picture:

America began as a sobering experience. The colonies were a disproving ground for utopias. In the following chapters we will illustrate how dreams made in Europe—the dreams of the zionist, the perfectionist, the philanthropist, and the transplanter—were dissipated or transformed by the American reality. A new civilization was being born less out of plans and purposes than out of the unsettlement which the New World brought to the ways of the Old.[41]

When he finally hit full form in his second volume of *The Americans,* Boorstin almost wholly abandoned concern for ideas and ideologies—devoting himself instead to people and things, a hustling America going about its business of becoming unique in the world. He focused on the underlying experience which a thinker like, say, Tocqueville handled on the level of ideas and explanation. He was intrigued by Frederick Tudor of Boston (the "Ice King"), and the development of the booster press and the booster college.[42] Boorstin's picture was thick with ambiguity—not in ideas, however, but in experience. And he claimed that here, if anywhere, you could find the real meaning of the country. "A great resource of America was vagueness," he declaimed.[43]

In his *Seedtime of the Republic,* Clinton Rossiter developed a similar picture. He was concerned to show that the American Revolution of 1776 was really the second of the country's historic revolutions, and actually less fundamental than the first. The first had ended by 1765; it was a revolution in the habits and practices of a people. Only because change had succeeded there could the second one—a revolution in ideas and politics—take full root and bloom. Again, as with Boorstin, it was experience, not ideas, which captured the meaning of America.

David Potter said something similar in *People of Plenty.* There he contended, "It was not our ordeal of democracy but our export of goods and gadgets, of cheap, machine-produced grain and magic-working medicines, which opened new vistas to the human mind and thus made us 'the terrible instigators of social change and revolution.' "[44]

Finally, Stanley Elkins focused on a time when this structural rootedness in American life was breaking apart; and he explained the brutality of the slave system as one result. It was brutal first because no stable institutions were around to channel and soften slavery. It was brutal second because even its critics offered inadequate methods for reforming it. "Intellectual[s] without connections," said Elkins, attacked slavery with a "harsh moral purity," but failed to offer any institutional alternatives to it.[45] Though he saw more thoughts aworld than did Boorstin or Rossiter, Elkins equally deplored the progressivist faith that certain kinds of ideas can connect straight into experience and remake it. And all three—Elkins, Boorstin, Rossiter—were committed to the organic continuity of American experience and were not much taken by efforts at radically uprooting life through projecting abstract visions of what the country ought to be.

At this point they joined back with their other counter-Progressive colleagues. Though they disagreed with the symbol-myth-image scholars on the role that ideas should play in life, they all agreed that there's much perverse power in ideas and that even the best and purest of them can do much mischief.

Progressives wouldn't accept that. Bad things come from bad ideas, and bad men, they said, good things come from good ideas and good men. But counter-Progressives saw good men doing bad things, and through good ideas. They do it not because their motives are ill, but because of *hubris*— they feel they know and are in control of things when in fact they aren't, and often can't be. Andrew Jackson unleased wild capitalistic energies not because he intended to, but because he tried to control by rhetoric things which wouldn't be tamed by words. Puritans hung witches in 1692 not because they were inveterate witch hunters, but because in open surroundings part of their ethic tended to erode another part of it, and they lacked the detachment or critical insight to face up to the consequences.

Where Progressives thought men could and should control things, counter-Progressives pointed out the paradoxes when they tried it. Progressives gained leverage on things by taking one idea and playing it off against its opposite. As a result, things in the world began to move. To Progressives, that movement was forward. Counter-Progressives looked again at the motion, and claimed it may not be forward at all. Also, they didn't seek leverage on things by playing off opposites. Rather, they took an idea and played it off against itself. As a result, things didn't move forward, but, instead, often circled back on themselves.

In his chapter "The Judges and the Judged," for example, Marvin Meyers pictured Americans busy consuming while at the same time denouncing consumption, busy making money while praising the ascetic virtues, and busy denouncing the Monster Bank for practices which were in fact their own. He concluded from this they were mighty sinners against their own jeremiads. They were hypocrites all, yet their rhetoric did offer them needed identity in trying times.[46] Their "persuasion" was not all of a piece; rather, part of it pushed them one way, another part pulled them another. Because they failed to acknowledge this ambiguity in their beliefs, they often involved themselves in ironies, intending one result, accomplishing its opposite.[47]

That's how counter-Progressives saw ideas—complicated and perverse, with a lot of built-in power. People should be careful how they handle them; sometimes, even the most innocent looking could go off and explode around their heads. Ideas are thus dangerous things for counter-Progressives, intriguing to watch and play with, but devilishly tricky, and seldom behaving quite the way people expect.

Unlike the counter-Progressives, *New Left* historians have not been much intrigued by existential uncertainty in life. In the counter-Progressive picture many things happened by accident, many more by irony—that is, through consequences which weren't intended in the original purpose. But the New Left has said that kind of explanation lets too many men and systems off the hook too easily. Accident and irony are the refuge men take because their intended consequences have come to light, not because their intents have somehow aborted.

Gabriel Kolko, for example, subtitled his *Roots of American Foreign Policy* "An Analysis of Power and Purpose"; and he meant we can best understand that policy by seeing how power is purposeful, not by explaining away accidents. Listen to Kolko's opening words in the book, as he comments on recent American experience:

For a growing number of Americans the war in Vietnam has become the turning point in their perception of the nature of American foreign policy, the traumatizing event that requires them to look again at the very roots, assumptions, and structure of a policy that is profoundly destructive and dangerous. Vietnam is the logical outcome of a consistent reality we should have understood long before the United States applied much of its energies to ravaging one small nation.

Kolko goes on, insisting we must develop an alternative explanation of such behavior:

We can only comprehend Vietnam in the larger context of the relations of the United States to the Third World, removing from our analytic framework superfluous notions of capriciousness, accident, and chance as the causal elements in American foreign and military policy. For the events in Vietnam expose in a sustained and systematic manner those American qualities that have led to one of the most frightful examples of barbarism of mechanized man against man known to modern history.

Then he concludes, challenging the counter-Progressive perspective on American experience: "The logical, deliberative aspects of American power at home and its interest abroad show how fully irrelevant are notions of accident and innocence in explaining the diverse applications of American power today, not only in Vietnam but throughout the Third World."[48]

Much New Left history has been written from such a perspective. Several of their studies focus on periods when uncertainty might seem to prevail in America—the dislocating times before the Civil War and foreign affairs in the twentieth century. At least these would be areas of uncertainty if seen through the counter-Progressive perspective.[49] But, in the New Left picture, what happened came from conscious intent; in its world, the events of American history have largely been willed by men, and men should be held responsible, directly responsible, for what they do.

There's been little of the stress of circumstance in New Left history. This is not because men are pure and simple masters of the world, but because they've compressed their world of experience into *systems*.

The counter-Progressive picture had a strain of radical Protestantism running through it—a lone individual confronting the stark universe and bending under the weight of such a mind burden (this part of the picture is clearest in Lewis' *The American Adam*). Myths and symbols and ironies resulted from men's efforts to shoulder that burden. New Left histories contain little of such an image, however. Instead, power systems mediate between persons and their world, and most of human experience takes place within these systems. A system is a kind of total interconnection of things— through social institutions, through ideological explanations, through the economic foundations of things—and it all issues forth in policies and events. If one wants to know why people act and think as they do, he must keep probing until he bares the system which puts it all together. Through these systems, men make for themselves a reality which is comprehensible to their minds and manageable for their wills.

Take William Appleman Williams and his *The Contours of American History*. Williams controlled that 500-page volume by locating the system component in each period he covered—"The Age of Mercantilism: 1740–1828," "The Age of Laissez Nous Faire: 1819–1896," "The Age of Corporation Capitalism: 1882–   ." In each period, he was after "the essential reality, assumptions, theory, and policies of the then accepted conception of the world."[50]

So also Eugene Genovese in *The Political Economy of Slavery*. Though Genovese was concerned with the economics of the system while Williams was more after ideas (what he called a *Weltanschauung*), both envisioned their particular focus within this broader system context. So too Stephen Thernstrom in *Poverty and Progress,* and Gabriel Kolko in *The Triumph of Conservatism* and *The Roots of American Foreign Policy,* and Walter LaFeber in *The New Empire*.

When New Left historians have looked out upon America's experience through these systems, they've seen massive concentrations of power, and haven't been much given to searching out areas of doubt in the psyches of the powerful. Their concern has mainly been with how public policies get made and implemented. And some of them have felt the counter-Progressive preoccupation with tracking down nuances diverted attention from the main events. The 1950s and 1960s, said Christopher Lasch, was "a generation that tended to confuse intellectual values with the interests of intellectuals as a class."[51] If counter-Progressives were able to convey a sense of human evil in books, they did it, the New Left implied, without disturbing the social order very much. Ambiguity in a novel—in, say, *Moby-Dick* or *The Great Gatsby*—might be a fascinating thing to watch and analyze. But ambiguity in a social order usually works to someone's unmerited benefit, and someone else's undeserved injustice. So have felt New Left historians.

Of the three explanation-forms under review here, the New Left has been least concerned with the distinctively "symboling" qualities of people (which is one reason we do less with them in this book). As we've seen, symboling was a major concern for counter-Progressives, and Progressives were also concerned with ideas and symbols of a sort (at least with progressive ones, anti-progressive ones they simply rejected). But New Left historians have seldom done straight intellectual history, save to see ideas as part of those larger power systems we've just noted.[52]

Where counter-Progressives sought to explain men's quests and images in America, New Left historians have searched more for "roots"—*The Roots of the Modern American Empire, The Roots of American Foreign Policy.* Quests and images bare the psychic impulses of men, roots bare systems of power. With quests, men *seek to* control their world through mind; with systems, men *do* control their world through power—economic power, political power, ideological power, social power, all interconnected. Where counter-Progressives spoke of an uncontrollable world of uncertainty outside human interests, New Leftists seldom have brought that world into their picture. To them, men have used ideas largely to protect and extend what they have, not to cushion the anxiety of change and protect themselves against future shock.

Counter-Progressives tapped the irrational in men and largely held it at that. But New Left historians have insisted that the irrational has a rational base in some dominant group's self-interest. Progressives saw similar things, but used their idea of progress as a lever to right the system. New Leftists have had no such covenant-salvaging faith. That's because they've not been as enamored of ideas as the Progressives. If Progressives connected some ideas back to interests, they used other ideas to transcend interests. New Leftists normally have not done this. In their perspective on man and the world, ideas have no self-generating power. Rather, ideas are determined by the larger structural forms which dominant groups and classes impose on their world. To change the ideas, to change the classes and the men, one must get to the system behind it all. That's the root of the New Left perspective. If one wants to do anything to alter reality in America, the system is the fulcrum point he must start from.

That should do for now as a preliminary survey of our subject—historians and their explanation-forms in twentieth-century America. We'll return to this subject again when we get to the case study chapters. In the meantime, we need to develop methods for handling such forms in a deeper, more controlled fashion.

NOTES

1. For the wider historical background within which these explanation-forms function, see especially John Higham's fine book, *History: Humanistic Scholarship in America* (Prentice-Hall, 1965). See also Robert Skotheim's *American Intellectual Histories and Historians* (Princeton University Press, 1966).

2. Morton White, *Social Thought in America: The Revolt against Formalism,* rev. ed. (Beacon, paperback, 1957).

3. James Harvey Robinson, *The New History: Essays Illustrating the Modern Historical Outlook* (Free Press, paperback, 1965—first published in 1912 by Macmillan), p. 265.

4. Charles Beard, *An Economic Interpretation of the Constitution of the United States* (Macmillan, paperback, 1961—first published in 1913 by Macmillan), p. xix.

5. Vernon Louis Parrington, *Main Currents in American Thought,* vol. 1 *The Colonial Mind: 1620–1800* (Harcourt, Brace and World, Harvest Book, 1954—first published by Harcourt in 1927), p. 62.

6. Perry Miller, *The New England Mind: From Colony to Province* (Beacon, paperback, 1961—first published by Harvard in 1953), p. 442.

7. Louis Hartz, *The Liberal Tradition in America* (Harcourt, Brace and World, Harvest Book, n.d.—first published in 1955), p. 32.

8. Stanley Elkins, *Slavery: A Problem in American Institutional and Intellectual Life,* rev. ed. (University of Chicago Press, paperback, 1968—first published by Chicago in 1959), p. 162.

9. John Higham, "The Construction of American History," in Higham, ed., *The Reconstruction of American History* (Harper, Torchbook, 1962), p. 9.

10. Howard Zinn, *The Politics of History* (Beacon, paperback, 1971—first published by Beacon in 1970), p. 10.

11. Christopher Lasch, *The Agony of the American Left* (Random House, Vintage Book, 1969), p. 27.

12. Eugene Genovese, *The Political Economy of Slavery: Studies in the Economy and Society of the Slave South* (Random House, Vintage Book, 1965), p. 7.

13. *Permanence and Change: An Anatomy of Purpose* (Bobbs-Merrill, paperback, 1965), p. 69 ff.

14. *Colonial Mind* (n.5 above), p. 62.

15. Ibid., p. 63.

16. Ibid., p. 19.

17. See, for example, John Higham, "Beyond Consensus: The Historian as Moral Critic," *The American Historical Review,* LXVII, no. 3 (April 1962), 609–25; J. Rogers Hollingsworth, "Consensus and Continuity in Recent American Historical Writing," *South Atlantic Quarterly* (Winter 1962), 40–50; and Dwight Hoover, "Some Comments on Recent United States Historiography," *American Quarterly,* XVII, no. 2, pt. 2 (Summer 1965), 299–318.

18. *New History* (n.3 above) p. 265.

19. *The Quest for Paradise: Europe and the American Moral Imagination* (University of Illinois Press, 1961), p. 38.

20. *The American Adam: Innocence, Tragedy, and Tradition in the Nineteenth Century* (University of Chicago Press, Phoenix Book, 1958), p. 5.

21. *Liberal Tradition* (n. 7 above), p. 7.

22. For further on Lewis and innocence/counter-innocence, see chapter 9.

23. See especially Richard Hofstadter's portraits of Jefferson and Jackson in *The American Political Tradition* (Random House, Vintage Book, n.d.—first published by Knopf in 1948), pp. 18–44, 45–67.

24. *Virgin Land: The American West as Symbol and Myth* (Random House, Vintage Book, n.d.—first published by Harvard in 1950), p. 3.

25. *The Great Evasion: An Essay on the Contemporary Relevance of Karl Marx and on the Wisdom of Admitting the Heretic into the Dialogue about America's Future* (Quadrangle, paperback, 1968—first published by Quadrangle in 1962), p. 12.

26. *Wealth and Power in America: An Analysis of Social Class and Income Distribution* (Praeger, 1962).

27. *The Triumph of Conservatism: A Reinterpretation of American History, 1900–1916* (Quadrangle, paperback, 1967—first published by the Free Press in 1963), p. 280.

28. *Agony* (n. 11 above), pp. 3–31.

29. "The New Deal: The Conservative Achievements of Liberal Reform," in Barton Bernstein, ed., *Towards a New Past: Dissenting Essays in American History* (Random House, Vintage Book, 1969—first published by Random House in 1968), pp. 264–65.

30. *Agony,* (n. 11 above), p. viii.

31. *Colonial Mind* (n. 5 above), p. 19.

32. *Economic Interpretation* (n. 4 above), pp. 17–18.

33. *New History* (n. 3 above), p. 247.

34. Robert Skotheim has written with much insight on this Progressive double standard on ideas. See his *American Intellectual Histories* (n. 1 above), pp. 77, 80–95, 131, 134–39.

35. *Colonial Mind* (n. 5 above), pp. 27, 53, 62. And *The Romantic Revolution in America: 1800–1860,* vol. 2 of *Main Currents* (Harcourt, Brace and World, Harvest Book, 1954—first published in 1927), pp. 54, 65, 138, 249.

36. *Romantic,* pp. 312, 114.

37. *The Jacksonian Persuasion: Politics and Belief* (Stanford University Press, paperback, 1964—first published by Stanford in 1957), pp. 3, 33, 121, 163, 185, 206, 234.

38. Ibid., p. 10.

39. Ibid.

40. *The Genius of American Politics* (University of Chicago Press, Phoenix Paperback, 1959—first published by Chicago in 1953), p. 186.

41. *The Americans: The Colonial Experience* (Random House, 1958), 1.

42. *The Americans: The National Experience* (Random House, Vintage Book, n.d. —first published in 1965 by Random House), pp. 10 ff., 124 ff., 152 ff.

43. Ibid., p. 219.

44. *People of Plenty: Economic Abundance and the American Character* (University of Chicago Press, Phoenix Paperback, n.d.—first published by Chicago in 1954), p. 135.

45. *Slavery* (n. 8 above), pp. 160, 27.

46. *Jacksonian Persuasion* (n. 37 above), pp. 121–41.

47. For further on this "ironic" explanation of intention, see the Reinhold Niebuhr and Perry Miller parts of chapter 9.

48. *The Roots of American Foreign Policy: An Analysis of Power and Purpose* (Beacon, paperback, 1969), pp. xi–xii.

49. The former not only *seems* an area of uncertainty, but in fact *is* in counter-Progressive scholarship. Witness Lewis' *The American Adam* and Meyers' *The Jacksonian Persuasion* and Marx's *The Machine in the Garden* and Ward's *Andrew Jackson: Symbol for an Age.* Like some New Left histories, all focused on pre-Civil War America (Marx also went beyond), but none talked much of slavery or events leading on to war. Instead, their concern was with how the culture identified and extended itself through its motivating symbols. And all saw these symbols functioning in one way or another as stays against confusion, in a time of radical disorder and unsettling change. That is not true of Smith's *Virgin Land,* which is partly on this period. Smith did say much about slavery and events leading to war. And of course Elkins' *Slavery* is wholly on that subject. Unlike New Left historians, though, Smith and Elkins both pictured these as radically uncertain times. And they noted that some of the greatest oppressions came precisely from men's inability to impose order and rationality on the transforming world about them. To them, it was an opening order, not a closed system, which characterized America during those years.

50. *The Contours of American History* (Quadrangle, paperback, 1966—first published by World in 1961), p. 22.

51. *Agony* (n. 11 above), p. 69.

52. This statement needs to be qualified. Some New Left works are almost pure intellectual history—notably Norman Pollack's *The Populist Response to Industrial*

America and Staughton Lynd's *Intellectual Origins of American Radicalism*. But these works seem to point backward to the Progressive tradition, and are not, I think, as distinctively "New" Left as are, say, Williams' and Kolko's and Lasch's. When Pollack closed his *Populist Response* with "Populism was more than a protest movement; it was a glorious chapter in the eternal struggle for human rights," (*The Populist Response to Industrial America: Midwestern Populist Thought* [Norton, paperback, 1966] p. 143) he might have gotten nods of agreement from Lynd and perhaps Howard Zinn, but certainly not from Genovese, Williams, LaFeber, Kolko, or Lasch. Not that these latter have been hostile to Populism; they just wouldn't talk about things that way. The New Left is divided on the role of ideas and power in life, but what seems "newest" in New Left history comes mostly from Williams and Kolko and Genovese and Lasch, and not so much from the works of Pollack and Lynd (save for Lynd's "oral history," but that's another matter).

BOOK II

Some Strategies for Grounded Inquiry

The therapist, on his side of the table, must not be too ready to impose his own preexisting personal construct upon the symbolism and behavior of the client. He will first have to compile a lexicon for dealing with the client.

> George Kelly
> *A Theory of Personality*
> *The Psychology of Personal Constructs*

As the physicist dissolves the hard table into whirling atoms, so the communication and information theorist dissolves the hard fact into messages filtered through a value system.

> Kenneth Boulding
> *The Image: Knowledge in*
> *Life and Society*
> (University of Michigan Press, 1956)

The most interesting and difficult issues of *method* usually begin where established techniques do not apply.

> C. Wright Mills
> *The Sociological Imagination*

5 Changes of Mind II: Some Strategies for Focus

The stuff of history is things that happen—
not things that are.
David Hackett Fischer
Historians' Fallacies

It is this lack of concern for the immediate
terms on which intellectual problems present
themselves to the makers of history that
accounts for our failure to get from Parrington
a feeling for the movement of ideas, their
change in function in different situations.
Richard Hofstadter
The Progressive Historians

Burke reduces the number of things to look
for but increases the number of ways to look
for them.
William Rueckert
*Kenneth Burke and the Drama of
Human Relations*

We've now got some alternative explanation-forms in front of us. Our next task is to explore how we might move beyond their outer surface and get down into them—trying, in effect, to see their world from the inside out.

We opened the last chapter with a brief, elementary *description* of the three forms—Progressive, counter-Progressive, New Left. We then passed to the next more complicated plane of *analysis,* taking the forms as general and set categories and glancing around at their several sides.

These first two planes are legitimate introductions to handling historians' ideas and explanation-forms. They familiarize us with the types under review, so we can see their several faces and compare one with another. Sometimes, though, historical inquiry concludes there. And it thus misses what I see as the deepest plane of intellectual inquiry—*grounded explanation.* On this plane, the general forms are focused down onto specifics, and we can gain some considerable mind control over them. That is, we can begin to use our model of functioning ideas from chapters 1 and 2. Here our concern is not so much with *what* questions—what do the forms look like?—but with issues of *how*—how were they created? how are they put together? how do they respond to this or that experience? how do they change?

On this third plane, our focus moves beyond the content of ideas to a concern for structure and function and process. Methodic questions will supplement substantive ones; and instead of taking a form as a finished product of mind, we'll try to enter it in process. In effect, we'll be attempting to picture the *behavior* of historians' explanation forms, just as in chapter 1 we were trying to picture the behavior of people's ideas.

In this chapter, we'll pinpoint some places where we can enter these forms, and generally suggest a few things to do once we get inside. In the case-study chapters later, we'll then try and put into practice what we suggest here. We'll also try there to select those particular strategies for inquiry appropriate to each place in a form.

II

To accomplish our purposes here, we'll need to work in a fashion different from what we did in the last chapter. There we assumed that the *issue* of form is basically unproblematic. Taking the forms as given, we simply filled in information about them. But now we'll make no such assumption about the givenness of forms. Instead, we'll take them as problematic, and we'll begin by posing some questions of them—to be specific, three kinds of questions: (1) *How do we name these forms, and should we in fact give such broad labels to them?* (2) *How and when do these forms change, and how does one explanation-form replace another?* (3) *How do historians' explanation-forms connect into the world around them?* These are not the only questions we need ask on this plane of grounded explanation, but they are some basic ones, and they might help focus our methodic concerns at this point. Let me briefly illustrate:

1. In chapter 4, we followed the normal historiographical procedure of treating the categories inside forms as solid and irreducible, something like atoms before scientists began breaking into them. There is value in that, for it enables us to generalize readily. And yet such a procedure does have severe limitations.

For example, I said things like, "The Progressives believed in progress. . . ." Quite true. And yet *how?* What did "progress" mean to them? When they used that idea, did it imply the same thing as it did for counter-Progressives? Were Progressives for progress anywhere and everywhere, or were they expressly for it sometimes and covertly against it others? Was there some kind of "unmoved mover" below the surface of their progress-form which occasioned why they should be for it here and against it there? And who exactly were these Progressives? Did they all believe in progress? How did that idea get into their minds? Did they communicate much with each other? Did they experience similar upbringings? Was there something "in the air" in those days which everyone imbibed and made them believe in progress as they did?

When we start pondering questions like this, we're quickly taken past the external face of historians' forms. Such questions point us inside toward the *experience* of ideas, rather than keeping us on their outer surface, or their abstract logic. But to get into that experience, we'll need some channels for entry, and some strategies for *grounding* our concerns. And that raises another series of questions.

Just how can we move into an explanation-form in some kind of controlled fashion? Through the individuals which comprise it? But how do individual thinkers make up such a form? How do they cluster together in such a way we can call them a "school" of historical explanation? Most discussions of American historical scholarship assume that schools of explanation exist, yet what exactly do we mean by this term? How much variation and how much consensus does it take before we can call a number of historians a school? Do, say, four or five historians writing on similar themes make for a school? But what if they differ on other themes? How do we establish the outer limits of a school? Is the New Left, for example, merely a variant of the old Progressive explanation form, or a whole new form?

Questions like that raise a vexing issue of labeling in history studies— *How do we apply names to collective groups?* In American historiographical scholarship, we have no very satisfactory answers to this question. We've just normally assumed that our group forms—Progressive, consensus, New Left, relativist, and so on—are basically unproblematic, and the only question is just who fits into what form. In short, we don't have very good *forms* to handle group forms.[1]

2. Any rigorous procedure for handling ideas and explanation-forms should have some way to explain *changes* of mind. We need to understand how patterns of seeing and of thinking are altered from one form to another. This gets us into one of the paradoxes of scholarship in American historiography. If historical study has anything distinctive going for it, it should be this concern for change, for the movement of things from one place or form to another. That, it seems, is what most distinguishes the historical enterprise from allied areas like sociology or political science or literature. Scholarship in American historiography has been true to this general sense of movement; we hear much about change of explanation-forms in history studies. Yet if we hear *that* explanations change among historians, we really don't know very much about *how*. We see one form here and another there, but we have only a vague notion of what happens in between. This is because we haven't constructed strategies for closely watching a change in the making.

To get inside such changes, we need some *focusing devices,* some ways of selecting out those points where changes of mind seem most imminent and for charting more precisely just how realignments in belief come about. By searching for a few of these "pivotal moments" in the life history of an idea, we may not yet be able to explain fully *how* people (or historians) change their minds; but we can at least locate some points *when* and *where,* and concentrate our attention more carefully on those points. At least they can give us a base to start from. And with this base we might begin connecting out into work from cognitive psychology and the sociology of knowledge and anthropological philosophy, where they're further along in such understandings than we are in history studies.

3. Finally, if we're to treat these forms as something more than floating categories of thought, we must find ways of seeing them in context, of connecting them in to things in the world. This gets to one of the most crucial problems of intellectual history studies—*how to relate the structure of mind to the stuff of experience?* To handle this issue, we'll need to involve ourselves not only in the externals of ideas—the times and the men around them—but also more deeply in their internal workings—how they distinctively respond to these times and these men.

In talking about such matters, intellectual historians have tended to speak of a broad "climate of opinion" informing a certain period, or a "spirit of an age." They claim that individual historians "reflect" that climate or spirit with their ideas. But how do such general ideas get inside people's minds? Should we assume everyone experiences these broad intellectual currents in exactly the same way? If so, how do we explain such uniformity? If not, how can we account for variations in the way people take in a general current of the times and respond to it?

Why, for example, does a historian seem to express a general theme one way one time, and another way another? Should we go on trying to talk about the *whole* of a historian's thought, or can we better center in on how his mind works by asking of each particular idea of his, "Where did he say it and when, and in response to what and whom?"

If we're to manage such questions, we'll need some sort of dialogic encounter model for how the individual mind engages its world. We already have broad outlines of such a model from chapters 1 and 2. Now we need ways of making these broad outlines more specific, and of rendering them usable in our historical inquiries. That is, we must take that model and refashion it into a *method*—an operative strategy for grounded inquiry.

During the remainder of this chapter, we'll explore some ways of handling these questions. The intent is to suggest a few tools for better controlling our materials in American history studies and for involving ourselves more fully inside the experience of them.

III

It is said that historians have no specialized jargon. I guess that's mostly true. In contrast to, say, the complicated terminology of economics, or philosophy, or sociology, or physics, the language of history can normally be understood by the proverbial man in the street. However much American historical scholarship may have become professionalized in the last three-quarters of a century, it still uses a generalized mode of discourse.

That, I think, is in history's favor. Yet there have been drawbacks. For if the language of historians is comprehensible to the man in the street, that is sometimes because they've borrowed their terms from him and have used them with little more self-awareness than he.

This first became an issue to me a few years back, when I had occasion to read through a debate of historians on whether America's past has been dominated more by "consensus" or by "conflict." Critics of the so-called consensus position argued that American histories written since World War II were generally conservative in substance and bland in temper (most of this was written before the rise of the New Left). As one historian wrote, "current scholarship is carrying out a massive grading operation to smooth over America's social convulsions."[2]

When we look into the language of this debate, we find the critics' case carried by words like: "ideology," "conservatism," "liberal," "conformist," "consensus," "conflict thesis of American history," "monolithic approach."[3] These are not uncommon words; they communicate to almost anyone literate enough to read them. Yet such words were used not only to communicate meanings in this debate, but to carry the critics' whole case against the histories they reviewed. Witness:

The reasons for this de-emphasis of conflict in the American past are numerous and obvious. Certain external circumstances make internal strife much less desirable and harmony much more valuable. Among these circumstances are the preoccupation with relationships with the communist countries and the resultant need for an ideology denying Marxian insights. Historians, consciously or unconsciously, have been influenced by this preoccupation and need. The McCarthy era, despite the resistance of many individuals in the intellectual community to pressure for conformity, took its toll also and made consensus seem more secure.

The critic then cemented his case, "Confronted with the climate of opinion favoring consensus, unwilling to admit the validity of extreme conflict or rigid class distinctions, historians have recently been interested in finding evidence to support social harmony or have worked in areas where concepts of conflict least apply."[4]

To make an argument like that stick, this critic had to assume that the meaning of his words and phrases—"de-emphasis of conflict," "internal strife," "harmony," "ideology," "McCarthy era," "pressure for conformity," "climate of opinion favoring consensus"—is self-evident and needs no further clarification. But words used in such fashion don't *lead on* to explanation of the histories under review, they *become* that explanation. And they replace any need for further inquiry. So critics in this debate swept over twenty to thirty-five books in the course of a 15–20 page essay, never pausing more than a paragraph or two for sustained analysis of any single historical work.

Later, in chapter 9, we'll inspect in more detail how this word "consensus" fits works so labeled. For now, let's just take note of how uncritically historians sometimes use their labels, and how, on occasion, they're tempted to let categories borrowed from the general culture substitute for close analysis of a historian's own text. Few words in this controversy were drawn out of the books under review; instead, they were imposed on those books by the critics' own deductive assumptions. What comes through are explanations paraphrased, not explanations rendered through the historian's own perspective on things.

Some of that is, of course, unavoidable in any debate. One argues with his own best tools and tries to make his case on home territory. Further, critics of "consensus" history may well have been correct, though I think not.

Correctness, however, isn't the point right now. The point is how we use our terms to establish correctness. If we borrow those terms from a generalized pool of words in the larger culture, then use such words to argue against others who may not think with these words at all, and if our whole case rests on everyone understanding those words in the same way, well, our explanations can get pretty disengaged from the experience of our "primary documents." That's one drawback of lacking a specialized, operational language in the history profession. Historians' debates are frequently unproductive, because their words don't always connect clearly into things in the world. Or rather, they don't connect in a way that's clear to both sides in the debate.

Take this word "consensus," for instance, and the critics' assumption that historians of the 1950s were cowed by the repressive American "climate of opinion" in the McCarthy era. On its face, this view seems logical. If we take words used in this debate and cluster them together in such and such a way, that's what we come up with. It was an age fostering consensus, histories written during that age were allegedly consensus histories; ergo, the historians reflect the age because they were repressed by it.

But couldn't we just as easily cluster these words together in the opposite way, and infer not a direct but rather an *inverse* connection between the 1950s "climate of opinion" and "consensus" histories? Couldn't we assume that especially those scholars prominent enough to write the shaping books of an era might not be silenced by a Joe McCarthy? Couldn't we say that they'd react defensively (or offensively) to McCarthy-like attacks on their own academic territory, so they'd go searching through America's past for ammunition to carry their case? Couldn't we "explain," say, Louis Hartz's *Liberal Tradition in America* or Richard Hofstadter's *Age of Reform* in this way too? That is, we could say they'd resent attacks on their own way of thinking, they'd seek to understand why Americans could be so repressive, so they'd go back to the culture's past to find out why. And having found out, to their own satisfaction, they could use this for intellectual('s) weaponry against McCarthyites. Both arguments seem equally credible. As long as we stay with the generalities of "consensus" and "climate of opinion," we can reason either way and not be wrong.

Not be wrong logically, that is. But we might be wrong empirically, and we'd do little in fact to clarify just how minds and words have functioned here in American historical thinking, or how particular minds connect into general cultural currents of the time. When we set out to relate things in the larger culture to the particular work of history, we can't do it by sticking with the general culture and general words all the time. We must sometimes journey down into the individual work, listen carefully to its distinctive words and moods and rhythms, and watch how it pictures that general culture in its own distinctive way. In short, we'll need to move inside its world and stay there for a while. As the literary critics say, "temporarily suspend disbelief."

Now an injunction like this would seem obvious. Normally, historians needn't be told to watch for particulars. That, for many, is the foundation stone of their field. But in historiography this is not so. Somehow, scholarship in American historiography has been dominated by general deductive categories (*that's* relativism, *this* is an economic interpretation, *that's* social science not history). And its broad survey critiques often pay scant attention to the individual work and its own unique modalities.

In chapter 3 we explored why this is true, and we'll return to this problem again in chapter 6.[5] For now, let's just assume it may be the case, and try to do something about it. One thing is to ask more self-conscious questions of the forming mind in history studies, of how historians apply words to things, and of the surrounding environments which affect the way they frame their pictures.

One such question has to do with the label "school," with our tendency to group historians together into general categories and to treat all inside a category as if they see things pretty much the same way. Which, by the way, is a procedure used in the last chapter. It's an *efficient* way to work with group forms, even if it's not always true to the facts.

For the moment, suppose it's all right to do that, suppose that historians do, in fact, arrange themselves into clusters and categories, and within each category they share common concerns. How can we explain this? How is it that persons widely separated in space and sometimes in time, coming out of diverse backgrounds and looking at different things in the world, nonetheless seem to hold similar pictures of how things work?

One way we've accounted for this is to assume that a broad "climate of opinion" pervades each period of history, and that historians writing in that period "reflect" such a climate. The climate becomes a kind of intervening variable between the historian and his world. And the term gives intellectual backing to the label "school" (i.e., a "school" is a particular "reflection" of a general "climate").

Like many working terms in the field, however, climate of opinion is more often used than dissected. Still, it's one of the reigning metaphors—perhaps *the* reigning metaphor—for handling ideas in the field. We've just seen it used in the consensus-conflict debate, and it informs much of John Higham's considerable scholarship in American historiography. Robert Skotheim also notes it as the basic idea behind his *American Intellectual Histories and Historians,* and he traces its usage in the profession back to Carl Becker, who in turn borrowed it from Alfred North Whitehead, who, according to Becker, lifted it from the seventeenth century.[6]

To my knowledge, no one has made a detailed study of this term's etymology, of how intellectual historians and historiographers have used it in various ways over the years. Someone should do that; it might illuminate some murky areas in the field, and show students of ideas something important about their own inherited forms for inquiry.

Lacking such a study, I can only hazard an impression; but I suspect this "climate" metaphor may be an unfortunate choice, for it calls up a picture of ideas as vaporous and airy things. And since climate in its original usage means "average weather," and weather is something that *happens to* us, it may also tend to homogenize individual nuances in belief, and suggest that ideas are things which envelop us rather than forms we dialogue with. Which, if my suspicions are correct, may account for a few of those generalized vagaries in the consensus-conflict controversy. Too often, I'm afraid, individual subtleties in belief and subschool variations have been evaporated into this overall "climate of opinion" concept, and further inquiry then gets blocked.[7]

It's imperative now that we raise some questions about this climate metaphor. If we look outside the history profession over to the social sciences, we might get some clues which could help us. For there we can find a much more dynamic, variable picture of how people's opinions relate to their environment.

That wasn't always the case. Two decades ago, *The Authoritarian Personality* studies employed general categories in much the same deductive way as some historiographers do now. And they justified their procedure thus: "There is reason to look for psychological types because the world we live in is typed and 'produces' different 'types' of persons."[8] *They* weren't responsible for the types, said the authors, *the world* was.

This conclusion came out of a broad-scale survey of 2,099 individuals. The authors seemed driven to "cover the field" with such a giant sample. And the only way they could order such a mass of data from such a mass of people was to "type" them into broad categories. But a study done a few years later—this time focusing on only ten subjects—challenged *The Authoritarian Personality* mode of categorizing. Probing down deep into single personalities and trying to take each person through his own distinctive perspective on experience, the authors of this later study commented,

One's opinions or attitudes serve as mediators between the inner demands of the person and the outer environment—the material, social, and, most immediately, the informational environment of the person. Figures of speech may be misleading, yet we do well to think of a man's attitudes as his major equipment for dealing with reality. This equipment is not a product solely of basic needs and defenses nor is it fashioned directly to the blueprint of the world in which the person finds himself. Nor is it simply borrowed ready-made from the groups to which he belongs or aspires. Something of all of these but not quite any of them, it is, essentially, an apparatus for balancing the demands of inner functioning and the demands of the environment.

The authors concluded from this: "One cannot predict a man's opinions by knowledge of his personality alone or of his environment alone. Both must enter into any predictive formula."[9]

Later studies in the social sciences confirm this conclusion. Focusing intently on a few individuals, they've discovered that people take their cues not from a single "block reality" (read "climate of opinion"), but from a great variety of intermediary information environments. From these environments, people receive messages and form opinions about life. Studies like this have urged inquiries in social science away from general deductive categories of thought and down to particularized ways of thinking. We in historiography and intellectual history studies might take heed of their example.[10]

Using these studies, we might query whether a school of historians is held together as much by broad cultural currents of thought as by particularized experiences in particularized subcultures. And if the latter, we might then raise some new questions: When and where should we look for these particular experiences? At the time when the historian expresses his thought? Back some time before when he was coming of intellectual age? Even further back when he was growing up? Obviously, there is no single answer to such questions; yet asking them should urge us past our assumption of broad cultural uniformities and stimulate us to seek out *more immediate, empirical connections* among thinkers in a group and between the thinker and his environment.

This injunction is not entirely new in history studies, of course. There's always been a kind of folk wisdom in the profession about schools and personal influences and such—a folk wisdom running counter to the unsociological climate-of-opinion idea. We assume for example that Henry Nash Smith and John William Ward and Leo Marx (and, later, Alan Trachtenberg) did much to cross-fertilize each other at Minnesota and that New Left history owes much of its rise to the influence of William Appleman Williams at Wisconsin. When we say (as we frequently do) that such and such a scholar or graduate department "produced" such and such a student, we acknowledge how important are personal and social influences in shaping people's beliefs. But little of this folk wisdom seems to reach print, maybe because it's difficult to do anything more than intuit influence of that sort.[11] So, when critics go to write about historians and their explanation forms, they frequently ignore what they may actually think about personal and social influences, and instead resort to broad "climate" or "spirit-of-an-age" metaphors to interpret their thoughts.

There are other questions we can ask about historians and their group categories. Does calling a group a "school" mean everyone in it shares all their pictures of reality? Obviously not. Yet how much must they have in common before they become identifiable as a school of historical explanation? Conversely, how much dissensus can a school tolerate before it ceases to be a school?

In the last chapter, for example, I claimed that Progressives held a one-dimensional view of ideas. But Carl Becker didn't, and he's usually labelled a Progressive. And I said counter-Progressives were much enamored of ideas. But that misses Daniel Boorstin, who once wrote, "It was life, and not thought, which would excel here."[12] And I said New Left historians share a "system" orientation toward historical reality. But that's not true of, say, Staughton Lynd, who—to the special disfavor of several New Left colleagues—generally rejects systems in favor of looking at ideas and individuals in the American past.

Such confounding of our conventional labels doesn't stop with a few negative deviations either. If we wanted to break apart the usual mode of clustering schools together and try rearranging the categories, we could come up with some interesting new combinations. Although they're supposed to "belong" to three different schools of historical explanation, Parrington, Ward, and Lynd share a similar picture of how ideas function in history (generally, ideas are not substantively grounded in that picture—theirs *are* mostly climate-of-opinion histories). Similarly, Beard, Boorstin, and Williams resemble each other on some points, sharing a picture not of ideas but of the importance of systems and institutions in America's past. And we can find an ironic temper running through the Progressive Becker, the counter-Progressive Perry Miller, and parts of the New Left historian Howard Zinn.

What then to make of these "trans-school" themes? We haven't been accustomed to clustering historians like that, and by crossing over time periods we confound the climate-of-opinion and spirit-of-an-age kind of explanation. But the comparisons are there to be made, and we might profitably spend some effort making them. Such comparisons might also cause us to ponder whether historians in fact fit so neatly into schools, or whether we've just found it convenient to label them like that so they can be handled more efficiently.

I'm not saying that schools of historical explanation don't exist at all, or that there are no group likenesses among historians. But by raising such questions, I do suggest that we mustn't go on just assuming these general types exist in the nature of things. We need to know much more about what comprises a historical type and why, and about the levels on which such generalized typing makes sense and on what levels it's simply nonsense.

What we need are some new-form ways of thinking about the problem. We need strategies which will take us past a few shared *pictures* of historians to look also for those shared *experiences* which help give life and shape to those pictures. In short, we need some more rooted, empirical ways of thinking about this issue of "school."

IV

Again, we can get aid by looking outside our own disciplinary boundaries —this time to Thomas Kuhn and his studies in the history of science. Kuhn's use of the "paradigm" form might help us to ground and focus our thinking on American historians, their collective groupings, and their explanation forms.

Since we've touched on Kuhn elsewhere in this book, and since his own sense of ideas resembles what we did in chapter 1, we can pass over the preliminaries of his model rather quickly. His first recognition is that everyone thinks down certain corridors; when people look at the world, they see not through completely open eyes, but through narrowed, focused ones. The world of outside experience—be that the experience of people or the experience of things—invariably comes to men filtered through mind.

Kuhn's special concern is for how these mind-filters function among practicing scientists; his term "paradigm" orders that concern. Among other things, a paradigm sets outer limits for seeing and thinking within a community of scholars. Since nature can't be taken in whole, the paradigm also serves to ward off information overload. It defines—or rather confines— what's salient from the whole world of nature, and it offers the working scientist a bounded space to think in. The paradigm, says Kuhn,

functions by telling the scientist about the entities that nature does and does not contain and about the ways in which those entities behave. That information provides a map whose details are elucidated by mature scientific research. And since nature is too complex and varied to be explored at random, that map is as essential as observation and experiment to science's continuing development.[13]

We might picture a paradigm as a kind of magnet, and the experiences of nature as metal filings. The scientist takes his magnet and runs it past the filings, and they get arranged into certain patterns, a magnetic field of sorts. Because each magnet is of a particular kind and shape and power (also each array of filings), and because each scientist runs it past the filings in a particular way, the resulting patterns will invariably be particular too. That is, they'll be arranged into certain configurations, or gestalts, by one magnet used in one way, and into different configurations with another magnet. Because no single magnet can ever get to all the filings of nature, there will always be some left over, falling outside any particular magnetic field. Facts selected within a paradigm thus inevitably crowd out other facts, and no paradigm can offer an all-inclusive patterning of nature.

So much for the moment on paradigm as an intellectual construct. Much of this should be familiar to us by now, since it resembles the basic thrust of our earlier chapters. What may not be so familiar, though, is how Kuhn probes for the existential base of these paradigms. It's here where he most seriously challenges our floating "climate of opinion" model of ideas in history. For his sense of paradigm is not so much intellectual as it is sociological; a paradigm builds and defines *community*.

To get their pictures of what the world is like, scientists look not only to nature, but to each other. Knowledge in science is thus socially as well as individually transacted, and paradigms function not only as mental constructs, but also as social institutions. As an institution, a paradigm's connections are not directly out to general forces in the culture, but to concrete subcultures, particular communities of people. To know why scientists picture things as they do, one must locate what special *reference groups* they form those pictures within. "A paradigm governs, in the first instance, not a subject matter but rather a group of practitioners," Kuhn writes. "Any study of paradigm-directed or paradigm-shattering research must begin by locating the responsible group or groups."[14]

In Kuhn's view, community norms govern the activity of scientists. They establish certain canons of propriety for scholarly work in the field. Through their acculturating procedures, initiation rites, and censoring devices, they socialize people into that community and legitimize its forms. Scientists learn and maintain their trade by listening to lectures, reading textbooks, doing laboratory exercises, attending conferences, reading and writing in the journals of their field, and so on. By doing all this, they not only pass in and on information, they also reinforce their community. From this community they imbibe their understanding of how nature behaves, and how they should behave as scientists in studying nature. It's also to this community— not to the general culture—that they address most of their work. The scientific subculture is the most salient of their reference groups; they seek out its rewards, and hope to avoid its punishments.[15]

At any moment in time, a paradigm expresses that community's consensus on some part of nature. Beyond its describing and explaining functions—telling what nature is and how—the paradigm offers identity and group solidarity to a community of scientists, plus a common language.

A while back we asked, "How much dissensus can a school tolerate before it ceases to be a school?" Now we might make a sociological response to this question. That is, we can look on a group of thinkers much as any other social grouping. Recognize they may be bound together not just by individual likenesses, but by communal norms too, and query how they'll respond when those norms are challenged. Any group, however tightly knit, must tolerate certain dissensus, so we can expect some degree of variation within it. What's crucial is whether those variations are inside the ongoing system—as with, say, Republicans versus Democrats in the American polity —or whether they pose a threat to the system itself. When they do, scientific communities—like political ones—are liable to respond by trying to silence their deviants. As Kuhn says,

Normal science, the activity in which most scientists inevitably spend almost all their time, is predicated on the assumption that the scientific community knows what the world is like. Much of the success of the enterprise derives from the community's willingness to defend that assumption, if necessary at considerable cost. Normal science, for example, often suppresses fundamental novelties because they are necessarily subversive of its basic commitments.[16]

Right here, Thomas Kuhn's functionalist sociological sense may cause us something of a jolt. For he's not especially disturbed that scientific communities attempt to suppress novelty. To him, these efforts are merely the institutions of group identity reacting to challenge. If they gave in to every challenge which confronted them, they'd lack the cohesiveness to maintain their group and carry on their work. And to Kuhn, it's through group maintenance that most progress in scientific understanding comes about.

Kuhn's position here is subtle, and easily misunderstood. On the one hand, he sees paradigms as serving a function like myths—not really true but quite useful in mobilizing people to think and do things. On the other hand, he doesn't reject them just because of that. In his view, a paradigm invariably restricts and forces inquiry, and that may confound our liberal intellectual sentiments. But he contends this is the only way to get much fruitful work done—besides, a paradigm community will normally generate its own anomalies and revolutions in form:

By focusing attention upon a small range of relatively esoteric problems, the paradigm forces scientists to investigate some part of nature in a detail and depth that would otherwise be unimaginable. And normal science possesses a built-in mechanism that ensures the relaxation of the restrictions that bound research whenever the paradigm from which they derive ceases to function effectively. At that point scientists begin to behave differently, and the nature of their research problems changes. In the interim, however, during the period when the paradigm is successful, the profession will have solved problems that its members could scarcely have imagined and would never have undertaken without commitment to the paradigm. And at least part of that achievement always proves to be permanent.[17]

Within a shared paradigm, inquiry can gain momentum down focused channels, and can thus get deep into the intricacies of things. Inside their own community, scholars can take certain things for granted, for they don't have to rebuild from the ground up every time they set out to do something. A scientist can *concentrate* his mental energies because, in a sense, he's working among friends and doesn't have to keep explaining his entire world to them all the time. Kuhn himself unwittingly hints what that can mean; in his preface he expresses gratitude to a colleague in the field—one Stanley Cavell —"the only person with whom I have ever been able to explore my ideas in incomplete sentences."[18]

"Normal" science—that is, science which functions wholly inside a paradigm—can penetrate to details of nature in a way not possible outside paradigm conventions. For that depth, however, it does exact the price of not questioning its own fundamentals. But at the same time, normal science—according to Kuhn—carries within it the seeds of its own destruction. If it may try and suppress a few dissenters along the way, it does get valuable work done. And when that dissent comes to be fundamental, then the whole paradigm community may have to give up its norms and reconstitute itself. Thus the logic—and socio-logic—of normality in science will lead in due time to revolution. "The very fact that a significant scientific novelty so often emerges simultaneously from several laboratories," says Kuhn, "is an index both to the strongly traditional nature of normal science and to the completeness with which that traditional pursuit prepares the way for its own change."[19]

V

With Kuhn as background now, and our perspective on ideas from chapters 1 and 2 setting a foundation, let's return to those questions we raised earlier about schools of historical explanation, and hazard a few answers. Or if not quite full answers, at least lines along which answers might be explored. We'll try two aproaches—first an intellectual response to this problem of school, then a sociological.

One of our earliest questions there was, "How do we name things?" We might translate that now into, "*Why* do we name things?" And we can respond that we name things not because things *are* what they're named, but because we want to *do* certain things with what we name. Names are not *in* things, *in* experience; rather, they come to life in what we're *doing with* experience. They're operative, dialogical, situational. Or ought to be.

When applying labels to historians, then, our question should not be "*Are* they grouped together?," but "*Can they be* grouped together?" This implies two things—(1) that the labeller himself groups them through an act of will, and (2) that the grouping therefore depends on what he's looking for. Schools are not inherent in the nature of history; they're created from an ongoing dialogue between the materials of historical interpretation and the minds of scholars who seek to order those materials.

Is Carl Becker a Progressive historian? It depends. He's a Progressive if we configure Progressivism one way, he's not a Progressive if we configure it another. The issue is not whether he *is* a Progressive; the issue is what we choose to include in our operative patterning of Progressive beliefs. And also what part of Becker we're looking at when we construct our pattern. If at his wry, ironic temper, then he probably wouldn't classify; I know of no other "Progressive" historian who had much of that sense. But if we're looking at Becker's early class-conflict model, then he would seem to be in; for almost all "Progressives" share in that part of the explanation.

A simple little dictum from psychology might help us here. Henry Murray once said (where I'm not sure), *"Each man is like all other men, like some other men, like no other man."* That is, if we look on some levels, no one is unique; rather, he's simply a member of the general species-human. On other levels, every one is unique; no one else in the species is exactly like him or her. On yet other levels, people come to be unique by their groupings. It all depends on which level we choose. When we're after the issue of "school," we should be looking on the second level—"like some other men." There we're concerned *just* for those ways in which people in a certain population resemble each other. On other levels, says Murray's dictum, these same people *don't* resemble each other at all. And on yet others, they *do* resemble each other, but they resemble everybody else too, so there's nothing distinctive in that. The point of the dictum is to keep our concerns self-consciously focused on the level we want. This idea of levels should help us, then, for again it offers an operative, dialogical sense of the labels we apply to things, also of the things (in this case people) we're labeling.

That, I think, should be our first priority for new-form naming in history studies—*an operative sense of our language.* We must recognize, for example, that there *is no* Progressive explanation, as a thing. Instead, the label "Progressive" is an abstraction from things, a mental construct, an ideal type, a way of condensing and distilling certain things from certain historians who wrote in certain ways in a certain period of time. It is a way of showing how *some* men resemble *some* other men, in *some* ways. We should also remember, though, that these same men resemble yet other men in yet other ways, and in some ways each one of them is not a type at all, but *sui generis.*

Maybe all this seems obvious. It is, I suspect . . . in theory. But it's not so obvious, or well heeded, in practice—as the consensus-conflict dispute and other such controversies over naming have shown. If critics in that debate had paused to define just what they meant by "consensus" and by "conflict," had then specified precisely where they were looking for each in America's experience, and had then used that operative sense to work carefully through a few selected works in the field, this debate might have offered us some more fruitful understandings.[20]

To be sure, we can get immersed in a good deal of needless hairsplitting in this impulse always to define our terms. We can get so wound up in dissecting our words that we never get to the world of experience they supposedly refer to. Philosophical ruminations like that can confuse as well as clarify our thinking, and on occasion can deflect us from our main purpose—

trying to explain historical experience. They present a potential danger zone in historiographical scholarship, a kind of metaphysical quicksand area. We should be on guard for that. Yet if a field doesn't have some commonly agreed-upon modes of discourse and—more important—some operative ways of connecting its language back to things in the world, then dialogue in historiography won't get very far. There are many reasons why scholarship in American historiography hasn't gotten very far to date and has had little impact on practicing historical research. But surely one major bottleneck is the haziness of our intellectual forms, and the undisciplined way we've applied words to things.

This *operative* sense is one way to sharpen our thinking on "school," for it can give us more flexible forms for handling ideas than does "climate of opinion." Another device we can use is the *sociological* sense—taking ideas out of the air and grounding the shared pictures of a historians' school in certain shared experiences and in structured institutions.

This is where Thomas Kuhn's "paradigm-community" model of scholarship comes in. His point is that when scientists approach nature, they do it through minds, and within communities. Scholarship contains an inescapable mirror-like quality, reflecting back on the scholar and the community doing it.

In using Kuhn for our own historical territory, though, we must make a few adjustments. Communities in history don't wholly parallel those in science. Few schools of historians, for example, are as tightly knit as Kuhn's scientific communities. Nor are historians normally as insulated from their times. Their subject matters tend to keep them more in touch with cultural forces around them, and make them somewhat less subject to promptings from their immediate professional surroundings.[21]

But if there are differences between the influences which affect historians and those affecting natural scientists, they're a matter of degree. Like scientists, historians do work in communities, they have group forms of initiation, rules, journals, conferences, rituals just as scientists do. They're also prone to believe that what they see is the actual truth of the world, and not a temporary consensus of their community.

With Kuhn's sociological sense, we might now better understand why this is the case. That is, we might try and explain how shared experiences underlie shared perspectives on reality, and how institutions of the historical community affect the way historians believe.

Through Kuhn, we can see that explanation-forms are not only mindforms, but institutionalized, experiential forms too. They're not just reflections of an abstracted "climate of opinion." They may be influenced by such general cultural forces, but they're influenced also by *intermediate references* between the individual historian and his culture. Some historians think like some other historians not only because they live in the same time, but also because they read each other's writings, are taught by each other, share ideas and gossip with each other, serve on convention panels with each other, write recommendations and reviews for each other, and visit with each other and each other's families. So when we inquire into historians' explanations, we should seek not only *intellectual modes* of such explanation, but *subcultures* or *communities* of explanation too.

For example, I'd once thought of subtitling the last chapter "Historians' Paradigms in Twentieth-Century America." But as I worked through Kuhn's *Structure of Scientific Revolutions,* I realized that if we were to use "paradigm" like he did, only the Progressive historians may really have had one. That is, for onto forty years a substantial community of scholars asumed their form was not simply *a* way of looking at reality in American history but, in fact, this is what reality *was.* And for those decades, textbooks, journals, reviews, exemplars of original scholarship, classrooms, conferences in history lent institutionalized support to that form.

We can't say this of either the counter-Progressives or the New Left. Maybe for a while at Harvard and Minnesota, a tiny group approached some kind of paradigm consensus inside the symbol-myth-image form; or maybe later at Wisconsin a few approached it within the New Left form. But neither group had the power to expand its form so that a whole array of general social structures in the profession supported and legitimized it. However zealous a symbol-myth-image or New Left historian might be, he'd frequently be made aware that his is only one among several ways of looking at the world.

We might better name these latter two *explanation-forms,* then, because they lack the cohesive social power of a community paradigm. They may be just as persuasive intellectually as the Progressive paradigm, but they've never been as firmly established institutionally. Just why this is so is beyond our scope in the present study. For to explain this matter in any depth would require a sophisticated sociology of historical knowledge. We need to develop such a sociology in the profession, and it's one of the intents of this study to raise questions which might point us in that direction. But what we do on that here is only suggestive; we need to know far more before we can say anything along this line with much confidence.

VI

Thus far we've used Thomas Kuhn for "normal" scholarship, for his view of scholarly communities as they function inside a paradigm consensus. But his book is aimed basically at "abnormal" science—that is, at science when its consensus is breaking apart. It's "the structure of scientific revolutions" which finally engages his attention. Here too we can find Kuhn of use.

At this point our question (and his) becomes, "What happens when one cluster of explanation commitments is given up, and another takes its place?" *How, in short, do minds change?*

Kuhn uses mainly sociological kinds of insights to explain the workings of normal scholarship. But he adds to these psychological insights when entering scholarship in revolution. Especially the psychology of perception.

For Kuhn, no paradigm allows the scientific community to slice through everything in nature. Because each paradigm directs attention to some compressed part of nature, there will always be experiences which fall outside its range. And, on occasion, those outside experiences will be connected to things which are inside the paradigm, and may affect them in ways the paradigm cannot account for. So the paradigm never has a perfect fit even with what falls inside its particular range of explanation.

Hence, any paradigm must allow for some margin of error. Within a firm paradigm consensus, it's assumed that such error is simply a failure in the scientist and his measuring instruments—a failure which time and progress in knowledge will correct. This is what Kuhn calls the "puzzle-solving" aspect of normal science—trying to solve puzzles thrown up by nature within the given paradigm.

But at some periods in the history of science, those puzzles may multiply at a rapid rate, putting strain on the core paradigm and its accepted way of explaining things. Gaps between nature and the given paradigm will be seen as "anomalies"; and if this anomalous state becomes acute enough, the community may be prepared for a complete overhauling of forms.

For Kuhn, a scientific community does not give off one paradigm and take up another merely because the facts of the world dictate it must. To be sure, a paradigm crisis may get precipitated because certain experiences in nature don't seem to fit that paradigm's range of explanation. But most scientists won't acknowledge this situation as a crisis. Instead, they'll see it as merely another complicated puzzle to be solved, and *inside* the reigning paradigm. The problem (as they see it) lies not in the general paradigm community, but in the individual scientist; it presents a challenge to his ingenuity and his instruments for research.

A few practicing scientists, though, may perceive the situation otherwise. As anomaly piles upon anomaly, their commitments to the established paradigm will be put under increasing strain. Something appears wrong. And their community of scholarship has no way to explain it. Some may begin looking *just* for those experiences which don't fit the paradigm, becoming fixated on anomalies between nature and scientists' explanations. In time, a few among them will sense they need not just more technical ingenuity—inventing new methods for solving the puzzle—but an exercise of creative imagination— picturing some part of nature through a whole new form.

At some point, someone (or ones) will then take such a leap of imagination and set forth a whole new way to cluster things together (this is what Kuhn calls "a change in visual gestalt").[22] Then a new candidate for paradigm gets launched. If this candidate is successful, the community will then set out to restructure its commitments, its procedures and apparatus for research, its textbooks, and so on. And that body of scientists will then enter a new reign of normality; what once was radical and suspect will now become conventional and seen by the comunity as simply "the way things are." Which means they will have settled into a new paradigm consensus.[23]

What Thomas Kuhn emphasizes is this: The revolution is in fact just that. If knowledge grows in evolutionary fashion through normal science, it takes discontinuous leaps during a scientific revolution. And these leaps are not necessarily forward. Mind doesn't perceive *more* during those times, it perceives *differently*. That's where Kuhn's use of gestalt psychology comes in. With it, he can suggest that paradigm change comes not through an accumulation of detail, but through mind patterning details in novel ways. The details may in fact be the same for both old and new paradigms, but how they're clustered is different.

In picturing normal science and its paradigm constructs earlier, we used the metaphor of *a magnet and metal filings*—each magnet arranging the filings into its own distinctive pattern. We might now picture a scientific revolution as something like *an earthquake*. What happens is this: Some time after adjustments in the ongoing system have settled in (the result perhaps of some prior earthquake), strains begin to build up in the form, usually along a fault-line. Existing alignments channel and harness some of those strains. But a few cannot be contained. At some point, the stress becomes uncontrollable, it passes over a critical threshold, and bursts through the old forms. A massive upheaval takes place then, shattering the contours of everything around it. For a few moments, all is blind chaos and uproar. Nothing holds together. There are no patterns or predictable behaviors, no continuities or recognizable coherences. After a time, though, things begin to take on recognizable shape again, they settle down into more enduring alignments, and make fresh kinds of interconnections. New solidarities and new channels for handling potential stress get formed, and for a while they function to hold things together. Until, that is. . . .

If we use this "earthquake" picture as a working metaphor for handling ideas, we should have some rather precise details to focus on now. Specifically, we can look for the strain points—or "fault-lines"—in an explanation form. This should help us pinpoint exact instants of mind change, so we can focus our attention on just how such a gestalt switch takes place. At this point, though, we may have to leave Thomas Kuhn. If he serves us well in his sociological sense of explanation-forms, he leaves us somewhat short in handling the detailed workings of change itself. In *The Structure,* he talks *about* revolutions in science, he doesn't take us down *inside* an actual one, to show us what a paradigm revolution looks like.[24]

What Kuhn shows instead are basically "before" and "after" *still* shots, plus some other still pictures labeled "during"—when old and new paradigms are in turmoil. There's value in that. It offers a sense of the "whats" of change. But it's also important to see change itself—a paradigm revolution at the moment of impact, if you will. For this, we need a strategy for catching explanation-forms in motion—that is, *something like a movie camera which can focus in right along a fault-line and record just how old alignments break under strain and how realignments get formed.*

This is something we don't have yet in American historiographical scholarship—a camera focused enough to catch the inner workings of an idea in transition. Lacking such a strategy, we can only say *that* explanations change; we cannot tell very clearly *when* or *how*. And this short-changes us in our scholarship; for if we're to deal with mind and ideas in any depth, we must come to grips with changes of mind—with how, at certain moments, ideas strain old forms, pass over critical threshold boundaries, and congeal into new patterns. Again, I think our conventional resort to "climate of opinion" may have blocked understanding here.

Normally, scholars in intellectual history and historiography have been content with tracing the route of ideas, and with charting their interconnections, their influence, and what has influenced them over time. This has predisposed scholars to stay on the outside of thoughts, concerned as they are to show them in impact with many different things around them. Such a procedure has resulted in much detail, and several competing crosscurrents affecting the thoughts under review. With all that, the whole picture might threaten to become unmanageable—save, that is, for one thing. It's all tied together by the controlling idea of each age, the climate of opinion.

Intellectual historians gain a certain coherence with a strategy like that. And they can show ideas as part of the living world around them. But they may also sacrifice getting very far into those ideas—seeing their precise inner makeup, and observing just how that makeup gets rearranged from time to time. Which means they have no rigorous procedure for handling changes of mind.

Take Vernon Parrington, for instance, and his Progressive explanation of experience. Now change—at least change perceived as progress—plays a vital role in his perspective on history. Parrington has a ready explanation for such change too; usually, it's stimulated by certain men and ideas in contact with "reality" and the future, and it's resisted by other men and ideas out of contact with same. Further, within his Progressive form, change is always happening; not much stands still for long in his picture of America. But if we inquire carefully into Parrington for change at the moment of its happening, for a picture of just how change looks, we're not likely to find it.

We might expect to see it, for example, in a place like "Changing Theory," chapter 3 of his third volume of *Main Currents*. But we look in vain. What we find instead are flat statements like "The change came in 1848" (with no further explanation), or broad assertions like "By force of gravitation the main stream of economic theory—like the main stream of political theory— poured into the broadening channels of capitalism, and only the lesser vagrant currents followed the old channels of agrarianism or the new channels of proletarianism."[25]

This paints a vivid picture of change all right. But it leaves unanswered—because unasked—just how one particular "current" leads into another one. Or precisely when.

Look also at William Appleman Williams' *The Contours of American History*, another study where change plays a central role. As we noted in chapter 4, Williams anchors his perspective on the American past to three dominant patterns of intellectual organization. He calls each a *Weltanschauung*. The first pattern—mercantilism—begins around 1740 and extends to 1828. The second—laissez nous faire—begins about 1819 and moves forward to 1896. The third—corporation capitalism—starts around 1882 and comes to the present. In his schematic mode of organizing this book, Williams includes a section within each *Weltanschauung* where he describes mind change from the present form into the form succeeding it. In all three parts of *The Contours,* he titles that section, "The Transformation of Reality and the Inception of New Ideas." These three sections total 98 pages, almost one-fifth of the whole text.

Here if anywhere in *The Contours,* we should find Williams' picture of mind-change in action. But we don't. Rather, we come across statements like, "The panic of 1819, which had been brought on by the mercantilists' fear of limiting private property too much (as well as by the pressure of special interests), had the ironic effect of touching off a vigorous drive to be done with mercantilism and replace it with the philosophy of laissez nous faire, 'let us do as we please.' "26

Which again, like Parrington, communicates a certain picture to the reader, and in this case does locate a specific moment of change (1819). But Williams drops the matter after noting that moment, he doesn't go on into it. Thus, he too falls short of picturing an actual historical idea in transformation.

The same is true—only more so—in historiography writing. Take John Higham's *History* and his chapter there on "The Crisis in Progressive History." In it he describes the Progressive explanation under strain, and supports his description—in 14 pages—with notation of some fifty books challenging the Progressive form. Higham ties these books together with phrases like "the general influence of the postwar disillusion" and "a declaration of independence from midwestern domination of progressive historiography."27 What's missing, though, are the precise fault-lines of strain, and the actual points where a historian's idea breaks out of an old form to construct a new one. There are several general themes, many books, and much strain in the old form; but there are no specific moments where all are brought together in concentrated focus, to picture changes of mind. Thus Higham gives us a detailed description of the fact of change, but he does not offer either a description or an explanation of *how.*

Now I'm not setting this up as some sort of final litmus test, insisting that any history proposing to handle ideas must show them in motion and in change. There are many things to be done with ideas, and this is only one of them. It is an important one, though. If it sounds like a rather tall order, it has been done in American intellectual history studies. And we might profit from examining just how.

VII

The clearest instance I know of is the second volume of Perry Miller's *The New England Mind*. It's an instructive book for us to look at in this chapter, for it confounds the conventional labels of American historians, especially those labels as they've been applied to Miller.[28] His works have been branded as too idealistic and too monolithic in their approach to Puritan history. That is (say the critics), they overemphasize the power of mind to affect events in New England, and they picture that mind as unchanging and homogeneous.[29]

If these labels were true, Perry Miller would be a notorious "climate-of-opinion" historian. Having concentrated on general themes and not locating points of change within these themes, he'd illustrate just what we're trying to counter in this chapter—broad and panoramic, floating, unfocused labels for the study of historical ideas. But I'm afraid Miller himself has been a victim of such broad-scale labeling. On occasion, these labels tell us more about the shortcomings of labeling in the profession than about the shortcomings of one P. Miller.

Not that these labels—idealistic, monolithic—are wholly untrue. Readers of Miller's first volume on *The New England Mind* may recall his foreword there:

My project is made more practicable by the fact that the first three generations in New England paid almost unbroken allegiance to a unified body of thought, and that individual differences among particular writers or theorists were merely minor variations within a general frame. I have taken the liberty of treating the whole literature as though it were the product of a single intelligence.[30]

"I have taken the liberty of treating the whole literature as though it were the product of a single intelligence." Now that's monolithic, climate-of-opinion thinking with a vengeance! When we read that book through, we'll find a few departures from this attitude—notably in its concluding chapter, "God's Controversy with New England."[31] But this volume goes on for more than 500 pages; to carry any "monolith" for that long is some chore. Perry Miller comes close; if he doesn't convince all his readers that the seventeenth-century Puritan mind *was* "a single intelligence," he should persuade them that he labored mightily to *picture* it that way.

But he doesn't do this in his second volume. There his strategy for handling ideas is almost directly contrary to his earlier one. In the 1939 volume—subtitled *The Seventeenth Century*—Miller had tried simply to put together the fundamentals of his New England mind, to construct a picture in his head (and ours) of what it was. In his 1953 study, however—subtitled *From Colony to Province*—he wants to show this same mind in transition, and in disintegration. And the picture he constructs of mind is not a finished product, an essence, but something ongoing, in motion. In the former volume, we see mind as generalized thought, in the latter it's mind as particularized process. Miller's strategy there is to catch ideas as they're moving, and show this movement as it's affected by things around it.

Such a procedure causes him not only to see and say things differently in the second volume, but to develop an alternative *form* for his study too. Volume 1 had focused around broad themes, intellectual currents running through England and New England. Its chapter titles reflect that—"The Augustinian Strain of Piety," "The Intellectual Character," "The Intellectual Heritage," "The Covenant of Grace." In structure at least, it's climate-of-opinion history (it's not climate-of-opinion in content, but that's another matter).

Miller's second volume has a wholly different organizing pattern, however. He's still concerned with "mind," but no longer in broad floating currents. Instead, it's minds confronting things in the world, in those public situations where Puritan leaders must bring their thought forms to bear on particular events. And his chapter titles convey this altered strategy. Thus: "The Expanding Limits of Natural Ability" (on and around the Anne Hutchinson controversy), "Half-Way Measures," "The Judgment of the Witches," "The Poison of Wise's Cursed Libel," "The Judgment of the Smallpox."

And, contrary to his critics, Miller doesn't assume mind *determines* events in this volume. In fact, it's almost the opposite (though not quite). Mind is so *belabored* by events in the New World that it gets distracted from its express concerns, and this becomes a major cause of its disintegration. It does participate in its own downfall, but the outside world helps it along too.[32]

A single instance may illustrate how Miller handles this. Take his chapter on Salem witchcraft—entitled "The Judgment of the Witches." The occasion is this: It's late September of 1692, and the hysteria and executions are over with. New England's intellectual establishment is compelled to speak its mind on the affair, to offer its official explanation of the colony's recent ordeal, and to justify why it behaved as it did. Cotton Mather—"peerless penman of the colony"—is chosen for the task.[33]

At this point in his chapter, Miller moves from writing on the general intellectual background for this event—telling us *about* mind—to showing us an actual mind at labor. He does this by getting inside the situation of that mind—Cotton Mather's—as he's obliged to confront the experience of witchcraft in the colony. Watch how Miller does this:

Cotton went to his study and, in fear and trembling, began to write. Leaving a blank page for the endorsement Stoughton [chief judge of the Salem court] was to supply him, this tortured soul blurted out his first sentence: "I live by Neighbours that force me to produce these undeserved Lines." If ever there was a false book produced by a man whose heart was not in it, it is *The Wonders [of the Invisible World]*.[34]

When Perry Miller moves in alongside Cotton Mather at this moment, there are three in that study—Miller, Mather, and the idea of national covenant. That idea—giving New England a special mission in the world—belongs to the general intellectual climate of the colony, and Miller has made much of it up to here in his book. It's also deeply imbedded in Mather's own mind, and Miller has made something of that too. But this is only background for the main action, which action is carried by the particular way Mather manipulates this idea (and gets manipulated in turn) in this particular moment of New England's history. Watch again as Miller narrates the clash between idea and event here, through the mind of Mather:

Once started, this man whose pen raced across paper at breakneck speed could not stop. His mind was bubbling with every sentence of the jeremiads, for he was heart and soul in the effort to reorganize them. And for days Stephen Sewall did not send the records [Sewall, clerk of the Salem court, was to supply Mather with an official transcript of the proceedings there, which transcript was to offer the documentary base for Mather's explanation]. Cotton might have waited; a man secure of himself would have waited; he was insecure, frightened, sick at heart (at the end of his manuscript he was again to betray himself; he had done "the Service imposed upon me"). He wrote an introduction, hoping that it would anticipate the records; like a criminal who protests his innocence, the more he scribbled, the more he disclosed. Still no word from Salem; he put in an extract from Perkins; he redacted a sermon . . . he had delivered on August 4; he devised a further jeremiad-like address to the country—and still nothing from Salem.[35]

Cotton Mather, as Miller pictures him, was becoming frantic. Though driven by an urge to explain this event and thus salvage his cherished national covenant, he'd not yet seen the documents upon which that explanation was to be based. Thus explanation was not tying into concrete experience here, but was spinning around wildly in Mather's own mind (a more extreme version of what we'll see with Frederick Jackson Turner in chapter 7). Miller goes on:

He ransacked his library for stories of apparitions, hoping that they might substantiate what he was about to receive. The book was already swelling much too big—he had to admit—and he had just transcribed the report of a trial before Sir Matthew Hale, when, to his immense relief, Stephen's packet arrived.

"He worked out a version of five of the twenty trials," Miller concludes, "wrote a few wearied and confused observations, and rushed the monstrous collection to a printer. The book was on the streets about October 15 [less than a month after the trials had ended]."[36]

Miller has thus given us a few of the outside forces affecting the idea inside Mather's mind; they establish certain pressures influencing him, some external conditions under which this idea would function. Having set the scene on this surface level, Miller then plunges into the actual workings of Mather's mind, embodied in the text of *The Wonders*.

He pauses beforehand to query, "Why did the poor devil not leave well enough alone, publish the reports, and throw into the fire everything he had poured out during the days of waiting."[37] In effect, Miller asks his readers to ponder this situation for a moment, and to let their minds play upon possible alternatives. "Don't take everything in the situation as a given just because it's over with," he seems to say. "Suppose this were not Cotton Mather here, and suppose the national covenant idea were not there putting enormous pressure upon his mind."

Once Miller has got his reader pondering the situation and considering alternatives without Mather and the idea, he may comprehend it better with them. So he moves on to answer his own question, again merging idea with event through laying open Mather's mind. But this time Miller adds another ingredient—*style,* or the impact of this idea at this moment on Cotton Mather's words:

He suffered from a monstrous lust for publication, that much is certain; but the fuller explanation, accounting for the discharge of both his conscious and unconscious motivations, is the compelling force of the jeremiad [one of the literary forms which the national covenant idea assumed in seventeenth-century New England]. He had to find a rationale for his country's ordeal and at the same time a modicum of peace with himself; he did both by forcing this wretched business into the traditional scheme of sin and retribution, which to him was the only form that would give conceivable significance either to New England's tragedy or to his own comprehension of it.

Miller then gets in his stinger: "He could not let a word he had written out of this trance go to waste; hence he, a stylist who kept even the sprawling *Magnalia* under some coherent control, published the most incoherent jumble he ever allowed to appear between covers."[38]

Miller then proceeds to detail this charge, going on for two pages of intricate textual analysis of *The Wonders*. He shows how Mather got his mind locked into the jeremiad-form, and how, once in the groove, Mather simply "went with the tide of his rhetoric."[39] Save for a single instance, that is, when Mather paused to face some unpleasant facts of the situation, and was momentarily to escape the grip of his ruling idea. "There was only one hitch," writes Miller, "and Cotton revealed it: the convictions had been secured 'notwithstanding the Great and Just Suspicion, that the Daemons might impose the Shapes of Innocent Persons in their Spectral Exhibitions upon the Sufferers (which may perhaps prove no small part of the Witch-Plot in the issue.)' "[40]

If Mather had stuck with this perception for long, he'd have questioned the whole procedure for conviction of the Salem court, and would thereby have failed to rationalize that Puritan establishment he was obliged to defend. By implication, he would also have questioned whether the national covenant-jeremiad formula would work here at all. For if persons had been falsely accused and wrongly convicted, could the hangings in fact be explained as just retribution for the colony's sins? That would be some considerable admission, especially for a Mather. For to admit this would be to undermine the Salem court's larger rationale for behaving as it did, plus Governor Phips's choice of Mather to issue a white paper on this experience, plus the entire inherited jeremiad-form which Mather had put upon his explanation.

Which, Miller is quick to note, didn't happen. Cotton Mather's flash of candor was brief; immediately after this uncharacteristic recognition, his inherited mind-forms took over from his eyes, and, in effect, he proceeded to deny he ever saw any such fault in the court's procedure. Miller rises to a peak of indignation in his response here, showing how not only fresh forms of historical analysis can be created from getting inside the moment of an idea, but fresh forms of moral judgment too:

Cotton salvaged what defense he could for a court in which he did not believe by the pitiful remonstrance: "Surely, they have at worst been but the faults of a well-meaning Ignorance." We avert our gaze while he, having made what he could of Stephen's notes, fled up the ladder of the jeremiad and soothed himself with fresh dreams of the New Jerusalem, "from whence the Devil shall then be banished, there shall be no Devil within the Walls of that Holy City."[41]

This is how Perry Miller manages his analysis of mind change in New England. We might call it a strategy of "fault-line focus" for handling ideas. In this case, the fault in the idea simply gapes a little wider and the pressure along it becomes a little more intense. The national-covenant idea does not change over into a new form, though the option for such change was opened by Mather's brief moment of recognition. By showing precisely how the New England mind (or at least Cotton Mather's New England mind) closed off that option, Miller pictures it in the act of laboring to maintain its identity, its hold upon events. And by focusing in close on this particular moment of strain, he's located the precise point where, if enough pressure is applied through enough events over enough time, that mind's idea is liable to break. As he puts it, "Henceforth there was, although for a time desperately concealed, a flaw in the very foundation of the covenant conception."[42]

Miller can say this because he's done his historical homework carefully, and he's made some imaginative connections among his facts. First, he's plotted in detail the external conditions under which Mather wrote—the increasing cultural strain on the idea of national covenant and its jeremiad form, the pressure for rationalizing the Puritan establishment put on Mather by Governor Phips and by Mather's own circle of friends, Mather's sense of his role as "peerless penman of the colony," the time press under which he labored (the whole thing took less than three weeks to write, from September 22 to October 11), the fact that he was forced (or forced himself) to write most of this report lacking the documentary evidence on which it presumed to be founded.[43]

These details are instrumental to how Miller explains Mather's behavior here; yet they're not at the core of his explanation. At the core are Cotton's own words, bound up in *The Wonders of the Invisible World*. By knowing the conditions of outside stress, Miller can better explain the inner turmoil which these words reveal. It's thus by merging inner with outer, word with situation, that Miller can put Mather's ideas into motion, and show the precise moments of their greatest strain.

This is what Perry Miller does throughout his *Colony* volume. By moving around both outside and inside ideas, he can show not only what an idea says, but how it works (or doesn't work). *Colony* is a study not of general thought in New England—not of "climate of opinion"—but of the inner workings of particular minds working through particular forms in particular moments at particular places responding to particular conditions. In short, it's just the kind of "perspectivistic" history we were calling for in chapter 2. Rarely has a work so escaped the categories—"monolithic," "idealistic"—of its critics.

Miller's special concern in *Colony* is for changes of mind, and he focuses his picture on those vulnerable points where change seems to be imminent. Hence his method works like a seismograph, detecting early tremors in Puritan mind-forms, and trying to measure just how intense each tremor is.

Thus we have a whole book structured around faults in the New England mind—from its opening prologue on Richard Mather's "generation-gap" dilemma to the epilogue whose closing words point toward Jonathan Edwards and the Great Awakening (and thus to Miller's earlier volume, *Jonathan Edwards*). The book thus confounds the labels of Miller's critics, and at the same time offers us in historiography-intellectual history studies a valuable new strategy for handling ideas.[44] We can find bits and pieces of such a strategy elsewhere in American intellectual history studies—say, Leo Marx's *The Machine in the Garden*, or R. W. B. Lewis' *The American Adam*, or Marvin Meyers' *The Jacksonian Persuasion*, or Bernard Bailyn's *The Ideological Origins of the American Revolution*, or Gordon Wood's *The Creation of the American Republic*. But it's in Perry Miller's *The New England Mind: From Colony to Province* where the whole pattern is worked out most fully.

VIII

If we now add these perspectives of Kuhn and Miller to where we were before in the territory, we've got two new words for our vocabulary. We've already spoken of "form," and "perspective," and "explanation," and "strategy for inquiry," and "school." Now we can add "pivotal moment" and "critical threshold."

"Pivotal moment" *specifies* "climate of opinion." It's a transitional point in mind forms. If we kept with the climate metaphor, we might call it a kind of front in the weather.

In pivotal-moment analysis, we assume that changes of mind take place at particular times, or at least they're most visible there. So we select out those momentous situations when something unusual seems to be happening with an idea, and we focus in closely to watch what's going on.

Not that mind always changes in these moments. In Cotton Mather, we have a case where it didn't. But the opportunity was there; Mather saw it, then backed off. The point of a pivotal moment is that, in it, mind can go either way. It's on a potential threshold of change—a fault-line—but it may or may not go over. This moment is simply an intensified kind of experience; that's because more pressures are impacting on mind, and more options are opened to it, than when it's working wholly inside a given explanation-form.

The term "critical threshold" merely adds a little more specificity to pivotal moment. The moment is the whole situation of stress, the threshold is the exact point of greatest stress. In the Mather example, the moment is the occasion of his writing *The Wonders of the Invisible World;* the threshold is that point where he questioned "spectral evidence," then backed away from what he saw.

It's on this threshold where actual change in a form may occur. It's right at 212 degrees Fahrenheit, say, where if we add any extra heat to water it becomes steam. Or it's at 32 degrees, where any less heat and water becomes ice. At a critical threshold, a tiny bit of pressure may tip one form over into another. All paradigms, or explanation-forms, can tolerate much discord within them. But on the threshold point, any further discord, and one explanation may get shattered and a new pattern starts forming.

By focusing on moments, then, we may isolate zones of vulnerability in each explanation form. In our concern with changes of mind, we can look for points where strains in a form seem greatest. For the Progressives, say, this is the point where historical change for them ceases to look like progress. It's where "experience" and "explanation" go in separate ways. As with Cotton Mather, their minds may tell them one thing, but their eyes see another. Their paradigm says all change must be placed along the progress-plane (i.e., it must be either progress or it's regress), but their experiences show them otherwise. That's the vulnerable point (or at least a vulnerable point) of the Progressives' explanation, and in chapters 7 and 8 we'll look closely at how they behave during moments like this.

We lack space for such detailed inquiry into vulnerable points of our other two explanation-forms. But we might say that counter-Progressives appear most vulnerable at the point where events fail to confirm their sense of coherence and continuity and complexity in American culture. And New Leftists appear most vulnerable at the point where the ongoing system in America shows enough flexibility to work through its problems.

But we needn't make too much now of these substantive points of strain. The intent of "moment" analysis is to serve basically as a strategy for inquiry —it should give us more control over detail when doing intellectual history-historiographical studies. It points out some highly concentrated experiences to look at, and it tells us that if we're concerned to understand changes of mind, we ought to focus in here. It also reduces information overload by suggesting that not all experiences in the history of an idea are equal, just as not all experiences in a person's life are equal. Some experiences may yield more results than others, and we might conserve our intellectual energies by concentrating on those with maximum potential yield.

IX

Two more new words, and we'll have completed our preliminary journey here into changes of mind. As we turned to Thomas Kuhn for help on "school" and to Perry Miller on "pivotal moments," here we'll turn to the literary critic Kenneth Burke. First, though, let's briefly go back and set up the questions which tie Burke's position into our own concerns.

We asked earlier in this chapter, "How does each historian relate to his times?" Up to now, we've suggested ways of connecting him to his school, and of finding points where the forms of that school are undergoing basic change. Here we'll be concerned with how he relates also to broader environmental forces around him.

We've already mentioned one way of doing this—through the "climate of opinion." In introducing his anthology *The Historian and the Climate of Opinion,* Robert Skotheim has clearly summarized this position:

What does the climate of opinion have to do with the way a scholar writes history? From the mass of records left by the past, the historian selects and interprets data on the basis of what is meaningful and important to him. In this process, he is reflecting his climate of opinion, for he studies the past from the perspective of the present. His sense of what is meaningful and important significantly derives from the climate of opinion in which he lives.

"This is not to deny that he honestly tries to understand the past," Skotheim concludes, "or to suggest that he intentionally distorts the past because of his present interests. It is only to insist that the historian cannot jump out of his intellectual skin."[45]

That's one way to look at this issue. It uses a kind of *mirror* model for handling ideas; the historian more or less passively reflects cultural currents in his environment. But it still leaves several questions unanswered. What do we mean when we say someone "reflects" his age, or its climate of opinion? How does an age get inside one, or reflect off one? Does the historian in fact *just* reflect the environment around him, or are there more active ways to picture how he relates to his world?[46]

These questions move us beyond historians as such to consider more general relationships—through ideas—between the individual mind and its larger environmental context. In handling this issue, scholars in history have normally tended toward one of two polar positions.

One, the so-called "intrinsic" approach to ideas, gets around the mind-environment dilemma by in effect ignoring environment. It approaches ideas where scholars readily find them—ordinarily in a printed text—and it tends not to ask how they got there. It's interested in the internal makeup of ideas; it's not much interested in connecting ideas to things in the world outside. It assumes that ideas are produced by mind, and it finds mind in individuals. There's little concern for collective mind in the intrinsic approach. It concentrates its energies on unit ideas, and frequently takes them apart with painstaking thoroughness. It's much into the *logic* of ideas.

The other, called the "extrinsic" approach, is more after the *utility* of ideas. This aproach is not much concerned with the idea itself, but rather with what's behind and around the idea. It interprets ideas not as causes but as effects or symptoms, and its focus usually strains outward from the individual mind to collective experiences. Mind, it says, is a product of environment; environment shapes it, it does little to affect environment in turn. Thus, the extrinsic approach always moves from idea to the world beyond idea. Where intrinsic scholars pretty much ignore environment to focus on the individual, extrinsic scholars see the individual pretty much determined by the environment surrounding him.

So much for the two positions as ideal types. No single historian, of course, wholly embodies either position; but American historians have normally leaned toward the extrinsic position more than the intrinsic. The latter has gotten a fuller hearing, though, in disciplines like literature and philosophy; historians who draw much from those disciplines are likely to be informed by some kind of intrinsic approach.[47]

But most historians rely less on such other disciplines, and are more inclined to use forms developed inside their own profession. These forms have normally urged scholars to look outward toward the environmental context of ideas rather than to spend much time probing their inner makeup. "Climate of opinion," we might note, is a variant of this environmentalist position.

But whether historians lean in one or the other direction, or occupy some median position between them, the polar extremes are still there, and most historiographers of ideas have been made conscious of them. This is especially the case after 1966 and Skotheim's *American Intellectual Histories and Historians*. For that rich and comprehensive study worked the categories of intrinsic versus extrinsic through the whole population of American intellectual historians, and summed up a fifteen-year methodology debate in the profession on same.

No clear consensus was reached on how to get out of this dilemma of internal versus external. The two positions became clearer as the debate progressed, but they tended to remain as polar opposites. The working historian still had to choose between two more or less incompatible positions—between seeing ideas as independent of environment or as determined by it.

This brings us to the point where Kenneth Burke can help us. In his book *The Philosophy of Literary Form,* Burke has wrestled with the same issue confronting these historians—how mind relates to environment. He wants to know, *How can we get into the life of ideas* (for Burke, it's the life of words) *without simply reducing ideas to the world around them?* That is, how can one protect the integrity of ideas as ideas, yet see them functioning also in environments outside themselves?

Burke works through this problem in literature—where the extreme of intrinsic analysis is the New Criticism and the extrinsic pole is represented by a form of sociological determinism. He proposes to collapse these polar opposites by developing a third alternative; he calls it *the "situation-strategy" approach.*[48]

Burke improves upon the historians by first reaching under the academic categories "intrinsic" and "extrinsic" to feel for some uncategorized life experiences below. His probes are not just for general life, however, but for something quite specific. That something is the experience of *words.* Words are Burke's focusing instrument. With that instrument, he cuts through much of the barrier separating outer from inner, extrinsic from intrinsic, in the handling of ideas. He does this by the simple trick of *picturing words as acts.*

Burke subtitles his book *Studies in Symbolic Action.* By doing this, he's trying to break through a massive schism in Western intellectual history—the schism which separates actions from thoughts, the externals of life from the internals. When they pictured ideas through the categories of extrinsic versus intrinsic, American historians were reflecting some of this action-thought dualism.

But Kenneth Burke rejects that kind of separation. To him there are "substantive" acts—that is, acts which involve people doing things. And there are "symbolic" acts—that is, acts which involve people thinking things. But both *are* acts to Burke—that is, they involve the whole human organism in motion. Contrary to the conventional action-thought dualism, he contends that the organism *is* acting when it's thinking, and it's acting manifestly when it's word-ing.[49]

Burke's point of departure, then, is neither of the two abstract categories "intrinsic" or "extrinsic," mind or environment. Rather, it's *the human self in motion, driven to order and express its experience through ideas and words.* He begins not by asking whether ideas are entities in themselves or products of environment. Instead, he starts with the existential self of persons, and he observes how that self encounters the world outside it. In short, he looks for a process not a thing. Thus "mind" and "environment" cease to be the more or less static entities of intrinsic and extrinsic, and both come alive, taking active roles in his dramatistic picture of experience.

Unlike the intrinsic critic of literature, Burke is not much interested in the idea or the word for itself. His concern rather is with what that idea or word suggests, what it points to, or connects with. At first glance, his procedure would appear extrinsic, for it strains outward from idea and word to what's beyond idea and word.

But where an extrinsic critic of ideas usually passes beyond them as a way of implying they aren't very important anyway, Burke reaches outside for entirely different reasons. His outward probes are not intended to locate what precisely out there "causes" ideas, but to find what it is in the world they're *responding to.*

Ordinarily, an extrinsic critic pauses with an idea only long enough to note its presence and perhaps its visible contours, then he passes on to the "really real" stuff of experience beyond.[50] But Kenneth Burke listens to ideas, and words, as carefully as does any intrinsic critic. This is not because he feels they're somehow autonomous, or have some kind of self-generating power. Rather, it's because he believes they offer a key to how people experience their world. To find that world, in its human dimensions, Burke insists we must go *through* idea and word. This is so because to him humans are the uniquely symbol-using species; they experience their world not directly, but through intervening filters set up by that distinctive trait of theirs—*language.* By working our way through the intricacies of how people use their words, Burke claims we're best able to reach their experience beyond words. In words, and in the ideas which words embody, are carried that dramatistic encounter between the inner self of perception and meaning and the outer world of stuff and things. Words are where we ought begin, then, when we set out to explore how people connect with the environment around them.

By separating thought from action, the conventional intrinsic versus extrinsic polarity sets the person off against himself. It relegates his ideas to one plane and his substantive experiences to another, then proceeds to argue which plane is more real. Burkean dramatism, though, sees man as acting even on his rhetorical plane and as expressive on his substantive one. So, by focusing on the drama of humans *in action,* it tends to collapse the polar extremes.

Or rather, by focusing on the drama of humans—through their words—in *inter-*action. For Kenneth Burke's is a dialogical model. This dialogic encounter is embodied, or takes place, in "situations," and the human word responses to those situations are "strategies." As his term *strategies* puts words into motion, his term *situations* shows us where to focus on these word movements. To compress all this into a phrase, we can say that *Burke's dialogical approach studies words in motion at the pressure points of their creation, in situations.*

"Every document bequeathed us by history," he claims, "must be treated as *a strategy for encompassing a situation.*"[51] To capsulize his model, a "strategy" is a "stylized symbolic act" for coping with a perceived "situation."[52]

And there we have it, our new method for inquiry. It's what I think can pull us free from the poles of the intrinsic-extrinsic dilemma, and can give us fresh ways of relating the historian to the environment around him. "Strategies" can make of ideas something more than a reflex action; it can also give them an energy which they lack in climate-of-opinion history. And "situations" can give us a focused arena for picturing where, and how, ideas confront the world of things and experience outside ideas.

These are our new terms—situation and strategy. What in fact may they show us? What leverage can such words give us to re-picture ideas, and to handle them differently? We might begin in our answer by taking the model of ideas developed from chapters 1 and 2 and applying these two terms to it. What comes out is a picture of human experience something like this:

Now and then people in cultures confront provoking "situations," when something in the world "out there" elicits a response from the mind "in here." Perhaps these people need to defeat some perceived enemy, or maybe build a highway, or express a political persuasion, or convey a love. By taking from historical tradition, from their culture's modes of identity, from their own experiences, associations, habits, references, moods, anticipations, and also taking from the situation itself, these people generate "strategies" for responding to those situations. Their strategies work more or less well in coping with these situations and in getting them out (or maybe not getting them out) of the dilemmas those situations present.

This process is historical, and takes place in time. Hence, it does not end with the first strategic response to the situation. For things in that situation often rebound on the responding strategies; usually, they alter them and sometimes cause unforeseen problems—for example how to govern the enemy you may have defeated, how to drive on a congested highway, or how to live with the politician you voted for or the lover you wooed. Consequences like this present further situations, which may occasion yet further strategic responses.

Thus we have an ongoing dialogic encounter between situation and strategy, through people. By seeing it *through* people, we carry the situation-strategy approach beyond the extrinsic interpretation of ideas. For we assume that people's perceptions play an active role in defining their situations. Mind does not merely "reflect" environment (as in climate of opinion); rather, it *engages* it. There may be urgencies in a historical situation, but there are few absolute necessities; there always seems to be more than just one way out. Hence people can use their power as symbol-creators, to re-form experience as it comes to them and transform things in their world (re our model from chapters 1 and 2).

But by picturing ideas in action and interaction, the situation-strategy approach moves past the intrinsic interpretation too. For it maintains that mind gets energized through contacting things outside it. The source of energy is not only in outside environment, but it's not only in mind either. Rather, it's *in the process of confrontation* between environment from one plane and mind from another. The planes do not lie inert, then, but continually encounter each other . . . in situations.

According to this strategic view, ideas are born under the stress of circumstance. *How* they respond to that stress is their own business, so to speak (that's where the intrinsic view still holds). But that they *must* respond, must connect their "in here" to environmental "out theres," is a basic tenet of the situation-strategy approach (and that's where the extrinsic view still holds).

X

These are some general outlines for the "situation-strategy" mode of analysis. Our next task is to see what we can do with it. We need now to make this model into a grounded strategy for handling historians and their explanation-forms. To do this, we might draw upon what we've already said of ideas in chapters 1 and 2, and of the "experience-explanation" strategy at the end of chapter 2. Much of situation-strategy is implicit there; we have only to add our new words now, and what was then a general *model* for inquiry (with experience-and-explanation) can become a working *method* (with situation-strategy). With that method, we can try and do the following in handling ideas:

1. First, we can redefine our basic unit, or process, of inquiry in intellectual history studies.   By picturing an idea as a "strategy," we give it energy and we put it into motion. That is, we make activity rather than repose its natural state. We also give it an inter-actional character, seeing it always in relation to something or other.

Thus we should look for ideas not at rest but in labor. Thus also our grammar for ideas might give off some of its more passive or inert "-ion" and "-ism" nouns—Puritanism, Transcendentalism, individualism—and develop more active verbs ending in "-ing." Like "symboling" and "minding."[53]

When one pictures intellectual history through the categories of intrinsic versus extrinsic, he may tend to ask, "Are ideas in the *mind,* or are they in the *world?*" And, "What *is* an idea?"

When we re-picture intellectual history through the situation-strategy method, we stop asking such questions. Instead, we see ideas as "in" neither mind nor world. And an idea is not an *is;* rather, it *does.* An idea is what happens when mind encounters world. And we look for it precisely at the point of encounter, in situations.[54]

2. We can also re-picture history, or intellectual history, as an ongoing series of problems or dilemmas which people must confront.   If one sees history as a sequence of events and thoughts which are already over with, then his task will be the retelling of what in fact happened. He'll strive for accuracy of detail most of all, and for getting the completed sequence straight.

But if we see history as an ongoing series of problematic situations, situations which provoke people's minds to respond, then we must do more than just tell what happened. We may also want to explore people's *perspectives* on these happenings (re chapter 2)—developing a sense of how men have tried to cope with the dynamic, kaleidoscopic world of their perceptions, and with the endless run of situations the world and their ideas have thrown up to their minds. We'll also want to know how their inherited pictures of reality have collided with events in the world, and just how those pictures have come out of each collision. We can't merely describe what happened, then; we've got to try and re-create people's pictures of experience at the time of happening. That is, we must not only show what *did* happen, we must also show *how people were seeing things as they were happening* (re Faulkner's strategy in *The Sound and the Fury*, or Miller's in *The New England Mind: From Colony to Province*). We're not after "thought," then, but rather "acts of mind-ing."

Thus, history, and especially the history of ideas, becomes not the story of finished things, but the analysis of problematic things. And we're not after ideas wholly as ideas—as "isms" or broad, floating "currents." Rather, we're after ideas coming hard up against the substance of things, in situations. By connecting these ideas back to their generating situations, and to other situations which they must confront through time, we concern ourselves not only with their logic, but their life history too. That's one reason to call ideas "strategies" here—to give them a living, experiential character.

Ideas are thus taken off the plane of givens in history, and are put into ongoing experience. We stop picturing them as complet*ions,* instead see them as people's efforts at complet*ing*—efforts which invariably fall short of their intent because, acting in history, ideas are never over with but always have a sequel. Hence the history of thought becomes for us a history of thinking. And we stop looking upon ideas as discrete unit entities, and begin to see them as *events*—mental events, as it were.

3. We can also look at the intrinsic-extrinsic dualism from a fresh perspective.   Some time back I mentioned that the situation-strategy approach collapses this dualism. That's not quite true. Rather, it attempts knocking off its polar extremes, and it tries to counter the "essentializing" tendencies those extremes have promoted.

Perhaps it's the dual functions of ideas which tempt us to explain them as one or the other, autonomous or instrumental. For ideas seem to play at least two contrary roles in people's experience. Humans, unlike other creatures, need not take their immediate environment as given. Instead, they can use ideas to imagine themselves beyond the here-and-now. Because of that, the intrinsic approach has some validity. People are not passive victims of the world around them; they may actively transcend that world. And they can do this through ideas. Clearly, then, their ideas give them some degree of self-generating power vis-à-vis environment.

But even in this act of transcending, people are still connected to their environment. They try to transcend certain kinds of things in their world, and they do it in certain ways. Environment seems to set at least minimal ground rules for people's responses to it.

The situation-strategy approach does not deny these opposing functions of ideas in human experience. In this sense, it acknowledges that intrinsic and extrinsic are still valid as hypothetical perspectives. But it's careful not to freeze these perspectives into essences, reifying them and making them things in themselves. It wants always to journey on past the analytic categories into people's experiences. Once there, it looks for ideas. Its point of focus is thus *ideas-in-experience*. And ideas in experience are what we're calling "strategies."

Situation-strategy analysis doesn't therefore collapse the whole dualism to the point where "mind" and "environment" melt into the same thing. The two remain different, but not as polarized essences. They're different rather as points of departure, temporary locations from which to look for things. And within the situation-strategy focus, what we're looking for is neither mind nor environment, but for ideas where they're at work, in situations.

This method of analysis further claims that when ideas impact in history they do so in specifics, in situations. Or at least that's where we find them. They may have started off elsewhere—maybe in the mind of some abstracted thinker, or perhaps they're products of certain structures in the polity or economy. But whatever their origins, they come to life in situations—in those public arenas where people bring their ideas to bear on the world around them, and where the world affects their ideas in turn (re Cotton Mather and his strategy for the witchcraft situation). It's *in situations* where ideas enter the life of history, and come to have living historical influence.

Through this situation-strategy approach, we thus redefine the intrinsic-extrinsic dualism not by moderating the extremes but by picturing the whole thing as a dialogic encounter. We can collapse the either-or of mind versus environment into a both/and, and we can look for the particular encounter of both mind and environment in historical situations.

4. *The "situation" can offer us a focus, a location, for inquiry in intellectual history-historiography studies.*   Ideas, as we've seen, can be vaporous things, hard to get a hold on. This is what makes focus—or how to get into your subject matter—a vexing problem for the student of ideas. As the field's guiding metaphor, "climate of opinion" is a case instance of how difficult it is to picture ideas and clearly focus in on them.[55]

Traditional narrative history, especially political history, has a built-in mode of focus. It points its story along the route of *events* as they pass through time. When the narrative historian wishes to gain depth on something, he simply pauses at one or another of these events and gives it a more thorough handling than the others. This also helps him emphasize the *unique* event, another characteristic preoccupation of the narrative technique.

But intellectual historians haven't had such a ready setup for them. However much ideas may in fact influence people's behavior, they don't seem to do it in any clearly structured fashion. That's one problem which must vex the student of ideas.

He's also concerned more with the *enduring theme* than with the unique event. These themes are not event-specific, but rather cross over several events spanning some length of time. Intellectual historians are usually after more general kinds of experience than their narrative colleagues.

This all makes for a dilemma of focus—how to handle these themes? Normally, intellectual historians have done it by downplaying the interplay of theme with event, and have tried managing ideas in other ways. One is the climate of opinion; we've already noted shortcomings in that. Another is simply to chart the theme as it's expressed by various individuals at different points in time. Yet another is to focus full on those individuals, through biographical portraits. But themes as such don't focus tightly and aren't easily manageable. Rooting them in individuals makes them easier to manage all right, but then they're more difficult to connect outward into history as public happening.

Take Parrington's *Main Currents*—say, his second volume on *The Romantic Revolution in America, 1800–1860*. This volume actually follows all three of the structures we've just mentioned. First, it's a model kind of climate of opinion history, with subsections organized around "The Mind of the South," "The Mind of the Middle East," and so on. Within these sections, it also charts themes—like "The Romance of the West," and "The Twilight of Federalism." And within these themes, Parrington's basic unit of focus is individuals—"John Taylor: Agrarian Economist," "Hugh Swinton Legare—Intellectual," "James Fenimore Cooper: Critic."

The book looks coherent, and its tight organizing structure may appear natural, unforced. But structurally, Parrington really has just two things going for him—an intuitive sense of his themes, and a number of individuals who more or less embody these themes. However, he lacks any method for connecting intellectual themes into the concrete experiences of history. That's because the structure of *Main Currents* keeps him from pausing long on any single event, or even on events in general. His themes thus float, uprooted. However much Parrington may quest for hard, substantial "reality"—praising thinkers who get there and damning those who don't—he's got no way of grounding his own analysis in such a reality. That is, his explanations don't move down into actual events, or into the interplay of theme, individual, social structure, and event.

That, I think, may be a key to why Parrington so often uses a "currents" metaphor for ideas. With nothing save his individual portraits to anchor ideas for him, he's forced back on broad-gauge thematic currents (realism, idealism, romanticism, democracy) to hold things in focus. But by doing this, he can't confront directly that substantial reality which he fervently wants to recapture.

One can make a similar (if more muted) comment about other major American histories of ideas—works like Richard Hofstadter's *Social Darwinism in American Thought,* or R. W. B. Lewis' *The American Adam,* or Louis Hartz's *The Liberal Tradition in America.* To be sure, these studies are not as compelled by "reality" as is Parrington. And there's much more subtle analysis of ideas in their work. But if there's subtlety of analysis, there's not much of public happening, at least not of happenings grounded in time and place, and responding directly to things in the world.

This doesn't make them bad histories. It simply leaves unsolved the question of how to focus with ideas. And when one is trying to show how ideas have had impact in history, this "currents-individuals" form has serious structural deficiencies.

That's where the "situational" focus can help. It offers a sort of halfway house between narrative history's grounded structure around events and intellectual history's less grounded structure around themes.

By using the situation as his base for focus, the student of ideas has a particular scene on which to fix his attention. It's an arena wherein he can root his subject matter in time and in place, and can watch carefully how it behaves. He may still be concerned with general, enduring themes. However, he sees them not merely in broad abstraction, but as they're refracted through unique and particular circumstances. Again, recall Cotton Mather and the witchcraft incident. Mather used a general theme there—the idea of national covenant. But he used it to cope with a particular event—witchcraft in Salem in 1692. What's significant in this situation (in Perry Miller's analysis of it anyway) is the *interplay* of theme and event, not either in isolation.

What a picture does for the visual eye, then, a situation can do for the intellectual eye. It offers the intellectual historian a way of getting at particulars, and of maybe catching subtleties in the experience of an idea which otherwise could get by the more broad-gauge thematic approach. By being grounded in situations, this kind of analysis can retain the sense of detail, of accident and circumstance and contingency, and of dramatic and ongoing action which characterize narrative event focus. But by its concern for strategic responses to those situations, it can also protect the analytic rigor and the philosophical depth of thematic focus. At least situation-strategy sets up a *structure* for doing this. It doesn't guarantee that it will all be done. That task is still up to the individual student of ideas, and how he manages his own particular talents.[56]

5. *Through the term "situation," we can also contextualize "environment," specifying more clearly its influence.*   In the intrinsic-extrinsic debate, one bottleneck was that environment came to be pictured as a more or

less monolithic thing, a wholly "out there" kind of reality. By definition, it tended to exclude ideas or symbols, which were supposed to reside "in here."

But situation-strategy analysis works against this block-environment assumption. It tries to de-homogenize environment by picturing the general "out there" through the eyes of particular "in heres." Its focus is not on environment as a whole (by implication, questioning whether "whole environment" is a workable construct); instead, it's on more particular slices of environment, on individuals' (or collectives') selective perceptions of it. A situation is not how environment *is*, it's mostly how people *see* it. In the language of chapter 2, it's a particular "perspectivistic" reality, not a holistic "objective" reality.

In thus perspectivizing environment, the situation-strategy approach contends the outer world works on people not holistically, but through intermediate references. To understand those references and how they'll impact, we must also understand where people let them in. And one place they let them in is through ideas, which serve as channels by which people communicate with the world outside them.[57]

"Strategies" gets beyond the environmental reductionism of the extrinsic approach by including ideas as *part of* the situation. Mind in a situation doesn't "reflect" the outer world, it *refracts* it, or part of it. That is, mind is not a mirror which sends back the world just as it comes to it. It's a *spectrum* which selects out part of the world, runs that part through its own inner structures, then sends it out altered from how it came in. In using the situation-strategy aproach, we must understand enough of conditions in the external environment to know just *what* mind is responding to. But we must also understand enough of mind's inner makeup to see just *how* it forms its own distinctive response. That's why neither of the polar approaches, extrinsic or intrinsic, will do by itself. Both are needed.

There's much yet to be done in clarifying what a situation may consist of and what opportunities might open for us through this alternative point of focus. But surely one immediate opportunity is to enrich our conventional sense of an "event" in history; and we can do this by the simple device of adding ideas and perspectives to it. By thus re-picturing external historical events to make them perspectivistic "situations," we could lay out whole new areas for inquiry in American historical scholarship. Every event which has conventionally been handled in chronological narrative, and every idea which we've normally handled through thematic analysis, might now be made available for a kind of merger in situation-strategy analysis.

Why not, say, explore Jefferson's "machine-garden" tension not only in passages of the *Notes on Virginia*? (as Leo Marx has done superbly) Why not also take those passages as a key to Jefferson's divided mind in public action? Look at his ironic strategies as president in the situation of the Louisiana Purchase or the Embargo. There we'd be exploring not only "mind," but mind as it acts in history and affects things around it.

Or we might look for "the Jacksonian persuasion" not only in the words of the Bank Veto (which Marvin Meyers has done superbly). We might also look for it in the strategic actions of Jackson as president in and around that veto. See how role and interpersonal transactions (e.g., Jackson's personal animosity toward Biddle) and other such influences in his immediate "situation" set up conditions to which that persuasion was a strategic response.

The opportunities are endless. To exploit them, we have only to confront theme with event—through the situation-strategy approach. In doing that, we might get to complexities in the career of an idea, and in the behavior of people through ideas, that we've not adequately handled before.[58]

XI

To recapitulate: The three methods proposed in this chapter—(1) the "paradigm-community" model of school, (2) the concept of "pivotal moments," and (3) "situation-strategy" analysis—are all *strategies for focus* in handling ideas. They're efforts to *ground* inquiry into historical explanation-forms, in contrast to the floating "climate-of-opinion" model.

Each takes us below the planes of description and analysis—our procedure in chapter 4—down to *methodic* and *explanatory* concerns. Their intent is not only that we observe ideas and take note of what they look like. Their intent rather is to provide instruments for the *doing* of people's mind-forms—for getting inside an idea to see how it's put together, how and when it may change, and how it connects to things around it.

The first strategy above—paradigm communities—offers a sociological grounding for the study of ideas. It asks of explanation-forms, "Who believed them?" "How did they get socialized into them?" "Who were their associates?" and "Through what social institutions did these associates communicate with each other?"

The second strategy—pivotal moments—offers a time-place grounding for the study of ideas. Or in this case, for the study of idea change. It asks of an explanation-form, "Where are its most vulnerable points, and when precisely is it liable to give up its established patterns under pressure?" It's a method for entering the inner workings of an idea in transition, for handling the *dis*-order of an idea, as it were.

The third strategy—situation-strategy analysis—gives a time-place grounding for the study of ideas too. But it also—through the "strategy" model—tries to suggest what ideas are and do for people. It asks first of an explanation-form not "What does it say?," but "Who said it?" "Where?" "When?" "How?" And, most important, "In response to what?" In effect, it wants to know, "What situation does the person see himself in when he says that?" Or, in Kenneth Burke's terms, "What is his *burden?*"[59]

Situation-strategy is a way not only of tracing intellectual themes over time, but of offering explanation to historical events. It asks of a historical idea, "What was the original situation out of which it grew, and through what situations was it altered?" It contends that historical ideas don't just grow out of other ideas, nor do they just reflect circumstances around them; instead, they come from precise moments of confrontation between idea and circumstance.

"Strategy" says ideas are not mirrors of the world, but efforts to maneuver it. And these efforts depend on how that world is perceived. Which perception is embodied in the term "situation," where the world is seen from the inside out—through people's experiential perspectives. In contrast to the climate-of-opinion approach, which looks at ideas from the location of environment, this approach imposes a kind of intervening variable between mind and environment, and that variable is the situation.

With these latter two methods—pivotal-moment analysis and situation-strategy analysis—we're trying to give *motion* and *location* to the model of ideas we set up in the earlier chapters.

Pivotal-moment analysis is intended as the major new strategy of this chapter, and maybe of the entire book. Without it, we'd lack substantive focus for our case studies to follow. And it's there where our strongest claim is made for a new territory in American historical scholarship.

With pivotal-moment analysis, we can put a microscope up to the picture of ideas we drew back in chapters 1 and 2. This strategy says we can best get into ideas at particular times, and we can most clearly see them in response to particular things. If we simply add "moments" to what we've said of ideas and of experience-explanation in the opening two chapters, we pretty much have our situation-strategy method.

And that method should be the next major contribution of this chapter. It, "perspectives," "experience-and-explanation," and "pivotal-moment" analysis are the four main "strategies for inquiry" offered in this book. They're the basic devices for grounding our own inquiries in the territory—"explanation in historical studies."

As the model of ideas from chapters 1 and 2 indicates what our subject matter is, situation-strategy offers clues for how we might get into it. It tells us where we can enter this dialogue-encounter between mind and world, explanation and experience, and how we might picture that interchange.

While pivotal-moment analysis grounds "climate of opinion" by specifying a *location* for ideas, situation-strategy analysis taps *energy* into the whole model. Climate of opinion sees the encounter between mind and environment in more or less stimulus-response fashion; environment takes the initiative, and mind simply follows along. But situation-strategy pictures it all *dramatistically*—both sides bring some energy to the encounter, but the real driving power comes from how (and when) the two confront each other. A strategy, then, is an explanation of one's experienced situation.

Finally, all these terms—explanation, perspectives, paradigm, paradigm strain, pivotal moment, critical threshold, situation, strategy—give us a *language* for use in American historiography studies. And with language we gain leverage to get things done.

All are focusing devices for getting at particulars, and for countering the dilemma of information overload in American historical scholarship. They set the forms for the remainder of this book.

From now on, we'll not be offering a narrative coverage of historians' explanation-forms in twentieth-century America; rather, we'll center in on a few intensified historical experiences for explanation. We'll look closely at selected moments in American intellectual history studies when something seems to be happening in an explanation-form—when it's being formed, under strain, altered, or dying. If there's any chronological thread holding these case studies together, it's wound around those moments. By this "moment" focus, we'll doubtless lose something in narrative continuity. But perhaps we'll gain some of it back in substantive grounding, and in control over our materials. At least that's the intent.

All of which readies us now to move on into the explanation-forms, and to watch how they behave. Or almost. . . . We need to add what we've said of books in chapter 3 to what we've said of idea-forms in this chapter, so we can develop some controlled strategies for analyzing a text. With such strategies, we should then be suitably prepared to go on in to the case studies.

NOTES

1. In his *A Behavioral Approach to Historical Analysis* (Free Press, 1969), Robert Berkhofer makes a suggestive beginning to this approach to group forms in history studies. See his chapter 4—"A Basic Orientation to Group Behavior"—which deals with criteria of membership in groups, group patternings, cultural uniformities, subcultural variations, and so on.

2. John Higham, "The Cult of the American Consensus: Homogenizing Our History," *Commentary* (February 1959), pp. 93–100. Reprinted in Richard Abrams and Lawrence Levine, eds., *The Shaping of Twentieth-Century America: Interpretive Articles* (Little, Brown, paperback, 1965), pp. 672–82. The quote is taken from the Little, Brown edition, p. 674.

3. See Higham, ibid., and "Beyond Consensus: The Historian as Moral Critic," *The American Historical Review* (April 1962), pp. 609–25; J. Rogers Hollingsworth, "Consensus and Continuity in Recent American Historical Writing," *South Atlantic Quarterly* (Winter 1961), pp. 40–50; and Dwight Hoover, "Some Comments on Recent United States Historiography," *American Quarterly* (Summer 1965), pp. 299–318.

4. Hoover, ibid., pp. 299–300.

5. One basic reason for the low stature of historiography should be obvious, though. To most in the profession, historiography studies are an avocation, not to be taken seriously as primary research. They're normally something to be done for release now and then. Thus they're not held to the same rigorous standards as is "real" history work.

6. See Becker's chapter "Climates of Opinion," *The Heavenly City of the Eighteenth Century Philosophers* (Yale University Press, paperback, 1959—first published in 1932 by Yale), pp. 1–31.

7. I shouldn't imply that climate-of-opinion studies need necessarily be vague and abstract. Certainly, Carl Becker didn't go after ideas in such generalized fashion. And his sensitivity to the details of word usage is exactly the kind of corrective I think historiography study needs now. See especially Becker's chapters on "Drafting the Declara-

tion" and "The Literary Qualities of the Declaration of Independence," *The Declaration of Independence: A Study in the History of Political Ideas* (Random House, Vintage Book, 1958—first published in 1922), pp. 135–93, 194–223.

8. T. W. Adorno et al., *The Authoritarian Personality* (Harper, 1950), p. 747.

9. M. Brewster Smith, Jerome S. Bruner, and Robert W. White, *Opinions and Personality* (Wiley, 1964—first published in 1956 by Wiley), p. 39.

10. See, for example, Robert Lane, *Political Ideology: Why the American Common Man Believes What He Does* (Free Press, 1961), and Milton Rokeach et al., *The Open and Closed Mind: Investigations into the Nature of Belief Systems and Personality Systems* (Basic Books, 1960).

11. There are exceptions, of course. For example, Burleigh Taylor Wilkins' fine study of Carl Becker and the immediate personal environments affecting him, *Carl Becker: A Biographical Study in American Intellectual History* (MIT, 1961). Or Richard Hofstadter's masterful study, *The Progressive Historians: Turner, Beard, Parrington* (Knopf, 1968). Or Edmund Morgan's "Perry Miller and the Historians," *Harvard Review*, 2, no. 2 (Winter-Spring 1964), 52–59. Or the fine essays in Marcus Cunliffe and Robin Winks, eds., *Pastmasters: Some Essays on American Historians* (Harper and Row, 1969).

12. *The Genius of American Politics* (University of Chicago Press, Phoenix Paperback, 1959), p. 186.

13. *The Structure of Scientific Revolutions* (University of Chicago Press, paperback, 1970), p. 109.

14. Ibid., p. 180.

15. Kuhn's study is intended as a *suggestive* picture of how networks of communication function in a scholarly subculture. For a more detailed, analytic study of a single community in action, see Warren Hagstrom, *The Scientific Community* (Basic Books, 1965). Historians who would like to do future such studies in their own field might well profit from Hagstrom's model. The best we have to date along such a line is Hofstadter's *The Progressive Historians;* however rich are Hofstadter's insights on individual thinkers, he's not done much to aid us plot out sociological lines of communication within this Progressive subculture. Hagstrom might help.

16. Kuhn, *Structure* (n. 13 above), p. 5.

17. Ibid., pp. 24–25. For a further refinement on Kuhn's position here, see his essay "Logic of Discovery or Psychology of Research?" in Imre Lakatos and Alan Musgrave, eds., *Criticism and the Growth of Knowledge* (Cambridge University Press, paperback, 1970), pp. 1–23.

18. *Structure*, p. xi.

19. Ibid., p. 65.

20. This, incidentally, is just about what Lee Benson has tried to do with the label "economic interpretation of history." It's a label which tended to accompany Progressive historical explanations, but not very self-consciously. Benson tries to lay bare some assumptions behind the economic explanation of experience, has put these assumptions together into a logical model, and has suggested alternative models for explaining the same experiences. In his work, and in Richard Hofstadter's *The Progressive Historians,* we can find a closely reasoned dialogue between Progressive and counter-Progressive versions of reality, a dialogue carried through clearly defined terms which connect back directly to particular experiences in history. Benson and Hofstadter might serve as models of what I'm urging of historians in this part of the chapter. For Benson, see especially his "Outline for a Theory of American Voting Behavior," in *The Concept of Jacksonian Democracy: New York as a Test Case* (Atheneum, paperback, 1964—first published in 1961 by Princeton), pp. 270–87. See also his *Turner and Beard: American Historical Writing Reconsidered* (Free Press, paperback, 1965—first published in 1960 by the Free Press). For Hofstadter, see *The Progressive Historians* (n. 11 above), especially his concluding chapter on "Conflict and Consensus in American History."

21. We shouldn't therefore throw out too much in objecting to climate of opinion here. The concept still has some value, if applied in the right places. The larger culture does of course influence all communities of scholars, some more directly than others. In this case, it would seem to affect historians more directly than most natural scientists. And the metaphor "climate of opinion" may still be of some value for picturing how.

22. *Structure,* (n. 13 above), p. 85.

23. For Kuhn's analysis of a scientific community under strain and in revolution, see especially his chapters on "Anomaly and the Emergence of Scientific Discoveries," "Crisis and the Emergence of Scientific Theories," "The Response to Crisis," "The Nature and Necessity of Scientific Revolutions," and "Revolutions as Changes of World View" (Ibid., pp. 52–135).

24. I am not faulting Thomas Kuhn here. What he has done in those 172 pages of text is remarkable. But he was working there under space limitations imposed by the *Encyclopedia of Unified Science*—which, he says, caused him "to present my views in an extremely condensed and schematic form." "This work," he writes, "remains an essay rather than the full-scale book my subject will ultimately demand" (ibid., p. viii). In a book written prior to *The Structure of Scientific Revolutions,* Kuhn did analyze a single revolution in considerable detail, but that was before he had his full model worked out. See *The Copernican Revolution: Planetary Astronomy in the Development of Western Thought* (Random House, Vintage Book, 1959—first published by Harvard in 1957).

25. *Main Currents in American Thought,* vol. 3, *The Beginnings of Critical Realism in America: 1860–1920* (Harcourt, Brace and World, Harbinger Book, 1958—first published by Harcourt in 1930), pp. 106, 103.

26. *The Contours of American History* (Quadrangle, paperback, 1966—first published in 1961 by World), p. 201.

27. *History: Humanistic Scholarship in America* (Prentice-Hall, 1965), pp. 198–212.

28. For more on how Perry Miller confounds the normal labels of historians, see chapter 9, section VIII.

29. For a comprehensive review of Miller's critics, see Michael McGiffert's splendid article, "American Puritan Studies in the 1960's," *William and Mary Quarterly,* 3rd ser. XVII, no. 1 (January 1970), 36–67. See also the penetrating study by Richard Reinitz, "Perry Miller's Irony: The Convergence of Intellectual and Social Histories of American Puritanism" (expanded version of a paper read at the American Historical Association convention, Washington, D.C., 1969). Karen Lystra is presently engaged in a book-length study of modes of thought used by Miller's critics.

30. *The New England Mind: The Seventeenth Century* (Beacon, paperback, 1961—first edition published in 1939 by Macmillan), p. vii.

31. Ibid., pp. 463–91.

32. For further on this view of change, see sections XI and XII of chapter 9.

33. *The New England Mind: From Colony to Province* (Beacon, paperback, 1961—first published by Harvard in 1953), p. 200.

34. Ibid., p. 201.

35. Ibid.

36. Ibid.

37. Ibid., p. 202.

38. Ibid.

39. Ibid., p. 203.

40. Ibid.

41. Ibid., p. 204.

42. Ibid., p. 207.

43. Ibid., p. 200.

44. See also the Miller part of chapter 9.

45. Robert Skotheim, ed., *The Historian and the Climate of Opinion* (Addison-Wesley, paperback, 1969), p. 2.

46. It's a tribute to Robert Skotheim's generosity of mind that he will characteristically raise the most serious questions of his own position. When I first began working with this Burkean approach a few years back, I'd not thought about it much as an alternative to climate of opinion. Skotheim, however, saw the connection immediately, noted further that the one is a passive model and the other more active, and encouraged me to develop the latter as an advance over climate of opinion. What follows owes much to conversations and correspondence with him. If on occasion I've criticized Skotheim's position in developing my own (or rather, my variant of Burke's), it's with

the utmost respect—amounting almost to awe—for a scholar who not only tolerates such criticism, but invariably seeks it out and helps give it shape.

47. See, for example, Arthur O. Lovejoy, *Essays in the History of Ideas* (Capricorn Book, 1960), and R. G. Collingwood, *The Idea of History* (Oxford, Galaxy Book, 1956).

48. See especially here Burke's title essay, "The Philosophy of Literary Form," *The Philosophy of Literary Form: Studies in Symbolic Action* (Knopf, Vintage Book, 1957 —first published in 1941 by Louisiana State), pp. 3–117. For a brilliant, comprehensive analysis of Burke's whole way of looking at the literary experience, and its connections to life outside, see William Rueckert, *Kenneth Burke and the Drama of Human Relations* (University of Minnesota Press, 1963).

49. Burke's position, it should be plain, closely resembles the "cognitive" scholarship we discussed in chapter 2.

50. See for example Skotheim's comment on Charles Beard "sketch [ing] ideas on the run, so to speak, rather than [settling] down with them in detailed analysis." *American Intellectual Histories and Historians* (Princeton University Press, 1966), p. 109.

51. *Philosophy of Literary Form* (n. 48 above), p. 93—italics in original.

52. Ibid. p. 111.

53. The term "symbolizing" is used in Leslie White's *The Science of Culture* (Evergreen, paperback, n.d.—first published in 1949 by Farrar, Straus and Cudahy). See especially White's first two chapters—"Science as *Sciencing*," and "The Symbol: the Origin and Basis of Human Behavior."

54. This picture of ideas resembles what Rush Welter ("The History of Ideas in America: An Essay in Redefinition," *Journal of American History*, LI, no. 4 [March 1965], 599–614) proposed in the historians' intrinsic-extrinsic controversy. Using Burke, I've called ideas "strategies"; using John Dewey, Welter called them "transactions." Beyond this, the differences seem to be minimal. Thus, Welter, unlike most historians in that controversy, did in fact construct an alternative to the polar opposites of intrinsic versus extrinsic. Where he pulled up short, I think, was in not grounding his transactional ideas *in history*. He didn't give them time and place, or show how they could be connected into events. That's where Burke's term "situations" adds something. It gives a location to ideas, a place to look for them, and to check out what they're responding to in the world. See especially pp. 607–14 of Welter's essay.

55. In his opening paragraph of *American Intellectual Histories and Historians,* Robert Skotheim quotes William Hesseltine, "Writing intellectual history is like trying to nail jelly to the wall" (p. 3).

56. The best working out of this I know of is Perry Miller's second volume of *The New England Mind*. Earlier, we used this volume to illustrate "pivotal moment" analysis. We might change the language some and make it a model of "situation-strategy" analysis also. Miller's whole book is structured around a succession of cultural situations, and people's strategic responses to them, through mind. It has the advantages of both narrative and thematic history. It's an example of how situation-strategy history might be written. For more on this, see the Miller sections of chapter 9.

57. Because of its emphasis on *modes of perception*—how people picture things— the strategic approach should encourage us to connect out across the boundaries of history into areas like cognitive psychology and the sociology of knowledge. It thus provides a channel for the "cognitive" scholarship on ideas we noted in chapter 2.

58. Of course, the situation-strategy model need not be restricted to just intellectual history. In a remarkably suggestive study, Robert Berkhofer shows how a situational grounding might help us refocus our studies of historical behavior. See *A Behavioral Approach to Historical Analysis* (n. 1 above), pp. 32–73. Berkhofer's behavioral agenda for the analysis of historical situations (p. 73) is almost precisely what Perry Miller carries out in *The New England Mind: From Colony to Province*.

59. *Philosophy of Literary Form* (n. 48 above), p. 16.

6 Historical Criticism and "The Strategic Journey"

It is in trying to decipher the semantics of utterances detached from their behavioral contexts that students of meaning have gone astray. Instead of asking what a statement, considered as an objective entity, means, we might better ask what this individual means (or intends) when he says thus-and-so, *and* what this statement uttered by so-and-so means to this listener. It is obvious that we have removed meaning from the level of the word to that of the utterance. Words do not have meanings, but functions.

> Joseph Church
> *Language and the Discovery*
> *of Reality**

Misplaced literalism makes a shambles of intellectual history.

> Jacques Barzun and Henry Graff
> *The Modern Researcher*

Some critics have quarreled with me about my selection of the word "strategy" as the name for this process. I have asked them to suggest an alternative term, so far without profit. The only one I can think of is "method." But if "strategy" errs in suggesting to some people an overly *conscious* procedure, "method" errs in suggesting an overly *"methodical"* one. Anyhow, let's look at the documents. . . .

> Kenneth Burke
> *The Philosophy of Literary Form*

Thus far, we've contended that the profession needs a subfield devoted to "explanation in historical studies," and we've sketched in parts of such a field. We suggested that it could use an anthropology of ideas (a "symbolic"), and we outlined a functional model for that in the opening two chapters. We also said this field needs some different strategies for handling ideas, and in chapters 4 and 5 (especially 5) we laid out a few possible ones. Further, we noted barriers in the profession which have inhibited such a field to date; and in chapter 3, when making a case for the "primary" consideration of "secondary" documents, we proposed ways around and through those barriers.

*Vintage Paperback, 1966; originally published 1961 by Random House.

What we need now is a device for bringing these several concerns to focus. Or rather, we need a *location* for bringing them to focus—an arena wherein we can control our inquiries into grounded ideas, and observe them behaving in response to things around them. That arena will be *the historical text*.

When we're working on "explanation in historical studies," the actual writings of historians should serve as our basic primary sources. It is there where we can control our investigations into the dialogue-encounter of explanation with experience and where we can chart changes in historians' idea-forms. The text should be our first location for watching the historian's mind in action, and it should be our last location for checking out interpretations of that mind. Between these opening and closing points of inquiry, we may wish to connect out elsewhere to locate influences upon mind—to the historian's life, his times, his professional community, and so on. But it's finally in the text itself where we can spot how those influences affect a historian's actual mind-work. The historical text should be our beginning point for inquiry in this field, and it should be our ending point.

In chapter 3, we suggested that historians have normally been so preoccupied with what they designate "primary" documents—getting to the facts *out there*—that they haven't been concerned much with how those facts get formed *in here*. We also suggested that historians haven't reflected much on their own "secondary" medium of expression—books and articles, and words within books and articles.

This shortcoming parallels what we saw with ideas in chapters 1 and 2. There we said historians have been preoccupied with the substantive *content* of ideas, largely ignoring their structure, function, and processes. The same holds true of historians and their documentary sources, primary as well as secondary. Historians have been preoccupied with the face-value content of documents, but they've shown little concern for how those documents are structured, what functions they perform, or what their strategic processes are.

This is not such a problem when historians are working on the "objective" plane of reality—which in chapter 2 we said included dates and names and things and statistics and such. There the concern is to establish publicly observable things and experiences in the world, and the conventional historians' procedure is well suited to do just that.

But such a procedure does become a problem when it handles evidence on the "perspectivistic" plane of historical reality—not the facts in the world "out there," but, as we noted in chapter 2, the world out there as filtered through particular experiences "in here." When historians use their conventional face-value procedure for such perspectivistic evidence, they impose a detached "objectivist" model on materials which are inherently subjective and situationally constructed.

To do the kind of historiography-intellectual history studies we want to do in this book, we need an alternative procedure for handling alternative kinds of evidence. For an instance of where this procedural dysjunction can put a strain on historical scholarship, and for a suggested alternative which might get us out of the dysjunction, let us now look into Darrett Rutman's book, *Winthrop's Boston.*

II

Winthrop's Boston is, as Rutman subtitles it, a *Portrait of a Puritan Town* during the years between the landing in 1630 and John Winthrop's death in 1649. The substance of this portrait is carried by a rich fund of "objective" information—on the structure of town government, on land dispersal, on church organization and membership, and other such details of social and political history in seventeenth-century Massachusetts Bay. Rutman has gone to much effort in collecting this information, and he has carefully controlled it for accuracy. It is hard to fault his procedure on the level of objective fact.

But if the substance of *Winthrop's Boston* is rendered from an almost "ideal historical-observer" position, its structure—also its effort at conscious drama—is built upon an objectivist reading of a "perspectivistic" historical document.[1] "The story," writes Rutman, "is cast in the form of a tragedy, the steady decline of what are discerned as Winthropian ideals and their eventual defeat in the light of the developments in the town and to a lesser extent the commonwealth."[2]

Tragedy, then, is the *pattern* which Darrett Rutman sets upon his facts. That pattern comes from his reading of John Winthrop's lay sermon, "A Modell of Christian Charity"—delivered in 1630 to the Puritan migrants on their passage over. From that sermon, Rutman constructs Winthrop's ideal hope for the colony; and from this base point he measures tragic decline in the two decades which follow. The fact of decline is substantiated by his objective data, but the pattern of decline comes from his perspectivistic data. Only Rutman doesn't interpret that data as perspectivistic. And therein lies a strain on his explanation.

Rutman sets out Winthrop's ideal in his opening chapter—"A Citty upon a Hill." He writes there,

The mind of one man at one place and time is clear to us . . . : that of John Winthrop. . . . En route across the Atlantic on the *Arbella,* the flagship of the 1630 migration—poised, as it were, between two worlds—Winthrop prepared a lay sermon, "A Modell of Christian Charity," which he delivered to his fellow passengers. In one phrase of the preoration he summed up his thought: "We shall be as a Citty upon a Hill."

Rutman continues, locating the central theme of Winthrop's sermon:

It would be a city . . . in the sense of a "City of God." Man would serve God here in all the ways that God demanded that He be served. . . . Men would serve their fellow men in this city as God would have them serve; men would fit into a society of men in such a way that the society would redound to God's credit, add luster to His crown.[3]

According to Rutman, Winthrop's ideal New World society was to be just the opposite of what he'd experienced in old England. Though not personally oppressed by conditions in England, Winthrop had been affronted by the moral disintegration around him, and he had emigrated mostly because of that. He hoped New England would become everything old England was not. "He dreamed of a better society," says Rutman, "and sought the New World to make it a reality. The 'Modell of Christian Charity' was his exposition of the nature of the new society he wished to establish in New England."[4]

That new society would be religious first of all, and would allow no other ideals to intervene between men and their God. It would also be a wholly integrated social order, with a deep sense of communal obligation one man for another. And it would gain energy and direction through being committed to a covenant between man and God; from this covenant, men could transcend the preoccupations of self and take on loftier responsibilities in the world.

But, says Rutman, Winthrop's ideal society was never to be realized—not in the colony generally, and not, certainly, in Boston. Rutman drives that point home in his closing chapter—"The City by the Water" (which is set off in dramatic contrast to his opening chapter, "A Citty upon a Hill"). Where, in 1630, Winthrop had envisioned an integrated godly community, by 1649 Boston had become a bustling commercial society. Business, not religion, was its main preoccupation, and in that pursuit self was not subordinated to community, but instead threatened to disintegrate it. Land was also dispersed so that private interests tended to dominate communal obligations, and Boston gained its identity not from being a covenanted city but from being a thriving international seaport. "In Winthrop's Boston," Rutman comments, "the ideal of the medieval community was transformed into the reality of modern society."[5]

Thus Darrett Rutman's "tragic" patterning of the facts in Massachusetts Bay. If there is to be tragedy in historical experience, however, there must be a tragic *perceiver,* someone who sees and feels it that way. Thus on the next to last page in his closing chapter, Rutman returns to the theme of his opening pages to ask, "And what of Winthrop? . . . did he sense the crumbling ideal which was all about him in Boston?"[6]

It's essential that John Winthrop *does* lament the disintegration of his ideal, else this story is not tragedy but simply change. So Rutman imagines what Winthrop must have felt near the end of his life:

Did he sometime during his last years stroll down to Town Dock on an evening constitutional and look outward, past the ships in the harbor, toward the Atlantic and the islands and ports around its rim—London, Tenerife, the unnamed rivers flowing into Africa's Bight of Benin, Antigua, and Barbados? Did he gaze across the harbor to Rumney Marsh with its rich farms and pastures?

"The farms and shipping lanes meant prosperity for Boston," says Rutman, "but by virtue of their temptation to men, his own failures as well. Home from his walk, did he sit among the books and carpenter tools of his study and wonder what his Boston had become, and would become?"

"Perhaps," Rutman continues. "At times there is a hint of disappointment in his writings, when he speaks of the wickedness among the settlers, or of too much self-love, or recounts the arguments in town, church, and commonwealth."[7] But Darrett Rutman respects his facts too much to hazard speculation beyond this. Lacking documentary evidence for Winthrop's disappointment, Rutman admits that "he never bewailed the whole as others were beginning to, never wrote of total failure."[8]

Which means that Rutman has thereby removed the tragic perceiver from his tragic pattern. For if John Winthrop doesn't sense this change as tragic, no one else in *Winthrop's Boston* can. So the book's closing words are set in strange contrast to its earlier organizing pattern. In these words, Rutman has Winthrop experience the change in New England not as tragic, but as simply the way God must have willed it:

One suspects that he was not fully aware of the extent of the failure, for he was never called upon to surrender all of the ideal all at once, only constantly required to surrender one small part of the whole in the interest of another part. In the end, he was more than likely content. If man had not come up to the optimistic expectations of the "Modell of Christian Charity," it was God's will. Having done his best with what his Lord had given him, Winthrop would turn to his Bible and find "comfort in God, and delight in heavenly things."[9]

III

Characteristically in *Winthrop's Boston,* Darrett Rutman will set the objective facts of the world up against John Winthrop's early vision for the colony, then claim that the one doesn't measure up to the other. And he constructs his pattern for this history—tragedy—from the apparent dysjunction between ideal and reality. Such a tragic patterning seems to hold throughout the book—until the last paragraph, that is, where Rutman admits he has little evidence for Winthrop's being disappointed in the outcome.

That admission puts a strain on the whole book—if not on its objective facts, then certainly on its tragic patterning of those facts. For if these events weren't tragic to Winthrop as he experienced them, was there indeed such a wide gap between his felt ideal and the actual facts of Boston? From this remove, we can hardly question the facts; Rutman has gathered them with care, and he shows time and again that Winthrop was aware of them. So we're led to question the ideal—*did John Winthrop wholly mean what he said in his 1630 sermon, "A Modell of Christian Charity"?*

We don't have to *know* what Winthrop actually meant to challenge Rutman's explanation. We just have to make that meaning *problematic,* rather than take it as given in the nature of his words. We can then thread our questions about those words back through *Winthrop's Boston,* aiming them at points where there seems to be a strain in Rutman's logic of explanation.

We've already found one point of strain—Rutman's last paragraph, where he admits that Winthrop was not alarmed by what was happening to his ideal. Recall he has Winthrop affirm there, "If man had not come up to the optimistic expectation of the 'Modell of Christian Charity,' it was God's will."[10]

But if Winthrop was characteristically so passive before God's will in such matters, why did he ever leave England in the first place? One might, of course, answer that he left there with ideals in mind, but that as he became prosperous and powerful in New England, he gradually sold out those ideals in the face of a beneficial reality. But, as Rutman notes, John Winthrop was prosperous and important in England too, and he had to give up much when emigrating to an uncertain New World situation. Even if we were to assume that Winthrop did sell out for power, then he couldn't have been entirely sincere in his "Modell" sermon, and thus Rutman's tragic explanation would be rendered suspect.

So Rutman's closing paragraph puts several strains on his pattern for interpreting the evidence. If one takes the tragic explanation, then he is confounded by the lack of evidence for it in Winthrop's life. If one takes the passive-acceptance-of-God's-will explanation, then he is hard put to account for why Winthrop ever pulled up stakes and left England. If one takes the sell-out-for-power-and-wealth explanation, then he must give up much of the contrary tragic explanation, and he must also explain why Winthrop abandoned his relatively sure status in England for an unsure one in the New World. Whatever explanation one uses here, it stumbles over certain evidence in Rutman's book, and it contradicts some other explanation used elsewhere in the study.

There is an additional point of strain early in *Winthrop's Boston,* where Rutman writes, "Winthrop's optimism that man could overcome his own nature—so illogical in view of his apparent Calvinism—was to prove sadly misplaced."[11] But to whom was this sad? To John Winthrop? Rutman later says not so. Then was Winthrop ever as optimistic as Rutman's reading of his ideal would suggest? Was "A Modell of Christian Charity" an "illogical" departure from his apparent Calvinism, or not?

We can't know for sure, at least not if we stick with our own "primary document" here—*Winthrop's Boston.* But we can take the evidence Rutman gives us in his book, and suggest an alternative patterning for it. We can do this by questioning how Darrett Rutman reads a historical document. All of the book's explanation strains, I think, come from *its tendency to take Winthrop's words at face value, and not question them beyond their surface meaning.*

Rutman assumes that "A Modell of Christian Charity" embodies the full meaning of John Winthrop's expectations for the colony. He not only assumes it as the *full* meaning of Winthrop's mind, he takes it as the *literal* meaning too. Read that way, all of Winthrop's "We shall's" are interpreted as "This is what I expect of us." To Darrett Rutman, Winthrop evidently *expects* the colony to become "a citty on a hill," he *expects* they will all be "knitt together as the fingers of one hand"; he does *not* expect, however, that the New World environment will offer temptations to self or pressures against the covenanted community. He does not expect that because Rutman doesn't show him *saying* he expects that.

What Winthrop says is thus taken literally to indicate what he believes. Taken that way, his words make him look naïve indeed, and they render his ideals vulnerable to the subsequent realities which tragically shatter them. But Rutman finds no evidence for such tragic disappointment in Winthrop. What then of the words? Were they so naïvely optimistic, or vulnerable to the New World, as they seem to the literal-minded observer?

What Rutman has done here is read "A Modell of Christian Charity" apart from its historical context—apart from the time and place it was delivered, apart from the audience it was delivered to, and, in a sense, even apart from the man who gave it (he cannot connect the optimistic words there into anything else of Winthrop). To be sure, Rutman is *aware* of all these contextual limitations, but they do not *operate* here in his reading of Winthrop's mind.

We might offer an alternative reading by posing an alternative set of questions. Rutman in effect asks of "A Modell of Christian Charity," "What did John Winthrop *say* in it?" We might ask in addition, "What *functions* did this sermon perform for the deliverer, and for the audience it was delivered to?"

Rutman's question leads him to assume that Winthrop said exactly what he meant, and what he meant was just what he expected to happen in the colony. Our alternative question assumes no such straight-line connection between word and meaning and between meaning and expectation.

Indeed, in this case, we might discover an almost inverse connection between word and expectation. That is, Winthrop's words may have functioned not as a direct indicator of his expectations, but indirectly as a *counter* to what he expected. Perhaps he anticipated full well what problems and temptations would beset these Puritans in the New World, and constructed his words as a challenge to those anticipations. He didn't expect that his words would wholly succeed; after all, men, to him, were creatures of temptation. Rather, he simply wanted to establish an ideal against which they might all (Winthrop included) judge their later behavior. That behavior never was to meet the ideal; but, if this kind of reading is correct, Winthrop never intended it to. He didn't expect that vision would *become* reality, he simply hoped it might *shape* it some.

What we're proposing here is a "situation-strategy" reading of Winthrop's words, a reading which takes off from our Burkean model of ideas in the last chapter. Instead of taking John Winthrop's 1630 words to indicate his full mind for some two decades thereafter, we're looking for part of his mind here as it functions in a particular situational context and responds with particular kinds of strategies. By this kind of reading, we don't assume that he intended to *describe* reality with his words; rather, we assert that he used those words as leverage to *affect* reality, doubtless realizing that reality would never wholly submit to his strategies.

Darrett Rutman's kind of reading makes for a one-way relation between mind and world. Mind is intended to *reflect* world; when it fails to, then it's seen to be out of joint. Such a reading also makes for a one-way relation between speaker and audience—speaker talks *to* audience, but there's no sense of audience responding. A "strategic" reading, however, asserts two-way relationships in such matters—mind encounters world but expects to get encountered in turn, and speaker wants to affect audience, but must direct and shape his words to where that audience is now and where he would like them to be some time hence.

Such a strategic reading may or may not recapture John Winthrop's actual meaning in "A Modell of Christian Charity." We'd have to go outside *Winthrop's Boston* to the full text and context of Winthrop's original words to determine that. But this reading does, I think, explain some of Rutman's facts better than Rutman's own pattern, and it alleviates points of strain in his book. With it, we may understand why Winthrop never became wholly disillusioned by later events in the colony, and why, sober Calvinist that he was, he could say what he did in 1630 and still not be naïvely optimistic about the colony's future. "A Modell of Christian Charity" might well be continuous with his Calvinist beliefs, not an "illogical" departure from them.

Why then does Rutman pattern his facts on such a shaky foundation? Because, I think, his procedure never obliges him to reflect on *the word as an expressive form,* or on the strategy of a historical text. Instead, he reads words and text on their face, then hurries out to "the facts" to see whether they fit or not. He is painstaking and rigorous in interpreting "objective" facts, but he is not given to such rigor with "perspectivistic" evidence. He reads perspectivistic documents as if they were repositories of abstract, floating ideas or themes—in this case "regeneration," and "community," and "moral obligation," and "the covenant"—and he fails to see them as the dynamic encounter of mind with particular situational dilemmas in the world.

Earlier, we noted a similar shortcoming in historians when they're handling ideas in history. We then tried to counter this shortcoming by proposing a *symbolic* for historical studies—a functional understanding of people's ideas as they interact with world. Now we note a like shortcoming when historians are handling words in documents. We might try and counter this shortcoming by proposing a *criticism* for historical studies—a functional understanding of people's words as they cluster together in documents.

IV

Darrett Rutman, it seems, has taken evidence from perspectivistic experience and has tried to handle it unperspectivistically. That is, he has looked at it from the outside in rather than approaching it from the inside out. He has thus relied upon the normal procedure of historians when dealing with such evidence—the procedure of quote-and-paraphrase, and of lifting general thematic currents from the materials.

Such a procedure puts a strain on this kind of evidence, as we noted in the last section. Its main shortcoming, I think, is its tendency to stick with the manifest appearance of perspectivistic materials and not move down inside them to try and see how they experience their world *at the moment they are constructed.*

What we need is an alternative procedure for handling perspectivistic experience—a procedure which will handle documents of such experience through the particulars of time and place and person and circumstance, and which will try and read their expressive forms from the inside out. The best procedure I know of this sort is the situation-strategy criticism of Kenneth Burke.

In the last chapter, we discussed Burke's picture of what ideas are and how they engage the world around them. That picture comes out of his technique for handling words and literary texts; so all we need now is to move one step further in Burke, and we should have our method of perspectivistic criticism.

In chapter 5, we said that Burke's model of ideas plays off against both the extrinsic and the intrinsic approaches. The same holds true for Burke's criticism of texts. At its extreme, extrinsic criticism stays wholly on the outside of texts, while intrinsic criticism remains wholly inside. Burke's approach, however, begins on the inside—with the words themselves—moves from there to the connecting context around the words—their author, his times, his situation, and so forth—then finally moves back into the words again to inspect how their connecting context affects them. In short, Kenneth Burke goes on a kind of "strategic journey" with a perspectivistic document. Through this journey, he gives such a document both a *textual* reading and a *contextual reading*—seeking to explain not only word but part of the world around and behind and under word.

Burke accomplishes this by doing with words what we saw him do with ideas before. He first takes what is ordinarily seen as passive and inert, and tries to put it into motion. With a text, he does this quite simply by *picturing words as acts.*

His is, as he calls it, "a reasoned method for treating art as act."[12] He means that word-forms don't serve simply as pointers to experiences and things in the world outside; they also function as experiences themselves, and help to create worlds of a sort. In short, they do not just passively represent active processes in the world, they have an energy of their own and are thereby actions of a kind.

Hence, for a Burkean critic, Darrett Rutman erred when he took John Winthrop's "Modell" as a literal platform for building some actual New England world. The Burkean critic might see the "Modell" as partly that, but he would more likely read it as a *re-action to* the situation around it. That situation would include (as Rutman has) Winthrop's more long-range concerns of past experience in old England and of future anticipations in New England. But it would also include (as Rutman has not) Winthrop's more immediate environment on the passage over, the state of his mind and the expressive forms available to him, his audience and the state of their mind and their expressive forms, and the reciprocal relations between Winthrop and his audience. Because Rutman has not considered the immediate situational context of Winthrop's words, he has no way to explain why his mind changed as the situation changed. Or rather, the Burkean critic would not say that Winthrop's *mind* necessarily changed after 1630, only that it took on different *forms* when acting on different things in the world.

It would be hard to observe all this if one remained wholly on the outside of John Winthrop's mind. But if one has a procedure for moving on inside and for seeing how his expressive forms are responses to the world *as he sees it at that time and at that place,* then one can account for change in Winthrop, and can weigh which changes are fundamental and last over time and which are situational and thus only temporary readjustments for him.

Such a procedure, I would contend, is a natural way to handle the expressions of mind, and to explain movement over time in those expressions. It is natural, I think, because it is what we do all the time in our everyday life experience. We encounter our own selves and others in particular situations, and we are accustomed to understanding spoken words in such situations—others' as well as ours—as very much shaped by time and place and mood and circumstance.

We are not much accustomed to taking the *written* word in this way, though, especially the written word in historical studies. There we're still influenced by the "ideal historical-observer" model, and tend to aim for a perfect correspondence of word with the objective world outside word. There may never be such a perfect correspondence, but it's still the ideal; and that ideal may block us from trying an alternative approach to the relation between word and world.

Kenneth Burke takes an alternative approach because he handles written words in literary texts much as most of us handle spoken words in our everyday lives. For him, all words—written or spoken—are simply *forms of human behavior.* A person behaves strategically when he constructs words in a text, just as he behaves strategically when he casts his vote in an election, or fixes his car, or fondles his lover. It's important to note that all these acts come through different expressive forms (unless, of course, one handles his lover as he does his car!); but it's equally important to note their fundamental human similarity *as* acts, by persons strategically responding to situations around them.

Words, then, are not set apart from other behavior for Burke. They're indeed the most distinctive of human behaviors, and to him the most important focal arena for checking what human experience is like. This is so because for him it is language (or symbolic action) which above all distinguishes man as man. As a student of Burke has written, to him, "Man is the specifically language-using or symbol-using animal, and . . . somehow the essence of man, human relations, and ultimate reality are to be derived from the dramatistic study of language and the various functions it performs for man."[13]

With such an attitude, a Burkean critic aims for the felt sense of experience out of which words are constructed; he wants to bring that experience to light and offer explanation to it. Words thus become an arena—or in Burkean terms a "scene"—wherein the encounter of mind with world is enacted, and perennially reenacted. As William Rueckert puts it, Burke's focus is "the drama of human relations as it is recorded in literature."[14]

Here again we can see how Burke differs from both extrinsic and intrinsic critics. Extrinsic critics deny that the drama of human relations takes place *inside* literature. They believe the motive forces for such a drama lie in the world outside; hence they're not prone to spending much time in the close analysis of texts, or of words in texts. Intrinsic critics are concerned almost entirely with words and texts alone and not with the larger human drama, so they aren't given to connecting words into other human experiences around them.

Kenneth Burke, however, takes the text as a particular arena to get at the general human drama, and he is reciprocally concerned with both text and drama. The one is a microcosm, filtered through its own special form, of the other. But to get at the larger drama, the critic must know the particular *medium* through which that microcosm is expressed. Thus he must study the forms of a text as well as its symbolic actions. As Burke states it in his foreword to *The Philosophy of Literary Form:*

Words are aspects of a much wider communicative context, most of which is not verbal at all. Yet words also have a nature peculiarly their own. And when discussing them as modes of action, we must consider *both* this nature as words in themselves *and* the nature they get from the nonverbal scenes that support their acts. I shall be happy if the reader can say of this book that, while always considering words as acts upon a scene, it avoids the *excess* of environmentalist schools which are usually so eager to trace the relationships between act and scene that they neglect to trace the structure of the act itself.[15]

V

That, basically, is Burke's model of how words function in the experience of people. We must now take this model and suggest how Burke makes a critical *method* of it, when he studies actual words behaving in literary texts. Kenneth Burke handles a literary text just as we noted him handling ideas in the last chapter. For him a text is the chart of a mind, and is to be understood as the *response* of that mind to something or other. As a critic, his task is to search for the mind behind the text, and to infer the experience which that mind is responding to.

Because he treats words and texts as "acts upon a scene," Burke handles his materials as if they were in motion, and is concerned to understand the context in which that motion takes place. In his terms, the words in motion are "strategies," the contexts of that motion are "situations." As he puts it,

We are reminded that every document bequeathed us by history must be treated as *a strategy for encompassing a situation.* Thus, when considering some document like the American Constitution, we shall be automatically warned not to consider it in isolation, but as the *answer* or *rejoinder* to assertions current in the situation in which it arose.[16]

Burke thus approaches a text as if there were a *conversation* going on in it—a conversation between mind and mind's sense of world, or between strategy and situation. On occasion, however, it may be strategic for the text's author to hide one or another sides in this conversation and make it look like something other than a dialogue. Sometimes—as in, say, a poetic text—only the strategy may be evident; and then the Burkean critic must try and re-create the inferred situation to which it is a response. At other times—as in, say, some history texts—only the world-situation is apparent, and the Burkean critic must then try and root out the masked strategy of response. In all cases, though, he must bring to light *both* sides in the conversation— that is, he must take what may look like a more or less completed monologue and re-create it as an ongoing dialogue.

With Burke, then, a text never comes out being simply "subjective mind" or "objective world"; rather, it's always a *dialogic encounter* between the one and the other. Where Darrett Rutman erred, from the Burkean point of view, was in treating mind and world in isolation from each other—setting the one off here (in Winthrop's "Modell") and the other off there (in the external facts of Boston's history), but not putting the two in continuing and active encounter with each other.

Later, in chapter 9, we'll see how Perry Miller *does* put Puritan minds and their world into an ongoing encounter. Miller's *The New England Mind: From Colony to Province* in effect does a Burkean critical reading of facts—

"objective" as well as "perspectivistic"—of seventeenth-century Puritan history. As we'll see, Miller does this by moving back and forth between words inside texts and the world outside texts. Because he sees each continually impacting on the other, he tries to read the world (or some of it) inside each text, and to detect each text (or some of them) acting outside in parts of the world. Which is precisely what Kenneth Burke would have the strategic critic do. Since he pictures word and world as invariably in conversation, neither looks quite as settled as when pictured in isolation from each other. Because it feels for the existential dynamic behind words, strategic criticism takes what may look like a finished conviction of mind, and shows it as a temporary strategy for coping with some situation in the world.

What a word or a text *says,* then, may not be wholly what it *means,* and what someone's mind means in one situation may not be at all what it means in another one. To trace the problematic connection between statement and meaning and between meaning in one situation and meaning in another, the critic must set out on a kind of "strategic journey" with words—a journey which, like Burke's and Miller's, moves back and forth inside and outside historical texts.

That, in essence, is what strategic criticism calls for. The actual workings of this criticism should become clearer soon as we proceed through the case studies in the three chapters which follow. But we might take a brief preliminary trek now, to indicate just where a critic goes when he takes a strategic journey with a historical text.

VI

Just as someone who sets out to travel in the world must *prepare* himself for what he's about to see, so also the historical critic who sets out to travel in a text. As the traveler seeks to gain experience in the world, so the critic must seek to gain experience in the text. In time, both traveler and critic may reshape that experience into their own forms; but if the experience is to affect those forms in any substantial way, it must be allowed to come through in its *own* forms first.

This is particularly true with the historical critic who handles perspectivistic evidence. The point of such evidence is that it must be experienced from the inside out. That is, what it says is bound up with the particulars of where it is and when and who and how; and the critic must move into these particulars if he's to make sense of such evidence. So it's crucial that the critic temporarily suspend his own forms and allow the forms of perspectivistic materials to speak in their own way.

Thus he should not ask first of a text, "Is it a true copy of the world?" In the beginning stages of his journey, the historical critic must be less concerned with whether a text is true to the world and more concerned with *just how it constructs its own version of the world.*

Like a literary New Critic addressing a novel, the historical critic must for a while practice a "willing suspension of disbelief" about the text, and go with his subject's mind in its own way. In time, he may come to judge that subject from his own world-position, but a long interior journey should come first.

Once the critic has prepared himself by suspending disbelief about the text's world and holding his own forms in abeyance, then he is ready to embark on his journey. Basically, that journey consists of three stages—(1) *moving into the text to experience what it says and how,* (2) *making a series of outward connections from the text to the world around the text, then* (3) *moving back into the text again, to check just how experiences from the outside world affect what's said and done in there.* Because text and world are intertwined in their encounter, these three stages are not entirely distinct but instead melt into each other. Nevertheless, it's possible to distinguish between them at least for purposes of analysis.

1. In the initial stages of this journey, the critic's basic concern is for *intricate textual analysis.* It is here where he should be most careful to suspend his own forms on the world and must allow the text to form its own world in its own way. In doing this, the critic should probe beyond the text's paraphraseable content to see it as a human construction, an imposing of form upon some part of experience. Since neither the form nor the experience are givens in the world, the text should be seen as problematic—that is, as incorporating a series of *choices* about how experiences may be constructed. The critic's job is to uncover what those choices are, and in time to try and explain why the text's author made those particular choices and not others.

To do this, the critic must in effect *un*-construct what the author once constructed. That is, he must try and tear the text all apart, so he can lay open just how it was put together in the first place.

To perform such a task, he will need tools. For strategic criticism, those tools might be *an agenda of questions* which one can use to address a book. Or, to return to the "journey" metaphor, such questions may function as guideposts to aid the historical critic in his travels.

One early guidepost will point to the text's *organizing patterns.* The critic will want to ask, "What is the text structured around?" (e.g., themes? individuals? chronology? regions? movements? institutions? situations?) He will also pay special attention to how an author opens a text, and how he closes it, for often these will provide a key to his basic organizing assumptions.

The critic will also want to know just how words and ideas are *clustered* in a text. Kenneth Burke has written, "The work of every writer contains a set of implicit equations. He uses 'associational clusters.' And you may, by examining his work, find 'what goes with what' in these clusters."[17]

Following up Burke's point here, the historical critic may ask questions like, "What are the text's pivotal terms, around which the others cluster?," and "What are the text's dramatic alignments?" (i.e., what goes *with* what in it, and what is set off *against* what?)

With such cluster analyses, the critic tries to establish the textual meaning of words and ideas not in essence, but in *relationship*. A word or idea in one text, associated with one cluster of perspectives on experience, may mean something quite different from the same word or idea in another text, where it fits into another cluster of terms. As Burke says, each term gains its distinctive meaning from " 'the company it keeps' in the utterances of a given writer or speaker."[18]

Such a method runs counter to the normal historians' procedure, where texts are handled through their paraphraseable content. This is what might be called the "in other words" mode of analysis. It is frequently used in historiographical writing, for it allows the historical critic to pass over several works in a relatively brief space, and thus "cover" the field. It has the advantage of efficiency; you can handle a lot at one time with such a procedure. But the Burkean critic insists that a text must be studied not in other words, but in *its own* words. For if words are to be used as a focal point for seeing mind in action, then we must know just *what* particular words that mind acts with, and *how* particularly it clusters its words into patterns of explanation.

There are other questions the critic might ask along this initial stage of the journey. Like "What is the basic mode of explanation in the text?" "What alternative explanations might be constructed for the same experiences?" "What kinds of experience does this explanation work best with?" "Worst?" "Are there strains, or fault-lines, in the author's explanation?" "How does an author behave when his explanation is under strain?" "How does he support his explanations?" (e.g., by appealing chiefly to facts? logic? sentiment? ideology? tradition?) "What are the text's most revealing moments?" (e.g., Benjy's bellowing when driven around the town square the wrong way, Charles Sellers' resort to "objective reality" in his closing sentence) "What strategies for focus, or devices for getting a handle on experience, does the author use?" "How does the author conceive his *role* vis-à-vis his materials, and vis-à-vis his audience?" (e.g., scholar? reformer? scientist? prophet? teacher? judge? chronicler? poet?) And, finally, "What seems to be the author's perceived 'situation' for this particular text, and how is the text a 'strategic response' to it?"

It's in this first stage where strategic criticism makes its distinctive contribution. Because so little has yet been done here in American historiographical scholarship, we'll concentrate our efforts on this stage in the book, and concern ourselves only incidentally with the other two. This is not to establish any hierarchy of importance—all three stages of the journey are important—it's only to try and right an imbalance of existing scholarship in the field.[19]

2. In the second stage of the journey, the critic's basic concern is for *making connections outward* from the text to the world around the text. It's

important that such connections go *through* the text, however, and not evaporate that text's particulars into the general "climate" of an age (as they were, I think, in the early 1960s "consensus-conflict" controversy).

In this second stage, and in the stage to follow, we have much to go on already in the field, and aren't obliged to construct a whole procedure of our own. If we add a few insights from Thomas Kuhn and from "cognitive" scholarship to the kind of observations, say, that Richard Hofstadter makes in *The Progressive Historians,* or John Higham in *History,* or Burleigh Wilkins in *Carl Becker,* or Robert Skotheim in *American Intellectual Histories and Historians,* or Thomas Pressly in *Americans Interpret their Civil War,* then we're about ready for work on this stage of the journey.

The historical critic might characteristically ask here: "What paradigm communities, or communities of explanation, does the author seem to work within?" "How much does he share with and how much does he depart from others in his explanation community?" "What are the significant features in his background, and does he share many of these with others whose explanations resemble his?" "Are there important crises, or turning points, in his life?" "What or whom does the author seem most to identify with?" (e.g., his profession? his culture? some subgroup in his profession or his culture?) "Who is his audience for the text, and how does he intend to affect them?" And finally, "What seem to be the major preoccupations and expressive forms of his times, and does he change at about the same pace as the times around him change?"

3. In the journey's third stage, the critic is concerned to *make connections back into* the text again, to see specifically how experiences from the world affect what happens there. The strategic journey begins with the text, then, and it ends there. The historical critic may find clues to the workings of mind in the outside world—in the life of the author, his times, and so on— but it's in the text itself where those workings must show up if we're to verify their influence.

Here the procedure is simply to take findings from the second stage, and work them back into our concerns on the first stage. For example, we might wish to check how some new personal association has affected the way a historian constructs his explanations. In chapter 8, we'll see that Arthur Schlesinger, Jr.'s contact with Reinhold Niebuhr influenced his transformation from the Progressive form to the counter-Progressive. And we can detect that transformation not only in general intellectual themes but in a distinctly Niebuhr-like way of writing which Schlesinger picked up (it shows in his 1949 book *The Vital Center*).

Here the critic must do just the reverse of what he did in the first stage. There he was concerned to tear the text down; here his task is to reassemble it. Only now, after he has experienced the text through *its* particular forms, he may use his *own* forms to try and put it back together again.

For on this third stage he is aiming at critical *explanation*—explanation of the historical word, and of the mind acting behind the word. He has the text before him where he can watch the visible workings of mind. He also has information from the outside to plug into that text. Now his job is the heady one of putting it all together—forming patterns and associations and connections, and thereby constructing his own explanation of what seems to be happening here between mind and world.

VII

In historical criticism, then, our basis for generalization is the historical text, and our strategic journey should begin and end with that text. In its intense concern for the text, this procedure may seem to resemble the New Criticism in literature. There is, however, a major difference between strategic criticism and New Criticism–if not always in procedure, then certainly in eventual goal. At its purest, New Criticism embodies the intrinsic principle of staying wholly inside the text; anything outside is felt to be extraneous. But strategic criticism looks into the text with quite different aims. It uses the text as a controlled laboratory in which to investigate how mind behaves as it tries to explain experience. The encounter of mind with world is its basic subject matter; the text is only its point of focus for managing that subject.

In the case studies immediately to follow, we'll take only part of the full strategic journey. We'll travel mainly on the first level—inside the text— and make only brief forays into the world outside. Or rather, we'll look at that outside world not through our *own* eyes, but only through the eyes of *others,* as they frame it in their texts. This reflects my own strategic decision that if any single study tries to do too much at once now in this sparsely worked area, it may quickly lose focus and control over its subject matter. Since we already have many fine extrinsic studies of historians' explanations, I think it imperative—at least for purposes of the present book—to stick closely to my "primary documents" here, the texts. This is not to give them an intrinsic reading, though, for such a reading never travels beyond the first stage of the journey. It's to give them *part of* a strategic reading, but to make plain there's more to come. It's also to connect leads out into the other two stages, leads which later studies in the field will hopefully follow up.

Eventually, we may be able to construct here *a working sociology of historical knowledge.* In its task of trying to explain the behavior of mind in context, such a sociology might move back and forth from general cultural forces to particular details of particular texts, and it might manage several intermediary levels of experience in between. But this kind of explanation model can't be constructed all at once. I see the present study as one step in that direction. In this, my initial step, I've chosen to begin from the inside of historians' explanations and work gradually out. Others in the field may choose to begin elsewhere. Hopefully, we may accomplish similar things; we'll just take them in a different order.

My mode of approach, then, is intended to be temporary—a beginning for historiographical inquiry, but not the full field. It is, in short, a particular strategy of inquiry for coping with a particular situation in American historical scholarship. Because historiographical studies to date have had no clearly defined field of focus, because they've lacked a way to ground their understanding of ideas, and haven't developed their own distinctive procedures for their own distinctive materials, I've aimed this study to counter those shortcomings. Its major concern is to gain more *focus* and *control* in our studies of American historians and their worlds.

Focus and control are not the only worthwhile qualities in historical scholarship, they're just what we lack now in historiographical studies. The several models and methods of these opening chapters—the "cognitive" model of ideas, the "perspectivistic" view of historical reality, the "experience-explanation" strategy, the case for a "primary" consideration of "secondary" documents, the Kuhnian concept of paradigm communities and communities of explanation, "pivotal-moment" analysis of ideas, Burkean "situation-strategy" analysis, Burkean "strategic" criticism—all should help us manage our inquiries with added rigor. And the case studies to follow offer a laboratory for testing and refining these methods.

With the historical texts in this laboratory, we have a defined population of materials to work with. That population sets boundaries for what we must cover, and may help us reduce the incidence of information overload. We'll further reduce this incidence by looking not for the whole life history of an explanation-form, but for particular moments when change in that form seems imminent, or when it's being pressured to re-form.

In historiography-intellectual history studies, "moment" analysis can afford us the same rooted base of operations as event analysis in regular history. And, within the Burkean model, it offers us some dramatized "scenes," where we can apply the situation-strategy method of the last two chapters.

So from here on out in this book, our concern will not be with the conventional question, "What, in essence, was this historian's thought?" Depending on where we may look in the corpus of a thinker's writings, we might find him saying most anything. Our concern, rather, will be, *"Given this particular historian in this particular situation responding through this particular form, how strategically does he put together his own explanation of experience?"*

In short, we're trying to analyze historians' explanation-forms as they behave in response to things in the world. Hence the case studies are intended to give us moving pictures of "strategic forms in action."

NOTES

1. See chapter 2, section II, for an analysis of this ideal historical-observer position.
2. *Winthrop's Boston: Portrait of a Puritan Town, 1630–1649* (University of North

Carolina Press, 1965), p. viii. Published for the Institute of Early American History and Culture.

3. Ibid., pp. 3–4.

4. Ibid., p. 7.

5. Ibid., p. 279.

6. Ibid., p. 272.

7. Ibid., p. 272–73.

8. Ibid., p. 273.

9. Ibid.

10. Ibid.

11. Ibid., p. 21.

12. *The Philosophy of Literary Form: Studies in Symbolic Action* (Random House, Vintage Book, 1957—first published by Louisiana State in 1941), p. ix.

13. William Rueckert, *Kenneth Burke and the Drama of Human Relations* (University of Minnesota Press, 1963), p. 129.

14. Ibid., p. 83.

15. Burke, *Philosophy,* p. vii.

16. Ibid., p. 93.

17. Ibid., p. 18.

18. Ibid., pp. 30–31.

19. If there has been little scholarship done on this level to date, we're not faced with a total vacuum. The best rationale I know for such scholarship comes in a splendid essay by David Levin, "The Literary Criticism of History" *In Defense of Historical Literature* (Hill and Wang, 1967). Levin has put his prescriptions to practice in a fine work of historiographical scholarship—*History as Romantic Art: Bancroft, Prescott, Motley, and Parkman* (Harcourt, Brace, Harbinger Book, 1963—first published in 1959 by Stanford).

BOOK III

Strategic Forms in Action: The Case Studies

This illustrates the first function of the enquiring laboratory. In brief, it is the replacement of illustrations only of conclusions by illustrations of problem situations.

Joseph Schwab
The Teaching of Science as Enquiry
(Harvard, 1964)

I began the analysis with three simple assumptions. First, not all beliefs are equally important to the individual; beliefs vary along a central-peripheral dimension. Second, the more central a belief, the more it will resist change. Third, the more central the belief changed, the more widespread the repercussions in the rest of the belief system.

Milton Rokeach
Beliefs, Attitudes, and Values:
A Theory of Organization and Change
(Jossey-Bass, 1968)

Literature is not words on the page but images in the head, and that head in society.

Leslie Fiedler
Review of Louis Kampf and Paul Lautner, eds., *The Politics of Literature*, in *Change* (Summer 1972)

7 "When Prophecy Fails": Turner, Progressives, and Paradigm Strain

The question is imperative, then, What ideals persist from this democratic experience of the West; and have they acquired sufficient momentum to sustain themselves under conditions so radically unlike those in the days of their origin?

Frederick Jackson Turner
The Frontier in American History

The effect of threat is to compel the client to claw frantically for his basic construct. Threat arouses the necessity for mobilizing one's resources. It should be borne in mind that the resources which are mobilized may not always be mature and effective. Therefore a threatened person may often behave in childish ways.

George Kelly
A Theory of Personality

How can a people progress if they have started near to perfection?

Richard Hofstadter
The Progressive Historians

All through this book we've been looking into ideas—what functions they may perform, and how and where we might study them. Here, in the first of our case study chapters, we'll focus on one particular kind of idea-behavior —*how mind responds to stress.* We're calling this behavior a "paradigm strain." Or rather, it's a paradigm strain with the Progressive historians, since their mode of explanation was so widely assumed and held over so many years that it seems to have reached the status of a Kuhnian paradigm. That's not true with either the counter-Progressives or the New Left, though, so we'll call theirs simply a "strain in explanation-form."

Just what is a paradigm strain, or a strain in explanation-form? It's a situ-

179

ation where mind and eye go in different directions, where one's forms for thinking don't jibe with what he sees. In our language, it's an explanation which doesn't manage the experience one's trying to make sense of.

In such a situation, mind—through its idea-forms—becomes unreliable as a guide to one's world of experience. This is so not necessarily because mind fails to explain the world of things outside. Rather, it's because mind gets entangled with itself. It goes after contradictory things, one precluding another. The strain is not basically between outer world and inner explanation, it's between competing behaviors inside mind itself, as it responds to world.

This strain becomes most intense at certain pressure points, or what in chapter 5 we called "fault-lines." Which fault-lines will be our special area of focus in this chapter. We'll watch how an idea moves along one of these lines of vulnerability, and we'll see how under pressure it gets stretched near the breaking point.

What we're after, then, is a fault-line for that historical "earthquake" which dislodged the Progressive patterning of ideas and brought in the counter-Progressive relocation. Through these next three chapters, we'll be investigating phases of this earthquake's natural history—studying points of strain here, some moments of revolutionary upheaval in chapter 8, and, finally, in chapter 9 the forming of a new kind of consensus.

II

In chapter 4, we saw something of the Progressive explanation-form. Further, there are now in print several excellent studies of Progressive historians. That should release us here from any burden of detailed coverage.[1] We needn't take much time, then, either to build up this Progressive historical form, or to analyze it now in any detail. But we can recall some of what we said in chapter 4, and add a little from other "secondary" (or rather, tertiary) studies. As a preliminary to our inquiry later into Progressives under strain, we might say this much now of these historians:

As we noted before, Progressives tried putting reality together so that experience became progress. They wanted to liberate men from their past; to do this, they had strategically to break them free from inherited forms of thought and behavior. Theirs was a missionary kind of "revolt against formalism," then, a battle for the new and the free and the dynamic against the old and the oppressive and the sterile.[2] Which also frequently meant setting off a New World America in their minds against an Old World Europe.

Progressives thus invested much of their identity in making prophecies about the future, and in proclaiming the basic goodness of things in the land. When things weren't looking so good, that was because something unnatural had interfered—perhaps this alien intruder was a kind of vestigial remain from Old World habits, or the entrenched self-interest of wealthy or greedy classes. In any case, it was an indication that things weren't as they should be.

Progressives didn't say that America's history *was* inevitably progress; rather, they said it *could* be, was *meant to be,* if only dedicated men worked to make it so. If Progress was their Master Good, apathy was their Master Evil—the worst men can do is give up. Much Progressive writing was thus devoted to showing that the fight was worth it, that America could become the history of progress if only enough effort were made in summoning men to do battle with injustice and reactionary interests. This then is one burden the Progressives took upon themselves—to regenerate a naturally democratic people and help guide them toward the good and just society.

III

Earlier, I said this Progressive explanation-form wielded enough power over enough years to be called a "paradigm" in the American historical profession. Really, that's only a suggestion. We'd require a lot more sociological understanding of historians' explanation communities before we could make a claim like that stick. We need such studies, though, and part of the reason I make that suggestion here is to encourage them. There are, however, a few scattered things we can say now; they might give us some circumstantial evidence in support of this contention, as a prelude to more sophisticated studies later.

Our first line of evidence here is perhaps the least reliable—it's the citing of authorities on the matter. Richard Hofstadter, who studied the Progressives more carefully than perhaps any other historian, has written, "Among writers on American history it was Turner, Beard, and Parrington who gave us the pivotal ideas of the first half of the twentieth century."[3] And John Higham, who's studied the mores of American historians as thoroughly as anyone, says in his *History:*

Between the two world wars progressive influence became so great in American historiography that it seemed for a time virtually to overwhelm all other conceptual possibilities. World War I neither interrupted nor diverted this widening stream of historical thought. Instead, the ideas of Turner, Beard, and their younger associates spread through the historical profession in the 1920's without any really sustained opposition. Certain new currents fed into the stream; and ultimately it grew vexed and turbulent. But these complications arose, for the most part, within the progressive tradition.[4]

A second line of evidence is a little more substantial—it's a poll taken of the American historical profession in the early 1950s. In this poll, respondents were asked to list their "most preferred" works in the field published during two periods—1920–35 and 1936–50. In both cases the list was topped by a work of Progressive scholarship—Parrington's *Main Currents* for the earlier period, Merle Curti's *The Growth of American Thought* for the latter. And in the 1920–35 years—when the form seems to have been at its strongest—six of the top eleven vote getters were Progressive historians. Turner's *The Frontier in American History* came in second (just one vote behind Parrington), the Beards' *Rise of American Civilization* was fourth, Becker's *The Declaration of Independence* was sixth, Arthur Schlesinger, Sr.'s *New Viewpoints in American History* was tenth, and John Hicks's *The Populist Revolt,* eleventh.[5]

The last line of evidence here is our most intriguing one—though it may or may not be representative of the historical profession at large. It's a presidential address to the Mississippi Valley Historical Association, and it calls on fellow historians to study "the democratic theme" in America's history. Though we shouldn't make too much of a single speech, it is a revealing instance of that *assumed* sense of reality which Thomas Kuhn says lies at the heart of the paradigm form. And the address becomes even more revealing when we note it was made by a winner of that poll just cited—Merle Curti.

Had this speech been given around, say, 1912—the year prior to Beard's *Economic Interpretation* and just before Parrington began work on his *Main Currents*—we might pass it by, or note it as an instance of the Progressive historical form in gestation. But the address was delivered to a gathering of colleagues in 1952, the same year of that poll showing how dominant Progressive explanations had been in the profession.

What makes it so fascinating a case of historical paradigm power is this: Almost four decades after the Progressive explanation began to take over in the profession, here is someone saying historians need to *try* just such an interpretation and lamenting that "the treatment of democracy in the American story has been for the most part peripheral rather than central"![6] Nowhere in his 26 pages does Curti mention there's ever been a Progressive school of historical explanation, though his address covers every major thinker in that school, and his own mind-set here works almost completely inside it.

Curti's basic strategy is to take this interpretation and raise it to public awareness among his colleagues. He does this by showing that many previous historians have in fact touched on aspects of "the democratic theme," but that no one has ever brought all their scattered ideas into a single pattern. Which is what Curti sets out to do in this essay.

So in the first 22 pages of his paper, he passes over some three dozen American historians, telling us how each was for or against democracy. Such a procedure involves Curti in some rather unique condensed versions of American historical scholarship, and some unlikely recruits to his new democratic school. Like: "Perry Miller accented the democratic aspects of New England Puritanism while locating these in the humanistic currents of the Renaissance."[7] Or, yet stranger: "From any point of view the *History* [of Henry Adams] was a conscious, sustained, and intellectually sophisticated effort to make democracy the central theme of the period between 1800 and 1818. It testified to Adams' use of our discipline as an instrument for understanding present and future."[8]

One might of course claim that Miller's and Adams' works are full-scale "democratic" interpretations of their subjects. But to do so as if it's the obvious common sense of the matter does give us pause. On the one hand, Curti laments that his colleagues have paid too little attention to this democratic theme, that American historians have given democracy only "peripheral" treatment. This would seem odd after four decades of little but Progressive explanations in American historical scholarship; but if it puts a strain on our empirical sense, at least it's logically possible. What puts a strain on our logical sense too is that Curti then extends his "democratic theme" so broadly as to make even Perry Miller and Henry Adams adepts of the form. On the one hand we have almost no democratic histories, on the other hand it appears that almost everybody's been writing them. Something seems to be awry.

We get a clue to what's happening in Curti's first and last paragraphs. His opening words warn that conservative interpretations of America are now coming to be heard in the profession; and in the final two paragraphs he observes that cold war repressions threaten to silence further inquiries into democracy. And he closes with this rallying cry to his colleagues:

I for one have faith that the democratic theme will continue to be explored by historians, who will continue to have not only the humility of scholars but the courage of patriots, and who because of this humility and this courage will keep on trying to rise above the pressures of their time, and, just as they find it and see it, present in their writings the truth about the history of democracy.[9]

Now one doesn't escalate rhetoric like that unless his stakes are high—higher probably than just some theme or other in his colleagues' explanations of their past. Curti evidently sees here not just a challenge to "the democratic theme in American historical literature," but to the historical enterprise itself. And when he says we need to "present . . . the truth about the history of democracy," he apparently means we need to present the truth about the history of America. It's axiomatic to him that the history of America is the history of democracy. What's at stake for Curti is continued inquiry into that history, which inquiry is being threatened by conservative interpretations from within the profession and cold-war pressures from without.

A paradigm is a "picture in the head" for which there seems no alternative among a community of scholars. Its power comes from being simply the assumed reality of things. So if within one's Progressive paradigm it's just assumed that good history is democratic history and that democratic history is good history, then it must follow that (1) challenges to democratic history are challenges to history itself, and (2) good histories like those of Perry Miller and Henry Adams are ipso facto democratic. And when assumptions like this are threatened, the paradigm adept may respond by simply reiterating them, trying to show that many others have held them too, and exhorting his colleagues to grasp onto them with renewed dedication. In such situations of threat, one will not pause to *define* or analyze "the democratic theme";

rather, one will rush out to *defend* one's own symbolic territory. Or, in Thomas Kuhn's words, one will do what paradigm adepts typically do—try to prove their position with the tools of that position: "When paradigms enter, as they must, into a debate about paradigm choice, their role is necessarily circular. Each group uses its own paradigm to argue in that paradigm's defense."[10]

Which response gives us a key not only to the power of the Progressive paradigm (at least in Merle Curti, in 1952), but to what seems a characteristic behavior of Progressives under strain. Because they believe their role as historians is to prophesy as well as to understand, they frequently interpret strain as simply a failure of will, and thus exhort themselves and others to try harder. They seek added leverage to get things moving back in the direction they want, and they tighten their paradigm commitment as a strategy for gaining that leverage. Which may help explain Curti's apparently contradictory logic of lamenting that we haven't had enough of this "democratic theme in American historical literature," then going out to claim doubtful supporters like Miller and Adams for the faith. Both strategies imply that the problem lies not with the paradigm itself, but with historians' inadequate understanding of it, and dedication to it. By strengthening that understanding and renewing their dedication, the problems which beset them can be overcome.

In this situation of course, that strategy didn't work. At the moment Curti was delivering his prophecy, Daniel Boorstin, and Perry Miller, and Louis Hartz, and R. W. B. Lewis, and others were well into their books which would signal the rise of a new kind of explanation in American historical and American Studies scholarship. Resistance to the old form was too far along then to be stilled by rhetoric.

In short, Merle Curti's prophecy failed. But the fact that such a figure could take such a tack at such a time indicates something of the holding power of the Progressive paradigm even in its dying moments.

IV

In this chapter, we're concerned with the question, *How does a mind behave under strain?* And in each of these case studies, we're also concerned not only to assert *that* mind behaves in such and such a way, but to show *how* —that is, to try and get inside mind, and see it in motion. We want to get involved in the *behavior* of historians' mind-forms. Thus our next task is to locate a place where we can observe this behavior, where the action of mind happens. And that should direct us right in to our fault-line, the vulnerable point (or at least *a* vulnerable point) of the Progressive paradigm.

Just where is this fault-line? Well, it should lie along the plane of most intense commitment in the paradigm. It's there where we should find its area of highest pressure build-up. Before, we noted that Progressives committed themselves to a picture that makes experience come out progress. But what happens when it doesn't? What if their prophecies about the future fail them, and experiences come out not looking like progress to them at all? It's at this point where the most revealing of strains should be opened in the Progressives' pattern of beliefs. I think it may be the basic fault-line in their whole paradigm. We'll investigate that fault-line here in Frederick Jackson Turner's book, *The Frontier in American History*.

Why Turner? Well, why not I suppose. Certainly he wasn't the only Progressive suffering strains in his explanation-form; yet our method of "strategic" criticism obliges us not to cover several historians but to focus in on one or two. So we'll take *a* mind as illustrative, and bring in others only incidentally.

Of the five most prominent Progressives, Becker and Robinson are out, at least for our central focus in this chapter (we'll make a few glancing remarks on them at the chapter's end). Becker often behaves more like a counter-Progressive than a Progressive, and Robinson wasn't all that influential. Besides, most of Robinson's substantive work was in European and not American history.

Which leaves us with Turner, Beard, and Parrington. I suppose if we wanted, we could make a reasonably good case for any of them. Of the three, Beard more nearly represents the political strain of American Progressivism, connecting most directly into public issues of his day. He thought more about political problems and involved himself more actively in them than did the other two. So if we went into Beard, we'd probably learn more things about the American Progressive movement in general than with any other historian in the school. But Beard wrote so many different and contradictory things over so many years that it would be hard to pinpoint one thing and focus in on it as a basic fault-line in his work. Not that it couldn't be done. It could, and David Marcell has made a suggestive beginning in a notable essay, "Charles Beard: Civilization and the Revolt Against Empiricism."[11] But to work it all out would take more space than we can use here.

Parrington is maybe the closest to being "modal" of all the Progressive historians, and we'll get substantially into him on that later. He wasn't as involved politically as Beard, nor was he as original a thinker. But if there's any single work which crystallizes what Progressive historical writing was generally up to, I suppose it's *Main Currents in American Thought*. It's a kind of composite Progressivist picture of American ideas. But Parrington's work came on the scene after much of the Progressive pattern had already formed. *Main Currents* served to condense the whole paradigm into a tightly interconnected cluster, moving it out into new areas (like literature), and applying it to the entire span of America's past. By the time Parrington did that (1927–30), however, strains in this Progressive form had grown acute. He may thus better illustrate the historiographical earthquake which destroyed this form than to express early strains building up inside it. Thus we'll take up Parrington in the next chapter, "A Paradigm Revolution in the Making."

Which leaves us with Turner. Who was first of the Progressive school, and there's something to be said for that. Who also wrote sparingly. There's something to be said for that too, at least when we're trying to hold our focus on a few things and not be overwhelmed by information overload. I've nothing against prolific historians—my favorite one was remarkably so. They can give headaches, though, to the historical critic who would prefer to take a limited universe of materials and work around thoroughly inside them. But I guess that can't be helped. Historians will write as they will; the critic can only sigh in relief when he comes upon some relatively sparse writer like Turner or Becker. And figure this is his just compensation for having also to tackle the bulky fellows like, say, Beard or Perry Miller.

But these are only incidental concerns, the last one somewhat frivolous, and most un-scholar-like. My basic reason for choosing Turner as a focus here is this: In his 1920 book, *The Frontier in American History,* we can watch a single mind worrying through the same problem time and again over some twenty-five years. The book consists of thirteen essays—beginning with his famous 1893 piece, "The Significance of the Frontier in American History," and ending with a 1918 wartime address, "Middle Western Pioneer Democracy." It also includes a revealing preface to the volume, written in 1920.[12]

Such a work offers us the advantage of time perspective—we can observe the same mind confronting the same dilemma over some duration, and we can see how its strategies develop through the years (or fail to develop, as the case may be). Of course this makes for a disadvantage too. A volume of essays is not as tightly constructed as is the usual kind of history work. Precisely because they carry different strategies to meet different kinds of situations, these essays won't give us quite the concentrated focus of the book-form we talked about in chapters 3 and 6.

But these are not just random essays gathered together either. Turner's most loyal supporter and his most penetrating critic both agree that he was uneasy with the book-form, and was more comfortable writing essays.[13] So when he was called upon in mid-career to express his full, matured position, Turner's response was to bring his major essays together into a single volume, *The Frontier in American History.*

It's significant that in his 1920 preface to this volume he chose neither to revise or even comment on his earlier positions. Instead, he simply repeated them. And later he was to write of this book: "On the whole I was rather pleased and surprised by the degree of continuity that appeared in the scattered essays brought into a single book, for which they were not originally intended."[14] So, given this continuity in position and given that we're not trying to handle the whole volume but only a single kind of fault-line within it, *The Frontier in American History* should serve our purposes here right well.

V

Turner's fault-line situation is set by the opening and closing scenes of his seminal 1893 essay, "The Significance of the Frontier in American History." That essay opens:

In a recent bulletin of the Superintendent of the Census for 1890 appear these significant words: "Up to and including 1880 the country had a frontier of settlement, but at present the unsettled area has been so broken into by isolated bodies of settlement that there can hardly be said to be a frontier line. In the discussion of its extent, its westward movement, etc., it can not, therefore, any longer have a place in the census reports." This brief official statement marks the closing of a great historic movement. Up to our own day American history has been in a large degree the history of the colonization of the Great West. The existence of an area of free land, its continuous recession, and the advance of American settlement westward, explain American development.[15]

And it closes:

What the Mediterranean Sea was to the Greeks, breaking the bond of custom, offering new experiences, calling out new institutions and activities, that, and more, the ever retreating frontier has been to the United States directly, and to the nations of Europe more remotely. And now, four centuries from the discovery of America, at the end of a hundred years of life under the Constitution, the frontier has gone, and with its going has closed the first period of American history.[16]

Frederick Jackson Turner is a Progressive, and Progressives are thought to be optimistic about the future. Yet here's a young Progressive launching a historical career not on a cheerful note but a tragic one. The frontier, he says, "explain[s] American development." But he also says that by the time of his essay, this frontier is over with. What then of the American future? How to explain it now, with its mobilizing force gone?

Earlier, we said a paradigm strain occurs in a situation where explanation and experience go in different ways. Well, here we have one. Turner's explanation of America is the *open* frontier. But his experience of the country —after his symbolic census date of 1890—is the *closed* frontier. This would be no paradigm strain if he then went on to devise some new kind of explanation for his post-1890 experience, or if he simply stuck with the pre-1890 experience and paid no attention to what happens afterward.[17] But Turner did neither. Time and again in this volume he worries over that dilemma. And in the doing he's able to pinpoint his problem precisely—*how to construct a new explanation when he sees the experience around him changing?* That's Frederick Jackson Turner's fault-line. *We* don't have to expose it for him—*he* sees it quite as clearly as we can. But seeing a rift in one's own mind is one thing, closing it off is quite another. As we'll learn in some moments, Turner was never able to do that. Not, at least, in *The Frontier in American History.*

His eyes thus show him one set of experiences, but his mind simply fails to go along. We might, in trying to capsulize this situation of strain, label the division here *Turner (I)* and *Turner (II)*—Turner (I) being his explanation of pre-1890 America with a still-opening frontier, Turner (II) being that explanation under stress, as it attempts to cope with his altered sense of America after 1890.[18]

If we put together Turner (I)'s picture of America, it might look something like this:

First, he'd probably welcome John Locke's claim, "In the beginning, all the world was America." In his 1893 "Significance" essay, Turner writes of "the originally simple, inert continent"; by that, he means America has been what the Old World is not.[19] Where the Old World is bounded in, America is open. Where the Old World is complex and convoluted, America is simple and pure. Where the Old World is oppressive, in America one can be free. In the Old World, people are always burdened down by tradition and by all sorts of interconnected obligations; but in America if one sets out to do something he can go straight on to do it. "America," says Turner, "became the land of European dreams" (1914).[20] And here dream could become actuality.

It is (or was) *the frontier* which makes America so distinctive to Turner (I). The frontier is an arena where people may go to regenerate themselves, to start all over again with life. Throughout America's past, we can find "a return to primitive conditions on a continually advancing frontier line"; and, he goes on to note, "This perennial rebirth, this fluidity of American life, this expansion westward with its new opportunities, its continuous touch with the simplicity of primitive society, furnish the forces dominating American character" (1893).[21]

For Frederick Jackson Turner, the frontier is a kind of transforming instant. Its initial impact is overwhelming, and *man* there is forced to give in to *thing.* Which giving in is the initial moment of his being re-born:

The wilderness masters the colonist. It finds him a European in dress, industries, tools, modes of travel, and thought. It takes him from the railroad car and puts him in the birch canoe. It strips off the garments of civilization and arrays him in the log cabin of the Cherokee and Iroquois and runs an Indian palisade around him. Before long he has gone to planting Indian corn and plowing with a sharp stick; he shouts the war cry and takes the scalp in orthodox Indian fashion. In short, at the frontier the environment is at first too strong for the man. He must accept the conditions which it furnishes, or perish, and so he fits himself into the Indian clearings and follows the Indian trails. (1893)[22]

But the frontier is not just savagery for Turner, nor the Indian the prototypical American. The prototypical American, rather, is the man of the Old World who's fled from the weight of tradition there, and has become transfigured by this frontier impact. What emerges from that moment of regeneration is a being midway between European civilization and Indian savagery, but morally superior to both. "Little by little," says Turner, this re-born man "transforms the wilderness, but the outcome is not the old Europe, not simply the development of Germanic germs, any more than the first phenomenon was a case of reversion to the Germanic mark. The fact is, that here is a new product that is American" (1893).[23]

The frontier thus offers opportunity for the rejuvenation of man by things. It's also open space, where a people can stretch out. And it's free land, land out there for the taking. Free land has offered opportunity not only for individual regeneration in America, but for a collective safety valve from oppressions building up in the more settled areas back East:

An area of free land has continually lain on the western border of the settled area of the United States. Whenever social conditions tended to crystallize in the East, whenever capital tended to press upon labor or political restraints to impede the freedom of the mass, there was this gate of escape to the free conditions of the frontier. The free lands promoted individualism, economic equality, freedom to rise, democracy. Men would not accept inferior wages and a permanent position of social subordination when this promised land of freedom and equality was theirs for the taking. (1903)[24]

"Who would rest content under oppressive legislative conditions," Turner queries rhetorically, "when with a slight effort he might reach a land wherein to become a co-worker in the building of free cities and free States on the lines of his own ideal?" (1903).[25]

Free land calls out the fundamental dreams of men, and the fundamental dreams of men are for democracy. With opportunity to start all over, men will naturally create democracies. This is proven by the fact that America is more democratic than Europe and the newer areas of America more democratic than the old.

And that's how Turner (I) measures "progress" in America's history. Progress is movement toward democracy; it's this kind of progress which the frontier stimulates. It gives grounding (literally) to democratic aspirations. "American democracy," writes Turner, "was born of no theorist's dream; it was not carried in the *Sarah Constant* to Virginia, nor in the *Mayflower* to Plymouth." Rather,

It came out of the American forest, and it gained new strength each time it touched a new frontier. Not the constitution, but free land and an abundance of natural resources open to a fit people, made the democratic type of society in America for three centuries while it occupied its empire. [1914][26]

The frontier has thus been the arena for democracy in America, and the country's motive force for progress. Because America equals democratic progress in Turner (I)'s explanation-form, the frontier comprises "the really American part of our history" (1893).[27] Which means those in contact with that frontier have the truest vision of the country's proper direction, and have had continually to reinstill this vision in those who've lost contact with it, and thus have forgotten the true America. Hence, "The men of the Mississippi Valley compelled the men of the East to think in American terms instead of European. They dragged a reluctant nation on in a new course" (1909).[28]

VI

That, in effect, is what Turner believes the frontier has done in America. We've now touched most of the high points in his (I)-form, at least those most relevant to our purposes in this chapter.

So we might try and pull all this together into a *Turner* (I)-*cluster*—a chart of what goes with what in his mind. We should first note something about the *structure* of that mind, though, before we go on to analyze content. Somewhat less so than his Progressive colleague Vernon Parrington but much more frequently than most counter-Progressives, Turner (I) tends to think in pairs. In the language of the cognitive psychologist George Kelly, Turner's constructs are "bi-polar"—that is, they run along set planes, and one end of each plane pushes off against its opposite.[29]

The most basic of Turner (I)'s polarities seems to run along a *New World/Old World plane*. The last paragraph of his preface to the *Frontier* volume begins by quoting these words: "An American is the born enemy of all European peoples." Those words were spoken by one M. Adet, a French minister to the United States. He said that in 1796. In 1920, Frederick Jackson Turner responds:

Obviously erroneous as are these words, there was an element of truth in them. If we would understand this element of truth, we must study the transforming influence of the American wilderness, remote from Europe, and by its resources and its free opportunities affording the conditions under which a new people, with new social and political types and ideals, could arise to play its own part in the world, and to influence Europe.[30]

The Frontier in American History takes off from there. Its thirteen essays are spread out over a quarter century, yet nowhere in them does Turner veer far from this position. All his essays are impelled by the question—*How is America distinguished from (and, by implication, better than) Europe?* This New World/Old World polarity is Turner (I)'s master construct; by it, he organizes much of the rest of his thinking. We might plot the resulting pattern like so:

Geographical

New World	*v.*	Old World
Open space	*v.*	Closed space
Frontier	*v.*	Routines of settled civilization
Expansion	*v.*	Static permanence
Isolation	*v.*	Interdependence
West	*v.*	East

Political

Opportunity	*v.*	Resignation or discontent
Freedom	*v.*	Servitude
Democracy	*v.*	Stratification
Individualism	*v.*	Collectivism
Competition	*v.*	Regulation
Weak government	*v.*	Strong government

Temperamental

Perennial rebirth	*v.*	Habitual routines
Progress	*v.*	Persistence in ancient ways
Optimism	*v.*	Resignation
Buoyant individualism	*v.*	Passivity and weakness
Self-sufficience	*v.*	Dependence
Directness	*v.*	Indirection

Metaphysical

Natural	*v.*	Artificial
Primitive simplicity	*v.*	Convoluted complexity
Organic ideals	*v.*	Abstract doctrines

VII

These are some of the core categories into which Turner (I) fits experience. By looking at the whole cluster and at his bi-polar procedure for organizing everything, we get a clearer view of Turner (I)'s basic form for picturing reality in the world, and of the role America and the frontier play in it.

What of Frederick Jackson Turner's role in this cluster? He doesn't lay it out for us here in so many words, but we don't have to dig too far to find it. What we find is yet another plane of bi-polar constructs—*prophecy versus narrative or detached chronicle.*

Turner says nothing explicitly about the historian's proper role in this *Frontier* book. But in his earlier essays it's plain he has little brief with the view of historian as mere chronicler of the past.[31] It's also plain from the *Frontier* volume that Turner is trying to work out a different sense of role for himself there as a historian. And he develops a role which fits into his entire configuration of beliefs about America and democracy and the frontier and progress. This role makes of the historian *a prophet of democracy*. Along the way in his work, such a historian may chronicle, he may criticize, he may analyze, he may philosophize. But all these are incidental to his *basic* role—to make clear his commitment to the forces of democracy in America, and to write history which re-energizes the democratic aspirations of people by bringing their experience to public consciousness. When that's done, then American history may genuinely become progress-ive.[32]

It's this sense of role which time and again stimulates Turner (I) to play off America against Europe, and to use his New World/Old World polarity to organize the rest of his constructs. What results is an interconnected cluster giving drama and energy to his history writing, and making it usable as a force for progressive democracy in America. Turner seems most buoyant in his writing when the entire pattern is holding together, when—to him at least—experience and explanation merge into a single natural whole, and each tenet in his belief pattern supports every other one. The passages we quoted a while back from Turner (I) express this sense of buoyancy.

But our main concern here is for what happens when that sense breaks down, when one category in his pattern doesn't fit so well with another, and when experience isn't coming out progress for him. This is where Turner (II) enters our analysis.

VIII

Turner (II) is Turner's explanation-form under strain, trying to cope with the situation of post-frontier America. When handling Turner (I), we've taken statements from most anywhere in his book, and haven't been much concerned to ground each of them in strategic context. This is because Turner (I) seems to vary little over the years in these *Frontier* essays, so the precise situational context of any given (I)-form statement is not that crucial. The context *is* crucial for Turner (II), however, since here we're looking not for a sustained, integrated pattern of beliefs but for *moments of temporary disintegration*. So we must move into Turner (II) in a more controlled fashion. And we can best do that by focusing on some particular text within the book.

For most purposes, that would be his 1893 essay, "The Significance of the Frontier in American History." This is his most famous piece, it was written during perhaps his most creative period, and its passages are the ones most often cited by other historians. For Turner (I), it *is* the most revealing of his essays. But for Turner (II) not so. True, there are a couple fault-line moments in the essay—the opening and closing paragraphs which we quoted at the beginning of section V. But his opening paragraph is not followed up and his closing one couldn't be, so this essay offers no instance where we can watch how Turner responds to strain (save by simple avoidance, which may indicate something I suppose).

For Turner (II), the most revealing moments in his *Frontier* book come in an essay published ten years later—"Contributions of the West to American Democracy." It was originally delivered as a Phi Beta Kappa address at Northwestern University, then published in 1903 in the *Atlantic Monthly*.

The essay begins in an analytic tone. Democracy, Turner claims, hasn't yet been understood properly:

Political thought in the period of the French Revolution tended to treat democracy as an absolute system applicable to all times and to all peoples, a system that was created by the act of the people themselves on philosophical principles. Ever since that era there has been an inclination on the part of writers on democracy to emphasize the analytical and theoretical treatment to the neglect of the underlying factors of historical development.[33]

Turner counters with a plea to search for the essential dynamics empowering the democratic form. He asks for what Morton White has labeled "cultural organicism"; it's a main tenet in what White calls the Progressives' "revolt against formalism."[34] It wants to probe below idea-forms to catch the underlying realities of life. As Turner says,

The careful student of history must . . . seek the explanation of the forms and changes of political institutions in the social and economic forces that determine them. To know that at any one time a nation may be called a democracy, an aristocracy, or a monarchy, is not so important as to know what are the social and economic tendencies of the state.

"These," he contends, "are the vital forces that work beneath the surface and dominate the external form."[35]

That statement sets the situation for the essay—or rather, for the first three-fourths of it. Turner continues this opening plea for a few paragraphs more; then, at the bottom of his second page, he brings us to his initial series of fault-line moments. Consistent with his beginning strategy of "cultural organicism," he notes, "We find ourselves at the present time in an era of such profound economic and social transformation as to raise the question of the effect of these changes upon the democratic institutions of the United States."[36]

In other words, what now if experience in America no longer comes out democratic progress? Turner faces his own question head-on, enumerating several changes in the prior decade (since 1890) which call American democracy into question. He lists four basic changes:

"First," he says, "there is the exhaustion of the supply of free land and the closing of the movement of Western advance as an effective factor in American development."[37] Second, "there has been such a concentration of capital in the control of fundamental industries as to make a new epoch in the economic development of the United States. . . . Side by side with this concentration of capital has gone the combination of labor in the same vast industries."[38] Third is "the expansion of the United States politically and commercially into lands beyond the seas."[39] And fourth, "the political parties of the United States now tend to divide on issues that involve the question of Socialism."[40]

That's not a Turner (I)–like picture of America anymore—a land and its people free, open, independent, individualist, distant from the embroilments of the world. So how will Turner (II) handle this? Clearly, he sees it as entirely changed situation. "It is doubtful," he says, "if in any ten years of American history [the decade since 1890] more significant factors have revealed themselves."[41] "Taken together," he goes on, "they constitute a revolution."[42]

A radically new experience, then, requires a radically new kind of explanation. Which is precisely what Turner (II) sets out to construct (until he gets sidetracked). And he intends this explanation again to be consistent with his opening plea for an organic understanding of democracy. He queries, "Is it not obvious, then, that the student who seeks for the explanation of democracy in the social and economic forces that underlie political forms must make inquiry into the conditions that have produced our democratic institutions, if he would estimate the effect of these vast changes?"[43]

It *is* of course obvious, if we've followed Turner up to here in the essay; so we're not put off (yet) when he temporarily switches back to his (I)-form to trace the evolving democratic experience in pre-1890 frontier America. We're not put off because he's simply doing what he said he'd do—that is, offering a historical explanation of American democracy, by grounding it in the social and economic forces which have shaped the form.

This back-tracking, we assume, is merely a prelude to his later explaining democracy (or its fall) in *post*-frontier, post-1890 America. Which explanation is presumably why he posed those fault-line questions in the first place. So we go along with Turner for some 13½ pages (a little over half the essay—it's 26 pages in all), while he traces the course of American democracy from colonial times up to 1890 and the disappearance of free land.

The frontier is of course the prime mover, and the whole Turner (I) cluster charted in section VI is put into play. He praises the great democratic leaders of America—Jefferson, Jackson, Lincoln—and baits anti-democratic conservatives like Alexander Spotswood and Timothy Dwight. He notes the "struggle between the classes of the interior and those of the coast," and makes plain the interior stood for democracy.[44] He mentions how the frontier was "free from the influence of European ideas and institutions," and how "The men of the 'Western World' turned their backs upon the Atlantic Ocean, and with a grim energy and self-reliance began to build up a society free from the dominance of ancient forms."[45]

Most all of Turner's (I)-form is there. His only discouraging note comes near the end of this 13½-page journey—when he observes that, following the Civil War, free lands came to be trans-Mississippi arid lands, and were not fit for the independent yeoman farmer. This presents a dilemma not on his (I)-form schedule. After briefly mentioning it, he postpones the problem for a page or two, until he arrives at his second series of fault-line moments.

It's in this series where his behavior is most revealing, and where we can see just how Turner's mind belabors under stress. Indeed right here (beginning at the bottom of the eighteenth page of a 26-page essay) is to be found the severest explanation strain in the entire volume.

Turner could hardly be more straightforward in facing his situation. After having taken on his old (I)-form temporarily to chart the experience of frontier America, he now changes course abruptly: "The question is imperative, then, What ideals persist from this democratic experience of the West; and have they acquired sufficient momentum to sustain themselves under conditions so radically unlike those in the days of their origin?"[46] Which is precisely the question we've been asking ourselves as we've worked along with Turner through his essay.

Up to this point in the essay, his whole pattern has held together. And for four more sentences it continues to. For in these sentences Turner takes his fault-line question and connects it back to his opening situation:

In other words, the question put at the beginning of this discussion becomes pertinent. Under the forms of the American democracy is there in reality such a concentration of economic and social power in the hands of a comparatively few men as may make political democracy an appearance rather than a reality? The free lands are gone. The material forces that gave vitality to Western democracy are passing away.[47]

Logically, Turner must now either admit that American democracy will wane along with the waning of its impelling forces, or he must come up with some new organic force which can take over from the frontier and keep democracy from falling. That is the situation Turner's logic has driven him into; and it's right at this moment where his strategies—so well controlled up to now in the essay—begin falling apart. Watch his next sentence: "It is to the realm of the spirit, to the domain of ideals and legislation, that we must look for Western influence upon democracy in our own days."[48]

But wait. If the open frontier closes off and the open frontier is the source for democracy in America and if democracy must be organically connected to roots in the life of people, then, by Turner's own logic, no unorganic "realm of the spirit" can bail it out. For spirit without roots is impotent, again by Turner's own words—those which opened his essay. The alternatives for him are clear—either democracy goes, or he must find a new grounded base for it.

No matter. Turner soars right along with his theme, ignoring logic, and following that "realm of the spirit sentence" with: "Western democracy has been from the time of its birth idealistic."[49] It's of little moment now that his whole strategy earlier in the essay was to reject this kind of uprooted reasoning—to show that the idealistic form has always been undergirded by an organic substatum in America, and therefore it's wrong to see it as merely a floating idea. By now, Turner has got himself so locked into the rhetoric of his (I)-form that the illogic no longer comes through to him; and he's evidently forgot what he said earlier about *post*-1890 America presenting a revolutionary new situation. For to get America out of its contemporary dilemma in 1903, he snaps right back into his Turner (I), *pre*-1890 form: "The existence of this land of opportunity has made America the goal of idealists from the days of the Pilgrim Fathers. With all the materialism of the pioneer movements, this idealistic conception of the vacant lands as an opportunity for a new order of things is unmistakably present."[50]

The frontier has been the only energy source for Frederick Jackson Turner's mind. Even though he says it's closed off after 1890, he's driven to keep drawing on it to perpetuate his ideal picture of America. Wandering even further away from the organic roots of his picture, he quotes a *British* poem to shore up his vision of *American* frontier democracy. It's Kipling's "Song of the English":

> We were dreamers, dreaming greatly, in the man-stifled town;
> We yearned beyond the sky-line where the strange lands go down.
> Came the Whisper, came the Vision, came the Power with the Need,
> Till the Soul that is not man's soul was lent us to lead.
> As the deer breaks—as the steer breaks—from the herd where they graze,
> In the faith of little children we went on our ways.
> Then the wood failed—then the food failed—then the last water dried—
> In the faith of little children we lay down and died.
>
> On the sand-drift—on the velt-side—in the fern-scrub we lay,
> That our sons might follow after by the bones on the way.
> Follow after—follow after! We have watered the root
> And the bud has come to blossom that ripens for fruit!
> Follow after—we are waiting by the trails that we lost
> For the sound of many footsteps, for the tread of a host.
>
> Follow after—follow after—for the harvest is sown:
> By the bones about the wayside ye shall come to your own![51]

Turner began this essay—"Contributions of the West to American Democracy"—sounding the need to root ideas in the world of things. Now, three-quarters of the way into it, he resorts to rootless ideas himself in order to keep democracy afloat in the land. He's got no other source of leverage; democracy for him has lost its underpinning in American life and now seems to inhabit some autonomous, self-generating sphere of its own.

And Turner's mode of analysis mirrors this change. Where before in the essay he'd structured his reasoning either by logic or by chronology, now it simply wanders rootless in search of the pure democratic idea. Which idea Turner is obliged to give us in disconnected bits and pieces. Like: "Hardly a Western State but has been the Mecca of some sect or band of social reformers."[52] "Even as he dwelt among the stumps of his newly-cut clearing, the pioneer had the creative vision of a new order of society."[53] The Middle West has meant "a destiny proportioned to the power that God had given [men]."[54] America "has furnished to this new democracy her stores of mineral wealth, that dwarf those of the Old World, and her provinces that in themselves are vaster and more productive than most of the nations of Europe."[55]

Once, Turner seems to sense that such words dodge the question he'd earlier posed for himself, and he tries to justify his behavior with reasoning like this:

It must be remembered that these democratic ideals have existed at each stage of the advance of the frontier, and have left behind them deep and enduring effects on the thinking of the whole country. Long after the frontier period of a particular region of the United States has passed away, the conception of the society, the ideals and aspirations which it produced, persist in the minds of the people.[56]

Now it's of course legitimate for a mind to reason that way. But it's a strain for Turner's mind to, since he's offered no explanation for why ideals can ever exist apart from the grounded experience of them (Plato could handle this, so also Hegel; not so Turner). He only proclaims the ideals, he never explains them. Whenever he does try to explain, it's back in his (I)-form, and that would seem to give little hope for democracy in America after 1890. For in the words of Turner (I), democracy is the result of a preeminently transforming *experience*—the regeneration which issues forth from immediate personal contact with the frontier. Without that experience, democracy in the land simply has no base.

Turner (I)'s is an *existential* explanation; experience must precede ideas, the frontier must precede democracy. Earlier in this "Contributions" essay, when he was following along his organicist strategy, he'd sought to correct the fact that "We have believed as a nation that other peoples had only to will our democratic institutions in order to repeat our own career."[57] But now Turner (II) is trying hard to believe just this, that democracy in America can survive on will alone.

Turner (II) is trying to give his audience the *word* and *idea* of democracy here without the grounded *experience* for it. Because democracy has been rooted in the frontier experience, and the frontier experience, after 1890, is over, people can no longer get into democracy first hand. Hence, by Turner's own logic, there's no place in the land to regenerate oneself anymore, save in memory and spirit. Thus, in an unwitting but enormous reversal of the whole radicalizing thrust of his (I)-form, he writes, "The problem of the United States is not to create democracy, but to conserve democratic institutions and ideas."[58]

Turner says that. But he offers no explanation for how it can happen. He merely makes America democratic by fiat, transforming his (I)-form existential explanation into an essentialist faith. No longer is his mind in radical revolt against abstracted formalism; now it's established a formalism of its own. And it's a formalism which lacks either grounding or vital energy.

It also involves Turner (II) in some peculiar revisions of Turner (I). Where before in this essay he'd scored the wealthy and raised doubts about the concentration of capital in a few hands, now he claims the masters of American industry are really only small democrats writ big. The John D. Rockefellers, the Mark Hannas, the Marshall Fields, the Andrew Carnegies —all "came from the midst of this [democratic] society and still profess its principles."[59] And, he writes of Carnegie, "Whatever may be the tendencies of [his] corporation, there can be little doubt of the democratic ideals of Mr. Carnegie himself."[60]

Where before he had claimed democracy as an immediate, regenerating experience available to everyone, now he writes, "If, indeed, we ourselves were not pioneers, our fathers were. . . . This experience has been wrought into the very warp and woof of American thought."[61]

The words go on like this pretty much undiminished, until, with some evident relief, Turner (II) closes his essay with this prophetic flourish: "Let us see to it that the ideals of the pioneer in his log cabin shall enlarge into the spiritual life of a democracy where civic power shall dominate and utilize individual achievement for the common good."[62]

IX

Here we can see a mind trying to move under strain—sensing new things, reaching out to explain them, but then snapped back into its old forms when the new threatens to overwhelm it. What we've been seeing is the experience of such a mind at such a time. Our next task is to try and offer explanation.

Up to now, our question has been, *How* does a mind react under stress? Here, we'll also ask the question, *Why?* Why does this mind behave as it does? Why questions are trickier than how ones; we're thus on shakier ground here than in the last section. So we'll follow our past procedure in this book when working in the territory of the tentative—listing a few possible "perspectives" on explanation, rather than giving one sure explanation of the whole matter.

1. First, we ought to note that what we've just seen of Frederick Jackson Turner is no isolated instance. That "Contributions" essay does offer the clearest and most extended case of Turner (II) in action, but it's not the only case by any means.

In charting this *Frontier* volume, I've counted some twenty-nine fault-line moments in it. Of these, nineteen could be called "pure" fault lines—where Turner recognizes that the frontier is over with and there's no more free land in America. The remaining ten are what could be called "partial" fault lines —that is, some variant of the above, like Turner's acknowledging labor strife in the country, or noting the pioneers' post-Civil War passage out onto arid lands in the West, or some such. When, for example, he writes in 1919, "With the end of free lands the basis of its democratic society is passing away," that we could say is a pure fault line.[63] But when he notes in 1910 that after the Civil War, "the farmer became dependent as never before on transportation companies," this is more of a partial fault line.[64]

In twelve of the nineteen pure fault-line situations in the book, Turner (II) responds with behavior resembling what we saw in the last section. That is, he pinpoints his problem, queries how he shall respond now, then he shies away from his own question with some rhetorical flourish from the (I)-form.

In his 1914 essay "The West and American Ideals," for example, Turner opens out a fault line thus: "Legislation is taking the place of free lands as the means of preserving the ideal of democracy. But at the same time it is endangering the other pioneer ideal of creative and competitive individualism." But two sentences further on, he closes this same fault line back off with:

It would be a grave misfortune if these people so rich in experience, in self-confidence and aspiration, in creative genius, should turn to some Old World discipline of socialism or plutocracy, or despotic rule, whether by class or by dictator. Nor shall we be driven to these alternatives. Our ancient hopes, our courageous faith, our underlying good humor and love of fair play will triumph in the end.[65]

That's one of the twelve fault-line responses I've noted. The other eleven are much like it. Of the seven responses (out of nineteen total) which aren't, three times he simply mentions the fault line, then goes on to something else (or ends his essay, as he did with his 1893 "Significance of the Frontier" piece); three other times he acknowledges that maybe government legislation can safeguard democracy now; but only once in the entire volume—in his American Historical Association presidential address of 1910—does he take the fault line as an indication not only that America has changed, but also that his (I)-form of explanation may need re-structuring. There he writes, "Time has revealed that these two ideals of pioneer democracy [individual freedom and democratic equality] had elements of mutual hostility and contained the seeds of its dissolution."[66] But this insight was never followed up in any later essays in the *Frontier* volume, so Turner (II) evidently didn't find it an adequate strategy for handling strain. His characteristic response in those later essays, rather, is to snap back in the old Turner (I) form.[67]

2. Note that we're not saying that there were "objective" experiences in the world which Turner's mind failed to see. Mind is invariably channeled, and can never see all that's there. Frederick Jackson Turner may have missed many things happening in the world around him, but that's not our concern here.

We're concerned instead with something Turner *did* see, something which begins his 1893 essay elevating him to historical prominence, something he returns to time and again thereafter in his writings. And this is the disappearance of free land, and what that implies for democracy in America. Repeatedly, Turner will see this problem, will define it as important, will try and explain it, but then under mounting strain will lapse back into his old mind-form.

His eyes will show him one thing, he'll then try to get his mind around what he sees, but he just can't. Turner (II) can *perceive* outside the Turner (I) explanation-form in this *Frontier* volume, but he cannot *conceive* outside it.

Or, in our language, he can "experience" post-frontier America, he cannot "explain" it. Rather, he can't explain it and at the same time protect his sacred vision of a democratic future for the country. He can note changes taking place in his America and on occasion can even recommend how to deal with them. But he has no sustained explanation for how to salvage democratic progress in this altered American situation.

So again, why? Well, for one thing, Turner (I)'s bi-polar constructs keep getting in the way. Recall the chart back in section VI. There we saw Turner (I)'s organizing levers on experience, with his New World/Old World polarity guiding the whole pattern.

In his pre-1890 form, all the bi-polar constructs held together neatly for Turner (I). Perhaps too neatly. For as he tries to rearrange a few things for his (II)-form, it looks as if everything in his world might be coming unstuck. He will characteristically start with his main fault-line—end of the free lands. Since closed space is opposed to open space in Turner's bi-polar constructs, he has to make that adjustment too. But then opportunity and rebirth and individualism are also connected to open space, and their bi-polar opposites are resignation or discontent, habitual routines, and collectivism. So those must be rearranged also. If all his constructs are interconnected in this way, pretty soon that core *New World/Old World* polarity will be threatened also, and this is more than Frederick Jackson Turner can handle. That polarity sets the outer boundary for his explanation-form (one might say for a good deal of his personal identity too), and he's simply unwilling to have it tampered with.

It's at this sensitive point—when the New World's unique virtues are close to being challenged—where Turner (II) is most inclined to snap back into his (I)-form, and fly off in some kind of rhetorical flourish. Which flourish says in effect, "After all, this *is* America, and we've got this great heritage of freedom behind us, and it can't let us down."

Here is one source of what we might call an "explanation lock" in Turner's mind. His bi-polar constructs are inter-linked so tightly that when he begins to revise individual pieces of the pattern, he gets just so far before it looks like the whole cluster might disintegrate—including, most importantly, its unmoved mover, New World versus Old World. Neither of the two Turners— (I) or (II)—is willing to let go of that.

3. Another source for this lock is a latent contradiction in Turner's sense of the frontier. There are many ambiguities in his use of this term "frontier," and Richard Hofstadter has detailed several of them in *The Progressive Historians*.[68] But one in particular is worth our attention here. It's a built-in ambiguity of Turner's (I)-form of explanation, and it threatens his sense of progress in the land right from the beginning.

We might say that in the explanation-form of Turner (I), America is what the earth was like before man began interfering with it. She symbolizes a fresh environment of *un-manmade things* for him, and the frontier is where this is most true. It's where men can come most intimately in contact not with other men but with things in their untouched purity.

It's this purity which gives Turner's frontier experience its transforming power. From the frontier, people gain opportunity to shuck off their past and start anew. For Turner, the frontier is a kind of perennial "future shock"— sans the shock, of course.[69]

Because of this frontier, people could be freed of European habits to commune with fresh things in the New World. And that's mainly how Turner (I) would measure progress in the land—progress is movement away from Old World confinements. As he wrote in 1918, "nature's revelations are progressive."[70]

But Turner catches himself in an inherent dilemma by such an explanation. For by definition, this kind of frontier experience is a transforming *instant* to Turner. And it requires *personal* contact, of man with thing. Once that instant is over, what then? How do you go on to live with such an experience in such a place? If you stay on the frontier for a while, invariably you'll have impact on it. You'll take its un-manmade things and try to make them over in your own image. In time, the land will begin showing traces of man. If this keeps on long enough, you may go on to build institutions, governments, industries, what have you. But those, in Turner's bi-polar cluster of constructs, are part of the *Old World* syndrome, what America is *not*. So it puts a strain on his explanation-form to call them "progress," for the Old World is supposed to represent regress. I think this is the dilemma Richard Hofstadter pinpointed when he queried of the American progressivist faith, "How can a people progress if they have started near to perfection?"[71]

A Charles Beard could get out of this dilemma (or at least some of him could), for his explanation of progress was connected not to un-manmade things but to technology and human community. But for most of Turner, not so (ditto Parrington). His explanation is always under strain when handling the products of human civilization.

For finally to Frederick Jackson Turner, democracy and progress mean *simplicity* (as to Trilling and Niebuhr in the next chapter they finally mean *complexity*). They mean breaking through convoluted Old World forms and penetrating to the primal New World essence below.

But however much he *sought* simplicity and purity, the contemporary *experience* of Turner (II) was coming to mean complexity. And ambiguity.

Even though he could sense this ambiguity—could in fact go along with part of it and cheer industrial growth, recommend certain kinds of government regulation, and so on—Frederick Jackson Turner had no *principle* to explain ambiguous experience. Nor did he take his experience of present ambiguity to indicate there might have been ambiguity in the American past too. Which could also imply built-in ambiguities in his (I)-form of explanation. Save for a single instance in his 1910 American Historical Association presidential address—where he admitted that democratic individualism may have been opposed all along to democratic equality—Turner never in this volume recognizes any chinks in his pre-1890 mode of explanation. That too may account for some of the strain in Turner (II)'s explanation-form. He just found it too tempting, it seems, to lapse back into the comfort of old forms.

4. Those are a few substantive reasons why Turner may have behaved as he did under strain. There are structural reasons too. One is tied to Turner's sense of *role*.

When Frederick Jackson Turner is under stress, he tends to assume the *prophetic* persona (he assumes it often when he's not under stress too). Within that persona, he becomes the voice of America's democratic aspirations, guiding the people onto the path of true progress. And he proclaims things like: "Let us dream as our fathers dreamt and let us make our dreams come true."[72] Or: "It is important that the Middle West should accomplish this; the future of the Republic is with her."[73] And: "As we turn from the first rough conquest of the continent there lies before us a whole wealth of unexploited resources in the realm of the spirit."[74]

This means we've an additional variable now in our picture of Turner and mind and world. For here is a historian not only trying to *explain* America, he's *taking responsibility* for it. Which puts added pressure of commitment onto his explanation-form. Doubtless this makes him behave differently than he might have otherwise. Just as a man with family may experience certain constraints which a bachelor doesn't, so also a historian who feels a nation's future on his shoulders.

This sense of role was strategically valuable in the Turner (I) explanation, when everything was meshing neatly for him. It gave him a lot of leverage on a lot of materials, and it made his historian's mission seem larger than just doing scholarship.

But precisely because this strategy worked so well for him in its (I)-form, it becomes hard to change in the Turner (II) situation. His bi-polar constructs—this versus that—fit neatly into the prophetic role for Turner (I). But when he tries rearranging some of those constructs for Turner (II), this sense of role keeps pulling him back. It will not allow him distance or leverage or perspective on himself and his new situation. Because he obliges himself to take on the prophetic role, Turner can't just "play" with experience for a time and experiment with new forms; the world (or at least the New World) weighs too heavily on him for that.[75]

Under such a mind-strain in such a time, a purely intellectual commitment might have soured, might have given up on a world which failed to behave according to its own explanation of things. But if it was Turner's prophetic faith in progress that got him in this bind in the first place, it also kept him from become cynical or complacent about life in America.

That's because his commitment is not purely intellectual here—and, under strain, not even mostly intellectual. Turner's first commitment is evidently to prophesying progress in the land, only secondarily does he try explaining that progress in a coherent, self-consistent manner. Prophecy, not explanation, claims his first loyalty at moments when the two conflict.[76]

And, as we've said, it's prophecy about *progress*. Progress is not only an explanation to progressivist Americans like Turner; it's also a kind of sheltering assumption, and can be used as an avenue for strategic escape. When all else fails—when logic is getting him in a bind and the facts don't seem to be going his way—he can always bail himself out with some glowing prophecy about the future of the republic.

This strategy will invariably work—with such progressivist minds—because of their abiding faith in what David Noble has called "the national covenant."[77] Under this covenant, the nation itself can never go wrong. Parts of it may veer off the straight path of progress, but these are only temporary aberrations. It *must* be that way because America has this mission to regenerate the world—especially the Old World—and if America's future begins to look bleak, what hope is there for mankind?

We saw a similar behavior back in chapter 5 (section VII), in Cotton Mather's effort to get his Salem court off the hook on "spectral evidence." Perry Miller wrote of Mather there:

Cotton salvaged what defense he could for a court in which he did not believe by the pitiful remonstrance: "Surely, they have at worst been the faults of a well-meaning Ignorance." We avert our gaze while he, having made what he could of Stephen's notes, fled up the ladder of the jeremiad and soothed himself with fresh dreams of the New Jerusalem, "from whence the Devil shall then be banished, there shall be no Devil within the Walls of that Holy City."[78]

Compare those last words of Mather with these of Turner: "Let us see to it that the ideals of the pioneer in his log cabin shall enlarge into the spiritual life of a democracy where civic power shall dominate and utilize individual achievement for the common good."[79] And, "Let us dream as our fathers dreamt and let us make our dreams come true."[80] Or:

It would be a grave misfortune if these people so rich in experience, in self-confidence and aspiration, in creative genius, should turn to some Old World discipline of socialism or plutocracy, or despotic rule, whether by class or by dictator. Nor shall we be driven to these alternatives. Our ancient hopes, our courageous faith, our underlying good humor and love of fair play will triumph in the end.[81]

If Cotton Mather "fled up the ladder of the jeremiad" in the late seventeenth century, Frederick Jackson Turner seems to have fled up the ladder of the national covenant some two centuries afterward. And, if we're not quite ashamed like Miller to "avert our gaze" (Turner, after all, was not quite condoning witch hanging), we may be somewhat embarrassed that, under pressure, he is so given to behaving like that. Almost invariably in such moments, he moves under the spell of prophecy, and is virtually reduced to incantation.[82]

We may now want to qualify some the title words of this chapter. With Turner, it's not quite "When *Prophecy* [about progress] Fails," it's "When *Explanation* [as a base for that prophecy] Fails."[83] Prophecy never really fails Frederick Jackson Turner. For when he can't predict progress through explanation, he always can make it through the national covenant. Prophecy at that point ceases to be an explanation, however, and becomes a kind of exhortation.

In Turner, it seems, there are two bases for prophecy, for predicting a future of democratic progress for America. His first base is explanation. Which is essentially the whole Turner (I) cluster we saw in section VI. It includes the frontier as the organic root for democracy in America, and all his bi-polar constructs (especially New World vs. Old World). This explanation strategy works fine for Turner (I). If he occasionally uses the prophetic voice under that form, it's still congruent with his basic way of explaining things, since the open frontier will guarantee a future of promise for America. Prophecy is thus *grounded* in the Turner (I) explanation-form.

It is not grounded in the strained explanation-form of Turner (II). Which is another way of saying prophecy goes in one direction for him, explanation in another. And prophecy—here sans roots—always prevails. If Turner can't explain progress organically through his own mind anymore, he'll let the abstracted national covenant do it for him. Which is his second base for prophecy. And this base invariably works for Turner; the American covenant is too near where he lives for him ever seriously to question it.[84]

So at the point where Turner lacks specific and grounded, operational ideas for explaining America's future, he lets the archetypal New World idea come to his rescue. At these moments, "progress" does not look like a confident prediction anymore, it looks like a sort of brake against despair, against the intellectual void of not understanding a discordant America around him. Thus like Cotton Mather two centuries before, Frederick Jackson Turner under strain elected to go "with the tide of his rhetoric," and sought to stay the course of American history with high-flying words.[85]

5. That last sentence may be severe. It does apply to Turner (II) when he's under the prophetic role. But he doesn't always assume that role when responding to stress. Occasionally, he'll take some other position. None of them is sustained long in his *Frontier* volume; mostly, they're mentioned in an essay or two, then never followed up again. But they are worth noting here, because they show a part of Turner (II) who grapples with explanation differently from what we've seen in these last few pages.

Several times in the book, Turner (II) will abandon his (I)-form polarity of individualism versus collectivism and, for a while, opt to cure post-1890 ills in America by *increasing government controls.* Usually, this tack will be sparked by some pressing problem in the West—arid lands, Populism, unfair railroad rates. At those moments, Turner comes to resemble a typical political Progressive of his times—acknowledging the failure of private initiative and calling for government regulation to guide the country toward greater social justice and rationality.

But at the point where this tendency would threaten his New World/Old World polarity—when more government controls would make America look like any other European country to Turner—he backs off and assumes the prophetic persona again.[86] That he started along this path so often suggests Turner kept touch with liberal political sentiments of his day. That he would go just so far suggests he didn't find this strategy wholly appropriate for closing off his fault-line. It was not a new explanation for him, I suspect, so much as an occasional bow to the Progressive political milieu around him. It seems to have been borrowed more than it was natural to him, and under even a little strain he was willing to give it up completely.

Less frequently in this book, but more coherently, Turner (I) poses *sectionalism* as a way out of his closed-frontier dilemma. This is especially the case in his 1909 essay, "The Ohio Valley in American History." He opens that essay with an unusual paragraph; it seems to contradict much of his (I)-form cluster:

In a notable essay Professor Josiah Royce has asserted the salutary influence of a highly organized provincial life in order to counteract certain evils arising from the tremendous development of nationalism in our own day. Among these he enumerates: first, the frequent changes of dwelling place, where the community is in danger of losing the well-knit organization of a common life; second, the tendency to reduce variety in national civilization, to assimilate all to a common type and thus to discourage individuality, and produce a "remorseless mechanism—vast, irrational;" [sic] third, the evils arising from the fact that waves of emotion, the passion of the mob, tend in our day to sweep across the nation.[87]

This looks like an entirely new strategy for Frederick Jackson Turner. In Turner (I), community and stability had been placed on the *Old World* side of his schema; but now he seems to be rearranging the polarities. And he *is,* but not quite as radically as those opening words might imply. For as we read on in this essay, it becomes clear that community and sectionalism are strategic devices for protecting his old form, not avenues for experimenting with a new one. He's still setting off the New World against the Old. Only now the Old World symbol is shifting ground for him; it's no longer just Europe, it's also the whole Eastern United States (this, by the way, just one year before Turner moved from Wisconsin to Harvard!)

So also, then, does Turner (II) shift ground in his defense of democracy. What began in 1893 as a commitment to process, the frontier, here has become a commitment to place, sectionalism. And not sectionalism in general but the American Midwest in particular. Turner has not given up on individualism or the other frontier virtues. He's simply using new devices to protect them, and to keep Old World traditions from invading their Midwestern, New World sanctuary.

Nor has Turner given up on his national covenant here, or the prophetic voice to proclaim it. In his next-to-the-last paragraph (sounding a defensive note about so often taking the prophetic pose), he writes, "Nor is it necessary that I should attempt to prophesy concerning the future which the Ohio Valley will hold in the nation." It may not be necessary, but Turner goes on to do it anyway, closing out his essay with these words:

Let us hope that its [the Ohio Valley's] old love of democracy may endure, and that in this section, where the first trans-Alleghany pioneers struck blows at the forests, where may be brought to blossom and to fruit the ripe civilization of a people who know that whatever the glories of prosperity may be, there are greater glories of the spirit of man; who know that in the ultimate record of history, the place of the Ohio Valley will depend upon the contribution which her people and her leaders make to the cause of an enlightened, a cultivated, a God-fearing and a free, as well as a comfortable, democracy.[88]

Those first three words—"Let us hope"—betray maybe a little worry in Turner, but not much evidently. His American vision still lives. Sectionalism—or rather Midwest sectionalism—is not really a new form of explanation for Turner (II) in this volume, since in later essays he neglects it for the (I)-form again. And even here, as we've seen, he'll still resort to prophecy and the national covenant at certain strategic moments. But if he's not quite broken over the threshold to a full new explanation, he comes about as close with sectionalism as with anything in this volume.[89]

Beyond these two—regulation by government and sectionalism—three other possibilities opened to Turner (II). Each claimed his attention briefly as a strategy to salvage democracy in post-1890 America. But none seems more than a momentary mood—a particular strategy used at a particular time, but seldom returned to again.

One strategy is simply *to glory in the nation's new industrial might*. This strategy can be found in his 1901 piece "The Middle West," where he writes,

A huge industrial organism has been created in the province,—an organism of tremendous power, activity, and unity. . . . The huge water system of the Great Lakes has become the highway of a mighty commerce. The Sault Ste. Marie Canal, although open but two-thirds of the year, is the channel of a traffic of a greater tonnage than that which passes through the Suez Canal. . . .

Turner continues in this vein,

This rapid rise of the merchant marine of our inland seas has led to the demand for deep water channels to connect them with the ocean road to Europe. When the fleets of the Great Lakes plow the Atlantic, and when Duluth and Chicago become seaports, the water transportation of the Middle West will have completed its evolution. The significance of the development of the railway system is not inferior to that of the great water way. Chicago has become the greatest railroad center of the world, nor is there another area of like size which equals this in its railroad facilities; all the forces of the nation intersect here. Improved terminals, steel rails, better rolling stock, and consolidation of railway systems have accompanied the advance of the people of the Middle West.[90]

For a while in this essay, that strategy seems to function well for Turner. Momentarily, he simply forgets about democracy and untamed nature, and indulges his pride in the country's massive material progress. And all the while he implicitly works the national covenant theme of New World versus Old World, glorying of course in the New.

But if Turner can be impressed by man-made things in America, he can't work up an explanation of democracy from them.[91] So after a time this pride in material growth begins to wear thin on him. Thus near the end of this "Middle West" essay, he pauses to note that Americans often need "the reminder that bigness is not greatness";[92] and his final words add a warning along with his usual closing cheer: "But if the ideals of the pioneer shall survive the inundation of material success, we may expect to see in the Middle West the rise of a highly intelligent society where culture shall be reconciled with democracy in the large."[93]

Once in this *Frontier* volume—in a 1910 essay entitled "Pioneer Ideals and the State University"—Turner (II) advances *the state universities* as a cure for the post-1890 ills of America. By this he means mostly the Middle Western state universities, so he hasn't abandoned all (I)-form hopes. But he does note that a spontaneous, unregulated individualism won't work anymore, that America now needs a pool of trained experts to help solve her national problems. As he puts it, "General experience and rule-of-thumb information are inadequate for the solution of the problems of a democracy which no longer owns the safety fund of an unlimited quantity of untouched resources."[94]

Now this is a major departure from his (I)-form. Where Turner (I) had seen democracy coming from the immediate, personal impact of frontier regeneration, here he sees democracy developing through the more collective, regulated growth of impersonal knowledge. And this is a knowledge which does not emerge from the people anymore. Turner sounds like a latter-day New Deal Liberal when he writes,

The industrial conditions which shape society are too complex, problems of labor, finance, social reform too difficult to be dealt with intelligently and wisely without the leadership of highly educated men familiar with the legislation and literature on social questions in other States and nations.

"By training in science, in law, politics, economics and history," he goes on, "the universities may supply from the ranks of democracy administrators, legislators, judges and experts for commissions who shall disinterestedly and intelligently mediate between contending interests."[95]

There is in this proposal, though, a little of that "up-the-ladder" behavior we noted before, so Turner hasn't completely broken free from his old forms. For one thing, he's still much into the American national covenant here and is exercised about threats to the republic from within. Thus, "Educated leadership sets bulwarks against both the passionate impulses of the mob and the sinister designs of those who would subordinate public welfare to private greed."[96]

For another, Turner doesn't quite explain how this educated leadership is to maintain its totally disinterested stance. He's appalled that stereotyped, Old World–like labels such as "the capitalistic classes" and "the proletariate" should be voiced so often in his day; and he wants his trained experts to overcome such class divisions by "disinterestedly and intelligently mediat[ing] between contending interests."[97]

But he never says *how*. Only that somehow the ideal of education is to guarantee their objectivity. Which ideal Turner voices in a most unorganic, "up-the-ladder" manner:

It is the function of the university to reveal to the individual the mystery and the glory of life as a whole—to open all the realms of rational human enjoyment and achievement; to preserve the consciousness of the past; to spread before the eye the beauty of the universe; and to throw wide its portals of duty and of power to the human soul.[98]

I doubt if a democracy (or any other polity, for that matter!) could survive long advised by men with visions like *this* in their heads. But we do know that Turner apparently didn't retain this vision in his own head for long. For in the four essays written after this in the *Frontier* volume, he never again returns to the theme of state universities as a guarantor of democracy. We get some insight on its temporary, "strategic" nature when we note it was given as an undergraduate commencement address, and at a state university too—Indiana. That may indicate why he said what he did then, and didn't say it again later—at least not in this book.[99]

Once in this volume—in a 1918 address on "Middle Western Pioneer Democracy"—Turner uses *war* as a way out of his post-1890 dilemma. Actually, this strategy doesn't get him out of the dilemma so much as it lets him forget it for a while. Democracy ceases to be problematic to Turner (as to many Americans) while his country is fighting for it.

Clearly, this is just a temporary out for Turner; but it does reveal how desperate can be his grip on the American national covenant, and how—during times of trial—his revulsion against the Old World can approach the grotesque. In a burst of Wilson-like chauvinism, he exclaims that in this war "The Prussian discipline is the discipline of Thor, the War God, against the discipline of the White Christ."[100] And he holds out the vision of a future day "where the *Pax Americana* furnishes an example for a better world."[101] Finally, Turner closes this essay—and the book—with:

This then is the heritage of pioneer experience,--a passionate belief that a democracy was possible which should leave the individual a part to play in free society and not make him a cog in a machine operated from above; which trusted in the common man, in his tolerance, his ability to adjust differences with good humor, and to work out an American type from the combinations of all nations—a type for which he would fight against those who challenged it in arms, and for which in time of war he would make sacrifices, even the temporary sacrifice of individual freedom and his life, lest that freedom be lost forever.[102]

X

When historians have studied changes of mind, they've normally set an explanation-form up against the objective facts of the world, then have claimed the former changed because it couldn't take account of the latter. There's something to be said for such a procedure. Using it, we might see Frederick Jackson Turner as a transitional figure from an agrarian order in America to an industrial one, and we might explain his mind strain as having been born in one order, but trying to live in another. In that case, we might note how symbolic it is that Turner was born in the opening year of the Civil War and died the year Franklin Roosevelt was elected. We might also note that it was during the 1930s—in a decade when the nation came full upon the consequences of industrialization—that Turner critics first got a wide hearing among American historians.

But as Thomas Kuhn has suggested, an explanation-form functions along other planes besides this truth/falsehood one; it helps build community too and provides identity for its holders. A political order, we know, is in jeopardy not just when it fails to answer objective needs in the world, but also when it begins doubting itself. So too an explanation form and an explanation community. When we're trying to see why mind-forms have changed in such matters, we should look not only for external stresses but for internal ones too. In the language of chapter 2, such stresses are "perspectivistic," not just "objective."

As we've seen in chapter 4 and again in this chapter, *change* is fundamental to the Progressives' explanation of experience. They're Progress-ives because they believe the most basic of changes in the world (or in America at least) must move in the direction of progress.

Using Alvin Toffler's terms, we can say that this idea of progress served as something of a "future shock absorber" for Progressive historians.[103] It not only explained what change *is* for them, it prescribed what change *should be*. And if some particular change should fail their prophecies about progress, they could always say, well, we've just momentarily lapsed from the American way, but tomorrow we'll work to put ourselves back on course.

With Turner, though, we've seen a situation where he can't resort to that kind of strategy. Or at least not without much strain on his mind. For, as he himself admits, change after 1890 sets America off on a radically new course. So, within his basic explanation-form, he's hard put to call these changes "progress." Thus the dilemma of Turner (II)—how to continue progressing when your explanation makes the future look bleak?

It's that question which does in Turner, in his *Frontier* book at least. It's a question his progress commitment and prophet's role drives him to ask— and ask continually—but his explanation-form is just not equipped to handle it.

What then can we learn from this case study of a historian's mind in action, and under stress? I trust we've learned something first of Frederick Jackson Turner, and how his mind responds strategically to different kinds of situations. By watching that mind in motion, we can see him framing different strategies for coping as his experience throws up different problems to him.

I hope we may also have learned something about mind-ing generally here. We should see that mind is not all of a piece, a straightforward rendering of completed thought. General historical categories—"liberal," "relativist," "consensus," "progressive," "conservative"—may hold together with neat logical consistency, but particular minds seldom do. Often they hold onto ideas which are logically contradictory, and they *see* many things which never get worked into their basic *forms* for explanation. They also sometimes double back on themselves, trying to close off gaps which they may sense in their own forms. Minds often betray doubt, then, at the very moment they're affirming themselves. The louder the affirmation, sometimes the graver the doubt. That's one lesson we can learn from a "strategic" reading of ideas.

We know this intuitively from our everyday life experience. We assume that people's ideas will occasionally be inconsistent and self-contradictory, and we can sense from a person's manner how confident he is in what he says. But if we know this from our everyday life, it doesn't always inform our historical scholarship. And this may be because our normal "climate-of-opinion" form tends to treat thought as end product, inert. It looks at mind after its work is completed, and thus fails to reach those inner stresses which may tear away at a person's mind while it's in motion, actively engaged in laboring over something.

With Turner, we've seen how he notes many things which never get patterned into his core explanation of democracy (e.g., the state universities, increased government legislation, and so on). His defenders have been quick to cite these—claiming they prove Turner's mind wasn't limited simply to the single frontier explanation. They prove no such thing. They only show that Turner's eyes sometimes ranged further than his mind-forms. *Taking note* of something, we should note, is not necessarily *explaining* it. If Turner occasionally voices the need for increased government intervention, for state universities to train a professional corps of political decision makers, for a rooted sectionalism to counter the effects of a mobile nationalism, if he sees all these as necessary to sustain democracy in the land, he does not explain *why*. And in his *Frontier* volume of essays, Frederick Jackson Turner *is* in fact limited to that single, frontier explanation. He does not explain his American experiences after 1890 in any other kind of self-consistent fashion. His mind is locked into a particular idea-form, and only in momentary flashes is he able to conceive of experience outside it.

XI

What we've seen of Turner here is simply *a* vulnerable point in the Progressive paradigm. It's not the only point by any means, as we'll see in the chapter to follow. But it's one of the more basic fault-lines in the whole paradigm, if not *the* most basic. At some time or other, every Progressive historian was plagued by the question, "How can you explain experience when it's no longer coming out progress?" Not all, though, behaved along that fault-line in the same way.

From what we already know of their writings and from existing scholarship on their lives and times, we can say *that* this is the case, that Progressives varied in their response to stress along this progress fault-line. We know, for example, that World War I was some kind of threshold situation for Carl Becker—that he entered it a committed Progressive, even writing anti-German propaganda for the Creel Committee on Public Information, but that he left this experience doubting not only the war aims and President Wilson but the idea of progress too and the whole Progressivist polarity of good men versus bad men and light versus unreason.[104]

If Becker went into that war a Progressive, he came out looking like some kind of counter-Progressive. Though his writings thereafter were not wholly counter-Progressive, they do reach out more toward alternative forms than does Turner. Ditto Charles Beard, whose later works (*The Republic, The American Spirit*) largely cast off the economic interpretation impelling his Progressive form, and again, like Becker's, point ahead to counter-Progressive historical forms.[105]

Even from our cursory knowledge, we can say *that* Progressives differed in their behaviors under strain. But only superficially yet can we say *how*. To deepen our understanding of how these various minds behave—how, say, Becker interprets his role differently from Turner and responds to stress situations with different kinds of strategies—we'd need to do some *controlled studies of comparative fault-line behavior*.

Here is a fine opportunity for future scholarship in American historiography; for our concerns here with cognitive psychology, with pivotal-moment and fault-line modes of focus, and with a situation-strategy reading of ideas, should prepare us well for such studies. To do them, we'd have to take two or more thinkers and locate a number of fault-line situations in a selected sample of their writings. Then we'd need to chart just how each behaved in each situation, setting their responses alongside each other and comparing and contrasting them. From such inquiries, we might gain a richer sense of variability in historians' mind work and a more detailed understanding of precise points of difference and similarity within groups of historians.

That could help us handle one issue we raised back in chapter 5—What constitutes a "school" of historical thinkers? How much consensus does it take to make a school and how much divergence before it ceases to be a school?[106] Too, such studies could show us how and when pressures build up along fault-lines in a paradigm (or explanation-form). From them, we might be able to gauge just how much pressure different fault-lines can withstand and what kinds of situations may topple existing forms and precipitate historiographical earthquakes. All this would get us deeper into "the structure of historians' revolutions," just as Thomas Kuhn has gotten into "the structure of scientific revolutions."

If this book were about three times as long as it is, we might undertake something like that here—enough, at least, to explain with more assurance than we can now how historians' mind-forms change. But to keep this book within manageable size, we're able to do only a few such inquiries. We'll be using these, plus what we know here and there from secondary sources, to hazard guesses about the rest. Future controlled inquiries, let's hope, will move us past this guessing stage to more rigorous explanations of such matters.

Such studies, I suspect, might show us that, of the major Progressive historians, Turner was the most resistant to change in his basic constructs, Becker was least resistant, and Beard and Parrington were somewhere in between. Turner's "up-the-ladder" behavior seems to be the most exaggerated in his school. This is partly because of certain apparent barriers set up in his mind, partly because he over-committed himself to the role of historical prophet, but mostly, I think, because Turner alone of these Progressives bound his explanation to a dated historical experience—the pre-1890 frontier. When that passed, so did the logic of his explanation. No other Progressive locked his fault-line so tightly to a given point in time, and thus each had more freedom of movement under changing circumstances.[107]

But if none besides Turner had the same kind of stress point, or quite fled up the ladder as often as he did under pressure, they all worked along this progress/regress plane. And they all suffered their own kind of strain when some important experience couldn't be explained as progress anymore. If Turner's behavior exaggerates the form, he only exaggerates what others in the school evidently felt too.

And they felt this so acutely because Progressive history was preeminently an *advocate* history. It not only explained things, it urged things to happen. What Progressives advocated was change, and change for them had to mean betterment. So even when one or another of their beliefs seemed to give way, this drive toward improvement would eventually snap them up again, pushing them back into the faith that experience *must* mean progress, and moving them along again in the old form. If Progressives were ever to abandon their sense of history as progress, then they'd give up their world to purposeless flux, and worse, moral complacency.

A Progressive might occasionally toy with such a mood, but rarely for long. Thus in the very period when Charles Beard was loosening his commitment to old Progressive norms—to his brand of economic determinism and to his past belief in an objective and knowable historical "reality"—his faith in human progress went on untouched. As he wrote in a 1931 introduction to J. B. Bury's *The Idea of Progress:*

Conceding for the sake of argument that the past has been chaos, without order or design, we are still haunted by the shadowing thought that by immense efforts of will and intelligence, employing natural science as the supreme instrumentality of power, mankind may rise above necessity into the kingdom of freedom, subduing material things to humane rational purpose.[108]

If Beard can consign the past to chaos—even if only "for the sake of argument"—he cannot do this with the future. Men can no longer control the past; but they can the future. It's still subject to human *will.*

And this future, through the exertion of will, *must* be progress-ive. For if it doesn't go in this direction, the sole alternative for Beard is regress. In the either-or structure of Progressive thinking, polar opposites negate each other —liberalism rules out conservatism, hope rules out despair, reason rules out dogma. But the converse is true too: dogma rules out reason, despair rules out hope, conservatism rules out liberalism. So, if progress goes, then regress is all that's left.

It's a historical paradox, then, that Progressive history—which got its impetus from the idea of progressive change as a revolt against static formalisms—eventually made progress itself into a formalism. By that idea, Progressives could reduce *other* experiences to critical investigation. But they were not willing to do the same with it. As James Harvey Robinson says, "It is clear enough today that the conscious reformer who appeals to the future is the final product of a progressive order of things."[109] After that, there'll evidently be no more need for new ideas.

And this, I think, gets us into a second fault-line of the Progressive paradigm. The first fault-line, as we've seen, centers on the question, "How do you explain experience when it's not coming out progress?" The second centers on the question, *"How do you explain ambiguous experience if you have no principle of ambiguity?"*

Progressives could recognize ambiguity all right. That we've seen even in Turner. But with the lone exception of Becker, their minds were not structured to explain it (and when Becker *was* explaining it, I'm not sure how

Progressive he was anymore). Instead, they were accustomed to taking experiences and following them down single tracks. When these tracks didn't always run in a straight line, that was not because of ambiguities inherent in the experiences themselves; it was because other experiences, running down other single tracks, had interfered.

In the next chapter, we'll observe this structure of mind more carefully in Parrington. Suffice it now to say that by recognizing it, we can better explain why Progressives were loathe to let go of their progress-form. It's not that they couldn't imagine any alternative idea. They could. *Regress.* And what came clustered along with regress in their bi-polar pattern of experience —apathy (as opposed to hope), resignation (as opposed to effort), injustice (as opposed to justice), unreason (as opposed to reason), the Old World (as opposed to the New). Progressives were not *just* cheerful and happy then; they *had to be* yea-sayers, they felt, else men would stop moving forwards and would slide back into a dark and dreary past.

Thus when Robinson writes, "History would seem . . . to condemn the principle of conservatism as a hopeless and wicked anachronism," he's not only expressing a low tolerance level for his opponents.[110] He's also saying that regress must be defeated if progress is to get anywhere in the world.

This may tell us something about the characteristic situations which have buoyed up Progressive faiths, the ones where their coping strategies seem to function best. Strategically, Progressive explanations were most successful in situations where massive formalisms had held people back from doing things, or from re-thinking things. To a Turner that formalism was the Old World, to a Beard it was stale and abstract political dogmas, to a Parrington it was old Federalist pieties, to a Robinson it was the whole pre-Progressive history of mankind.

Their Progressivist strategies were framed in response to such situations, and they'd originally been designed to cut through the formalism and re-invigorate life. Which they did. But at a price. To cut through such traditions, they needed hard and fast and straight and narrow ideas. And they had to concentrate their energies *on* the cutting; they couldn't tarry for long to question whether the formalism was as monolithic as they thought, or ask whether the world would be just as they planned it if they were successful. If they just stuck to the job ahead, they'd probably get it done—that is, they would break through the formalism.

But the very success of such strategies in formalistic situations made them less pliable for other kinds of situations. What can Turner do when he's not able to set off New World against Old, but must show both worlds responding to similar problems (e.g., the need for governmental controls over industrialization)? What can Beard do in situations where abstract political doctrines are not a barrier to democracy, but seem the best means of protecting it (e.g., against foreign totalitarianism in the 1930s and 1940s)?

These are not formalistic situations, where one cluster of ideas battles another. They are instead *ambiguous situations*—where ideas run in more than one direction at a time, and opposites don't quite negate each other. Here the strategic problem is not to take hard cutting tools and break through crusty barriers. Rather, it's to take opposing principles and hold them in some kind of balanced tension. And one keeps that balance by constantly playing these principles off against each other—not so that liberalism can eventually cancel out conservatism, or freedom cancel out control, or the New World the Old, but so that *both* sides of each polarity can sustain and give energy to each other through their opposition.

Increasingly, Progressives were to experience this sort of ambiguous situation—as the nineteenth-century world passed into the twentieth, and as they tried to explain World War I and the 1920s and the Depression and the New Deal and the rise of totalitarianism and, finally, World War II. On occasion, one of them might make it over the threshold into an alternative form, and handle some particular ambiguity by loosening his either-or bipolar opposites. But however much a single Progressive historian could get his mind around one or another ambiguous situation, the whole barrage of paradoxical experiences finally became too much for the form. The pressure of experience upon explanation, events upon mind, finally dislodged the old forms, precipitating an intellectual earthquake which brought in a whole new pattern of historical categories. In this new pattern, paradox and ambiguity and irony were not seen as historical anomalies to be set aside as departures from the norm, but these kinds of experiences were perceived *as* the norm. How this came about, and when and through whom, is the subject of our next chapter.

NOTES

1. With these Progressive historians, I may have to moderate somewhat my earlier strictures about the poverty of American historiographical scholarship. Much really admirable work has been done on Progressives—biographical portraits, empirical testing of their theses, studies of them in the context of their times, and even a little of that "literary" analysis we asked for in chapters 3 and 6.

Partly, I suppose, Progressives have been studied so much because more than any other grouping of American historians they fall into a fairly tight "school" of explanation, and are themselves more readily explained than, say, the more formless and perhaps more complicated group of counter-Progressive thinkers. The shaping Progressives —Turner, Beard, Robinson, Becker, Parrington—all were born in the Midwest, and within a decade and a half of each other (Turner, the oldest, was born in 1861; Beard, the youngest, in 1874). All had similar formative experiences, all were small-town boys who journeyed East for their education, and they came of intellectual age during years of reformist ferment. And all in some way or other gave voice to reformist sentiments.

They connect rather directly to their times, then, and we can move back and forth from their writings to their age without too much shifting of intellectual gears (this is most true with Beard, who was more actively involved in his times than any other of his school; it's perhaps least true with Becker, who ordinarily responded to his times only from some considerable distance). Which means we can get directly into the history of the times when we're looking at these Progressives. Thus, their works are more like "primary" documents of the era than, say, works of counter-Progressive scholars in the 1950s and 1960s.

This school has also been much studied in the post-World War II years, because many historians writing then were raised under progressivist assumptions, and were obliged to work them out of their system, so to speak, before they could go on to construct their own intellectual identity. Progressivism has been the dominant explanation form in twentieth-century American historical scholarship, and historians who've sought alternative forms have found it necessary to use the Progressive one as a sort of moving off point.

This is manifestly the case with the finest of these studies—Richard Hofstadter's monumental work, *The Progressive Historians: Turner, Beard, Parrington* (Knopf, 1968). That book culminates a scholar's odyssey of some third of a century with Progressives; as Hofstadter describes it, his work is "a reprise of that perennial battle we wage with our elders, particularly with our adopted intellectual fathers." "If we are to have any new thoughts, if we are to have any intellectual identity of our own," he says, "we must make the effort to distinguish ourselves from those who preceded us, and perhaps pre-eminently from those to whom we once had the greatest indebtedness" (p. xiv).

It's a tribute to the intellectual character of Richard Hofstadter that he can take such a personal identity search and build it into the richest study ever made of a school of American historians. It's also a testimony to the possibilities of historiography in American historical scholarship. After *The Progressive Historians,* it should be harder for members of the profession to dismiss historiography as not being "real" scholarship.

For these Progressives, the best full study is of course Hofstadter. One of the most useful brief introductions is Charles Crowe, "The Emergence of Progressive History," *Journal of the History of Ideas,* 27, no. 1 (January-March 1966), 109–124. See also the bibliographical references in both.

For the Progressives under stress, or in conflict with counter-Progressives, see Hofstadter, "Conflict and Consensus in American History," in *Progressive Historians,* pp. 437–66; John Higham, "Crisis in Progressive History," *History: Humanistic Scholarship in America* (Prentice-Hall, 1965), 198–211; Robert Skotheim, "Challenges to the Progressive Tradition," in *American Intellectual Histories and Historians* (Princeton, 1966), 173–255; Arthur Mann, "The Progressive Tradition," in John Higham, ed., *The Reconstruction of American History* (Harper and Row, Torchbook, 1962), pp. 157–79; Cushing Strout, "The Twentieth-Century Enlightenment," *The American Political Science Review,* XLIX, no. 2 (June 1955); David Noble, *The Paradox of Progressive Thought* (Minnesota, 1958), and *Historians against History: The Frontier Thesis and the National Covenant in American Historical Writing since 1830* (Minnesota, 1965); and my "Political 'Reality' in Recent American Scholarship: Progressives v. 'Symbolists,'" *American Quarterly,* XIX, no. 2, pt. 2 (Summer 1967), 303–28; and "Implicit Irony in Recent American Historiography: Perry Miller's *New England Mind,*" *Journal of the History of Ideas,* XXIX, no. 4 (October-December 1968), 579–600.

2. See Morton White, *Social Thought in America: The Revolt against Formalism,* rev. ed. (Beacon, paperback, 1957).

3. *The Progressive Historians* (n. 1 above), p. xii.

4. *History* (n. 1 above), p. 190. It's interesting to ponder why the Progressive mind-set suffered so few setbacks among American historians in the 1920s—at a time when political Progressivism was certainly on the wane, and when intellectuals outside the historical profession were entertaining all kinds of doubts about the Progressive faith. Again, we must inquire more into the sociology of particular intellectual sub-communities before we can begin to explain why. Resort to general "climate-of-opinion" or "spirit-of-an-age" explanations won't help much here.

5. John Caughey, "Historians' Choice: Results of a Poll on Recently Published American History and Biography," *Mississippi Valley Historical Review,* XXIX (September 1952), 289–302.

6. "The Democratic Theme in American Historical Literature," *Mississippi Valley Historical Review,* XXXIX (September 1952), 25.

7. Ibid., p. 24.

8. Ibid., p. 12.

9. Ibid., p. 28.

10. *The Structure of Scientific Revolutions* (University of Chicago Press, paperback, 1970), p. 94.

11. "Charles Beard: Civilization and the Revolt Against Empiricism," *American Quarterly*, XX, no. 1 (Spring 1969), 65–86. In this essay, Marcell traces Beard's movement from a militantly Progressive position to what we would call a "counter-Progressive" one. And he locates a "pivotal moment" for the change too. He writes, "I am convinced that the process of writing *The Rise of American Civilization,* as much as any single thing, led Beard toward the multi-causation approach to history and away from economic determinism. Although *The Rise* takes a strongly economic tack, before its writing Beard never evinced a consistent interest in the role of ideas in history; afterward, he never ceased to be concerned with the problem" (p. 71). Marcell doesn't move down into *The Rise* to show us just how this change comes about, though he does go some into Beard's later writings to note his evolution toward a "consensus"-like position.

12. This was one of only two books Turner finished in his lifetime. His other book —*Rise of the New West, 1819–1829*—was published in 1906. A third—*The United States, 1830–1850: The Nation and Its Sections*—was incomplete at his death in 1932. It was later put together and published in 1935 by Turner's friends.

13. See Ray Allen Billington's foreword to Turner's *The Frontier in American History* (Holt, Rinehart and Winston, paperback, 1962), pp. xii–xiv. (Copyright 1920 by Frederick Jackson Turner, 1948 by Carolyn M.S. Turner, 1962 by Holt, Rinehart and Winston, Inc. Reprinted by permission of Holt, Rinehart and Winston, Inc.) See also Hofstadter, *Progressive Historians* (n. 1 above), pp. 111–17.

14. Quoted by Billington in Turner, *Frontier*, p. xiv. For Frederick Jackson Turner, the secondary scholarship is immense, and I'll mention only a small part of it here. One of the best brief introductions is Howard R. Lamar, "Frederick Jackson Turner," in Cunliffe and Winks, eds., *Pastmasters: Some Essays on American Historians* (Harper and Row, 1969), pp. 74–109. A useful survey of secondary scholarship on Turner is Gene Gressley, "The Turner Thesis—a Problem in Historiography," *Agricultural History*, 32, no. 4 (October 1958), 227–49. For the background of the frontier idea up to Turner, see Henry Nash Smith, *Virgin Land: The American West as Symbol and Myth* (Random House, Vintage Book, n.d.). Smith's concluding chapter, "The Myth of the Garden and Turner's Frontier Hypothesis" (291–305) gives indication of why Turner found it so difficult to let go of his ruling idea.

For how Turner drew upon the intellectual milieu around him, see Lee Benson, "The Historial Background of Turner's Frontier Essay," *Turner and Beard: American Historical Writing Reconsidered* (Free Press, paperback, 1965), pp. 41–91. For what impact the frontier idea has had on the general intellectual community in America, see Warren Susman, "The Useless Past: American Intellectuals and the Frontier Thesis," *Bucknell Review,* 11 (1963), pp. 1–20.

Beyond the above, three anthologies have gathered together much valuable scholarship in and around Turner: George Rogers Taylor, ed., *The Turner Thesis Concerning the Role of the Frontier in American History* (Heath Paperback, 1956); Ray Allen Billington, ed., *The Frontier Thesis: Valid Interpretation of American History?* (Holt, Rinehart and Winston, paperback, 1966); and Richard Hofstadter and Seymour Martin Lipset, eds., *Turner and the Sociology of the Frontier* (Basic Books, paperback, 1968).

15. Turner, *Frontier,* p. 1.

16. Ibid., p. 38.

17. We might then say his explanation-form is *irrelevant* to the changed times; but an irrelevant explanation is not the same as an explanation strain. In the former, the problem is *external*—the form doesn't fit things outside (e.g., Barry Goldwater's *The Conscience of a Conservative*). In the latter, the problem is *internal*—the form is inconsistent with itself. And that form's holder feels the strain in his own mind. Again, it's not just a strain *between* mind and world; it's also a strain between contradictory behaviors *inside* mind, as it responds to the world. In our language of chapter 2, it's not an "objective" strain so much as it is "perspectivistic."

18. We could go on to say that *Turner (III)* might stand for a new strategic explanation for his changed American situation. But, as we'll see, he almost never pulls that off. Mainly the old explanation simply lies in strain, just below the threshold of change. Only occasionally does Turner pass over his own threshold to glimpse some new form for thinking about experience. And then he's not persistent enough to hold onto it for long. At least not in this *Frontier* volume.

19. Turner, *Frontier*, p. 15. In this section, when I'm citing a quotation from Turner, I've put the date of each statement in parentheses. That's because in making up this composite of Turner (I), I've taken passages from pretty much anywhere in the book. It doesn't look as if Turner (I) changed much over the years, at least not in any steady progression which can be charted from this *Frontier* volume. By noting the date of each statement, I'm trying to illustrate the generally enduring quality of his beliefs here about the pre-1890 New World.

20. Ibid., p. 301.
21. Ibid., pp. 2–3.
22. Ibid., p. 4.
23. Ibid.
24. Ibid., p. 259.
25. Ibid.
26. Ibid., p. 293.
27. Ibid., p. 4.
28. Ibid., p. 185.

29. *A Theory of Personality: The Psychology of Personal Constructs* (Norton, paperback, 1963—first edition published in 1955), pp. 61 ff., 106 ff. Kelly contends that all human thinking is basically bi-polar. That is, a person who's given to talking much about love is doubtless implying much about its opposite too—hate. We'd not just say of this person that he or she was oriented toward love, then. We'd say rather that a good part of their thinking was constructed along a love/hate plane. And as a critic (or, in Kelly's case a therapist), we'd be concerned why they choose to construct their thoughts so much along this plane rather than along other planes—say, cheerful/sad, adventure/security, and so on.

Kelly thus urges us to look for the *planes* along which people think, and not simply for individual datums of thought. He also insists that logical opposites—love-hate, aggressive-passive, courage-fear—are not psychologically opposite at all. Rather, in human personality they always come linked in pairs. When we see one, the other is invariably close by. I'm not certain I'd agree with Kelley that *all* our thinking is bi-polar. But he does get us to looking for implied or covert ideas, ideas which we might not see right off if we stuck only to the face of someone's thoughts. And if this bi-polar idea may not fit all thinking, it does seem to fit certain styles. The ideological style is one, the prophetic another. And since, as we'll see, much of Turner's thinking under strain is in the prophetic style, I believe Kelly's idea may serve as a valuable key for us here.

30. *Frontier*, p. xx.

31. See especially his essay of 1891, "The Significance of History." It's reprinted in Ray Allen Billington, ed., *Frontier and Section: Selected Essays of Frederick Jackson Turner* (Prentice-Hall, paperback, 1961), pp. 11–27.

32. "Democracy," Turner wrote as an undergraduate in 1883, "is waiting for its poet" (in Hofstadter, *Progressive Historians,* [n. 1 above], p. 63). There is reason to believe he felt he could be that poet.

Eight years later he wrote as a young professor, "Historical study has for its end to let the community see itself in the light of the past, to give it new thoughts and feelings, new aspirations and energies" (in *Frontier and Section,* p. 27). There's also reason to believe Turner aimed his own historical studies to do just that.

33. *Frontier* (n. 13 above), p. 243.
34. *Social Thought in America* (n. 2 above), p. 12.
35. *Frontier*, p. 243.
36. Ibid., p. 244.
37. Ibid.
38. Ibid., p. 245.
39. Ibid., pp. 245–46.
40. Ibid., p. 246.
41. Ibid.
42. Ibid., p. 244.
43. Ibid., p. 247.
44. Ibid., p. 248.
45. Ibid., p. 253.
46. Ibid., pp. 260–61.

47. Ibid., p. 261.
48. Ibid.
49. Ibid.
50. Ibid., pp. 261–62.
51. Ibid., p. 262. Turner's use of poetry in this *Frontier* volume is intriguing. Six times he quotes poetry here, always to illustrate the spirit of the American frontier. Yet only two of his citations are from American poets—one each from Lowell and Whitman. Three are from English poets, two from Kipling and one from Tennyson, the remaining one is unnamed. Five of the six times he uses poetry in the book, it's in response to some strain situation. And he invariably uses it for moral uplift. This suggests that Turner sees poetry only as some sort of strategic release, an inspirational out when pressures mount up in the world of pedestrian things. ("A Song of the English" from *Rudyard Kipling's Verse*, Definitive Edition. Copyright 1907 by Rudyard Kipling. Reprinted by permission of Mrs. George Bambridge and Doubleday & Company, Inc.)
52. Ibid.
53. Ibid., p. 263.
54. Ibid.
55. Ibid., p. 268.
56. Ibid., p. 264.
57. Ibid., p. 244.
58. Ibid., p. 266.
59. Ibid., p. 264.
60. Ibid., p. 265.
61. Ibid., p. 264.
62. Ibid., p. 268.
63. Ibid., p. 202.
64. Ibid., p. 276.
65. Ibid., p. 307.
66. Ibid., p. 320.
67. In matters of mind, counting is a risky business. One must be somewhat arbitrary in defining what he's looking for, and there are always hazy borderlines which may confound one's numbering scheme. Some of these fault-line moments, for example, are rather extended ones; should we call each of them a single moment, or break them down into several? Generally, I've done the former, but there's a certain amount of subjectivity involved. By counting here, I'm not trying to deny this necessary subjectivity in handling ideas. Rather, I'm merely attempting to make public my subjective biases, revealing the criteria for my explanations. When we intellectual historians use qualifiers like "frequently" and "often" or "seldom"—as we invariably do in studies of mind—we're implying numbers. I just prefer to make my numbers more explicit, also my criteria for arriving at them. For anyone who'd like to explore this matter further, what I've called "pure" fault-line moments appear on the following pages in Turner's *Frontier* volume—xix, 1, 37, 38, 39, 155, 202, 219, 221, 239, 244, 245, 262 (2), 293, 300, 307, 311, 316.
68. See "The Frontier as Explanation," *Progressive Historians* (n. 1 above), pp. 118–64.
69. At an 1896 dedication address given at his home town high school in Portage, Wisconsin, Turner was moved to declare of the frontier, "Here was a magic foundation of youth in which America continually bathed and was rejuvenated" (in Henry Nash Smith, *Virgin Land* [n. 14 above], p. 297).
70. *Frontier*, p. 341.
71. *Progressive Historians*, p. 7.
72. *Frontier*, p. 301.
73. Ibid., p. 155.
74. Ibid., p. 309.
75. George Kelly has remarked, apropos of the overcommitted mind in this kind of situation, "A person who is completely and continually involved in the ultimate consequences of his acts is in no position to experiment with new ideas" (*Theory of Personality,* [n. 29 above], p. 170).
76. We ought to note, though, Turner's varying audiences here, and his acute sense of same. Two essays in this *Frontier* volume were given first as undergraduate com-

mencement addresses and a third was made to dedicate the State Historical Society of Minnesota. These are fit occasions for the prophetic voice, they're not so fit for the analytic. The most sustained analytic tone in the entire book comes in Turner's AHA presidential address of 1910, "Social Forces in American History," given to an audience of his professional colleagues. Thus, sometimes Turner resorts to the prophetic voice simply because he's speaking, and to a nonprofessional audience, and on occasions when he might normally be expected to try and raise their spirits. We shouldn't make too much of this, however. It's just one variable which may help us understand why he does what he does in a few essays. I'm not sure it helps much for others, where he takes on the prophetic voice on seemingly "unprophetic" occasions.

77. *Historians against History: The Frontier Thesis and the National Covenant in American Historical Writing since 1830* (n. 1 above).

78. *The New England Mind: From Colony to Province* (Beacon, paperback, 1961), p. 204.

79. *Frontier*, p. 268.

80. Ibid., p. 301.

81. Ibid., p. 307.

82. As we noted before, in twelve of his nineteen "pure" fault-line situations, Turner resorts to "up-the-ladder" strategies. This is also true of his essay *conclusions*. Of the thirteen essays in the book, 10 close in a tone which either boasts of America's successes (especially the Middle West's), or cheers her on to greater ones in the future. The only exceptions, as I see it, are his "Significance of the Frontier" piece, which ends on a kind of tragic note, and his essays "The Old West" and "Social Forces in American History," which conclude in an analytic voice.

83. I've taken this title from a book of the same name—*When Prophecy Fails,* by Leon Festinger et al. (Harper and Row, Torchbook, 1964—first published in 1956 by Minnesota). *When Prophecy Fails* is a study in what psychologists call "cognitive dissonance." Cognitive dissonance is a psychological state where items in a person's belief pattern conflict with each other. This psychological state parallels the intellectual state we've been calling "explanation strain."

84. There is an interesting kind of paradox here, though. If we follow the metaphor of Turner (II) "fleeing up the ladder of the national covenant," then the logic of Turner (I) has already kicked that ladder out from under him! For if American uniqueness is dependent on the frontier, when that frontier goes after 1890, so goes the covenant. Needless to say, Turner never fully confronted that paradox.

85. Miller, *Colony* (n. 78 above), p. 203.

86. See for example the passage we quoted a few pages back, from Turner's p. 307. It's the one which begins, "It would be a grave misfortune," and it ends, "our underlying good humor and love of fair play will triumph in the end."

87. *Frontier,* p. 157.

88. Ibid., pp. 175–76.

89. In subsequent essays, though, this "sectionalism" construct did give Turner leverage to break completely out of the Turner (I)-Turner (II) dilemma, so he could move on into what we could call a Turner (III)-form. We never see a Turner (III)-form in his *Frontier* volume of 1920, but later we can find instances of it. In an essay published in 1922, for example—"Sections and Nation"—Turner again advances the sectional idea; but here he's only updating his 1909 "Ohio Valley" form. That is, he's still setting the New World off against the Old; and he writes of "the evil path of Europe," and scores Old World nations for engaging in "sinister combinations." He also says of America: "The American section may be likened to the shadowy image of the European nation, to the European state denatured of its toxic qualities." (*Frontier and Section* (n. 31 above), pp. 153, 139, 137.

But in a 1925 essay—"The Significance of the Section in American History"—Turner does almost break free from the dualism of New World versus Old. And if the American national covenant is still there in his mind, it's now held in check by other concerns. Thus he writes things like: "We are more like Europe, and our sections are becoming more and more the American version of the European nation" (ibid., 115–16).

Nor does Turner here resort to the prophetic voice at moments when his logic seems to threaten sacred beliefs about America. Maybe that's because he's merely calling for new analytic constructs, and not trying to salvage the republic anymore. He has not obliged himself to guard the national covenant, nor to stir lagging spirits in his audience. Instead, he's just asking that they look at things through fresh forms. Thus, on his last page he writes, "The significance of the section is that it is the faint image of a European nation and that we need to reexamine our history in light of this fact" (ibid., p. 135). What was dark and "shadowy" in 1922 has three years later become just "faint," and there's no reference to "sinister" or "toxic" any more.

I'm not sure what to make of this. It's a different Turner from what we've seen in his *Frontier* volume; and it suggests there were times when he was completely free from stress, or at least when he could use stress to construct new explanations from new kinds of experience. Why he didn't do this earlier, or why he couldn't hold onto it for long, is still a puzzle. But I suspect Turner's strong sense of *role* may help solve part of the puzzle. When he's in the prophetic role, he can never pull away from old forms for long. But when—for some reason or other—he's able to take up the analytic role, it gives him leverage to experiment with new forms (for a time at least). If that's true, it may help explain why Turner's former students always claim he was so remarkably open, while those who know him only through his writings don't think so at all. Perhaps with his students he kept away from that prophetic voice?

90. *Frontier*, pp. 149–50.

91. A half-century later, David Potter would try updating Turner on democracy and man-made things with his *People of Plenty: Economic Abundance and the American Character* (University of Chicago Press, Phoenix Books, 1960—first published by Chicago in 1954).

92. *Frontier*, p. 155.

93. Ibid., p. 156.

94. Ibid., p. 284.

95. Ibid., p. 285.

96. Ibid., p. 286.

97. Ibid., p. 285.

98. Ibid., p. 288.

99. It's also intriguing to note that Turner gave this address in 1910, the very year he left one of the best state universities—Wisconsin—for Harvard.

100. Ibid., p. 357.

101. Ibid., p. 338.

102. Ibid., pp. 358–59.

103. *Future Shock* (Random House, 1970), p. 339.

104. Writing to a friend in mid-1920, Becker noted that the war "is the result of some thousands of years of what men like to speak of as 'political, economic, intellectual, and moral Progress.'" "If this is progress," he queried in Henry Adams-like fashion, "what in Heaven's name would retardation be!" (cited in Burleigh Taylor Wilkins, *Carl Becker: A Biographical Study* [MIT, 1961], p. 132).

For a study of World War I as a fault-line situation in Becker's thought, see Phil Snyder, "Carl Becker and the Great War: A Crisis for a Humane Intelligence," *Western Political Quarterly*, 9 (1956), 1–10.

105. For a fuller study of Beard's change from the Progressive to a kind of counter-Progressive form, see David Marcell, "Charles Beard" (n. 11 above).

106. Did Becker, for example, mostly stop being a Progressive after World War I? I think so. But we'd need a lot sharper sense of what we mean by "Progressive" and "counter-Progressive," and of points in between, before we could say that with much assurance.

107. The strange thing is why Turner chose to rest so much of his case on this symbolic date—1890. Of course it *is* the date of the census report. But that report—even the part of it quoted by Turner—doesn't say what he claims it says. It doesn't say the whole frontier has closed, only that there's no longer any single frontier *line*. Given Turner's obvious anguish with the closed frontier idea, it's odd that he never quibbled with or even read very carefully his own factual base for this idea. For more on the

circumstances surrounding this strange behavior, see Lee Benson, "The Historian as Mythmaker: Frederick Jackson Turner and the Closed Frontier," in *Toward the Scientific Study of History* (Lippincott, paperback, 1972), pp. 175–89.

108. Beard's introduction to J. B. Bury, *The Idea of Progress: An Inquiry into Its Growth and Origin* (Dover, paperback, 1955—first published by St. Martin's in 1932), p. xl.

109. *The New History: Essays Illustrating the Modern Historical Outlook* (Free Press, paperback, 1965—first edition published by Macmillan in 1912), p. 264.

110. Ibid., p. 265.

8 A Paradigm Revolution in the Making: Parrington and the "Moments" of Lionel Trilling and Reinhold Niebuhr

One has always to reckon with the generation that has gone before. I think where one gets one's real intellectual impetus is reacting against ideas one has felt strongly.
Richard Hofstadter
"Interview: 1960"

What comes into being when two contradictory emotions are made to confront each other and are required to have a relationship with each other is . . . quite properly called an idea.
Lionel Trilling
The Liberal Imagination

Man's capacity for justice makes democracy possible; but man's inclination to injustice makes democracy necessary.
Reinhold Niebuhr
The Children of Light and the Children of Darkness

The practice of normal science depends on the ability, acquired from examplars, to group objects and situations into similarity sets. . . . One central aspect of any revolution is, then, that some of the similarity relations change. Objects that were grouped in the same set before are grouped in different ones afterward and vice versa.
Thomas Kuhn
The Structure of Scientific Revolutions

It's such a principle of ambiguity which Lionel Trilling catches up on in 1950, in his preface to a volume of essays on *The Liberal Imagination*. In that preface, and in several of the essays which follow it in the book, Trilling aims to update the liberal mind-form. In effect, he is after a new kind of strategy for what he sees as a new kind of situation. What we have here is a paradigm revolution in the making, or part of one.[1]

The Liberal Imagination is thus one of those threshold moments marking the transition from Progressive explanations to counter-Progressive ones. In a little while, we'll place this volume in a wider context; for now, let's watch just how Trilling passes over the threshold of an old form into a new one.

In 1912, James Harvey Robinson had claimed, "History would seem . . . to condemn the principle of conservatism as a hopeless and wicked anachronism."[2] Lionel Trilling starts off in 1950 as if Robinson had got his way, and four decades later conservatism as a principle has died out in the American mind. "In the United States at this time," he writes, "liberalism is not only the dominant but even the sole intellectual tradition. For it is a plain fact that nowadays there are no conservative or reactionary ideas in general circulation."[3]

That's a giant step away from Robinson, and from most other Progressives (including Merle Curti of 1952). Where they picture a liberalism beleaguered, and exhort their listeners to go out and break through old "formalisms," Trilling takes an entirely different perspective. He assumes the liberal persuasion has already won his audience's mind—"I know that I will not be wrong if I assume that most of us here are in our social and political ideas consciously liberal and democratic"—and he's concerned to go on and ask in effect, *"What price have we paid for our victory?"*[4]

Lionel Trilling calls himself a liberal. Yet clearly he's restive with this triumph of the liberal form. And herein he departs from the Progressives who preceded him. As we've seen in chapters 4 and 7, Progressives tended toward a two-party system in matters of experience. One party takes you in one direction, the other the opposite way. You cast your commitment with one or the other, and you work for the victory of your own side.

But Trilling rejects such a picture. One thing (almost the basic thing) he has go at here is the Progressive-liberal belief in straight lines of experience. He pictures ideas, for example, not as unidirectional but as moving in more than a single way at a time. They contain their own counter-tendencies. As he writes later in the book, "What comes into being when two contradictory emotions are made to confront each other and are required to have a relationship with each other is . . . quite properly called an idea."[5]

Progressives want victory; they strive to defeat the other side, and they frame their strategies accordingly. But Trilling's strategy is different; he tries to structure a *debate*. He doesn't want either side to win. Rather, he proposes that they engage each other in dialogue. He pictures experience not as a dualism—*either* this or that—but as a dialectic encounter—*both* this and that. If one or the other side should go on to win in this encounter, that would be lamentable to Trilling. But this, he feels, is precisely the situation of contemporary liberalism. In matters of mind, it reigns unchallenged. "It is not conducive to the real strength of liberalism that it should occupy the intellectual field alone," Trilling maintains. "The intellectual pressure which a [conservative opponent can] exert would force liberals to examine their position for its weaknesses and complacencies."[6]

In the absence of any conservative opposition, Trilling proposes to take on that role himself, or some of it. Where Progressives had often taken the prophetic role—urging liberals faster and further down lines they're already on—Lionel Trilling, following Kenneth Burke some two decades earlier, will issue a "counter-statement."[7] He does that because, as he says, "a criticism which has at heart the interests of liberalism might find its most useful work not in confirming liberalism in its sense of general rightness but rather in putting under some degree of pressure the liberal ideas and assumptions of the present time."[8]

Again, Trilling pictures a situation entirely altered from that of his predecessors. Progressives, as we've seen, tended to function best in "formalistic" situations, and they used ideas as hammers to break through those formalisms. But Trilling doesn't picture here an old formalistic Establishment needing regeneration by a fresh, new body of ideas. Rather than urging mind to go out and fight against brittle power structures, he insists that it take pause and critically reflect on itself. And he does this because he believes mind—the liberal-progressive mind—has been fighting so long that it's not considered what such a battle strategy may have done to its sense of experience.

At this point, Trilling draws a clear picture of the altered situation, and the need for an alternative strategy of response. We should get this picture clear in our own minds now, since it underlies much of what later counter-Progressives want to "counter" in the Progressive explanation.

Liberalism, according to Trilling, has let itself become too politicized over the years. It has truncated its sense of experience, driving it down those lines which, under pressures of the moment, seem most efficient for doing battle against conservatives. As he phrases it,

It is one of the tendencies of liberalism to simplify, and this tendency is natural in view of the effort which liberalism makes to organize the elements of life in a natural way. And when we approach liberalism in a critical spirit, we shall fail in critical completeness if we do not take into account the value and necessity of its organizational impulse.

He continues, noting how mind and imagination can get constricted amid the organizing necessities of politics:

But at the same time we must understand that organization means delegation, and agencies, and bureaus, and technicians, and that the ideas that can survive delegation, that can be passed on to agencies and bureaus and technicians, incline to be ideas of a certain kind and of a certain simplicity: they give up something of their largeness and modulation and complexity in order to survive.

"The lively sense of contingency and possibility," he concludes, "and of those exceptions to the rule which may be the beginning of the end of the rule— this sense does not suit well with the impulse to organization."[9]

II

That's how Lionel Trilling senses the general situation of American liberalism in 1950. When he moves that sense into specifics in *The Liberal Imagination,* he settles down first on Vernon Louis Parrington. Trilling's opening essay in the book—"Reality in America"—is one of the most powerful of early assaults on the Progressive explanation-form. It has also been one of the more influential.[10]

Trilling chooses Parrington because for him he's a case illustration of the American liberal mind. "Parrington," he writes, "formulated in a classic way the presuppositions about our culture which are held by the American middle class so far as that class is at all liberal in its social thought and so far as it begins to understand that literature has anything to do with society."[11]

Parrington not only represents the American liberal mind to Trilling, he has also helped shape it: "It is possible to say of V. L. Parrington that with his *Main Currents in American Thought* he has had an influence on our conception of American culture which is not equaled by that of any other writer of the last two decades."[12]

Trilling does not tarry long in getting to his sense of Parrington's problem. On his second page he writes, "He had after all but a limited sense of what constitutes a difficulty."[13] And that's because, according to Trilling, Parrington's sense of experience is too thin and "rather too predictable to be continuously interesting."[14]

Again, we see what we noted of Progressives in the last chapter: their tendency to picture experience traveling down straight lines, and to think in bi-polar opposites. With such a tendency, says Trilling, Parrington assumes that there is reality and there is unreality, and the critic's duty is to break through the one into the other. As Trilling describes it,

> Parrington does not often deal with abstract philosophical ideas, but whenever he approaches a work of art we are made aware of the metaphysics on which his aesthetics is based. There exists, he believes, a thing called *reality;* it is one and immutable, it is wholly external, it is irreducible. Men's minds may waver, but reality is always reliable, always the same, always easily to be known. And the artist's relation to reality he conceives as a simply [sic] one. Reality being fixed and given, the artist has but to let it pass through him.[15]

To Trilling, Parrington praises only those artists—like, say, Theodore Dreiser—who let that reality pass directly through them. But he rejects writers who block that passage, or deflect it, or who fix their gaze on other, less "real" spheres of experience. Henry James, for example, or Nathaniel Hawthorne.

Trilling cites Parrington's objection that Hawthorne was "forever dealing with shadows, and he knew that he was dealing with shadows."[16] "Perhaps so," Trilling responds, "but shadows are also part of reality and one would not want a world without shadows." Besides, he adds, a world lacking shadows "would not even be a 'real' world."[17]

For Lionel Trilling, it seems, reality is what people experience. If they experience shadows, or demons, then those experiences are real in their consequences. It will not do simply to declaim against them, or opt for a picture of man, and of reality, which tries to deny them. A picture of experience denying shadows would not be "reality"; it would be only a *wish* picture of reality.

Here we can see Trilling pointing out toward the fugitive, the subjective, the ambiguous, the not easily capturable in the experience of people. Because Trilling's Parrington cannot recruit Hawthorne into his "main currents in American thought," he rejects him, and implies that his art "contributes nothing to democracy, and even . . . stands in the way of the realization of democracy."[18]

Trilling is put off by such a conception. Dissenting sharply from the Progressives' strategic sense of their role (especially with their tendency to play the prophet), he comes to Hawthorne's defense:

> If what Hawthorne did was certainly nothing to build a party on, we ought perhaps to forgive him when we remember that he was only one man and that the future of mankind did not depend on him alone. But this very fact serves only to irritate Parrington; he is put out by Hawthorne's loneliness and believes that part of Hawthorne's insufficiency as a writer comes from his failure to get around and meet people.[19]

Trilling's Parrington seeks straight lines for experience, Trilling himself goes after multiple, convoluted ones. Parrington pictures the world as a track, or often dual tracks, the two running in opposite directions. But Trilling's world of experience resembles a net, with all sorts of crisscrossing and interconnecting lines. Which accounts for his objection to the progressive-liberal conception of ideas. "Too often," he writes, "we conceive of an idea as being like the baton that is handed from runner to runner in a relay race." "But," he contends, "an idea as a transmissible thing is rather like the sentence that in the parlor game is whispered about in a circle; the point of the game is the amusement that comes when the last version is compared with the original."[20]

This brings us to another basic tenet of counter-Progressives. To Lionel Trilling, and to many counter-Progressive historians, a culture should be characterized not by what it *is,* but by what it *talks about.* Thus Trilling's "parlor game" metaphor over the "relay race." Thus also his *spectatorial* role of "amusement," rather than the *participant's* role of racing with the idea-baton, and passing it on, intact, to the runner just ahead.

"Parrington's characteristic weakness as a historian," says Trilling, "is suggested by his title, for the culture of a nation is not truly figured in the image of a current." "A culture," he counters, "is not a flow, nor even a confluence; the form of its existence is struggle, or at least a debate—it is nothing if not a dialectic."[21]

Parrington goes to the polity for his basic categories of experience. One sense of life there is Jeffersonian, the other Hamiltonian. Life's drama, the American drama, is embodied in the ongoing battle between the two.

In contrast, Trilling looks to the world of literature for his categories of experience. Where Parrington would inject political categories into literature, Trilling injects literary categories into politics. And he merges them both into the larger construct of *culture*. "It is no longer possible to think of politics," Trilling says, "except as the politics of culture."[22]

Literature, he feels, points nearer to the heart of a culture than does politics. That's why he substitutes a "dialectical" picture of experience for Parrington's "alternating currents" (read parties *in* power, and parties *out of* power). And that is why he urges us to re-consider those American writers who embody such a dialectic, precisely the kind of thinker who most confounded Parrington:

In any culture there are likely to be certain artists who contain a large part of the dialectic within themselves, their meaning and power lying in their contradictions; they contain within themselves, it may be said, the very essence of the culture, and the sign of this is that they do not submit to serve the ends of any one ideological group or tendency.

Trilling then concludes, "It is a significant circumstance of American culture, and one which is susceptible of explanation, that an unusually large proportion of its notable writers of the nineteenth century were such repositories of the dialectic of their times—they contained both the yes and the no of their culture, and by that token were prophetic of the future."[23]

Here is one of those exact moments where counter-Progressives move over the threshold past the Progressive form. It is just this paradox of yes-and-no, this "significant circumstance of American culture," which Progressive historians did not find "susceptible to explanation" at all. Turner, as we've seen, couldn't handle it, Beard couldn't either, at least not consistently, and, as we'll see soon, it gave Parrington trouble too.

But it's this sense of paradox which counter-Progressives—handling both affirmations and counter-affirmations within the same form of explanation—thrived upon and made central to their picture of experience in America. What Trilling says above points directly to R. W. B. Lewis a few years later in *The American Adam*. It also gets to much of Leo Marx in *The Machine in the Garden*, Marvin Meyers in *The Jacksonian Persuasion*, Charles Sanford in *The Quest for Paradise*, Henry Nash Smith in *Virgin Land*, and William Taylor in *Cavalier and Yankee*. And it touches upon basic themes of Richard Hofstadter in *The Age of Reform*, Perry Miller in *The New England Mind*, Stanley Elkins in *Slavery*, Louis Hartz in *The Liberal Tradition in America*,

Merrill Peterson in *The Jefferson Image in the American Mind,* and David Noble in *Historians against History.* And that constitutes a pretty large part of the counter-Progressive roster.

For counter-Progressives, in contrast to Progressives, experience *is* basically paradox. Characteristically, they will begin with some affirmation which had been simply self-evident within the Progressive paradigm (like, say, history = progress, or human nature = goodness). Then they'll go on to show how it contains inside itself all kinds of concealed contradictions and negations. They do this because their own characteristic situations—in short, their sense of what is "normal" in human experience—differ radically from those of Progressives.

III

Before we move on into the counter-Progressives' strategy of response, we might pause for a moment and consider just what *were* their characteristic experiences, and thus their sense of the altered situation. We might do this by starting with an essay of Daniel Bell, published in his 1960 book, *The End of Ideology.* It's titled "The Mood of Three Generations," and it focuses on intellectuals who came of age in America during the 1930s, 1940s, and 1950s. Our special concern is with Bell's opening section of the essay— sub-titled "The Once-Born, the Twice-Born, and the After-Born."

Starting off with the experience of his own generation, Bell reflects that "we . . . are sadder and perhaps wiser than the first political generations of the century."[24] Though few intellectuals in his day approach the stature of a Dewey, a Beard, a Holmes, a Brandeis, yet "to read these men today is to be struck by their essential optimism, . . . which was based upon an ultimate faith in the rationality or common sense of men."[25] They were, in his terms, a "once-born" generation—they set out their lines for experience early, then simply followed straight along those lines with their lives and their minds.

Bell's own generation, in contrast, is "twice-born." They too started off down certain lines (often those set by the Deweys, Beards, et al.); but at some crucial point along the way they found those lines blocked. Some enormous obstacle kept them from moving straight ahead—or even, like Turner in the last chapter, from veering off on some extended detour. So they were forced to go back and begin all over—in effect, having to be *re*-born. This time they took their journey along quite different lines, and in a much different manner. That's because in their second life they carried with them a memory of blocked hopes in the first. Hence, "Ours, a 'twice-born' generation, finds its wisdom in pessimism, evil, tragedy, and despair." Says Bell, "We are both old and young "before our time.' "

The signal figures of this reborn generation are, for Daniel Bell, Lionel Trilling and Reinhold Niebuhr; and the pivotal moment of rebirth is the situation of the late 1930s. That generation began "intense, horatory [sic], naive, simplistic, and passionate." But, Bell says, "after the Moscow Trials and the Soviet-Nazi pact, [they became] disenchanted." Out of that disenchantment they went on to construct different patterns of life from their liberal-progressive predecessors, and tried to generate different patterns of thought too. Thus, from these twice-born intellectuals "and their experiences we have inherited the key terms which dominate discourse today: irony, paradox, ambiguity, and complexity."[26]

A "situation," as we suggested in chapter 5, can be a paradigm-shattering experience. For this generation of American intellectuals, *totalitarianism* seems to have presented the bottleneck situation. That, for many, was the barrier they couldn't get through or around, the one so massive they had to go back and re-pattern their whole sense of what life is like in the world.[27]

It hit them on both sides of their political spectrum. Accustomed to dividing the world of experience into left and right with an uncrossable line drawn somewhere down the middle, many intellectuals first saw left-wing totalitarianism as simply a more extended form of their own liberal faith. Within their bi-polar construct pattern, this all seemed quite logical. Since everything on the left is presumed to oppose everything on the right, and since experience runs down straight lines, it follows that communism is simply a point along the same line as progressive liberalism, but somewhat past it.

And for those in that generation who inclined toward the role of prophet and who sought something more wholly regenerating than a moderate liberal persuasion, communism seemed a perfect faith. Indeed, for those who took the faith full, it appeared to offer a complete merger of explanation with experience, mind with world. Witness Arthur Koestler, writing of his experience of Communism in *The God that Failed:*

To say that one had "seen the light" is a poor description of the mental rapture which only the convert knows (regardless of what faith he has been converted to). The new light seems to pour from all directions across the skull; the whole universe falls into pattern like the stray pieces of a jigsaw puzzle assembled by magic at one stroke. There is now an answer to every question, doubts and conflicts are a matter of the tortured past—a past already remote, when one had lived in dismal ignorance in the tasteless, colorless world of those who *don't know.*[28]

This had been Koestler's sense of experience in the early 1930s—before the Spanish Civil War, the Moscow Trials, and the Nazi-Soviet Pact. These three events, however, forced to his attention something which had laid fugitive and repressed in his mind before. That something was *paradox*—the paradox, in this case, that experiences can cross over the polar categories, and that left-wing regimes as well as right-wing ones can suppress and brutalize human existence. That paradox was symbolized in the Nazi-Soviet Pact of 1939, where the political extremes of right and left joined, in defiance of Progressivist bi-polar categories.

Arthur Koestler had of course *experienced* paradox before; until the late

1930s, though, he did not have to pattern it into an *explanation*. But by then, these paradoxes were no longer seeming to be exceptions to the rule, but perhaps were becoming the rule itself. So Koestler and his colleagues had to try and re-cluster the rules of life through different forms. In Thomas Kuhn's terms, they had to take such paradoxes out of the realm of "anomaly" and bring them to center mind. When they did that, they drove out of their minds the old patterns and clusters, and tried to build up counter ones. Such a task was not easy or pleasant for them, as the poignance of *The God that Failed* essays shows. For to be twice-born you have to *die* once. As Richard Wright says when his totalistic faith rejects him, "For a moment it seemed that I had ceased to live."[29] And for those who'd once experienced such a holistic vision, such an all-encompassing explanation of experience, their second life could never be as personally exhilarating as the first. As Wright goes on to say after his faith had waned:

I remembered the stories I had written, the stories in which I had assigned a role of honor and glory to the Community Party, and I was glad that they were down in black and white, were finished. For I knew in my heart that I should never be able to write that way again, should never be able to feel with that simple sharpness about life, should never again express such passionate hope, should never again make so total a commitment of faith.[30]

Most liberal-progressive intellectuals did not give themselves so wholly to a doctrinaire faith. Hence the process of shock, rebirth, and repatterning was not quite so traumatic for them. But what the comparatively few "god-that-failed" thinkers experienced *in extremis,* many more underwent in moderation. And those who could barely get by this frontal assault on their liberal explanation-form from the left, were even harder pressed by a more devastating attack from the right.

The left-wing assault—climaxing in the late 1930s—questioned this generation's faith in certain kinds of men and ideas. The right-wing assault—climaxing in Nazism during World War II—put to question their faith in ideas and man himself. For Nazism revealed depths of bestiality in the human species never lighted by the Progressive explanation. Under the pressure of such a demonic force, minds were driven to ask, "How do you explain such bestiality without simply picturing man *as* bestial, and giving everything over to despair?"

Not everyone, of course, saw the situation as so radically different. Some pictured Nazism as merely an extension of those old formalisms which progressives had battled all along, and they called for a rededication to their time-proven strategies.

Sidney Hook, for example, took a stance similar to Merle Curti's in the last chapter. That is, he branded the liberals' trauma as simply a "failure of nerve," and hinted that their anguished response to the malaise of the times sometimes abetted the irrational obscurantism of Adolf Hitler. Like Curti,

Hook called for a renewal of commitment to precisely those qualities which the situation had put under strain—the qualities of reason and of hope:

Not until a democratic, freedom-and-welfare planning economy is built out of what is left of our world, in which stable traditions can absorb the conventions of revolt of political man and the experiments of growth of individual men, will these intellectual excesses subside from epidemic to episodic proportions. Until then it is necessary to prevent the intellectual hysteria from infecting those who still cling to the principles of rational experiment and analysis.[31]

But as with Curti, so with Hook. His very mode of reasoning betrayed his uneasiness. The liberal-progressive explanation was no longer the obvious common sense of the matter (as with an unquestioned paradigm), but was now put on the defensive to justify itself. It had been relegated to one among competing modes of thinking in the intellectual community, it was no longer the only acceptable one. In short, this was a time of paradigm crisis among progressive-liberal intellectuals. It's what we're calling a "critical threshold" situation.

Some would halt before the threshold, look both forward and backward, and decide that the old forms still worked. But others would feel these old forms in an ill fit with their new experiences. And these experiences, they believed, were simply so pressing that they must become part of any future explanation. Thus they, like the god-that-failed writers, would try and break apart their old mind sets, would pass over the threshold, and rechannel their minds into new patterns.

For these thinkers, life seemed to be moving in more than one direction at a time; so they sought forms which would manage the ambiguity of their experience. A Reinhold Niebuhr, for example, would try and re-found his liberal faith on *both* optimistic and pessimistic perspectives on man, would write "Man's capacity for justice makes democracy possible; but man's inclination to injustice makes democracy necessary," and would construct a book-length essay around that statement.[32]

Or an Arthur Schlesinger, Jr.—whose 1945 *Age of Jackson* is one of the last American histories written inside an unreconstructed Progressive faith—would pass over the threshold in 1949 by opting for a "vital center" which rejects the polar opposites of both right and left. Schlesinger would substitute a *circular* model for the left-right lines of the Progressive explanation. Communism and Fascism—representing the more violent approach to human affairs—would meet at the circle's bottom; Liberalism and Conservatism—representing the more moderate approach—would meet at the top.[33] Though it's clear that Schlesinger still opts for the liberal over the conservative alternative, his circular model makes either one preferable to the violent extremes at the bottom—fascism and communism. These extreme forms, not conservatism, are now seen as the liberals' real enemy.

This was an era of realignments, then, when minds were taking things all apart and putting them back together again in different ways. What emerged were not only new pictures of experience, but new kinds of loyalties—some who were thought to be friends in the past no longer seemed so, others who were seen as enemies now came to look like friends. Which is exactly what happens when a paradigm community undergoes upheaval. As Thomas Kuhn says, "A revolution is . . . a special sort of change involving a certain sort of reconstruction of group commitments."[34]

IV

In chapter 5, we asked, *What does a paradigm revolution look like?* Well, here we are in one now, and we might pause and look around for a while to consider just what is to be said of such situations. We should begin to learn something of the general appearance of paradigm revolutions before we move further inside this particular one. Or rather, we ought move back and forth now from the particular to the general, so we can build up a working picture of "the structure of historiographic revolutions," as Kuhn has with "the structure of scientific revolutions."

Let's begin by recalling what we said in chapter 5. There we were concerned with the question, "How do people change their minds?"; and we suggested that to explain *how* we must first locate *when* and *where*. We then drew upon Thomas Kuhn's idea of "paradigm revolutions" to structure our inquiries, but noted that Kuhn—in *The Structure of Scientific Revolutions,* at least—stopped with that when and where, and didn't show us much of how. Or rather, he didn't focus on an actual revolution in the making, to get inside the moment of an idea as it's undergoing upheaval. In short, he didn't picture a paradigm revolution *in motion,* just at the point when it's altering forms.

To supplement Kuhn at this point, we brought in three of that chapter's controlling terms—"situation-strategy" analysis, the "earthquake" metaphor of mind change, and the idea of "pivotal moments." Each was introduced as a focusing device, a way of controlling inquiry into ideas and idea change.

The concept of a *situation* was our key there, our basic strategy for focus. It's there where we can watch most closely just how ideas behave, for in a situation the accumulated stress of dislocations in an idea-form comes to surface. It's there too where we can locate the rebalancing of ideas, the patterning into new forms, and setting off in new directions. Situations—or some kinds of situations—can thus be seen as stress points, like fault-lines in an earthquake.

And that was our second major term from chapter 5—the *earthquake* metaphor of idea change. Through that metaphor, we can watch how greater and greater strain builds upon along a fault-line, or series of fault-lines (the plot of chapter 7). Occasional slippage (e.g., Turner's "up-the-ladder" strategy) may relieve some of the strain; but if the surrounding pressure becomes intense enough, only a major relocation can release it. And then we have an earthquake—where surrounding forces break through the old forms and there is a massive upheaval, altering the contours of the ground around it.

We picture idea change as a seismic shock, then, and the exact time of change—or just before the change—is our *pivotal moment*. It's in this pivotal moment, or critical threshold situation, where everything is especially sensitive. In "normal" times, when the old forms are held in balance and the pressures are not acute, an explanation-form can tolerate much discord within it. Thus a Henry Adams—or, later, much of Carl Becker and parts of Charles Beard and Vernon Parrington—could depart some from dominant Progressive categories without disturbing the core historical community much. In normal situations, a paradigm community may simply absorb the dissent, or ignore it, because there are few available channels where that dissent can build up much momentum.

But if that's true in normal times, it's not the case in "revolutionary" times, in a critical threshold situation. In these kinds of situations, everything which is said or done becomes crucial, for the balances are so precarious that even a little pressure may topple the forms. So even if someone should voice the same kind of idea which had been said and absorbed some time before, here it may provide the spark for revolution. The historian who looks at such an idea at such a time and says, "Well, that's not really new; X said it back in ——" misses the point. The point is not that it's new or even different; the point is that in this particular time and in this particular situation, it may make the tiny added push or pull which shatters the old balance. In that sense it may be "revolutionary"—whether new or not.

So when we're inquiring into a critical threshold situation, we've got to look at things with special care, since certain kinds of ideas are likely to exert more power there than at perhaps any other moment. The really difficult question, thought, is *"Where do you look?"* For at this point our earthquake analogy is not wholly appropriate.

Unlike earthquakes in nature, historians' revolutions don't ordinarily happen all at once. If they did, our task in this chapter would be made easier. We'd simply locate the obvious moment of upheaval, then train our eyes in close on that situation and watch what happens and how.

We can of course say that under the impact of new kinds of situations in the 1930s and 1940s, the Progressive paradigm began to disintegrate, and that by the middle 1950s it was all but gone. But we can't very well locate one single moment and say, *"This* is the actual point where everything changed." For if we're looking at the movement from Progressive to counter-Progressive in the explanation of America's experience, we can find pivotal moments dotted all across the intellectual scene—some from within the history profession, but most, it seems, from without.

This gets us to a basic difference between historians and the scientists described by Kuhn. Historians are generally less insulated from the surrounding culture, and from other intellectual subcommunities. Thus, many of their signals come from outside the profession. Because of this, and *because there are differential rates of change in different subcultures,* the number and range of variables in each situation is compounded. During the 1930s and 1940s, any historian who looked outside to, say, literature or theology for his cues was less likely to be caught up in the Progressive mind-set than one working wholly inside the profession, or who took cues from politics. Thus Perry Miller—who came of intellectual age in the 1920s and wrote or edited three major studies in the 1930s—never came under Progressive domination (though he also didn't exert much influence on historians until the late 1940s, when others in the profession were turning to the same cues as Miller).

We ought not picture historians as wholly caught up in the moment either, or in their culture's contemporary "climate of opinion." Precisely because they're historians, they have an expanded time sense beyond the immediate situation. Or ought to. If an Arthur Schlesinger, Jr. would support his progressivist present—in *The Age of Jackson*—by looking back upon a past which he thought resembled it—a Miller would journey to a past—in *The New England Mind: The Seventeenth Century*—which to him didn't look like the American present at all. In fact, it was precisely because this Puritan past was so different that Miller, in his 1939 volume, found it so engaging.

All this might caution us from overcompressing our materials, and from making a community of inquirers seem more unified than they in fact are. However much we may chart Progressive disintegration in the late 1930s and 1940s, we ought not forget that when American historians were queried in 1952 on their "most preferred" work of the 1936–50 years, a Progressive history—Merle Curti's *The Growth of American Thought*—took first place.[35] And perhaps the most important study done in the 1940s—Schlesinger's militantly Progressive *The Age of Jackson*—continued to influence historians for some considerable time thereafter.

Pivotal moments are not single and all of a piece, then. Rather, they're multiple. Which brings a problem to issue: *Just what moments do you focus in on when you're trying to chart a paradigm revolution in the making?*

V

Because this issue of focus is problematic, we're obliged to make clear just what we're trying to *do* with these moments. And, almost more important, what we're *not* trying to do.

1. Ideas, as we've contended before, have been treated too abstractly in American intellectual history studies. They have not been brought down into situations enough, to watch them get knocked around. It's in situations, or in this case moments, where we can best handle ideas not as inert "thought," but as dynamic "strategies."[36]

We'll make no claim that the cases we focus on here are the *only* significant moments of transition; and we can make only a disputed claim that they're even the *best* ones for charting this historical movement from Progressive to counter-Progressive. But we can claim this: students of ideas should begin to look *for* moments, as a strategy for getting at particulars. Moments can become for us *intensified* experiences, where something unusual appears to be happening with an idea. By moving into idea change through a few selected pivotal moments, we're attempting to ward off information overload in the study of historical experience in America. We're also attempting to counter the assumption, normal in history studies, that any one moment is equal to any other.

2. All moments are not equal in the life of ideas; some are in fact "better" than others. This is so not because there's some abstract, superhistorical judge which measures one moment weightier than another. It's because when we've developed an operational sense of just what we're looking for in an explanation pattern, then some moments of an idea in fact come to be more revealing than others.

As we need to use moments as a strategy for focus with ideas, so we need to develop such an *operative* sense of what we're looking for and why. With such a sense, we can make more reasoned selections in our moments for focus.

Here George Kelly's "plane" construct can help us. As we noted in the last chapter, Kelly urges us to break general belief patterns down into particular planes—say, love/hate, or abstract/concrete, or permanence/change, or dynamic/passive—and to watch how ideas move along these planes.[37] If we're looking at one particular plane of an explanation pattern, then we can best locate it in certain historical moments; if we're looking for another plane, then other moments are preferable. Each plane has its most revealing moments, also its own vulnerable points and critical threshold situations.

In each case, what we want is to break a pattern of ideas down into something manageable. We can do that first by looking *for* moments, we can do it second by developing an operative sense to guide our choices for focus.

3. When we've done that—have taken our explanation pattern and have isolated its various planes, their particular moments and their accompanying stress points—then we can bring into action those "literary" devices which we noted in chapter 6. In short, we've got our intensified "experience," and we've sorted it out from several other experiences which—from our operational sense—are not as intense. With everything incidental to our purposes sorted away, we should have before us a historical "text"—an article, a book, a chapter, a passage, a paragraph, a sentence, a phrase, a word. Our next task is to give this historical text-experience "explanation."

In (Kenneth) Burkean terms, that text can now be used as a "scene," where we can observe the drama of mind wrestling with itself and with the world.[38] In these scenes, ideas are being formed, under strain, altered, or dying.

These moments, or scenes, may or may not reveal the *causes* of such idea change. And when we move from one moment to another we can't tell yet whether the two are necessarily linked, one being cause, the other effect. We will try to draw a few connections between moments in these case studies; but such connections are mostly hypothetical. We've chosen our cases and their moments—Turner, Trilling, Parrington, Niebuhr, R. W. B. Lewis, Miller—mostly for their expressive power, not (necessarily) for their causal influence. We'll use our literary devices here to try and find out just what are their characteristic modes of expression, and how they behave in what kinds of situations. From this, hopefully, scholars can move on later to explain more of what influences what, and when, and how. But that will come much later in American historiographical studies; we have much preliminary work to do first.

4. However much we may try and rationalize our choices, then—and we'll do that in the three sections coming up—we can make no solid case that the historical texts we've selected are in fact those most "representative" of their times. Perhaps over time we'll learn enough of how intellectual subcommunities function—of lines or nets of communication within them, and ways they connect outward into other communities—to justify such selections in a more empirical fashion. We're not ready for that yet, though. What we know of such behaviors is only fugitive and scattered now; we can only grope some here and there, hoping to frame a few of the right questions now so others can go on to make better connections later.

But if we're in largely uncharted territory, we're not entirely without cues. We know we're trying to understand points where mind changes, we have Thomas Kuhn's suggestions on how scientific communities function and move from one form to another, and we have Kenneth Burke's situation-strategy tools, plus a few of our own. We also have much scholarship in American history around us; if it hasn't always asked exactly the questions which concern us here, it has provided a lot of data and insights which we can now try and use for our own purposes. Most important, we have our "primary documents" intact—the works of history and American Studies on which, finally, our explanations must be based.

If we know that ours aren't the only moments, or perhaps even the best ones, they are at least *some* moments. And if our choice of some here provokes others to counter with better choices of their own, that will lead to exactly what we need now in American intellectual history-historiography studies—*an ongoing dialogue about ideas which is grounded in the specifics of time and place and situation, and is focused on particular historical texts.*

VI

Now that we've admitted that the choice of any particular moment is somewhat arbitrary, we're still left with the question, "What particular particulars do we choose?" We've tried to hold out the possibility of alternatives with all those caveats, now it's time to get on with the business of justifying our selections.

The choices are Lionel Trilling and Reinhold Niebuhr, the texts Trilling's *The Liberal Imagination* (1950) and Niebuhr's *The Children of Light and the Children of Darkness* (1944). In the section to follow, we'll try and explain why. But because there are multiple moments into the counter-Progressive form, because there is so little secondary (or tertiary) scholarship on counter-Progressives, and because this whole book is a study in process which attempts to open out alternative lines for future inquiry, we might pass briefly over a few other moments which could bear following up later.

In chapter 7, we looked some at the later Carl Becker and Charles Beard, and noted a few themes in their thinking which might be labeled "counter-Progressive." In the future, we need some pivotal moment studies which would begin with the full counter-Progressive form of the 1950s, then would plot back to Becker and Beard in the 1930s and 1940s (in Becker's case, on back into the 1920s too). Such studies would need to isolate planes along each form, then chart on which planes Becker or Beard most nearly approached the counter-Progressive explanation, and on which they appear most distant from it. David Marcell, for example, suggests that Beard's 1942 book *The American Spirit* was essentially counter-Progressive (he uses the term "consensus") in its sense of "civilization"; but it seems to remain Progressive in its sense of "progress."[39]

For such studies, we already have the raw material of Becker's and Beard's writings, plus several fine interpretive works. All we need is to ask some new questions of these materials, and we should be able to plot Becker and Beard along this Progressive/counter-Progressive fault-line.[40]

If we were to focus on the American Studies strain of the counter-Progressive form, another moment might be F. O. Mattiessen's classic 1941 study, *American Renaissance*. There we could watch part of the American Studies symbol-myth-image form in the making. We could also see how Matthiessen uses that form to counter Vernon Parrington—especially Parrington's progressivist picture of how literature relates to ideas and to culture. Matthiessen writes,

Although I greatly admire Parrington's elucidation of our liberal tradition, I think the understanding of our literature has been retarded by the tendency of some of his followers to regard all criticism as "belletristic trifling." I am even more suspicious of the results of such historians as have declared that they are not discussing art, but "simply using art in a purpose of research." Both our historical writing and our criticism have been greatly enriched during the past twenty years by the breaking down of arbitrary divisions between them, by the critic's realization of the necessity to master what he could of historical discipline, by the historian's desire to extend his domain from politics to general culture.

"But," Matthiessen warns,

you cannot "use" a work of art unless you have comprehended its meaning. And it is well to remember that although literature reflects an age, it also illuminates it. Whatever the case may be for the historian, the quality of that illumination is the main concern for the common reader. He does not live by trends alone; he reads books, whether of the present or past, because they have an immediate life of their own.[41]

In those words, we can detect several themes which later come to preoccupy counter-Progressive American Studies scholars—their tendency to treat literary works as having "an immediate life of their own," their search for a work's "meanings" over its "uses," above all, their insistence that a work of art or ideas "illuminates" a culture as well as "reflects" it. In F. O. Matthiessen, we can thus see an early instance of how New Critical techniques have gotten merged with broader cultural analysis in American Studies scholarship. And his painstaking dissection of ideas stands in sharp contrast to the Progressive tendency to "sketch ideas on the run."[42]

It's no coincidence, then, that both focal figures for our next chapter, on counter-Progressives—R. W. B. Lewis and Perry Miller—were much influenced by Matthiessen. Lewis writes in *The American Adam,* "My debt to F. O. Matthiessen's *American Renaissance* will be evident on many pages; more important and less evident is a debt to the man himself, to a wise and dedicated teacher and an unforgettable friend."[43] And Miller has acknowledged Matthiessen's influence in his first two books—*Orthodoxy in Massachusetts* and *The Puritans.* So also has Daniel Aaron acknowledged Matthiessen in *Men of Good Hope.* And Leo Marx has written in *The Machine in the Garden:* "My way of thinking about literature and society was formed, years ago, when I was a student working with F. O. Matthiessen and Perry Miller. I have made no attempt to specify my debts to them. Anyone who knew them, or who knows their work, will have encountered their quite different influences everywhere in this book."[44]

Within the community of professional historians, the two most often seen as transitional figures from the Progressive form to the counter-Progressive are Arthur Schlesinger, Jr., and Richard Hofstadter. Schlesinger is perhaps the most dramatic case of explanation change. In four brief years from 1945 to 1949, he was transformed from an aggressively Progressive stance to an early variant of the counter-Progressive position.

Schlesinger's 1945 book, *The Age of Jackson,* opens with a progressivist epigraph from George Bancroft:

"The feud between the capitalist and laborer, the house of Have and the house of Want, is as old as social union, and can never be entirely quieted; but he who will act with moderation, prefer fact to theory, and remember that every thing in the world is relative and not absolute, will see that the violence of the contest may be stilled."[45]

And it closes with the characteristic Progressive tendency to claim liberalism as distinctively "American," while rejecting conservatism as something unnatural to the country:

Every great crisis thus far in American history has produced a leader adequate to the occasion from the ranks of those who believe vigorously and seriously in liberty, democracy and the common man. . . .

In the past, when liberalism has resolved the crisis and restored tranquility, conservatism has recovered power by the laws of political gravity; then it makes a new botch of things, and liberalism again must take over in the name of the nation.[46]

By 1949, however, and *The Vital Center* Schlesinger has given off his belief that conservatism is the main enemy of liberty, has abandoned his progressivist left-right model for that circle we noted a few pages back, and has urged liberals to join with conservatives to combat a new enemy which threatens them both—totalitarianism. What intervened between 1945 and 1949 was Schlesinger's growing sense of a totalitarian threat to liberty, his early work in the Americans for Democratic Action, and, perhaps most important, his association with Reinhold Niebuhr.

Schlesinger first became acquainted with Niebuhr in late 1946, when the two began working together in the early years of the Americans for Democratic Action. "Initially impressed and charmed," Schlesinger later recalled, "I then began reading his books. I suppose that *The Nature and Destiny of Man* . . . had more influence on me (and my attitudes toward history) than any other single book."[47]

Schlesinger also was much influenced by Niebuhr's wartime book, *The Children of Light and the Children of Darkness.* He writes of that book:

Niebuhr's rendition of the Christian interpretation of human nature, his sense of the frailty of human striving along with the duty none the less to strive, his sense of the tension between history and the absolute—all these things gave form to my own gropings about human nature and history and showed me how skepticism about man, far from leading to a rejection of democracy, established democracy on its firmest intellectual basis.

Schlesinger continues, "Niebuhr also . . . confirmed my sense that irony was the best human and historical stance—an irony which does not sever the nerve of action." "Also, through the years," Schlesinger was to write in 1968, "Niebuhr more than anyone else I have known has served as the model of a really great man."[48]

When we look into *The Vital Center,* this Niebuhrian impact is quite visible. Schlesinger has not only borrowed Niebuhr's sense of man and democracy there—the "great tradition" of American liberalism is now revised to include Nathaniel Hawthorne as well as Andrew Jackson—he has also taken on Niebuhr's characteristic mode of talking about things.[49] After citing Niebuhr's famous "Man's capacity for justice" statement, for example, he goes on to write,

The image of democratic man emerges from the experience of democracy; man is a creature capable of reason and of purpose, of great loyalty and of great virtue, yet also he is vulnerable to material power and to spiritual pride. In our democratic tradition, the excessive self-love which transforms power into tyranny is the greatest of all dangers. But the self-love which transforms radicalism from an instrument of action into an expression of neurosis is almost as great a danger. If irresponsible power is the source of evil, and irresponsible impotence, the source of decadence, then responsible power—power held for limited terms under conditions of strict accountability—is the source of wisdom.[50]

"Creature," "spiritual pride," "self-love," "evil," "wisdom"—those words were penned by Arthur Schlesinger, Jr.; but, as we'll see soon, they come in the form of Reinhold Niebuhr. They also come in the form of ambiguity, which leads straight into the counter-Progressive explanation.[51]

Schlesinger's subsequent concerns have been too politicized for him to remain wholly counter-Progressive (adepts of the form have not been notably political). But, since the mid-1940s, his writings have not returned to the old Progressive polarities either.

Finally, there is Richard Hofstadter, whose 1948 study, *The American Political Tradition,* is sometimes cited as the first full-scale effort to move outside the Progressive framework. It's one of the originals in the counter-Progressive school, maybe *the* original.

Like many counter-Progressive historians, Hofstadter started off as a Progressive. Unlike Schlesinger, though, his movement from "once-born" to "twice-born" does not seem directly the result of some outside personal influence, or of involvement in political action. Rather, it seems to have come from a continuing (and what was to amount to a lifelong) dialogic engagement with his Progressive predecessors.[52] As he was to say in a 1960 interview, "One has always to reckon with the generation that has gone before. I think where one gets one's real intellectual impetus is reacting against ideas one has felt strongly."[53]

Hofstadter's initial historical impetus came from Charles Beard. "It was Beard," he says, "who got me excited about American history." "Turner never did," he goes on, "I'm too much of an Easterner."[54] Hofstadter took from Beard his economic explanation of experience, an explanation which made sense of his own world in the 1930s. "My generation," he writes, "was raised in the conviction that the basic motive power in political behavior is the economic interest of groups."[55]

But in a 1941 essay on "Parrington and the Jeffersonian Tradition," Richard Hofstadter gave hint of where his mind would settle in the years to come. He criticized Parrington's work for being too neatly schematic, and also challenged his agrarian interpretation of Jefferson. But he would still reaffirm the basic Progressive form by writing there, "That early American politics centered about a struggle between agrarian and capitalist interests is not likely to be questioned."[56]

By 1948 and *The American Political Tradition,* however, Hofstadter had given up that class-struggle picture of American experience. "Although the Jeffersonians and Federalists raged at each other with every appearance of a bitter and insoluble opposition," he writes, "differences in practical policy boiled down to a very modest minimum when Jefferson took power, and before long the two parties were indistinguishable."[57]

Hofstadter had thus broken with the Progressives' "polar opposites" model by this time. He was also trying to counter Progressive categories. Witness the built-in ambiguity of his chapter titles: "Thomas Jefferson: The Aristocrat as Democrat," "Andrew Jackson and the Rise of Liberal Capitalism," "Woodrow Wilson: The Conservative as Liberal."

By thus confounding Progressive linkages, by putting together what they'd held apart, Hofstadter emphasized what he called "the common climate of opinion" in the country—"a unity of cultural and political tradition, upon which American civilization has stood."[58] He felt previous historians had been too caught up by the rhetoric of battle to detect these underlying commonalities, and he called his colleagues to "a reinterpretation of our political traditions which emphasizes the common climate of opinion."[59]

Hofstadter's emphasis upon "consensus" at this point prefigures Louis Hartz (and indeed some of the New Left) rather than Daniel Boorstin. For he didn't like these uniformities in the American polity; mostly, at this time he deplored them. "American traditions . . . show a strong bias in favor of equalitarian democracy," he wrote there, "but it has been a democracy in cupidity rather than a democracy of fraternity." And it "has always been bounded by the horizons of property and enterprise."[60]

Hofstadter's next major study, *The Age of Reform* (1955), is wholly within the counter-Progressive form. Indeed, it's one of the clearest examples in the historical literature of that form.

Like the Progressives before him, Hofstadter was interested in American reform and reformers. But he would not take their anti-formalistic strategy and play off these reformers against conservatives. Instead, he would argue that the reformers themselves were conservatives of a sort. Especially the Populists (less so, the Progressives and New Dealers).

Hofstadter's stance was not anti-Progressive, though. Rather, it's what we've been calling "counter"-Progressive. That is, he would take certain progressivist assumptions about experience, bring them up to light, turn them around, invert a few, challenge this or that, but he would not reject the whole mind-set out of hand. As he wrote in his introduction, "The place of the progressive tradition . . . is so secure that it should now be possible to indulge in some critical comments without seeming to impugn its entire value.[61]

Drawing upon Lionel Trilling and *The Liberal Imagination,* Hofstadter contended that liberals must criticize their own tradition, since they can get no intellectual challenge from conservatives. Merging Trilling's dialogue prescription with Niebuhr's skeptical realism, he wrote,

To the degree that I have been critical in these pages of the Populist-Progressive tradition, it is criticism that aims to reveal some of the limitations of that tradition and to help free it of its sentimentalities and complacencies—in short, to carry on with a task so largely shirked by its opponents that it must be performed by its supporters.[62]

Hofstadter's 1968 volume, *The Progressive Historians,* is a rare occasion in American historical scholarship—an effort to revise a tradition of historical interpretation by engaging directly *with* that tradition. (The normal procedure is to make a few glancing remarks about the dominant interpretation, which may serve to stereotype it as much as type it, then substitute one's own "true" explanation of the facts for the "erroneous" version of the old form.) It's the fullest sustained dialogue we have of counter-Progressive with Progressive, and it's a gold mine for the student of these two forms. In its 466 pages of text is to be found the most comprehensive picture of a paradigm community in American historical scholarship, and the most serious effort to counter such a paradigm with an alternative explanation-form.

What makes *The Progressive Historians* so remarkable—beyond its obvious qualities of mind- and leg-work—is Hofstadter's candid historical self-awareness. "I have asked myself why I wrote this book," he says, "and why at this time."[63] His answer is revealing, for it takes us deep into this Progressive–v.-counter-Progressive dialogue about experience:

I started this book out of a personal engagement with the subject, out of some sense of the incompleteness of my reckoning with my intellectual forebears, out of the feeling I have about this and other subjects that I do not quite know what I think until I have written it, and the conviction that if I did not write about these men now the clarification that I hoped for from such a reckoning might never take place.

Hofstadter goes on, telling how his generation started off in its "once-born" stage: "At the point at which I began to have some identity as a historian, it was the work of these men, particularly Beard and Parrington, that interested me as supplying the guiding ideas to the understanding of American history." When he entered his "twice-born" stage, however, these ideas would not serve as guides any longer; mostly, they had become roadblocks for him. "Later, at a time when my own conceptions of our history were beginning to take form, I found myself impelled to write again about all three of these men and to take some note of their critics."

He concludes, capturing almost perfectly what I intend by the word "counter" in the label counter-Progressive:

A good deal of what has gone into this book is then a reprise of that perennial battle we wage with our elders, particularly with our adopted intellectual fathers. If we are to have any new thoughts, if we are to have an intellectual identity of our own, we must make the effort to distinguish ourselves from those who preceded us, and perhaps pre-eminently from those to whom we once had the greatest indebtedness. Even if our quarrels are only marginal and minor (though I do not think that can be said of the differences discussed here), we must make the most of them.[64]

VII

These are a few moments when minds have wrestled with Progressive dilemmas and then have gone over the threshold to suggest a new kind of explanation for experience in America. With world enough and time, we could explore each moment with care. A natural history of this Progressive/counter-Progressive earthquake would include shock waves in the later Beard and Becker and Parrington, then a detailed account of the early relocation of forms in thinkers like Schlesinger, and Hofstadter, and Matthiessen.[65]

But time and space keep us from doing that. Instead, we're concentrating our energies on the moments of Lionel Trilling and Reinhold Niebuhr. The reasons for this choice are instructive, for they tell us something important about communities of explanation in history, and how they may differ from those in science.

If paradigm revolutions always happened along straight lines, then our task here would be simple. We'd just move directly from the later Beard, Becker, and Parrington to the counter-Progressives who followed them, staying in or near the profession most all the time. But if we did that now, we'd not get very deep into this particular revolution; for it was much affected by forces well *outside* the profession. Neither Trilling nor Niebuhr was professionally trained in history, nor did either, to my knowledge, ever even attend a professional historians' convention. Yet I think it is these two—one a literary critic, the other a theologian—who more than any others signal this paradigm revolution in American historical writing.

When I first began planning this study a few years back, I thought to plot this historians' earthquake along lines running mostly inside the profession. That is: Here was the Progressive form under strain, and here were Parrington, Beard, and Becker bending under that strain and reaching out for new forms, but always (or most always) being pulled back by their idea of progress, or by their prophetic role.

Then (so went my logic) here were the early counter-Progressives, less committed to a faith in progress and to the role of prophet. They'd push the old form a little further, until at some point it would break, and they would pass over the threshold into an entirely new form. With a situation like that, those late Progressive historians and early counter-Progressives would not be incidental to this chapter, they would be our main focus. We'd not be looking much at Niebuhr and Trilling, but would be staying closer to the profession.

But as I read further in counter-Progressives, I discovered an intriguing fact. They didn't seem much affected by the later Beard at all (save negatively, in his foreign-policy books), and only a little by the later Becker (this influence is clearest in, say, David Noble, Cushing Strout, and Robert Skotheim). Nor did they seem to be influenced by Parrington when he's under pressure, especially as he begins to doubt his own form in the final volume of *Main Currents.* When counter-Progressives wrote of Progressives, it was not of the later form, under strain, it was of the early form, when most everything in it fit together.

Like New Left historians some years afterward—who would overcompress their predecessors into the "consensus" form—these early counter-Progressives would overcompress their Progressive predecessors, building themselves a solid base to move off from. And mostly, that base would be a *negative* launching point; positively, they'd look elsewhere for their cues about experience in America. That elsewhere was to the general intellectual community, where the anguish of explanation crisis seems to have been felt more acutely than inside the history profession. It's here where we can locate those who came to be "significant others" for the early counter-Progressives.

To select our particular moments, then, we're obliged not only to plot forward, but backward too—what, in retrospect, later counter-Progressives seem most to have drawn from the years during and right after World War II. If we look there for the counter-Progressive form in gestation, two experience-explanation planes seem to stand out—one runs along conceptions of *democracy,* the other along conceptions of *reality.* On both planes the Progressives had clear and strong positions; and on both, counter-Progressives took them and gave them a kind of counter-twist.

These two planes help us narrow our range of possible moments. Within that range, along these two particular fault-lines, Niebuhr's *Children of Light and Children of Darkness* and Trilling's *Liberal Imagination* most clearly signal what's to come in the years just ahead.

Daniel Bell, as we've seen, calls his a "twice-born" generation. And we're calling them a "counter"-generation, with a counter-strategy for explaining experience. When Progressives tried to explain things, they took their signals from politics. Their polarizing of experience into conservative and liberal, their concern for the "uses" of ideas, their passionate commitment to democracy as a party thing, indeed their very name—Progressive—were all drawn from the categories of politics.

To get leverage for constructing an alternative strategy, several counter-Progressives looked away from the world of politics toward literature and religion. Not that they abandoned politics. They just didn't *start* there in looking for cues to explain life in America. Instead, they took their basic categories from outside politics, then worked them back into politics and to other areas of American experience. John Higham catches this tendency when he writes,

Perhaps a keynote to contemporary historiography may be found in the frequent attempt to combine such antithetical principles as consensus and conflict without entirely negating either alternative. *Like modern literary critics and theologians,* many present-day historians seem to say that life is ambiguous. America, therefore, becomes a realm of paradox: a nation born of revolt that was moderate, yet genuinely revolutionary; a society that is liberal in its ideals, yet conservative in its behavior; united in its divisions, and divided in its unity.[66]

In neither literature nor religion did counter-Progressives seek specific doctrines or bodies of knowledge. They looked rather for underlying attitudes—embodied in such terms as "symbol," "ambiguity," "tragedy," "innocence," "paradox," "evil," "irony," and "myth."

On the literary side, this caused a widening of America's intellectual tradition to include the "non-party" thinkers of our past—like Jonathan Edwards, Fenimore Cooper, Hawthorne, Melville, Poe, and Henry James. And it would detect hidden contraries in the "party" writers and doers—like Jefferson, Emerson, Jackson, Whitman, Wilson. Even such a political counter-Progressive as Schlesinger would thus be prompted to write, "In the years after the Second War Americans began to rediscover the great tradition of American liberalism—the tradition of Jackson and Hawthorne, the tradition of reasonable responsibility about politics and a moderate pessimism about man."[67] This tendency would also extend a bridge over from history to literature, so that the American Studies strain of counter-Progressivism would become a natural outgrowth of its basic sense of life.[68]

On the religion side, counter-Progressives sought an attitude toward man which would take them deeper than did the old Progressive form, which would help explain why they had to be "born" a second time, and which would add direction and meaning to their trans-formed life. They found this (or part of it) not in religious faiths or institutionalized religion, but in the kinds of questions which critical religion had characteristically posed of life. In the 1930s, 1940s and 1950s, these questions were most sharply pointed in the writings of Reinhold Niebuhr, and they helped counter-Progressives to root their pessimism not in anomic despair and resignation but in an integrated vision of man and of history.[69]

VIII

It remains now to consider briefly just how direct and widespread were these impacts of Trilling and Niebuhr among counter-Progressives. As we noted before, it is not our major concern here to claim Trilling and Niebuhr as *influences*. But there's enough fugitive evidence available to give us a few hints. And that will have to do until we know more about how to trace out sociologies of historical knowledge, and about how to chart nets of intercommunication within and among intellectual subcommunities.

Lionel Trilling's influence is in a few cases direct and traceable. In *The Machine and the Garden,* for example, Leo Marx cites Trilling's dialectical theory of culture as having shaped his own thinking, and adds, "Trilling's definition has proven remarkably useful in the interpretation of American writing in the nineteenth century."[70] Stanley Elkins in *Slavery* and David

Noble in *Historians against History* and *The Eternal Adam and the New World Garden* also cite the influence of Trilling. And we've already noted that Richard Hofstadter drew upon Trilling in *The Age of Reform*. Further, we've mentioned Daniel Bell's statement that the two most "representative" figures of his twice-born, 1930s generation are Trilling and Niebuhr.[71]

Beyond that, no other major counter-Progressive work, to my knowledge, cites Trilling as a direct influence. Other studies—like, say, R. W. B. Lewis' *The American Adam* and Marvin Meyers' *The Jacksonian Persuasion*— are informed by a Trilling-like sense of culture. But, lacking further evidence, all we can say is that these are just parallel resemblances, not cause-and-effect influences.

With Niebuhr, we have a little more to go on; for where his direct impact has been felt, it's usually been deep. This is clearest with Schlesinger, and we've already mentioned that Niebuhr directly influenced his metamorphosis from Progressive to counter-Progressive. We've also noted that Schlesinger dedicated his 1957 volume, *The Crisis of the Old Order,* to Niebuhr. And his 1956 essay, "Reinhold Niebuhr's Role in American Political Life and Thought," suggests the Niebuhrian impact beyond the world of academe.[72]

Niebuhr also influenced Perry Miller. In a 1958 review of *Pious and Secular America,* Miller wrote, "It is by now somewhat difficult to recapture the shock many of us felt when we first encountered the ideas of Reinhold Niebuhr back in the 1930s." He went on to include himself among a group of "atheists for Niebuhr," who have "copiously availed themselves of Niebuhr's conclusions without pretending to share his basic and, to him, indispensable premise."[73]

And C. Vann Woodward has drawn from Niebuhr in his book, *The Burden of Southern History.* Niebuhr's influence there is especially clear in Woodward's closing essay, "The Irony of Southern History."[74]

Beyond this, Niebuhr's impact on counter-Progressives is hard to catch. That's either because it's just not there, or, more likely, because Niebuhr is one of those shaping thinkers whose influence is so widespread that it's sometimes redundant to acknowledge it. Such thinkers help form their age because the situation of the age is so ripe for them. As Arthur Mann has written, "Niebuhr has been a teacher of his times because he is a barometer of them."[75] To trace cause-effect connections in such cases is well-nigh impossible.

How much, for example, did Niebuhr's thinking affect the "end to innocence" strain in counter-Progressive thinking—a strain Robert Skotheim has detected in works of Henry May, Leslie Fiedler, Louis Hartz, William Leuchtenberg, R. W. B. Lewis, David Noble, Rogert Osgood, Schlesinger, and Cushing Strout?[76] How much did Niebuhr influence the "ironic" explanations of, say, Marvin Meyers in *The Jacksonian Persuasion,* or Perry Miller in *The New England Mind: From Colony to Province?* Elsewhere, I've claimed that this latter volume of Miller embodies a Niebuhrian kind of irony; but again, as with Trilling, the resemblance seems to be parallel not cause-effect.[77]

But parallel or cause-effect, they *are* resemblances. And, as we'll see through this chapter and into the next, those resemblances are often striking. That, finally, is why Lionel Trilling and Reinhold Niebuhr serve as our pivotal moments here. And it's why, as I've said, these two more than any others seem to signal this paradigm revolution in American historical-cultural writing.

IX

When Lionel Trilling wanted to argue with, or counter, the Progressive picture of experience, he felt he could best get to it by having go at Vernon Louis Parrington. Trilling, in effect, believed that Parrington was a kind of "modal" Progressive; and taking him apart was a shorthand way to challenge the whole progressivist sense of reality in America.

In chapters 4 and 7, we also suggested that Parrington could be seen as a modal Progressive. No one of course is fully typical or representative of anything, so taking the part for the whole always involves risk. But whether Parrington is in fact the modal Progressive historian, several counter-Progressives acted as if he were—including, beyond Trilling, Richard Hofstadter, John Higham, David Noble, Merrill Peterson, and Charles Crowe.[78]

If we're to get a detailed sense of just what counter-Progressives felt they must counter—what was their first-life experience which they had to be "re-born" out of—it might pay us to consider Parrington now as a sort of composite Progressive. We'll do this (1) to get a working picture of the Progressive configuration which, through this chapter and the next, counter-Progressives set out to re-pattern and (2) to locate precisely those abnormal experiences in the Progressive picture which come later to be normal with counter-Progressives. For Vernon Louis Parrington not only seems to represent the Progressive explanation in its core form, he also embodies its characteristic strains.[79] Those strains came from encountering experiences which his explanation wasn't designed to handle. Thomas Kuhn calls this kind of experience an *anomaly*—that is, "a phenomenon for which his paradigm had not readied the investigator."[80] By isolating such anomalies in this modal Progressive, we can see more clearly how a fault-line moves over from the fringe of a form to its center, from being an exception to the rule to becoming the rule itself. That line should take us from Parrington up through Trilling and Niebuhr and beyond, to R. W. B. Lewis, Perry Miller, and other counter-Progressive thinkers. In this chapter and the next, it will become our focusing device as we move back and forth from the Progressive form to the counter-Progressive.

Lionel Trilling was wrong about Parrington. Or rather he was half right, maybe a little more. His picture does explain the progressivist Parrington who divided the American world into Jeffersonian and Hamiltonian, who criticized Hawthorne and Henry James for departing from "reality" and praised writers like Theodore Dreiser and James Branch Cabell because they reflected reality, who dismissed Jonathan Edwards as an "anachronism," and who called most everyone he liked "a child of Jean-Jacques."

But Trilling's Parrington is not the Parrington who wrote that post–Civil War America is "an excellent example of what human nature will do with undisciplined freedom."[81] Nor is he the Parrington who once said, "A just and liberal government is an excellent idea, but it is one for which few amongst the mass of men greatly care."[82] Or, "Every realist knows that 'the people' is a political fiction."[83] Nor is he the Parrington who once claimed that men are "half-God," but "half-devil" too, and who would therefore scorn those with "a childlike ignorance of *Realpolitik*."[84]

Trilling's picture does not explain the Parrington who regrets, ironically, that "the custodianship of America by the middle class has brought unsuspected consequences in its train."[85] Nor the one who expresses a surprisingly ambiguous sense of experience when commenting on James Russell Lowell: "Life puzzled him, as it puzzles every serious mind."[86]

Finally, Lionel Trilling's critique doesn't begin to approach the Parrington who—incredibly, for a Progressive—once blurted out, "It is a misfortune that America has never subjected the abstract idea of progress to critical examination"![87]

In these words, we see Parrington as variously conservative, pessimistic, skeptical, ironical, intrigued by complexity, and a critic of progress. And none of these fits our usual pattern of Progressive categories. Though the tone of Parrington's words is still Progressive here, their content points toward the counter-Progressive form. What can we make of this?

It seems we have something resembling our picture of Frederick Jackson Turner in the last chapter. That is, there's a *(I)-form* and a *(II)-form* with Parrington. The (I)-form is the core paradigm, his basic Progressive explanation of experience. This is the Parrington who Trilling went after in his "Reality in America" essay, and it's the Parrington who usually comes to mind when we think of him. The (II)-form, however, is that explanation under strain, running along fault-lines in Parrington's mind, and pressured by anomalies between his sensed experience and his characteristic mode of ordering things. We know much about his (I)-form way of thinking, but not so much about his (II)-form.

So we'll do with Parrington now some of what we did with Turner before —we'll gather together his (I)-form cluster of categories, then watch carefully how his (II)-form behaves under the stress of anomaly. Since our interest in Parrington here is only instrumental—we're using him *just* for perspective on counter-Progressives—we needn't analyze his mind-work quite as thoroughly as we did Turner's. We're not concerned with all his behaviors, only with those which help us trace lines forward to Trilling, and Niebuhr, and Lewis, and Miller, and beyond.

X

The general Progressive picture we drew back in chapter 4 owes much to Parrington, for, as we've said, he put together the broad sweep of the paradigm. So we've already seen something of him, especially in his (I)-form.

To chart Parrington (I) further, all we need do is open the pages of his first volume, on the 1620–1800 period in American thought. Most all the pattern is there, solid and working well. This pattern also retains through much of volume 2 (1800–60), with only a few cracks here and there. By his third volume (1860–1920), though, those cracks are beginning to gape wide, so wide that it's hard to detect any consistent mode of explanation in it at all (this apart from the fact that the book was unfinished at his death).

We can best manage our analysis of these (I)- and (II)-forms by breaking down Parrington's thinking into its various "planes" of explanation, and looking at polar opposite categories lying along each plane. We'll explore four such planes here—reality/unreality, liberalism/conservatism, change/permanence, order/disorder.

Turning first to his *reality/unreality* plane (which Trilling, recall, saw at the heart of it all), we see a picture that confirms Trilling in its essentials. As Parrington says in the introduction to his second volume, he strives "to penetrate critically to the intellectual core of a period, to weigh this romance in realistic scales, to take off the outer wrappings and lay bare the inner truth." And, he warns, such an endeavor "is no May-day undertaking."[88]

In his first volume—*The Colonial Mind: 1620–1800*—reality/unreality had been subservient to the liberalism/conservatism plane which we'll look at in a few moments. But by volume 2—*The Romantic Revolution in America: 1800–1860*—reality/unreality has become the dominant plane of his thinking, more so than liberal/conservative. This, I think, is because Parrington does so much with creative literature here, and in literary study he is trying to effect an anti-formalistic revolution. Which gets to one important part of his perceived "situation," and his strategy for responding to it.

The study of American literature, Parrington believes, had been uprooted from reality—becoming disconnected from where people actually live and feel and think. In his words, it is "narrowly belletristic."[89] He "lays bare the inner truth" of this formalistic situation in his introduction to *The Colonial Mind:*

Our literary historians have labored under too heavy a handicap of the genteel tradition—to borrow Professor Santayana's happy phrase—to enter sympathetically into a world of masculine intellects and material struggles. They have sought dantier fare than polemics, and in consequence mediocre verse has obscured political speculation, and poetasters have shouldered aside vigorous creative thinkers.[90]

That, in short, is the academic formalism which Parrington seeks to break out of. And "reality" functions as his cutting tool. Reality, he assumes, is more fundamental than literature; it is cause, literature is effect. "The main divisions of the study," he says, "have been fixed by forces that are anterior to literary schools and movements, creating the body of ideas from which literary culture eventually springs."[91] Many of Parrington (I)'s characteristic judgments are connected to his sense of this situation, especially that kind of judgment which most irritated Lionel Trilling.

Thus Parrington on Poe: "Apart from his art he had no philosophy and no programs and no causes." Because Poe lacked such politicized commitments, Parrington judges that "The problem of Poe, fascinating as it is, lies quite outside the main current of American thought, and it may be left with the psychologist and the belletrist with whom it belongs."[92] Which psychologist and which belletrist deal not with reality, but with distortions of reality. And these the historian of the "main currents" must either avoid, or correct.

Hawthorne is treated in like manner. Parrington writes of Hawthorne's "temperamental aloofness from objective reality," and is puzzled by his inability to take in the bustling world of activity around him:

For a man gifted with imagination to fail to lift his eyes to the horizon beyond which the hurrying ships were seeking strange markets, and instead to turn them in upon a shadowy world of half real characters; to overlook the motley picturesque in the foreground of the actual, in order to brood over an old adultery and twist it into theological sin, can be explained only on the ground that Hawthorne was concerned with ethical rather than romantic values, that he was interested rather in the problem of evil than in the trappings of romance.[93]

Which places him, like Poe, outside the "main current" of America. "How characteristic of a mind long fed on symbols," Parrington exclaims of Hawthorne, "to turn away from the wealth of reality and prefer a shadow!"[94] Those who look at shadows merely obscure things for Parrington (I), unless, of course, they connect shadows to the real world beyond. Had Hawthorne "grappled with economics as Thoreau did," he might have been able to manage his shadows.[95] But he did not, so Parrington concludes his portrait of him, "He was the extreme and finest expression of the refined alienation from reality that in the end palsied the creative mind of New England. Having consumed his fancies, what remained to feed on?"[96]

Parrington would also write, "The explanation of the curious career of Henry James, seeking a habitation between worlds and finding a spiritual home nowhere, is that he was never a realist."[97] He titles his section on James "Henry James and the Nostalgia of Culture"; and he comments that though James tried, "it was impossible to barricade himself securely against the intrusion of the unpleasant."[98] And so Henry James fled from America to the Old World, to a world of insubstantial "culture," there to preoccupy himself with trivial problems of artistic technique. "He was concerned only with *nuances*," Parrington concludes.[99] And nuances, it is plain, are not "reality" to Vernon Louis Parrington.

We could go on along this reality/unreality plane—noting that Parrington titles his section on the literature of the American Revolution "Literary *Echoes*," that he scorns those who "have done no serious reading in economic theory," and that he says, "It is absurd, of course, to expect an aesthete to concern himself with ideas, or to care greatly about what goes on outside his ivory tower."[100] We could take all these statements and expand on them, but the essential outlines should be clear by now. Picturing himself in a formalistic situation, girded to battle "unreality" with "reality," Parrington (I) is suspicious of anything which wanders far from his own sense of the main line. That, a quarter-century afterward, counter-Progressives would take these wanderings and make them the core culture suggests just how radical was the revolution of the 1940s and 1950s which brought in a new perspective on reality in America.

Liberalism/conservatism is the basic plane we've looked at all along in our consideration of Progressives, so we need give it only a passing glance now. This plane runs throughout Parrington's three volumes, but it's most prominent in volume one, especially in his treatment of the Puritans.

His opening section in that book is titled "Liberalism and Puritanism," and it's plain that for him the one must be opposed to the other. The intellectual history of seventeenth-century New England is dramatized in the "clash between a liberal political philosophy and a reactionary theology."[101] Parrington (I) connects liberalism with altruistic social sentiments; thus, Roger Williams is "perhaps more adequately described as a Puritan intellectual who became a Christian freethinker, more concerned with social commonwealths than with theological dogmas."[102] And conservatism is connected with a crabbed selfishness: "The historian need not wander far in search of the origin of the theocratic principle; it is to be found in the self-interest of the lay and clerical leaders."[103]

As we move on through Parrington (I), we discover that the history of American liberalism embodies a kind of simultaneous past. All liberals in America's past seem to be speaking to each other. Or rather, they are all made to say much the same thing. Here we see those straight lines of experience we've mentioned before:

> The line of liberalism in colonial America runs through Roger Williams, Benjamin Franklin, and Thomas Jefferson. . . . Over and against these protagonists of liberalism must be set the complementary figures of John Cotton, Jonathan Edwards, and Alexander Hamilton, men whose grandiose dreams envisaged different ends for America and who followed different paths.[104]

This long line of Progressive heroes all hold similar pictures of America and her democratic potential. All are "children of Jean-Jacques," all have faith in the basic worth and dignity and goodness of men, and all envision a day when the common man will receive his just rewards in the world. With such futuristic visions in their heads, liberals are frequently misplaced in their own times. But the future always proves them right. Thus: "The gods, it would seem, were pleased to have their jest with Roger Williams by sending him to earth before his time. In manner and speech a seventeenth-century Puritan controversialist, in intellectual interests he was contemporary with successive generations of prophets from his own days to ours."[105] That is one thing "progress" meant to Progressives—being vindicated by history.

If we now merge this liberalism/conservatism plane with reality/unreality, we can begin to detect a pattern in Parrington's (I)-form. He doesn't fully show us what reality *is* in this form, but he does tell us who sees it, and how.

Thomas Paine, for one, sees it: "A thoroughgoing idealist in aim, generous and unsparing in service to humanity, he was a confirmed realist in the handling of facts. He refused to be duped by imposing appearances or great reputations, but spoke out unpleasant truths which gentlemen wished to keep hidden."[106] Increase Mather, however, does *not* see it. Like most conservatives in America, Mather is blinded to true reality: "He closed the windows of his mind against the winds of new doctrine, and bounded the fields of speculative inquiry by orthodox fences. He was of the succession of John Cotton rather than Thomas Hooker, a priestly theocrat, though never a shuffler like Cotton, less troubled by free inquiry, less by the intellectual." "All his life," Parrington concludes, Mather "was inhibited from bold speculation by his personal loyalties and interests."[107]

For Parrington (I), then, the true realist is not opposed to the true idealist along this reality/unreality plane. Rather, both join in common cause against the escapist—he who would distort reality or never see it at all. This type may escape reality because, like Increase Mather, he has narrow loyalties or self-interests. Or, like Poe or Hawthorne or Henry James, he may escape because he lacks the generous liberal sentiments to face out to the world. Either way, the escapist misses not only what the world *is,* but what it might *come to be.*

And the realist-idealist catches *both* is and might be. Parrington's true realist doesn't truckle under to reality, or rest satisfied that what is is what ought to be—like, say, Alexander Hamilton or Daniel Webster. Rather, he behaves like a Tom Paine and seizes reality in line with some progressive purpose. Similarly, the true idealist does not ignore reality. Instead, he bores deeply enough into it so he can perceive its essential possibilities, then he tries to turn reality full in the direction of those possibilities. Which, in a word, means "progress."

"Reality," to Parrington (I), is not so much a fact or a thing or a place as it is a process—the process of breaking through stale and conservative formalisms, and pointing in the direction of a liberal future. Unlike the escapist, the realist-idealist who perceives reality has opened the windows of his mind. He's a realist because that opening has allowed him to see things. He's an idealist because he sees not only what is there, but what could be, what should be, if only men would seize the progressive vision and make it an actuality.

This gets us to our third plane from Parrington (I)—*change/permanence.* Like most everything else in his bi-polar categories, with change/permanence Parrington (I) is for the one side, against the other. In this case, he's for change, against permanence. And he's most at home in situations which are bounded by the two—dualistic situations which set one off against the other. Like that of early eighteenth-century New England, where "Dogma was face to face with rationalism."[108] Or New England a century later, whose culture he sees through the crabbed figure of Fisher Ames: "Of this testy little world that clung to its smallclothes and tie-wig, refusing to adopt the Jacobin innovation in dress and manners and politics, declining to temper its prejudices to the gusty whims of a leveling age, Fisher Ames was the universal counselor and oracle."[109] Or the situation which set up this brittle old Federalism against the rising spirit of a "renaissance" in New England:

But at last the old barriers gave way, and into this narrow illiberal world, that had long fed on the crusts of English rationalism and Edwardean dogmatism— dry as remainder biscuit after voyage—broke the floods that had been gathering in Europe for years, the waters of all the streams of revolution that were running there bank-full. Before this inundation the old provincialisms were swept away, and for the first time in its history, and the last, the mind of New England gave itself over to a great adventure in liberalism.[110]

These are "formalistic" situations. The entire (I)-form cluster holds tightest in places where Parrington can thrust off a generous, liberalizing future against locked-in Establishments "founded on the solid granite of . . . prejudice."[111] Change for Parrington (I) is not merely change, then, nor merely permanence. Rather, in his bi-polar configuration, change is linked with reality and liberalism to come out progress, permanence is linked with unreality and conservatism to come out regress, a backward sliding into the unenlightened past. When those linkages begin breaking apart (as we'll see soon), then the Parrington (I)-form is in trouble.

Our last plane of concern with Parrington (I) is *order/disorder,* and here we begin to feel some slight tremors in the paradigm. Quite apart from any anomalies vis-à-vis the world outside, there are internal, "perspectivistic" contradictions in Parrington's behavior along this plane. It's here, then, where we get some hint of what's to come with Parrington (II) and explanation-strain.

The most basic internal contradiction comes from the impulse to abstraction in Parrington's mind. This is an impulse which pulls him away from that substantial "reality" which also impels him. Parrington never found any device for getting his ideas out of the air and onto the ground, though that's where he *said* they were. He couldn't get them there because his abstracting impulse always got in his way. With this abstracting impulse, Parrington is driven to write sentences like: "But with the spread of the philosophy of intuitionalism, the negative individualism of Unitarianism became positive, broke with the respectable conservatism of commercial congregations, and overflowed in a rich and generous faith."[112]

When Parrington's mind is functioning like this, no experience is seen for itself alone; rather, all experiences must be abstracted into some general -ism or other. At times (as in the above sentence), experience seems nothing more than an intermixture of such -isms; so, despite himself, Parrington unwittingly behaves like a Platonist of sorts. Ideas beget ideas which go on to beget other ideas, without touching much of anything in the world outside. One can read for long stretches in *Main Currents* without stumbling across a concretion of any sort.[113]

Part of this is of course a functional necessity, given the job Parrington set out for himself. *Main Currents in American Thought* is the most gigantic organizing task in the entire history of American intellectual history. For Parrington strove there to bring order from the whole sweep of American ideas. It's been noted that he was the first to undertake such a task. We might note that he was the last too. No one since has ever tried to take in such a wide scene, has tried to cover so much over so long a period of America's intellectual history.

Regardless of Parrington's other preoccupations as a Progressive historian, this task alone obliged him to create organizing types, schemas, isms, categorical levers, devices for compressing and focusing and holding onto the bulky project so it wouldn't get out of hand (or head).[114] But it also made him vulnerable to more focused minds like Trilling's—who would charge that compressing and delegating and administering experience like this can fence in the genuinely liberal imagination, inhibiting its free expression of "variousness, possibility, complexity, and difficulty."[115]

What is most basic with Parrington along order/disorder is what's been implied in all these planes—his *bi-polar* mode of thinking. Parrington (I) goes to the past with two things in his mind at a time; whenever he finds one thing, its opposite is around too (this is more true with Parrington even than it was with Turner in the last chapter). It's here—along order/disorder— where he's most given to compressing experience, and where, in his (II)-form, he comes to be most vexed by ambiguity.

With this tendency to compress experience, Parrington has a penchant for naming things, and for keeping his names short. His names of things also have single meanings, and they don't change. Thus: "John Cotton: Priest," "Roger Williams: Seeker," "Nathaniel Hawthorne: Skeptic," "Andrew Jackson: Agrarian Liberal," "Herman Melville: Pessimist."

By labeling things like this, Parrington is able to compress experiences tightly so they will slide into his bi-polar clusters, which bi-polar clusters constitute the core (indeed almost the whole) of his (I)-form of explanation. A composite Progressive schema from Parrington (I)—a chart of what goes with what in his mind—might look something like this:

Anthropological

Innocent man	*v.*	depraved man
Altruism	*v.*	selfish interests
Broad-minded	*v.*	narrow-minded
Conscience	*v.*	greediness

Political

Progress	*v.*	static society
Individual	*v.*	the state
Liberal political philosophy	*v.*	reactionary theology
Equality	*v.*	hierarchy
Democracy	*v.*	aristorcracy (or oligarchy)
Freedom	*v.*	absolutism
Majority will	*v.*	minority interests
Common people	*v.*	gentlemen

Intellectual

Robust creativity	*v.*	stale formalism
Vigorous thought	*v.*	genteel *belles lettres*
Rationalism	*v.*	dogma
Idealism	*v.*	economic determinism
Romance ⟷	*v.* ⟷	realism
Realism ⟷	*v.* ⟷	idealism
Romantic	*v.*	mundane and petty
Critical	*v.*	romantic
Economics	*v.*	unreality

Historical

The future	*v.*	the past
Lutheranism	*v.*	Calvinism
English Independency	*v.*	Presbyterianism
Freeholds	*v.*	feudalism
The frontier and backcountry	*v.*	coastal cities
Yeomanry	*v.*	Royalist interests
Agrarian majority	*v.*	Constitution-makers
French Jacobins	*v.*	Federalists
Jefferson	*v.*	Hamilton
Homespun and coonskin	*v.*	tie-wig and smallclothes
Agrarianism	*v.*	capitalist manufacturing interests
Unitarianism	*v.*	Calvinist dogmas
French liberalism	*v.*	English rationalism
Transcendentalism	*v.*	Federalism[116]

With such an explanation schema, clustered in such a way, Parrington can bring shape to an enormous mass of materials. And he can trace out particular lines in the American past, separating things off one from another. There's a certain kind of aesthetic purity in being able to order history around this way—saying things like: "In banishing the Antinomians and Separatists and Quakers, the Massachusetts magistrates cast out the spirit of liberalism from the household of the Saints"; or, "Such progress as Massachusetts made towards freedom and tolerance was gained in the teeth of theocratic opposition; New England democracy owes no debt to her godly magistrates"; and, "There was not a grain of liberalism in [Cotton Mather's] make-up."[117]

Occasionally, the categories may cross over—as in the move from Anne Hutchinson's liberalism in the seventeenth century to Thomas Hutchinson's conservatism in the eighteenth. But this can be explained by moving around Parrington's schema to catch up some other linkage of categories (in this case the link between conservatism and material well-being):

> The career of the last royal governor of Massachusetts affords a suggestive study in the relation of material prosperity to political principles. Descended in the fourth generation from the Antinomian enthusiast, Mistress Anne Hutchinson, whom all the authorities of Boston could neither terrify nor silence, but who suffered contumely and exile rather than submit her will to official censors, Thomas Hutchinson reveals in his stiff conservatism the common change that follows upon economic well-being.[118]

The Hutchinsons, then, are exceptions which prove the rule, not exceptions to the rule. And the rule is that in Parrington (I) an idea goes in no more than one direction at a time, and always down straight lines. That should prepare us for the anomalous world of Parrington (II), where experiences move in more than a single direction at once, and not always down straight lines.

XI

Thomas Kuhn has written,

> Discovery commences with the awareness of anomaly, i.e., with the recognition that nature has somehow violated the paradigm-induced expectations that govern normal science. It then continues with a more or less extended exploration of the area of anomaly. And it closes only when the paradigm theory has been adjusted so that the anomalous has become the expected. Assimilating a new sort of fact demands a more than additive adjustment of theory, and until that adjustment is completed—until the scientist has learned to see nature in a different way—the new fact is not quite a scientific fact at all.[119]

This seems to be just what happened in the movement from Progressives under strain to the early counter-Progressives. Something was wrong, the Progressives could recognize that all right. They would even go past recognition to *say* things are wrong. But they'd rarely go beyond the saying to explain *why*.

For to do this they'd have to admit that the new facts of American experience—what Kuhn calls *anomalies*—had outmoded their existing forms for explanation, requiring them to invent new forms. As Kuhn notes, paradigm adepts are not so easily thrown off track. "By themselves," he writes, anomalies "cannot and will not falsify that . . . theory, for its defenders will do what we have already seen scientists do when confronted with anomaly. They will devise numerous articulations and *ad hoc* modifications of their theory in order to eliminate any apparent conflict."[120]

That's a fair description of Parrington (II)'s behavior. *Main Currents in Thought* is riddled with anomalies—with flaws in his (I)-form pattern—and they get more numerous as Parrington approaches his twentieth-century American present. At first, as they emerge early in volume 2 (volume 1 is pretty much anomaly-free), they're nothing more than minor tremors—not sufficiently powerful to disturb the existing form at all, just strong enough to show that *some* experiences for Parrington don't get bound into his core Progressive form. By volume 3, though, anomaly has become almost *the* significant experience. Throughout the whole book, Parrington worries over the question, "*Where did American go wrong?*" It's a good place to watch the mind of Vernon Louis Parrington laboring under stress, and beginning to come apart.

Because Parrington's (I)-form is put together as it is, these anomalies are not *merely* exceptions to the rule. There are, we might say, *rules* for why exceptions are exceptions to the rule. Or if not rules, then at least reasons. By exploring these reasons, we may know better why such experiences move from their anomalous state with Progressive historians over to center form with counter-Progressives.

In the preceding section, we took Parrington (I) and broke his explanation pattern down into four planes—reality/unreality, liberalism/conservatism, change/permanence, and order/disorder. We'll do the same now with Parrington (II), and add to each plane its accompanying anomaly. We'll thus look at four anomalies along these planes—the "reality-anomaly," the "goodness-anomaly," the "progress-anomaly," and the "ambiguity-anomaly."

We've already seen a few internal strains building toward the *reality-anomaly*. In the last section, we noted Parrington's tendency to run experience through a filter of -isms, and suggested that this pulled him away from what he claimed was "reality" in the world. He would condemn a Hawthorne for dealing only with shadows and symbols, then go on to talk about some experience or other through a haze of symbolic abstractions.

Early in *Main Currents,* this is merely an internal contradiction in Parrington (I), a rift between the substance of his thought and the procedure of his thinking. It remained internal as long as the reality of America (or rather *his* reality of America) confirmed his predictions—as long, that is, as his reality revealed the blindness or hypocrisy of some group of power wielders, and pointed to a juster, more liberal future.

Mostly, in volumes 1 and 2, reality did just that for Parrington. It's pretty easy to tell who's speaking for the future and who's not in those two volumes. Hence Parrington was enabled to do what he was evidently most comfortable with—"to take off the outer wrappings and lay bare the inner truth."[121] In baring this underlying truth of experience, Parrington could show how appearances deceive people, how the Establishment claimed things were thus and so, but really they were not. By revealing precisely where the fault lay in the system and what was "real" and what "unreal," Parrington could help liberals seize the day and work to make things better in the future. So his unmasking was instrumental there, a device for improving things. That, in short, was Parrington (I)'s strategy for cutting through formalism; "reality," as we've said, was his cutting tool.

By volume 3, however, reality is no longer going Parrington's way. There's no easily visible formalism to break through and no underlying liberal "main current" which reliably points to a more progressive future. Instead, the lines of experience in America have gotten all crossed and tangled. And for much of that volume, something more than a formalistic breakthrough is needed to right things. The American promise seems to be exiting for him, and reality is failing to confirm his predictions.

Enter Parrington (II). Parrington (I), we saw, pictured himself battling effete intellectuals, "poetasters" of the "genteel tradition." He, in contrast, would "enter sympathetically into a world of masculine intellects and material struggles."[122] But when he gets to volume 3, Parrington betrays doubt about this vigorous life. For vigor in his post–Civil War America is expressed not only by progressive intellects, but by the captains of industry, by the Babbitts, by all those compelled to "make it" in the American land of promise. This, to Parrington (II), is where "progress" is tending in the land, and it gives him pause about the inherent liberality of those "masculine intellects and material struggles."

It gives him pause because it's no longer just the privileged few who are selling out his American dream, here it's become the many. The few he could manage. He'd expected that. His (I)-form had a place for "selfish interests"; he'd clustered them along the same pole with "minority interest," and "altruism" along with "majority will." But this situation is confounding those categories, for here the *majority* are behaving selfishly, and they are selfish merely because they're trying to take advantage of America's opportunities. They are working to make real the American dream, at least that part which applies to *them*. Like good anti-formalists, they *are* abandoning old restraints, and catching on to the underlying energies of the land. Only they aren't being altruistic about it at all. And to a saddened Parrington (II), they offer "an excellent example of what human nature will do with undisciplined freedom."[123]

It's hard for Parrington to label such actions "conservative"; it's harder yet to call on "the people" to throw the rascals out. For here the people *are* the rascals. Parrington (II) doesn't give up his liberal vision in despair, but he certainly does narrow its range. "A just and liberal government is an excellent ideal," he writes in chagrin, "but it is one for which few amongst the mass of men greatly care."[124]

"The people" have now become "the mass" for Parrington (II). He'll not call on them to salvage the republic anymore; they're making too much off it, "getting on," as he calls it.[125] Salvation must come, *if* it is to come, not from the many but from the few. If these few are not out there vigorously working in reality, they're at least free, and "freedom" has evidently replaced "reality" as Parrington's most cherished vision in volume 3. This vision has been pared down from a regeneration of the whole American system—in the name of the people—to merely looking for signs, disconnected signs, of spiritual revolt among a few lonely artists and intellectuals. "It is the men of letters," he writes, "—poets and essayists and novelists and dramatists, the eager young intellectuals of a drab generation—who embody the mind of present-day America. . . . They at least decline to block the path to the Promised Land with retainer-fees." "They at least are free souls," he says, "and in the measure of their abilities, free thinkers."[126]

This is a long way from condemning the "poetasters" of Parrington's volume 1. There, a bustling material reality had rendered men of letters mostly irrelevant. But here they hold America's only hope for transcending that reality. There they were merely "echoes"; here they've become beacon lights, spiritual shafts for Parrington in the material wilderness of contemporary America:

> It is to [the men of letters] therefore that one must turn to discover the intellectual currents of later America—to their aspirations as well as their criticisms. Literature at last has become the authentic voice of this great shapeless America that means so much to western civilization. [To] the intellectuals, the dreamers, the critics, the historians, the men of letters . . . one may turn hopefully for a revelation of American life.[127]

And so Vernon Louis Parrington moves in the direction of the counter-Progressive form, where literature and ideals don't passively "reflect" reality, but actively transcend it too. In this third volume, his sense of "reality" is so tenuous that a retreat into literary "unreality" doesn't seem so bad, given the unpleasant economic realities around him. Parrington (II) is still some remove away from the symbol-myth-image form of the 1950s and 1960s, but to the degree that he begins doubting his economic explanation of experience here, he reveals an anomaly which counter-Progressives will later pick up and make basic to their own explanations. That, in brief, is Parrington's response to the reality-anomaly along the reality/unreality plane of experience.

Anyone who claims people and things are basically good has got a problem: how to explain what is not good. This leads to Parrington's *goodness-anomaly*. Through much of volumes 1 and 2, he got around that problem by a characteristic liberal strategy—labeling some men and some ideas good and some not good. The good are basic and natural, however, the bad are alien and doubtless will wither away in time. At moments when the bad seems to be firmly established in America, some prophet (or prophecy) of light would come along and work to uproot it, uproot it in the name of reason and justice and humanity. Progress would guarantee that no particular evil could dominate things for long. This Progressivist principle explains why Calvinism eventually fell in New England, why liberalism triumphed in the American Revolution, why Jefferson won out over Hamilton, and why Transcendentalism broke through the staid old tie-wig Federalism. It also explains why, for Parrington, so many "children of Jean-Jacques" were loose in the land. Man himself was basically good, American man doubly so; evil one could account for by the self-interested few who schemed to exploit the rest. But they wouldn't last long if only good men worked for liberalism.

Granted, there were a few hitches in this strategy, but they were minor. When he was working in the political world, for example, Parrington would invariably praise "the people," and those who worked for them. But when he was looking at politics from some outside perspective—say, through the eyes of critical Transcendentalists—then he might occasionally drop his guard and let slip some phrase about "the cheap praise of the gullible public."[128] But it was clear—or seemed so—that Parrington felt this "gullible public" could be enlightened in time, and the Transcendental vision of man would eventually merge with the actual condition of Americans.

It seemed clear, anyway, through volumes 1 and 2. But by volume 3, Parrington will speak of "an undisciplined generation rioting in its new freedoms," and of "a huge symphony in praise of human perfectibility that assaulted American ears in the Gilded Age."[129] His tone here shows that he's not wholly taken with the idea of freedom anymore, or the assumption of man's perfectibility (Jean-Jacques is now put on probation). At least these qualities are no longer just assumed in his paradigm, as they had been before.

Parrington's opening section in volume 3 is labeled "Free America"; and it's obvious he's no longer cheering on freedom here. Indeed, sometimes he seems to be mocking it, choosing his label "Free America" with purposeful ambiguity. "Children of Jean-Jacques" are conspicuously absent from this volume, and he holds in little respect here "uninstructed idealists with no understanding of *Realpolitik*."[130] And where he's said hardly a discouraging word about Jacksonian democracy or Transcendentalism in volume 2, in volume 3 he writes of them:

The old Jacksonian leveling had been negative; its freedoms had been individual, its anarchism selfish and unsocial. The great ideal of the fellowship had been lost in the scramble for rights. Even transcendental democracy had narrowed its contacts. The hermit Thoreau in his cabin at Walden Pond was no symbol of a generous democratic future. In the struggle for liberty and equality the conception of fraternity had been denied and the golden trinity of the Enlightenment dismembered.[131]

That's not the full counter-Progressive form yet, but it's not far from it either—from the counter-Progressive picture of Jacksonian democracy drawn by, say, John William Ward in *Andrew Jackson: Symbol for an Age* or Marvin Meyers in *The Jacksonian Persuasion.* By the mid-1950s, though, Ward and Meyers would have available to them several liberal cushions against despair—cushions provided earlier by thinkers like Trilling and Niebuhr. Parrington in the late 1920s didn't. Or at least he had fewer. So when men in his day turn out to be worse than he hoped, he's paradoxically tempted to nostalgia—to turn back and look upon the good old days earlier in the republic. When his liberal virtues fail him, he evidently has no option but to turn in a conservative direction. That's one consequence of either-or thinking; when the either fails, then all you've got is the or. Parrington never becomes a right-out conservative, or at least if he does he'd never admit it. But watch him describe Federalist New England in volume 3, picturing fondly what he'd declaimed against in the preceding volume.

It was an excellent heritage—that old culture. Never richly creative, never endowed with a fleshly paganism, it possessed nevertheless a solidity got from long wrestling with eternities, a pleasantly acrid flavor got from crotchety old books, and a sober morality got from contemplation of the sinfulness of the children of Adam. It was as native to New England as Boston brown bread, and it issued in self-respecting and dignified character.

Where before Parrington had perceived this New England founded on "the solid granite of prejudice," now he uses the same metaphor but alters its meaning: "Underneath all transcendental and other eruptions it had lain unmoved like the granite foundations of the New England fields; and now after those eruptions had subsided it provided the solid footing on which later culture might rear its chaste temples."[132]

That attitude goes well past the counter-Progressive form, toward a Burkean (Edmund, this time) view of human experience. It honors the solid virtues over the creative and dynamic ones, it praises sobriety over innocence, and it respects the dull but sustaining qualities of men over the invigorating ones. This is one tack Parrington (II) takes when his faith in human nature falters. It's not his only tack, as we'll see later. But lacking any sense that a liberal polity might be founded on a pessimistic view of man, Parrington is forced to restrain his liberal faith when his optimism gives way. That's how he responds to his goodness-anomaly along the liberal/conservative plane of experience.

Parrington (I) had believed men were good not merely because of how they actually behaved around him, but by his sense of their potential too— what they *might* do if only the environment were made right for them. When that sense gave way, when his confidence in the future began to wane, he started to question whether men are in fact so good. Goodness and the future had been linked in his (I)-form; in his (II)-form they are simultaneously put under strain. And this leads to his *progress-anomaly*.

That anomaly pinpoints one of the more intriguing paradoxes in the Progressive explanation-form, a paradox we detected in Frederick Jackson Turner too. So long as Parrington is working in the remote past—with the Puritans, say, or Federalist New England—his view of the future is invariably rosy. Confidently, he will play off a vigorous (and generous) idea of progress against one formalism after another, and in time those formalisms all topple. But as this future approaches actuality and he nears his own present (which, according to the straight doctrine of progress, should be the *best* of all times), Parrington becomes progressively more troubled about his world, and not certain of the future any more at all. Earlier liberals— Williams, Franklin, Paine, Jefferson, Jackson, Whitman, and others—all point forward to the twentieth century. But when America really comes to that century, Parrington begins to wonder if maybe we should go back and start all over again.

Or, if not completely start over, then at least radically (or conservatively) reassess those forces which caused America to move so rapidly out of her past. Like, first, the idea of progress: "It is a misfortune that America has never subjected the idea of progress to critical examination."[133] Then that ever-opening frontier which Turner had rhapsodized about: "If in one sense the conquest of the continent is the great American epic, in another sense it is the great American tragedy. The vastness of the unexplored reaches, the inhospitality of the wilderness, the want of human aid and comfort when disaster came, these were terrifying things to gentle souls whom fate had not roughhewn for pioneering."[134]

In Burkean (Edmund again) fashion, Parrington goes on to lament that "the social fabric is being torn rudely across by a changing economics," and he speaks out in favor of "the sober restraints of aristocracy, the old inhibitions of Puritanism, the niggardliness of an exacting economy." Which restraining virtues, he says, are being overwhelmed in post–Civil War America "with the discovery of the limitless opportunities for exploitation."[135] This exploitation is coming not from the privileged and self-interested few, but from the many, and a many now entertaining both liberal and conservative ideas in their heads. Parrington (II) almost shatters his tight (I)-form cluster when he writes, "The doctrine of preemption and exploitation was reaping its harvest. The frontier was having its splurge, and progress was already turning its face in another direction."[136]

Here is ambiguity, evidently conscious ambiguity, where good ideas harbor and produce bad ideas, and bad consequences. No longer do all good things cluster around one pole, all bad ones around the other. Gone also are those unambiguous formalistic situations of his first two volumes, and the old Establishments to bait. In volume 3 there are no tie-wig Federalists or

Puritan priests; instead, it's just a confusing "welter that is present-day America."[137]

Before, Parrington (I) had bailed liberals out of some unlovely presents by projecting lines forward to more progressive futures. Now Parrington (II) lifts himself out of a yet more unlovely—and confusing—present by projecting lines *backward* into the past. Through this device, he hopes to get perspective on his times and gain leverage to criticize them. But such leverage is no longer progressive-liberal, it's become *conservative*. Witness:

How much was lost in the break-up of the excellent culture of the eighteenth century the children of the seventies neither knew nor cared. Generations of growth had gone to its shaping. It had been formed by the needs of men and women conscious of the ties that linked them with the past. It was bound back upon the rich cultural life of medieval times, and in the aristocratic eighteenth century it had come to flower in forms of fine distinction and dignity.

He continues in this same loving tone,

Touch that century on any side—dress, architecture, furniture, manners, letters, and the same note of refinement, of grace, of balanced and harmonious form, is everywhere evident. The culture of the times of the Coffee House Wits was all of a piece, held together by an inner pervasive unity. The formality of the wig and the heroic couplet was symbolic of a generation that loved dignity, and the refinement of the Chippendale sideboard, wrought in slender Honduras mahogany, was the expression of a society that cultivated the graces of life.[138]

"Generations of growth," "the ties that linked them with the past," "the rich cultural life of medieval times," "fine distinction and dignity," "balanced and harmonious form," "an inner pervasive unity," "the graces of life." Odd fare for a militant Progressive. But there it is, not just an isolated phrase or two, but a whole pattern of unrelieved nostalgia.

When Vernon Louis Parrington loses his moorings in the future, he has to return—or retreat—to the past for his roots. A cynic might say that underneath it all he is *essentially* a conservative anyway, always had been. I'm not sure that's true.

A truer—or at least fairer—judgment might go something like this: Parrington's (I)-form had been founded on uncriticized hopes for the future. These hopes were almost totally out front, with no defenses built around them. When his vision of the future begins to look less and less like progress, however—when it veers away from the progressive line of light and reason and justice and becomes simply a welter of change and bigness and exploitation—Parrington has nothing in his belief pattern to fall back on. Everything in this pattern had been aimed in one direction only; when that direction gets blocked, his whole (I)-form is put in jeopardy.

In Alvin Toffler's terms, Parrington (II) is suffering from "future shock." His shock is made worse because his Progressive form here has no built-in "future shock absorbers."[139] Parrington is not so much *essentially* a conservative, then, as he is *situationally* one—in situations where his belief pattern gives him nothing else to fall back on. In such situations, his explanation-form is rendered defenseless against a pessimistic future, and is put under enormous pressure. That's Parrington (II), then, and his dilemma with the progress-anomaly along the change/permanence plane of experience.

Finally, there is the *ambiguity-anomaly,* which runs along the order/disorder plane of Parrington's thinking and which underlies all the other anomaly-planes in his (II)-form. By now, it should be clear that ambiguity is not Vernon Parrington's forte. In his (I)-form, he hadn't had to face ambiguity much; his bi-polar clustering and his tendency to see experience through abstracted -isms held him away from the internal complexities of a particular idea, or from an idea going in more than one direction at a time. In his (II)-form, though, he does face ambiguity, but never with evident ease. Ambiguity always seems to have made Parrington uncomfortable, as it did most Progressive historians.

That's because, as we've said, Progressives were accustomed to handling formalistic situations. In such situations, their "either-or" structure of mind held things together, helping them break through the formalism to the liberalizing reality below.

But an either-or kind of mind is ill structured to cope with ambiguous situations. It's Parrington's response to this kind of situation which caused Lionel Trilling to write of him, "He had after all but a limited sense of what constitutes a difficulty."[140] This limitation became evident when Parrington's (I)-form addressed the thinkers of "contraries" in American intellectual history—*non*-bipolar minds like Edwards and Cooper and Hawthorne and Melville.

Such thinkers confounded Parrington. His one-way labels—"The Anachronism of Jonathan Edwards," "James Fenimore Cooper: Critic," "Nathaniel Hawthorne: Skeptic," "Herman Melville: Pessimist"—caught only a single side of their minds. Hence, these thinkers of contraries slipped between the categories of Parrington (I), his labels couldn't catch hold of them.

He did on occasion recognize this, though, and didn't just wholly compress them into the forms he'd set up for them. But he behaved as if they *should have* fit those labels; when they didn't it was *their* fault, not the label's. Thus he wrote of Jonathan Edwards in volume 1: "There are inconsistencies in his thought as there were in his pastoral life; and we shall understand his position only when we recognize the contrary tendencies which confused him."[141] And of Cooper in volume 2:

> Fenimore Cooper is one of the puzzling figures of his generation. In his substantial character was embodied what may well appear no more than a bundle of contradictions. Romancer and social critic, feudal-minded yet espousing a republican faith, he pretty much baffled his own generation in its testy attempts to understand him, as he has pretty much baffled later times.[142]

Parrington (I) was similarly confounded by contrary *events*—where an idea evidently produced its opposite result. He would recognize the double experience, but give it a single-minded explanation. Like Marvin Meyers some thirty years later, for example, Parrington noted how ironic were the consequences of Jacksonian democracy. But unlike the counter-Progressive Meyers, Parrington excused his liberal Andrew Jackson from any responsibility for those conservative consequences:

Perhaps the rarest bit of irony in American history is the later custodianship of democracy by the middle class, who while perfecting their tariffs and subsidies, legislating from the bench, exploiting the state and outlawing all political theories but their own, denounce all class consciousness as unpatriotic and all agrarian or proletarian programs as undemocratic.

"But," Parrington insisted, "it was no fault of Andrew Jackson if the final outcome of the great movement of Jacksonian democracy was so untoward; it was rather the fault of the times that were not ripe for democracy."[143]

Thus Parrington (I) on contraries. He could not, with the measuring instruments at his command, get his mind around materials which were tangled and multi-directional. They remained anomalous for him, experiences that wouldn't fit into his core paradigm. A generation after Parrington, counter-Progressives would take such anomalies and incorporate them into their new form. They would do that basically by picturing experience, or at least American experience, not as this-*versus*-that, but as *both*-this-and-that—a balanced tension of polar opposites. And they would thrive on just those thinkers who had baffled Parrington—like Edwards and Cooper and Hawthorne and Melville. Contrary to Parrington, they wouldn't place them outside the "main current" of American thought at all.[144]

That's the ambiguity-anomaly, as handled through Parrington's (I)-form. This anomaly didn't seem to worry Parrington much in his first two volumes, since the few ambiguities there were evidently incidental exceptions to the rule—to a rule he held so firmly that he didn't bother even to question it. Indeed, he was so confident of this rule that occasionally he would relax his tight form and say an encouraging word of some non-liberal thinker like John Adams or John C. Calhoun or even Alexander Hamilton. But he never let his core (I)-form explanation be touched by these exceptions. So even though he might pause to applaud Hamilton's effort to found government on people's self-interest and note that "this was not a pose of . . . cynicism, but a sober judgment confirmed by observation and experience," that slight pause never caused Parrington to temper anything he wrote of Tom Paine or Thomas Jefferson or any other anti-Hamilton liberal in volumes 1 and 2.[145] Like Frederick Jackson Turner, Parrington (I) could *see* some things which ranged outside his core form, but he would not allow them to disturb the form itself.

Such anomalies *do* disturb him in volume 3, though, for here he no longer feels so removed from the strain of ambiguity in American life. Those ambiguities are beginning to push in on Parrington in this volume—pressuring his core form and threatening to upset his sense of what is normal and what's alien in the experience of Americans.

As we've already seen, Parrington (like other Progressive historians) begins to lose his intellectual gyroscope when his studies get closer to the present. American experience is getting away from him; no longer do his bi-polar clusters seem to manage things. Though sometimes he'll respond to these ambiguities by simply moving from one side of a polarity over to its opposite—as in his liberal-to-conservative reversal on Federalist New England—he doesn't appear entirely satisfied with that tack either. Thus, right after those nostalgic passages on eighteenth-century New England we cited earlier, Parrington scorns Thomas Bailey Aldrich for holding similar values in post-Civil War America. Where just a few pages before he'd been writing fondly of "good taste," "traditional standards," "balanced harmonious form," "the graces of life," now he complains that Aldrich "sturdily combated all literary leveling," and "of social economics he knew nothing."[146] And Parrington has evidently snapped wholly back into his (I)-form again when he baits Aldrich thus:

In such literary judgments the arch-conservative is engaged in defending the genteel tradition against every assault, convinced that the portals of creative literature open into the past and that in following in the footsteps of the dead we shall come upon a living world. The sterility of his own refined craftsmanship is perhaps sufficient commentary upon his faith.[147]

In short, Vernon Louis Parrington in volume 3 seems bewildered. He wanders back and forth across his anomaly planes, now stopping at this position, now at that, but never resting comfortably anywhere for long. There are deep fissures in his (I)-form, and powerful tremors give warning of a major earthquake soon to come.

He is wounded, grievously. But he is not destroyed. Parrington (I) and Parrington (II) are not Parrington "first-born" and Parrington "twice-born"; they're Parrington first-born, and Parrington first-born under stress. Unlike counter-Progressives, he never gives off the old form, dies symbolically, then comes to be re-born into a new form.[148]

For despite the stress, despite the doubts, despite his sustained moments of nostalgia, Parrington still hangs on to his faith in man and hope for the future. Which means that these pressuring experiences *remain anomalies* for him, still exceptions to his basic form. Sometimes he must fight desperately to keep them anomalies, but he does.

XII

This is nowhere better revealed than in two essays which come near and at the end of volume 3, and which we'll use as our closing texts in this discussion of Parrington. They both adopt a kind of "jeremiad" strategy—first berating the sins of Americans, and seeming to give up all hope by tabulating one evil after another in the land, but then, at almost the moment of total despair, suddenly reversing course and moving (or fleeing) up the ladder of faith.[149]

The first of these essays is on Sinclair Lewis. Lewis evidently had some considerable impact on the later Parrington. As we've seen, Parrington (II) was becoming much disaffected from middle-class America, and Lewis seems to have contributed to that disaffection. So what Parrington writes of Lewis may reflect back on himself.

In the passage I've chosen for focus, he begins on a low note: "In the great American mass . . . human nature is certainly foolish and unlovely enough. It is too often blown up with flatulence, corroded with lust, on familiar terms with chicanery and lying; it openly delights in hocus-pocus and discovers its miracle-workers in its Comstocks and Aimee Semple Mc-Phersons." This is what's come of the American dream of Roger Williams and Thomas Jefferson, in an age when speed seems to have replaced progress for Parrington, and greed replaced social justice.

"But," he continues, "for all its pitiful flabbiness human nature is not wholly bad, nor is man so helpless a creature of circumstance as the cynics would have us believe. . . . There are Martin Arrowsmiths as well as Elmer Gantrys, and human nature, if it will, can pull itself out of the trap."[150]

As he proceeds in this essay, Parrington draws himself up into his full Progressive (I)-form, seeming to regain faith as he writes. "Bad social machinery," he declaims, "makes bad men. Put the banker in the scullery instead of the drawing-room; exalt the test-tube and deflate the cash register; rid society of the dictatorship of the middle class; and the artist and the scientist will erect in America a civilization that may become what civilization was in earlier days, a thing to be respected." Finally, with a hint of that old fighting spirit which had energized his first two volumes, Parrington concludes, "For all his modernity and disillusion learned from Pullman-car philosophers, Sinclair Lewis is still an echo of Jean-Jacques and the golden hopes of the enlightenment—thin and far off, no doubt, but still an authentic echo."[151]

All of America's blemishes are freely admitted, then, but they don't cause Parrington to abandon hope. So long as even a faint glimmer of light can show itself, he'll be armed for the good progressivist battle.

The second essay for our focus closes out volume 3. It's entitled "A Chapter in American Liberalism," and Parrington addresses it to the generation of intellectuals just coming of age.

The strategy of that address is intriguing; indeed, it's perhaps the most revealing instance we have of Parrington (II) in a controlled, reflective mood responding to pressures on his form. Had he held that form in full confidence, and felt a similar progressive confidence in the young, he might simply have exhorted them to keep the faith intact, listing all its glories and accomplishments, and outlining for them what is left to be done for America. The situation might, in short, have been a kind of passing on of the Progressive covenant.

But Parrington doesn't take that strategy—at least, not straight on. Instead, he goes at it in a convoluted way. He doesn't begin with it, but rather starts off on a defensive note. The younger generation worries him. And his own faith worries him a little too. So he's doubly anxious, about his generation and theirs. Thus his opening words sound like some contemporary old liberal trying to make his case before a group of skeptical young radicals. He pleads his own cause, but simultaneously scores them for their youthful brashness:

Liberals whose hair is growing thin and the lines of whose figures are no longer what they were, are likely to find themselves in the unhappy predicament of being treated as mourners at their own funerals. . . . It is hard to be dispossessed by one's own heirs, and especially hard when those heirs, in the cheerful ignorance of youth, forget to acknowledge any obligations to a hard-working generation that laid by a very substantial body of intellectual wealth, the income from which the heirs are spending without even a "Thank you."[152]

Ungrateful they are. But also bright and sophisticated, more so than he, he admits. And they're also more dedicated "revolters against formalism." "They have far outrun their elders," Parrington grants, "in the free handling of ancient tribal totems."[153] If Establishment-baiting is all that's required of liberals, then this generation of rebels are superbly qualified. They've inherited that strategy from their liberal-progressive fathers, and have set it on to new heights.

But revolting against formalism is not enough, says Parrington as he begins to change pitch in his essay; rebellion must have some larger purpose in mind. Here he sets down hard on the young. For he sees them aimlessly attacking things, without knowing why: "Gaily engaged in smashing *bourgeois* ideals, the young intellectuals are too busy to realize that it was the older generation that provided them with a hammer and pointed out the idols to be smashed." But that, he laments, "is the way of youth."[154]

Nonetheless he, as an elder, won't resign himself to their unknowing ways. Instead, he sets out to instruct these wayward youth, those for whom "there is no past . . . beyond yesterday."[155] He'll try and put them back on the proper progressive course into the future by lighting for them the tradition they've come out of. As he begins to chart this tradition—the tradition of his own generation—Parrington abandons that defensive tone which opened the essay. He's proud of what he looks back upon, and his whole (I)-form begins to emerge in full splendor.

His generation, he says, "went to school to excellent teachers"—they were instructed by Darwin, Spencer, Mill, Marx, Haeckel, Taine, William James (but *not* brother Henry), and Henry George.[156] This school was "richer in intellectual content . . . than any the younger liberals have frequented," and it was "dedicated to the ideals of the Enlightenment and bent on carrying through the unfulfilled program of democracy."[157]

Parrington seeks to recapture the spirit of this school in phrases like: "the flood of light," "a reexamination of the American past in order to forecast an ampler democratic future," "the great movement of liberalism," "a democratic renaissance," "to put away all profitless romanticisms and turn realist," "ceaseless conflict between the man and the dollar."[158]

It's all onward and upward, a progressive revelation of faults in the American reality and of bright hopes for reforming them. Then Parrington arrives at World War I. Comes the upheaval. And the shattering of this Progressive faith—giving birth to a new generation of rebellious cynics which threaten to turn his own generation out to pasture. Listen:

Then the war intervened and the green fields shriveled in an afternoon. With the cynicism that came with post-war days, the democratic liberalism of 1917 was thrown away like an empty whiskey-flask. Clever young men began to make merry over democracy. It was preposterous, they said, to concern oneself about social justice; nobody wants social justice. The first want of every man, as John Adams remarked a hundred years ago, is his dinner, and the second his girl.

"If the mass—the raw materials of democracy—," he continues, "never rises much above sex appeals and belly needs, surely it is poor stuff to try to work up an excellent civilization, and the dreams of the social idealist who forecasts a glorious democratic future are about as substantial as moonshine." "It's a discouraging essay," he laments.[159]

But those are not Parrington's last words in this essay. Not quite. He's got three sentences left. Just as, near the moment of total hopelessness, he had rescued the liberal faith earlier through Sinclair Lewis, so also here. The faith is wounded, no doubt of that. Never again can it be regained whole, no doubt of that either. But it's all we progressives have got, Parrington implies. So like Frederick Jackson Turner before him (though somewhat less confidently), Parrington rejects an attitude of total despair, and tries to reinvigorate the old form with these final words:

Yet it is perhaps conceivable that our current philosophy—the brilliant coruscations of our younger intelligentsia—may indeed not prove to be the last word in social philosophy. Perhaps—is this *lése-majesté*—when our youngest liberals have themselves come to the armchair age they will be smiled at in turn by sons who are still cleverer and who will find their wisdom as foolish as the wisdom of 1917 seems to them today. But that lies on the knees of the gods.[160]

XIII

"On the knees of the gods." This is not quite Turner's "fleeing up the ladder of the national covenant," but there are resemblances. Parrington might momentarily fall away from form and write of "the children of those who are now half-devil," and of "a childlike ignorance of *Realpolitik*,"[161] but he would not go further than that. And when the world really began to look bleak, then his "bad social machinery makes bad men" or "the knees of the gods" might be brought along to push things back into line.

Because Progressives were driven to unmask realities, they often saw men at their most brutal and depraved. But they never allowed that man himself is brutal. Only his lesser, and unnatural, self. And particular selves too—maybe sometimes Puritan priests, or Federalists, and certainly Robber Barons. Not man in general, though; man in general is naturally good.

Progressives were kept from radically revising their estimate of man, it seems, from a lurking suspicion that to do so would be a sellout, a failure of nerve, a giving up the battle to their enemy the conservatives. For their cheerful picture of man was not simply good cheer or serene confidence, it was also a strategy for keeping their minds together while in the heat of conflict. If they changed this strategy, they'd be admitting that conservatives had been right all along, and the people are unfit for basic reform. To a Progressive, such an admission was finally unthinkable.

A decade and a half after Parrington died, the theologian Reinhold Niebuhr would pick up on this same goodness/evil plane, and would make it his base for reconsidering the liberal-progressive explanation of experience. What was anomalous to Parrington before the stock market crash and the Depression, before the rise of totalitarianism, before World War II, has become the base situation for Niebuhr by the mid-1940s. *Can liberals any longer believe that man is good by nature? If so, how can they square that with the world around them? If not, how can they salvage the liberal faith?* This is the dilemma for liberals in Niebuhr's time. In *The Children of Light and the Children of Darkness* (1944) he constructs an answer, trying to offer the liberal mind a brake against mounting despair.

He does this through a whole new strategy of approach. Parrington had looked out upon experience largely through political categories. Occasionally, he would broaden these to include economics and sociology. But he tried to keep away from sustained probings into psychology, which he thought deflected one away from "reality." Parrington had been put off by the "perpetual turning-in of the mind upon itself, the long introspective brooding over human motives."[162]

But Reinhold Niebuhr would make such broodings the core of his own alternative explanation-form. He would center his whole thrust on psychological questions which Parrington had asked only obliquely. A half-decade before *The Children,* Niebuhr had opened his Gifford Lectures, "Man has always been his most vexing problem. How shall he think of himself?" And he followed this with, "Every affirmation which he may make about his stature, virtue, or place in the cosmos becomes involved in contradictions when fully analyzed. The analysis reveals some presupposition or implication which seems to deny what the proposiiton intended to affirm."[163] That is how

Niebuhr would launch his massive, 630-page inquiry into "The Nature and Destiny of Man"—his most sustained effort at explaining what he thought were the fundamentals of human experience.

Parrington had been driven to unmask "reality." On occasion, he might be pushed to question human nature along the way, but that was not on his main route. He'd do so only under intense pressure. And if he found contradictions there in his picture of man, they would come as a shock to him, something anomalous and unexpected.

To Niebuhr, however, the heart of man's experience lies not in those external political forms which preoccupied Parrington, but in *the human self*. So when Niebuhr sets out to unmask reality, it's the inner self of man which he seeks to lay bare. Questioning that self comes not as a by-product of some other task, it's his main concern. And he's not shocked to find contradictions in the nature of man, for to him the nature of man *is* contradiction. So it's not accidental that Reinhold Niebuhr should open his most comprehensive work —*The Nature and Destiny of Man*—with a question probing into the human self, nor that his first answer to this question should picture that self as problematic.

Niebuhr's intent in this work was twofold: to get strategic leverage on a new kind of world situation by reassessing the human self, and to connect larger political and cultural abstractions back into that self. He felt this inner self had been obscured in the externalist concerns of progressive liberals, and he proposed to re-open psychological questions which they had closed off. Thus his whole first section of that book is titled, "Man as a Problem to Himself."[164]

The Nature and Destiny of Man enters our analysis now because, published in 1941–43 (and based on lectures given in 1939), it prepares ground for his 1944 book, *The Children of Light and the Children of Darkness*. Which later study will be our point of focus here with Niebuhr. *The Nature and Destiny of Man* is thus a kind of "pivotal moment into a pivotal moment," as it were, developing the psychology which Niebuhr then plugs into political democracy in *The Children*. Future studies of the counter-Progressive form in genesis should do more with *The Nature and Destiny,* for it's one of the fullest statements available of basic counter-Progressive assumptions about the dialectical nature of man. For our purposes now, it's enough to say that in this work Niebuhr opened the way to a re-formed explanation of experience in America; and he did it by moving onto the goodness/evil plane, but traveling along it in a direction different from Progressives before him.

XIV

We've explored at some length the Progressives' characteristic sense of the American situation, the situation for which their (I)-form strategies had been devised. It was a situation where the inertial force of alien interest groups tried to block vigorous, forward-looking visions of society. If the latter had "reality" on their side, the former was buttressed by *power*. And power was in a sense complicity to Progressives. It meant victimizing the people, manipulating their weaknesses, gaining strength for a minority of power wielders by taking strength away from the majority.

But when Progressive liberals broke through these old power structures, they would not go on to rule through power themselves. Instead, they would govern by just and humane ideals, and the people would gain in strength through a fresh influx of light, hope, and equality. Power situations were not quite natural to Progressives, however numerous they may have been in their world. Their basic strategies were framed to do away with the complicity of power, substituting the ideal justice of liberal democracy.

Eight years before *The Children of Light and the Children of Darkness,* Reinhold Niebuhr set down his own criticism of this progressivist strategy. What he came up with does not wholly parallel what we've seen in Parrington and the Progressive historians, but it does resemble them at crucial points. And it sets a negative reference point for Niebuhr's own counter-strategy later in *The Children.* Here is Niebuhr's phrasing of "the liberal creed":

a. That injustice is caused by ignorance and will yield to education and greater intelligence.

b. That civilization is becoming gradually more moral and that it is a sin to challenge either the inevitability or the efficacy of gradualness.

c. That the character of individuals rather than social systems and arrangements is the guarantee of justice in society.

d. That appeals to love, justice, good-will and brotherhood are bound to be efficacious in the end. If they have not been so to date we must have more appeals to love, justice, good-will and brotherhood.

e. That goodness makes for happiness and that the increasing knowledge of this fact will overcome human selfishness and greed.

f. That wars are stupid and can therefore only be caused by people who are more stupid than those who recognize the stupidity of war.[165]

In 1936, it had been plain to Niebuhr that this creed would not do. By 1944 and *The Children,* it has become doubly plain. The advent of totalitarianism, and the outbreak of war, have for him outmoded the old liberal-progressive strategy. "The fury of fascist politics," he writes, "represents a particularly vivid refutation of the democratic view of human nature."[166]

It is a drastically altered situation to Niebuhr, and he insists that a wholly different strategy of response is needed if mind is to keep on with its effort to make sense of world. Like the Progressives before him, he pictures a democracy beleaguered, but not by any stale formalism. "The demonic fury of fascist politics" is hardly formalistic; indeed, it's more vigorously anti-formal than any liberal strategy could ever be.[167] It's also more driven to uproot "realities." Fascism is not, to Niebuhr, merely some further extension along the conservative plane—an extreme form of seventeenth-century Puritanism, say, or of New England Federalism. Nor can it be overcome, as they were (for Parrington), by breaking through to a world of light and justice beyond.[168]

For Niebuhr, this fascist threat cannot be met simply by reaffirming the democratic faith against power structures, and calling for more of it. Democracy must be defended, there's no question of that to Niebuhr. But not, not any longer, by a merely qualitative extension. Instead, it requires a radical re-thinking and an entirely new rationale. Thus Niebuhr subtitles his *Children* book "A Vindication of Democracy *and* a Critique of Its Traditional Defense."

The problem is not just to break down the complicity of power anymore; to Niebuhr it's more complex than that. Power is simply there. It is a reality of human experience, inescapably so. You cannot answer power merely by affirming ideals, you must answer it by exercising *counter*-power. To do this effectively, though, you have to comprehend what power is, and see its roots deep in the nature of man. Progressive innocence, Niebuhr feels, had obscured those roots. It had done this because it believed power is unnatural to man, at least to liberal man. So it expended its efforts in declaiming against power, or in using power in fact but pretending it was something else.

To Reinhold Niebuhr, though, power is simply written into the human situation, and thus into the situation of democracy. So also is ambiguity. Men shouldn't merely give in to power—on that Progressives had been right. But they'd been wrong in feeling that power is somehow undemocratic. What's needed is a new picture of power and a new strategy for handling it; and these must take into full account the ambiguities of power in a democracy. Niebuhr expresses his altered sense of the situation:

Democratic theory . . . has not squared with the facts of history. This grave defect in democratic theory was comparatively innocuous in the heyday of the bourgeois period, when the youth and the power of democratic civilization surmounted all errors of judgment and confusions of mind. But in this latter day, when it has become important to save what is valuable in democratic life from the destruction of what is false in bourgeoise civilization, it has also become necessary to distinguish what is false in democratic theory from what is true in democratic life.[169]

Niebuhr feels the old strategy of democracy is not only inadequate— "false," as he calls it here—but it causes men to vacillate between hope and despair about their condition. We've already seen this vacillating behavior in Turner (II) and Parrington (II). At one moment they'll be issuing gloomy reports on the health of the republic, at the next they'll snap back into the old faith, claiming things aren't really so bad after all.

They did this, Niebuhr would claim, because they had too heady a hope for man's potential to transcend himself. When man fails their hopes—as, for

Niebuhr, he invariably will—they had nothing to fall back on save blind faith. However much that faith may have worked in earlier—and simpler—times, it's now become a shaky support for vindicating a democratic polity. "The consistent optimism of our liberal culture has prevented modern democratic societies both from gauging the perils of freedom accurately and from apreciating democracy fully as the only alternative to injustice and oppression," Niebuhr writes. "When this optimism is not qualified to accord with the real and complex facts of human nature and history, there is always a danger that sentimentality will give way to despair and that a too consistent optimism will alternate with a too consistent pessimism."[170] Which, in such precarious times, could be fatal to democracy. For, as he contends, "both moral sentimentality in politics and moral pessimism encourage totalitarian regimes."[171]

What had gotten Progressives into this bind, from Niebuhr's perspective, was their tendency to think in bi-polar opposites. Had *they* set out to write on "the children of light and the children of darkness," assuredly they would have sided *with* light and *against* darkness. In a sense Parrington's *Main Currents* did just that. Throughout America's history it pictured sinister combinations of conservatives, their power dark and subterranean; and it arrayed against them open groupings of liberals, their motives pure and clear, and their strength thoroughly above board. Parrington's dramaturgy in *Main Currents* set up the strength of light versus the power of darkness. Whenever a liberal got in trouble in his day, Parrington could always bail him out by claiming he helped light the path to a clearer future. Progress and light were linked in Parrington's (I)-form, as were conservatism and darkness.

But Niebuhr's *The Children of Light and the Children of Darkness* does not set off light *against* darkness. In one sense, it rejects both light and darkness; in another sense, it's for both. What it really says, though, is that this light-versus-darkness dramaturgy sets up the problem, but it does not give a workable answer. It does not give a workable answer because in such an ambiguous situation, either-or thinking simply confounds the issue. What men must do instead is take the either-or polar extremes and collapse them into some third alternative.

Niebuhr would thus agree with Progressives that the goodness/evil plane gets to the issue; he would not agree that one should work along that plane simply by opting for goodness against evil. "It is an illusion of idealistic children of light," he says, "to imagine that we can destroy evil merely by avowing ideals."[172]

Previously, we saw Parrington trying to do just that (also Turner in the last chapter, with his up-the-ladder behavior). When Parrington called someone "a child of Jean-Jacques," he meant they had seen the light and would use it to overcome darkness. And by adopting this *child* metaphor, he set up the situation perfectly for Niebuhr's counter-strategy to follow in *The Children*. For in using "child" as he did, Parrington meant to say that the innocence of light would get us out of the problem; but by using "children" as *he* does, Niebuhr means to say that the innocence of light *is* our problem.

Like the Peanuts comic strip, Reinhold Niebuhr takes the American idolization-of-children theme and inverts it. Children are not wholly innocent to him, nor is innocence wholly praiseworthy. One must have a certain kind of courage to take self-evident truths and fight to make them real. Progressives had that kind of courage. But one must have a certain kind of perverse wisdom to take self-evident truths and claim they're really falsehoods, or at best half-truths. It's that kind of perversity which drives Niebuhr in *The Children.*

Picture the situation: Here is a culture in mid-war still compelled by certain liberal-progressive ideals, still honoring its Jeffersons and its Paines, still reading Progressive histories, and still believing itself the light of the world (especially while it's doing battle with the dark furies of fascism). But here is Reinhold Niebuhr telling it things like: "Our democratic civilization has been built, not by children of darkness but by foolish children of light." Or: "The children of light have not been as wise as the children of darkness."[173] He associates these builders of American democracy not with the progressivist qualities of "reason" and "justice" and "goodness"—as Parrington had—but with "blindness" and "stupidity" and "illusions."[174]

Clearly, Niebuhr's categories cluster together differently than Parrington's, at least in Parrington's (I)-form. What connects with "light" for Niebuhr is not "reason," but "stupid," or some variant like "foolish" or "illusory" or "naive." Niebuhr has rearranged this pattern by doing something Progressives seldom did. All their planes characteristically ran down straight lines. But Niebuhr's planes frequently cross over each other. What he's done here is cross the light/darkness plane with another plane—*innocence/wisdom.* On this latter plane Niebuhr *does* tend to think in either-or fashion. He's manifestly for wisdom over innocence. Because of that, he can reject the progressive choice of light versus darkness. And he can warn that America's idealistic children of light had better grow up. For their light is not strong enough, he says, nor good enough, to continue illuminating the darkness any more.

XV

By taking these two planes now—light/darkness and innocence/wisdom —and watching just how Niebuhr has crossed them, we might better understand what he means by his core terms "children of light" and "children of darkness." We can also see how he's structured ambiguity into the terms, and note how this ambiguity is quite intended, part of his operating sense of experience.

Niebuhr's title is taken from Luke 16:8: "The children of this world are in their generation wiser than the children of light." He proceeds to build upon this text: "We may well designate the moral cynics, who know no law beyond their will and interest, with a scriptural designation of 'children of this world' or 'children of darkness.' " "The children of darkness are evil," says Niebuhr, "because they know no law beyond the self. They are wise, though evil, because they understand the power of self-interest."[175]

Conversely, "The 'children of light' may . . . be defined as those who seek to bring self-interest under the discipline of a more universal law and in harmony with a more universal good." But "the children of light are virtuous because they have some conception of a higher law than their own will. They are usually foolish because they do not know the power of self-will."[176]

The forces of darkness are mostly represented by fascism in this book. Niebuhr aims a few words directly at them, but most of his ammunition here is used on children of light. If the forces of darkness are more reprehensible than those of light, they don't comprise Niebuhr's American audience for this book, and he doesn't choose to preach to the converted. They might tolerate someone calling them "naive," or even "stupid" or "blind," if he'd at least acknowledge their motives were pure. They might let him get at their heads if he'd still grant the goodness of their hearts and wills. But Niebuhr won't allow his American children of light even that tiny satisfaction:

It must be understood that the children of light are foolish not merely because they underestimate the power of self-interest among the children of darkness. They underestimate this power among themselves. The democratic world came so close to disaster not merely because it never believed that Nazism possessed the demonic fury which it avowed. Civilization refused to recognize the power of class interest in its own communities. It also spoke glibly of an international conscience; but the children of darkness meanwhile skilfully set nation against nation. They were thereby enabled to despoil one nation after another, without every civilized nation coming to the defense of each.

"Moral cynicism," he concludes, "had a provisional advantage over moral sentimentality. Its advantage lay not merely in its own lack of moral scruple but also in its shrewd assessment of the power of self-interest, individual and national, among the children of light, despite their moral protestations."[177]

This, then, is the situation for contemporary America to Niebuhr. The democratic forms are still intact; but the mind which justifies those forms is dangerously mis-informed. Niebuhr's situation parallels what we saw in Lionel Trilling earlier—where the liberal administration functions efficiently, but the liberal imagination has become impoverished. Trilling counters this situation by proposing an alternative picture of reality, also by advocating a dialogue sense for the liberal mind. And Niebuhr adds to that his sense of man as radically evil.

To him, liberals have got themselves in a bind because they don't *know* evil. They don't know evil because they don't know freedom. Or rather, their bi-polar minds have barred them from seeing the inescapable connections between the one and the other. Here again Niebuhr mixes planes of experience. Progressives had set good across from evil in their schema, and freedom across from oppression—thus separating evil from freedom. But Niebuhr connects the two planes. If good comes from freedom, he says, so also does evil.

We've seen Parrington (II) under stress on precisely this point. In his volume 3, Parrington *saw* that the business exploiters and the Babbitts were acting "freely" in post–Civil War America. But he didn't know what to make of it. Freedom was supposed to lead to reason and charity and justice and equality, yet here it was causing exploitation and greed and ignorance. Parrington (II) suffered much anguish on this, and he finally had to record it as an anomaly—a consequence of freedom all right, but in this situation an abnormal consequence.

To Niebuhr, though, such behavior is not abnormal or anomalous at all, for he *expects* that freedom will be abused by men. This abuse is not just a good idea being corrupted, used improperly. The abuse is *attached to* the idea, part of its existential makeup. Abusive freedom is just as normal as creative freedom for men; there's no way of guaranteeing the one without risking the other.

The difference here is not only substantive, it's procedural too, expressed in how the two positions address the problem. When Progressives wrote about men's freedom, they did so characteristically in the prophetic voice. Usually, it came when some tyranny or other was oppressing people, and "freedom" was the Progressives' strategy for challenging that tyranny. Freedom was not something they paused to analyze in such situations, freedom was something they rushed to proclaim. It was assumed, self-evident, as the Declaration of Independence had said. That document, in fact, almost perfectly embodies the Progressives' strategy of freedom. Freedom itself is unproblematic, the only problem is how to get it.

But if the problems of freedom are anomalous to Progressives, freedom itself is problematic to Reinhold Niebuhr. He makes it so by taking Progressive anomalies, and asking *"How come?"* How come, he wants to know, can "an essentially harmless individual" do so much harm in the world? "How is it," he queries, "that an essentially good man could have produced corrupting and tyrannical political organizations or exploiting economic organizations, or fanatical and superstitious religious organizations?"[178]

Niebuhr is familiar with the usual liberal answer to this; and in conveying it he catches almost exactly what Frederick Jackson Turner did in his flights up the ladder of the American national covenant. "Whenever the democratic idealists were challenged to explain the contrast between the actual behaviour of men and the conception of it," he writes, "they had recourse to the evolutionary hope; and declared . . . that human history is moving toward a form of rationality which will finally achieve a perfect identity of self-interest and the public good."[179]

Reinhold Niebuhr will have none of that. So he—a theologian—challenges this essentially transcendental argument with a secular sort of response. "History," he writes in counter to the liberal idea of progress, "is creative but not redemptive":

There is indeed progress in history in the sense that it presents us with continually larger responsibilities and tasks. But modern history is an almost perfect refutation of modern faith in a redemptive history. History is creative but not redemptive. The conquest of nature, in which the bourgeois mind trusted so much, enriches life but also imperils it. The increase in the intensity and extent of social cohesion extends community, but also aggravates social conflict.

"The bourgeois surrogate for religion," Niebuhr concludes, "is . . . a sorry affair."[180]

We have seen Turner (II) wrestling with the problem of freedom in post-1890 America . . . and losing. But his pre-1890 picture of freedom was quite clear. Freedom in America was produced by the frontier. It came from a transforming instant, that instant where the closed heritage of the Old World encountered New World surroundings which were open and natural. To Turner (I), freedom was a gift of that instant.

For Niebuhr, however, freedom is not just a gift but a *burden* too. And it is basically not the product of special kinds of environments; rather, it's a universal species-quality. By transmuting freedom from a gift, or some regenerative vision, into a lifelong existential burden, Niebuhr can take it out of the realm of Progressive prophecy, and *analyze* it. And in the analysis he can assert the necessary connection between human freedom and human evil.

By such an assertion, Niebuhr tries to make of evil, or sin, a *radical* not a conservative idea. Sin comes not because man is degenerate and therefore incapable of governing or improving himself, as conservatives had claimed. Sin comes because man is free, radically free, so free that he can choose either good and evil, or both. He is not just free enough to be good. He is free, period. Here Niebuhr—calling man a sinner—allows people more freedom than his liberal opponents, who would prefer that men be limited to just good things.

The good is always fragmentary to Reinhold Niebuhr, *some* good, never *the* good. When he says this, he aims it not only at conservative Establishments (which Progressives had done), but at liberals too. Notice how he challenges, implicitly, one of the favorite and most enduring documents of liberal-progressives—the Declaration of Independence:

Even if a particular age should arrive at a "disinterested" vision of justice, in which individual interests and passions were completely transcended, it could not achieve a height of disinterestedness from which it could judge new emergents in history. It would use its apparatus of "self-evident truths" and "inalienable rights" as instruments of self-defence against the threat of the new vitality.[181]

There is a note of cynicism running through Niebuhr here, of seeming despair or resignation at any effort by humans to improve their lot. He takes the pose of a skeptical irritant to reformers, countering their liberal visions with a "Yes . . . but" kind of response. Seen through the Progressive bi-polar typology, he looks like a conservative. That is, he's a critic of liberal reform, and critics of liberal reform are presumed to be conservatives.

But seen through his own typology, Niebuhr intends to be a radical of sorts. He asserts man's limited nature not as a strategy to keep men from doing anything, but as a prod to keep them dissatisfied with *any* kind of human particularity, conservative *or* liberal. He's almost as suspicious of virtue as he is indignant at vice.

"It is man's nature to transcend nature," Niebuhr writes, "and to elaborate his own historical existence in indeterminate degree."[182] This is odd fare from someone who also calls man a sinner. But to Niebuhr it all fits together.

For him, man's limited nature is an empirical fact, even apart from Christian doctrine. It is as much a fact as the near-blindness of someone groping in a darkened cave. But this fact of human limitations is not what Niebuhr means by original sin. It's their *response* to those limitations which makes men sinners.

Original sin to Niebuhr is not so much a taint *written into* human nature; instead, godliness is *written out* of it. Humans commit evil not basically through a presence but through an absence. They are pulled into sin, not pushed.

They are pulled because, not being gods, they nonetheless pretend that they are. They take their own partial perspectives on experience, and try to universalize and "objectify" them, freezing life's vitalities in the process. They'll propose some universal brotherhood of men, but invariably it will exclude people from another class, or race, or nation, or sex, or world view. They'll reason their way out of some vexing cultural dilemma, but fail to understand that reason alone cannot cure problems which unreason has helped create. They'll set out to explain the history of man, but always from the location of their own special time.

It is not just the self-interested few who do this—as Progressives had claimed. For Niebuhr everyone does it. If the children of light are normally less greedy about their own particularities than, say, the children of darkness, they're also more liable to be blinded to the form of self-interest they do have. And in some situations their blind innocence can be more dangerous than the children of darkness' outright greed. Where Parrington (I) had set off liberalism against self-interest, Niebuhr sees a healthy and an unhealthy self-interest in all people, whatever their political creed. Though the unhealthy self-interest cannot be separated from the healthy, it's clear that the unhealthiest self-interest of all is the human effort to deny self-interest. *That,* for Reinhold Niebuhr, is original sin.

Look back now at the statement from Niebuhr we just quoted: "It is man's nature to transcend nature and to elaborate his own historical existence in indeterminate degree." If we read this through the Progressive persona, it would look like a version of the idea of progress, envisioning man's progressively more ennobling future. It also looks like a liberal's strategy for breaking through the conservative forces of restrain and inertia.

But Niebuhr does not write this in the prophetic voice; he means it rather as an analytic comment. "Transcend nature," "elaborate his own historical existence," "indeterminate degree" are not meant as rallying cries for freedom. Rather, for Niebuhr they're sober (and sometimes sad) observations on man's perennial restlessness. Those transcending powers don't always impel men forward to reason and justice and charity; they drive them every which way, sometimes forward, sometimes backward, sometimes sideways or in circles, but rarely for long down straight, progressive lines.

It's precisely this power to transcend things which gets people into trouble. It's not only the source of men's freedom and nobility, it's the root of their oppressions and brutalities too. Man is brutal not because he is part animal to Niebuhr, man is brutal because he is so wholly *man*. His brutalities always have a transcending, spiritualizing quality to them, giving them a special vehemence which animal brutalities lack:

Man, being more than a natural creature, is not interested merely in physical survival but in prestige and social approval. Having the intelligence to anticipate the perils in which he stands in nature and history, he invariably seeks to gain security against these perils by enhancing his power, individually and collectively.

"Possessing a darkly unconscious sense of his insignificance in the total scheme of things," Niebuhr continues, "he seeks to compensate for his insignificance by pretensions of pride." Therefore, he concludes, "The conflicts between men are . . . never simple conflicts between competing survival impulses. They are conflicts in which each man or group seeks to guard its power and prestige against the peril of competing expressions of power and pride."[183]

Progressives didn't ignore evil. As we've seen, they expended much of their energy along this goodness/evil plane. But their strategy for handling evil was to particularize it—locating it in particular men and particular ideas and particular institutions.

Niebuhr believes that kind of strategy is escapist. It deflects men from fully confronting their own radical sin; for it points to others for the fault, and it points to the future for the solution. Sin is in man not in men, claims Niebuhr. Paradoxically, he'll use this disparaging conclusion to build up a theory of tolerance, one man for another; and it will become the working base of his new rationale for democracy.

It underlies Niebuhr's most famous single statement, wherein is embodied his core insight in *The Children:* "Man's capacity for justice makes democracy possible; but man's inclination to injustice makes democracy necessary."[184]

By that statement, Niebuhr reveals the heart of his counter-strategy to

Progressives. By it also, he reveals a strategy for handling "contraries." Progressives would doubtless have agreed with his first clause—"Man's capacity for justice makes democracy possible." The second clause, however, would have confounded them—"but man's inclination to injustice makes democracy necessary."

We saw earlier how, when Parrington began to doubt the justice of man, he began to doubt democracy too. That democracy could ever come directly out of people's injustice was inconceivable to him. But to Niebuhr, democracy responds to *both* sides of human nature. That it's an expression of man's finer qualities seems obvious to him, and he belabors it little. But that it might serve as a brake against man's baser qualities needs emphasis, he believes, and this is where Niebuhr concentrates his energies.

All men, he claims, incline to injustice—"good" men as well as bad, "wise" men as well as foolish, leaders as well as followers, "men of light" as well as men of darkness. Because of this universal inclination to injustice, no man—or group of men—should be trusted with too much power. Most authoritarian political theories are flawed by a double standard on goodness/evil. They're overly pessimistic about the mass of men, but unduly optimistic about the leaders:

In all non-democratic political theories the state or the ruler is invested with uncontrolled power for the sake of achieving order and unity in the community. But the pessimism which prompts and justifies this policy is not consistent; for it is not applied, as it should be, to the ruler. If men are inclined to deal unjustly with their fellows, the possession of power aggravates this inclination. That is why irresponsible and uncontrolled power is the greatest source of injustice.[185]

Progressives had detected *seeds* of democracy in the past and in the present; but mostly they projected democracy some distance into the future. Democracy was an ideal possibility for them, a part of their future Good Society. In short, Progressives threw all their weight on the side of Niebuhr's first clause—"Man's capacity for justice makes democracy possible."

But, as we've seen, they were left defenseless when real experiences in America seemed to veer away from their hopes. They became confused; sometimes they just ignored the ambiguities of their experience, sometimes they grew to despair, but rarely did they develop any strategy which might get them through their confusion. We've seen their plight in Turner (II) and Parrington (II). Niebuhr addresses such a plight when he writes,

A too consistent optimism in regard to man's ability and inclination to grant justice to his fellows obscures the perils of chaos which perennially confront every society, including a free society. In one sense a democratic society is particularly exposed to the dangers of confusion. If these perils are not appreciated they may overtake a free society and invite the alternative evil of tyranny.[186]

There's no evidence that Progressive histories ever looked for tyranny as a way out of their confusion. That's just Niebuhr's own added warning, facing fascism as he is in 1944. But beyond that, he's located precisely the Progressives' vulnerable point along this goodness/evil plane, and he's described the situation when their (I)-form begins to disintegrate.

Progressives had got themselves into such a bind, according to Niebuhr, because they'd staked so much on the future. They'd risked everything on democracy as a human *possibility,* a progressive hope for man. But they failed to see its function also as a present *necessity,* a counter to the very ambiguities which drove them to despair of man.

To Niebuhr, democracy is not only or even primarily a way of reaching for the good. It's more fundamentally a means of decentralizing or fragmenting the bad. It's not just an expression of man's ideal hopes, it's also a way of handling his very real fears and suspicions. It's not only a way of doing good things, it's a way too of challenging those who would gain the power to do any things, good or bad. It is, in addition to *straight* lines toward justice and reason and light, *counter*-lines too—counter-justice, counter-reason, counter-wisdom, counter-power. It is trusting and not trusting, believing and disbelieving, working for a goal and being skeptical of that goal. But for Reinhold Niebuhr it is, most of all, not resting satisfied with any human particularity, never claiming *a* way is *the* way, and always trying to avoid self-righteous illusions. "Democracy," he says, "is a way of finding proximate solutions to insoluble problems."[187]

Niebuhr tries to prepare men for those (to him) inevitable moments when some ultimate solution turns out to be just proximate, when hopes are raised only to be shattered by their consequences. In earlier days of the American republic, an opening future was always there as a safety valve from present discontents. So when hopes were on occasion dashed, men could still say, well, tomorrow. . . .

But in latter days, that future has seemed less a distant hope and more a looming reality, and thus it's lost much of its appeal as a safety valve. This is not only Niebuhr's counter-Progressive perspective, it was the Progressives' perspective too (or part of it). We've seen both Turner (II) and Parrington (II) growing dismayed about the future. As they approached their own times in their histories, they were not so inclined to chart a straight line of progress running from the past through the present on into the future. In short, they were slowly losing grip on their sense of America as an innocent, wholly new kind of experience in the world—where the age-old burdens of power, complicity, evil, ignorance, and coercive authority could be overcome.

They were giving up their picture of America as innocent, a *New* World. But they had nothing to replace it. Lacking any alternative picture, and tying their sense of innocence so tightly to the democratic form, Progressives allowed their hopes for democracy to wane along with their waning sense of innocence.

This is where Reinhold Niebuhr enters the American intellectual scene. His initial strategy is to try and break apart this progressive-liberal connection between democracy and innocence. Picturing America not in a situation of *innocence* but in one of *power,* he insists that mind can handle this situation only by giving up its straight-line, bi-polar schemas of experience, and developing a manageable sense of ambiguity. In Niebuhr's picture, America is in a transition stage where its old innocent mind has got itself, willy-nilly, hooked up with new kinds of power realities in the world. It can cope with these realities only by tempering its past vision of "light" with a strong new dose of "darkness." "The preservation of a democratic civilization," Niebuhr warns, "requires the wisdom of the serpent and the harmlessness of the dove":

The children of light must be armed with the wisdom of the children of darkness but remain free from their malice. They must know the power of self-interest in human society without giving it moral justification. They must have this wisdom in order that they may beguile, deflect, harness and restrain self-interest, individual and collective, for the sake of the community.[188]

XVI

What is peculiar and distinctive about any form of explanation is not usually its individual tenets, but the *configuration* of those tenets. To understand that configuration, we must chart what connects with what in a mind-form, *and* . . . with what degree of emphasis. One can find passages in Parrington which sound just like Niebuhr, or Trilling, or Henry Adams, or Edmund Burke. And one can use those passages to make a case that Parrington wasn't essentially Progressive at all. But when we break his thinking down into its constituent planes, then cluster those planes together into patterns, these isolated passages can take on a different coloration. They're not departures from the Progressive form so much as efforts by that form to handle anomaly.

Through this dual process of *analysis*—taking ideas apart—and *synthesis* —clustering them back together again—we can make some sense of these apparent exceptions to the norm. We may begin to see *why* they're exceptions, by tying them down to the existential particulars of time and place— or, in our terms, to their distinctive "situation," and their "strategy" for coping with it.

With such a procedure, we can see that when Parrington most resembles later counter-Progressives, he's not simply making random variations from his normal form. He's trying to cope with the unexpected. In Thomas Kuhn's terms, he's addressing anomalies—experiences for which his normal form had not prepared him.

For Progressives, the most basic of these anomalies was *ambiguity.* They could see ambiguities, but they had no working model of them, no strategy for managing them in their minds. In short, ambiguity did not fit into their pattern of what connects what with in the world. Their main strategy had been devised to handle unambiguous formalistic situations; for them, this was the characteristic American experience. When formalistic situations became less frequent in their experience and ambiguous situations more frequent—that is, when the uncharacteristic in America tended to become characteristic—Progressives were left burdened with an unworkable strategy.

So when we want to locate vulnerable points in the Progressive form, we should look for ambiguous situations, where experiences aren't moving along straight lines, and note how Progressives try and cope with them. In our analyses of Turner and Parrington, we've seen them stumbling over such situations, for they just couldn't get through them by the normal procedure of paradigm-induced "puzzle solving."

When Niebuhr and Trilling take up the same kind of situation some years afterward, they address it not as anomalous, something unexpected in American experience, but as a form of experience so frequent and so characteristically human that it presses hard upon mind for explanation. So what was at fringe form for Turner and Parrington and the Progressives moves to center form for Niebuhr and Trilling and the counter-Progressives. Their form is in a sense "programmed" to handle life's dissonances.

Thomas Kuhn has characterized what seems to be happening here. "When . . . an anomaly comes to seem more than just another puzzle of normal science," he writes, "the transition to crisis and to extraordinary science has begun." By "crisis" and "extraordinary science," Kuhn means something close to what we're calling a "critical threshold situation." He continues,

The anomaly itself now comes to be more generally recognized as such by the profession. More and more attention is devoted to it by more and more of the field's eminent men. If it still continues to resist, as it usually does, many of them may come to view its resolution as *the* subject matter of their discipline. For them the field will no longer look quite the same as it had earlier.[189]

What we have in Turner (II) and Parrington (II) are points of mounting strain in the old form, where the pressure of anomaly has become acute. What we have in Niebuhr and Trilling are pivotal moments in the revolution, where an upheaval comes to shatter the old form and clears the ground for a new one. And what we'll have with R. W. B. Lewis and Perry Miller in the next chapter are moments when the new form comes to settle in, and begins applying its explanations to new kinds of "characteristically American" experiences.

XVII

Counter-Progressives deal with many of the same particulars as Progressives, but through a new gestalt, a new picture of how things cluster together in the world. Because of their different strategy for patterning experiences, they can cope with kinds of stresses which Progressives couldn't handle. In concluding this chapter, it might do now briefly to list just wherein

Trilling and Niebuhr, in their mutual moments, have re-done the Progressive form. This can help us recapitulate where we've been in this chapter and the preceding one; and it may prepare us for our plunge into the full counter-Progressive form in the chapter which follows.

First, all four of our case thinkers—Turner, Parrington, Niebuhr, Trilling —are concerned here with *the situation of democratic liberalism*. That's the base situation they all address, and each tries to construct strategies for handling it.

For the Progressives, the initial strategy is to break through established power structures, and all their (I)-form categories have been clustered to that end. They want to accomplish this efficiently and quickly, so they compress all their tenets into clear, simple form. They also frequently assume the prophetic voice; through that, they can support progressivist causes in the past. Thus Parrington can cite Jefferson's "I have sworn upon the altar of God eternal hostility against every form of tyranny over the mind of man," and take such a declaration at face value.[190]

No counter-Progressive would ever let something like that get by straight. For they believe that the true democratic strategy should not be simply to advance liberal democracy, but to re-think it. So they're not as inclined to the prophetic voice, at least not the same kind of prophecy as Turner or Parrington. Their characteristic voice is critical-analytic rather than prophetic, and when they do prophesy it's not a proclamation of good things to come so much as a warning to reconsider things now. Counter-Progressives are characteristically individuals who, like Niebuhr, were once nourished on Progressive assumptions, but have come to sense life is more complicated than that, and have gone on to use this "moment of truth" as the base point in their thinking.

To counter-Progressives, then, democracy is finally complexity, and an appreciation of same. Democracy is also *process* to them, where to Progressives it is basically *substance*. For Progressives, democracy is freedom and justice and reason and equality; for counter-Progressives, it's critical dialogue and channels where any affirmation can be challenged by some counter-affirmation.

Second, and following from the first point, all four are concerned *to draw a clear picture of what reality is like, and then use that picture to suggest what fellow liberals should do about it.* But they differ sharply in what such a picture looks like, and in their prescription for liberals.

Progressives picture a reality of straight lines, with two opposing sides grouping to control it. If liberals are to avoid being bested in this battle, they must band together against conservatives, and they must go out and win new supporters to their cause. Which cause is to defeat conservatism. Genuinely liberal progress can begin when conservatism is over with. So the historian's task is to make his Progressive platform clear and appealing, and hope he can persuade others of its justice.

Niebuhr and Trilling begin with a different sense of their audience. They assume this audience was long ago converted to the liberal cause. Rather than try and persuade their listeners to strengthen their commitments, or act-ivate them, they warn them to take a second look. They take what they believe are their listeners' main assumptions, and try and counter them.

They don't want to demolish those assumptions. Rather, they just want to get to their audience's liberal commitments, and set them into sharp dialogue. They think liberalism has grown lax without an effective conservative challenge; so they propose such a challenge, but within the liberal persuasion.

They support this procedure by their sense of reality. They think things live by challenge and dialogue, so instead of straight lines of experience they draw crossing lines. Since an idea can go in more than one direction at a time, Niebuhr and Trilling look not only for where it's heading now, but for its *contrary* direction too. They think it the historian's duty, and the culture critic's, always to be on the lookout for the counter side of an experience.

So they're always turning things over and around. Trilling does this because he thinks liberalism has gotten frozen into channels of activism, and is too busy doing things to take full account of "variousness, possibility, complexity, and difficulty."[191] Niebuhr does it for a similar reason. To him, nothing is ever done once and for all. This is what radical freedom means to him—that humans will (and must) perennially unfasten things which seem to be fastened down once and for all. So both Trilling and Niebuhr urge the liberal mind to pause and reflect on itself and its commitments; and they draw a dialectical picture of man (and of reality) which gives direction to that kind of mind.[192]

Third, all address man and experience *along the goodness/evil plane.* Progressives set off good against evil—good man versus evil institutions, altruistic man (the many) versus self-interested men (the few). The duty of the good is to overcome evil.

Niebuhr and Trilling counter that good cannot overcome evil this way, for the two are inseparable. Further, evil is ineradicable in human nature, for it (like good) is an outgrowth of man's radical freedom.

We've already noted how Niebuhr bases his rationale for democracy not only on "man's capacity for justice," but on his "inclination to injustice" too. And Trilling stresses the value of "a judicious belief in the existence of demons."[193]

Unlike Progressives, Niebuhr and Trilling don't look for just good or bad motives in people, but see some demonic impulses in everyone. They're more given to psychological probing than are Progressives, and are less inclined to believe that external rearrangements can cure men of those internal irrationalities.

Fourth, both sides *work from the ongoing situation.* In this sense, they all employ "counter-" kinds of strategies.

Progressives inherit formalistic explanations, and respond with counter-formalistic strategies. Counter-Progressives inherit Progressive explanations, and respond with counter-Progressive strategies.

And both require ongoing assumptions to push off from. Progressives need conservatives to bait, in facing their characteristic formalistic situations; and counter-Progressives need Progressives to bait, in facing their characteristic ambiguous situations. Both frequently resort to the "not . . . but" device of countering the expected.

What they say, and how they say it, depends in large part on who comes before them—on what is inherited in the situation. To try and comprehend either view apart from this, to treat them in isolation from their predecessors, is thus to miss the (negative) reference base which gives drama to much of their thinking. That's why some kind of "situation-strategy" procedure is imperative to understanding just what they're up to.

Finally, all four thinkers *arrange experience into numbered constructs.* The Progressives characteristically work in twos—this versus that. But Niebuhr and Trilling tend to work in threes—this versus that, *plus* an added alternative, this-*and*-that.

If Progressives' constructs are bi-polar, then, counter-Progressives' tend to be *triadic.* This tri-polar mode of clustering will become clearer when we get to R. W. B. Lewis in the next chapter, but it's already implicit in Trilling and Niebuhr.

Trilling takes the polar opposites of liberal and conservative, and adds to them the principle of ambiguity. If he doesn't fully spell out *what* this principle is, he does say *where* we can look for it—in literature and in literary categories.

He pictures a situation for mind where the *political* tradition is controlled by liberal ideas, but where the *literary* tradition is dominated by anti-liberal ideas—the ideas of Yeats, Eliot, Proust, Lawrence, and others. He asks that ideas from the conservative realm—literature—be injected into the liberal realm—politics—and hopes that some new alternative will emerge from the encounter.[194]

Niebuhr's third alternative hasn't been wholly worked out by 1944 and *The Children of Light and the Children of Darkness.* He clearly opposes the progressivist polarity of light versus darkness; and much of his position is implicit in how he negates this dualism. But it's not fully explicit yet. By 1952, though, and *The Irony of American History,* that new alternative has become visible in Niebuhr. It will provide our point of departure in the chapter to come.

NOTES

1. More precisely, it's a paradigm revolution from one end only—the Progressive. From the other end—the counter-Progressive—it's a revolution in explanation-form. As we've suggested before, it seems proper to call the Progressive form a "paradigm," but the counter-Progressive one just an "explanation-form."

2. *The New History* (Free Press, paperback, 1965—first published in 1912 by Macmillan), p. 265.

3. *The Liberal Imagination: Essays on Literature and Society* (Doubleday, Anchor Book, 1957—first published in 1950 by Viking), p. vii.

4. Ibid., p. 291.

5. Ibid., p. 288.

6. Ibid., p. viii.

7. See Burke's *Counter-Statement* (University of Chicago Press, Phoenix Books, 1957—first published in 1931).

8. *Liberal Imagination* (n. 3 above), p. viii.

9. Ibid., p. xii.

10. Richard Hofstadter has remarked of this essay, "In point of its timing and influence, no Parrington criticism was more important than Lionel Trilling's essay, 'Reality in America,' in *The Liberal Imagination* (1950)" (*The Progressive Historians: Turner, Beard, Parrington* [Knopf, 1968], p. 492). A shorter version of this essay was published a decade earlier, in the *Partisan Review* (January-February 1940). This was mainly the Parrington part of the essay, its first half. Trilling added another part later, in 1946 (*The Nation*, April 20), which concentrated on Henry James and Theodore Dreiser. We're using the 1950 combined version here because, being included in *The Liberal Imagination*, it's set in the context of his preface and subsequent essays. It also seems to have had a wider impact on the American intellectual community than did the two shorter versions.

11. *Liberal Imagination*, p. 1.

12. Ibid.

13. Ibid., p. 2.

14. Ibid.

15. Ibid., pp. 2–3.

16. Ibid., p. 6.

17. Ibid., pp. 6–7.

18. Ibid., p. 5.

19. Ibid., p. 6.

20. Ibid., p. 186.

21. Ibid., p. 7.

22. Ibid., p. ix. That statement of 1950, incidentally, prefigures Marvin Meyers' counter-Progressive study of seven years later, *The Jacksonian Persuasion*. It also characterizes Richard Hofstadter's similarly counter-Progressive position in his 1955 book, *The Age of Reform*. And it's part of what Leo Marx is after in his 1964 study, *The Machine in the Garden*.

23. *Liberal Imagination*, p. 7.

24. *The End of Ideology: On the Exhaustion of Political Ideas in the Fifties* (Collier Book, 1961—first published by the Free Press in 1960), p. 300.

25. Ibid.

26. Ibid.

27. Robert Skotheim has worked out with considerable care the impact of totalitarianism on American intellectuals in the 1930s and 1940s, and I am much indebted to him for my analysis here. See his *Totalitarianism and American Social Thought* (Holt, Rinehart and Winston, paperback, 1971), especially chaps 2 and 3, "The Discovery of European Totalitarianism in the 1930s," and "Progressivism in Eclipse: A New Conservatism in the 1940s and 1950s."

28. In Richard Crossman, ed., *The God that Failed* (Bantam, paperback, 1965—first published by Harper and Bros. in 1950), p. 19.

29. In ibid., p. 143.

30. Ibid., p. 146.

31. "The New Failure of Nerve," *Partisan Review*, X (January-February 1943), 2–23. This essay is reprinted, in abridged form, in Chester Eisinger, ed., *The 1940's: Profile of a Nation in Crisis* (Doubleday, Anchor Paperback, 1969), pp. 352–62. The quote is from p. 352. Eisinger has reprinted here several essays in and around this "failure of nerve" controversy—from Hook, Granville Hicks, Morris Cohen, Arthur

Schlesinger, Jr., and Lionel Trilling. See his section on "The Failure of the Left," pp. 335–88.

32. *The Children of Light and the Children of Darkness: A Vindication of Democracy and a Critique of Its Traditional Defense* (Scribner's, paperback, 1960—first published by Scribner's in 1944), p. xiii.

33. *The Vital Center: The Politics of Freedom* (Houghton Mifflin, 1949), p. 145. Schlesinger's irritation at the old politicized simplifications of experience parallels Trilling's. He writes, "This ingenious solution [the circular model] does reformulate the right-left classification in terms which correspond to the complexities of this ghastly century. But the . . . formula does not lend itself to the shorthand of mass communications—to the simplifications of the headline writer, for example, who hardly has time or space to plot his characterizations with a compass along the circumference of a circle" (ibid.). That circle, incidentally, comes in a chapter titled "The Restoration of Radical Nerve." Though Schlesinger doesn't mention Sidney Hook by name in it, his chapter looks like a direct counter to Hook's "failure of nerve" charge.

34. *The Structure of Scientific Revolutions* (University of Chicago Press, paperback, 1970), pp. 180–81.

35. John W. Caughey, "Historians' Choice: Results of a Poll on Recently Published History and Biography," *Mississippi Valley Historical Review* (September 1952), p. 300.

36. "Moments," as we're defining them here, are just more restricted "situations." For an expansion on this point, see chapter 5, sections VI, VIII, and XI.

37. See Chap. 7, section VI and footnote 29 there.

38. See Burke's *The Philosophy of Literary Form* (Random House, Vintage Book, 1957), pp. 3–117; and William Rueckert's *Kenneth Burke and the Drama of Human Relations* (Minnesota, 1963), 128–62.

39. "Charles Beard: Civilization and the Revolt Against Empiricism," *American Quarterly*, XX, no. 1 (Spring 1969), 65–86.

40. See, for example, Phil Snyder, "Carl Becker and the Great War: A Crisis for a Humane Intelligence," *Western Political Quarterly*, 9 (1956), 1–10; Cushing Strout, "Liberals in Crisis," *The Pragmatic Revolt in American History: Carl Becker and Charles Beard* (Cornell University Press, paperback, 1966), pp. 115–62; Burleigh Taylor Wilkins, "Becker and World War One: Involvement and Disillusionment," "Becker during the 1920's and 1930's: The Social Thought of a Tired Liberal," and "Becker and World War Two: The Recovery of Faith," *Carl Becker: A Biographical Study in American Intellectual History* (MIT, paperback, 1967), pp. 125–73, 210–29; David Noble, "Becker: The Covenant Replaced by Civilization," *Historians against History: The Frontier Thesis and the National Covenant in American Historical Writing since 1830* (Minnesota, 1965), pp. 139–56; and Marcell (n. 39 above).

41. *American Renaissance: Art and Expression in the Age of Emerson and Whitman* (Oxford, Galaxy Book, 1968—first published by Oxford in 1941), pp. ix–x. Lionel Trilling cites Matthiessen's critique in his own essay on Parrington. See *The Liberal Imagination* (n. 3 above), p. 12.

42. Robert Skotheim, *American Intellectual Histories and Historians* (Princeton University Press, paperback, 1966), p. 109.

43. *The American Adam* (University of Chicago Press, Phoenix Books, 1958), p. iii.

44. *The Machine in the Garden* (Oxford, 1964), p. 385.

45. *The Age of Jackson* (Little, Brown, 1945), p. vii.

46. Ibid., pp. 521–22.

47. Quoted in Marcus Cunliffe and Robin Winks, eds., *Pastmasters: Some Essays on American Historians* (Harper and Row, 1969), p. 363.

48. Ibid.

49. *Vital Center* (n. 33 above), p. 165.

50. Ibid., p. 170.

51. Schlesinger was to repay some of his debt to Niebuhr by dedicating to him the first of his *Age of Roosevelt* volumes—*The Crisis of the Old Order* (1957). He also wrote a brilliant article on Niebuhr's influence—"Reinhold Niebuhr's Role in American Political Life and Thought," in Charles W. Kegley and Robert Bretall, eds., *Reinhold Niebuhr: His Religious, Social, and Political Thought* (Macmillan, paperback, 1961—first published in 1956), pp. 126–50. It's interesting to note that as Schlesinger

listed the "prophets" of his own generation in 1949, he was to name, in addition to Niebuhr, no less than three writers from *The God that Failed* book—Ignazio Silone, Andre Gide, and Arthur Koestler. These three, plus Niebuhr, make up four of the seven on his list. The remaining three are Ernest Hemingway, George Orwell, and Edmund Wilson. These were prophets for Schlesinger because "they refused to swallow the fantastic hypocrisies involved in the defense of totalitarianism" (*Vital Center,* p. 147). That's untrue, of course. They did indeed "swallow" those totalitarian "hypocrisies," almost to a man. But then, like Schlesinger, they changed their minds.

52. Though there was no single figure like Niebuhr who signaled Hofstadter's transformation from one position to the other, nonetheless he was affected by the literary critics Edmund Wilson and Lionel Trilling, and by the sociologist of knowledge Karl Mannheim. For a remarkable essay on Hofstadter's life and thought, which traces his move from Progressive to counter-Progressive, see Arthur Schlesinger, Jr., "Richard Hofstadter," in Cunliffe and Winks, (n. 47 above), pp. 278–315.

53. Quoted in ibid., p. 280.

54. Ibid., p. 279.

55. Ibid.

56. "Parrington and the Jeffersonian Tradition," *Journal of the History of Ideas,* 2 (October 1941), 391.

Hofstadter in 1960 commented of this essay, "That helped me get Parrington out of my system. . . . I suspect that to some degree Parrington influenced me. I don't think much of him now" (in Schlesinger, "Hofstadter" [n. 52 above], p. 282).

57. *The American Political Tradition, and the Men Who Made It* (Knopf, Vintage Book, n.d.—first published in 1948), p. ix.

58. Ibid., pp. vii, x.

59. Ibid., p. vii.

60. Ibid., p. viii.

61. *The Age of Reform: From Bryan to F.D.R.* (Knopf, Vintage Book, 1960—first published in 1955), p. 19.

62. Ibid., p. 15.

63. *Progressive Historians* (n. 10 above), p. xiii.

64. Ibid., pp. xiii–xiv.

65. For interpretations of American historical writing during this period of transition, see Arthur Mann, "The Progressive Tradition," in John Higham, ed., *The Reconstruction of American History* (Harper Torchbook, 1962), 157–79; Charles Crowe, "The Emergence of Progressive History," *Journal of the History of Ideas,* 27, no. 1 (January-March 1966), 123–24; Higham, "Crisis in Progressive History," in *History* (Prentice-Hall, 1965), pp. 198–211; Robert Skotheim, "Challenges to the Progressive Tradition," in *American Intellectual Histories,* (n. 42 above), pp. 173–255; J. Rogers Hollingsworth, "Consensus and Continuity in Recent American Historical Writing," *South Atlantic Quarterly,* LXI (Winter 1962), 40–50; Dwight Hoover, "Some Comments on Recent United States Historiography," *American Quarterly,* XVII, no. 2 (Summer 1965), 299–318; Richard Hofstadter, "Conflict and Consensus in American History," in *Progressive Historians* (n. 10 above), pp. 437–66; and two articles of mine, "Political 'Reality' in RecentAmerican Scholarship: Progressives v. Symbolists," *American Quarterly,* XIX, no. 2, pt. 2 (Summer 1967), 303–28, and "Implicit Irony in Recent American Historiography: Perry Miller's *New England Mind,*" *Journal of the History of Ideas,* XIX, no. 4 (October-December 1968), 579–600.

For an imaginative effort to set all this in a larger, world civilization context, see C. Vann Woodward, "The Age of Reinterpretation," *American Historical Review,* LXVI, no. 1 (October 1960), 1–19.

66. "The Construction of American History," in Higham, ed., *Reconstruction* (n. 65 above), pp. 23–24 (my italics).

67. *Vital Center* (n. 33 above), p. 165.

68. It's no coincidence, I think, that later New Left historians—renewing a concern for the political and economic in American experience—have withdrawn this bridge from history over into literature. New Left history is thus not as natural a base for American Studies–type integrations—not, at least, as we've known these integrations in the past.

69. For the religious background of Niebuhr's thinking, see William Lee Miller, "The Rise of Neo-Orthodoxy," in Arthur M. Schlesinger, Jr. and Morton White, eds., *Paths of American Thought* (Houghton Mifflin, 1963), pp. 326–44, and Donald Meyer, *The Protestant Search for Political Realism, 1919–1941* (California, 1960).

For the impact of this religious renaissance on American historical writing, see Henry May, "The Recovery of American Religious History," *American Historical Review,* LXX (October 1964), 79–92. May opens this article, "For the study and understanding of American culture, the recovery of American religious history may well be the most important achievement of the last thirty years" (p. 79).

70. *Machine in the Garden* (n. 44 above), p. 342.

71. *End of Ideology* (n. 24 above), p. 302. Trilling's impact on Bell has been so strong that his 1966 book, *The Reforming of General Education,* was dedicated to him.

72. In Kegley and Bretall, eds., *Reinhold Niebuhr* (n. 51 above). This essay has also been reprinted in Schlesinger's volume, *The Politics of Hope* (Houghton Mifflin, 1964), pp. 97–125.

73. "The Influence of Reinhold Niebuhr," *The Reporter,* May 1, 1958, pp. 39, 40. Niebuhr later returned the "atheists for Niebuhr" compliment by calling Miller "a believing unbeliever." In "Perry Miller and Our Embarrassment," *Harvard Review,* II, no. 2 (Winter-Spring, 1964), p. 50.

74. In *The Burden of Southern History* (Knopf, Vintage Book, 1961), pp. 167–91.

75. "The Progressive Tradition," in John Higham, ed., *Reconstruction* (n. 65 above), p. 167.

76. " 'Innocence' and 'Beyond Innocence' in Recent American Scholarship," *American Quarterly,* XIII, no. 1 (Spring 1961), 93–99.

77. See my "Implicit Irony in Recent American Historiography: Perry Miller's *New England Mind*" (n. 65 above). See also chapter 9 here.

78. See Hofstadter, *Progressive Historians,* p. 352; Higham, *History,* p. 197; Noble, *Historians against History,* p. 98; Peterson, *The Jefferson Image in the American Mind* (Oxford, 1960), p. 329; and Crowe, "The Emergence of Progressive History" (n. 65 above), p. 121. Crowe, for example, has written: "Virtually all [Progressive] assumptions and presuppositions were made completely overt in the Summa Theologica of Progressive history, V. L. Parrington's *Main Currents of American Thought* [sic], a book which thrust a systematic and formalized account of Progressive notions into all the major aspects of American thought and every corner of national life" (p. 121).

79. The secondary scholarship on Parrington, though rich, is not nearly as extensive as on Turner. A good place to begin is Ralph Gabriel's brief intellectual biography—"Vernon Louis Parrington," in Cunliffe and Winks (n. 47 above), pp. 142–66. The most extensive treatment in the literature to date is Richard Hofstadter's, in *Progressive Historians* (n. 10 above), pp. 349–434 (including a good bibliography).

See also Robert Skotheim and Kermit Vanderbilt, "Vernon Louis Parrington: The Mind and Heart of a Historian of Ideas," *Pacific Northwest Quarterly,* 53, no. 3 (July 1962), 100–13; James L. Colwell, "The Populist Image of Vernon Louis Parrington," *Mississippi Valley Historical Review,* 69 (1962), 52–66; Merrill Peterson, "Parrington and the Jeffersonian Tradition," in *The Jefferson Image in the American Mind,* pp. 321–29; Arthur Ekirch, "Parrington and the Decline of American Liberalism," *American Quarterly,* III (Winter 1951), 295–308; and David Noble, "Vernon Louis Parrington: the Covenant and the Jeffersonian Jeremiad," in *Historians against History* (n. 40 above), pp. 98–117.

80. *Structure of Scientific Revolutions* (n. 34 above), p. 57.

81. *Main Currents in American Thought,* vol. 3, *The Beginnings of Critical Realism in America: 1860–1920* (Harcourt, Brace and World, Harbinger Book, 1958—first published in 1930 by Harcourt), p. 17.

82. Ibid., p. 167.

83. *Main Currents,* vol. 2, *The Romantic Revolution in America: 1800–1860* (Harcourt, Brace and World, Harvest Book, 1954—first published in 1927 by Harcourt), p. 71.

84. *Critical Realism,* pp. 86, 122.

85. Ibid., p. xix.

86. *Romantic Revolution,* pp. 451–52.

87. *Critical Realism*, p. 19.
88. *Romantic Revolution*, p. xiii.
89. *Main Currents*, vol. 1, *The Colonial Mind: 1620–1800* (Harcourt, Brace and World, Harvest Book, 1954—first published by Harcourt in 1927), p. ix.
90. Ibid., p. xii.
91. Ibid., p. ix.
92. *Romantic Revolution*, pp. 55, 56.
93. Ibid., p. 437.
94. Ibid., p. 441.
95. Ibid.
96. Ibid., p. 442.
97. *Critical Realism*, p. 240.
98. Ibid., p. 239.
99. Ibid., pp. 240–41.
100. *Colonial Mind*, p. 253 ff.; *Critical Realism*, p. 164; ibid., p. 57.
101. *Colonial Mind*, p. x.
102. Ibid., p. 64.
103. Ibid., p. 19.
104. Ibid., p. xii. It was this quality in Parrington which occasioned Richard Hofstadter to write, "In *Main Currents* ideas do not develop, they only recur." *Progressive Historians* (n. 10, above), p. 400.
105. *Colonial Mind*, p. 62.
106. Ibid., p. 347.
107. Ibid., p. 100.
108. Ibid., p. 152.
109. *Romantic Revolution*, p. 271.
110. Ibid., p. 309.
111. Ibid., p. 272.
112. Ibid., p. 320.
113. Parrington is 6½ pages into his Transcendentalists, for example, before he ever pauses to take note of anything around their ideas. And then it's only a passing mention of "a Yankee world given over to materialism." (ibid., p. 377).
114. In his introduction to Parrington's third volume of *Main Currents,* E. H. Eby makes a revealing comment on how Parrington went about his work, and especially on this passion for order in his mind: "He habitually began with his thesis—a phrase, a sentence, or a revealing figure. This was examined and stripped of its implications as one would peel an onion layer by layer. So imperious was the habit of this procedure that his ability to write would be blocked until he had in mind a perfectly crystallized concept expressible at the maximum in one sentence." Eby goes on to note how Parrington was blocked from writing on post-Civil War America until he could *label* it. When he finally came up with "The Great Barbecue," then Parrington was freed to go on with his work.
115. *Liberal Imagination* (n. 3 above), p. xiii.
116. A word or two in explanation of this chart. Because Parrington's sense of experience is so politicized and at the same time organically whole, any division into categories is bound to be somewhat arbitrary. Thus we can't really isolate the political off from everything else. By labeling one set of clusters "Political" and another "Historical," I'm merely trying to distinguish those categories which are more or less continuous through time from those which are contingent upon time and place.
The double arrows ⇆ on romance/realism and realism/idealism mean that Parrington (I) can go either way with those clusters. Sometimes, he's for romance over realism, sometimes for realism over romance. But he's never, let us note, for both simultaneously. The lines don't go two ways at once—as in an ambiguous model. They go one way this time, the opposite way the next. When we get into his (II)-form and ambiguity, *then* we'll see Parrington being pulled in two directions simultaneously. But not here, in his (I)-form.
117. *Colonial Mind*, pp. 15, 50, 114.
118. Ibid., pp. 198–99.
119. *The Structure of Scientific Revolutions* (n. 34 above), pp. 52–53.

120. Ibid., p. 78. For further on anomaly and paradigm crisis in Kuhn, see his three chapters, "Anomaly and the Emergence of Scientific Discoveries," "Crisis and the Emergence of Scientific Theories," and "The Response to Crisis," in ibid., pp. 52–91.

121. *Romantic Revolution*, p. xiii.

122. *Colonial Mind*, p. xii.

123. *Critical Realism*, p. 17.

124. Ibid., p. 167.

125. Ibid., p. 27.

126. Ibid., p. xvi.

127. Ibid.

128. *Romantic Revolution*, p. 417.

129. *Critical Realism*, pp. 26, 201.

130. Ibid., p. 138.

131. Ibid., p. 76.

132. Ibid., pp. 50–51.

133. Ibid., p. 19.

134. Ibid., p. 388. Parrington had titled his section on the frontier in volume 1, "The Frontier: Land of Promise." But here in volume 3 he writes of "the huge wastefulness of the frontier," and of a people "busily intent on squandering the resources of the continent" (*Critical Realism*, p. 15).

Leaving no doubt that it's *Turner's* frontier he's referring to, he goes on to say, "Very likely we should have felt the tragedy of the frontier long ago if we had been as much concerned with inner experience as with outward act, if we had been psychologists as well as chroniclers. But we have been too prone to romanticize the objective reality and disguise slatternly ways with the garb of backwoods independence" (*Critical Realism*, pp. 388–89).

135. *Critical Realism*, pp. 117, 17.

136. Ibid., p. 26.

137. Ibid., p. xxvi.

138. Ibid., pp. 48–49.

139. *Future Shock* (Random House, 1970), p. 339.

140. *Liberal Imagination* (n. 3 above), p. 2.

141. *Colonial Mind*, p. 156.

142. *Romantic Revolution*, p. 214.

143. Ibid., p. 145.

144. For how counter-Progressives have handled these "contrary" thinkers, see Perry Miller on Edwards in *Jonathan Edwards* (William Sloane, 1949); Henry Nash Smith, R. W. B. Lewis, and Marvin Meyers on Cooper, in *Virgin Land* (Random House, Vintage Book, n.d.), 64–76, 256–60; *The American Adam*, pp. 98–105; and *The Jacksonian Persuasion* (Stanford Paperback, 1967), 57–100; and Lewis and Leo Marx on Hawthorne and Melville, in *American Adam*, 110–26, 127–55, and *The Machine in the Garden*, pp. 11–19, 27–33, 265–77, 278–319.

145. *Colonial Mind*, p. 304.

146. *Critical Realism*, pp. 48–49, 54, 60.

147. Ibid., p. 57.

148. It's interesting to wonder, though, whether Parrington could have withstood the pressure of much more ambiguous experience before his old Progressive form would have given way and toppled. He died June 16, 1929, just 2½ months before the stock market crash. His third volume was only half complete at the time. Suppose he'd lived long enough to finish that volume—say, a couple of years into the Depression. Given the direction he was heading, and the speed he was evidently moving, it seems possible that he might have wholly abandoned his old explanation. But whether, at that late date (he was fifty-eight at his death), he could have delivered up some new explanation is doubtful. More likely he would have come out with a study in unrelieved disillusion, rather than a study in ambiguous disillusion.

149. For an extended treatment of this "jeremiad" strategy, see Perry Miller, *The New England Mind: From Colony to Province* (Beacon Paperback, 1961)—especially his chapter on "The Jeremiad," pp. 27–39. David Noble has applied the jeremiad-national covenant idea to Parrington in his "Vernon Louis Parrington: The Covenant and the Jeffersonian Jeremiad," *Historians against History* (n. 40 above), pp. 98–117.

150. *Critical Realism*, p. 367.
151. Ibid.
152. Ibid., p. 401.
153. Ibid.
154. Ibid., pp. 401–402.
155. Ibid., p. 401.
156. Ibid., p. 402.
157. Ibid., p. 403.
158. Ibid., pp. 402, 403, 404, 406, 409, 410.
159. Ibid., pp. 412–13.
160. Ibid., p. 413.
161. Ibid., pp. 86, 122.
162. *Romantic Revolution*, p. 437.
163. *The Nature and Destiny of Man: A Christian Interpretation*, vol. 1, *Human Nature* (Scribner's, paperback, 1964—first published in 1941), p. 1.
164. Ibid., pp. 1–25.
165. In Kegley and Bretall (n. 51 above), pp. 130–31.
166. *Children* (n. 32 above), p. 24.
167. Ibid., p. 23.
168. For a latter-day progressivist effort to draw certain parallels between Puritanism and fascism, see Thomas Jefferson Wertenbaker, *The Puritan Oligarchy* (Grosset's Universal Library Paperback, n.d.—first published in 1947 by Scribner's)—especially his chapter 10, "The Elect Lose the Fasces," pp. 292–338.
169. *Children* (n. 32 above), p. 40.
170. Ibid., p. xiv.
171. Ibid., p. viii.
172. Ibid., p. 142.
173. Ibid., p. 10.
174. Ibid., pp. 13, 29, 138.
175. Ibid., pp. 9–10.
176. Ibid., pp. 10–11.
177. Ibid., pp. 11–12.
178. Ibid., pp. 18, 17.
179. Ibid., pp. 30–31.
180. Ibid., p. 132.
181. Ibid., p. 72.
182. Ibid., p. 78.
183. Ibid., p. 20.
184. Ibid., p. xiii.
185. Ibid., pp. xiii–xiv.
186. Ibid., p. xiii.
187. Ibid., p. 118.
188. Ibid., pp. 40–41.
189. *The Structure of Scientific Revolutions* (n. 34 above), pp. 82–83.
190. *Colonial Mind*, p. 361.
191. *Liberal Imagination* (n. 3 above), p. xiii.
192. For a view of Niebuhr diametrically opposed to my own here, see Morton White's Epilogue to *Social Thought in America: The Revolt Against Formalism* (Beacon Paperback, 1957—first published in 1949)—entitled "Original Sin, Natural Law, and Politics," pp. 247–80. After treating progressivist thinkers as "revolters against formalism" in the body of his book, he goes on to handle Niebuhr as part of a formalist counter-revolt. As opposed to the Progressivist "process" philosophy, Niebuhr's is, he feels, an "essence" philosophy—with reified categories like "original sin" and "radical evil." Needless to say, I think White is dead wrong on Niebuhr.
193. *Liberal Imagination*, pp. xi–xii.
194. See here especially Trilling's last essay in *Liberal Imagination*, on "The Meaning of a Literary Idea," pp. 272–293.

9 A New "Consensus" Forms: R. W. B. Lewis, Perry Miller, and the Counter-Progressive Explanation

For the notion of original sin draws its compelling strength from the prior notion of original innocence.
R. W. B. Lewis
The American Adam

Mather's is a curious way of backing into modernity; yet the charting of his crablike progress is one of the best methods for understanding how a middle-class, empirical, enterprising society could emerge out of an aristocratic, teleological order.
Perry Miller
The New England Mind: From Colony to Province

What we want is [sic] *not terms that avoid ambiguity, but terms that clearly reveal the strategic points at which ambiguities necessarily arise.*
Kenneth Burke
A Grammar of Motives

In *The Irony of American History,* Reinhold Niebuhr confronts head-on the Progressives' anomaly-dilemma. As we've watched it develop over the last two chapters, that dilemma poses the question: *How do you respond when you begin with one set of purposes but end up with a contrary set of results?* How, in short, do you manage incongruity? Do you just consign incongruities to the realm of anomaly and exception, then quickly pass over them? Do you take the cynical pose, and resign yourself to the inevitable failure of good intents? Or what?

In 1944 and *The Children,* Niebuhr had rejected these polar extremes of "light" and "darkness." It was not entirely clear, though, what he would put in their place. But by 1952, he's developed an operative instrument for moving beyond rejection to a new, more positive position. That instrument is *irony*—which he offers doubly as an explanation of American experience and as a critic's role for voicing that explanation.

As an explanation, irony is aimed at certain kinds of connections between intention and consequence in the life history of ideas. With irony as an instrument, Niebuhr proposes to explain why some ideas, used by some people in some situations, may stumble over themselves and produce their contrary results.

He defines irony by contrasting it with two other kinds of connections along this intention/consequence plane—pathos and tragedy. "Pathos," Niebuhr writes, "is that element in an historic situation which elicits pity, but neither deserves admiration nor warrants contrition. Pathos arises from fortuitous cross-purposes and confusions in life for which no reason can be given or guilt ascribed. Suffering caused by purely natural evil is the clearest instance of the purely pathetic."[1]

In a *pathetic* situation, disparities between intent and consequence are produced by outside forces, beyond human control. Men are not responsible for what happens in pathetic situations; and they can do little to resolve them, save to lament the suffering and the damage, try to repair what they can, extend aid to the victims, then work to gain more control over the causes of pathos in the future. In the past, hurricanes and floods and earthquakes have produced what Niebuhr calls pathetic situations.

In Niebuhr's *tragic* situation, people have slightly more control over their destiny. They can make choices, and they can act in accord with those choices —powers they lack in pathetic situations. Still, men are not wholly responsible for what they do there, since again—as in pathos—some external force intervenes between what they intend and what they produce by their acts. "The tragic element in a human situation," says Niebuhr, "is constituted of conscious choices of evil for the sake of good."

If men or nations do evil in a good cause; if they cover themselves with guilt in order to fulfill some high responsibility; or if they sacrifice some high value for the sake of a higher or equal one they make a tragic choice. Thus the necessity of using the threat of atomic destruction as an instrument for the preservation of peace is a tragic element in our contemporary situation.

"Tragedy," he writes, "elicits admiration as well as pity because it combines nobility with guilt."[2] In a tragic situation, men are noble as well as guilty because they willingly choose some less-than-desirable consequence. They do this because certain inevitabilities are built in to the situation, and they are forced to bide by those inevitabilities.

But in Niebuhr's *ironic* situation, men are fully in control of their choices, and are thus directly and wholly responsible for the outcome of their acts.

Irony is not built in to the outcome, it comes only because humans make certain kinds of choices in essentially open circumstances. When intention here fails to produce the desired consequence, then it's *people* who must bear the burden of failure. The ironic connection is, for Reinhold Niebuhr, a radically human one, whereas in pathos and tragedy extra-human forces always intervene, and account for the blockage of intent.

"Irony," he writes, "consists of apparently fortuitous incongruities in life which are discovered, upon closer examination, to be not merely fortuitous."[3] In pathos, incongruity is not explainable at all in human terms, and in tragedy it's only partly explainable. But in irony the sources of incongruity lie in the minds and behaviors of men, so irony *is* potentially explainable in human terms. With an ironic situation, we thus look for the roots of incongruity not outside the situation but inside:

If virtue becomes vice through some hidden defect in the virtue; if strength becomes weakness because of the vanity to which strength may prompt the mighty man or nation; if security is transmuted into insecurity because too much reliance is placed upon it; if wisdom becomes folly because it does not know its own limits—in all such cases, the situation is ironic.[4]

In the last chapter, we saw how Vernon Parrington responded to incongruity through his Progressive form. Looking at Jacksonian democracy along the intention/consequence plane, he noted that its results were out of line with its intents. But, he insisted, "it was no fault of Andrew Jackson if the final outcome of the great movement of Jacksonian democracy was so untoward; it was rather the fault of the times that were not ripe for democracy."[5]

Though Parrington was to label this contrary outcome "ironic," he would not connect it back to the original motives of Jackson. Instead, he severed any possible link there between liberal intent and conservative consequence —claiming that Andrew Jackson bore no responsibility for what happened to his idea.

Parrington's behavior here is characteristic of his form. Progressives work along this intention/consequence plane by starting with certain principles, then justifying those principles wholly on the basis of their *motives*. If the motives are good, what they produce must be good too. When on occasion it isn't, then they'll resort to the "progress"-explanation; the times are not ripe yet. In due time they will be, of course; but in the meantime, Progressives say, we can hardly fault good motives for being burdened with backward times. Instead, we just exhort men of good will to try harder—trusting that with sufficient effort good motives will out, and will eventually produce their intended results.

Where Progressives work the *intent* side of this plane, Reinhold Niebuhr works the *consequence* side. With his irony explanation, he's concerned for the "after-effects" of ideas. And he insists that good intents frequently miscarry not because of bad times, but because of concealed chinks in the intents themselves, and in the way they're acted upon.

Hence motive is not sufficient to justify the act for Niebuhr. More than Progressive historians, he is concerned with what happens to an idea *between* motive and act, between intention and consequence. To him ironies are produced not by bad men with bad principles, but by apparently good men with good principles who act too innocently and too self-righteously on those principles. "Our moral perils are not those of conscious malice or the explicit lust for power," he writes. Rather, "They are the perils which can be understood only if we realize the ironic tendency of virtues to turn into vices when too complacently relied upon; and of power to become vexatious if the wisdom which directs it is trusted too confidently."[6]

Niebuhr is especially vexed by the progress-explanation of incongruity, the faith that we can escape life's dissonances by trusting to the future. "Every nation has its own form of spiritual pride," he notes. "Our version is that our nation turned its back upon the vices of Europe and made a new beginning."[7]

To Niebuhr, this "new beginning" mind-set has had pernicious effects. It has kept Americans from carefully investigating their own principles, or from understanding that they cannot beg off bad consequences by claiming the innocence of their intentions. This progressivist mind-set has blocked critical self-understanding, according to Niebuhr, because it perpetually claims the future will bail Americans out of their present discontents. Whenever they get in trouble, they always try and free themselves simply by working harder, tightening their commitments, producing more, renewing their faith. "Progress" guarantees that over time they'll succeed.

According to Niebuhr, that strategy tends to substitute blind faith for critical explanation. And in this case it blocks genuine historical understanding with the progress-dogma. From his view, it refuses to investigate the life history of an idea as it moves over time from intent to consequence. Instead, it cares only about intent. When consequence varies from intent, that's not the fault of the idea itself, but only with times which have not yet caught up with it. So the idea need not be reassessed, nor the motives behind it investigated. Rather, both idea and motive need only to be reaffirmed, and acted upon the more strenuously, so they can mutually progress toward a future when intent and consequence *will* be merged (re Turner's "up-the-ladder" exhortations in chapter 7).

Seen from Niebuhr's ironic perspective, this Progressive explanation assumes a certain timeless quality in ideas. Ideas—or at least progressive ideas—are not in fact outgrowths of particular historical situations, nor do they change over time as they move from vision to actuality. Instead, they're in some sense functionally autonomous from the historical flux—serving as levers to change things in the world, but being essentially untouched by change themselves.

In contrast, Reinhold Niebuhr emphasizes the *historicity* of ideas. He insists that an idea in intent may not look at all like the same idea in consequence. So when we go to picture ideas, we must consider them through their natural history—tracking them as they move from one location to another.

Hence Niebuhr, with irony, prepares the way for a new explanation of intellectual and cultural *change* in America. Progressives, as we've seen, explained the motive force behind change in progress-terms; change is produced by certain men and ideas envisioning a more enlightened, juster future. Niebuhr doesn't doubt that men see it this way all right, especially "children of light" in America. But he does question whether they always produce in line with their visions. Listen to him counter the progress-explanation of America's history:

That we should be less innocent as a nation than our fathers hoped; that we should be covered with guilt by assumption of the very responsibilities which express virtue; that we should become less powerful in relation to the total historical pattern as we become more powerful in given historical issues; that the happiness which our fathers regarded as the true end of life should have eluded us, all this fits very well into the pattern of ironic failure.[8]

II

Niebuhr's explanation of ironic change is not tightly controlled, and he frequently resorts to religious prophecy when critical analysis might have served the purposes of explanation better (he concluded the passage just above with: "In all of them human limitations catch up with human pretensions").[9] But if he doesn't offer up a carefully worked out theory of intellectual change in America, he does at least hint what such a theory might look like. Shortly, we'll see how Perry Miller fills in Niebuhr's schematic outline, and develops a more coherent explanation of how ironic change comes about.[10]

In preparing for Miller, and in concluding this discussion of Niebuhr, we might now put together a few basic assumptions behind this ironic explanation of experience:

As pictured by Niebuhr, *an ironic situation occurs when the consequences of an act are diametrically opposed to its intentions, and the fundamental cause of the disparity lies in the actor himself and his original purposes.*[11]

As ideas journey across the intention/consequence plane from one end to the other, what happens is this: Men establish purposes. They act from those purposes. Because ideas don't always travel down straight and narrow lines, these actions may have unforeseen consequences, some contradicting their earlier intent. Thus far we have merely incongruity, a disparity between intent and consequence. Incongruity is transmitted into irony if adepts of these purposes try to handle the disparity by simply renewing their original dedication, which may then cause further contradictory consequences, to which they may respond by even more fervently renewing their dedication, and so on.

There are certain requisites to an ironic situation. Ironies are liable to abound in cultures or subcultures (1) which function in open enough environments where their actions will produce results, (2) which have their identity tied closely to rhetorical, rationalized purposes (as opposed to cultures whose sense of direction comes through, say, unrationalized habit and tradition), (3) which are dedicated to instrumental activism, to doing things and not merely accepting things as they are, and (4) which tend to examine their successes and their failures in essentially moral and teleological rather than causal or functional terms.

What's basic here is that ironies occur in relatively open situations (as opposed to the one-way-out, "formalistic" situations of Progressives), and that to discover them one must be alert to possible connecting links between intents in such situations and their consequences over time. So when Reinhold Niebuhr finds himself in a situation like Parrington (II)—where liberal principles seem to have aborted and ambiguities are proliferating—he does not respond by trying to reaffirm the principles. Nor, failing that, is he tempted like Turner and Parrington to turn conservative. Instead, he hunts for *the ambiguous connection*—the concealed link which, when found, reveals where intention may have veered off the main line, starting one place but ending another. That link is what Niebuhr calls *irony*.

As a key to the counter-Progressive historical form, *The Irony of American History* is important not because of its general interpretation of America's past, nor even because of its incipient explanation of intellectual change. In its present form, the former is too broad scale to be of much serious use to historical scholarship; and the latter, as we've said, is not yet carefully enough worked out. What's most important here is the critical *role* which Niebuhr manifests for the historian trying to manage an ambiguous situation. Where Progressive historians, conceiving their role as prophets of progress, tended to despair in such situations, Niebuhr's role here offers a counter to despair. That's because he speaks not as a liberal prophet of American progress, but as a radical critic of the culture's main assumptions.

When Progressives encountered the anomaly-dilemma which opens this chapter—how to respond when you begin with one set of purposes but end up with a contrary set of results—they took this question personally. Such a dilemma was an insult to their best hopes; it threatened not only their country but themselves too. They'd staked all they had on America's future, and when it failed, so (they felt) did they. This is how they interpreted their role vis-à-vis their country; and in chapters 7 and 8 we've seen how they behaved in response to such a threat.

Reinhold Niebuhr, in a similar situation, behaves differently because he conceives his role differently. When the culture is embroiled in ambiguities and incongruities, he doesn't conceive his first task as trying to bail it out, but rather as critically investigating how it got there in the first place. Though there's some feeling of urgency in Niebuhr (more so than in most other counter-Progressives), it's not a sense that people must *act* quickly to avert crisis. Rather, it's a sense that they must pause and *reflect* deeply—putting off precipitate action until they think out what their actions may lead to. Otherwise, they may produce even more ambiguities and incongruities, adding yet further to "the irony of American history."

This role does not make Niebuhr a passivist, though he (like most counter-Progressives) is somewhat less inclined to sound the call for action than are Progressives. He's more concerned rather to place a critical task of mind in front of acting. And that task, as phrased by Kenneth Burke in the statement which precedes this chapter, is to create terms that will "*not . . . avoid ambiguity, but terms that clearly reveal the strategic points at which ambiguities necessarily arise.*"[12]

Niebuhr's core term here—irony—is borrowed from literature, and it's a literary kind of role which he offers for the student of history. That role demands considerable self-control by the historian, control especially over his moral judgments and personal sympathies. Handling the ironic role, according to Niebuhr, requires "an observer who is not so hostile to the victim of irony as to deny the element of virtue which must constitute a part of the ironic situation; nor yet so sympathetic as to discount the weakness, the vanity and pretension which constitute another element."[13] Because that kind of balance is hard to maintain consistently, the detection of irony is usually reserved "for observers rather than participants."[14]

Such a stance is taken more in literary studies—where the critic or author need feel no moral responsibility for his fictional characters—than it is in history study—where the student is dealing with real people. Because of this need for detachment, irony has sometimes been associated with an icy, reserved voice which pokes fun at human foibles and resists all efforts at social reform or change.[15] But such a voice needn't accompany irony. As we'll see soon with R. W. B. Lewis and Perry Miller, an ironic voice can be just as deeply involved with its subjects as can a Progressive. But where Progressives involve their *wills* as strongly as their minds and emotions (sometimes more so), counter-Progressives channel their form of involvement through mind and emotion, keeping their wills mostly free from the direct action. That is, where Progressives try and make things happen differently in the American past, counter-Progressives seldom do that.

This, I believe, is Reinhold Niebuhr's chief legacy to counter-Progressives in *The Irony*—his altered sense of the historian's role. Written in the early 1950s, *The Irony of American History* is too much a cold-war document for Niebuhr to hold his ironic balance throughout the study. But as he articulates this role in his preface and concluding chapter and as he intermittently implements it in the book's body, he's caught much of what later American historians and culture critics have countered in the Progressive voice. This combination of sympathetic engagement with critical detachment, held together by an ironic mode of analysis, is almost exactly the role Miller assumes in *The New England Mind: From Colony to Province,* and Marvin Meyers in *The Jacksonian Persuasion*. It also gets to much of Lewis' voice in *The American Adam*, David Noble's in *The Paradox of Progressive Thought* and *Historians against History*, Charles Sanford's in *The Quest for Paradise*, Leo Marx's in *The Machine in the Garden*, Louis Hartz's in *The Liberal Tradition in America*, and Richard Hofstadter's in *The Age of Reform*.

III

In chapter 4, we suggested something of the *variety* of positions among counter-Progressives, and we'll briefly return to that later in this chapter. But our main focus here will be on two of the most *intense* expressions of the form—R. W. B. Lewis' *The American Adam* and Perry Miller's *The New England Mind: From Colony to Province*. As before in our case studies, we must raise the question of selection. Why these two?

In justifying our choices, we're on shakier ground here than we were with Progressives. At least with Progressive historians, we have consensus among scholars that there was such an explanation-form, that "Progressive" is the proper name for it, that it prevailed for some forty years in the profession, and that a few dominant figures—notably Turner, Beard, Becker, and Parrington—did most to shape and represent its thinking. There also is wide agreement that the form is worth studying; hence there's been much critical scholarship on thinkers in and around this school (topped recently by Richard Hofstadter's distinguished study, *The Progressive Historians*). So when we want to focus down on something within the form, we have what's been done before as a base to move off from.

We've got almost none of that with counter-Progressives. For one thing, there's been little scholarship analyzing the form—no book-length studies at all, and only a half-dozen or so articles trying to handle these thinkers as a group. For another, there is little agreement even on what to call them. The only commonly used label has been "consensus." But however useful that may be as a brand, it doesn't hold up well under critical analysis. To my knowledge, the name we've used—counter-Progressive—appears here for the first time in print. I think the term is appropriate for most of this group of thinkers most of the time, and I've tried to suggest why. But still we must admit that with these counter-Progressives (or whatever it is they should be called), we're working in a critical vacuum of historiographical scholarship, and at this elementary stage any label and any selections to "represent" the form are mostly arbitrary.

There are of course other potential candidates besides Lewis and Miller. There's Richard Hofstadter, whose *The American Political Tradition* (1948) is often cited as first in the form, whose *The Age of Reform* (1955) is one of its most noted and controversial studies, and whose *The Progressive Historians* (1968) is perhaps the last book-length expression of counter-Progressive scholarship in American historical writing. There's Henry Nash

Smith, whose *Virgin Land* (1950) began a sequence of American Studies symbol-myth-image counter-Progressive works (unless, of course, we count F. O. Matthiessen's 1941 *American Renaissance,* in which case he becomes a candidate too). There are Daniel Boorstin and Louis Hartz, whose *The Genius of American Politics* (1953) and *The Liberal Tradition in America* (1955) worked the form through the broad sweep of America's past (though with contrasting conclusions—Boorstin liked what he saw, Hartz didn't). There are also Edmund Morgan, Marvin Meyers, Leo Marx, Stanley Elkins, David Noble, John Higham, Lee Benson, (parts of) Arthur Schlesinger, Jr., and so on.

But with such a paucity of previous scholarship on these thinkers, it would take most of a whole chapter just to detail why each should be considered as a candidate for focus, but why nonetheless I've chosen Lewis and Miller over them. Maybe the best strategy in such a situation is simply to make what claims one can for one's own candidates, hope these claims will be challenged by others with counter-claims, then further hope that these counter-claims will help fill up the vacuum of critical scholarship on counter-Progressives.

My first claim is almost wholly impressionistic. Counter-Progressive explanations have been most distinctively expressed through the literary strain of American Studies scholarship, and through intellectual history studies. Within these two strains, *The American Adam* and *The New England Mind: From Colony to Province* constitute peak moments of scholarship I believe— the former in the American Studies symbol-myth-image school, the latter in the intellectual history strain. They are, I feel, simply the finest expressions of their respective genres.

My second claim is a little less intuitive and a little more rational (or at least rationalized). Lewis and Miller concentrate on precisely those experiences which most confounded Progressives. Thus what Progressives took as anomalous, these two picture as normal.

In the preceding chapter, we detected four anomaly-planes in Parrington (II)—the reality-anomaly, the goodness-anomaly, the progress-anomaly, and the ambiguity-anomaly. Were we to be really schematic about our case studies, we might say that Lionel Trilling picks up from Parrington on the *reality* plane, Niebuhr picks up on the *goodness* plane, Miller on the *progress* plane, and Lewis on the *ambiguity* plane. In each instance, they take what's anomalous for the Progressives and move it to the heart of their own form. So in these four cases we have a rather full answer to what most bothered Progressives.

That's probably over-schematizing our cases, but there is some justification for such a claim. We've already seen Trilling responding to Progressives on reality/unreality, and Niebuhr on goodness/evil. With Miller, we'll be concerned mostly with his counter-progress view of change ("crablike progress," he calls it), while in Lewis we'll be looking at how he launches head-on into ambiguity in American experience.[16]

Further, both Lewis and Miller can be seen as moving directly out of the earlier pivotal moments of Trilling and Niebuhr. Lewis acknowledges the influence of Trilling, and Miller of Niebuhr, and those influences are visible in their work. Lewis further extends Trilling's dialogue-culture idea, and "irony" is his own express position in *The American Adam*. Miller in *Colony* handles Puritan New England not as a single "mind" (as he had in his 1939 study, *The New England Mind: The Seventeenth Century*), but as a dialogue culture too; and his analysis of change in that culture is mostly ironic (in content as well as in voice).

Our main focus in this chapter is with Miller; we'll be using Lewis mostly to set the stage for him. Which isn't to put down Lewis, but merely to say that nothing in the form can touch Perry Miller. *The New England Mind: From Colony to Province* is the consummation of counter-Progressive scholarship. More than any other work in the form, it sets a counter to the Progressive perspective on experience—to its picture of "reality" in America, to its unidirectional view of ideas, to its characteristic confusion in the face of ambiguity, to its prophetic voice, most of all to its sense of historical change as progress. In the whole corpus of American historical scholarship, *Colony* is perhaps the subtlest study we have of cultural change over an extended period of time (in this case the century following 1630 in Massachusetts Bay). And it's the most painstakingly thorough effort in the field to construct an alternative to the progress-explanation of change.

For these reasons, and for others which will develop in the studies themselves, R. W. B. Lewis and Perry Miller have been cast to represent the counter-Progressive form—Miller to do the main acting, and Lewis to be brought in for a supporting role.

IV

Unlike Parrington, R. W. B. Lewis doesn't let ambiguity confound him. This is because he pictures the ambiguous in life as something more than mere confusion. He does this by structuring ambiguity into a manageable form, then he goes on to plot some of the exact points at which lines begin to veer off course, and cross, and get entangled in human experience.

Lewis' strategy is not to look first at ambiguities in particular American ideas, but to frame a picture of the broader culture surrounding those ambiguities. In other words, he prepares himself for convolutions in the particular by first sorting out lines of the general. His Prologue to *The American Adam*—entitled "The Myth and the Dialogue"—offers the clearest, most vivid sense in the form of how counter-Progressives have re-pictured *culture* after Progressives.

As we've seen, Parrington's picture of culture in America is drawn from the *polity*—there are liberals (Jeffersonians) and there are conservatives (Hamiltonians), and they are battling for control of the country and its future (the "main currents"). But Lewis's form for culture resembles a *forum,* or perhaps a *seminar.* There are not just two sides but several— "voices," he calls them. And the point of it all is not victory, but inquiry and dialogue—to get ideas up in the air, to investigate them, and to encourage everyone to hear out perspectives which vary from their own.[17]

In effect, Lewis has picked up on and extended Trilling's and Niebuhr's dialogue-prescriptions from the last chapter. As Karen Lystra has remarked, "Culture and dialogue are synonomous in Lewis' lexicon."[18]

Where Parrington had pictured culture as running down certain lines in America and had defined these lines as the main currents, Lewis—like Lionel Trilling—conceives culture as varying perspectives around a central problem, or theme. He writes, "I want . . . to suggest an analogy between the history of a culture—or of its thought and literature—and the unfolding course of a dialogue: a dialogue more or less philosophic in nature and, like Plato's, containing a number of voices."[19]

Through these voices—not through any particular one but through all in concert—the culture gains its sense of direction. It is what it is by *debate.* It is not an affirmation of some single belief, it is an arena for controversy:

The debate, indeed, may be said to be the culture, at least on its loftiest levels; for a culture achieves identity not so much through the ascendancy of one particular set of convictions as through the emergence of its peculiar and distinctive dialogue. (Similarly, a culture is on the decline when it submits to intellectual martial law, and fresh understanding is denied in a denial of further controversy.)[20]

Hence the student of culture should look not only for what is said, but who said what in response to whom. Correctly handled, cultural-intellectual history "exposes not only the dominant ideas of a period, or of a nation, but more important, the dominant clashes over ideas."[21]

At its heart, Lewis's counter-Progressive strategy for handling ambiguity is really quite simple. He pictures culture *as* ambiguity. By constructing such a general picture in his mind, he's ready to manage particular ambiguous experiences when they begin to move through his form.

We've seen how convoluted lines of experience upset Vernon Parrington. They upset him because within his form a culture ought to stand for something clear and direct—in the case of America, Progressive liberalism. When America failed that, when it pointed not only in the Progressive direction but in other directions simultaneously, this confounded Parrington's expectations, and put strains on his mind.

But R. W. B. Lewis expects that a culture will point in several directions at once. For that's what a culture *is* to him—multi-perspective responses to experience. From the entire range of human variables, the culture *will* direct its attention toward some small region of salience. But a vital culture will not dictate all the specific responses to that region—who says what, and how, in the culture's ongoing conversation.

In the early nineteenth century, says Lewis, the particular region of salience for American culture—what set "the cultural conversation of the day"—was focused around "the peculiar capacities of the inhabitant of the new world."[22] That's what the "voices" in the dialogue were talking about.

Lewis detects three such voices, countering the Progressive assumption that American thought goes forth by twos. His first two voices are straight-line Progressive—the forward-looking and the backward-looking (he calls them "Hope" and "Memory").[23] Had Progressives got their way, these two would be the only cultural spokesmen. Progressives would further hope that Hope might eventually replace Memory, and then *the* genuinely American voice could, without interference, get everything in the country moving in the right direction. As Lewis says of Emerson (from whom he got these two terms), "[He] saw no dialogue at all, but only a 'schism,' a split in culture between two polarized parties."[24] And Emerson (or Lewis' Emerson) would heal the split by having the voice of memory die away.

But in Lewis' dialogue-culture, such a result is impossible. Hope, he contends, *requires* Memory to push off from. And vice versa. "The parties of Hope and Memory virtually created each other," he maintains. "The human mind seems by nature to be 'contrary,' as by nurture it becomes dialectical."[25]

Now that's a striking observation. Lewis is not just saying what even a Progressive would admit—that things often get so confounded you've got to put up with both sides whether you want to or not. Nor is he saying quite what Lionel Trilling was in the last chapter—that each side needs the other's challenge in order to keep stimulated. He's claiming rather that the two parties in effect *produce* each other—that in situations where one finds Hope, Memory must be around too. We don't think in direct lines, Lewis insists; rather, we're always rebounding off of things. Our minds run in angular fashion, sometimes triangular, but not (for long) down straight planes.

Lewis is also saying (and by it moving even further away from Progressives) that the two parties not only produce each other, but, quite outside their conscious intentions, they help create yet a third party from their encounter. Where Hope and Memory see things in either-or terms—either us or them—this third alternative sees things as both/and—both Hope and Memory, in some kind of compound mixture.

Hope and Memory are easily labeled—Lewis simply lifts his names from the Progressive form, through Emerson. But his third party does not submit to such ready naming. That's because it embodies *doubleness* in its vision of life, so a single-meaning name won't do for it. It's a kind of "counter-party" party, distinctively "counter-Progressive" in its picture of experience. So Lewis gives it a label almost by indirection. "For the third party," he says, "there is no proper name: unless we call it the party of Irony."[26]

Lewis briefly explains what he means by his three party labels. Hope:

As an index to the "hopeful" stand on national morality, I cite the editorial (of 1839) which hailed the birth in America of "a clear conscience unsullied by the past." The national and hence the individual conscience was clear just because it was unsullied by the past—America, in the hopeful creed, had no past, but only a present and a future. The key term in the moral vocabulary of Emerson, Thoreau, Whitman, and their followers and imitators consequently was "innocence."

Memory:

To the "nostalgic"—that is, to the party devoted to Memory—the sinfulness of man seemed never so patent as currently in America. As the hopeful expressed their mounting contempt for the doctrine of inherited sin, the nostalgic intoned on Sundays the fixed legacy of corruption in ever more emphatic accents; and centers of orthodox Calvinism, like Andover and Princeton, became citadels of the old and increasingly cheerless theology.

Irony:

But the ironic temperament—as represented, say, by the elder Henry James—was characterized by a tragic optimism: by a sense of the tragic collisions to which innocence was liable (something unthinkable among the hopeful), and equally by an awareness of the heightened perception and humanity which suffering made possible (something unthinkable among the nostalgic).[27]

Hope. Memory. Irony. That's how Lewis re-clusters things after Progressives. He's taken the Progressive *dualism* and re-formed it into a *triad,* and he contends that "American culture has traditionally consisted of the productive and lively interplay of all three."[28]

By this re-clustering, by his picture of culture not as a straight-line affirmation but a variable-perspective conversation, and by locating a third American party of "contraries," R. W. B. Lewis has readied himself to move along the simplicity/ambiguity plane of experience and to take what was puzzling and anomalous for Progressives and offer coherent explanation to it.

V

All parties in Lewis' conversation respond to a particular cultural situation. This situation serves as a kind of magnet for their voices—attracting them, though not dictating the specific route of their approach. The situation is one of new historical beginnings, stimulated by a sense that "the race was off to a fresh start in America."[29]

Lewis begins his cultural conversation just after the War of 1812, opening with a chapter on "The Case against the Past." And he writes that,

The American myth saw life and history as just beginning. It described the world as starting up again under fresh initiative, in a divinely granted second chance for the human race, after the first chance had been so disastrously fumbled in the darkening Old World. It introduced a new kind of hero, the heroic embodiment of a new set of ideal human attributes. America, it was said insistently from the 1820's onward, was not the end-product of a long historical process . . . ; it was something entirely new.[30]

This cultural situation also has its corresponding character type. What Vernon Parrington, responding to a similar situation, had called "children of Jean-Jacques," Lewis calls original "American Adams":

It was not surprising, in a Bible-reading generation, that the new hero (in praise or disapproval) was most easily identified with Adam before the Fall. Adam was the first, the archetypal, man. His moral position was prior to experience, and in his very newness he was fundamentally innocent. The world and history lay all before him. And he was the type of creator, the poet par excellence, creating language itself by naming the elements of the scene about him.[31]

In short, it was a situation for creating things, where mind had opportunity to begin all over in thinking about world (or felt it did). And this, to Lewis, is the larger meaning of his American dialogue: "the purpose of a cultural conversation, to judge from our American example, is not simply to settle the terms of discussion. It goes beyond that to provide materials for the creative imagination."[32]

Here we're at a point where I think R. W. B. Lewis has been misunderstood by critics. Discussion of *The American Adam* has been preoccupied with content—the American *as* Adam, and how important relatively is this idea for understanding American culture.[33]

Clearly, the American as Adam is Lewis' *theme*—just as, say, the American as liberal is Parrington's theme. But where theme is almost the whole point to Parrington, it is not to Lewis. Theme is instrumental for him— allowing him to get at *form* and *process,* or the drama of mind and imagination in action. Which drama provides the motivating energy for *The American Adam.*

More than any other work in counter-Progressive scholarship, *The American Adam* is a lineal descendent of F. O. Matthiessen's *American Renaissance.*[34] And Matthiessen—reacting against Parrington and much influenced by the New Criticism—had claimed in that book, "The critic's chief responsibility . . . is to examine an author's resources of language and of genres, in a word, to be preoccupied with form."[35]

Lewis is not so concerned with the American *as* Adam in his book, but with the American *imagined* as Adam. He's also concerned with what this Adamic image stimulated, bound up in the creative visions it released, through the expressive form of language. To Lewis, the Adamic image is important because of its usage for the American writer—it impels him to create words through fresh forms.

Hence, Lewis' focus is not basically on the *content* of certain ideas, or what they point to directly in American culture (as with, say, Leo Marx's "machine" and "garden" symbols, or H. N. Smith's "virgin land," or Charles Sanford's "paradise"). Instead, it's on *the American mind in the act of creation*.

It's of course an empirical question whether this Adamic idea was very important for American culture in the early nineteenth century. If it wasn't, then Lewis' larger base for generalizing is demolished. Critics thus properly question that base. But Lewis' main purpose in *The American Adam* is not to *show* that this idea had wide influence in America. His purpose, rather, is to say in effect, "*Assuming* that it did, here's how it may have affected certain sensitive minds of the time."

Thus Lewis takes the whole period as a kind of artist's canvas, an arena where visions get created. And his subject is not just or even primarily the American as a new Adam, but rather *the American thinker imagining himself as a new kind of God*. This thinker creates the world, then goes around naming his creations.

Or at least that's what the "Hopeful" do. Thus Lewis calls Whitman's *Leaves of Grass* "a Yankee Genesis: a new account of creation in the world."[36] And he writes of Whitman:

"I reject none, accept all, then reproduce all in my own forms." The whole spirit of Whitman is in the line. . . . It is the creative phase, in that sense of creativity which beguiles the artist most perilously into stretching his analogy with God—when he brings a world into being. . . . In the case of Whitman, the type of extreme Adamic romantic, [it's as though he] really were engaged in the stupendous task of building a world that had not been there before the first words of his poem.[37]

In those of "Ironic" voice, this God-role is more subdued. But the act of creating is still the point of their thought, in Lewis' analysis. Thus he says of Hawthorne:

The Marble Faun is a novel explicitly about the hero as Adam; but it is no less a novel about the heroine as artist. In it, Hawthorne's sense of the analogy between human creativity and human conduct—so evident elsewhere in his fiction—receives its most thorough and complex expression. The artistic dimension of *The Marble Faun* is neither secondary nor peripheral; it is precisely the dimension in which the story's chief "epiphany" is clinched.[38]

Lewis also writes of Melville: "Experience fulfilled and explained itself for Melville only and finally in language. He was the writer above all others who could have asked Forster's question: " 'How do I know what I think till I see what I say?' "[39] And when he goes on to analyze *Moby-Dick,* Lewis is concerned less with the novel's content than with the mode of its creation (and its vision of creation).

For R. W. B. Lewis, then, the fundamental issue is: *"What kind of experience stimulates the creative imagination in America?"* For the Hopeful, it's the experience of new beginnings, where all life is fresh and new and innocent, untainted by the past. And on the main line of his analysis, Lewis treats the Hopeful—Thoreau, Whitman, Emerson—much like Parrington does (though his treatment of them doesn't always parallel Parrington along his *by*-lines).

But where Lewis departs from Parrington is on his handling of Ironists— especially Hawthorne and Melville. As we've seen, these thinkers confounded Parrington; they confounded him because he tried using his characteristically straight-line approach on them, and it wouldn't work. He couldn't understand why Hawthorne wasted his mind away on shadows and memories, and why Melville got so sidetracked wrestling with Evil.

Because Parrington was of the hopeful persuasion, he was unable to comprehend how imagination might be released by anything *but* hope. Lewis, however, suggests that for the Ironists it is *hopes dashed* which stimulate mind to create. For them, men begin with hope, they move innocently along that line until they experience a "fortunate fall," *then* they can start to live and think creatively. As Lewis says of Melville, "It is hard to resist the inference that creativity for Melville was closely, dangerously, associated with the monstrous vision of evil. You have to go through hell, he suggests, either to get the oil or write the book."[40]

Here, with those of Ironic voice, we see R. W. B. Lewis at his most fundamentally counter-Progressive. For in his chapters the ironic imagination, not the progressive, represents what is most characteristic in America's experience.[41] And it's *irony* which stimulates the work of great American imagination, neither hope nor memory do.

Parrington, as we've seen, was uneasy with the "contrary" themes of American literature. He couldn't cope with those of ambiguous vision— Edwards, Cooper, Hawthorne, Melville, Poe, Henry James—and he ended by calling them confused, or anachronistic. But Lewis' schema implies that Parrington had never suffered a "fortunate fall"; he'd lived all his life just once-born, and thus hadn't plumbed the profoundest depths of human experience. Had he stumbled and fallen like, say, Melville, then perhaps he could have handled these characteristically American thinkers of contraries.

Hence for Lewis the most revealing vision of Adam is embodied not in Walt Whitman—who extended fresh Adamic innocence to its furthest extreme in the American dialogue—but in Herman Melville—who took that hopeful innocence, cast it down into his fiery "Try-Works," then tempered it out to something fine and hard. Where Parrington had titled his chapter on Melville, "Herman Melville: Pessimist," Lewis' is ironically titled, "Melville: The Apotheosis of Adam." And he writes there:

By the time he wrote *Moby-Dick,* Melville had dissociated himself in scorn from what he now regarded as the moral childishness of the hopeful. But he was not blinded to that hypnosis by evil which a bankrupt Calvinism had visited upon the nostalgic. . . .

Melville, that is to say, had penetrated beyond both innocence and despair to some glimmering of a moral order which might explain and order them both. . . . like the elder Henry James, Melville had moved toward moral insight as far as he had just because he had begun to look at experience dramatically. He had begun to discover its plot; and Melville understood the nature of plot, plot in general, better than anyone else in his generation. For Melville was a poet.[42]

VI

If the *range* of Lewis' counter-Progressive explanation doesn't quite equal Perry Miller's, the *term* "counter-Progressive" more fully applies to him than to Miller—indeed, to Lewis more than to any other thinker in the form.

This is the case first because when he chooses, R. W. B. Lewis can be the most "Progressive" of all counter-Progressives. He's more receptive to what he's countering than any of his colleagues in the form; and he builds his own perspective on an acknowledged Progressive base.

Most counter-Progressives insist on a view of life as complex and ambiguous, and are thereby put off by indications of naïveté and innocence in the American mind. But Lewis is not so put off. On occasion he'll assume the full Progressive voice himself, and write (as he does in his opening paragraph) of "the authentic American as a figure of heroic innocence and vast potentialities, poised at the start of a new history," or (as he does in his closing paragraph) of "the indestructible vitality of the Adamic vision of life."[43]

Yet we've seen how Lewis can challenge this Progressive view too; and in this he resembles his counter-Progressive colleagues. If a Frederick Jackson Turner were to proclaim what Lewis did—"the authentic American as a figure of heroic innocence and vast potentialities, poised at the start of a new history"—he'd likely take that vision straight (in fact, he *did,* that's what his frontier theory is all about). R. W. B. Lewis will start with it straight, but then he'll go on to chart the perils of such historical naïveté.

He can exhilarate in the sense of freshness released by the new American Adam, while being pretty sure that the "old Adam" still lurks around somewhere. His first section in *The American Adam* is titled "The Danger of Innocence," and his handling of Cooper, James (Sr.), Horace Bushnell, Hawthorne, and especially of Melville, seems to promote and extend Lionel Trilling's point about the need for a "judicious belief in the existence of demons."[44]

We listen to Lewis speak of the "illusory myth of the American as Adam," and we expect next to hear him scorn that myth.[45] But he does not. He can look at these American innocents and neither be beguiled like Parrington into calling them "children of Jean-Jacques" nor angered like Niebuhr into calling them "stupid children of light." Lewis has more tempered control over his sympathies than either of his two predecessors. It's the kind of control which Niebuhr calls for in *The Irony,* but it's Lewis not Niebuhr who is able to manage it through an entire book.

That control doesn't wholly disengage him from his subjects. Nor does it mean he simply refrains from judging anything. R. W. B. Lewis is passionately involved in this strenuous book—especially in his epilogue, where he moves his analysis up to the present day.

But the direction of his involvement differs sharply from that of Progressives. They would measure involvement by the depth of their commitment to one side in the debate and to one vision of life and of America's future. But Lewis' involvement is measured by his commitment to the *dialogue,* and to the fresh creative visions which issue from it.

Here again Lewis comes through as *counter*-Progressive, and counter-Hope—not *anti*-Progressive, nor anti-Hope. Where Niebuhr's most characteristic counter-Progressive observation is his "Man's capacity . . ." statement, Lewis' is: "For the notion of original sin draws its compelling strength from the prior notion of original innocence."[46] He wants to protect notions of *both* sin and innocence—not for themselves alone, but because of the illumination which results when these two visions encounter each other. This encounter is most fully embodied in the ironic voice, and Lewis conveys its particular brand of hope in the words which close the book's body: "The shared purpose of the party of Irony was not to destroy the hopes of the hopeful, but to perfect them."[47]

Lewis adds an epilogue to these concluding words, because he feels his own counter-Progressive hope for the dialogue is threatened by forces in contemporary American culture. To him, these are the forces of skepticism, a further extreme along the goodness/evil plane beyond Niebuhrian realism. This skepticism threatens to still the dialogue, causing Americans—in an "age of containment"—to "distrust . . . experience," and "huddle together and shore up defenses."[48]

"The contemporary picture is not a dishonest one," says Lewis. "It contains many remarkable and even irreversible psychological, sociological, and political insights." "But," he continues, "it remains curiously frozen in outline; it is anything but dialectical and contains within it no opposite possibilities on which to feed and fatten."[49]

In this picture there is no hope; it does not refresh life and word but instead deadens them. Consequently, the potentially ironic perspective has nothing to counter, and it flattens out "in mere mordant skepticism." "Irony," notes Lewis, "is fertile and alive; the chilling skepticism of the mid-twentieth century represents one of the modes of death."[50]

Lewis tries to counter this skepticism by a new, more sobered vision of hope—a vision which (in 1955) he finds in novels like *Invisible Man, The Catcher in the Rye,* and *The Adventures of Augie March.* It's a vision which, above all, is willing to risk experience, as were the hopeful and the ironic of the early nineteenth century.

In my graduate methods seminar on "Explanation in American Studies," someone once queried why a full-scale study of this Adamic theme was so late coming in American scholarship—it seemed such an obvious way of threading through part of the culture's experience. After much collective pondering, we finally gathered that the theme had been around for quite some time—that Parrington's "children of Jean-Jacques" were manifestations of it, as were Niebuhr's "foolish children of light." But, we felt, somehow it had to be run through both the Parringtons and the Niebuhrs, both the exaltation and the revulsion, before it could issue forth in the controlled penetration of an R. W. B. Lewis. One student then capped the discussion by remarking that, in a way, *The American Adam* is an ironic effort to salvage what's left of Parrington after Trilling and Niebuhr had got through with him.[51]

VII

The American Adam concentrates on a situation which has captivated the American Studies symbol-myth-image imagination. It's a situation, as thinkers in this school define it, empowered by a sense of openness and possibility in American culture—where, beyond any previous period in the country's past, old ideas and institutions were being swept away and new ones had opportunity to be born. They see it as a time when Americans set out to make themselves distinctively *American,* thrusting off against their Old World heritage. Such a situation stimulated many of the most noted symbol-myth-image studies—including, beyond *The American Adam,* John William Ward's *Andrew Jackson: Symbol for an Age,* Marvin Meyers' *The Jacksonian Persuasion,* William Taylor's *Cavalier and Yankee,* and much of Henry Nash Smith's *Virgin Land* and Leo Marx's *The Machine in the Garden* and Charles Sanford's *The Quest for Paradise.*

As they picture it, the culture was then sparked by the myth of the New World—a myth given expression in John Locke's "In the beginning, all the world was America."[52] It was also stimulated by an accompanying ritual of rebirth, embodied in Crevecoeur's query, "What then is the American, this New Man."[53]

As their name implies, scholars in this school have handled the situation mainly through symbols and myths and images, not basically through substance. That is, they say little relatively of actual functioning institutions, or of social practices or of political interests, or of technological developments, or of historical events; but they do say much of the ideas which (they feel) mobilized Americans at the time. As we noted in chapter 4, there's a strain of the Gatsbyesque "world's foundation on a fairy's wing" in these thinkers—

expressed at its most extreme in Sanford's claim: "The Edenic myth, it seems to me, has been the most powerful and comprehensive organizing force in American culture."[54]

In Lewis, for example, we find little of the world of experience outside written expression. For all its talk of "culture," *The American Adam* is basically a study of themes in high literature—with an accompanying theory of culture but only a tiny representation of that culture itself. And even his theory suggests that a culture realizes itself not through particularized interests or unarticulated traditions, but only through the generation of ideas and active talk.

There's a similar lack of substantive grounding in other symbol-myth-image studies. Ward's *Andrew Jackson: Symbol for an Age* says little of the political institutions through which Jacksonian symbols are channeled, or of political interests affecting those symbols. Meyers' *The Jacksonian Persuasion* is aware of the interests, but it too shows little of the institutions (namely, how Jackson's "persuasion" is colored by the way he functions through the institutional restraints of the presidency).

In short, in most of these symbol-myth-image studies, we get only a loose sense of how symbols interact with substance in the world.[55] Not being rooted in substantive concretions, or in public events as they happen through time, these works fail to connect into the experience of *movement* in America. Nor do they give us a narrative of *public action*.

By concentrating on myths and symbols, by tracing them back into ancient origins in time and into psychic roots in human personality, scholars in this school emphasize the *enduring* qualities in American experience, the permanences. If they recognize that there are variations on these enduring themes, and that they've altered some over the years, symbol-myth-image thinkers have developed no controlled method for handling those alterations. Mostly, they just say here the culture was then and there it was later, then they hypothesize about what happens in between, and where, and how.

In essence, their picture of American experience has been taken largely with a *still* camera. By thus (like, say, Tocqueville) suspending the culture in space (and, often, in time), they can note subtleties in outline and nuances in balance which previous pictures had glossed over. But they cannot show, in controlled detail, how that culture has moved through time in America, and is jolted by men and events and environment.[56] It has remained for someone in the form to take this counter-Progressive sense of subtlety and nuance and ambiguity, expand it into the public culture of a particular period, and put the whole picture into motion. This is the task Perry Miller set for himself in *The New England Mind: From Colony to Province.*

VIII

It is not ordinarily thought so. It is ordinarily thought that Miller is the example *in extremis* of the scholar who takes thought as the whole of man, and whose conception of mind in Puritan America is largely monolithic, and static.[57]

That, I think, is because many critics have gotten snagged on some of Miller's more outrageous statements from his book prefaces. Like: "I have been compelled to insist that the mind of man is the basic factor in human history."[58] Or: "I hope . . . that the book [*The New England Mind: The Seventeenth Century*] will stand against the assaults of those who . . . deny the importance of ideas in American history, as a way of excusing their own imbecility."[59] Or Miller's oft-cited scorn of "bathtub and stove" social historians who have no sense of ideas.[60]

Critics read these statements, then take Alan Simpson's objection that Miller "has told us too much about the Puritan mind and not enough about the Puritan's feelings" as a proper rejoinder, and they fail to move on into what Miller means by "mind" in his actual history-work.[61] Perry Miller pictures ideas as so powerful that they rule and sometimes victimize men. But, like Reinhold Niebuhr with irony, he believes it is still *men* who do their own ruling and victimizing, and he is at much pains to show how.[62]

The common conception of Miller does, though, fit much of his first volume on *The New England Mind,* published in 1939 (fourteen years before the second volume, which will be our main concern in this chapter). His strategy there was to structure "the New England Mind" as a more or less finished thing; he wanted to put the thoughts of a whole century together and treat them as a unity. Hence he rather presumptuously commanded time to stand still in that volume—trying in effect to re-enact John Winthrop's 1630 *Arbella* injunction to his fellow Puritans: "We must be knitt together in this worke as one man."

Miller justified this presumption by writing in his foreword there:

My project is made more practicable by the fact that the first three generations in New England paid almost unbroken allegiance to a unified body of thought, and that individual differences among particular writers or theorists were merely minor variations within a general frame. I have taken the liberty of treating the whole literature as though it were the product of a single intelligence, and I have appropriated illustrations from whichever authors happen to express a point most conveniently.[63]

Historians might properly object that things don't happen this way, and that it's an enormous distortion of time and of the variability of human experience to pretend they do. Nonetheless, Miller did so pretend, through most of his 491 pages of text in that volume. He made few concessions to time there, and he went on for full chapters at a time without ever mentioning any human event outside a thought.[64] One historian was so offended by Miller's procedure that he dismissed the whole volume as an "autistic performance"![65]

But Miller did try to make plain in this volume (again, in his foreword) that he didn't think things *actually* happened this way, but that he was picturing them *as if* they did, for temporary strategic reasons. As he wrote there (in his opening paragraph):

The title which I have given this work may appear presumptuous in the light of its actual contents, for the book is rather a topical analysis of various leading ideas in colonial New England than a history of their development. I must plead in extenuation that I offer this as the first volume in a projected series upon the intellectual history of New England to extend through the eighteenth and early nineteenth centuries, that I conceive of it as setting the stage or furnishing points of departure for the subsequent account, and that in the portion to follow I shall begin the narrative with the decade of 1660 and there undertake a more sequential tracing of modifications and changes.

Miller concluded, "The present work, therefore, is to stand as a preliminary survey, as a map of the intellectual terrain of the seventeenth century, disregarding for the moment occasional and chronological phases."[66]

Which, in 1939, pretty much predicts what Miller was to do a decade and a half later in his second volume on *The New England Mind* (except that he doesn't begin his narrative with the decade of 1660, but some years before). Where he took ideas as more or less completed products in his earlier volume, in the latter one he pictures them as *problematic.* This study does not reveal a unified "New England Mind" so much as a community of people addressing themselves to certain common dilemmas. Thus Miller re-creates "mind" here not basically through finished thoughts lifted from the pages of books and Harvard theses (as in his 1939 study), but through anxious thoughts as people tried translating them into public actions—in election sermons, in court trials, in colony-wide synods, and so on. Hence Miller is concerned here with mind under strain, the strain which comes when people seek to live by their thoughts—in community with others seeking the same thing. Not the *logic* of ideas, but their *experience,* is what Miller is into here (his critics to the contrary notwithstanding).

His focus is thus on mind in public, under stress, and responding to the experience of attempting to realize itself in the world. And because it's a history, this volume is concerned with how that mind gets passed on from time to time. Where *The New England Mind: The Seventeenth Century* analyzes statics and the structure of Puritan thought, *The New England Mind: From Colony to Province* is impelled by dynamics and change.

It all takes place in the century following 1630 in Massachusetts Bay— between John Winthrop's *A Modell of Christian Charity* delivered in mid-Atlantic on the Puritans' passage over, and Jonathan Edwards' 1731 lecture, *God Glorified in the Work of Redemption, by the Greatness of Man's Dependence upon him, in the Whole of it.* Miller's purpose is to chart what happened in the movement from early seventeenth century to early eighteenth. Within this purpose his strategy is dual—to *describe* that movement in intricate detail, and to try and offer *explanation* to its underlying patterns.

Vernon Louis Parrington had explained such a movement by claiming the triumph of light over darkness. One set of principles—pointing toward the Enlightenment—replaced another—a vestigial remain of reactionary Calvinism (only Parrington didn't choose Jonathan Edwards to represent the culture in 1731—he, recall, had dismissed Edwards as an "anachronism").[67] But Perry Miller rejects such a straight-line explanation. Instead, he sees change, willy-nilly, seeded in the colony's early principles. One set of values didn't *replace* another; rather, *one grew out of its own inherited forms and into another,* despite itself. As Miller describes it,

From Colony to Province *may be imagined as taking place, so to speak, inside* The Seventeenth Century. *While the massive structure of logic, psychology, theology stands apparently untouched, the furnishings of the palace are little by little changed, until a hundred years after the Great Migration the New England mind has become strangely altered, even though the process (which, all things considered, was rapid) was hardly perceptible to the actors themselves.*

"A hundred years after the landings," he concludes, "they were forced to look upon themselves with amazement, hardly capable of understanding how they had come to be what they were."[68]

In other words, Miller works with precisely the question which opened this chapter—how to respond when you begin with one set of purposes but end up with a contrary set of results. To handle this issue, he engages in the characteristically counter-Progressive practice of tracking down incongruities, and he tracks them down the *intention/consequence plane.* Intention is always Miller's base point, especially the early Puritan intentions embodied in Winthrop's *Arbella* speech—"we must be knitt together in this worke as one man," "we shall be as a Citty upon a Hill, the eies of all people are uppon us."[69] When he is concerned with consequences later in the book—the Half-Way Covenant of 1662, the witchcraft tragedy of 1692, the land-bank controversy of the early eighteenth century, smallpox in 1721—Miller is always concerned that they be "measured against the background of the original expectation" (with frequent incongruous results).[70] Unlike Parrington with Andrew Jackson, he does not sever consequence from intent, but is always looking for how the one connects up with the other.

Miller's basic problem, then, is: *How do you put intellectual form on this change?* Parrington had put form on the movement from seventeenth century to eighteenth by calling it "progress." John Higham, looking at Miller's contrary interpretation, merely inverted Parrington's categories and called *Colony* "an epic of unrelieved defeat."[71]

But if there is decline in Miller's New England (what he calls "declension"), there is not quite "unrelieved defeat."[72] Miller's categories, like R. W. B. Lewis', are not *anti*-Progressive; rather, they're *counter*-Progressive. As Lewis won't wholly reject the Progressive sense of "innocence," so Miller doesn't wholly reject its sense of "progress."

There *had* been progress in New England, Miller affirmed. But it wasn't quite what Progressive historians had hoped for, nor did it come about in just the way they claimed. As Reinhold Niebuhr's most representative counter-Progressive observation is his "Man's capacity . . ." statement, and Lewis' is his "original sin-original innocence" one, so Perry Miller's is: "[Cotton] Mather's is a curious way of backing into modernity: yet the charting of his crablike progress is one of the best methods for understanding how a middle-class, empirical, enterprising society could emerge out of an aristocratic, teleological order."[73]

Colony, then, is where Miller works out an alternative to the Progressive picture of change. He contends that though substantial, and visible, *social* changes had occurred during the century after 1630 in New England, its *intellectual* changes were largely covert, lying hidden beneath the surface of its official identity. Only the trained eye and the sensitive ear, knowing where to burrow in and what to listen for, could detect the precise route of this kind of change.

Miller's procedure for doing this brings to mind an observation by Lionel Trilling. "Too often," says Trilling, "we conceive of an idea as being like the baton that is handed from runner to runner in a relay race." Countering this progressivist sense of how ideas move, he goes on to say, "But an idea as a transmissible thing is rather like the sentence that in the parlor game is whispered about in a circle; the point of the game is the amusement that comes when the last version is compared with the original."[74]

Hence Miller, in addition to looking for explicit expressions of mind in New England, probes also for the covert, the repressed, the hints between the lines. In doing this, he gets so deeply into ideas that he almost *hears* them, like spoken words in a conversation. And he pays attention not only to *what* people say, but their inflections, pauses, accents, and so on. At one point, he even pretends to overhear "tavern whispers," and at another he makes much of a twenty-nine–year silence from New England's official "mind" on the witchcraft affair.[75] By testing ideas for tone and nuance and temperature as well as for face-value content, he can infer (of John Wise): "His heart was really in this portion of the book," or: "Those who have become acquainted with the personality of Cotton Mather know that when he talks this way he is about to betray somebody."[76]

Thus when Miller writes here of mind-change in New England, it's not broad assertions *that* change somehow took place, but minute descriptions of precisely *how* (after he's first located when and through whom and under what conditions). "To proceed successfully from the intellectual to the social pattern," he says, "requires of the historian—and the reader of histories— a sensitivity to the nuances of ideas at least as delicate as that of the best intellects of the period."[77]

Miller not only tries to describe and explain *this* change—in the Puritans, in Massachusetts Bay, in the century after 1630—he wants *to create a working picture of intellectual and cultural change in general* (or at least in America). Perry Miller is often called an "artist" as historian. There is truth in that. But there is also (and simultaneously) a strain of the "scientist" in him—of the urge to hypothesize about the general through controlled testing of the particular.

Thus he uses Massachusetts Bay as a kind of "laboratory" for the study of how ideas and cultures function (and dysfunction). As he writes in his foreword to *Colony:*

Frankly, did I regard this investigation as no more than an account of intellectual activity in colonial New England I would long since have given it over as not worth the effort. But the fascination of this region, for the first two hundred years of its existence, is that it affords the historian an ideal laboratory. It was relatively isolated, the people were comparatively homogeneous, and the forces of history played upon it in ways that can more satisfactorily be traced than in more complex societies. Here is an opportunity, as nearly perfect as the student is apt to find, for extracting certain generalizations about the relation of thought or ideas to communal experience. I believe profoundly that the story herein recounted is chiefly valuable for its *representative* quality: it is a case history of the accommodation to the American landscape of an imported and highly articulated system of ideas.

"What I should most like to claim for this study," Miller concludes, "is that it amounts to a sort of working model for American history."[78]

IX

To carry out such a laboratory analysis in *Colony,* Miller makes several basic assumptions about "mind" in New England—what it is, and does, and how to get into it. We'll need to look at these now, as a preliminary to seeing his counter-Progressive explanation of change.

First, Miller is concerned here largely with *collective* mind, or rather mind as it's addressed to collective situations ("what was said and done publicly").[79] In *Seventeenth,* he'd been almost purely an intellectual historian—locating intellect there in the mind of individuals. By *Colony,* however, he has become a cultural historian too—culture residing in the experience of human collectivities. Where *Seventeenth* was on the logic of mind, *Colony* is more into the socio-logic of culture. It's concerned not only with ideas, but with the public interplay of idea and world, through time.

Second, Miller is concerned with mind *in action* in this volume. A while back, we noted that what's missing in most counter-Progressive symbol-myth-image books is any experience of public action in American culture. There is much private experience—like, say, R. W. B. Lewis' Adamic creations—and some public rhetoric—like Jackson's bank veto in Marvin Meyers or Daniel Webster's speeches in Leo Marx—but there is little of mind on the firing line, acting publicly in response to events in the world, and having to face the consequences of those actions over time.

In *Colony,* Miller moves beyond these preoccupations of symbol-myth-image scholars. He pictures mind not only as it privately creates words and ideas, but as it frames them under the stress of public circumstance. His express purpose is not simply to chart intellectual themes, but "to get on with an analysis of events as they befell."[80]

Miller's sense of mind and culture is characteristically counter-Progressive, resembling what we've seen of Lewis in *The American Adam.* That is, mind is sparked by the challenge of opposition, and reveals itself through an on-going dialogue. But where Lewis is concerned just with how mind and imagination behave *inside* that dialogue, Miller moves on *outside* too, showing how mind (and on occasion, imagination) go on to interact with events in the world. His concern is thus with "voices" who are obliged not only to speak, but to act too, and to live with the consequences of their actions.

Third, Miller pictures mind somewhat as Thomas Kuhn does a paradigm —it sets *form* for a community's understanding of the world (and of itself). In his words, it bounds in "the horizon of consciousness."[81]

For Miller, mind in New England functions so that "intelligence could cope with events."[82] It's a device people use for explaining experience, through particular channels. David Hackett Fischer has charged that Miller deals only with "narrowly rational thought" in New England.[83] But that is not true. Miller—in *Colony* at least—studies thought not so much as a rational experience itself, but as a mechanism for rationalizing experience outside it. People may try and rationalize what's not in fact rational; indeed, they're often driven to rationalize precisely those things which *aren't* worked into their understandings. If what they say and think looks to be "narrowly rational," then it's incumbent upon the historian to search for what lies behind the face of its thought. Which Miller does. Like Kenneth Burke, he is concerned to pierce the logic of thought so that it comes out "strategies."

Karen Lystra has written, "There is a fascination in [intellectual history] —a fascination that could spell-bind Perry Miller—the drama of men struggling to make sense of their experience, and also and maybe even more important struggling to experience what made sense and only what made sense."[84] I think Lystra has caught precisely what Miller is up to here. Time and again he pictures the Puritans struggling to "make . . . events intelligible."[85] But he also notes that this struggle is with a "bewildering reality" in New England.[86] Mind invariably strives to cope with and manage this reality. But Miller doesn't take the officially sanctioned "New England mind" for the whole reality of New England. If sometimes the leaders in Massachusetts Bay seek to limit *the* world to *their* world, Miller won't allow them that pretense for long. Much of *Colony*'s drama comes at precisely this point

—Miller periodically showing how enormous is the gap between the world pictured by the official Puritan mind and the world of experience outside that mind.

Which leads to the fourth of Miller's working assumptions about mind. If mind largely controls *responses to* events in New England, it does not control *events themselves*. *Colony* outdistances other intellectual histories by explaining how a purposive people compelled to live by ideas cannot thereby make their life into those ideas. The non-ideational world of things and stuff and unarticulated experience still resists and lies largely outside the forms of mind.

In the foreground for Perry Miller—always—are ideas, principles, beliefs, dogmas. But in the nearly visible background—in *Colony* anyhow—is that vast, unpredictable, and unformed world of experience beyond ideas (what he calls a "buzzing factuality").[87] It's a world which men seek to comprehend and manage, but which they never quite successfully carry off. Occupying center stage in this book, then, is Miller's title focus—"the New England mind." But lurking just beyond sight are that mind's silent (and often unwelcome) partners—*past experience* in Old England, and *present environment* in the New World. Much of Miller's intrigue comes from his subtle reminders of those silent partners, reminders coming at just those moments when Puritans seem most tempted to forget them.

We've noted that there's little of the world outside verbal expression in R. W. B. Lewis. This is not the case with Perry Miller. If he gives us little of that outside world in fact, he continually brings it in by inference, suggesting how environment and events belabor mind and put obligations on it to respond. *Colony* is thus a study of "the intellect in predicament."[88] This intellect is in predicament because finally it's answerable not only to itself, but to the world of experience outside (though it seems often to prefer otherwise).

The fifth of Miller's operating assumptions is this: by watching carefully how mind behaves, he hopes to *reconstruct experience around and behind and under (and sometimes in front of) mind*. His concern is not so much with thought itself, but with the existential context of thinking.

In *Seventeenth,* Miller was driven to explain the Puritan idea-forms, and to him this task was sufficient in itself. That volume is an example par excellence of an "intrinsic" analysis of ideas, concerned mostly with mind's internal logic. By *Colony,* however, mind has also become instrumental for Miller; through it, he infers much of the life in New England outside mind. As one of his most insightful critics, Bernard Bailyn, has remarked, Miller has "run far ahead of his interference, . . . extemporiz[ing] a social history far subtler than any yet written."[89]

Whether he's in fact done that of course awaits the social history. The question is properly important, but it is not our concern here.[90] Our concern is that Miller *believes* he can get to the world of things and behavior outside mind by going through mind. That is, he assumes that, over time, experiences in New England will bear themselves up into ideas, and ideas into words. Thus by looking at words, their interconnections and strategies, and their behavior in repose and under stress, he feels he can infer much of the world situation beyond words.

We've already noted Miller straining to overhear "tavern whispers"; and in his quest for mind in New England he even cites a 70-page tract against masturbation (hardly Fischer's "narrowly rational thought"!) "It accounts for many veiled passages in the sermons," he remarks.[91] By listening thus to people's thoughts, Perry Miller assumes he can reconstruct a good deal of their behavior surrounding those thoughts, and of the world surrounding their behavior.

Sixth, to picture mind as he does, Miller develops a distinctive procedure for handling ideas, and that procedure is what before we've called "situation-strategy" analysis.[92] Through this mode, Miller studies not only ideas in New England, but what ideas carry along with them—intentions, consequences, lurking suspicions, suppressed fears, significant silences, and so on. Mind, it seems, "emotes" in Colony—Alan Simpson to the contrary notwithstanding.

As we've noted, Miller's 1939 volume on The New England Mind: The Seventeenth Century was structured around broad themes—intellectual currents running through Puritan New England. Thus its chapter titles: "The Augustinian Strain of Piety," "The Intellectual Heritage," "The Nature of Man," "The Plain Style," "The Covenant of Grace." Seventeenth is an illustration, an unusually well-controlled illustration, of one sort of "climate-of-opinion" history.

Some of Miller's chapter titles in his 1953 volume, The New England Mind: From Colony to Province, seem to suggest a similar thematic orientation—"The Jeremiad," "The Protestant Ethic," "Profile of a Provincial Mentality," "The Experimental Philosophy." But other titles imply a more chronological, event-oriented structure—"Half-Way Measures," "The Judgment of the Witches," "The Poison of Wise's Cursed Libel," "The Judgment of the Smallpox," "The Death of an Idea."

When we move beyond titles to what Miller actually does in these chapters, however, we see that his organizing scheme is neither thematic nor chronological; rather, it's situational. And his titles are meant to suggest not floating currents of ideas, nor single events in time, but cultural dilemmas, and the Puritans' strategic responses to those dilemmas, through mind.

Thus, Colony is structured around neither theme nor event, but around the interplay of theme and event in situations. For Miller, a historical situation is a succession of events linked together by what appears to be a theme. But these themes are so intertwined with events, so knocked around by them and thereby altered in shape and direction, that it seems more appropriate to call them "dilemmas" or "strategies." Themes float, but dilemmas or strategies connote engagement; and it is engaged ideas which move through Colony.

In this book, then, a situation is where an idea collides with events. Out of this collision comes a strategy, or cluster of strategies. But no sooner does a strategy emerge from one situation than it collides with another. And a strategy appropriate for one situation may not be suited for the next. Thus, over time, rifts develop between situations and strategies in the colony, and in these rifts lie what (for Miller) are the "identity crises" of the New England mind.[93] That is, they reveal the culture's continuing battle with the world to maintain its own sense of meaning and direction.

The entire book can be read as a series of efforts by Miller to locate some pressing cultural dilemma in a situation—Anne Hutchinson and the debate over "preparation," controversy surrounding the Half-Way Covenant, charter loss, witchcraft, smallpox—then to marshal ideas, books, sermons, personalities, parties around that situation. He thus gives each dilemma a substantive location in time and space, and, by "strategizing" mind there, he tries to put it all into motion.

What results is a succession of case studies of the New England mind in operation . . . and in transition. When Miller's method is working, we can see in these cases not only the fact of intellectual transitions in the colony, but some *precise moments* of alteration ("pivotal moments," in our language).[94]

Which leads into the seventh of Perry Miller's working assumptions about mind. In *Colony,* he is preeminently concerned to explain *changes of mind* in New England. And again, "situation-strategy" is his method for doing this.

Richard Hofstadter has written, "In his love of counterposing ideas Parrington has all too often neglected to get them into motion."[95] One reason for this is Parrington's lack of situational grounding for ideas. He was passionately concerned to get at the substantial "reality" behind ideas; but he never developed any procedure for doing this, for moving outward from idea into the world around idea. In short, Parrington never was able to break his "reality" down into anything manageable—like, for example, "situations." Thus, only rarely in *Main Currents* do we actually *see* an idea encounter things and events in the world.

But such encounters are Miller's main concern in *Colony;* his intent is to show the "trying out" of ideas in historical experience. Because of this, ideas move there, and they change. They move because they're pictured not just as floating currents, but as strategic responses to things in the world. They change because in historical situations their abstract logic comes to have actual consequences for people (as we'll soon see when we get to Miller on irony).

Thus, by grounding mind in situations, Miller hopes to capture moments of intellectual change in Massachusetts Bay. These situations—for example, the controversies over salvation and preparation, over infant baptism and criteria for church membership, over leadership of Harvard College, over inflation and its impact on minister's salaries—are all held together by the thread of Miller's central plot in *Colony*. That plot too can be defined in situation-strategy terms: it poses the question, *"What happens when a system of strategies generated out of one situation is applied to another?"* By aiming this question time and again at his New England mind, Miller pinpoints the movement of change in that mind, and the dislocations between mind and world which are both cause and consequence of that change.

The eighth of Miller's operating assumptions is this: to handle in intricate detail both mind itself and the conditions for change in that mind, he must employ methods of narrative as well as of analytic history. *Colony* is thus almost a new genre in American historical writing—*a narrative of intellectual action.* Which genre merges the intense probing and logical rigor of symbol-myth-image analysis with the sense of motion and substantive grounding of chronological narrative history.

Most American intellectual histories have tried to analyze an idea (or ideas) rather than tell a story. But by choosing a people where an idea *is* the story (or so he claims), Perry Miller tries to do both simultaneously.

Unlike most other intellectual histories, *Colony* is not only a study *of* ideas, it's a kind of immersion *in* ideas. That's so because, as we've said, Miller seizes upon an idea at the precise moment of its birth, or death, or alteration, and he uses that moment as a window through which to view the existential conditions surrounding it. Miller thus tries to involve his readers inside the drama of idea as public action, as R. W. B. Lewis does in the drama of idea as private creation.

Hence Miller not only attempts to give explanation to experience in *Colony;* like any skilled storyteller, he tries also to give experience to his explanations. By picturing mind as he does, he re-creates through a dramatistic medium what Lewis in another context has called "the how of thinking . . . the intellectual drama of which the idea is the temporary denouement."[96]

X

That is Perry Miller on mind. Our main concern, however, is with Miller on mind-*change,* especially his counter-Progressive explanation of change.

In *Colony,* Miller's most basic assumption about mind-change is this: Mind is formed in response to concrete experiences in the world. When one mind-form, framed in response to one kind of experience, tries to cope with an entirely different experience, the situation is ripe for change in mind.

There is of course nothing distinctive about that. No Progressive historian would take exception with Miller up to here. Where Miller differs is not in his sense of the situation for change, but in the precise nature of that change. For him, such changes are seldom straightforward, mind simply adjusting to the evident demands of new experience (which is how Progressives would picture it). For Miller, mind (or at least the New England mind) usually tries to protect and defend its established forms even while responding to altered circumstances. Out of these contrary tendencies—*to defend the old and respond to the new*—come the peculiar characteristics of cultural change in Puritan New England (and thus Miller's counter-Progressive explanation of it).

Rephrased in our own terms, the problem is what we noted before as the underlying plot of *Colony:* What happens when a system of strategies generated out of one situation is applied to another? The basic situation in Massachusetts Bay is a novel and unfamiliar environment of space and time, and both are *open* relative to what Puritans had experienced in the Old World. Their basic strategy of response is to try and *bound in* this New World space and to transmit their values intact over time. That is, they seek change, but not *too* much; they want to use their ideas as levers to alter things around them, but they don't want the levers themselves to be altered. They *are* altered nonetheless, though few recognize how. *Colony* is an account of how —of what happens between situations and strategies throughout a century's experience in the New World, as a succession of unanticipated problems puts strain on mind to maintain itself whole.

A Progressive historian would see the resulting changes (at least the *liberal* changes) as more or less conscious and planned. But Miller doesn't see it that way at all. The colony's original purposes are conscious and planned all right, and the environment is open enough so that people can act on those purposes. But their actions don't always bring about just the changes they anticipate. For Perry Miller, even an open environment (*especially* an open environment) has a way of intervening between intent and consequence so that the one doesn't simply move in a direct line to the other.

All these points come to focus in Miller's prologue to *Colony.* That prologue sets the base situation for the whole volume. In the historical "scene" therein, Miller seizes upon the Bay Colony at the precise moment when, according to his strategic logic, the future direction of its mind is most problematic. This is the moment when all the founding leaders are dying off, and, somehow, their strategies must be passed on intact to a younger generation who've never experienced either life in the Old World, or the drama of migrating to the New. It's the time when mind is most in danger of losing direction, since its original grounding experience is almost gone. Witness Miller's opening words in this prologue:

John Winthrop, Governor of Massachusetts Bay, died in 1649, as did Thomas Shepard. . . . Two years before, Thomas Hooker, magisterial founder of Connecticut, who could put a king in his pocket, preceded them. In 1652, John Cotton, foremost scholar and official apologist of the New England Way, died in Boston, his name a mighty one wherever Protestant learning and erudition were revered. These had been the spokesmen, and with them a generation ended.

. . . By the sixth decade of the century only one remained from the pantheon of great founders—Richard Mather of Dorchester. Only he, principal architect of *The Cambridge Platform* (by which in 1648 orthodox New England published to the world its distinctive constitution of church government), only he could pronounce the admonition and benediction of the fathers.

By the tenth of April 1657, almost deaf and blind in one eye, he felt the time had come to speak *A Farewel-Exhortation to the Church and People of Dorchester in New England*. . . . He and his colleagues had invested property, energy, life; now others must carry on, children who, like his youngest son Increase, knew nothing of heroic days in England when King Charles darkened the skies by dismissing Parliament and when Laud's "visitors" told Richard to his face that he better have begot seven bastards than to have preached without a surplice. Into this valedictory, Richard Mather poured the experience of a generation, strove by main force to warn of what in their eyes, despite the miraculous achievement, were evident dangers.[97]

Indeed, it seems, almost *because of* "the miraculous achievement." For this founding generation, in Miller's view, have succeeded in many of their visions; they've succeeded so well that they pass on a world entirely altered from what they'd grown up in, and out of which they'd formed their own strategies. Would a strategy framed in the Old World, against a situation of dissent, work for a situation where, essentially, dissenters are now getting their own way and have built at least the basic structures of the New World they want? How, in short, to cope with an environment where people may accomplish what they envision, but where accomplishment brings unique problems of its own? As Miller says of John Winthrop, "he knew the danger to be not failure but success."[98]

Miller's purpose in this prologue is to dramatize the gap—to him an unbridgeable gap—between the lived experience of things and abstracted ideas about them. When he pauses later in the volume to query, "How could experience be shipped across the Atlantic?" he emphasizes how difficult it is to re-create an experienced situation through ideas and words alone.[99]

Miller is intrigued by the way his New England mind confronts its most vexing early dilemma—*how to recapture the founders' experience of one kind of world, through ideas and words, so that it can motivate sons and daughters who've lived all their lives in another kind of world.* This situation dramatizes a classic kind of "generation gap" in the colony—and a gap doubly widened because it's not only in time but in space too, a breach not just between then and now but between there and here, that side of the Atlantic and this.

A third force widens it yet more. It's not only a "situation" gap (time, space), it's a "strategy" gap as well. For what the founding generation strove to recapture and pass on is not merely *an* experience, but a kind of intensified experience like few ever have in life. "Leaders of the first generation," says Miller, "were participants in a great world."[100] As a strategic response to what they felt was the degenerating situation of the Old World and the opportunities of the New, the fathers had labored against enormous odds to found a plantation. As Miller describes it, this was a mighty act. But what could the sons do for an encore? Their fathers had been offered the challenge of high drama, but the sons' problems were becoming those of routine. By this time, "New England was no longer a reformation," remarks Miller, "it was an administration."[101]

We've noted that Miller tries to re-create historical experiences as he gives explanation to them (thus tackling, at some remove, the same problem besetting the Puritan fathers). In doing this, he focuses the dilemmas of general mind down into particulars—particular men, particular events, particular environments. Thus, like Kenneth Burke, he pictures the encounter of mind with world as *acts upon a scene*—acts by particular actors who envision the general scene through their own special, "perspectivistic" locations in time and space.

Hence in Miller's prologue to *Colony*, we see not a generalized "New England mind" responding, but instead a situation-specific act—through someone whose ideas have been shaped by distinctive kinds of experience, who is located in time and in place, and who frames strategies for responding to the special predicament he feels himself in at this moment in history. That mind is Richard Mather's; his predicament is his sense of imminent death and his awareness that, as the last surviving founding leader, when he dies an idea may go with him. Reacting to his own imagination of impending death (he was in fact to live twelve more years), and to the actual deaths of his colleagues, Mather tries to frame words which will stay the death of their ideas too. He doesn't want the New England mind to go down with the framers of that mind. Mather is thus an ideal case for picturing right off in *Colony* Miller's New England mind in predicament.

This mind, through Richard Mather, is in predicament mostly because of the situation's externals—the various "gaps" we've just noted. But it's also under strain because of its own inner makeup. Here Miller explains the workings of a historical idea as a consequence neither of the inner structure of "mind" nor of the outer forces of "environment," but of the dialogic encounter between them. New England's is a historical mind, and thus has been channeled by past experiences. It therefore responds to this second-generation New World situation not with everything potentially at its disposal, but through built-in filters.

It's at this point where the whole inner logic of Puritanism which Miller had constructed in his previous volume—*The New England Mind: The Seventeenth Century*—becomes immediately relevant. If Richard Mather's purely pragmatic problem vis-à-vis his audience is vexing enough—how to "supply them with an experience they had missed"—the inherited forms of Ramist logic serve to compound his dilemma.[102] For those forms keep Mather, and all other New England ministers in the early decades, to what was called "the plain style." Fearful lest congregations be seduced by a rhetoric which moves their emotions but by-passes their understanding, the plain style cautions ministers to aim their words directly at mind. They must move their listeners by logic, and not attempt to subvert mind by going under it to work up emotions. The Ramist form, says Miller,

restricted Richard Mather to a logical statement of enumerated points, here and there embellished by a rhetoric which took care not to lay too direct a hold upon emotions lest it become enthusiastic. With this instrument he was endeavoring to prove that the children were required to know anxieties which nothing in their life, except their parents' tales, had ever conveyed to them.[103]

Richard Mather's dilemma is how to teach his younger listeners by logic what their own experience has not taught them, and cannot. They are "a population who had grown up with victory already accomplished and institutionalized," and Mather must somehow address their present needs, yet still pass on to them values from the past.[104]

Thus, the situation for Perry Miller's prologue in *Colony:* It dramatizes, through Richard Mather, the dilemma of re-creating a lived experience through ideas and words alone (an especially vexing dilemma when those ideas and words are restricted by the Ramist form).[105] It also dramatizes, through Mather's audience, the dilemma of native experience in apprehending Mather's largely imported ideas. Finally it dramatizes, for the colony, the dilemma of devising a new accommodation of idea to experience—strategy to situation—and doing it so that the original power of Puritan beliefs can be revivified and rendered usable.

XI

That new accommodation (of which Mather's *Farewel-Exhortation* of 1657 is an early version) was to take shape after a decade or so into a native New England mind-form. Miller calls this form *the jeremiad.* For the Puritans, this jeremiad—following along Richard Mather's dilemma—becomes "a way . . . of making intelligible order out of the transition from European to American experience."[106] For Perry Miller, the jeremiad becomes an instrument for tracking changes of mind through the first century's experience in the New World, and for setting down on some of mind's strain points.

"Instinctively," writes Miller, the Puritans "responded to the demands of the situation," framing a strategy to resolve Mather's generational dilemma.[107] As "the one literary type which the first native-born Americans inevitably developed," the jeremiad would attempt for these native-born what the migration had been for their English-born fathers.[108] It would also attempt collectively (especially on fast days and election days) what could not be done by a succession of individual conversions to the faith.

If the jeremiad, at least in its early stages, is restrained by Ramist logic from playing on emotions directly, it can still appeal to the founders' original purposes, and especially to people's sense of guilt for having betrayed those purposes. It can't re-create the founding experience, we've noted that in the last section. But it can take an experiential impossibility and make it into a strategic opportunity. It can do this simply by lamenting, time after time, in situation after situation, that they've *lost* the old values and are a disgrace to their fathers. Their very humiliation might become a lash for arousing them to action.

Thus the jeremiad has a three-staged purpose vis-à-vis its audience: It tries to show (1) that the present generation has allowed New England to degenerate, so that it's become almost as bad as the Old World which their fathers had left, (2) that the situation is in some senses worse, for God has chosen them for a special errand, and they are betraying him as well as themselves, (3) but that, despite all this, New England may still become the Lord's best hope for the world if only her sons and daughters will give up their dissolute ways and return to the original path of their fathers.

So, following his prologue where he shows the dilemma of passing on an idea without the experience of it, Miller then explains how the jeremiad-form comes to cope with this dilemma. In part that form looks back to bygone experiences; in this sense it's still bound into Mather's dilemma. But it also connects into the experience of contemporaries; it does this by listing all their discontents, then insisting that they're caused by their failure to uphold the old beliefs. By invoking remorse about present discontents and connecting that remorse to their betrayal of the fathers, the jeremiad makes clear what must be done. They must repent, must take this sense of guilt and apply it to their wills, and immediately change their ways. It is *almost* too late, but not quite, the jeremiad warns. By a massive reorganization of their faculties, they may yet save themselves. And more important, they may yet save the colony and its covenanted mission.

As Miller describes it, the jeremiad is a useful strategy for reinvigorating a community of will, and for using guilt as a device to bind people together in common purpose. "These communities preserved their personalities," he says, "as long as they possessed a framework which validated their reason for being."[109] The jeremiad does just that for Puritans. It may not stop all their suffering, but it does give a reason for it—"The federal covenant does not shield a federated people from the wrath of God: it makes that wrath intelligible."[110] Nor does this jeremiad allow them wholly to control their experience with their minds. But it does pinpoint wherein their ignorance lies, so when they don't understand things they at least know where they must exert more effort. Thus "by grieving over the incomprehensible, it provided a method of endurance."[111]

The jeremiad, then, is the Puritans' basic idea-form for coping with change. It's also Perry Miller's idea-form for charting that change. He focuses on the New England mind mainly through "the frame of the jeremiad," and he watches how this jeremiad encounters one situation after another through the colony's history.[112] *He thus plots the movement of mind along a succession of change moments in Massachusetts Bay, which moments pinpoint the encounter between native mind-form and world.* By focusing through the jeremiad, the cultural historian can map the route of change in New England; "taken in succession," Miller says, these jeremiads provide "a chronology of social evolution."[113]

Colony is thus pointed along the trail of these change moments and the identity crises they reveal—the early fast days, the Synod of 1679 and its call for *The Necessity of Reformation,* the conflict over charter autonomy with England, loss of that charter and the imposed regime of Sir Edmund Andros (when, significantly, domestic jeremiads ceased), witchcraft in 1692, the credit controversy of the 1710s, the smallpox epidemic of the 1720s. It's this mode of organization which makes *Colony,* as we've said, almost a new genre in American historical studies—a narrative of intellectual action. The identity crises and change moments form Miller's narrative, the jeremiad response his intellectual action.

Thomas Kuhn has noted that we not only see different things through our different paradigms, we also see *through* different things. That is, our pictures of the world differ because we use different *instruments* for looking at it.[114]

Vernon Parrington had detected progressive change in Puritan New England by looking through ideas of liberals, and by locating these ideas in floating "currents" of thought. But Miller measures change in the colony by looking through the jeremiad, and by locating these jeremiads in cultural "situations." By this procedure, he picks up on changes that Parrington never got to; the jeremiad-form plays no role at all in *Main Currents,* and, as we've said, Parrington didn't set his ideas down in situations.

Because of this different measuring instrument, Perry Miller catches ambiguities which Parrington had not looked for. And with this instrument, he tries to manage his alternative to the Progressive explanation of change.

What happens with jeremiads in these New World situations is this: As each new dilemma presents itself to mind, a different part of the inherited strategy is pulled out for response. In the original Puritan belief system, everything had been held together by an intricately balanced structure of interlocking polarities (or so Miller claimed, and he'd taken 491 pages of text in *The New England Mind: The Seventeenth Century* to build up his claim). But this system comes to be unlocked and unbalanced as its varying emphases are applied to each successive New World situation. This is what Miller refers to when he writes in his foreword to *Colony:*

From Colony to Province may be imagined as taking place, so to speak, inside *The Seventeenth Century.* While the massive structure of logic, psychology, theology stands apparently untouched, the furnishings of the palace are little by little changed, until a hundred years after the Great Migration the New England mind has become strangely altered, even though the process (which, all things considered, was rapid) was hardly perceptible to the actors themselves. A hundred years after the landing, they were forced to look upon themselves with amazement, hardly capable of understanding how they had come to be what they were.[115]

What results by the early eighteenth century is not so much a *manifest alteration* of the original Puritan belief system, but a *latent explosion* of that system. The system itself is intact, or looks so on its surface, but its inner connections have all been blown apart. Thus, a century after the colony's beginnings, Miller's New England mind has become "an intricate system of interacting stresses and strains . . . a time-bomb, packed with dynamite, the fuse burning close."[116]

Everything is still there from what the founders brought over. If we use the normal historians' procedure and look just at the system's face, nothing much seems altered. But if we have instruments for burrowing down under mind, as it were, getting at it from the bottom up, then we can detect enormous change (potential as well as actual). To Miller, change in New England comes not in the manifest *content* of beliefs; change comes rather in how tenets in the belief system are *configured,* how they're connected one with another. New values come to mind in the colony (e.g., "works" over "faith," external over internal) not because they were completely missing from the original system, but because earlier they had not been emphasized *in that particular way.*

One doesn't discover this simply by looking at what's there in a system of beliefs. One also needs a precise apparatus for measuring its intensity, and for gauging how much relative weight it puts on each of its individual tenets. That's what Miller tries to do with his jeremiad-situational instrument of focus.

If it's through this situational focus that Miller attempts to reveal stresses and changes in mind, it's through their jeremiad strategy that Puritans seek to conceal them. Or if not always conceal them, at least manage them in such a way as to maintain a hold on their original identity. For the strategy of the jeremiad is to stay admission of lasting changes—to deflect unmanageable guilt about declension by acknowledging that there has indeed been decline, but it's not irreversible. Whatever change has taken place is only temporary, and unnatural, and can be reversed with the proper dedication. No change can be admitted as fundamental in the jeremiad; it must be seen as a temporary lapse of heart and will, never a basic alteration in mind.

But if the student of mind comes to read these jeremiads as strategic not literal, and if he can ground them in those situations which occasion mind to behave as it does, then—for Miller—he may detect changes which mind itself desperately tries to conceal. Thus:

[Jeremiads] were releases from a grief and a sickness of soul which otherwise found no surcease. They were professions of a society that knew it was doing wrong, but could not help itself, because the wrong thing was also the right thing. From such ceremonies men arose with new strength and courage: having acknowledged what was amiss, the populace could go back to their fields and ships, trusting that a covenanted Jehovah would remember His bond. When again they grew apprehensive, they could look into their own hearts, find what was festering there, and hasten once more to cleanse their bosoms of poisonous stuff by public confession.

"Although jeremiads and the Reforming Synod [of 1679] called for an alteration of social habits," Miller continues, "the result was only more days of humiliation." Puritans, as we'll see in the next section, try to manage a problem of social structure by locating its cause in their hearts. "Knowing their impotence," Miller concludes, "the people needed a method for paying tribute to their sense of guilt and yet for moving with the times. Realizing that they had betrayed their fathers, and were still betraying them, they paid the requisite homage in a ritual of humiliation, and by confessing iniquities regained at least a portion of self-respect."[117]

XII

The jeremiad does two things for Perry Miller. It enables him to track mind changes, as we've just seen. It also gives focus to his counter-Progressive explanation of such changes. And that explanation is largely *ironic*.

Miller's ironic mode of explanation resembles what we saw earlier with Reinhold Niebuhr. That is, it works along the intention/consequence plane of experience, and it enables him to manage the Progressive anomaly dilemma which opened this chapter—How do you respond when you begin with one set of purposes but end up with a contrary set of results? In short, it's a way of coping with ambiguity.

Where Niebuhr theorizes about irony but doesn't control it very well in his analysis, Miller controls it throughout most of *Colony* but doesn't theorize about it much. His ironic explanation is mostly implied; and the historical critic is thus obliged to take what Miller does in his history and make it explicit.[118]

First, Miller, like Niebuhr, sees ironies occurring in relatively *open situations*. Recall that Niebuhr pictured tragic and pathetic incongruity in closed situations, where extra-human forces account for the disparity between intent and consequence. But ironic incongruities, he says, take place in open situations, where men have control over what they do.

So also for Perry Miller. There are few ironies in his 1939 volume, which concentrated mostly on the Puritans' experience in England and on the Continent, where opportunity for them was limited. Only when the Puritan creed is transported from the Old World to the New do ironies begin to happen. Time and again in *Colony* we'll hear Miller say, "This conclusion, even though it can be found potentially in European drafts . . . was forced into the open by American experience."[119]

What is only potential in Europe—in a perceived situation of narrow boundaries—can become actuality in America—where opportunity seems boundless. But for Miller opportunity doesn't mean people will always accomplish what they set out to do. Opportunity means that the side consequences of intents, and the wholly unanticipated ones, will proliferate along with the consciously planned ones. So a situation of opportunity offers more perils of a sort, and more temptations to irony, than do situations bounded in by inevitables. This is what Miller means when he writes of John Winthrop, "he knew the danger to be not failure but success."[120]

Second, for Miller, ironies abound in an open environment because *strategies formed out of one situation may be ill formed for another.*

Because situations in the New World are open and multiple, they offer men choices. Theoretically, they might in each instance choose a strategy wholly appropriate to the situation, and thus for the most part avoid ironies.[121] But mind in New England has been filtered through past situations, so it addresses each new situation not as a blank but through channels built up over time. On occasion, the hold of these channels may tighten under strain and become "vise"-like—locking mind in so that instead of responding directly to the situation at hand, it desperately clutches onto its existing forms (for example, Cotton Mather and his witchcraft strategy in chapter 5).[122]

In these instances, men are locked in not by the situations, but by their own minds. Their dilemma is compounded by the very openness of things in the New World. For in an environment of opportunity, more—and more variable—situations are thrown up to mind, sometimes overloading it.[123] The mind liable to irony, we might say, is an over-busied mind—burdened by an oversupply of situations and hard put to invent strategies appropriate for every one. Thus, Miller continually says of his New England mind, as it's confronted by some new situation, "Here was the predicament in which the intelligence of the community found itself.[124]

Mind's predicament is made more vexing when it's impelled by powerful purposes, by an inherited sense of mission which it is driven to maintain. Under such a mission, mind in New England strains to protect its original identity, yet also respond to changing events in the world. It's both conservative and liberal; and if this gives it a richness and a sustaining power, it also tempts it to irony. Thus Cotton Mather (Miller's most noted instance of the ironic mind in Puritan America): "With a sweep of his hand he would wipe away all theological scruples, and cry aloud, 'EXPERIENCE! EXPERIENCE! 'tis to THEE that the Matter must be Referr'd after all; a few Empiricks here, are worth all our Dogmatists.' And yet, perhaps in the very next moment, this superpragmatist would feel his mind gripped in the vise of the jeremiad."[125]

"Superpragmatist" and "the vise of the jeremiad"—much of the drama in *Colony* comes from mind's veering between these two poles. Miller often shows how a strategy ingeniously devised to meet one situation gets locked in to mind, causing it to misfire in some other one.

Ministers soon after 1689, for example, employ the jeremiad to explain why they had lost their charter in 1684, and had for three years after 1686 been punished by the imposed royal regime of Sir Edmund Andros.[126] According to the jeremiad explanation, "The people had lost 'the most happy and easy Government in the world' because they frequented taverns; the possibilities of divine correction now included, in addition to plagues and crop failures, such a political regime as Andros', which has 'by the most impartial men been confessed to have become intolerable.' "[127]

This is a satisfying strategy for helping the Puritans understand a severe (if temporary) setback in the colony's hopes, for thrusting off against an Old World devil which everyone had experienced, and for regrouping forces after they regain power. In short, the jeremiad strategy makes them believe they can exorcise external evil by exerting their wills. It also helps them, in a sense, to re-experience the kind of high drama of Old World versus New which impelled their founding grandfathers two generations before.

But when this same strategy is applied in 1692 to rationalize the Salem court, it miscarries. For it explains their affliction as simply another invasion of evil, this time in the form of a New World devil. And it justifies exorcism again—executing that Devil's minions—as a necessary proof of their will and dedication.

The jeremiad form looks at the disparity between intention and consequence, and says in effect, "Try harder." It doesn't ask mind to reconsider itself, it asks it rather to act with more dedication and fervor. Incongruity, according to the jeremiad, lies not in *intent;* it lies rather in failure to exercise the necessary *will* upon intent. This "try harder" syndrome seems to work for 1689, as it explains the three years' punishment of Andros. Puritans had been punished because they hadn't been dedicated enough; and punishment stops—after 1689—because they have gotten back on the right track.

But "try harder" in 1692 gets translated through the jeremiad form into "punish the unrepentant," and "punish the unrepentant" into "execute unconfessing witches" (confessing witches got off free). And all this with ironic results. What's intended as a strategy to *protect* existing mind-forms has, in Miller's words, "fatally soiled" them.[128] He comments on the ironic outcome:

Henceforth there was, although for a time desperately concealed, a flaw in the very foundation of the covenant conception. The doctrine that afflictions are punishments to be dispelled by confession had produced at least one ghastly blunder; repentance had been twisted into a ruse, and the civil magistrate, by a vigorous exercise of his appointed function, had become guilty of hideous enormities. . . . The meaning of New England had been fixed, by Winthrop and the founders, in the language of a covenant; if henceforth there was so much as a shadow of suspicion upon that philosophy, in what realm of significance could the land hold its identity?[129]

Third, Miller is able to detect ironies because, like many counter-Progressives, he's always looking for *the counter side of an idea.*

For Progressives, an idea is just what it seems, a more or less straightforward expression of some intent or other. When an idea doesn't turn out as it should, then some other idea must have deflected it from its intended course.

But for counter-Progressives, ideas have their own counter-tendencies buried within them. So when an idea gets knocked off course, it may have knocked itself off. Richard Hofstadter speaks in characteristic counter-Progressive fashion when he remarks of Parrington, "In seeking for the causes that overthrew Puritanism from without, Parrington and many of his contemporaries passed up the profound changes that were taking place within."[130]

Miller, on the other hand, concentrates on the changes from within rather than from without, and he locates causes of change in the unseen ambiguities of Puritan ideas. He searches often for "the hidden drift of the conception," and notes time and again that "the New England mind found itself, wholly within the circumference of its straightforward assumptions, entangled in contradictions."[131]

Because of his effort to open out the underlying rifts in ideas, Miller frequently makes observations like: "The ministers copiously denounced Arminianism even while expanding the covenant in every direction, and they could continue to do so, until one should arise to accuse them of having become, to all practical purposes, Arminian—although by that time they would no longer be capable of understanding what their accuser meant."[132] Or: "Thus in the first years of the eighteenth century multiplicity continued to grow out of simplicity; the covenant theology, having conceived and cradled the principle of voluntary consent, set the New England mind at work destroying that theology. The whelps were eating up the dam."[133] Or:

The husbandmen and traders were doing nothing but what they had been told to do. They worked in their callings—and brought multiplicity out of unity. There were perceptibly "more divisions in times of prosperity than in times of adversity." . . . The more everybody labored, the more society was transformed. The more diligently the people applied themselves—on the frontier, in the meadows, in the countinghouse or on the Banks of Newfoundland—the more they produced a decay of religion and a corruption of morals, a society they did not want, one that seemed less and less attractive.[134]

Miller's Puritans don't realize that when they set forth their *mission* in the New World, *energy* and *opportunity* will be unleashed too. If they can more or less control mission (at least they have a clear model from the founding era), they tend to be confounded by energy and opportunity. When, through their jeremiad form, they react to every sidetracked expression of energy and opportunity by calling for a renewed commitment to mission, they produce ironies.

This is so because every movement forward (i.e., toward mission) covertly stimulates side movement too (i.e., toward the release of energy and opportunity). If the jeremiad can shame Puritans to action, it cannot—in an open environment—always predetermine the course and consequence of this action. Thus, in his chapter on "The Protestant Ethic," Miller writes of the jeremiad as an engine of ironic change:

While the ministers were excoriating the behavior of merchants, laborers, and frontiersmen, they never for a moment condemned merchandizing, laboring, or expansion of the frontier. They berated the consequenecs [sic] of progress, but never progress; deplored the effects of trade upon religion, but did not ask men to desist from trading; arraigned men of great estates, but not estates. The temporal welfare of a people, said Jonathan Mitchell in 1667, required safety, honesty, orthodoxy, and also "Prosperity in matters of outward Estate and Livelyhood."

Miller continues, locating precisely the point of ironic incongruity in the Puritans' jeremiad strategy:

In fact, in the ecstasy of denunciation, Jeremiahs enthusiastically indorsed those precepts of pious labor which from the beginning had been central in Calvinism. Merchants, farmers, and shipbuilders increased "cent per cent," and the consequence appeared to be a decay of godliness, class struggles, extravagant dress, and contempt for learning; New England seemed to be deserting the ideals of its founders, but preachers would have deserted them even more had they not also exhorted diligence in every calling—precisely the virtue bound to increase estates, widen the gulf between rich and poor, and to make usury inevitable.[135]

Fourth, Puritans breed so many ironies, in Miller's analysis, because *the jeremiad form locks them into moralized strategies for responding to structural situations.*

By this I mean the Puritans—when working through the jeremiad—are prone to diagnose all problems as moral, to be cured by moral nostrums (e.g., a change of heart, a rededication to the old ways, exorcising evil, and so on). They don't see their dilemmas as structural too—sociological, economic, political. And thus they fail to note that money lusting and wig wearing and tavern frequenting are not only aberrant acts of individuals, but perhaps functionally normal behavior in collectivities at certain historical stages of development.

This is where the jeremiad's "try harder" syndrome breeds ironies. Because it reacts to every incongruous consequence only by restimulating early intent, it sets into motion further consequences which become even more incongruous. For the jeremiad encourages on the level of *motive* the very seeking out of opportunity which it condemns in *result*. It thus releases forces it can neither comprehend nor control. And, ironically, it cannot comprehend or control these forces precisely because it's so busy stimulating them at one end of the intent/consequence plane, and then berating them at the other.

In short, the jeremiad blocks mind from seeing certain kinds of interconnections among things. It may, as we saw earlier, connect the colony's loss of their charter with the frequenting of taverns. But it does not connect its "try harder" nostrum to the building of taverns in the first place. Nor to frontiering. Nor to accumulating wealth. Nor to the wearing of wigs. Nor to any of the other manifold opportunities offered to a people driven to action in a novel and opening world.

Because the jeremiad "labors under an inherent necessity to pile up its tale of woe," it blinds mind to basic reasons for its discontent.[136] By the early eighteenth century, according to Miller, the jeremiad "could no longer pretend to control a process it did not understand. Its technique, its very vocabulary, was limited to itemizing the surface manifestations of a reality which was not a matter of morals but of finance."[137]

Irony itself is not inevitable in Perry Miller's New England. Irony comes only because men make certain kinds of *choices*. But when mind invariably responds to events through the jeremiad form, it almost guarantees that ironies will result. For the jeremiad, in open situations, has a built-in, self-defeating quality. It encourages mind to act, but it blocks mind from pondering what results from those actions. So action—as opposed to apathy—assumes a moral quality of its own for Puritans, becoming in a sense self-justifying. This is one reason why, for Miller, behavior in New England is so characteristically ironic. As he comments on the Puritan ministers: "They would not understand what I mean, but actually in this fashion they were becoming Americanized—all the more speedily because, not obtaining the results they desired, they had to redouble their endeavors."[138]

Fifth, in Perry Miller's ironic world, *forward motion is not always impelled by forward-looking motives.* Sometimes people move into the future looking backward; this is what he means by "crablike progress."[139]

We've noted that when Parrington saw change as forward motion, he inferred that someone must have *planned* it that way. Thus, progress in New England came because progressive liberals like Roger Williams, Thomas Hooker, Anne Hutchinson, Solomon Stoddard, John Wise, Robert Calef held visions of a juster, more humane, and enlightened society, and they labored to translate that vision of a future world into actuality. As they worked for progress, they were fought all along the way by John Winthrop, John Cotton, and Increase and Cotton Mather, conservatives who feared change and used their entrenched powers to block it.

Miller doesn't disagree that what results by the early eighteenth century in

New England can be labeled "progress." Nor does he disagree that Puritan liberals help produce it. But he does disagree that they always have their eyes set on a progressive future when they do what they do. He also disagrees that conservatives resist that future at every point. Progress for Miller doesn't often come about in straightforward ways.

The jeremiad itself, as we've seen, stimulates a more open, variable society. Yet this is hardly its intent. It builds its opener future all the while looking backward to a more homogeneous, stratified order. Its intent is conservative, but its consequence is frequently, and ironically, progressive.

Just as conservative intents can lead to progressive consequences, so progressive ideas don't always grow out of progressive motives. Parrington had looked at New England's incipient rationalism of the early eighteenth century, and explained it as dynamic and aggressive and forward looking. He also saw it as wholly opposed to reactionary interests and dogmas led by the Mathers, Increase and Cotton.

Perry Miller is hardly an apologist for the Mathers. He has little good to say of Increase, and some of the most damning words ever written about Cotton were penned by him. Yet, in Miller's explanation, Cotton Mather is not only the most irrational reactionary in Massachusetts Bay, he's also the colony's most committed rationalist. More than anyone else in New England, Miller's Mather is conversant with the new eighteenth-century forces of reason and science. In this respect, he's the most forward-looking man of his time.[140]

Further, the gentler, more tolerant expressions of rationalism at the time come not from committed, forward-looking liberals but from those whose minds are simply exhausted with all the colony's theological squabbles. Thus Benjamin Wadsworth:

Wadsworth had . . . shown, since his ordination in 1696, a superlative genius for stating the obvious, a gift that was to elevate him eventually, through a series of the dullest utterances in the period, to the Presidency of Harvard College. . . . calling for meekness, forbearance, good manners, Wadsworth said that were all things really searched to the bottom, "we should scarce find two Christians in the whole world exactly of the same mind in all particulars." He ventured to propose that the original assertion of New England—the pure Biblical polity—was actually of less importance than the fact "that we are men, rational Creatures of the same Species, or kind," wherefore we should be induced "to live peaceably and quietly."

"With a simplicity which, in the circumstances, amounted to genius," Miller remarks, "he asked 'why should any man impose his particular notions or opinions upon mee, or I impose mine upon him?' "[141]

Progress is a given for counter-Progressive historians. On this point they don't quibble with their Progressive predecessors. They are not conservatives or reactionaries; most seem to want a society of justice and reason and tolerance and charity. However much they may try and counter Progressive liberalism, they're still men of a liberal persuasion.

Where they disagree with Progressives is not on what progress *is*, but on how you get there, on how progressive change *comes about* in the world. Counter-Progressives don't see change toward justice and reason and tolerance and charity proceeding in straightforward ways. Rather, progress comes in roundabout fashion, conservatives sometimes looking to the future and liberals to the past. Liberal societies don't always come because people planned it that way, they frequently come despite people's plans.

With his ironic explanation, Perry Miller works off the Progressive form. He agrees mostly with the Progressives' beginning and ending points in New England; he just disagrees about how mind changes from the one to the other. As he says, "a society's (like an individual's) image of itself does not stand in so simple a relation to how it behaves."[142]

Sixth, Miller handles ironic change in New England by *taking later consequence and connecting it back to earlier intent.* This makes of irony a distinctively *historical* explanation; it studies the life history of ideas as they move from intent to consequence in the world, through situations.

Progressives saw situations as characteristically "formalistic." In such situations, there was only one way out for them—forward. In a formalistic situation, Progressive historians were not inclined to take an idea there and trace it back to its earlier intents. They were inclined rather to urge it forward, so it could build up sufficient momentum to break through the formalism.

Thus Parrington looked at Jacksonian democracy and saw some of its results as ironic. But he did not—like, say, Marvin Meyers—take these results as a cue to reinvestigate its original intents. He took them instead to indicate that the formalism was imposing, and liberals must renew their efforts to break through it.

Perry Miller, however, takes the early founding intents as his base situation for the New England mind. This is why Richard Mather's *Farewel-Exhortation* opens *Colony;* it sets the original experience and intent of the founders, and shows us the last of the founding leaders straining to reinstill those intents.

In *Colony,* Miller time and again takes some later experience and measures it "against the background of the original expectation."[143] Thus: "By this time [the late 1660s], there were families in Boston, the city on a hill, who no longer spoke to each other."[144]

By thereby detecting the remote consequences of ideas (also the remote intents of consequences), Miller gains what Kenneth Burke has called "perspective by incongruity."[145] Each of mind's acts has a sequel (rather, a sequel of sequels) in the colony. And with his ironic sense of change, Miller not only charts the sequels which follow from each act, but the acts which have preceded each sequel. That is, he writes history both forward and backward. By this procedure, he can keep clear the interconnections between intent and consequence in a historical idea, which interconnections are necessary to his ironic explanation of change.

Seventh, and finally, Perry Miller is enabled to do all this because he assumes a different *role* from Progressive historians. It's distinctively a role for managing ambiguity.

When Progressives saw ambiguity, they strained to cut through it, so they could go on to *do* something, or urge others to. Hence they struck the prophetic persona.

Ambiguity, they felt, paralyzed people. And paralysis was anathema to them—they couldn't just sit back and let things happen. The worst thing people can do is nothing. The point was to be up and doing, and the liberal historian should frame his strategies accordingly. So Progressive histories often took on a latter-day variant of the jeremiad form—pointing to evils in America so people would be stimulated to correct them.[146]

The jeremiad is the main key to Miller's *The New England Mind: From Colony to Province*. But the volume itself is not a jeremiad, not in the Puritan sense at least. It does not galvanize its readers to action, nor is it any manifest effort to project forward some vision of the Good Society and urge Americans to work for it. Miller does not counsel apathy in *Colony*. But he does show time and again how apathy's opposite—*moral intensity*—hung up the Puritans. So where Progressive historians often took on the prophet's role, Miller almost never does. He does make judgments and he frequently takes sides, but they're not the judgments and sympathies of Progressive prophecy.

Miller's role is difficult to label (as are many things in his work); but it seems to manifest that balance of detachment with sympathy which Niebuhr prescribed in his conclusion to *The Irony of American History*. We can see this role at work (if we cannot quite label it) in Miller's chapter "The Judgment of the Witches."

Salem witchcraft was a favorite whipping event for Progressive historians, since it confirmed their worst suspicions about Puritans. It gave them opportunity to reject the whole Puritan order of things, and it put their critics in the untenable position of seeming to defend witch hunts.

Miller, however, believes the progressivist judgment on Salem is simply unhistorical, and the anti-progressivist judgment too apologetic. He proposes a stance outside both parties:

Critics of the Puritan priesthood—often children of that caste—have wrenched the story from its context; sober historians, trying to restore the true setting, slide into the accents of apology and gloss over a crime. One may appreciate that witchcraft was as real an offense in 1692 as murder or treason and yet remain profoundly convinced that what went wrong at Salem is something for which Puritanism and New England are justly to be indicted, not in terms of a more "enlightened" age, but specifically in their own terms—in those of the covenant.[147]

Somewhat like a literary New Critic, Miller takes the order Puritans imposed on reality, and works within that. He doesn't say this is a desirable order, nor even one he would like to live in. He simply says it's *their* order, and he holds them to their word.

He does sympathize with the *problems* of the colony in establishing and maintaining itself, even though he's not concerned to sympathize with Massachusetts Bay as an ideal social order. His concern is to give Puritans a full hearing as they address their dilemmas, in situations; and he rejects "irrelevant intrusions of modern criteria."[148] Paradoxically, Miller rejects modern criteria because they would let Puritans off the hook. Seventeenth-century minds could hardly be held responsible for values which only later centuries had come to know. Their actions would not then be ironic, but tragic, or pathetic, or something else.

In interpreting the witchcraft situation, Miller will not allow sympathy for its victims to jolt him from his core focus on *mind*. He is appalled at what the Puritans did there. He accuses Judge Stoughton's court of murder, and he describes the atmosphere of hysteria much as a Progressive might: "Prisons became crowded, every man's life lay at the mercy of any accuser, brother looked sidewise at brother, and the friend of many years standing became a bad security risk."[149] But Miller's real indignation is not that Puritans did un-progressive or illiberal things back in 1692; it's that they did *un-Puritan* things. For they severely damaged their own cultural identity—the covenant —in their too-intense efforts to defend it (Miller's chapter "Salvaging the Covenant" immediately precedes "The Judgment of the Witches").

A few pages back we saw Miller judging how the witchcraft strategy affected the New England mind. "The real effect of the tragedy," he says, "is not to be traced in the field of politics or society, but in the intangible area of federal theory, and in the still more intangible region of self-esteem." He went on to remark,

Henceforth there was, although for a time desperately concealed, a flaw in the very foundation of the covenant conception. . . . The meaning of New England had been fixed, by Winthrop and the founders, in the language of a covenant; if henceforth there was so much as a shadow of suspicion upon that philosophy, in what realm of significance could the land hold its identity?[150]

And in chapter 5, we looked at Miller judging Cotton Mather's part in this situation. Recall:

Cotton salvaged what defense he could for a court in which he did not believe by the pitiful remonstrance: "Surely, they have at worst been but the faults of a well-meaning Ignorance." We avert our gaze while he, having made what he could of Stephen's notes, fled up the ladder of the jeremiad and soothed himself with fresh dreams of the New Jerusalem, "from whence the Devil shall then be banished, there shall be no Devil within the Walls of that Holy City."[151]

With judgments like these, Perry Miller can be *in* a culture without being *of* it. He can sympathize with its problems without letting those sympathies bind him to its solutions. By such judgments, Miller approaches that ideal critic's role which John Higham spelled out in 1962, when calling for a moral history "beyond consensus."[152]

I'm still not sure what to call this role. It's neither wholly engaged with its subjects, nor wholly detached either. Rather, it's a compound mixture of both. It judges the past by that past's own standards, not by modern criteria. Yet it maintains a perspective outside those standards too, for it doesn't simply write history as apology—saying that whatever happened was right, or inevitable. Its point of focus is on the colony's leaders, yet its sharpest barbs are aimed *at* those leaders.

But whatever we might call it, Miller's role in *Colony* is clearly intended to detect ambiguity and manage it—especially ironic ambiguity. And if this role has any pragmatic uses, it's to counter the pretensions of mind which produce such ironies. Miller's role seems to grow out of a sense of life, and of America, which Reinhold Niebuhr has made manifest in *The Irony:* "Our moral perils are not those of conscious malice or the explicit lust for power. They are the perils which can be understood only if we realize the ironic tendency of virtues to turn into vices when too complacently relied upon; and of power to become vexatious if the wisdom which directs it is trusted too confidently."[153]

XIII

Counter-Progressive historians are often accused of promoting "consensus" in their explanation of American experience. As one of their early critics wrote of them, "The conservative frame of reference is giving us a bland history, in which conflict is muted, in which classic issues of social justice are underplayed, in which the elements of spontaneity, effervescence, and violence in American life get little sympathy or attention."[154]

This accusation breaks down at some basic points, and we'll get into that soon. But it does hold for a few works in the counter-Progressive form, and it catches moments or themes in others. The consensus label is wholly appropriate, I think, for Daniel Boorstin's *The Genius of American Politics.* It's also right for Louis Hartz's *The Liberal Tradition in America—if* we acknowledge that Hartz deplores the uniformity he finds in the nation's past.

Other works in the form have tended to downgrade conflict in their explanation of American experience. Richard Hofstadter, for example, notes in his introduction to *The American Political Tradition:* "The following studies in the ideology of American statesmanship have convinced me of the need for a reinterpretation of our political traditions which emphasizes the common climate of opinion. The existence of such a climate of opinion has been much obscured by the tendency to place political conflict in the foreground of history."[155]

And Stanley Elkins writes in *Slavery:* "If . . . there were such a thing as a pure 'innocence situation,' it might look very much like nineteenth-century America. There, space and mobility prevented the development of a tight social structure in which one had to accept exploitation, aggression, lust, and avarice as a daily problem."[156] Marvin Meyers also notes in *The Jacksonian Persuasion:* "America has never experienced that raw struggle of rich and poor, few and many, recognized at least since Plato as a fundamental source of conflict and change in political society."[157] And in *People of Plenty,* David Potter argues that opportunity and affluence, not conflict between rich and poor, most characterize America's past.

We can find strains of such a position in other counter-Progressive works too—most notably Hofstadter's *The Age of Reform,* Clinton Rossiter's *Seedtime of the Republic,* John William Ward's *Andrew Jackson: Symbol for an Age,* and Lee Benson's *The Concept of Jacksonian Democracy.* Though none of these studies wholly denies conflict in American experience, they don't place it at the center of their picture either. And when they do see conflict, it's rarely between rich and poor, or conservative and liberal. They're not, then, given to the Progressive kind of polarizing.

If consensus *must* logically lie at the opposite pole from polarized conflict, then counter-Progressive works do indeed tend toward consensus. Unlike Progressive histories, they don't dramatize the conflict of polar opposites in the American past; ergo, they must show consensus.

But for most works in the form, this kind of logical deduction doesn't hold up. It doesn't hold up because counter-Progressives don't work with a consensus-versus-conflict model of American experience. Rather, they work with a *counter-balanced* model, where consensus needn't necessarily preclude conflict.

Opposites are linked in the counter-Progressive picture of culture. And their characteristic labels show this paradoxical linkage. Thus Miller projects a picture of "crablike progress" in America's history; and Meyers pictures "the venturous conservative," Lewis "the fortunate fall," Marx "the machine in the garden." And Hofstadter's chapter titles in *The American Political Tradition* express this interconnection of logical opposites—"Thomas Jefferson: the Aristocrat as Democrat," "Andrew Jackson and the Rise of Liberal Capitalism," "Theodore Roosevelt: the Conservative as Progressive," "Woodrow Wilson: the Conservative as Liberal."

But if opposites are linked together in the counter-Progressive form, they're never wholly merged. That is, they still oppose each other, but here *within* the same person (or idea, or movement). Where Progressives set off one thing against another, counter-Progressives picture things set off against themselves. Their sense of America is not so much a uniform consensus, then, but *linked opposites in conflict.*

This picture grows out of the counter-Progressive sense of *role.* The "consensus" label implies that scholars in this form are either detached from the vital realities of life in America, or cowed by political repressions or cultural conformities of the 1950s and 1960s.

Critics have offered little grounded evidence for these charges, however, and they don't stand up well under close reading of works in the form. Several counter-Progressive studies—for example, Hartz's *Liberal Tradition* or Elkins' *Slavery* or Sanford's *Quest for Paradise* or Smith's *Virgin Land* or Ward's *Andrew Jackson*—are written out of profound discontent with America. There's no evidence that they are pressured—or pressured themselves—into muting their criticism because they somehow fear reprisal.

There *is* evidence, though, that they never worked their criticisms into any agenda for social action. The consensus critique implies these scholars are disengaged from the culture. I think that is untrue. They are engaged all right, deeply engaged. The intense passion of their works shows that. But they're engaged as private selves, not as prophets of a social program.

The Progressive role, tending toward historical prophecy, pointed to what was wrong in America, and called for people to *do* something about it. The counter-Progressive role also points to what is wrong, but it rarely frames a strategy for action. Counter-Progressives are not satisfied with things, then, but they don't say how we should move from here to there, from awareness of wrongs to correcting wrongs.

Their quietist role seems to grow out of several moods. Occasionally, it indicates a mood of despair—a sense that America's dilemmas are so overwhelming that there's no visible way out. This role is a strategic counter against Progressivist optimism, and Progressives' faith that every problem has a ready solution. Thus Louis Hartz: "The liberal society analyst is destined in two ways to be a less pleasing scholar than the Progressive: he finds national weaknesses and he can offer no absolute assurance on the basis of the past that they will be remedied. He tends to criticize and then shrug his shoulders, which is no way to become popular, especially in an age like our own."[158]

On other occasions, this quietist role comes from a sense that acting in America is too often hasty, and involves oversimplifying things. Which can breed ironies. Thus Richard Hofstadter: "The most prominent and pervasive failing [of American political culture] is a certain proneness to fits of moral crusading that would be fatal if they were not sooner or later tempered with a measure of apathy and of common sense."[159]

Most often, though, counter-Progressive quietism comes from a feeling that Americans need radically to re-think things; *reflective thought,* they believe, is a necessary prerequisite to acting. Thus they concentrate on re-forming pictures in people's minds, rather than framing programs for social action. Such attitudes are most readily found in the concluding words of counter-Progressive books.

Thus Henry Nash Smith closes *Virgin Land* with:

The capital difficulty of the American agrarian tradition is that it accepted the paired but contradictory ideas of nature and civilization as a general principle of historical and social interpretation. A new intellectual system was requisite before the West could be adequately dealt with in literature or its social development fully understood.[160]

And Leo Marx closes *The Machine in the Garden* with:

We require some new symbols of possibility, and although the creation of those symbols is in some measure the responsibility of artists, it is in greater measure the responsibility of society. The machine's sudden entrance into the garden presents a problem that ultimately belongs not to art but to politics.[161]

And Richard Hofstadter closes *The Age of Reform:*

Much of America still longs for—indeed, expects again to see—a return of the older individualism and the older isolation, and grows frantic when it finds that even our conservative leaders are unable to restore such conditions. In truth we may well sympathize with the Populists and with those who have shared their need to believe that somewhere in the American past there was a golden age whose life was far better than our own. But actually to live in that world, actually to enjoy its cherished promise and its imagined innocence, is no longer within our power.[162]

And Louis Hartz closes *The Liberal Tradition in America:*

Can a people "born equal" ever understand peoples elsewhere that have to become so? Can it ever understand itself? These were the questions which appeared at the beginning of this book; inevitably also they are the questions which appear at the end.[163]

And Marvin Meyers closes *The Jacksonian Persuasion:*

To men of the Jacksonian generation the Old Republic was just out of reach; was seen in something like the full design that Jefferson had drawn; was still directly relevant to their condition. As the image grows remote and small, the Jacksonian persuasion tends to lose either its power or its worth; its power when the appeal to the past turns merely cranky and archaic; its worth when nothing remains but the righteous wrath.[164]

XIV

The counter-Progressive role is designed for a situation sans urgency, where the need for re-forming in America is fundamental, but it needn't be done immediately. So counter-Progressives take their time about it, leisurely turning things over and around, picking up nuances and paradoxes that the more hurried eye might miss.

Where Progressives are readied to participate in the drama of American regeneration, counter-Progressives function more like theater critics. They're intensely concerned with how things are done, but they don't serve as doers themselves. Like Leo Marx in the passage just above, they separate doers off from thinkers, actors from critics, and strive to keep the two roles distinct. Their own role is critically to take apart old pictures of America and occasionally to project new ones. But what these new pictures may mean programmatically is not their job; that's up to the doers and actors, they feel.

Critics charge that this role reflects the bland conformity of Americans during the Eisenhower era, and the political repressions of McCarthyism. It is passive, they say, because it fears the repercussions of doing anything.

As I said before, there is scant evidence for this charge. Further, it ignores the social functioning of academic subcommunities. McCarthyism may have cowed high school teachers, or professors at the more vulnerable state colleges and fundamentalist religious institutions. But scholars at Harvard and Minnesota and Yale and Berkeley and Michigan are not likely to be that vulnerable to outside pressures. Their home institutions can serve as a buffer for them, so also their national professions. This may not insulate them from all outside influences. But it does give them distance and leverage, so they can usually respond to such influences in their own way, and often in their own time.[165]

Counter-Progressives did *respond* to the "climate of opinion" in America during the 1950s and 1960s. Their intent was not to accept that climate, however, but to counter it (save for Daniel Boorstin). To them, America was not an apathetic or tyrannical culture so much as it was *innocent.* They saw innocence as the nation's first failure, and the first thing which needed correcting. Charles Sanford catches this counter-Progressive sense of the American situation as he opens *The Quest for Paradise:*

Kenneth Boulding . . . once told members of an American Studies Association that if he could "explain" President Eisenhower satisfactorily, he would hold the key to the meaning of human history. One sensed in his statement the unspoken assumption that, somehow the entire history of mankind was summed up in the collective experience of the United States of America and projected through the public image of the President. However fanciful and exaggerated this suggestion may appear, it is worth entertaining, for through its short history the United States has notably been a land of quests, and philosophies of history have been largely the studies of quests: the quest for adventure, for riches, for salvation, for power, for survival.

Sanford goes on, tying this general explanation into contemporary American experience:

In a very real sense President Eisenhower personifies an America which has turned its back upon the provincial isolationism which dominated its earlier history and has accepted global responsibilities in the world of nations. But the unaccustomed perplexities and frustrations attending this new outlook have made Americans impatient, baffled, confused. . . . Where one most needs a patient, mature, realistic approach to problems, one meets instead an irrational, immature demonology. This situation relates to the paradox that although Eisenhower is a representative of one of the most advanced, industrial nations on earth, his chief appeal seems to be a naive simplicity which recalls America's preindustrial past.[166]

In the 1950s, one could believe counter-Progressives all the more because Eisenhower was president and John Foster Dulles secretary of state, just as a decade later one could believe New Left historians because Lyndon Johnson (or Richard Nixon) was president and the United States was at war in Viet Nam. To counter-Progressives, America was an innocent culture moving into a situation of world power, where to the New Left America was an authoritarian nation in a situation of empire. The former wanted to bring the culture to self-consciousness, through ending its innocence; the latter wanted to burst the nation's pride, through attacking its injustices. The latter also wanted to bare the "system" structure harboring these injustices, and they sought to create a new, juster system. Hence while the latter is concerned with institutional rearrangements, the former concentrates on mind.

In chapters 7 and 8, we explored vulnerable points in the Progressive form. Basically, it seems, Progressives had most difficulty explaining *recent* American experience, experience near their own times. So also the counter-Progressives, at least in their latter days. If they caught the cultural climate of the 1950s, they failed to anticipate the 1960s. Their explanations hardly got a full hearing among scholars before a rapid succession of events—the assassination of President Kennedy, war in Viet Nam, the black revolt, university confrontations—threatened to outmode it. When things *were* happening, or when things *did* need to be done, then the counter-Progressive role looked much too passive and accepting. And when injustices seemed unambiguous —as in Viet Nam or with the blacks—then the counter-Progressive search for paradox and nuance looked like the wilfull self-indulgence of a leisure class. As Peter Blau said in framing a 1960s intellectual response to the 1950s: " 'Why talk in subtleties,' Tolstoy wrote when criticized for abandoning the complexity of art for the bluntness of polemic, 'when there are so many flagrant truths to be told.' "[167]

A while back we noted Reinhold Niebuhr setting the scene for the counter-Progressive ironic role. "Our moral perils," he asserted, "are not those of conscious malice or the explicit lust for power."[168] Niebuhr wrote that in 1952. But events of the next decade seemed to date him, for America's moral perils *did* then appear to come from conscious malice and the explicit lust for power.

Which is where New Left explanations enter the American scene. Counter-

Progressives had framed no "usable past" to handle those types of experiences. Their strategies had been programmed for ambiguities and ironies and the unanticipated consequences of innocent intents. Conscious malice, explicit power grabbing, overt oppression, unambiguous situations were mostly "anomalous" for the counter-Progressive form. Just as counter-Progressives took Progressive anomalies and moved them to the center of their own form, so the New Left would take counter-Progressive anomalies and move them to the center of *their* form.

New Left historians insist that some situations *are* unambiguous, that reality *can be* hard and substantial as well as symbolic, that explicit power *is* a fact of American life, that some injustices *are* real not imagined, and that things *must* be done to right these injustices. Counter-Progressives, they feel, have clouded over these harsh realities with their concern for symbols and nuances and ironies. Thus Christopher Lasch writes of the counter-Progressive mood:

The defection of intellectuals from their true calling—critical thought—goes a long way toward explaining not only the poverty of political discussion but the intellectual bankruptcy of so much recent historical scholarship. The infatuation with consensus; the vogue of a disembodied "history of ideas" divorced from considerations of class or other determinants of social organization; the obsession with "American studies" which perpetuates a nationalistic myth of American uniqueness—these things reflect the degree to which historians have become apologists, in effect, for American national power in the holy war against communism.[169]

XV

We've concentrated on vulnerabilities and strain points in only one form in this study—the Progressive. We've done that because we're not trying to chart a full history of these three explanation-forms. We're just trying to illustrate something of the *structure* and *process* of mind-change among American historians and cultural analysts. Our intent is to be *suggestive* about twentieth-century historical explanations here, not inclusive.

A fuller history would look also for strain points in counter-Progressive explanations, and for pivotal moments from the counter-Progressive form into the New Left. We might find some of these moments along a *straight-line/ambiguity* plane, and along the plane of *action/quietism*.

The Progressive strategy, as we've seen in chapters 7 and 8, was formed in reaction to unambiguous formalistic situations, and it urged straight-line action to break free from those formalisms. But it couldn't handle ambiguous situations, where such straight-line action might double back on itself and produce ironies.

The counter-Progressive strategy, as we've seen in chapter 8 and this one, was formed in response to experiences Progressives couldn't handle. Counter-Progressives devised a strategy for managing ambiguity, and for explaining change as something other than progress. They pictured themselves in an age of consequences—where ideas must not only be fought for, but lived with. Hence they counseled against straight-line action, showing how frequently it produced ironies.

But as the Progressive form was bound by its founding strategies, so also the counter-Progressive. If counter-Progressives could manage ambiguity and nuance and subtlety and irony in America's experience, they couldn't so effectively handle massive power structures, gross injustice, and situations which cried out for men to do things, quickly and with firm commitments.[170]

So we seem to have come full circle by the mid-1960s—when we hear Warren Susman issue a new radical call for a "usable past" to break Americans free from the formalisms of today. And we may recognize something of the Progressivist prophet's role when we hear Susman say, "Perhaps there will yet be a reawakening, as there was in the 1890s, to the other real need and function of history in our kind of society. Perhaps there will even be another kind of social order."[171]

This may *look* to be a full-circle return to the Progressive situation. And some have even called New Left historians "neo-Progressives." But I think that label is about as appropriate as is "consensus" for the counter-Progressives. It's somewhere around half true, maybe a little less.

To explain wherein New Left historians differ from Progressives, and why, and how, would involve us in another detailed series of "anomaly-planes," "fault-lines," "pivotal moments," and such. And this time not with just two forms but three. Back in chapter 4, we gave hint of these three explanation-forms—Progressive, counter-Progressive, New Left—as they were set up alongside each other. Beyond that we cannot go here. Otherwise, we'd be trying to explain too much historical experience for just one book. And that would be ironic for a study which opened by protesting the burden of information overload in American historical scholarship.

NOTES

1. *The Irony of American History* (Scribner's, paperback, n.d.—first published by Scribner's in 1952), p. vii.

2. Ibid., pp. vii–viii.

3. Ibid., p. viii.

4. Ibid.

5. *Main Currents in American Thought,* vol. 2, *The Romantic Revolution in America, 1800–1860* (Harcourt, Brace and World, Harvest Book, 1954), p. 145.

6. *Irony* (n. 1 above), p. 133.

7. Ibid., p. 28.

8. Ibid., p. 162.

9. Ibid.

10. It's not my first intent here to *promote* an ironic interpretation—only to show how Niebuhr (and later, Perry Miller) have used it. But irony, properly controlled, does hold promise as *a behavioral explanation of the unanticipated in human experience.*

For leads here which might be followed up, see Robert Merton, "The Unanticipated Consequences of Purposive Social Action," *American Sociological Review* (December 1936), 894–904; my "Implicit Irony in Recent American Historiography: Perry Miller's *New England Mind*," *Journal of the History of Ideas*, XXIX, no. 4 (October-December 1968), 579–600; and a forthcoming book-length study by Richard Reinitz, *Ironic America: A Present Vision of the Past.*

11. In putting together this picture of Niebuhr's irony, and in the discussion of Miller later in the chapter, I've drawn freely from my article "Implicit Irony in Recent American Historiography" (ibid.). The *Journal of the History of Ideas* has granted permission for this use.

12. *A Grammar of Motives and A Rhetoric of Motives* (World, Meridian Book, 1962), p. xx (italics in original).

13. *Irony* (n. 1 above), p. 153.

14. Ibid.

15. See here the discussion in Charles Walcutt, "Irony: Vision or Retreat?" *Pacific Spectator* (Autumn 1956), pp. 354–66.

16. *The New England Mind: From Colony to Province* (Beacon, paperback, 1961—first published in 1953 by Harvard), p. 442.

17. *The American Adam: Innocence, Tragedy, and Tradition in the Nineteenth Century* (University of Chicago Press, Phoenix Books, 1958—first published by Chicago in 1955), p. 7.

18. Case Western Reserve Graduate Seminar Paper (Fall 1969).

19. *American Adam* (n. 17 above), p. 1.

20. Ibid., pp. 1–2. Like the cognitive psychologist George Kelly, R. W. B. Lewis looks for the *plane* of thinking with an idea, not the isolated datum of thought.

21. Ibid., p. 2. Lewis, by the way, goes on to cite Perry Miller here as a model for this kind of cultural analysis. In a footnote he writes, "An excellent example of intellectual history seizing upon the dialectical and dramatic qualities of its subject has been the volumes on the New England mind by Perry Miller" (ibid.).

22. Ibid., pp. 155, 2.

23. Ibid., p. 7.

24. Ibid.

25. Ibid. It's not clear why Lewis uses a "party" metaphor for these views. "Voices" is literary in connotation, and that suits his main concern. But "party" is political, and politics is hardly where *The American Adam* points. Party sounds like a Progressive category, not a counter-Progressive one. But Lewis' usage is still counter-Progressive, if his naming is not. When he writes generally of dialogue-cultures in his opening pages, he speaks of voices, but when he goes on to label those voices for early nineteenth-century American culture, he calls them parties. However, he doesn't *handle* them in party-like fashion later in his case analyses. Unlike Parrington, Lewis treats each thinker as an individual voice, not just as a representative of his party. Why he should call them parties, then, is a puzzle. Perhaps he's subtly parodying the Progressives? I don't know.

26. Ibid.

27. Ibid., pp. 7–8.

28. Ibid., p. 7.

29. Ibid., p. 45.

30. Ibid., p. 5. The sense of having a uniquely American "second chance" here is just the reverse of what Daniel Bell meant by "twice-born" in the last chapter. There it was *innocence* which caused death in the first life, and the need for rebirth; and the second life was tempered by a haunting memory of tragedy and paradox. Here it is *tragedy* and *paradox* and *the burden of memory* (Old World habits) which cause death and the need for rebirth; and the second life is to be regenerated by innocence.

31. Ibid.

32. Ibid., p. 3.

33. See for example Richard Sykes' curt dismissal of Lewis' Adamic theme in "American Studies and the Concept of Culture: A Theory and a Method," *American Quarterly*, XV (Summer 1963), 253–70.

34. Recall what was noted of Lewis in the last chapter: "My debt to F. O. Matthies-

sen's *American Renaissance* will be evident on many pages; more important and less evident is a debt to the man himself, to a wise and dedicated teacher and an unforgettable friend" (*American Adam* [n. 17 above], p. iii).

35. *American Renaissance: Art and Expression in the Age of Emerson and Whitman* (Oxford, 1941), p. xi.

36. *American Adam* (n. 17 above), p. 45.

37. Ibid., p. 49.

38. Ibid., p. 117.

39. Ibid., p. 130.

40. Ibid., p. 139.

41. Lewis doesn't mean by irony exactly what Reinhold Niebuhr does, but there are resemblances. Like Niebuhr, Lewis sees life normally as in a state of balanced tension, and through irony he wants to hold a vision of "the doubleness of things" (ibid., p. 24). But unlike Niebuhr, Lewis does not preach that irony is an avoidable product of human pretensions, nor is he so quick to damn "stupid children of light." Where Lewis and Niebuhr most resemble each other, though, is on their shared picture of experience as *ambiguous*. It's on this simplicity/ambiguity plane where they take the opposite position from Progressives.

42. Ibid., pp. 132–33.

43. Ibid., pp. 1, 198.

44. *The Liberal Imagination* (Doubleday, Anchor Book, 1957), pp. xi–xii.

45. *American Adam*, p. 89.

46. Ibid., p. 9.

47. Ibid., p. 193.

48. Ibid., p. 196.

49. Ibid., pp. 195–96.

50. Ibid., p. 196.

51. Seminar comment of James Gilreath, April 8, 1971. The question was originally posed by Dan Velucci, on the same evening.

52. Lewis, for example, cites Locke's dictum as a characteristic faith of his party of hope. *The American Adam*, p. 42.

53. This question opens Smith's *Virgin Land,* the original of the symbol-myth-image school. *Virgin Land: The American West as Symbol and Myth* (Random House, Vintage Book, n.d.—first published in 1950 by Harvard), p. 3. Lewis cites Smith in *The American Adam,* saying that *Virgin Land* "is rich in suggestive information about the historic notions of the new Eden and the new Adam" (p. 100). Smith is also cited by Ward, Meyers, Taylor, Marx, and Sanford—in short, all the symbol-myth-image authors noted above. Out of such intercommunications are "paradigm communities" built (though this one never sustained enough momentum to become quite a paradigm, I think).

54. *The Quest for Paradise: Europe and the American Moral Imagination* (University of Illinois Press, 1961), p. vi.

55. A notable exception is Alan Trachtenberg's *Brooklyn Bridge: Fact and Symbol* (Oxford, 1965). By focusing on a particular, rooted thing—the Brooklyn Bridge—Trachtenberg is enabled to take experience on its least abstract level. On this level, the bridge is simply a *thing,* a mode of transportation and a phenomenon of structural engineering. But he can also move to the bridge at its most abstract symbolic level in the culture—as an expression of "the peaceful mastery of nature" (p. 8) and the last link in "Columbus' efforts to find a passage to India" (p. 76). And Trachtenberg handles it on levels in between too—the pragmatics of promoting and financing, the machinations of power politics and political corruption, and so on. Hence *Brooklyn Bridge: Fact and Symbol* gives us the experience of this bridge on several different levels—from Tammany Hall on the one end to Hart Crane on the other, and to the Roeblings moving back and forth in between. A Charles Sanford will abstractly *tell* us that a cultural symbol functions on many levels simultaneously; but Alan Trachtenberg goes on to *show* us, in concrete, manageable detail. It's the most focused, and grounded, of all the symbol-myth-image works.

56. For my critique of the symbol-myth-image school here, I have profited by discussions with Rush Welter, and from reading Welter's fine article, "The History of

Ideas in America: An Essay in Redefinition," *Journal of American History,* LI (March 1965), 599–614.

57. For critics' pictures of Perry Miller, see Michael McGiffert's comprehensive article, "American Puritan Studies in the 1960's," *William and Mary Quarterly,* 3rd ser. XXVII, 1 (January 1970), 36–67. McGiffert notes what critics have said of Miller on "mind":

"Everett H. Emerson avers that 'we now recognize Puritanism as much less unified than Miller made it out to be.' Similarly, John M. Bumstead holds that 'there is no such animal as "New England" or "American" Puritanism as a monolithic intellectual religious, or ecclesiastical entity.' Sydney Ahlstrom refers to 'the Puritan Mind' and 'Massachusetts "Orthodoxy"', as 'fallacious concretions'; Kenneth Silverman sees only heterodoxy in Massachusetts—'a welter of uncertainty among Puritans themselves regarding practically every religious, political, literary, and social notion entertained' in seventeenth-century New England (pp. 40–41)."

All of which sounds reasonable enough. Save for one problem. From Everett Emerson down through Kenneth Silverman, the critics above mistake a historians' stereotype of "mind" for what Perry Miller means by it. As I hope to show in the pages which follow, Miller pictures mind in a way much different from our normal preconceptions in American historical scholarship. I wish to thank here my colleague in Miller studies, Karen Lystra, for radically redirecting my own preconceptions about the meaning of mind in Perry Miller, and for thus saving me from some grievous errors. Lystra is now engaged in a book-length study of Miller's critics which, when completed, should go well beyond things I've only suggested here.

58. *Errand into the Wilderness* (Harper, Torchbook, 1964—first published by Harvard in 1956), p. ix.

59. *The New England Mind: The Seventeenth Century* (Beacon, paperback, 1961—first published in 1939 by Macmillan), p. xii. The statement is from Miller's 1961 preface to the paperback edition.

60. It's odd that this is the most notable instance of Miller's notorious contempt for non-intellectual history, yet his actual words are not so much scornful as favorable. What he said was: "I am the last to decry monographs on stoves or bathtubs, or tax laws, banks, the conduct of presidential elections, or even inventories of artifacts. All this is the warp and woof of American history. . . . Even so, I was condemned to another (I do not say a better) sort of quest" (*Errand,* pp. vii–viii). Anyone familiar with Miller's writing knows that of course he *does* mean better. But here (for once) he was polite enough not to say so.

61. Alan Simpson, *Puritanism in Old and New England* (University of Chicago Press, Phoenix Books, 1961—first published by Chicago in 1955), p. 21.

Miller, I fear, is one of the more notable victims of the poverty of historical criticism in the profession. His works are vulnerable to challenge on many levels, and scholars like Darrett Rutman, Kenneth Lockridge, Edmund Morgan, John Demos, Philip Greven, and Stephen Foster are doing much to update Miller's interpretations, and correct errors in them. But a scholar has a right to be challenged for his own errors, and stereotypes, not for someone else's. *Winthrop's Boston,* for example, may demolish what Darrett Rutman conceives as "mind" in early New England, but only tangentially does it get to Perry Miller's conception. Alan Simpson may believe that by concentrating so much on mind one must necessarily ignore feelings, but Miller doesn't buy that mind-emotions dualism; and anyone who reads his work with care should see why. And David Hackett Fischer, who has a fine enough mind to know better, uses Miller as an example of "the idealist fallacy" in history studies. Citing two statements from Miller's prefaces, then echoing Simpson's criticism for support, Fischer writes that "both volumes of the *New England Mind* tend, in the fashion of idealist history, to consider narrowly rational thought. . . . Miller made much—too much—of fine-drawn dichotomies, but not enough of the emotional cement which was the inner bond of Puritan belief" (*Historians' Fallacies: Toward a Logic of Historical Thought* [Harper and Row Torchbook, 1970], p. 198).

Which makes one doubt if Fischer ever went into *The New England Mind* beyond its prefaces, or beyond what Simpson charged of Miller. Could anyone actually watch Miller handling the Mathers—Richard, Increase, Cotton—or Solomon Stoddard or

John Wise or Benjamin Wadsworth or the Half-Way Covenant or the witchcraft tragedy, and still claim he deals with "narrowly rational thought"? Miller himself is partly at fault for these misunderstandings. For his prefaces are so energetic that they offer critics a visible target for attack, and ridicule. Some critics, I suspect, never get beyond these prefaces. In any case, Miller's critics too frequently attack *the profession's* categories of "mind" and "idealism" and "emotions," and fail to investigate Miller's own, as they develop in his histories.

Because there is no powerful ethic in the profession insisting that we *read* full history works, and carefully, and through *their own* categories, we seldom get far into the minds of those who would re-arrange these categories of ours. We are urged instead to read "original" documents, not "secondary" histories. And thus a Perry Miller—like Melville in Miller's own *Raven and the Whale*—falls through the slats between categories too narrow to support him, and too inflexibly wooden to catch him.

Miller is a rebuke to a history profession which persists in believing that its subject matter is only "out there," not a dialogue between "out there" and "in here," and which thereby locates its "primary" documents wholly in the external world, seldom in the historian's mind which perceives that world. The first failing of Miller criticism in the profession is clear—*it simply hasn't gone to the primary sources and inspected them with enough care,* primary sources in this case meaning the books and articles Perry Miller wrote.

62. The best brief introduction to Miller and Miller studies is Robert Middlekauff's fine essay—"Perry Miller," in Marcus Cunliffe and Robin Winks, eds., *Pastmasters: Some Essays on American Historians* (Harper and Row, 1969), pp. 167–90.

For useful reviews of the critical scholarship in and around Miller, see McGiffert, "American Puritan Studies in the 1960's" (n. 51 above), and Richard Schlatter, "The Puritan Strain," in John Higham, ed., *The Reconstruction of American History* (Harper and Row, Torchbook, 1962), pp. 25–45.

See also, for critical studies of Miller, David Hollinger, "Perry Miller and Philosophical History," *History and Theory* (Fall 1968), pp. 189–202; Edmund Morgan, "Perry Miller and The Historians," *Harvard Review,* II, no. 2 (Winter-Spring 1964), 52–59; Alan Heimert, "Perry Miller: An Appreciation," *Harvard Review,* II, no. 2 (Winter-Spring 1964), 30–48; Richard Reinitz, "Perry Miller and Recent American Historiography," *Bulletin of the British Association of American Studies,* 8 (June 1964), 27–35; and my "Implicit Irony in Recent American Historiography" (n. 10 above).

63. *Seventeenth* (n. 59 above), p. vii.

64. This is especially the case with Miller's 90 pages on Ramist logic, which make for some of the most abstract writing anywhere in American historical scholarship. Save for a few pages at the beginning of this analysis, and a page or two at the end, the reader wonders if he's stumbled into a treatise on systematic philosophy, not a work of history (ibid., pp. 116–206).

65. Reported by Peter Gay in *A Loss of Mastery: Puritan Historians in Colonial America* (California, 1966), p. 142.

66. *Seventeenth,* p. vii.

67. I've described at some more length a Progressive explanation of this change in my "Implicit Irony in Recent American Historiography" (n. 10 above). Only there I used Thomas Jefferson Wertenbaker's *The Puritan Oligarchy* as my case example, not Parrington.

68. *The New England Mind: From Colony to Province* (n. 16 above), foreword.

69. "A Model of Christian Charity," in Edmund Morgan, ed., *Puritan Political Ideas, 1558–1794* (Bobbs-Merrill, paperback, 1965), pp. 92–93.

70. *Colony,* (n. 16 above), p. 248.

71. *History: Humanistic Scholarship in America* (Prentice-Hall, 1965), p. 227.

72. Of the four "Books" in *Colony,* the first three are titled "Declension," "Confusion," and "The Splintering of Society."

73. *Colony,* p. 442.

74. *Liberal Imagination* (n. 44 above), p. 186.

75. *Colony,* pp. 326, 191.

76. Ibid., pp. 297, 314.

77. Ibid., preface to the 1961 Beacon paperback edition.

78. Ibid., p. foreword to original 1953 edition.
79. Ibid.
80. Ibid.
81. Ibid., p. 367.
82. Ibid., p. 178.
83. *Historians' Fallacies,* p. 198.
84. Raymond College American Civilization Journal (May, 1969).
85. *Colony,* p. 159.
86. Ibid., 1961 preface.
87. Ibid.
88. Ibid., p. 206.
89. Review of *The New England Mind: From Colony to Province,* in *New England Quarterly,* 27, no. 1 (March 1954), p. 116.
   In his 1961 preface to the paperback republication of *Colony,* Miller petulantly dismisses this observation of Bailyn, saying it "implied that therefore that construct ['the New England mind'] was floating in thin air, like some insubstantial island of Laputa." Which is simply false. Perry Miller was evidently so girded for critics who misunderstood him that he wasn't prepared to understand an understanding one.
90. For how subsequent Puritan scholarship has confirmed or disconfirmed Miller, see McGiffert, "American Puritan Studies in the 1960's" (n. 57 above).
   See also the forthcoming study by Karen Lystra, *Perry Miller and His Critics,* and two brilliant papers by Richard Reinitz, "Perry Miller's Irony: The Convergence of Intellectual and Social Histories of American Puritanism," and "Irony as a Strategy for American History" (the first delivered at the December, 1969 convention of the American Historical Association, in Washington, D.C., the second at the April, 1971 convention of the Organization of American Historians, in New Orleans).
91. *Colony,* p. 330.
92. See the fuller description of situation-strategy analysis in sections IX and X of chapter 5. I've drawn freely here, and in chapter 5, from two unpublished conference papers of mine on the situation-strategy method. The first, "Strategy for American Studies," was read at a northern California American Studies Association meeting, held at the Davis campus in October, 1968. The second, "Handling Ideas 'Strategically': Perry Miller, Intellectual History, and the 'Situational' Approach," was read at a convention of the Organization of American Historians, held in New Orleans in April, 1971. My discussion here has benefitted from the responses of H. Bruce Franklin, Richard Reinitz, and Larzer Ziff, who served as critics of the first paper, and from Jurgen Herbst, who served as critic of the second. I've also been much informed by the criticisms of Robert Skotheim, Rush Welter, and Karen Lystra, who read those papers in draft.
93. I'm indebted to Karen Lystra for suggesting that Erik Erikson's term "identity crises" might be applied to Miller's "situations" in *Colony.*
94. It was in mulling over *Colony* that I first came to see the opportunities of "pivotal-moment" analysis for the understanding of historical idea-change.
95. *The Progressive Historians* (Knopf, 1968), p. 401.
96. "Spectroscope for Ideas," *Kenyon Review,* XVI (Spring 1954), 316. "Situation-strategy" is not only Miller's method for handling *others'* ideas in *Colony,* I suspect it helped him hold his *own* mind under control too. There is a strain in Perry Miller towards reifying mind—giving it a self-generating power and making it almost a species of its own. Through his situational method, however, Miller counters this drive, pulling his abstractions back down toward the concrete, forcing them to move in the world among men and things and events. What we have in *Colony* is a working out of these two strains—one impelling his mind toward the abstract, the other pulling it back into the concrete. We can read the book as a kind of dialectic revelation of Miller's own mind, then. It thrusts powerfully in one direction toward ordering and generalizing and continually proclaiming something or other "commence[s] a new chapter in the history of the provincial mind" (p. 296). But it thrusts just as powerfully (or almost) in the opposite direction too—trying to convey the rich, uncategorized details of life and world in New England.
   Miller controls this dialectic in *Colony* by straining his generalizations through what

is sometimes a bewildering maze of detail. Characteristically, he'll begin a chapter by pointing to some dilemma besetting the Puritans. Then he'll move into an actual situation where they must confront that dilemma head-on, and he'll describe all the complexities and convolutions and incongruities there (not only actual ones but potential ones too). He'll do this in such a profusion of names and events and hints and opaque references that even the alert reader can get hopelessly lost. Then at about the point where it seems Miller is lost too and has forgotten his original dilemma, he pulls back out of the maze to explain just how the Puritans responded to this dilemma with their strategic ideas. He'll also go on, in that chapter or some later one, to chart how those strategies got snagged on some other situation which they were compelled to respond to, but which they were ill-formed to handle. His procedure here is an example of the "experience-explanation" strategy we noted at the end of chapter 2.

It's this procedure which makes *Colony* so long and involved (and which may explain why some of Miller's critics evidently never got much beyond his prefaces). Some of Herman Melville's readers have had the same problem, objecting to his mass of detail on whaling in *Moby-Dick*. But the details, I think, serve similar strategic functions for both Melville and Perry Miller—not merely to convey an imposing run of facts, but to give substance and variation (what R. W. B. Lewis calls "coloration") to their generalizing symbols, and thus to control the general by immersing it in the particular and to elevate the particular by pulling it out toward the general.

97. *Colony*, p. 3.

98. Ibid., p. 5.

99. Ibid., p. 122.

100. Ibid., p. 5.

101. Ibid., p. 11.

102. Ibid., p. 13.

103. Ibid., p. 14.

104. Ibid., p. 11.

105. Richard Mather's dilemma here parallels that of Frederick Jackson Turner in chapter 7—how to transmit an idea when the grounded experience for it has passed?

106. *Colony*, p. 31.

107. Ibid., p. 28.

108. Ibid., p. 29.

109. Ibid., p. 178.

110. Ibid., p. 24.

111. Ibid., p. 51.

112. Ibid., p. 275.

113. Ibid., p. 40.

114. *The Structure of Scientific Revolutions* (University of Chicago Press, paperback, 1970—first published by Chicago in 1962), p. 111 ff.

115. *Colony*, foreword to original 1953 edition.

116. Ibid., p. 484.

117. Ibid., p. 51.

118. For further on this, see my "Implicit Irony in Recent American Historiography: Perry Miller's *New England Mind*," (n. 10 above). See also Richard Reinitz, "Perry Miller's Irony: The Convergence of Intellectual and Social Histories of American Puritanism" (n. 62 above).

119. *Colony*, p. 65.

120. Ibid., p. 5.

121. I say "for the most part" because no strategy could possibly manage all the contingencies in any open situation.

122. *Colony*, p. 366.

123. See Alvin Toffler on future shock and information overload. *Future Shock* (Random House, 1970), 305–26.

124. *Colony*, p. 364.

125. Ibid., p. 366.

126. Domestic jeremiads ceased during those three years, by the way. This reveals an important "strategic silence" in the New England mind. The jeremiad strategy works

when people can control their own destiny. When they lose this control, as in the Andros interregnum, then the jeremiad strategy simply won't work. For it has no way of addressing people who can't cure evils by their own will (or feel they can't).

127. *Colony*, p. 179.

128. Ibid., p. 204.

129. Ibid., p. 207.

130. *Progressive Historians,* p. 422.

131. *Colony*, pp. 212, 363.

132. Ibid., pp. 214–15.

133. Ibid., p. 67.

134. Ibid., p. 51.

135. Ibid., p. 40.

136. Ibid., p. 179.

137. Ibid., p. 309.

138. Ibid., p. 214.

139. Ibid., p. 442.

140. See here Miller's chapters on "Do-Good," "Reason," and "The Experimental Philosophy," ibid., pp. 395–446.

141. Ibid., p. 248.

142. Ibid., p. 164.

143. Ibid., p. 248.

144. Ibid., p. 107.

145. *Permanence and Change: An Anatomy of Purpose* (Bobbs-Merrill, paperback, 1965), p. 69 ff.

146. For more on this jeremiad strategy in progressivist histories, see David Noble, *Historians against History: The Frontier Thesis and the National Covenant in American Historical Writing since 1830* (Minnesota, 1965).

147. *Colony*, pp. 191–92.

148. Ibid., p. 192.

149. Ibid., pp. 204, 195.

150. Ibid., p. 207.

151. Ibid., p. 204.

152. "Beyond Consensus: The Historian as Moral Critic," *The American Historical Review*, LXVII, no. 3 (April 1962), 609–25.

Higham writes here, "The historian is not called upon to establish a hierarchy of values, but rather to explore a spectrum of human potentialities and achievements. While maintaining its own integrity, while preserving the detachment that time and distance afford, he must participate in variety, allowing his subjects as much as possible to criticize one another. . . . In the simplest sense, the historian commits to moral criticism all the resources of his human condition. He derives from moral criticism an enlarged and disciplined sensitivity to what men ought to have done, what they might have done, and what they achieved" (pp. 614–15). This seems precisely what Miller set out to do in *Colony*—and what, for the most part, he achieved.

153. *Irony* (n. 1 above), p. 133.

154. John Higham, "Beyond Consensus" (n. 152 above), p. 616. This "consensus" critique has a fascinating life history—indeed, at times almost an ironic one. The critique began in 1959, with an article by Higham in *Commentary*. Charging that a "cult" of consensus had developed in American historical writing, Higham said that recent historians were "carrying out a massive grading operation to smooth over America's social convulsions." He closed his article by calling for renewed "appreciation of the crusading spirit, a responsiveness to indignation, a sense of injustice" ("The Cult of the 'American Consensus': Homogenizing Our History," XVII, *Commentary* [February 1959], pp. 96, 100).

This 1959 article by Higham seems to be one of the "pivotal moments" in the movement from counter-Progressive to New Left in American historical explanations. For the "consensus" label soon caught momentum—pressuring the counter-Progressive form at certain vulnerable points, and preparing the way for an alternative form. The label's history is at times ironic, though, for the initial push against consensus came from *within* the counter-Progressive form. It was begun by counter-Progressives who dissented from some of their colleagues on some things, but who were not prepared for a radically new form.

Three years after his "Cult" piece, Higham urged historians to reach for a moral stance "beyond consensus." And that same year, in an article criticizing the "consensus-continuity" position, Rogers Hollingsworth predicted that "it will not be long before historians . . . again stress the variety, change, and conflict which have made American history so rich in human experience" ("Consensus and Continuity in Recent American Historical Writing," *South Atlantic Quarterly* [Winter 1962], p. 50).

Hollingsworth's prediction proved correct. For soon New Left historians would do just what he said, and in the doing dissent yet further from "consensus" history. In a slashing attack on Richard Hofstadter's *Age of Reform,* for example, Norman Pollack contended that "the consensus framework and McCarthyism are, far from being at opposite poles, actually one and the same trend." Detecting "an unmistakable sign of stereotypic thinking" in consensus historians, Pollack claimed their works expressed "a desire to eliminate uncertainty from one's existence." "It is difficult to escape the conclusion," he said, "that the critics of Populism . . . exhibit the very traits of authoritarianism they impute to others" ("Fear of Man: Populism, Authoritarianism, and the Historian," *Agricultural History,* 39, no. 2 [1965], 7–8).

Three years after Pollack, Barton Bernstein introduced a collection of New Left essays by pushing off against "consensus" history. He closed this introduction by referring back to Higham's 1962 article: "We have, by necessity, moved beyond objective history to the realm of values. In this venture we are . . . responding in a modest way to the call issued a few years ago to move 'beyond consensus' " (Bernstein, ed., *Towards a New Past: Dissenting Essays In American History* [Random House, Vintage Book, 1969—first published by Pantheon in 1968], p. xiii).

In the meantime, John Higham was having second thoughts. In his 1965 book *History,* Higham moderated his earlier attack on consensus histories, and in 1969 he wrote, "The whole fuss about 'consensus' and 'conflict' has become stale and hackneyed, and the sooner it subsides the better." A year later, Higham noted of his 1962 "Beyond Consensus" article, "Writing at the height of the conservative reaction against progressive history, I feared it would go too far. It did go too far, and we are now in the throes of an impetuous reaction against that reaction." This "impetuous reaction"— the New Left—dismayed Higham. He felt there was little distinctive in the New Left explanation save its hostility to liberalism, and he noted that it was "sustained by a common American tendency to associate boldness and energy with innovation." He also noted, "It has tended to be casual or superficial in accounting for social change."

Personal communication from Higham, January 19, 1969; *Writing American History* (Indiana University Press, 1970), pp. 138, 167, 168.

The history of this "consensus-conflict" controversy might make for an interesting case study in historians' labeling, and in the tendency of these labels sometimes to move beyond their framers' intents. For more on the New Left reaction to "consensus" histories, see Irwin Unger, "The 'New Left' and American History: Some Recent Trends in United States Historiography," *American Historical Review,* LXXII (July 1967), 1237–63. For case studies in the "consensus" school, see my "Implicit Irony in Recent American Historiography," and "Political 'Reality' in Recent American Scholarship: Progressives v. Symbolists," *American Quarterly,* XIX, no. 2, pt. 2 (Summer 1967), 303–28. In these studies, I reject the consensus label. Finally, for a superb brief review of the whole counter-Progressive–consensus framework, see John Higham's chapter "A Search for Stability," in *History,* 212–32.

155. *The American Political Tradition, and the Men Who Made It* (Knopf, Vintage Book, n.d.—first published in 1948 by Knopf), p. vii.

156. *Slavery: A Problem in American Institutional and Intellectual Life* (University of Chicago Press, paperback, 1968—first published in 1959 by Chicago), p. 162.

157. *The Jacksonian Persuasion: Politics and Belief* (Stanford Paperback, 1960— first published in 1957 by Stanford), p. vi.

158. *The Liberal Tradition in America* (Harcourt, Brace and World, Harvest Book, n.d.—first published in 1955), p. 32.

159. *The Age of Reform: From Bryan to F.D.R.* (Random House, Vintage Book, 1960—first published in 1955), p. 15.

160. *Virgin Land* (n. 53 above), p. 305.

161. *The Machine in the Garden: Technology and the Pastoral Ideal in America* (Oxford, 1964), p. 365.

162. *Age of Reform* (n. 159 above), p. 328.

163. *Liberal Tradition* (n. 158 above), p. 309.

164. *Jacksonian Persuasion* (n. 157 above), p. 275.

165. For an empirical study supporting this contention that professors were not so cowed by McCarthyism, see Paul Lazarsfeld and Wagner Thielens, Jr., *The Academic Mind* (Free Press, 1958).

166. *Quest for Paradise* (n. 154 above), pp. 1–2. For more on this "innocence" explanation in counter-Progressive scholarship, see Robert Skotheim's review essay, " 'Innocence' and 'Beyond Innocence' in Recent American Scholarship," *American Quarterly*, XIII, no. 1 (Spring 1961), 93–99.

167. "Relevance: The Shadow of a Magnitude," *Daedalus*, 98, no. 3 (Summer 1969), p. 657.

168. *Irony* (n. 1 above), p. 133.

169. "The Cultural Cold War: A Short History of the Congress for Cultural Freedom," in Bernstein, ed., *New Past* (n. 154 above), p. 323.

See also, for Lasch's response to counter-Progressive thinking, "The Anti-Intellectualism of the Intellectuals," in *The New Radicalism in America, 1889–1963: The Intellectual as a Social Type* (Knopf, 1965), 286–349. See especially his comments on Reinhold Niebuhr there—pp. 299–306.

170. Stanley Elkins' *Slavery* is an exception to these comments. That book *does* handle a situation where gross injustice is perpetrated by a massive power structure. *Slavery* is a sort of half-way study between the counter-Progressive form and the New Left. Or rather, it's a characteristically counter-Progressive explanation applied to a characteristically New Left kind of experience.

171. "History and the American Intellectual: Uses of a Usable Past," *American Quarterly*, XVI, no. 2, pt. 2 (Summer 1964), 263.

APPENDIX

Appendix: Taking a "Strategic Journey": Some Questions for Inquiry

"Historical evidence is not a previously known entity, like a continent; when it emerges, it comes in response to questions which need it."
Cushing Strout, "Ego Psychology and the Historian," *History and Theory* (1968)

"There is some heuristic value in suggesting that a given literary text is analogous to a response to an interview schedule for which the questions have been lost. The text embodies the response in a complex form, and the meaning of the work may be specified, in part, by reconstructing the 'questions' to which the author was responding."
Gordon Kelly, "Literature and the Historian," *American Quarterly* (May, 1974)

In keeping with the conversational mode of this inquiry, I thought to include for this edition a sample checklist of questions that may help readers initiate a dialogue with their authors. The questions are based on assumptions developed in chapters 3 and 6, that a book or article is a form of human behavior, acts of a particular person putting a particular construction upon reality. The inquisitive reader, then, is asked to discover how that construction is put together—in effect, to try and re-enact the human choices that led to this distinctive construct-ing of reality rather than some other.

The questions are intended as tools for the reader, offering leverage in this effort to simulate an ongoing conversation with the author. Their function is close to what Gordon Kelly has suggested in the epigraph above—that is, a book can be taken as the completed response to an interview schedule for which the original questions are missing, and it is up to the book's critic to re-enact the questions to which the text is in effect a response.[1]

The list below is not intended as comprehensive. Rather, it is a brief sample suggesting some kinds of questions a reader might pose of a book or article (or a poem, play, painting, or material artifact, allowing for adjustment in medium). In keeping with the "journey" metaphor of inquiry outlined in chapter 6, I have separated the questions into three stages—(1) doing close literary analysis inside the text, (2) connecting outward from the text to worlds and lives around the text, and (3) moving back into the text again to check specifically how outside realities affect the constructed reality inside.

The three stages of the journey are not totally discrete of course, thus some questions apply to more than one stage at a time. This is because the intent of the questions is *to cultivate a textual-contextual habit of reading* that respects the integrity of both the text and the outside world, yet also studies arenas of interconnection between them. The questions thus point toward a criticism at once literary and cultural, founded in both humanistic and social scientific strategies for inquiry.

(1) The Constructed World Inside the Text

—What seems to be the author's perceived "*situation*," to which the book or essay is a "*strategic response*"? That is, for what purpose do you think the author wrote the book? (or, in Kenneth Burke's terms, what is the book's "burden"?)

—What are the author's *basic constructs* for ordering experience? (substitute "categories of explanation," "components of reality," or whatever) What clusters with what in the author's constructs? What clusters against what? Along what *planes* do the constructs run? (e.g., love/hate, order/disorder, freedom/constraint—see the chart on Vernon Louis Parrington, p. 256)

—In the cognitive psychologist George Kelly's terms, do the author's constructs tend to be relatively *permeable*, or *impermeable*? (e.g., Frederick Jackson Turner's and Quentin Compson's are relatively impermeable—that is, more or less closed off to disconfirming experience; Perry Miller's, Dilsey's, Carl Becker's, and Martin Duberman's are relatively permeable)

—Does the author have some kind of "*unmoved mover*" in his/her mode of explanation, something that makes everything else go? (e.g., for Richard Hofstadter in *The Age of Reform*, ideas; for Daniel Boorstin in *The Americans*, the pragmatic actualities of American life; for Robert Wiebe in *The Search for Order*, the power of impersonal institutions)

—Are there major *strains* in the author's characteristic mode of explanation? If so, where precisely are they, and do they recur throughout the work? Does the author seem to be aware of the strain, or not? How does the author cope with strain? (see for example the analysis in chapter 7, "'When Prophecy Fails': Turner, Progressives, and Paradigm Strain.")

—What kinds of experiences is the author best attuned to explaining? Least?

—How does the author conceive his/her *role* in the work? (i.e., what persona or mask does the author wear?—detached scholar? social reformer? prophet? chronicler? judge? citizen . . . of the world? . . . of the nation? . . . of some subgroup in the world or nation?)

—What *mood* or *tone* does the author write in? Does this mood or tone change depending on the particular situation inside the work? (e.g., Reinhold Niebuhr often assumes the tone of an angry prophet; Frederick Jackson Turner is sometimes the professorial explainer, sometimes the elevating poet, sometimes the dry chronicler, sometimes the anxious cultural cheer-leader)

—What or whom does the author most identify with? (e.g., the academic profession? [John Snell, in *History as a Career*] the larger American culture? [Daniel Boorstin in *The Genius of American Politics*] the human race? [Barry Commoner in *The Closing Circle*] some subgroup in the culture? [John Blassingame in *The Slave Community*].

—Who does the author think is his/her *audience*, or "readers-to-be"? Do you think the author in fact reaches the audience he/she intends to reach?

—How *detached* or *committed* is the author? How self-aware is he or she of same? (e.g., Norman Pollack in *The Populist Response to Industrial America* is committed but not self-aware; Martin Duberman in *The Uncompleted Past* is committed *and* self-aware)

—What is the author's *praxis*—that is, what does he/she want the reader to do upon finishing the work? (e.g., research the matter further? sympathize with one side or another in some historical drama? vote for one party over another in the next political election?)

—What is the function of historical-cultural explanation for the author? (e.g., for Parrington, to vitalize the liberal spirit; for Carl Becker in "Everyman His Own Historian," to pay his coal bills intelligently; for Lionel Trilling, to convey a sense of life's infinite complexities)

—What, for the author, is *the basic locus of cultural reality*, or, in the contemporary vernacular, how does the author locate "where the action is"? (e.g., for R. W. B. Lewis, in the dialogue of ideas; for Philip Greven, in the impersonal functioning of collective institutions; for Tom Wolfe, in the drama of personal life-styles; for Kai Erikson, in dynamics of the cultural scene)

—How does the author think a culture is put together, and how does it continue to function? (e.g., by a willing contract of the people? by force and manipulation? by persuasion? by habit and custom? by commitment to certain cultural ideals?)

—Does the author see the culture under review working on several different levels, or is it pretty much all of a piece? Is the culture *homogeneous,* or *heterogeneous*?

—Does the author prefer *strife,* or *tranquillity,* in a culture? *Justice,* or *order*? How much of each?

—Does the author think *change* a good thing, or does he/she like things pretty stable? If change, how much, and how would he/she prefer it be brought about? If not change, does the author suggest how to cope with forces that nonetheless promote change?

—What *single word* (phrase, sentence, paragraph, chapter, section) best represents or crystallizes the work? Why?

—What are the author's *code terms* or phrases? (e.g., with R. W. B. Lewis, "innocence," "evil," "irony"; Alexis de Tocqueville, "democracy," "equality") What terms rally around each other? What terms push off against each other? (see for example the charts on pp. 191, 256)

—Is there anything revealing in how the author *opens* the book or essay? *Closes* it? (see for example the discussion of Frederick Jackson Turner's "Frontier" essay, pp. 187 ff.)

—Where are the book's most revealing *moments*? (e.g., in *The Sound and the Fury,* Benjy's bellowing at being driven around the town square backward; in Parrington, his lament in Volume III that young radicals seem to be displacing old liberals these days)

—What *strategies for focus,* or devices for getting a handle on experience, does the author use? (e.g., Perry Miller in *Colony* uses situations; Parrington uses individuals and regional "minds"; John William Ward uses intellectual themes in *Andrew Jackson: Symbol for an Age*)

—How well does the author *control* his/her subject matter? (e.g., Tocqueville, Arthur Schlesinger, Jr., Tom Wolfe, and Hannah Arendt exercise remarkable control over their materials; Reinhold Niebuhr, Alvin Toffler, and Gordon Wood [in *The Creation of the American Republic*] sometimes lose control and let their materials lead them around—as do many authors of doctoral dissertations)

—Is there *fat* in the work? Could sections and ways of doing things be squeezed out? (e.g., for T. W. Adorno et al. in *The Authoritarian Personality,* yes; for R. W. B. Lewis in *The American Adam,* no)

—What "population" does the author take his/her observations from? Does the author make the sources plain to the reader?

—How does the author employ his/her sources? Quotation? (Robert Skotheim) Paraphrase? (Parrington) Total recreation? (Tocqueville) Quotation and close textual analysis? (Leo Marx and Perry Miller) Statistical citation? (Philip Greven)

—How much of the work presents concrete detail and how much abstract generalization, and what strategies does the author employ for connecting the two? (e.g., Daniel Boorstin in *The Americans: The Democratic Experience* is strong on detail; Tocqueville in *Democracy in America* is strong on generalization; Perry Miller in *Colony* is strong on both, and on situational contexts for relating the two)

—How does the author *support* his/her explanations? By appeal chiefly to facts? Logic? Ideology? Sentiment? Tradition?

—Is the author to be trusted? That is, does he/she say things and offer evidence in such a way that you are inclined to believe what is said?

—What kinds of *connections* does the author make among disparate levels of experience? And how? (e.g., literature with history, politics with art, high literature with popular literature, the individual with the social structure, an event with its intents and consequences, ideas with manifest behavior)

—How *self-aware* is the author of method, of how he/she is doing what he/she is doing? (e.g., Alvin Toffler is quite unself-conscious, Stanley Elkins very self-aware)

—How much and in what way does the author draw upon materials or methods outside the conventions of academic history or American Studies?

—What *propels* humans for the author? (e.g., articulated ideals? unarticulated greed? drive for power? unarticulated custom?) What holds humans back, or in? (e.g., conventional roles? oppression by others? habit? the impersonal power of institutions? the yet more impersonal power of environmental resources?)

—What is the author's estimate of the human species? Are there strains or contradictions in that estimate? (see for example the analyses of Parrington and Niebuhr, chapter 8)

—How does the author handle the problem of *evil*? (e.g., deny it altogether? locate it in the soul of man? in alien peoples? in alien ideologies? in institutions? in tradition? in particular people?)

—Where is the work weakest? Strongest? Are there apparent reasons why some parts are weak, some strong?

—What important questions does the author leave out? Are there other relevant materials the author should have used? Other relevant methods?

—What *alternative* kinds of explanations might be used for the experience under review?[2]

(2) Worlds and Lives Outside the Text

—What are the significant features in the author's *background*? Does he/she share many of these features with others whose explanations are similar? (see for example Richard Hofstadter's analysis of Turner, Beard, and Parrington in *The Progressive Historians*)

—Are there important crises, or turning points, in the author's life?

—To what "social generation" does the author belong, and what are the distinctive experiences of that generation? (see for example Malcolm Cowley's portrait in *Exile's Return: A Literary Odyssey of the Twenties*)

—Are there larger communities of explanation within which the author works? (e.g., Progressives, counter Progressives, new social historians)

—If the author does work in a larger explanation community, how was he/she *socialized* into that community?

—How much does the author share and how much does he/she depart from others in his/her explanation community?

(3) From the Context Outside Back into the Text Again

—In what way(s) does the work express contemporary issues in the wider culture and social structure? Contemporary issues in the culture and social structure of academe? (if an academic book; if not, then in its own appropriate communal context)

—Is the author's mode of explanation shaped by distinctive experiences of region? social class? race? ethnic group? sex? age? Are strains in the author's mode of explanation connected to these demographic factors?

—Who are the author's "significant others"? (that is, with whom does the author most identify? against whom?) To what degree do these significant others affect the author's own sense of his or her role?

—If the author is an academic, does his/her particular academic affiliation shape what is said? (e.g., Roy Harvey Pearce in "American Studies as a Discipline" [1957] is patient about American Studies not yet having developed as a discipline, perhaps because he lived in a department of English when he wrote the essay; Richard Sykes in "American Studies and the Concept of Culture" [1963] is less patient, perhaps because he was residing in an American Studies program at the time he wrote)

—Is the work's pattern of explanation affected by the availability of funding sources? (in the case of *Time on the Cross*, for example, manifestly yes; in the case of *Main Currents in American Thought*, no, although the study was 14 years in the making)[3]

NOTES

1. Recent scholarship in anthropology suggests that Kelly's analogy not only has heuristic value as a device for the imagination, but may in fact forecast an area of future integration between literary criticism on the one hand and fieldwork in anthropology and sociology on the other. For the "new ethnography" of the last decade pays special attention to the distinctive language of its respondents, and requires a sensitivity to interpreting the ethnog-

raphic interview analogous to what New Critics have asked readers of a literary text. I am not aware of actual borrowing from one discipline to another, but the potential is there, and both fields could benefit from the interchange.

See James Spradley and David McCurdy, *The Cultural Experience: Ethnography in a Complex Society* (Science Research Associates, 1972); Evan Jenkins, "The New Ethnography: Language as the Key to Culture," *Change* (January, 1978), pp. 16–19; and Spradley, *The Ethnographic Interview* (Holt, Rinehart, and Winston, 1979).

2. As noted earlier (see pp. 174–175), I have concentrated on stage (1) of the journey in this book, touching on (2) and (3) only incidentally. That emphasis is reflected in this Appendix too. In my planned sequel to this volume—to be titled *American Historical Explanations II: From Intellectual History to Cultural History*—I hope to do more justice to the second and third stages of this "strategic journey" of inquiry.

3. As I have indicated throughout the volume, I believe Kenneth Burke's "situation-strategy" method of criticism provides the best way of connecting up text to context, of moving from inside the literary or historical work to worlds and lives outside. I have also indicated that I believe scholars and students in the field have made too little use of Burke or of any other explicit models for doing historical-cultural criticism.

As with any generalization, there are exceptions, and I urge the interested reader to consult the following for excellent suggestions on how to do historical criticism: Hayden White, "The Historical Text as Literary Artifact," *CLIO* (June, 1974), pp. 277–303; David Levin, "The Literary Criticism of History," *CLIO* (October, 1971), pp. 42–45; Gordon Kelly, "Literature and the Historian," *American Quarterly* (May, 1974), pp. 141–159; and Lark Hall, *Vernon Louis Parrington: The Genesis and Design of Main Currents in American Thought* (Case Western Reserve University Doctoral Dissertation, Spring 1979). See also the many fine critical essays published in the journal *Reviews in American History* (1973–).

INDEX

Index

373

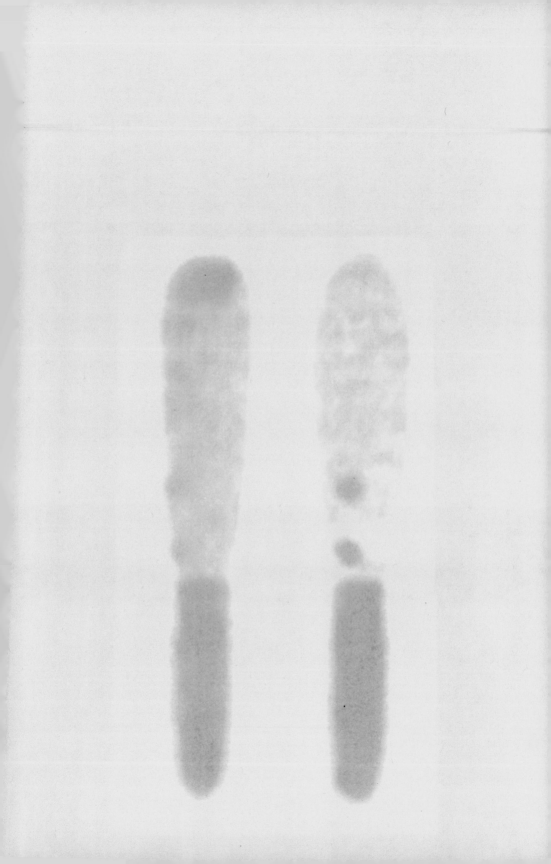